Communications in Computer and Information Science 2937

Rationale

The CCIS series is devoted to the publication of proceedings of computer science conferences. Its aim is to efficiently disseminate original research results in informatics in printed and electronic form. While the focus is on publication of peer-reviewed full papers presenting mature work, inclusion of reviewed short papers reporting on work in progress is welcome, too. Besides globally relevant meetings with internationally representative program committees guaranteeing a strict peer-reviewing and paper selection process, conferences run by societies or of high regional or national relevance are also considered for publication.

Topics

The topical scope of CCIS spans the entire spectrum of informatics ranging from foundational topics in the theory of computing to information and communications science and technology and a broad variety of interdisciplinary application fields.

Information for Volume Editors and Authors

Publication in CCIS is free of charge. No royalties are paid, however, we offer registered conference participants temporary free access to the online version of the conference proceedings on SpringerLink (http://link.springer.com) by means of an http referrer from the conference website and/or a number of complimentary printed copies, as specified in the official acceptance email of the event.

CCIS proceedings can be published in time for distribution at conferences or as post-proceedings, and delivered in the form of printed books and/or electronically as USBs and/or e-content licenses for accessing proceedings at SpringerLink. Furthermore, CCIS proceedings are included in the CCIS electronic book series hosted in the SpringerLink digital library at http://link.springer.com/bookseries/7899. Conferences publishing in CCIS are allowed to use our online conference service (Meteor) for managing the whole proceedings lifecycle (from submission and reviewing to preparing for publication) free of charge.

Publication process

The language of publication is exclusively English. Authors publishing in CCIS have to sign the Springer CCIS copyright transfer form, however, they are free to use their material published in CCIS for substantially changed, more elaborate subsequent publications elsewhere. For the preparation of the camera-ready papers/files, authors have to strictly adhere to the Springer CCIS Authors' Instructions and are strongly encouraged to use the CCIS LaTeX style files or templates.

Abstracting/Indexing

CCIS is abstracted/indexed in DBLP, Google Scholar, EI-Compendex, Mathematical Reviews, SCImago, Scopus. CCIS volumes are also submitted for the inclusion in ISI Proceedings.

How to start

To start the evaluation of your proposal for inclusion in the CCIS series, please send an e-mail to ccis@springer.com

Kevin Daimi · Hamid R. Arabnia ·
Leonidas Deligiannidis
Editors

Security and Management, Wireless Networks, Software Engineering Research and Practice

24th International Conference, SAM 2025, 24th International Conference, ICWN 2025, and 23rd International Conference, SERP 2025, Held as Part of the World Congress in Computer Science, Computer Engineering, and Applied Computing, CSCE 2025
Las Vegas, NV, USA, July 21–24, 2025
Revised Selected Papers

Springer

Editors
Kevin Daimi
University of Detroit Mercy
Detroit, MI, USA

Hamid R. Arabnia
University of Georgia
Athens, GA, USA

Leonidas Deligiannidis
Wentworth Institute of Technology
Boston, MA, USA

ISSN 1865-0929 ISSN 1865-0937 (electronic)
Communications in Computer and Information Science
ISBN 978-3-032-22207-7 ISBN 978-3-032-22208-4 (eBook)
https://doi.org/10.1007/978-3-032-22208-4

This Springer imprint is published by the registered company Springer Nature Switzerland AG
The registered company address is: Gewerbestrasse 11, 6330 Cham, Switzerland

Preface

It is our great pleasure to introduce this collection of selected papers presented at the 24th International Conference on Security & Management (SAM 2025), the 24th International Conference on Wireless Networks (ICWN 2025), and the 23rd International Conference on Software Engineering Research & Practice (SERP 2025).

These conferences were held as part of the federated 2025 World Congress in Computer Science, Computer Engineering, and Applied Computing (CSCE 2025), which took place from July 21 to July 24, 2025, in Las Vegas, Nevada, USA.

The CSCE 2025 Congress brought together papers from a diverse array of communities, including researchers from universities, corporations, and government agencies. Accepted papers are published by Springer Nature, and the proceedings showcase solutions to key challenges in various critical areas of Computer Science, Computer Engineering, and Applied Computing.

Computer Science (CS) is the study of computational systems, data processing, information management, and automation. Many applications in CS focus on solving problems that would be impossible or extremely difficult to address without the use of computers. It serves as a bridge between computational science and other scientific fields. The interdisciplinary nature of CS involves leveraging computers to understand and solve complex challenges, making it the science of using computers to advance scientific discovery. Computer Engineering (CE), on the other hand, integrates aspects of computer science, electronic engineering, and electrical engineering. It encompasses the design and production of computer hardware, such as chips, servers, supercomputers, embedded systems, and communication systems, among others.

Considering the above broad outline, the CSCE 2025 Congress was composed of the following focused conferences:

Applied Cognitive Computing (ACC); Bioinformatics & Computational Biology (BIOCOMP); Biomedical Engineering (BIOENG); Scientific Computing (CSC); eLearning, e-Business, Enterprise Information Systems, & e-Government (EEE); Embedded Systems, Cyber-physical Systems, & Applications (ESCS); Foundations of Computer Science (FCS); Frontiers in Education (FECS); Grid, Cloud, & Cluster Computing (GCC); Health Informatics (HIMS); Artificial Intelligence (ICAI); Data Science (ICDATA); Emergent Quantum Technologies (ICEQT); Internet Computing & IoT (ICOMP); Wireless Networks (ICWN); Information & Knowledge Engineering (IKE); Image Processing, Computer Vision, & Pattern Recognition (IPCV); Modeling, Simulation & Visualization Methods (MSV); Parallel & Distributed Processing Techniques & Applications (PDPTA); Security & Management (SAM); and Software Engineering Research & Practice (SERP). The scope of each track can be found at: https://www.american-cse.org/csce2025/conferences.

The primary objective of the CSCE Congress and its associated conferences is to foster opportunities for cross-fertilization between the fields of Computer Science (CS) and Computer Engineering (CE). The CSCE Congress is deeply committed to promoting diversity and eliminating discrimination, both in its role as a conference organizer and as a service provider. Our goal is to create an inclusive culture that respects and values differences, promotes dignity, equality, and diversity, and encourages individuals to reach their full potential. We are also dedicated, wherever possible, to organizing a conference that represents the global community. We sincerely hope that we have succeeded in achieving these important objectives.

The Steering Committee and the Program Committees would like to extend their gratitude to all the authors who submitted papers for consideration. This year's conferences received submissions from 58 countries, with approximately 50% of them coming from outside the USA. Each submitted paper underwent a rigorous peer-review process, with at least two experts (an average of 2.4 referees per paper) evaluating the submissions based on originality, significance, clarity, impact, and soundness. In cases where reviewers' recommendations were contradictory, a program committee member was tasked with making the final decision, often consulting additional referees for further guidance. The Congress followed the guidelines of COPE (Committee on Publication Ethics):

- Typical submissions underwent a single-blind peer review process, in which the authors remained unaware of the identities of the reviewers, while the reviewers were informed of the authors' identities.
- Papers authored by one or more members of the program committee, including co-chairs, were subjected to a double-blind peer review process, ensuring that neither the authors nor the reviewers were aware of each other's identities or affiliations.

The SAM 2025 Conference received a total of 186 submissions, of which 38 papers were accepted, resulting in a paper acceptance rate of 20%. For this volume we selected only 23 of the papers accepted at SAM. The ICWN 2025 Conference received 33 submissions, of which 8 papers were accepted, resulting in a paper acceptance rate of 24%. For this volume we selected only 5 of the papers accepted at ICWN. The SERP 2025 Conference received 49 submissions, of which 8 papers were accepted, resulting in a paper acceptance rate of 16%. In addition, the book contains 1 poster paper.

This volume includes 37 of the accepted papers from SAM 2025, ICWN 2025, and SERP 2025.

We are deeply grateful to the many colleagues who contributed their time and effort to organizing the Congress. In particular, we extend our thanks to the members of the Program Committees, the Steering Committee, the referees, and the Chairs and organizers of individual sessions and conferences. We would also like to express our appreciation to the primary sponsor of the conference, the American Council on Science & Education. The list of members of the Program Committee for each track can be found at: https://www.american-cse.org/csce2025/committees.

We extend our heartfelt gratitude to all the speakers and authors for their valuable contributions. We would also like to thank the following individuals and organizations for their support: the staff at the Luxor Hotel, the staff of Springer Nature, Soheyla Amirian (Pace University), Farzan Shenavarmasouleh (Medialab Inc., USA), and Farid Ghareh Mohammadi (Verify Radiology Images Consultants, LLC, USA) for their assistance in various aspects of the event.

We are pleased to present a curated selection of papers from the SAM 2025, ICWN 2025, and SERP 2025 conferences. These proceedings represent a collection of outstanding research contributions that reflect the diversity and depth of work in core areas of Security & Management, Wireless Networks, and Software Engineering Research & Practice.

August 2025

Kevin Daimi
Hamid R. Arabnia
Leonidas Deligiannidis

Organization

Steering Committee – Co-chairs (CSCE 2025)

Hamid R. Arabnia	University of Georgia, USA
Leonidas Deligiannidis	Wentworth Institute of Technology, USA
Fernando G. Tinetti	Universidad Nacional de La Plata, Argentina
Quoc-Nam Tran	Southeastern Louisiana University, USA

Co-editors of SAM 2025, ICWN 2025, and SERP 2025 Proceedings – Publication Co-chairs

Kevin Daimi	University of Detroit Mercy, USA
Hamid R. Arabnia	University of Georgia, USA
Leonidas Deligiannidis	Wentworth Institute of Technology, USA

Members of Steering Committee (CSCE 2025)

Babak Akhgar	Sheffield Hallam University, UK
Abbas M. Al-Bakry	University of IT & Communications, Iraq
Nizar Al-Holou	University of Detroit Mercy, USA
Hamid R. Arabnia	University of Georgia, USA
Rajab Challoo	Texas A&M University-Kingsville, USA
Chien-Fu Cheng	Tamkang University, Taiwan
Hyunseung Choo	Sungkyunkwan University, South Korea
Kevin Daimi	University of Detroit Mercy, USA
Leonidas Deligiannidis	Wentworth Institute of Technology, USA
Eman M. El-Sheikh	University of West Florida, USA
Mary Mehrnoosh Eshaghian-Wilner	University of California, Los Angeles, USA
David L. Foster	Kettering University, USA
Henry Hexmoor	Southern Illinois University at Carbondale, USA
Ching-Hsien (Robert) Hsu	Chung Hua University, Taiwan
James J. (Jong Hyuk) Park	SeoulTech, South Korea
Mohammad S. Obaidat	University of Jordan, Jordan
Marwan Omar	Illinois Institute of Technology, USA
Shahram Rahimi	University of Alabama, USA

Gerald Schaefer	Loughborough University, UK
Fernando G. Tinetti	Universidad Nacional de La Plata, Argentina
Quoc-Nam Tran	Southeastern Louisiana University, USA
Shiuh-Jeng Wang	Central Police University, Taiwan
Layne T. Watson	Virginia Polytechnic Institute & State University, USA
Chao-Tung Yang	Tunghai University, Taiwan
Mary Yang	University of Arkansas for Medical Sciences, USA

Research Tracks – Co-chairs (CSCE 2025)

Abeer Alsadoon (Co-chair, Health Informatics)	Charles Sturt University, Australia
Soheyla Amirian (Co-chair, Computer Vision & AI)	Pace University, USA
Hamid R. Arabnia (Co-chair, HPC)	University of Georgia, USA
Kevin Daimi (Co-chair, Security)	University of Detroit Mercy, USA
Leonidas Deligiannidis (Co-chair, Imaging Science, AI)	Wentworth Institute of Technology, USA
Richard Dill (Co-chair, Military and Defense Modeling)	US Air Force Institute of Technology, USA
Ken Ferens (Co-chair, Cognitive Computing & AI)	University of Manitoba, Canada
David de la Fuente (Co-chair, Information Management)	University of Oviedo, Spain
Shanzhen Gao (Co-chair, Artificial Intelligence, Education)	Virginia State University, USA
Farid Ghareh Mohammadi (Co-chair, Computer Vision & AI)	Verify Radiology Images Consultants, LLC, USA
Michael R. Grimaila (Co-chair, Military and Defense Modeling)	US Air Force Institute of Technology, USA
Douglas D. Hodson (Co-chair, Military and Defense Modeling)	US Air Force Institute of Technology, USA
Masahito Ohue (Co-chair, Mathematical Modeling)	Tokyo Institute of Technology, Japan
Peter M. Maurer (Co-chair, Theoretical Computer Science)	Baylor University, USA

Program Committees of SAM 2025, ICWN 2025, and SERP 2025

Refer to the lists at: http://sam.udmercy.edu/sam25/organization_com.html, http://sam.udmercy.edu/sam25/program_com.html, https://www.american-cse.org/csce2025/committees.

Contents

Poster Research Papers

Cybersecurity - Defensive and Offensive Strategies, and Related Issues

The Human Factor in Cybersecurity: A Conceptual Model Integrating Cognitive Biases

Roberto Andrade[1](✉), María Fernanda Cazares[2], and Daniela Cordova-Pintado[3]

[1] Colegio Politécnico, Universidad San Francisco de Quito, Quito, Ecuador
randradep@usfq.edu.ec

[2] Universidade Lusófona, Lisboa, Portugal
a22411590@alunos.ulht.pt

[3] Departament d'Enginyeria de la Informació i de les Comunicacions, Universitat Autònoma de Barcelona - UAB, Barcelona, Spain
daniela.cordova@uab.cat

Abstract. This paper advances cybersecurity by proposing a cognitively grounded framework that explains how human biases and decision-making limitations contribute to security vulnerabilities. By first establishing a strong foundation in classical decision theory and then integrating insights from cyberpsychology, the study offers a nuanced model that not only identifies why users make risky choices, but also guides the design of adaptive interventions-such as serious games-that improve cognitive skills and reduce susceptibility to attacks. This dual-theoretical and empirical approach bridges the gap between technical defenses and human-centered security strategies, promoting more resilient digital behavior.

Keywords: Cybersecurity · Human Factors · Cognitive Bias · Phishing

1 Introduction

Cybersecurity is no longer solely a technical problem, but increasingly a human-centered challenge. While technical infrastructures have evolved to mitigate system-level vulnerabilities, social engineering attacks-especially phishing continue to bypass sophisticated defenses by targeting users' cognitive biases and emotional responses [1,2]. The persistent success of such attacks reveals the limitations of security models that presume rational, compliant, and well-informed users.

Traditional frameworks in cybersecurity are predominantly built on technical and rule-based assumptions, where users are expected to recognize threats and act accordingly. However, research in cognitive science and behavioral economics shows that individuals frequently rely on heuristics-mental shortcuts that

K. Daimi et al. (Eds.): CSCE 2025, CCIS 2937, pp. 3–13, 2026.
https://doi.org/10.1007/978-3-032-22208-4_1

enable fast but error-prone decisions [3]. In phishing contexts, these heuristics are exploited through urgency cues, authority mimicry, or emotional triggers, leading users to act before engaging in reflective reasoning.

Table 1 presents a structured comparison between traditional cybersecurity and cyberpsychology, highlighting a paradigm shift in the understanding and mitigation of cyber threats. Traditional cybersecurity operates under the assumption that threats are primarily technical and that users behave rationally, whereas cyberpsychology acknowledges that human behavior is bounded, driven by heuristics, and influenced by emotions. This distinction is reflected in the focus of interventions: technical defenses such as firewalls and encryption versus behavioral strategies like cognitive training and user modeling. The typical attack vectors addressed also diverge, with traditional approaches targeting malware and privilege escalation, while cyberpsychology focuses on phishing, social engineering, and decision fatigue. Notably, the user is reframed from being the weakest link to an adaptive agent whose behavior can be studied and influenced. Theoretical foundations expand from cryptographic and architectural models to psychological frameworks such as dual-process theory and the Fogg Behavior Model. Although each approach has its strengths and limitations, the table underscores the importance of integrating both perspectives to effectively enhance digital security in diverse real-world contexts.

2 Theoretical Foundations

The online context introduces several factors that alter perception, attention, and emotional salience [4]):

1. Interface overload leads to alert fatigue, causing users to ignore even critical warnings.
2. Digital trust heuristics emerge from prior experience with brands or platforms, leading to overreliance on surface cues.
3. Social validation mechanisms can reinforce unsafe actions.

In classic decision theory, humans are assumed to act rationally when presented with risks or choices. However, bounded rationality, as proposed by Simon [5], suggests that individuals operate within constraints of time, information, and cognitive capacity. Rather than performing exhaustive risk calculations, they rely on heuristics-mental shortcuts that simplify decisions but increase the likelihood of systematic error. Phishing attackers exploit these heuristics by embedding cognitive traps within message structure and timing. For instance:

- The availability heuristic leads users to overestimate the legitimacy of familiar logos or names.
- Heuristic authority causes users to comply with messages seemingly issued by figures of power (e.g., managers or IT).
- The urgency framing effect manipulates users into acting impulsively, bypassing deliberation.

Table 1. Traditional Cybersecurity vs Cognitive Security

Dimension	Traditional Cybersecurity	Cyberpsychology
Core Assumption	Threats are primarily technical; users are rational actors	Human behavior is bounded, heuristic-driven, and emotionally influenced
Focus of Intervention	Technical defenses: firewalls, IDS/IPS, encryption, access control	Behavioral defenses: cognitive training, simulation, user modeling
Typical Attack Vector Addressed	Malware, zero-days, privilege escalation	Phishing, social engineering, decision fatigue
User Role	Often viewed as weakest link or liability	Viewed as adaptive agent whose behavior can be understood and shaped
Theoretical Foundations	Cryptography, network architecture, Zero Trust, access control models	Dual-process theory, Protection Motivation Theory, Fogg Behavior Model
Strengths	High automation, scalable, protects infrastructure	Context-aware, improves resilience, supports education and awareness
Limitations	Ignores human fallibility, assumes compliance, rigid to changing behavior patterns	Requires contextual adaptation, scalability challenges, less standardization
Measurement Strategies	Logs, system alerts, forensic traces	Interviews, cognitive tests, simulation logs, emotional/cognitive indicators
Real-world Applicability	Critical systems, enterprises, infrastructure	End-user behavior, SME environments, education/training

These biases align with Dual Process Theory [3], which distinguishes between:

1. **System 1:** fast, emotional, heuristic-driven decisions.
2. **System 2:** slow, effortful, logical thinking.

Phishing attacks are effective when they trigger System 1 under emotionally loaded conditions, preventing System 2 from intervening. This dynamic makes users especially vulnerable to deception when messages provoke urgency, fear, or familiarity.

Empirical studies reinforce these theoretical insights by demonstrating how users actually behave during phishing encounters. Alsharnouby et al. [6] conducted an in-depth analysis of user interactions with simulated phishing websites and found that participants correctly identified only 53% of phishing attempts. The study highlights how users often rely on visual familiarity-such as logos, layout, and trusted domain appearance-over deliberate analytical processes. Even participants with basic cybersecurity knowledge made errors under cognitive load or emotional pressure, underscoring the role of bounded rationality and affective bias in real-world phishing susceptibility.

These findings align with the dual-process framework and support the need for psychologically informed security strategies. Rather than relying solely on technical defenses or awareness campaigns, effective interventions should address the cognitive and emotional mechanisms that shape decision-making under uncertainty. This lays the foundation for integrating neuropsychological principles into cybersecurity models, as explored in the following section.

3 Emotional and Executive Systems Involved in Phishing-Related Decision-Making

Building upon the theoretical and empirical foundations outlined above, this section delves into the underlying neuropsychological mechanisms that influence phishing-related decision-making. Understanding which brain systems are activated-and how they interact-helps explain why individuals often fail to resist phishing attempts despite having security knowledge.

Figure 1 illustrates a neuro-psychological model that captures the interplay of emotional and executive systems involved in phishing-related decision-making. The process begins with a phishing attempt, which triggers activation in the amygdala-the brain's key structure for detecting threat and processing fear-related stimuli [7]). This fast, automatic emotional response is part of what Daniel Kahneman would label "System 1," and it can occur prior to conscious deliberation. Simultaneously, information about the perceived threat is processed by the prefrontal cortex (PFC), which is responsible for executive control and inhibitory regulation [8]). If the PFC is under cognitive strain or influenced by emotional overload, its ability to regulate behavior is diminished, making it less likely to suppress an impulsive click or override emotional urges.

The insula, at the center of the diagram, plays a crucial role in integrating interoceptive signals-internal bodily sensations such as tension, discomfort, or arousal-and translating them into subjective experiences of risk and trust [9]. The insula essentially evaluates the "gut feeling" about whether something feels off and contributes to the final phishing decision. Although not explicitly labeled in the diagram, the anterior cingulate cortex (ACC) is functionally involved in conflict monitoring, detecting mismatches between expected and actual outcomes [10]. This entire loop demonstrates that phishing decisions are not simply the result of cognitive knowledge deficits but rather emerge from a dynamic interaction between emotional salience, bodily awareness, and executive inhibition-a view supported by the Somatic Marker Hypothesis [11] and Neurovisceral Integration Theory [12]. In this way, the model provides a compelling foundation for emotion-aware and neurocognitively informed security training.

Phishing susceptibility is deeply rooted in the interplay between distinct brain regions responsible for emotional salience, executive control, and habitual action. The amygdala plays a central role in detecting threats and processing fear, making it highly reactive to urgency or danger cues commonly

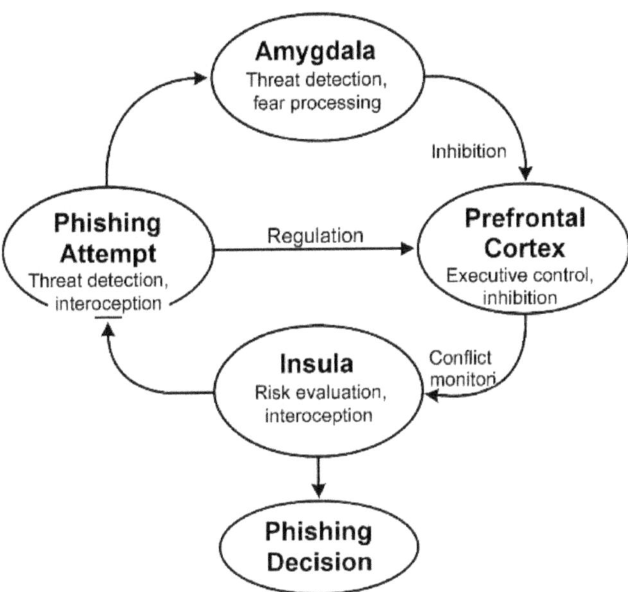

Fig. 1. Mental process related phishing detection.

found in phishing messages [7]. This activation can trigger automatic emotional responses before conscious deliberation occurs. In contrast, the prefrontal cortex (PFC) is responsible for executive functioning, including inhibition and controlled decision-making. Its role is to regulate impulsive reactions initiated by the amygdala; however, doing so requires cognitive effort and time, which are often unavailable in phishing scenarios designed to provoke immediate action [8]. When emotional load is high, the anterior cingulate cortex (ACC), responsible for conflict detection and error monitoring, may also be bypassed, limiting the individual's ability to recognize inconsistencies between the message content and expected patterns [10]. The insula further contributes to phishing vulnerability through its role in risk perception and interoception-the awareness of internal bodily states such as discomfort or doubt. It enables individuals to make "gut-level" judgments, which are particularly influential in ambiguous or uncertain contexts [9]. A phishing message that appears legitimate may not trigger discomfort in the insula, reducing the chance of critical evaluation. Finally, the basal ganglia and associated habit systems facilitate automated behavior, such as clicking without conscious thought. These neural circuits are shaped by repetition and reward, meaning users conditioned to respond to similar-looking emails may do so habitually, even when risk is present. Together, these systems form a neuro-cognitive substrate that explains why users may succumb to phishing attempts despite awareness, revealing the need for interventions that target both cognitive control and emotional regulation (Table 2).

Table 2. Relation between brain regions and phishing susceptibility

Brain Region/System	Function	Role in Phishing Susceptibility
Amygdala	Emotional salience, fear processing	Reacts to urgency/threat cues in phishing messages
Prefrontal Cortex (PFC)	Executive function, inhibition, decision-making	Supposed to inhibit emotional responses-but requires time/effort
Anterior Cingulate Cortex (ACC)	Conflict monitoring, error detection	Detects inconsistency, but can be bypassed under high emotional load
Insula	Risk perception, emotional awareness	Influences gut-level decisions under uncertainty
Basal ganglia/Habit systems	Automated behavior patterns	Facilitates habitual clicking or response patterns

Applied Case Scenario

To illustrate how these systems operate in practice, consider the following realistic scenario:

A university employee receives an urgent email purportedly sent by the institution's IT department. The message warns that their credentials have expired and urges them to click a provided link within the next 15 min to avoid account suspension.

The phishing stimulus triggers immediate emotional arousal. The amygdala reacts to the perceived threat and urgency, activating a stress-based fear response. The email's formatting-familiar logos, tone, and authoritative signature-engages heuristic processing via System 1. As a result, the user's reflective system (System 2) may not activate to evaluate the message critically.

Meanwhile, the prefrontal cortex (PFC) attempts to exercise executive control, but its functioning may be impaired by cognitive load (e.g., multitasking, time pressure). This reduces the user's ability to inhibit the automatic impulse to comply. The insula processes internal sensations such as tension or anxiety but may fail to signal discomfort if the email aligns too closely with legitimate past communications.

The anterior cingulate cortex (ACC) could detect subtle anomalies-like an odd sender address-but its conflict monitoring is compromised under emotional overload. If the user has previously clicked similar messages without consequence, the basal ganglia may reinforce a habitual "click-through" pattern.

This neurocognitive cascade reveals that phishing susceptibility stems not from ignorance alone, but from the convergence of emotional priming, diminished executive regulation, and habitual behavior. Interventions must therefore address emotional resilience, decision pacing, and reflective awareness-not merely increase technical knowledge.

4 Cyberpsychological Decision-Making Model

Figure 2 represents a cyberpsychological decision-making loop, composed of four core phases: Perception & Salience Evaluation, Cognitive Appraisal & Trust Calibration, Action Selection, and Post-Decision Rationalization. Each phase is associated with specific cognitive biases (e.g., availability heuristic, overconfidence, status quo bias), consistent with the Dual Process Theory [3], where System 1 (fast, intuitive, emotionally driven) overrides System 2 (slow, reflective) during phishing attempts. This cyclical model shows how digital decisions are not isolated acts, but part of a feedback system where previous experiences (rationalization) inform future perceptions, reinforcing habitual biases. Importantly, the presence of trust calibration aligns with Protection Motivation Theory [13], where users assess threat severity and self-efficacy before acting-often impaired by cognitive distortions.

From a cyberpsychological standpoint, the model also highlights the environmental modifiers surrounding the decision loop: Interface Design, Digital Fatigue, and Social Validation. These contextual variables are well-documented in the field [4], where interface overload and habitual alert exposure lead to desensitization and decision fatigue, reducing the user's ability to detect deception. The model's inclusion of Social Validation acknowledges that digital behavior is influenced by perceived group norms and social reinforcement, echoing constructs from social cyberpsychology and digital trust studies. Overall, the model integrates cognitive and affective dimensions within realistic digital contexts, offering a comprehensive framework for understanding-and eventually intervening in cybersecurity behavior.

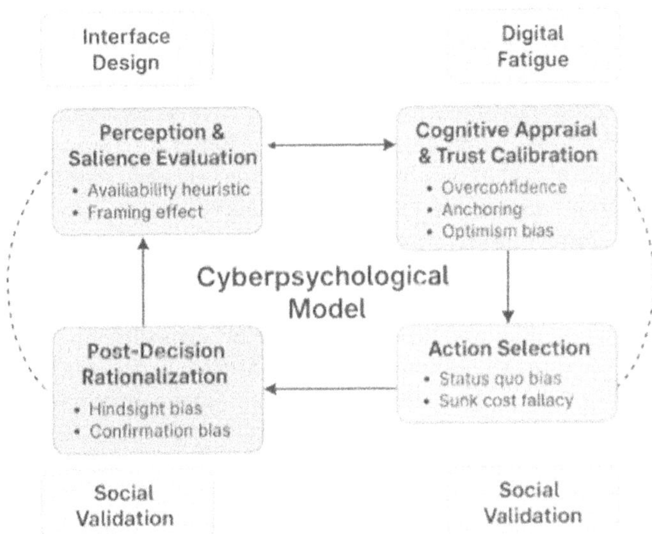

Fig. 2. Cyberpsychological Model.

Phishing attacks frequently exploit neurobiological vulnerabilities, particularly the role of the amygdala in processing emotionally charged stimuli such as fear, urgency, and social threat. The amygdala is activated by cues signaling danger or loss, which in phishing manifests as alarming language ("Your account will be locked"), imminent consequences ("Respond within 10 min or lose access"), or hierarchical social pressure ("Your manager needs this file now"). These emotional triggers bypass rational deliberation by activating System 1 processing [3], thereby weakening the inhibitory function of the prefrontal cortex, which would otherwise allow users to reflect, verify, and resist malicious cues. Understanding this neurological pathway is essential not only for behavioral modeling but also for designing technically sophisticated phishing simulations that mirror real-world manipulative strategies. From a technical perspective (Table 3), these affective manipulation strategies correspond directly to several techniques within the MITRE ATT&CK framework, particularly under the Initial Access and Execution tactics. Techniques such as [T1566.001: Spearphishing Attachment], [T1566.002: Spearphishing Link], and [T1566.003: Spearphishing via Service] often deploy emotionally charged content that is specifically crafted to excite the amygdala. Additionally, [T1204: User Execution] capitalizes on users' habitual and impulsive clicking behavior, which is strengthened by emotional priming. These mappings reveal that the success of many real-world phishing campaigns is neurocognitively predictable, and that defenders should account for these emotional vectors when designing detection tools, behavioral analytics, or training platforms. For example, Natural Language Processing (NLP) could be used to flag messages containing high-arousal emotional content, while serious games or simulated attacks could train users to recognize and regulate amygdala-triggered impulses.

5 Conceptual Model for Phishing Behavior

The proposed conceptual model integrates cognitive, emotional, and neuro psychological mechanisms to explain user susceptibility to phishing attacks and guide the design of behaviorally adaptive interventions Abril T, et al. [14], propose that personalizing the experience and feedback in cybersecurity training programs improves their effectiveness. Central to the model is the interplay between emotional reactivity-particularly the amygdala's response to threat cues-and executive inhibition managed by the prefrontal cortex (PFC). When phishing messages evoke urgency, fear, or social authority, the amygdala triggers rapid affective responses, often before reflective processes in the PFC can engage [3,7]. At the same time, interoceptive risk signals, processed by the insula, influence users' intuitive judgments about trust and safety [9]. If the stimulus is sufficiently ambiguous or emotionally primed, the likelihood of impulsive action increases. Additionally, the anterior cingulate cortex (ACC) plays a role in detecting conflicts between expectations and input-such as recognizing inconsistencies in a suspicious email-but can be bypassed under high emotional load [10]. This neurocognitive loop illustrates why secure behavior often fails, even among

Table 3. Relation between brain regions and MITRE ATT&CK

Brain Region/System	Function	Phishing Exploit Vector	MITRE ATT&CK Technique
Amygdala	Emotional salience, fear processing	Urgency, fear-inducing language ("Account locked", "Security breach")	T1566.001: Spearphishing Attachment T1566.002: Spearphishing Link
Prefrontal Cortex (PFC)	Inhibition, executive function, decision-making	Overloaded by cognitive/emotional stress, reducing rational control	T1204: User Execution (impulsive click execution)
Anterior Cingulate Cortex (ACC)	Conflict monitoring, error detection	Conflict between appearance and internal doubt ignored under pressure	T1566.003: Spearphishing via Service
Insula	Risk perception, interoception, emotional awareness	Gut-level feelings overridden by familiarity or manipulated trust	T1204 + T1566: Emotional manipulation bypassing risk signals
Basal Ganglia/Habit Systems	Automated behavior, pattern repetition	Habitual clicking from overtraining in similar environments (e.g., clicking on daily emails)	T1204: User Execution

users with technical knowledge. In parallel, the model introduces key behavioral and contextual dimensions critical for experimental operationalization and serious game design. It incorporates the role of habit systems (basal ganglia) in shaping automatic clicking behaviors, particularly under high email exposure or repetitive task patterns [8]. The model also accounts for external influences-such as interface design and social cues-that reinforce decision-making biases through visual formatting, sender identity, and hierarchical pressure. Drawing on frameworks from cyberpsychology [4] and Protection Motivation Theory [13], the model supports the creation of adaptive simulations that replicate real phishing conditions while allowing for the capture of physiological, cognitive, and behavioral metrics. These attributes make the model suitable for both experimental research (e.g., with think-aloud protocols and psychometric tools) and the development of serious games that target cognitive bias awareness, emotion regulation, and decision-making under uncertainty (Fig. 3).

This conceptual model contributes to a more comprehensive understanding of phishing susceptibility by uniting cognitive biases, emotional triggers, and habitual responses within a neuropsychological framework. It serves not only as

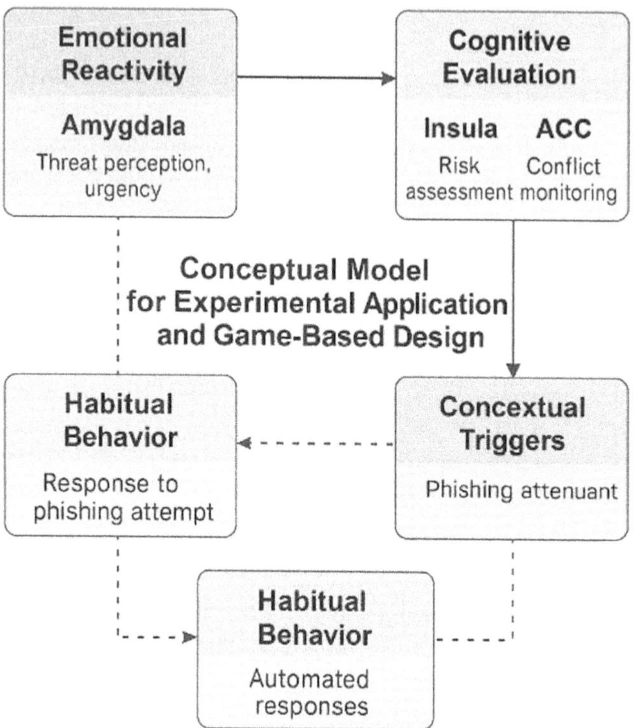

Fig. 3. Habitual Behavior related with phishing response.

a diagnostic lens but also as a blueprint for designing personalized and adaptive training tools. By operationalizing this model in experimental studies or serious game environments, researchers and practitioners can better measure, predict, and ultimately mitigate risky user behaviors in cybersecurity contexts.

6 Conclusion

This paper presents a conceptual and neuropsychological framework that bridges classical decision theory, cognitive biases, and emotional processes to explain why users fall for phishing attacks. By integrating insights from cyberpsychology and neuroscience, the study moves beyond conventional rule-based security models to offer a more human-centered approach.

The proposed model highlights the importance of emotional salience, executive control, and habitual behavior in shaping digital decisions under pressure. It demonstrates that phishing susceptibility is not solely a matter of user ignorance but arises from bounded rationality and affective vulnerability. This understanding informs the design of adaptive, behaviorally grounded interventions such as serious games, emotion-aware interfaces, and realistic phishing simulations.

Future work may further operationalize this model through empirical testing, including user stratification, and personalized feedback mechanisms. Ultimately, aligning cybersecurity practices with cognitive and emotional realities promises to foster more resilient user behavior and more effective defense strategies in complex digital environments.

References

1. Parsons, K., McCormac, A., Butavicius, M., Pattinson, M., Jerram, C.: Determining employee awareness using the human aspects of information security questionnaire (hais-q). Comput. Secur. **42**, 165–176 (2014)
2. Furnell, S., Clarke, N.: Power to the people? The evolving recognition of human aspects of security. Comput. Secur. **31**(8), 983–988 (2012)
3. Kahneman, D.: Thinking, Fast and Slow. Farrar, Straus and Giroux, New York (2011)
4. Greene, G., Shapiro, M.: Cyberpsychology: implications for the future of security. Secur. J. **28**(2), 116–130 (2015)
5. Simon, H.A.: Bounded rationality. In: Eatwell, J., Milgate, M., Newman, P. (eds.) Utility and Probability, pp. 15–18. The New Palgrave, Macmillan, London (1990)
6. Alsharnouby, M., Alaca, F., Chiasson, S.: Why phishing still works: user strategies for combating phishing attacks. Int. J. Hum Comput Stud. **82**, 69–82 (2015)
7. LeDoux, J.E.: The Emotional Brain: The Mysterious Underpinnings of Emotional Life. Simon & Schuster, New York (1998)
8. Miller, E.K., Cohen, J.D.: An integrative theory of prefrontal cortex function. Annu. Rev. Neurosci. **24**(1), 167–202 (2001)
9. Craig, A.D.: How do you feel-now? The anterior insula and human awareness. Nat. Rev. Neurosci. **10**(1), 59–70 (2009)
10. Botvinick, M.M., Braver, T.S., Barch, D.M., Carter, C.S., Cohen, J.D.: Conflict monitoring and cognitive control. Psychol. Rev. **108**(3), 624–652 (2001)
11. Damasio, A.R.: Descartes' Error: Emotion, Reason, and the Human Brain. Avon Books (1994)
12. Thayer, J.F., Lane, R.D.: A model of neurovisceral integration in emotion regulation and dysregulation. J. Affect. Disord. **61**(3), 201–216 (2000)
13. Rogers, R.W.: A protection motivation theory of fear appeals and attitude change. J. Psychol. **91**(1), 93–114 (1975)
14. Abril, T., Gamito, P., Motta, C., Oliveira, J., Dias, F., Pinto, F., Oliveira, M.: The role of ecological simulations on cybersecurity risk behaviors. In: Exploring a Novel Approach to Cybersecurity (2024). In Review

Competency-Based Cybersecurity Education: Developing Industry-Aligned Curriculum Modules

Major Houston[1], Jing Chen[1](✉), and Darren Waldrep[2]

[1] Department of Mathematical, Computer, and Applied Sciences, Athens State University, Athens, AL, USA
mhousto1@my.athens.edu, Jing.chen@athens.edu
[2] Department of Management, Athens State University, Athens, AL, USA
Darren.waldrep@athens.edu

Abstract. This paper aims to develop competency-based education (CBE) modules for cybersecurity at Athens State University, focusing on risk management, encryption, and communications security management. Aligned with industry standards like those from NIST, the competencies emphasize hands-on learning and performance-based assessment to better prepare students for real-world cybersecurity roles. Survey feedback from academic and industry participants supports the relevance and effectiveness of these competencies, while also suggesting the inclusion of areas like the Privacy Framework and end-user awareness. This paper lays a foundation for ongoing academic-industry collaboration and future curriculum integration. The findings address the cybersecurity skills gap and highlight the need for continuous curriculum refinement in response to evolving threats and workforce demands.

Keywords: Cybersecurity Education · Survey · Risk Management · Encryption · Communications Security Management

1 Introduction

This paper aims to design and develop competency-based education (CBE) modules for the cybersecurity program at Athens State University, focusing on three critical technical areas: risk management, encryption, and communications security management. The goal is to align academic content with established industry standards such as those from the National Institute of Standards and Technology (NIST) and the National Initiative for Cybersecurity Education (NICE). By emphasizing hands-on learning, performance-based assessments, and personalized learning paths, the paper seeks to equip students with practical skills that are directly applicable in the cybersecurity workforce.

To achieve this, the paper outlines a structured process for developing clear and relevant competency statements for each focus area. It involves analyzing current job roles and industry requirements, gathering input through surveys from both students and industry professionals, and designing performance-based assessment tools to measure

K. Daimi et al. (Eds.): CSCE 2025, CCIS 2937, pp. 14–23, 2026.
https://doi.org/10.1007/978-3-032-22208-4_2

student proficiency. Personalized learning paths will be proposed to support individual skill development, and continuous feedback mechanisms will be established to refine and improve the curriculum. It is important to note that this work is limited to the development of the CBE framework and competencies; it does not include implementing these modules into existing courses or exploring topics beyond the three identified cybersecurity domains.

The significance of this paper lies in its contribution to addressing the cybersecurity skills gap by shifting from traditional, knowledge-based instruction to a competency-driven model. By aligning educational outcomes with real-world expectations and fostering collaboration between academia and industry, this approach enhances graduate employability and ensures curriculum relevance. Additionally, the framework developed here offers a scalable model that other institutions can adopt to modernize their cybersecurity education programs.

2 Literature Review

The rapid evolution of cybersecurity threats has led to a growing demand for skilled professionals who possess not only theoretical knowledge but also practical, hands-on experience. However, traditional education models often fall short in preparing students for the real-world challenges they will face in the cybersecurity workforce (Mammi & Ithnin, 2012). As a result, educational institutions are increasingly adopting competency-based education (CBE) to better align academic programs with workforce requirements.

CBE focuses on the mastery of specific skills or competencies, rather than time spent in class, offering students a personalized learning pace and performance-based assessments (Voorhees, 2001). This approach is especially valuable in cybersecurity, where job roles demand demonstrable skills in risk management, encryption, and communications security. According to the National Institute of Standards and Technology (NIST), the cybersecurity workforce must be capable of identifying, protecting, detecting, responding to, and recovering from threats (NIST, 2017). The National Initiative for Cybersecurity Education (NICE) Framework further emphasizes the alignment of education with job roles to meet evolving cybersecurity challenges (NICE, 2020).

Several studies support the effectiveness of CBE in bridging the cybersecurity skills gap. Watkins et al. (2018) argue that by designing curricula around industry-endorsed competencies, institutions can produce graduates who are immediately job-ready. Similarly, Ewell (2013) highlights that performance-based assessments allow students to demonstrate their capabilities through real-world applications, increasing their employability.

Despite these advantages, implementing CBE presents challenges. It requires significant restructuring of curriculum, faculty training, and buy-in from industry partners to validate competencies (Dragoo et al. 2016). Additionally, continuous feedback from employers and students is necessary to ensure the relevance of developed competencies. Nonetheless, institutions like Athens State University are taking proactive steps by developing cybersecurity modules focused on critical domains, informed by surveys and input from both students and industry professionals.

This literature underscores the importance of integrating CBE into cybersecurity education to ensure that graduates possess the practical skills demanded by employers.

By aligning academic outcomes with frameworks such as NIST and NICE, and incorporating feedback from key stakeholders, institutions can better prepare students for dynamic and high-stakes cybersecurity roles.

3 Methodology

Surveys are an efficient method for collecting data from large, diverse populations and are particularly effective for capturing both numerical trends and rich, subjective viewpoints when using mixed-question formats (Fink, 2013). The promise of anonymity encourages more honest and reflective responses (Singer & Couper, 2017), and standardized question formats support reliable cross-group comparisons.

To improve survey reliability and engagement, pilot testing was first conducted to identify unclear questions, aligning with standard validation practices (Presser et al., 2024). Gamification techniques and incentives were used to increase participation. A mixed-method approach involving follow-up interviews added qualitative depth, and adaptive questioning was incorporated to tailor follow-up questions based on initial responses. Data validation mechanisms, such as automated checks for inconsistencies, were implemented to further enhance data quality.

Efforts to increase survey completion included designing a concise questionnaire and emphasizing the research's significance. Reminders and small incentives were also considered, reflecting best practices for maximizing survey participation (Dillman et al., 2014). Collected data were subjected to a cleaning process to remove incomplete, duplicate, or inconsistent entries, a critical step in ensuring data quality (Van den Broeck et al., 2005). Quantitative responses were analyzed using basic statistical methods to uncover patterns and trends, while qualitative responses were coded thematically to extract recurring themes and opinions (Braun & Clarke, 2006). Comparative analysis was conducted across different demographic groups to examine variations in cybersecurity understanding and engagement, a method that enhances the depth of interpretation (Creswell & Creswell, 2018).

In the context of cyber education, they provide insights into students' knowledge, perceptions, and engagement with cybersecurity concepts. This methodology section outlines the process of designing, distributing, and analyzing survey data while discussing the advantages and limitations of using surveys in cyber education research. Additionally, improvements made to enhance the reliability and effectiveness of the survey method are highlighted.

The survey was developed to evaluate multiple dimensions of cybersecurity education, including awareness of cybersecurity threats, comprehension of core principles, perceived effectiveness of teaching methods, and the ability to apply knowledge in real-world contexts. These aspects reflect widely recognized learning objectives in cybersecurity education. The instrument included a combination of multiple-choice, Likert-scale, and open-ended questions. Quantitative items were used to generate measurable data, while open-ended responses allowed for qualitative insights, a recommended approach in educational survey research (Creswell & Creswell, 2018).

Participants were chosen from a pool of individuals actively involved in cyber education programs, such as high school and college students, educators, and cybersecurity professionals. This purposive sampling method ensured diverse perspectives, which is essential for generalizing findings across educational levels (Etikan et al., 2016). The survey was distributed through several channels: online platforms (e.g., Google Forms, Microsoft Forms), official school communication systems (email and LMS), in-class QR codes, and paper-based formats in areas with limited digital access. Multi-channel distribution has been shown to increase response rates and inclusivity (Wright, 2005).

To enhance participation, respondents were assured of anonymity and data confidentiality, which is critical in minimizing response bias (Singer & Couper, 2017). Reminder emails were also employed, a practice linked to improved response rates in digital surveys (Fan & Yan, 2010).

Table 1 shows all survey questions used in this research.

Table 1. Survey Questions

Question Number	
1	Consent to Participate in Survey
2	What is your age?
3	What is your gender?
4	What is your Affiliation?
5	Please indicate your highest education?
6	Please indicate level of experience.
7	Based on the significance within your industry, please Rate Risk Management 1 to 5.
8	Based on the significance within your industry, please Rate Encryption 1 to 5.
9	Based on the significance within your industry, please Rate Communications Security Management 1 to 5
10	Please suggest any other relevant competencies or additional input to this competency list.

4 Results

There are 30 participants to evaluate the relevance and effectiveness of cybersecurity competencies. The participants ranged in age from 27 to 62 and represented various sectors and levels of experience. This diverse sample was intentionally selected to minimize bias and ensure a well-rounded perspective on the competencies being assessed.

Question 1 is to make sure we have consent from somebody taking the survey. All participants agreed to take this survey. Question 2 asks for the age of participants, and the ages range from 27–62 years old.

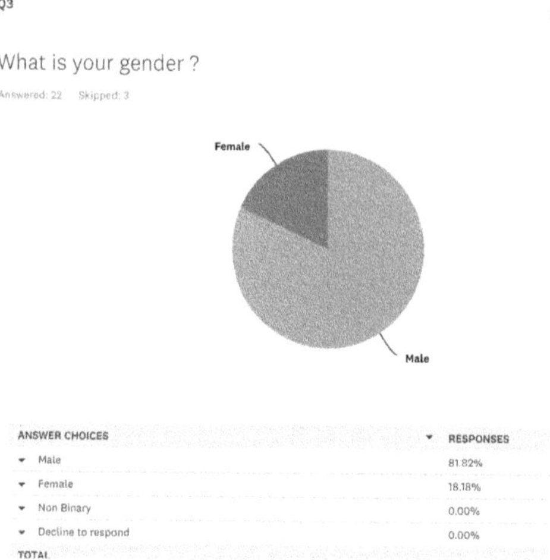

Fig. 1. Gender Distribution

Figure 1 shows the result of question 3. Almost 82% of them are male, and only 18% are female.

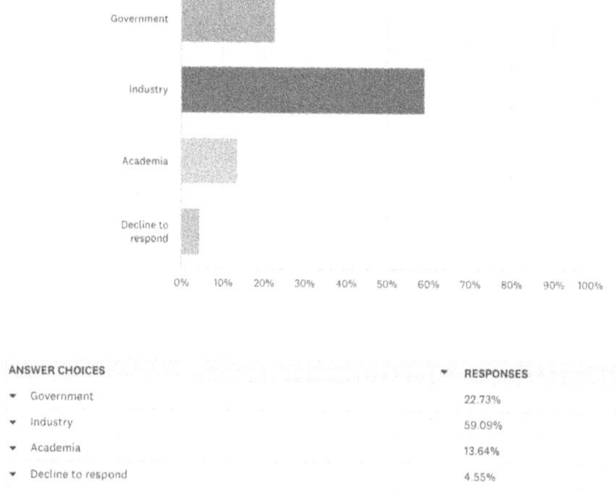

Fig. 2. Affiliations Distribution

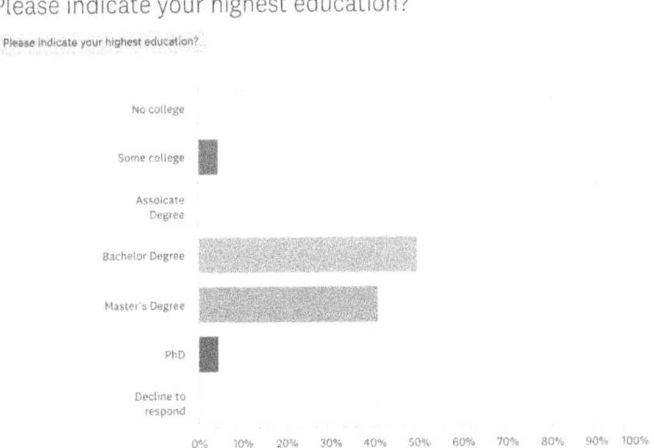

Fig. 3. Education Level Distribution

Figures 2 and 3 are from questions 4 and 5, respectively. Almost 60% participants are from the industry. Participants with a bachelor's degree make up 50%. Although the participants were chosen at random, many colleagues in the academic field completed the survey.

Question 6 collects the information on the experience level of participants. There are three levels of experience, which are entry-level, mid-level, and senior level, listed in Table 2.

Table 2. Level of Experience

Experience	Years of experience	Description	Skills have/ possessed
Entry-Level	0–2 years	• Learning and training in company processes and industry standards. • Performing basic tasks under supervision. • Assisting teams with papers and administrative work. • Communicating and collaborating with team members. • Developing skills through hands-on work. • Following guidelines and instructions closely.	• Basic knowledge of relevant tools, software, or industry practices. • Strong willingness to learn. • Good communication and teamwork skills. • Time management and organization.

(*continued*)

Table 2. (*continued*)

Experience	Years of experience	Description	Skills have/ possessed
Mid-Level	3–7 years	• Managing papers or tasks with minimal supervision. • Leading small teams or mentoring junior employees. • Problem-solving and decision-making within assigned areas. • Implementing strategies and optimizing processes. • Communicating with clients, stakeholders, or cross-functional teams.	• Strong expertise in field-specific tools and processes. • Leadership and problem-solving abilities. • Effective communication and collaboration. • Ability to work independently and make informed decisions.
Senior-Level	8+ years	• Managing teams, departments, or company divisions. • Setting strategies and making high-level business decisions. • Handling complex problem-solving and decision-making. • Mentoring mid and entry-level employees. • Representing the company in high-stakes meetings or negotiations.	• Advanced expertise in industry and business strategy. • Strong leadership, coaching, and mentoring skills. • High-level problem-solving and decision-making.

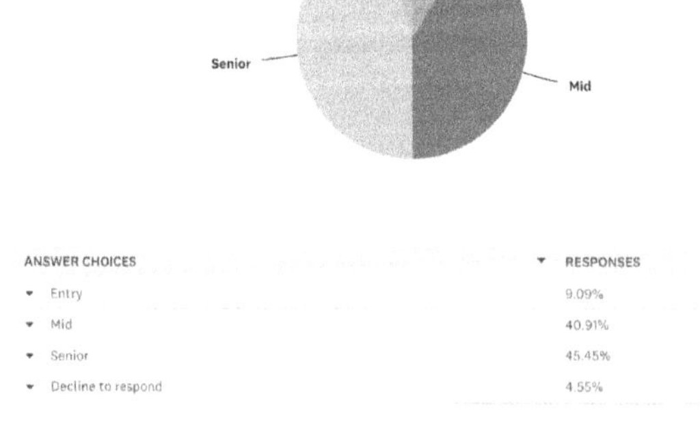

Fig. 4. Experience Level Distribution

More than 85% of participants have mid-level and senior-level experience, as shown in Fig. 4. Their feedback helps us to understand the gap between cybersecurity education and real-world needs.

Questions 7 to 9 ask participants to rate three aspects of cybersecurity based on their experiences.

- Risk Management
  Effective risk management is fundamental in cybersecurity education as it equips individuals with the skills to identify, assess, and prioritize risks, allowing them to implement effective strategies to protect information systems and mitigate potential threats. By identifying and reducing possible risks to an organization's financial, intellectual, and physical assets, effective risk management helps protect such resources.
- Encryption
  Encryption is crucial for securing sensitive information because it transforms data into an unreadable format that can only be accessed by authorized users with the appropriate decryption key, thereby protecting it from unauthorized access and cyber threats. This ensures confidentiality, integrity, and trust in digital communications and data storage.
- Communications Security Management
  Securing communications is vital for protecting sensitive information in transit because it prevents unauthorized access and interception, which can lead to data breaches and misuse of confidential data. To ensure that data remains confidential and integrity is maintained throughout transmission, in addition to having the data encrypted, secure protocols must be in place.

The scales are from 1 to 5. This five-point Likert scale measures how important respondents consider specific items, ranging from 1 (least important) to 5 (most important). It helps quantify subjective opinions and identify priorities based on perceived relevance (Table 3).

Table 3. Range from the lowest to the highest

	Lowest	Highest	Average
Risk Management	3	5	4.63
Encryption	2	5	4.46
Communications Security Management	3	5	4.3

The results closely aligned with the expectations. Many participants expressed strong support for the NIST competencies we proposed and agreed that they should be taught. Additionally, they provided valuable feedback on other important competencies that should be included in cybersecurity education. Among the suggestions were the Privacy Framework, end-user awareness training, and change management, both of which were highlighted as critical areas for improvement.

The survey also assessed the perceived importance of specific cybersecurity domains, with participants providing the following average scores on a 5-point scale.

Overall, respondents found the survey to be quick and easy to complete. Their feedback not only reinforced the significance of the competencies but also provided valuable insights into additional areas that could enhance cybersecurity education.

5 Conclusion and Future Work

The findings from this paper underscore the importance of competency-based education (CBE) in cybersecurity and reaffirm the necessity of aligning curricula with industry needs. By focusing on three critical areas—Risk Management, Encryption, and Communications Security Management—this initiative ensures that students develop the practical skills required to thrive in cybersecurity roles.

The survey results demonstrate strong industry and academic support for these competencies, with participants highlighting the relevance of NIST-aligned competencies and advocating for the inclusion of additional areas such as the Privacy Framework and end-user awareness training. The consistently high ratings for all three domains further validate their significance in cybersecurity education.

Moreover, the feedback gathered highlights the value of a hands-on, performance-based approach to learning. Traditional knowledge-based assessments often fall short in preparing students for real-world cybersecurity challenges, whereas competency-based learning fosters skill mastery through practical application. By integrating these competency statements into cybersecurity programs, educational institutions can better equip students with industry-relevant expertise, making them more competitive in the job market.

While this paper successfully developed competency statements and assessment strategies, its impact extends beyond curriculum development. It establishes a foundation for ongoing collaboration between academic institutions, industry professionals, and students, ensuring that cybersecurity education remains dynamic and responsive to evolving threats and workforce demands. The paper has several limitations: it does not implement the developed competencies into existing courses, focuses only on three cybersecurity areas, and depends on active participation from industry and students, which may be difficult to achieve. It may also face delays due to IRB approval requirements, and the fast-changing cybersecurity landscape will require continual updates to keep the competencies relevant.

Future work could involve piloting these competencies in actual coursework, integrating them into cybersecurity certifications, and expanding research to explore additional competencies that may emerge as cybersecurity threats continue to evolve. Additionally, fostering stronger academic-industry partnerships will be crucial in refining these competencies and creating adaptive, real-world learning experiences for students.

Ultimately, this paper contributes to bridging the cybersecurity skills gap by fostering a competency-driven, hands-on learning model that aligns with both employer expectations and the ever-changing landscape of cybersecurity. Through continuous feedback, refinement, and collaboration, this initiative will serve as a stepping stone toward a more resilient and well-prepared cybersecurity workforce.

Despite its strengths, the paper has several limitations. It does not include the actual implementation of the developed competencies into the university's existing courses, which may delay the immediate impact on student learning outcomes. The paper is also limited to three core areas within cybersecurity, potentially excluding other important domains. The effectiveness of the paper relies on active participation from industry professionals and students, which could be a challenge to secure at scale. Lastly, due to the rapidly evolving nature of cybersecurity threats and technologies, ongoing updates and refinements will be necessary to maintain the long-term relevance of the developed competencies.

References

Mammi, H., Ithnin, N.: Competency-based education (CBE) for IT security: towards bridging the gap. In: Proceedings of IEEE International Conference on Teaching, Assessment, and Learning for Engineering (TALE), pp. 20–23, Hong Kong, China (2012)

Ewell, P.: The Lumina Degree Qualifications Profile: implications for assessment. National Institute for Learning Outcomes Assessment (2013)

Watkins, A., Tobey, B., David, H., O'Brien, C.: Applying competency-based learning methodologies to cybersecurity education and training: creating a job-ready cybersecurity workforce. Infragard J. **5**(1), 1–14 (2018)

Dragoo, A., Barrows, R.: Implementing competency-based education: challenges, strategies, and a decision-making framework. J. Contin. High. Educ. **64**(2), 73–83 (2016). https://doi.org/10.1080/07377363.2016.1172193

National Institute of Standards and Technology (NIST).: Framework for improving critical infrastructure cybersecurity (Version 1.1), 2017,. https://nvlpubs.nist.gov/nistpubs/CSWP/NIST.CSWP.04162018.pdf

National Initiative for Cybersecurity Education (NICE).: Workforce Framework for Cybersecurity (NIST SP 800–181 Rev. 1), 2020, https://doi.org/10.6028/NIST.SP.800-181r1

Voorhees, A.: Creating and implementing competency-based learning models. New Dir. Inst. Res. **110**, 83–95 (2001). https://doi.org/10.1002/ir.13

Braun, V., Clarke, V.: Using thematic analysis in psychology. Qual. Res. Psychol. **3**(2), 77–101 (2006). https://doi.org/10.1191/1478088706qp063oa

Creswell, J., Creswell, J.: Research Design: Qualitative, Quantitative, and Mixed Methods Approaches, 5th edn. SAGE Publications (2018)

Dillman, D., Smyth, D., Christian, L.: Internet, Phone, Mail, and Mixed-Mode Surveys: the Tailored Design Method, 4th edn. Wiley (2014)

Etikan, I., Musa, S., Alkassim, R.: Comparison of convenience sampling and purposive sampling. Am. J. Theor. Appl. Stat. **5**(1), 1–4 (2016). https://doi.org/10.11648/j.ajtas.20160501.11

Fan, W., Yan, Z.: Factors affecting response rates of the web survey: a systematic review. Comput. Hum. Behav. **26**(2), 132–139 (2010). https://doi.org/10.1016/j.chb.2009.10.015

Fink, A.: How to conduct surveys: a step-by-step guide, 5th edn. SAGE Publications (2013) 2013

Presser, S., Couper, M., Lessler, J., et al.: Methods for testing and evaluating survey questions. Public Opin. Q. **68**(1), 109–130 (2024). https://doi.org/10.1093/poq/nfh008

Singer, E., Couper, M.: Some methodological uses of responses to open questions and other verbatim comments in quantitative surveys. Methods Data Analyses. **11**(2), 115–134 (2017). https://doi.org/10.12758/mda.2017.01

Van den Broeck, J., Cunningham, S., Eeckels, R., Herbst, K.: Data cleaning: detecting diagnosing, and editing data abnormalities. PLOS Medicine. **2**(10), e267 (2005). https://doi.org/10.1371/journal.pmed.0020267

Wright, K.: Researching internet-based populations: advantages and disadvantages of online survey research, online questionnaire authoring software packages, and web survey services. J. Comput. Med. Commun. **10**(3), JCMC1034 (2005). https://doi.org/10.1111/j.1083-6101.2005.tb00259.x

Composing Cyberattacks: Sequential Composition with Communication

Ke'Asia Fearn and Katia Maxwell(✉)

Athens State University, Athens, AL, USA
katia.maxwell@athens.edu

Abstract. The rapid development of technology has established cybersecurity as a fundamental field for research and development. The use of modeling and simulation tools including Petri Nets and their extension Petri Nets with Player, Strategies, and Costs (PNPSC) are used to analyze different cyberattack scenarios. While it is easy to focus on a single cyberattack and analyze its impact on a system and organization, in today's day and age an extensive system attack which focuses on more than a single cyberattack can be debilitating to an organization. PNPSC models have been studied to be composed together in the means of parallel compositions and sequential composition to represent a more comprehensive system attack that goes beyond a single cyberattack. This study expands on the sequential composition method. The theoretical structure of the method is discussed along with a proof of concept based on a practical walkthrough exercise.

Keywords: Cyberattacks · Model Composition · Petri Nets · PNPSC models · SQL Injection · Cross-Site Scripting

1 Introduction

The rising deployment of networked systems with digital infrastructure makes cybersecurity an essential research and development field. Modern cyberattacks continue to become more complex while occurring with greater regularity which creates substantial threats to users, commercial and public entities, and governmental institutions. The current systems require strong security measures which detect and block attacks to protect both the system's integrity and resilience. Security in cyberspace relies heavily on modeling and simulation methods that enable professionals to study attack behaviors and test defensive approaches to create resilient security systems.

Petri Nets is one technique that is used to model cyberattacks due to its mathematical modeling language which enables effective description and analysis of dynamic systems. Cybersecurity domains support Petri Nets because attack situations within this field consist of multiple interconnected real-time processes. The modeling approach using Petri Nets allows experts to create systematic models of cyberattack vectors which enables simulation of propagation and system vulnerability detection.

An extension of Petri Nets that enables dynamic modeling of cyberattacks to monitor system status while executing defensive strategies automatically is Petri Nets with

K. Daimi et al. (Eds.): CSCE 2025, CCIS 2937, pp. 24–36, 2026.
https://doi.org/10.1007/978-3-032-22208-4_3

Players, Strategies and Cost (PNPSC) [13]. The models can be analyzed to determine crucial information for protecting complex interconnected networks including critical infrastructure, software systems, cloud systems, and Internet of Things (IoT) to name a few.

This research focuses on cyberattack modeling by demonstrating a complete framework to represent different attack paths and equivalent attack tactics which enable attackers to move between attacks. The methodology expands a pre-defined composition method, sequential composition, introduced by Mayfield et al. [12]. The expansion unifies two independent attacks into one framework with community between the two models to improve the understanding of how techniques to perform attacks can lead to multiple outcomes. This study contains and evaluation of existing research about cyberattack modeling alongside Petri Nets and PNPSC models. In addition to the evaluation, the structure to expand the composition method is discussed. A proof of concept through a case study analysis provides information on the effectiveness of the composition method to help cybersecurity professionals improve their research and development of secure systems.

2 Background

There are many different methods that can be used for the purpose of modeling and simlulation. When it comes to modeling cyberattacks, there are several studies that have been done through the use of Petri Nets and extensions on Petri Nets that have been defined to be able to better design models based on the scope of the research. It has also been evident through research and documentation that some of the most vulnerable systems are those that are associated to the web, where everyone with an Internet connection can have access to it, if it is front facing. Documentation created by the Open Worldwide Application Security Project (OWASP), and the Common Attack Pattern Enumeration and Classification created by MITRE Corporation, are foundational sources that provide details on cyberattacks [4].

2.1 Petri Nets

Petri Nets are not a new concept, it has actually been around since the early 1960s when it was first designed to represent and assess systems characterized by collaboration, coordination, and resource sharing [1]. Petri Nets, with its mathematical underpinning and visual depiction, shown in Fig 1, have demonstrated their utility in understanding the dynamics of complex developing systems. Petri Nets have been adapted for use in representing various applications, such as weather forecasting, network diagrams and cyberattacks. In the realm of cybersecurity, Petri Nets offer a robust framework for depicting and assessing events related to attack scenarios.

Hamadi and Benatallah demonstrated Petri Nets as a tool for modeling and analyzing online service composition [2]. The visual and formal features provided by Petri Net models allow for the analysis of systematic service operation, interaction and dependency within the model [2]. The results of their research established multiple formalisms for composing separate Petri Nets into a single model. Their work, became a foundation

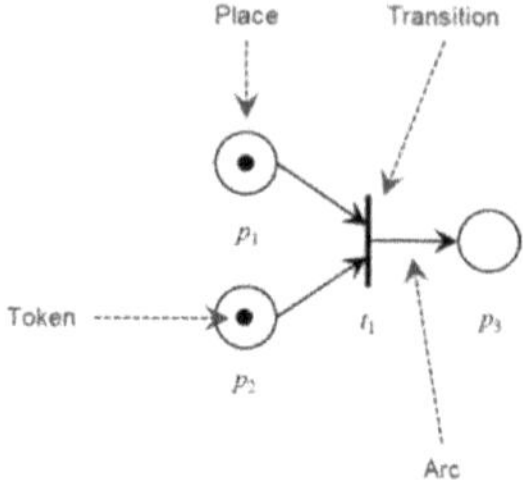

Fig 1. A simple Petri net - Basic components [21]

for the work conducted by Mayfield et al., which in return became a foundation for this study [20, 23]. The methods for composing models together with methods for evaluating system behavior across different conditions created a framework to examine collective outcome of the models. This framework was later adopted by Mayfield et al. with the composition of cyberattack models, and will be further expanded in this study [23].

2.1.1 PNPSC

An extension of Petri Nets was proposed by Zakrewska and Ferragut that was specific to the modeling of cyberattacks [20]. Their work described a model that extended a Petri Net with Players, to also include Strategies (PNPS). Their main focus on the extension was based on three ideas that support cyberattacks. The first is that players represent either an attacker or a defender and the associated actions that the player would take. Second is that each player has a goal, and within the Petri Net, that goal is attained when a token is found within the place in the model which represents that goal state. Third, is the idea that there are places that are observed and play a role in the decision that the attacker or defender will make in association to their strategy.

Petty et al. further extended on Zakrewska's and Ferragut's research by adding the of cost to a PNPS, therefore creation Petri Nets with Players, Strategies, and Cost (PNPSC). The cost that was proposed is based on a calculation of the cost of the attack on an organization. While these components are utilized for simulation purposes, this study focuses on the modeling of the cyberattacks and expands on the method of sequential composition of PNPSC modes, defined by Mayfield et al. [23].

2.2 Web Application Security

OWASP is a non-profit organization that is dedicated to improving the security of software [17]. They are well known for their Top 10 list, which highlights the most critical security risk to web applications. As part of that top 10 list, Cross Site Scripting (XSS) and SQL Injection are part of #3. XSS attacks inject malicious scripts into web pages through input validation vulnerabilities which allow attackers to steal personal information and take control of user sessions. SQL Injection attacks use harmful inputs to manipulate database queries which enable attackers to access and modify or delete vital data.

The analysis by Adhyaru's examines multiple attack methods which target online applications through SQL Injection and XSS and Cross-Site Request Forgery (CSRF) and session hijacking [5]. The research demonstrates how cyberattacks become more complex while showing the difficulties of protecting modern interconnected systems. The research by Ludinard et al. identifies and develops countermeasures against web application attacks that compromise data integrity and confidentiality and availability [6]. The authors introduce a detection approach which merges real-time system monitoring with precise behavioral specifications to detect security threats. Their detection approach relies on anomaly identification through the evaluation of system and data interaction discrepancies which reveal vulnerabilities such as SQL Injection and XSS. The research demonstrates the necessity of resolving data-centric vulnerabilities to defend web applications from modern cyber threats.

With XSS and SQL Injection being part of the OWASP Top 10 list for multiple years, it is important to be able to fully understand, analyze, and develop applications that are not susceptible to these types of attacks. Through the use of emulators and simulations, analysis are capable of recreating attack behaviors and system interactions. By doing so, XSS and SQL Injection attacks become easier to understand, however when an analyst begins to consider a larger and more complex sequence of actions taken as part of a system attack it can become more challenging to fully understand all the intricacies involved. Through the use of creation models with PNPSC nets, and composing those models together to represent these more complex attacks, an analyst will have a basis for additional research to determine how to better protect their system against a more comprehensive cyberattack.

2.3 Modeling

Through modeling and simulation capabilities organizations can duplicate cyberattacks by using systematic methods to study attacker behaviors and their targeted system vulnerabilities. Modeling enables researchers to study complex system interactions through controlled abstraction which produces simplified representations of systems and attack scenarios and processes. Cyberattack models show the fundamental elements of an attack which include entry points, propagation routes, and system responses. These models enable researchers to evaluate both offensive and defensive cybersecurity aspects through analytical methods.

The research by Erden et al. presents a detailed evaluation of functional modeling approaches used in engineering and system design [7]. The research evaluates multiple system modeling approaches through graphical and mathematical methods to demonstrate their ability to show system component relationships and behavioral connections and planned outcomes. The authors study function modeling usage through product design, system engineering, and process optimization domains. The authors stress that function modeling enhances design process clarity and communication and innovation capabilities. This research demonstrates PNPSC models for complete cyberattacks through graphical representations of attack process interactions and transitions based on the evaluated approaches. The attack model composition method supports the integration of multiple functionalities into a unified framework.

2.4 Composition

The structure of cyberattack models enables the analysis of security mechanisms interactions and their defense enhancement capabilities as well as attacker methods to combine multiple exploits for system compromise. A properly designed security framework includes preventive measures which decrease system vulnerabilities while improving resistance capabilities. The process of choosing and combining cyberattack models to create a composite attack model for target systems based on specified characteristics is known as composition [8]. To fully understand the process of composing two or more PNPSC models to represent a system attack, it is important to understand the methods that have been developed to allow for this composition to occur.

Petty et al. studied the implementation of extended Petri nets for both modeling and evaluating cyberattacks [11]. The authors describe a method which combines multiple research initiatives to improve reinforcement learning-based approaches for attacking or defending computer systems. The research extends basic Petri nets through additional features which allow for complex modeling of attack sequences and system vulnerabilities and defensive tactics. The research supports the development of formalized cyberattack models which are simulated to analyze different attack methods and their consequences. While reinforcement learning is the end goal of the research initiative, an intermediary phase was that of the composition of PNPSC models. Mayfield et al. defined two methods of composition that can be applied to PNPSC models, those were sequential composition and parallel composition [23].

One of the important aspects of composing models together is that the selection and composition process is a problem that is considered to be NP-complete problem. However, this can be addressed when heuristics are put into place and there are defined characteristics that are taken into consideration. Maxwell documented a set of heuristics rules that can be used to select different cyberattack models [8]. By following these heuristics to narrow down the number of models to work with, composition can then be done between the PNPSC models either sequentially or in parallel. Sequential composition can be summarized as a simulation running through one model, and when it reaches the end of the first model it automatically continues to the second model, following the same process for as many models as were composed together by adding an arc to the PNPSC model from one to the next. The parallel composition has additional heuristic requirements because portions of the attack flow are required to be identical. This allows for the models to be composed together in parallel where one or more attack is taking place, but the execution requirement that is identical between the two is only performed once and the result is used to continue the simulation of both models at the same time.

The proposed composition for this study expands on the previously defined sequential composition but also takes into consideration aspects of parallel composition with the fact that part of the execution flow must be identical between attacks that are being composed into a system attack model.

3 Sequential Composition with Communication

Research shows that cyberattacks can be carried out simultaneously by multiple attackers or sequentially if the first attack does not succeed which allows the attacker to launch a second attempt [8]. This research expands the sequential attack concept by adding communication functionality between the first and second attacks. When analyzing CAPEC, as part of the execution flow, techniques that are used are documented [4]. The heuristic that is established for this composition is based on the models that are being composed together having an identical attack technique within the same phase of the execution flow. The hypothesis is that the attacker can start one attack before using the common technique to pivot into attempting the second attack before finishing the first attack. Mayfield et al. present the formal mathematical definition of a PNPSC net in their work [12]. The formal definition of a PNPSC net is taken into consideration in the construction method of a sequential composition with communication model. The following is an explanation of how the construction of the composed model takes place.

Sequential Composition with Communication Construction Method:

1. Extract Components: Retrieve the sets of places, transitions, arcs, entry states, and exit states from both input Petri Nets.
2. Create a Communication Place (p_c): This place will act as the handoff point between N_1 and N_2.
3. Create a Communication Transition (t_c): This transition will control whether the process moves from N_1 to N_2.
4. Modify $PNPSC_1$: Redirect the final common technique transitions of N_1 to transition into added communication place p_c.
5. Modify $PNPSC_2$: Introduce a new transition (t_c) from pc to the place of N_2 that begins the next phase of the execution flow.
6. Combine the Elements: Merge the updated places, transitions, and arcs into a single Petri Net [13].

Due to the fact that PNPSC models can be very large, Figs. 2 and 3 illustrate a generalized design of the Explore phase of the Execution flow of two PNPCS nets. The Execution flow of cyberattacks as documented by CAPEC can have up to three phases, Explore, Experiment, and Exploit. In Figs. 2 and 3, the nodes of the PNPSC model highlighted in bold represent the techniques that are common to both attacks during the same phase of the execution flow.

As described in the construction method, to compose the two models together an extra state to enable the transition from one attack technique conclusion to the corresponding place in the second attack is required. This will place a token in the model where it can progress onto the next phase of the execution flow, known as the Experiment phase of the second attack. This means that the attacker can start the second attack without having finished the full execution of the attack that they first started with. When modeling PNPSC nets, transitions lead to states, and a question that may arise from this construction method is "why does the transition at the end of the first attack not go directly to the state at the beginning of the next phase in the second attack?" While this research does not focus on the simulation for the model, the model must be designed with the expectation that the simulation will be executed. Therefore, the inclusion of the

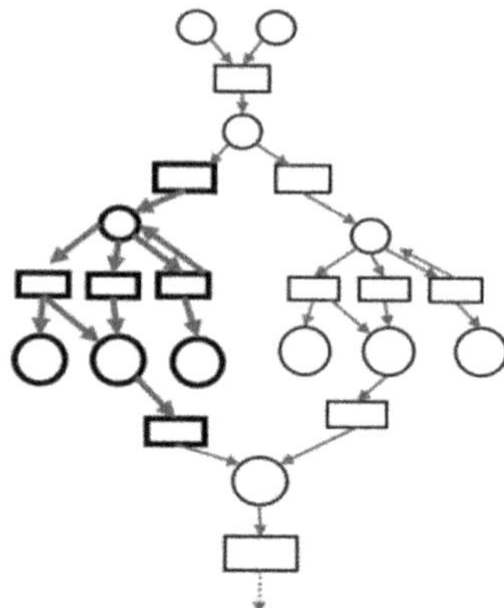

Fig. 2. Diagram of $PNPSC_1$ Explore Phase [13]

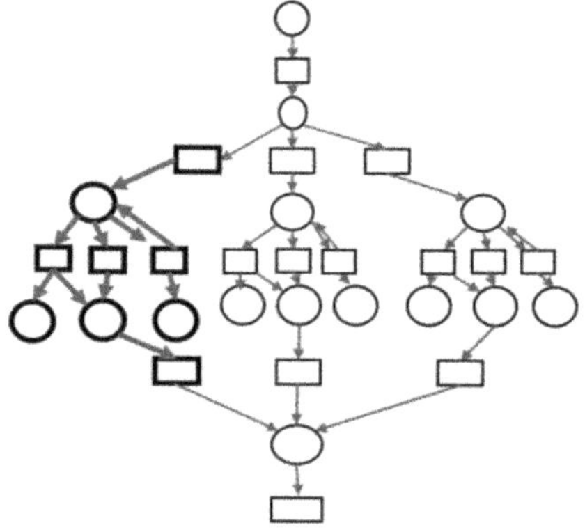

Fig. 3. Diagram of $PNPSC_2$ Explore phase [13]

displayed state and transition allow for expanded data tracking and analysis. The new state allows the person executing the simulation to see the "choice" made by an attacker to "pivot" to a different attack instead of sticking with the first one. This is done by being able to track how many times the token traverses the model through the added place and transition. Figure 4 shows the visual representation using the two partial models shown in Figs. 2 and 3.

An example scenario of this type of composition can occur if there is an attacker that is looking to conduct a system attack by performing SQL injection and XSS attacks. Both of these attacks have an Explore phase technique of using a spidering tool to find vulnerabilities in the system. Based on the construction method and the visual representation given in Fig. 4, one can assume that the attacker begins a SQL Injection attack, and after conducting the spidering technique and obtaining results chooses to no longer perform a SQL Injection attack but instead a XSS attack. While theoretically and visually represented, a basic simulation through a walkthrough process is required to make sure that the theory is also applicable.

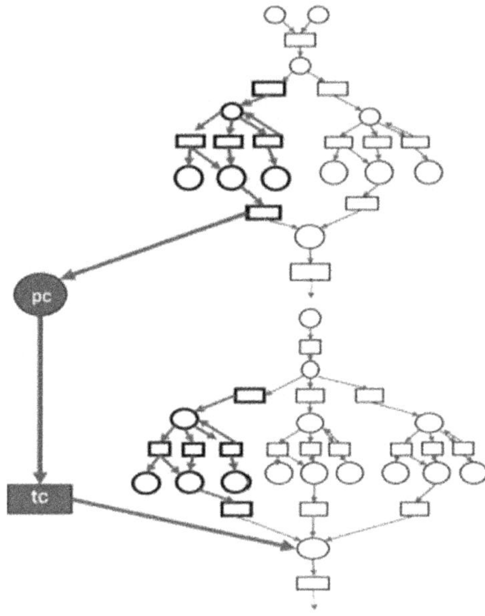

Fig. 4. Combination of $PNPSC_1$ and $PNPSC_2$ [13]

4 Walkthrough and Results

The walkthrough was performed in accordance with the process defined in the theoretical model to demonstrate the proof of concept from a practical point of view. The first thing was to identify a software platform that would enable the performance of the cyberattacks. In addition to choosing the testing platform, it was important to confirm that the chosen platform would allow for the execution of both SQL Injection and XSS attacks and that crawling of the system could be done through Spidering The identified platform was Metasploit and the vulnerable target was Metasploitable2. A Kali Linux virtual machine was set up in VMware Workstation [14]. Mutillidae, a vulnerable web application, within the Metasploitable2 framework, has vulnerabilities identified in the OWASP Top Ten, specifically the login.php page, which is listed in the Mutillidae support materials as being susceptible to SQL Injection and XSS attacks [15, 16].

After setting up the virtual environment and installing the necessary software, the first thing to do was to ensure that both Metasploitable 2 and the Mutillidae directory were accessible and had the login.php page necessary for the walkthrough. After verifying that the file existed on Metasploitable2, the next step was to confirm that the file could be accessed from Kali Linux.

After verifying the presence of the files, the next step was to run the application using Linux, Apache, MySQL, PHP (LAMP) to ensure that the testing environment for the walkthrough was fully set up [22]. The command "sudo opt/lamp/lamp start" started the Apache and MySQL servers on the LAMP stack for localhost access. Once LAMP was up and running, the environment was set up to look like a real system that an attacker would target. After the installation was done, the next thing to do was to go through the walkthrough from the perspective of the attacker. Upon opening Firefox on Kali Linux and getting to the Mutillidae web page, login.php, the next action was to crawl the system. Spidering was done using the OWASP ZAP tool which was installed on the virtual system [17]. OWASP ZAP is a tool that uses a systematic way of identifying URLs within a web application that is being scanned by crawling through the different browsing paths. The attacker has to select the target URL, modify parameters and then start the scan to start spidering using the OWASP ZAP tool.

Figure 5 shows OWASP ZAP in a running state. The left panel displays the Sites Tree, which provides a logical structure of the web application URLs and resources that are scanned and allows the user to control the scans and view the identified vulnerabilities. The right pane allows the user to set specific parameters associated to the attack, while the bottom section shows the ongoing scanning of the machine.

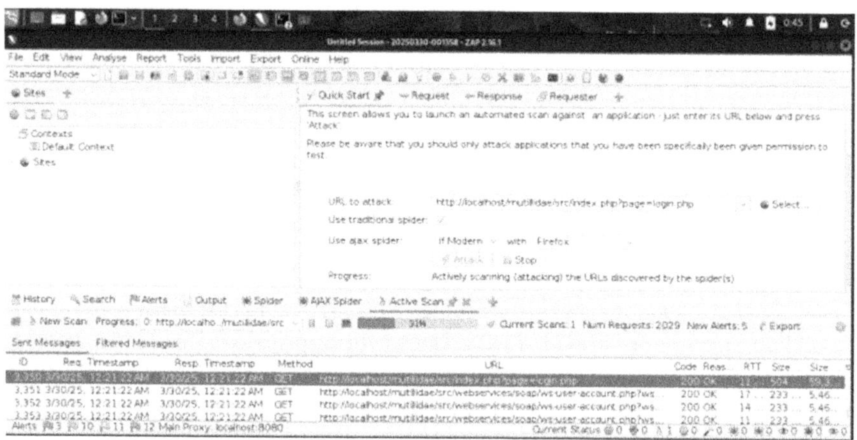

Fig. 5. OWASP ZAP- Spidering

Once the scan is completed and the vulnerable URLs are identified at the bottom of the OWASP ZAP tool the attacker can choose which URL to work with. The first attack considered in this walkthrough is SQL Injection. The login.php page operates on localhost. Figure 6 shows the initial attempt of a SQL injection attack. The SQL Injection payload ' OR 1=1 --, is a common attack used to avoid authen-tication on a login page by exploiting vulnerabilities in SQL queries that are not properly secured. The query "SELECT * FROM users WHERE username = " OR 1=1 #' AND password = ";", could allow unauthorized access, due to 1=1 always evaluat-ing to true. The '--' comment stops password verification by disregarding the remaining words of the query. This in turn, highlights the potential vulnerability of this web application to SQL Injection attacks [18].

Figure 7 shows that utilizing the SQL query described within the Username granted access to the attacker as an Admin, shown by the arrows in the figure. As a result the attacker is now able to perform tasks on the system that only those with administrative privileges are given permissions to perform.

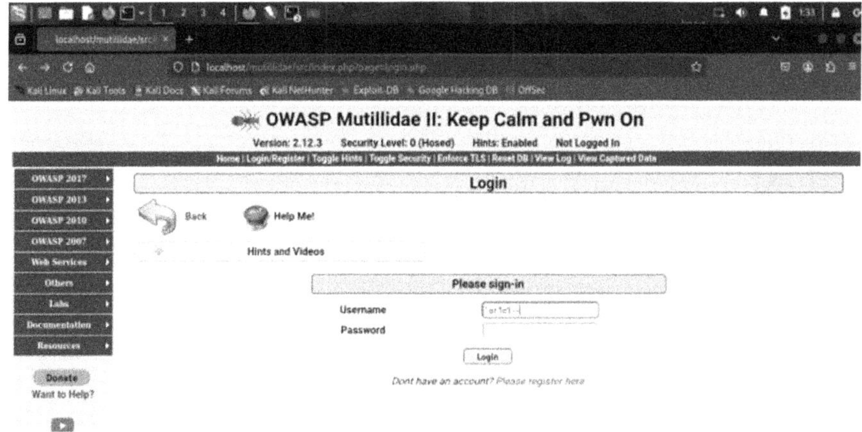

Fig. 6. login.php Mutillidae page

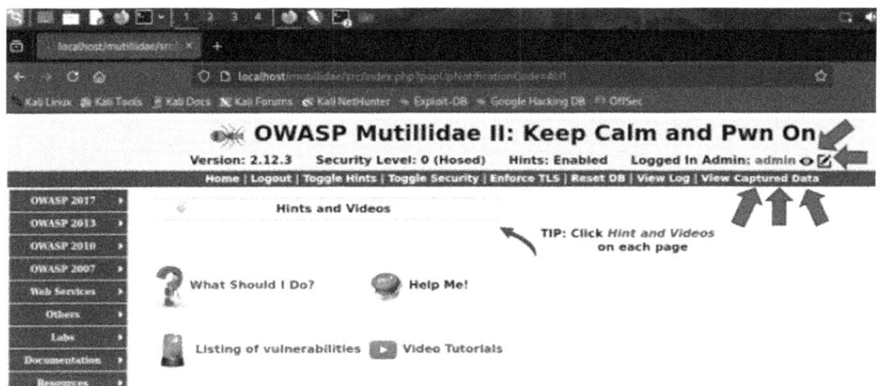

Fig. 7. Logged in as Admin on Mutillidae

The result of spidering also serves as the basis for a XSS attack during this proof-of-concept walkthrough. The login.php page from the SQL Injection attack also serves as the basis for the attempt to inject malicious scripts through XSS as shown in Fig. 8. The payload entered into the Username field contained "' or 1=1 ; <script>alert("XSS Attack")</script?" [19].

The attacker performed a successful XSS attack after clicking Login as shown in Fig. 9. A warning message showing "XSS Attack" confirms that the script is executed when the user enters Login without having provided a password. The attack demonstrates a security flaw in the login interface functionality.

From the walkthrough provided, it can be seen that the spidering technique produces multiple attack possibilities\. The practical application of theoretical concepts presented in this research becomes evident through this guide. An attacker starts with one attack before using a technique which allows them to deviate from the initial attack. The results obtained enable attackers to execute different attacks that use the same method within the

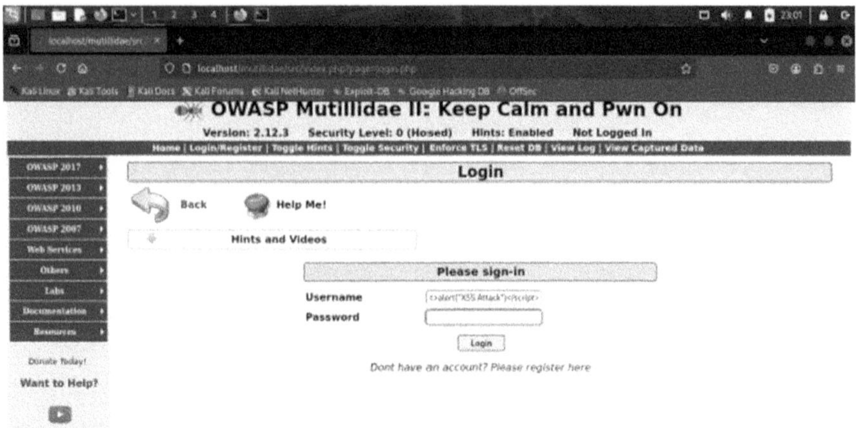

Fig. 8. XSS script input on login.php

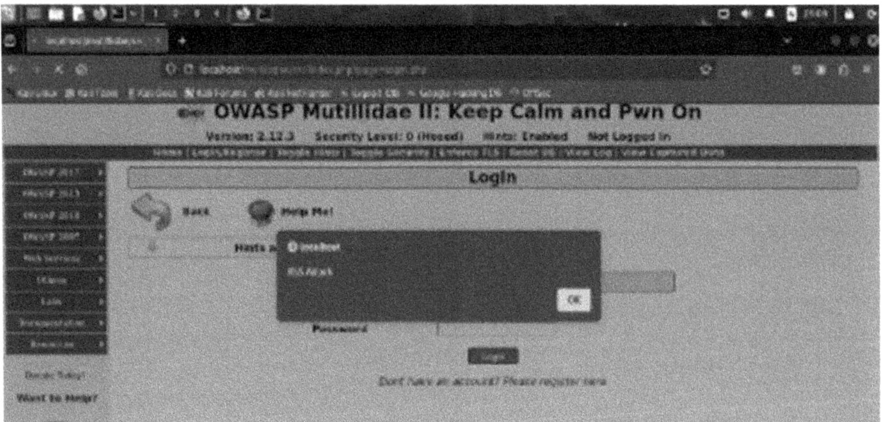

Fig. 9. Successful XSS attack at the Login page

same execution flow phase. Sequential composition with communication functions as an attack modeling approach to analyze attackers who modify their initial attack strategy during an ongoing attempt.

5 Conclusion and Future Works

This research contributes to a wider project on the composition of cyberattacks through the establishment of a new composition method and practical evaluation of the process by following the process established by the model. The research demonstrates how attackers can begin a system attack by performing a SQL Injection attack before making the decision to pivot to a XSS attack by using the results of an attack technique that was performed. This research documents a multi-step attack sequence through the development of the sequential composition with communication modeling approach. The construction method of the composition and the walkthrough demonstrate the need for proactive security measures to reduce both individual and collective cybersecurity risks.

The results of a widespread strategy allow attackers to pivot between attacks, therefore emphasizing the need for additional research to evaluate alternative attack methods. Attackers could utilize compromised systems to form a botnet as part of their attack tactics. The analysis of distributed attacks becomes essential because attackers can use one technique's results to launch another attack.

References

1. Giua, A., Silva, M.: Petri nets and automatic control: a historical perspective. Annu. Rev. Control. **45**, 223–239 (2018)
2. Hamadi, R., Benatallah, B.: A petri net-based model for web service composition. Australasian Database Conf, 191–200 (2003)
3. Bearss, E.M., Petty, M.: A deep reinforcement learning technique for PNPSC net player strategies. In: Proceedings of the 2023 ACM Southeast Conference 2023, pp. 96–103
4. MITRE.: Common Attack Pattern Enumeration and Classification (CAPEC). 2022. https://capec.mitre.org/
5. Adhyaru, R.P.: Techniques for attacking web application security. Int. J. Informat. Sci. Tech. **6**(1/2), 45–52 (2016)
6. Ludinard, R., et al.: Detecting attacks against data in web applications. In: 2012 7th International Conference on Risks and Security of Internet and Systems (CRiSIS). IEEE (2012)
7. Erden, M.S., et al.: A review of function modeling: approaches and applications. Ai Edam. **22**(2), 147–169 (2008)
8. Maxwell, K.P.: Selecting and Composing Cyberattack Component Models. The University of Alabama in Huntsville (2022) https://louis.uah.edu/uah-dissertations/246
9. Xiong, P., Fan, Y., Zhou, M.: A petri net approach to analysis and composition of web services. IEEE Trans. Syst. Man Cybern. Part A Syst. Humans. **40**(2), 376–387 (2010)
10. Cantrell, W.A., Maxwell, K.P., Petty, M.D., Whitaker, T.S.: Matrix reduction verification of extended petri nets. In: Proceedings of the 2020 ACM Southeast Conference, pp. 296–299 (2020)
11. Petty, M.D., et al.: Modeling cyberattacks with extended petri nets. In: Proceedings of the 2022 ACM Southeast Conference, pp. 67–73 (2022)
12. Mayfield, K.P., Petty, M.D.: Petri nets with players, strategies, and cost: a formalism for modeling cyberattacks. In: Proceedings of the 17th International Conference on Security and Management (SAM), Las Vegas, NV (2018)
13. Fearn, K.S.: Modeling and simulation of cyber attacks focusing on the composition of models. ProQuest. (2025) https://www.proquest.com/docview/3194436860
14. VMware.: VMware workstation for windows. TechSpot. (2025). https://www.tech-spot.com/downloads/189-vmware-workstation-for-windows.html#google_vignette
15. Metasploitable 2 exploitability guide.: Metasploitable 2 Exploitability Guide | Metasploit Documentation. (n.d.). https://docs.rapid7.com/metasploit/metasploitable-2-exploitability-guide#mutillidae
16. Yakup Seker.: Mutillidea GET Method SQL Injection Login (Level:Low). (2020). YouTube. https://www.youtube.com/watch?v=g87_Ylj0Ibc

17. Download zap.: ZAP By Checkmarx. (n.d.). https://www.zaproxy.org/download/
18. Codingbolt: Injection vulnerability allowing login bypass. Medium SQL. (2024) https://medium.com/@codingbolt.in/sql-injection-vulnerability-allowing-login-by-pass-7f1de7d77a6a
19. PseudoTimeXSS Reflected Login Form Low Security Level.: YouTube (2022). https://www.youtube.com/watch?v=RuwGUEmq_bo
20. Zakrzewska, A.N., Ferragut, E.M.: Modeling cyber conflicts using an extended petri net formalism. In: 2011 IEEE Symposium on Computational Intelligence in Cyber Security (CICS), pp. 60–67. IEEE (2011)
21. Petty, M.D., Whitaker, T.S., Bland, J.A., Mayfield, K.P.: Modeling cyberattacks with petri nets: research program overview and status report. In: AlaSim International Conference, Huntsville, AL (2017)
22. Yang, K., Heidi, E.: How to install Linux, Apache, MySQL, PHP (LAMP) stack on ubuntu. DigitalOcean. (2024) https://www.digitalocean.com/community/tutori-als/how-to-install-lamp-stack-on-ubuntu
23. Mayfield, K.P., Petty, M.D., Whitaker, T.S., Bland, J.A.: Composition of cyberattack models. In: Proceedings of the 31st International Conference on Computer Applications in Industry and Engineering (CAINE), pp. 8–10. New Orleans, LA (2018)

AI-Driven Deepfakes: Exploring Exploitation Risks and Cybersecurity Responses

Brianna Geiger[1], Mei Li[1], Anjali Desai[1], Rui Zhu[2], and Huirong Fu[1](✉)

[1] Oakland University, Rochester 48309, MI, USA
{briannageiger,meili,ahdesai,fu}@oakland.edu
[2] Kettering University, Flint 448504, MI, USA
rzhu@kettering.edu

Abstract. Deepfakes, which are powered by artificial intelligence, have emerged as a formidable cybersecurity challenge with far-reaching implications. This paper provides a comprehensive analysis of deepfakes and their implications for cybersecurity, focusing on the evaluation of existing deepfake detection systems. The paper specifically examines how deepfakes pose significant security threats, including identity theft, fake news, and other cyberattacks. The security analysis is conducted on the attacks across various domains, such as politics, government, finance, entertainment and social media. Existing detection tools include machine learning, blockchain-based verification, digital watermarking, and evaluation for their effectiveness and limitations in combating deepfakes. Finally, the paper discusses potential improvements in detection methods, emphasizing the need for AI-based countermeasures, collaborative systems, public awareness, and regulatory measures to mitigate these risks.

Keywords: AI · Cybersecurity · Deepfake · Deepfake Detection · Machine Learning · Blockchain · Watermarking

1 Introduction

In recent years, the number of fake videos, news, and images are not only increasing but they are also getting more realistic than ever before due to deepfakes. Deepfakes are a form of AI-generated media that can change images, sounds, or videos to create highly realistic but fabricated content. Deepfakes have the potential to manipulate and threaten individuals, corporations and governments, raising significant concerns in the field of cybersecurity. Powered by Generative Adversarial Networks (GANs), deepfakes utilizes two neural networks: "generator" and "discriminator", which together make up a GAN architecture. The generator creates new, fake images that closely resemble real data, while the discriminator tries to distinguish between real data and the fake data generated by the generator. This iterative process enables the production of increasingly realistic outputs. Deepfakes also employ deep learning models like autoencoders and GANs to detect facial expression and features from an image or a video frame and replace that with a target person's face. Although this technology seems to affect information only online, it entails high risks to people, corporations, and other important entities.

K. Daimi et al. (Eds.): CSCE 2025, CCIS 2937, pp. 37–54, 2026.
https://doi.org/10.1007/978-3-032-22208-4_4

The major contributions of the work are three-fold:

- Analyzes how deepfakes can be exploited for cyberattacks, misinformation campaigns, and identity fraud.
- Assesses existing deepfake detection tools, including machine learning models, blockchain-based verification, and digital watermarking, and highlighting their limitations in combating deepfakes.
- Explores potential advancements to enhance deepfake security mechanisms.

The rest of this paper is organized as follows: Sect. 2 provides a background on deepfakes. Section 3 conducts security analysis and their implications. Section 4 evaluates existing deepfake detection systems. Section 5 discusses potential improvements for building secure systems to counter deepfake threats. Section 6 presents case studies, and Sect. 7 concludes the paper.

2 Background

The term "deepfake" was first coined in late 2017 by a Reddit user of the same name. This user created a space on the online news and aggregation site, where they shared pornographic videos that used open-source face-swapping technology [1]. The term has since broadened to include "synthetic media applications" that predate the Reddit page, as well as newer innovations such as StyleGAN, which generates highly realistic still images of fictional individuals, according to Henry Ajder, head of threat intelligence at the deepfake detection firm Deeptrace.

Since its inception, deepfakes have grown exponentially more sophisticated and applicable. Initially limited to micro-communities, it has become widely accessible due to the advances in AI, user-friendly tools, and open-source platforms. Deepfakes are now capable of swapping someone's face to a targeted person's face, mimicking voices, and even changing video content in real-time. Just like other technologies we have seen in the past, deepfakes have developed rapidly and have been adopted in various fields such as entertainment, marketing, and virtual reality. Nonetheless, its use in disinformation campaigns, identity theft, and impersonation attacks has placed the technology in the spotlight.

Deepfakes are currently one of concerns in cybersecurity as they are becoming more commonplace. Such synthetic media assets can avoid normal authentication mechanisms, take advantage of the weakness in the biometric identification process, and weaken the confidence of the people in the information they see online. Recent events have shown the increasing ability of deepfakes to become politically motivated, fraudulent, and provide tools for bullying. As technology continues to advance, it makes fake news harder to identify and therefore, deepfake detection and prevention are essential in enhancing cybersecurity.

Furthermore, the ethical implications of deepfakes need to be addressed as well. Beyond technical challenges, deepfakes pose significant social risks that necessitate multi-stakeholder response from technologists, policymakers, and industry representatives, including threats to privacy and the reliability of journalism and public information. It's vital to comprehend this technology's past and possible future to formulate the right approach to address its malicious application and to use the innovation appropriately.

3 Security Analysis of Deepfakes

3.1 Threat Landscape

The ever-increasing use of deepfakes in today's world poses a great threat to different domains in politics, finance, social media, and cybersecurity. In politics, deepfakes are part of the reason for the widespread disinformation about public leaders because they show people having supposedly said or endorsed something that they really have not. The goal of creating deepfakes like these is to diminish public trust in leaders, ultimately affecting their reputation and possibly election results.

In finance, deepfakes are used in a similar manner as they can create false statements from company representatives or financial analysts that undermine public trust. In one instance, a video of a CEO advertising a financial scheme was proven to have synthetic audio through the use of AI based detection tools [2]. Deepfakes may also be used as a social engineering tactic in scams that request your private information or bank account details to exploit you or even steal your money.

Deepfakes are used across the Internet to spread misinformation about people as a form of cyberbullying. Specifically, they can be used to create inappropriate or pornographic content of real people that can spread easily across social media when platforms such as Instagram are pushing AI content towards the user but are lacking in content moderation and cybersecurity measures [3].

In cybersecurity, deepfakes can be used in a variety of ways by attackers who want to impersonate or manipulate a victim into giving away information through social engineering attacks. Attackers may be able to create a deepfake that can trick biometric identification systems into falsely authenticating them or another unauthorized individual. Deepfakes often make cyberattacks much more effective and social engineering more convincing, so it is important that organizations take the proper steps to be able to detect deepfakes and take immediate action to minimize security risks (Table 1).

Table 1. Threats and Impacts

Threat Category	Brief Description	Impact
Political Manipulation	Deepfakes are used to spread misinformation about public leaders, fabricating statements or endorsements.	Undermines public trust, damages reputations, and influences election results.
Financial Fraud	Attackers use deepfakes to impersonate executives or financial analysts, leading to scams and fraudulent transactions.	Causes financial losses, erodes trust in digital transactions, and enables large-scale fraud.
Social Media & Cyberbullying	Deepfakes create false or inappropriate content, including non-consensual imagery, that spreads quickly online.	Leads to reputational damage, emotional distress, and privacy violations.

(*continued*)

Table 1. (*continued*)

Threat Category	Brief Description	Impact
Cybersecurity Threats	Attackers use deepfakes for social engineering, impersonating individuals to bypass security measures.	Enables unauthorized access to sensitive systems, making cyberattacks more effective.
Social Engineering Attacks	Realistic deepfakes are used in phishing, impersonation, and pretexting attacks.	Increases success rates of scams, leading to data breaches and financial losses.
Disinformation Campaigns	Deepfakes spread fake news and manipulated media to mislead the public.	Influences public perception, destabilizes societies, and threatens media integrity.
Biometric Authentication Exploits	Attackers use deepfakes to bypass facial and voice recognition security measures.	Compromises secure authentication systems, leading to identity fraud and unauthorized access.
Vulnerabilities in AI & Detection Systems	Lack of standardized verification tools and evolving deepfakes make detection difficult.	Increases the risk of undetected synthetic content, weakening cybersecurity defenses.

3.2 Social Engineering Attacks

Social engineering is a strategy used by attackers to manipulate and lure victims into giving away their personal information or other private data through phishing, impersonation, pretexting, or insider threats. The use of deepfakes enable attackers to have greater success in performing these attacks because deepfakes are more realistic and persuasive than they are [4]. Attackers will send phishing emails, phone calls, or messages to victims pretending to be a legitimate company or bank that needs your information urgently and can be targeted. Sharing this information with attackers is a breach of confidentiality and can lead to further attacks that could hurt the availability of systems and the integrity of data on them if the attacker uses this information to gain access to important systems.

In [5], a new hire for the company KnowBe4 turned out to be a North Korean spy who had malicious intentions to infiltrate the systems and steal sensitive data to sell to the DPRK government. He was able to successfully pass interviews and background checks using a false photo and a stolen identity. Once he was hired into this remote position, he was sent his work computer, but the computer was actually sent to an "IT laptop farm" located in the US. The employee used a VPN from North Korea to log on and immediately started downloading malware onto it. Luckily, the attacker was not able to do any real damage since he was caught quickly.

3.3 Disinformation Campaign

There is a substantial amount of deepfakes that have been spreading for quite some time and this can result in the mass spread of misinformation as we all know. There are many consequences that we will discuss that in this day and age can be very dangerous and detrimental to the integrity of the media industry and everyone alike. These can have a serious impact on democracy, the spread of deepfake porn, politically edited videos, and much more.

One instance of this occurred during the Slovakia elections in September of 2023. There was a fake audio clip of Michal Šimečka, who is the leader of the liberal Progressive Slovakia party, discussing possible electoral fraud with a prominent journalist. This was shared on social media by his opponents and eventually was denied and credited as fake. This clip was already viral on many platforms hence it was already too late to stop the damage that would be done. Even an audio clip that turns out to be a deepfake could have a severe consequence on the outcome of his election [6]. Though these can only be speculations as to why he did not perform well in the election compared to his components, the viral spread of this audio clip in such a short time truly is dangerous. Again, this can be one of the many factors given Slovakia's historical climate [7].

3.4 Financial Fraud

Financial fraud can also be an instance where deepfakes can spread information or contribute to promoting scams that can have adverse effects on consumers financially. Again, with the use of more advanced technology now, there are many more cases of these phishing scams that are available to the public. One such case occurred in Hong Kong, there was a finance worker who allegedly paid around $25 million to scammers who were posing as the chief financial advisor of the company. This was done using a form of deepfake via a video call. This adds to the situation of a reminder that employees must be more careful when discussing with others [8]. The Hong Kong police made six arrests for scams similar to this case. It is another implication of how easily deepfakes can be dangerous in the financial industry as this has occurred more than once but was a first to be heard of in Hong Kong [9]. Adding on, deepfakes can falsify contracts, testimonies, and in some cases surveillance footage. There can also be an undermining of trust like the worker who was prompted to trust the chief financial advisor who turned out to be a fraud. All of these are individual incidents that have occurred, however the already plethora of deepfake-enabled scams can erode confidence in digital transactions.

3.5 Vulnerabilities

Deepfakes also exploit critical vulnerabilities in current AI systems, media platforms, and authentication mechanisms. These can facilitate weaknesses such as the spread and acceptance of manipulated media. There is a lack of standardized verification tools that can detect synthetic content effectively. There is a strong dependence on biometrics such as voice or facial recognition that are used in banking or secure systems. Voice cloning can already be employed to exploit these authentication systems. According to [10], when it comes to machine learning methods, there is a 98% accuracy for these specific methods; however, a vulnerability or weakness could be that it was only for relying on datasets, selected features, and alignment between their train and test sets. The article states how using a similar dataset can also obtain higher results. However, an unrelated dataset would drop the performance to nearly 50%. The current GANs, which are the backbone of deepfake creation, are constantly evolving [10]. Machine learning models that train using public datasets are vulnerable to being exploited for better deepfakes. The models that use GANs may also become ineffective if they become vulnerable to adversarial attacks.

4 Evaluation of Existing Deepfake Detection Systems

4.1 Machine Learning Models

In [11], GAN was discussed to generate deepfake films by swapping two actors' faces. A type of deepfake face-swapping technology called an autoencoder is a neural network designed to compress data and then reconstruct it. It uses variational autoencoder (VAE) to handle variations like facial expressions. In face-swapping, the encoder-decoder architecture learns to map one face into another using shared encoding and dedicated decoders for reconstruction. Autoencoders alone are effective but not able to produce realistic or sharp images. GANs play a role because they consist of a generator which can create fake images, and a discriminator which can evaluate their realism to lighting, texture, and fine details. By starting with lower resolutions and gradually increasing depth over training, GANs may reach great degrees of realism [11]. GAN and VAE compete each other and improve the generator's output over time.

Another method to identify deepfake from facial expression is to use computer vision models and machine learning. It's particularly focusing on anomalies in eye blinking. The way it works is that the model would observe eye-blinking behavior to see if any suspicious or unrealistic patterns occur. Normally, AI-generated faces often lack realistic eye-blinking behavior because most training datasets used in deepfake generation do not include images of faces with closed eyes. The absence or unnatural frequency of eye blinking is a key indicator that a video may be synthetically generated rather than captured by a real camera. Several methods had been proposed to detect and analyze eye-blinking patterns. Pan et al., Sukno et al. Divjak et al. are the AI developers who developed frameworks to infer eye closeness during blinking, and highlighting deviations from natural blinking behavior, measuring vertical distance between eye contours using Active Shape Models, providing a basic to evaluate eye motion patterns. Using optical flow to detect and track dominant vertical eye movements across videos which helps identify unnatural or absent blinking. Soukupova et al. introduced a scalar value calculated from facial landmarks to describe the eye's state. This method aims to observe from each part of the face areas like lips, nose, jaw, right and left eyebrows and right and left eye to predict unusual behaviors.

Among the above methods, the research team identifies the Ear Method – Eye Aspect Ratio-Support Vector Machines (EAR-SVM) approach as the most effective. This method can identify synthetic faces that fail to replicate this natural behavior. When integrated with temporal analysis and other facial detection techniques, the EAR-SVM method becomes a powerful tool for spotting deepfakes, providing a robust mechanism for analyzing eye movements and ensuring video authenticity. The eye locations are identified for frames. Using the dlib library, we can extract 68 facial landmarks on a face. Of those, 12 points are used to localize the left and the right eye. The EAR value is mainly calculated based on the coordinates of these 12 eye points, between the eye's height and breadth [11]. The EAR value remains constant when the eye is open and approaches zero when the eye is closed. What is common in synthetic videos is unnatural blinking patterns or absence of blinks.

Unlike GAN, VAE, and GAN + VAE hybrid, which are typically used to create or analyze facial imagery, EAR-SVM focuses on identifying abnormal eye-blinking patterns using Eye Aspect Ratio (EAR) and classifying them through a Support Vector Machine (SVM). The strength of this method lies in its ability to effectively capture temporal emotion patterns and provide accurate classification, even when deepfakes attempt to replicate subtle facial dynamics. EAR-SVM achieved the highest accuracy of 0.98, outperforming the EAR method at 0.93 and LRCN model at 0.70 [11]. It may struggle with real-time processing due to computational overhead and requires careful feature selection to avoid overfitting during training. Nevertheless, in controlled testing environments, EAR-SVM consistently outperformed other models by reliably detecting both excessive and missing blink events, making it a robust tool for deepfake forensics [11] (Table 2).

Table 2. Deepfake Detection with GAN and VAE Models

Model	Components	Strengths	Limitations
Autoencoder	Encoder-Decoder architecture	Compresses and reconstructs faces effectively.	Cannot produce highly realistic or sharp images.
Variational Autoencoder (VAE)	Encoder-Decoder with probabilistic encoding	Better at handling facial variations.	Less realistic compared to GAN-based approaches.
Generative Adversarial Networks (GAN)	Generator and Discriminator	Generates realistic images through adversarial training.	Requires intensive training and large datasets.
GAN + VAE Hybrid	Both generator (GAN) and encoder-decoder (VAE)	Combines strengths of both models, improving realism and handling variations.	Complex and computationally intensive.
EAR-SVM	EAR with temporal windowing and SVM with	Effectively captures temporal emotion patterns and provides accurate classification using SVM.	May struggle with real-time processing and requires careful feature selection to avoid overfitting.

4.2 Blockchain Verification

Blockchain verification can employ a variety of techniques and methods to ensure secure and efficient data management. Public blockchain offers a robust framework that is done by enabling decentralized verification and record-keeping media authenticity. By leveraging blockchain's cryptographic features, stakeholders can ensure media files are validated against trusted sources thus, promoting accountability and reducing the spread of manipulated content. The blockchain method not only enhances the trust of digital ecosystems but empowers users with secure tools to combat deepfakes.

To add on, [10] discusses how blockchain is one of the most appropriate tools to combat deepfakes. There is an approach that is proposed that they discuss, "Hasan and Salah proposed a blockchain-based generic framework to track suspected video's origin to their sources. The proposed solution can trace its transaction records, even though the material is copied several times." The main contributions quoted in the article are: "presents a generic framework based on blockchain technology by setting up a proof of digital content's authenticity to its trusted source, presents the proposed solution's architecture and design details to control and administrate the interactions and transactions among participants, integrates the critical features of IPFS decentralized storage ability to blockchain-based Ethereum Name service." Again, this emphasizes the main point of utilizing public blockchain as its validity shows promising results when it comes to a more detailed system. A main point that was proposed in the article by the authors was utilizing Hasan and Salah's approach was the features like IPFS that work to provide the necessary framework to approach decentralization of storage which is pivotal to how blockchain works [10]. The article also suggests another approach from another literature, "Chan et al. proposed a decentralized approach based on blockchain to trace and track digital content's historical provenance (i.e., image, videos, etc.)." In LSTM Convolutional Neural Network (CNN) models, the contents are hash encoded and the high dimensional features are coded in a binary structure. This is then stored in a permission-based blockchain in which only the owner has rights [10].

Both approaches cover how well blockchain can offer secure storage which in the case of deepfake detection is ideal. Both approaches offer a transparent history of transactions and allow for simple verification. Another important point, both can eliminate a single point of failure allowing for more security against hacks and data loss. Blockchain can handle multiple contributors and consumers verifying data integrity in real-life cases.

While the application of blockchain in combating deepfakes is promising, it is important to acknowledge the challenges, such as scalability and user adoption. Blockchain's decentralized verification and consensus algorithms can be costly and slow, hindering mass adoption among content creators and media companies. Another key challenge is establishing a universal standard for global adoption, which requires collaboration between governments, corporations, technical leaders, and the platforms with which blockchain will be integrated. Furthermore, blockchain alone cannot detect deepfakes; it must work alongside AI tools. Additionally, energy consumption—especially when handling large transaction volumes for deepfake detection—can become a significant barrier to large-scale adoption due to the environmental impact and the cost of running these systems.

4.3 Digital Watermarking

Quantum image watermarking techniques leverage quantum properties and robust image processing algorithms to embed imperceptible watermarks into host images. Unlike cryptography, watermarking aims to hide the existence of information within otherwise seemingly harmless data, making it less likely to be detected or suspected [12]. There are several ways that this technology detects deepfakes. When a deepfake manipulates an image or video, it disrupts embedded watermarks. By analyzing the watermarked image or video, discrepancies caused by tampering can signal the presence of a deepfake. This is done by the quantum watermarking techniques such as NEQR, LBB, DCT and Wavelet embedding. This technique also has a high capacity to enable embedding unique identifiers or authentication keys. These can be checked against a database to verify the authenticity of the content. Deepfake detection systems can extract these identifiers to confirm if the content has been altered or if the watermark has been removed.

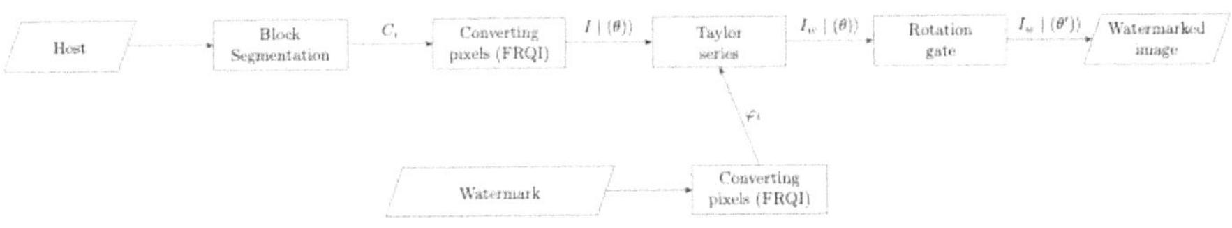

Fig. 1. Watermark embedding

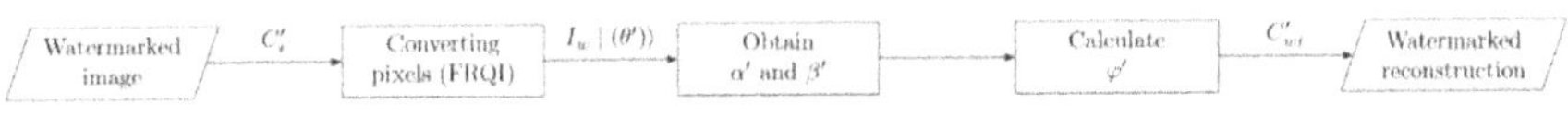

Fig. 2. Watermark extraction

The watermarking system detects deepfakes through the embedding and extraction of watermarks in quantum-encoded images. Figure 1 shows the process of watermark embedding [12]. Grayscale host and watermark images are segmented into blocks, and images are converted into quantum representations using Taylor series. Then the watermark pixels are normalized and embedded into the host image blocks via encoding and rotation gate transformations. The next step is to extract the watermark in order to separate it from the host image by decoding the quantum-encoded watermark pixels. Figure 2 shows the process of extraction [12].

This research introduced a quantum watermarking scheme using amplitude elevation decoding with Taylor series and rotation gate X, achieving high imperceptibility (PSNR-H) and robust watermark detection (PSNR-W). This paper provides contribution to the field of quantum watermarking, offering a robust method that not only ensures content authenticity but also holds potential for deepfake detection through its tampering resistant watermarking scheme. The use of amplitude elevation decoding and rotation gates demonstrates a novel integration of quantum computing techniques for watermarking.

Table 3. Performance Evaluation of Quantum Watermarking

Taylor Order	Host Image	PSNR-H (dB)	PSNR-W (dB)	Imperceptibility	Robustness	Watermark Visibility
1	Peppers, Boat, Airplane, Peacock	<30	15.61 (Peacock)	Poor	Low	Watermark readable
2	Peppers, Boat, Airplane, Peacock	−30	11.61 (Peacock)	Moderate	Low	Still slightly visible
3	Peppers, Boat, Airplane, Peacock	>30	19.85	Good	Good	Slight to no visibility
4	Peppers, Boat, Airplane, Peacock	−62-79	−20	Very Good	Good	Not visible
5	Pepper + Others	−84.25	−20	Excellent	Good	Invisible
6–10	Peacock	∞ (from order 6)	19–21	Perfect	Good	Invisible
11–15	Peacock	∞	Drops to 0–5	Perfect	Poor	Distorted or unreadable

According to [12], and based on their reported results, we constructed a performance matrix to summarize the quantum watermarking system's imperceptibility, robustness, and visibility across different Taylor series orders as shown in Table 3. The performance matrix demonstrates that quantum watermarking using Taylor series and rotation gates can embed watermarks with high imperceptibility and reasonable robustness, indicating strong potential for detecting deepfakes. The high PSNR-H values suggest that the quantum watermark does not visibly degrade the host image, making it difficult to detect and therefore ideal for tamper-proofing. Meanwhile, stable PSNR-W readings (approximately 19–21 dB) acro Taylor orders 3 to 10 show that the quantum watermark remains steadily detectable even after slight modifications. This implies that any false modification to the image would be noticeable, it can cause disruption or missing or signaling manipulation. Therefore, this quantum watermarking approach offers a promising method for authenticating digital images and videos and identifying potential deepfakes by spotting irregularities or absent embedded markers. It also offers a comprehensive analysis supported by detailed simulations and algorithms, giving a clear insight into the algorithm's behaviors.

While the paper successfully demonstrates a robust quantum watermarking scheme, there are certain limitations, such as the dependency on host images, that merit further exploration. Additionally, while quantum watermarking presents a novel and promising approach, real-world applicability is presently hindered by the limited availability of quantum hardware. Most proposed schemes, including the one discussed in this paper, are being implemented on classical systems as of now, which limits their everyday application in real-life scenarios. Addressing these hardware constraints is critical for enabling scalable, secure, and practical quantum watermarking solutions in the future.

4.4 Limitations of Current Systems

The current deepfake detection systems are based on machine learning techniques that use deep neural networks like GANs and VAEs to train the models. However, these systems are not perfect; they can often make mistakes and have limits on what they can detect. The accuracy of these systems depends on if the models are trained with high quality and diverse datasets that are regularly updated [13]. Real-time detection systems also require many resources and expenses to provide accurate and up to date results.

Blockchain verification is a tool that allows social media content to be authenticated and traced back to its origin and identify whoever posted it. This technology is helpful in detecting deepfakes because it can determine if the content is reliable or possibly suspicious depending on if the source it came from is trustworthy and if the data has been altered. The goal of blockchain verification is to analyze the integrity of the data using stored hash values. Since blockchains will detect content changes, it discourages people from creating fake content as their actions can be traced and they can be held accountable.

However, we cannot rely on blockchains as the only method for the detection of deepfakes because they can only detect if a piece of content is original or if it was modified [13]. If the content was already fake to begin with, blockchain will not be useful. If the original content is lost, the blockchain will not be able to compare with the original since it does not store the content but rather the hash values that will change if the content is altered [14]. Additionally, if harmful deepfakes are detected on the blockchain, they cannot be easily removed, so this may cause the entire blockchain to need to be deleted, causing major losses to the platform [14]. The scalability of blockchain is limited as well.

Digital watermarking also provides authenticity and traceability like blockchain verification, but in a different way. This technology achieves this through embedding imperceptible information into a quantum-encoded image that is undetectable by the human eye. Still, watermarks may be altered or removed without permission, leading detection systems to falsely identify images. Watermarks may also not be able to be detected if they are very secure and robust. They may also reduce the quality of images in some instances (Table 4).

Table 4. Limitations of Current Systems

Limitations	Description
Dependence on Training Data	Models may fail to detect new deepfakes if not regularly updated based on the training data.

(*continued*)

Table 4. (*continued*)

Limitations	Description
False Positives & False Negatives	Real content may be misidentified as fake, or vice versa, reducing trust in the system.
Resource-Intensive and Expensive	Real-time detection requires significant resources and is costly to maintain.
Vulnerability to Adversarial Attacks	GAN-based models can be tricked by malicious attacks, leading to misidentifications.
Blockchain Verification	Blockchain only checks if content is altered. It does not help with detecting deepfakes that are created from scratch or when the original content is lost.
Immutability of Blockchain	Harmful deepfakes on blockchain cannot be easily removed, risking major losses.
Scalability Issues	Blockchain faces scalability challenges, limiting large-scale use in detection.
Digital Watermarking	Watermarks can be altered or undetectable and may degrade image quality.

Over the past few years, deepfakes have already evolved so much that it is hard for the human eye to detect. Although some countries have begun to introduce regulations, there are still major gaps in tackling the worldwide issues caused by deepfakes.

Deepfakes pose serious ethical dilemmas, particularly in balancing their potential for creativity and education while ensuring rules and protections are in place to prevent misuse. Current legal frameworks struggle to address deepfake-related harm due to their anonymity, global reach, and rapid dissemination. Existing laws, such as defamation, copyright, privacy, and cybersecurity laws offer partial solutions but were not designed for deepfakes and often fail to address their full impact. Proving harm and enforcing regulations across jurisdictions remain significant obstacles. As deepfakes continue to evolve and become more realistic, they will be much more difficult to discern even with detection systems, so we must work together to combat them with better and scalable detection models and training.

5 Enhancing Existing Systems for Deepfake Detection

5.1 Overview of AI-Based Deepfake Detection Tools

There are various AI based detection solutions that are already available to the public for free. They each have their own strengths and weaknesses and differ in what they can be used for. These include:

FakeCatcher: Developed by Intel and offers 96% accuracy for detecting deepfake videos [15].
Sensity AI: All-in-one detection tool that detects deepfake images, videos, and audios with 98% accuracy. Is free but requires users to sign up [16].

TrueMedia: Allows users to detect deepfakes in social media posts via its URL whether it is an image, video, or audio. User sign up required [17].
Hive AI: Provides AI generated image, video, and audio detection [18].
ElevenLabs: Detects AI generated audio using their platform [19].
Hiya: Detects AI generated audio in videos using deep learning solutions. Free Google Chrome extension that requires user sign up [20].
DeFake: Ongoing research project to create the best machine learning solution for deepfake detection. Studies and training on adversarial examples and multiple detection methods that analyze inconsistencies between video frames and fakeness in audio. The project's goal is to help journalists in combating disinformation with a user-friendly, accurate tool [21].

5.2 Strengthening Deepfake Defenses: AI Robustness, Public Awareness, and Policy Interventions

Deepfake detection has a long way to go before we can achieve consistently reliable and accurate results. One of the primary challenges is the vulnerability of detection systems to adversarial attacks, were small, imperceptible perturbations in images or videos can deceive AI models into misclassifying fake content as real [22]. To counter this, adversarial training can be incorporated into machine learning models to improve their robustness and resistance to such attacks. Additionally, developing shared frameworks and standardized training datasets will enhance model consistency and reliability across different applications. Stronger collaboration between tech organizations, researchers, and policymakers is essential in advancing the effectiveness of deepfake detection systems.

Public awareness and education play a crucial role in mitigating the risks posed by deepfakes. Many people are unaware of how convincing AI-generated media has become, making them more susceptible to misinformation. It is vital to educate individuals on how to critically evaluate digital content and recognize the telltale signs of deepfakes, such as inconsistencies in facial expressions, unnatural speech patterns, or mismatched shadows. With the growing prevalence of deepfakes, media literacy programs should be widely implemented to help the public develop skepticism towards suspicious content. Furthermore, organizations should enforce stronger authentication measures, such as multi-factor authentication (MFA) and zero-trust security models, to reduce the risks associated with deepfake-powered fraud and identity theft.

Government regulations and policy interventions are crucial in curbing the malicious use of deepfakes. There is an urgent need for laws that regulate the creation and distribution of deceptive AI-generated content, ensuring that individuals and entities responsible for harmful deepfakes are held accountable. In response to this growing threat, several governments have begun enacting legislation.

In the United States, the 2025 bipartisan "Take it Down Act" establishes federal penalties for non-consensual intimate imagery (NCII), including AI-generated deepfake pornography. It also mandates that social media platforms and other websites remove such content within 48 h upon receiving victims' requests [23]. This bill marks a significant step forward in protecting victims, especially women and girls, and upholding the privacy and dignity of the US residents. It also has the potential to prevent severe emotional hard and may help reduce suicide risk among affected individuals. This act demonstrates a significant federal effort to standardize protections against deepfake abuses.

At the state level, Texas introduced House Bill 366, which calls for criminal prosecution of releasing manipulated political media without appropriate disclosure. The bill aims to ban the distribution of deceptive political content [24].

Internationally, similar efforts are underway. The European Union's Artificial Intelligence Act, effective from February 2025, requires transparent labeling of synthetic media and classifies certain deepfakes as prohibited AI contents. Spain has reinforced this regulation by imposing fines of up to €35 million on companies that fail to properly label AI-generated content.

Collaboration between governments, law enforcement agencies, and the tech industry can establish ethical guidelines for deepfake detection and usage. Additionally, privacy concerns must be addressed, as machine learning models rely on both real and synthetic data for training. The ethical dilemma of using real human likenesses without consent raises important questions: Should AI-generated content be labeled? How should personal data be protected? Policymakers must strike a balance between technological innovation and privacy rights to develop fair and transparent regulations that safeguard individuals from deepfake exploitation.

6 Case Studies

6.1 Real-World Examples: Deepfakes in Political Manipulation

According to [25], deepfakes were involved in an unethical use in the political year 2024 when a fake robocall with the voice of President Joe Biden, misled voters in New Hampshire. The specific robocall in New Hampshire encouraged people not to vote in the primary election to subjugate the results of the election to such information. The robocall message was that "Your vote makes a difference in November, not this Tuesday". While the call was not a deepfake video of the president – it did include a false voice taking the call. White House press secretary Karine Jean-Pierre affirmed that the call was indeed a fake one, and it was not recorded by the president. This case shows that deepfakes are dangerous in political manipulation as they can be used to mislead the voters, subvert the democratic process, and disseminate falsehood at sensitive occasions such as elections. Such cases make it increasingly important to employ various security measures to counter harmful deepfake incidences.

Impact on individuals: The direct effects of the fake Biden robocall on individuals are the potential to mislead and confuse voters. For individuals receiving the call, the risk was that they would decide not to vote because of the misleading message or they would doubt the credibility of the election. The cost to the citizens could be high, in terms of handling stress and anxiety they feel when they have lost faith in the programs meant to enable them to vote.

Impact on society: On a broader societal level, using deepfakes to send misleading information for the election could be an alert for the public to undermine public trust in democratic processes. Deepfakes that create false messages with the purpose of engaging voters' participation give rise to confusion, fracture, and doubt regarding the election process. Where there is high political polarization as in most democratic societies today, the incidence of such events increases the spread of fake news and weakens the public's confidence in both political leaders and the electoral process.

6.2 Real-World Examples: Deepfakes in Individual Financial Scams

Deepfakes have emerged as a formidable tool for executing financial scams. In [26], the video was posted on November 24, 2024, Heidi Swan, a 62-year-old, who is a healthcare worker became a victim of an elaborate advertisement that involved a deepfake of Elon Musk. The video that went viral on social media showed Musk involved in an advertisement of an investment in cryptocurrencies. Having identified the deepfake to have the physical appearance of Musk and his voice, Swan really believed that it was Musk and felt that because he is the richest individual on earth, it was right to follow Musk's advice on finance. Swan spent more than $10,000 on what she thought was a real and legitimate business. But the video turned out to be fake and made by cybercriminals. Unfortunately, Swan fell into the trap and lost her hard-earned savings just in a few hours. After realizing the loss, Swan went back and watched the video again and again and she still thought the video looked legitimate. The cybercriminals used AI tools to cut out Musk and replace with a deepfake of him. According to the CBS reporter Brian New, a study found that Musk is the most common celebrity to be used to create deepfake scams. One of the reasons that there are so many deepfakes of Musk is that he does a lot of interviews. The more content there is online, the easier it is to make a deepfake. New emphasized the importance of taking a moment to critically evaluate the content you see online, considering who posted it and what they are asking for, before taking any action. This approach can serve as a critical line of defense against falling victim to deepfake scams.

Impact on Individual: Swan lost her money in a matter of hours. This could increase significant emotional distress which would lead to feelings of helplessness and guilt for having fallen victim to the scam. She might tell everyone around her, and those who hear her story may feel that the internet is not trustworthy.

Impact on Society: On a societal level, people will be less engaged and less trusting in digital media, even from credible sources. Such loss of trust can slow down implementations of new innovations such as smart contracts, and other developments of new digital economies.

6.3 Detection Efficacy of Machine Learning Models

In one study, different machine learning algorithms, including CNNs, SVMs, and hybrid CNN-SVMs, were trained and tested on a set of 1000 real and fake images and a set of 500 real and fake videos. Each model was analyzed for highest accuracy using different performance metrics, including their accuracy, precision, and recall rates and their F-1 score. The accuracy rate is how many images or videos the model correctly guessed. Precision is the ratio of how many true positives vs. false positives there were. Recall is the ratio of how many true positives vs. false negatives there were. F-1 score balances precision and recall, so it will show how accurate the model is but also take into account how many false positives and false negatives there are. The CNN model outperformed SVM model with an F-1 score of 95% compared to 92% for image detection and an

F-1 score of 91% compared to 88% for video detection [27]. However, the accuracy of one model depends on many factors like training datasets and model complexity, so one model may be better than another in different situations. CNNs are typically more efficient at handling large datasets and feature recognition while SVMs are more efficient at handling high-dimensional datasets and image classification. That being said, the combined CNN-SVM model showed even greater accuracy than each individual model with an F-1 score of 97% for image detection and 94% for video detection [27]. Using different features from both of the CNN and SVM models allowed for the most robust model with the highest accuracy rate with the lowest false positives and negatives. This is because the CNNs were better at analyzing and extracting specific features from the input images and the SVMs were better at classifying the input data as real or fake by finding the optimal hyperplane and ignoring possible outliers.

7 Conclusion

Deepfakes, powered by AI models, have rapidly evolved, presenting both innovation and severe risks. Through our research and case studies, we explored how deepfakes are being weaponized for political manipulation and financial scams, demonstrating their ability to mislead voters, undermine trust in political systems, and cause substantial financial losses.

Our findings underscore the need for robust cybersecurity measures, public awareness, and the development of advanced detection and prevention tools to combat the escalating dangers of deepfakes. Our evaluation of detection systems revealed potential solutions, including GAN and VAE based models, the EAR-SVM methods, blockchain verification, and quantum watermarking. Of these, the EAR-SVM approach holds potential since it has the ability to combine face feature extraction with a machine learning classification procedure to detect deepfakes. It utilizes the SVM's ability to classify data points by their features which allows it to recognize the characteristic traits of deepfakes.

Nevertheless, no single solution is sufficient. The limitations of current systems, such as dependence on training data, vulnerability to adversarial attacks, and substantial computational, memory, and energy requirements needed to run deepfake detection models effectively. Many of these technologies require high-performance GPUs and high-bandwidth infrastructure to handle the processing of multiple volumes of video or audio information. Real-time detection, in particular, puts additional pressure because it requires low-latency inference and fast data pipelines, which are costly to provide and difficult to scale across hardware. The high costs and technical demands of these detection systems may not be practical to implement in lower-resource environments, such as developing countries, small organizations, rural areas, or even some social media platforms. Providing more affordable deepfake detections for these groups of community needs to be improved. Improving the accessibility and affordability of deepfake detection technologies for these communities is a critical area that needs further development.

Ultimately, addressing deepfake threats requires a multilayered defense: incorporating technical resilience, public education, ethical protection, and governmental intervention. Through interdisciplinary collaboration, we can create scalable, dependable, and proactive solutions to combat the misuse of synthetic media and build a safer digital ecosystem.

Acknowledgments. This work was supported in part by NSF grant DGE-2146280. Any opinions, findings, conclusions, or recommendations expressed in this work are those of the authors and do not necessarily reflect the views of the NSF.

References

1. Somers, M.: Deepfakes, explained. MIT Sloan. https://mitsloan.mit.edu/ideas-made-to-matter/deepfakes-explained Accessed 1 June 2025
2. Sarkar, D., Bhattacharya, D.: Video of Gautam Adani endorsing a financial scheme is fake. Deepfake Analysis Unit.. https://www.dau.mcaindia.in/blog/video-of-gautam-adani-endorsing-a-financial-scheme-is-fake. Accessed 1 June 2025
3. Laczi, S., Póser, V.: Impact of deepfake technology on children: risks and consequences. In: 2024 IEEE 22nd Jubilee International Symposium on Intelligent Systems and Informatics (SISY), pp. 215–220. IEEE, Pula, Croatia (2024). https://doi.org/10.1109/SISY62279.2024.10737593
4. Alahmed, Y., Abadla, R., Ansari, M.: Exploring the potential implications of AI-generated content in social engineering attacks. In: 2024 International Conference on Multimedia Computing, Networking and Applications (MCNA), pp. 64–73. IEEE, Valencia, Spain (2024). https://doi.org/10.1109/MCNA63144.2024.10703950
5. Sjouwerman, S.: How a North Korean fake IT worker tried to infiltrate us. KnowBe4. https://blog.knowbe4.com/how-a-north-korean-fake-it-worker-tried-to-infiltrate-us. Accessed 1 June 2025
6. Nadal, L., Jančárik, P.: Beyond the deepfake hype: AI, democracy, and "the Slovak case". Harvard Kennedy School.. https://misinforeview.hks.harvard.edu/article/beyond-the-deepfake-hype-ai-democracy-and-the-slovak-case/. Accessed 1 June 2025
7. Helmus, T.: Artificial intelligence, deepfakes, and disinformation. RAND Corporation.. https://www.rand.org/content/dam/rand/pubs/perspectives/PEA1000/PEA1043-1/RAND_PEA1043-1.pdf. Accessed 1 June 2025
8. Chen, H., Magramo, K.: Finance worker pays out $25 million after video call with deepfake 'chief financial officer'. CNN.. https://www.cnn.com/2024/02/04/asia/deepfake-cfo-scam-hong-kong-intl-hnk/index.html. Accessed 1 June 2025
9. Gandhi, A., Sharma, S.: Deepfakes in financial fraud: a comprehensive exploration. Mondaq.. https://www.mondaq.com/india/white-collar-crime-anti-corruption%2D%2Dfraud/1400570/deepfakes-in-financial-fraud-a-comprehensive-exploration. Accessed 1 June 2025
10. Rana, M., Nobi, M., Murali, B., Sung, A.: Deepfake detection: a systematic literature review. IEEE Access. **10**, 25494–25513 (2022). https://doi.org/10.1109/ACCESS.2022.3154404
11. Garde, A., Suratkar, S., Kazi, F.: AI-based deepfake detection. In: 2022 IEEE 1st International Conference on Data, Decision and Systems (ICDDS), pp. 1–6. IEEE, Bangalore, India (2022). https://doi.org/10.1109/ICDDS56399.2022.10037286
12. Refiyanti, M., Budiman, G., Novamizanti, L.: Quantum image watermarking based on quantum state modification using rotation gate. In: 2024 International Conference on Artificial Intelligence, Blockchain, Cloud Computing, and Data Analytics (ICoABCD), pp. 178–183. IEEE, Indonesia (2024). https://doi.org/10.1109/ICoABCD63526.2024.10704405
13. Puri, B., Kumar, J., Mukherjee, S., Bhaskar, S.V.: Analysis of deepfake detection techniques. In: 2023 International Conference on Circuit Power and Computing Technologies (ICCPCT), pp. 71–76. IEEE, Kollam, India (2023). https://doi.org/10.1109/ICCPCT58313.2023.10245532

14. Wei, X., Zhang, W., Bai, G., Li, B.: Research on technology against deepfake. In: 2023 3rd International Conference on Mobile Networks and Wireless Communications (ICM-NWC), pp. 1–5. IEEE, Tumkur, India (2023). https://doi.org/10.1109/ICMNWC60182.2023.10435749
15. AI generated or real? FakeFinder.: https://fakefinder.ai/. Accessed 1 June 2025
16. All-in-one deepfake detection.: Sensity. https://sensity.ai/. Accessed 1 June 2025
17. Identifying political deepfakes in social media using AI.: TrueMedia. https://www.truemedia.org/. Accessed 1 June 2025
18. AI to understand, search, and generate content.: Hive. https://thehive.ai/. Accessed 1 June 2025
19. AI speech classifier.: ElevenLabs. https://elevenlabs.io/ai-speech-classifier. Accessed 1 June 2025
20. AI voice detection.: Hiya. https://www.hiya.com/products/protect/ai-voice-detection. Accessed 1 June 2025
21. Wright, M., Hickerson, A., Kong, Y.: DeFake Project. https://docs.google.com/presentation/d/1Haqyz-8P08zEoe6z8RVpeYp3r9F4j84BgOC8OaYpBJM/edit#slide=id.p1. Accessed 1 June 2025
22. Fan, L., Li, W., Cui, X.: Deepfake-image anti-forensics with adversarial examples attacks. Future Internet. **13**(11), 1–14 (2021). https://doi.org/10.3390/fi13110288
23. U.S. Senate Committee.: TAKE IT DOWN Act passes the House, heads to President Trump's desk. https://www.commerce.senate.gov/2025/4/take-it-down-act-passes-the-house-heads-to-president-trump-s-desk. Accessed 1 June 2025
24. Phelan, D.: Texas house bill 366. Texas State Legislature.. https://legiscan.com/TX/text/HB366/id/3197809. Accessed 1 June 2025
25. Pezenik, S., Shepherd, B.: Fake Biden robocall urges New Hampshire voters to skip their primary. ABC News.. https://abcnews.go.com/Politics/fake-biden-robocall-urges-new-hampshire-voters-skip/story?id=106580926. Accessed 1 June 2025
26. New, B., Salazar, L., Lozano, M., Fralicks, S.: Deepfakes of Elon musk are contributing to billions of dollars in fraud losses in the U.S. CBS News.. https://www.cbsnews.com/texas/news/deepfakes-ai-fraud-elon-musk. Accessed 1 June 2025
27. Stankov, I., Dulgerov, E.: Detection of deepfake images and videos using SVM, CNN, and hybrid approaches. In: 2024 XXXIII International Scientific Conference Electronics (ET), pp. 1–5. IEEE, Sozopol, Bulgaria (2024). https://doi.org/10.1109/ET63133.2024

Harnessing Machine Learning and Artificial Intelligence in Cyber Security: A Deep Dive into Threat Detection, Anomaly Detection, Intrusion Detection, and Malware Analysis

David Dorsaima, Lisa Kovalchick, and Weifeng Chen(✉)

Department of Computing and Engineering Technology, Pennsylvania Western University, California, USA
{kovalchick,chen}@pennwest.edu

Abstract. Machine Learning (ML) and Artificial Intelligence (AI) have shown great promise in several areas of cybersecurity. They can learn from patterns, make predictions, and adapt to new situations, making them ideal for identifying threats, detecting anomalies, and discovering intrusions. ML and AI techniques can enhance threat detection in cybersecurity through anomaly detection, predictive analytics, automated threat hunting, phishing detection, malware detection, and user behavior analytics. In this article, we investigate how ML and AI could be integrated to detect Phishing, Malware, Insider Threats and Intrusion Detections. We also study several real-life cases that utilize ML and AI to enhance cybersecurity. Finally, we present a prototype of an ML- and AI-based cybersecurity system.

Keywords: Machine Learning · Artificial Intelligence · Phishing · Malware · Insider Threats · Intrusion Detection

1 Introduction

Machine Learning (ML) and Artificial Intelligence (AI) have shown great promise in several areas of cybersecurity. They can learn from patterns, make predictions, and adapt to new situations, making them ideal for identifying threats, detecting anomalies, and discovering intrusions [1]. ML and AI techniques are highly complex, emerging discipline with numerous potential applications to the monitoring and security of large-scale data systems. They can enhance threat detection in cybersecurity through anomaly detection, predictive analytics, automated threat hunting, phishing detection, malware detection, and user behavior analytics.

ML's core advantage in cybersecurity lies in its ability to learn and adapt. Traditional, rule-based systems operate based on pre-defined rules and heuristics, and while they're effective in dealing with known threats, they often struggle with zero-day threats for which no rule exists. ML algorithms, on the other hand, can learn the typical behavior of a system, user, or network by analyzing historical data. Once a baseline of "normal"

K. Daimi et al. (Eds.): CSCE 2025, CCIS 2937, pp. 55–66, 2026.
https://doi.org/10.1007/978-3-032-22208-4_5

behavior is established, the algorithm can then monitor ongoing activities and flag any significant deviation from the norm. This behavior-based anomaly detection method is particularly effective in discovering novel threats. This is particularly useful in detecting zero-day attacks and Advanced Persistent Threats (APTs).

Zero-day attacks refer to exploits that take advantage of software vulnerability on the same day that the vulnerability becomes publicly known, hence the term "zero-day". These attacks occur before the software developers have had a chance to develop and distribute a patch, making them particularly hard to defend against. ML algorithms can provide robust defense against zero-day attacks by identifying abnormal patterns in system behavior, even if the specific threat has never been encountered before.

Advanced Persistent Threats (APTs) are sophisticated, often state-sponsored cyber-attacks in which the attacker gains unauthorized access to a network and re-mains undetected for an extended period. APTs are typically targeted at organizations with high-value information, such as government entities and large corporations. Since APTs do not follow predictable, rule-based patterns and often employ novel techniques to evade detection, ML algorithms are often a potent tool in detecting and mitigating such threats. By continuously learning and adapting to what is "normal" within a network, these algorithms can flag unusual network traffic, unusual user behavior, or unfamiliar file types that might indicate an APT.

AI and ML models have revolutionized the field of cybersecurity by adding predictive capabilities to security systems. They analyze past data and patterns to predict and prevent future security incidents. AI and ML models are trained on large amounts of past security data, such as network traffic logs, historical security incidents, and known threat patterns. These models learn from this data to understand patterns associated with security incidents. For instance, an unusual pattern of network traffic might indicate a Distributed Denial of Service (DDoS) attack, or multiple failed login attempts could signify a brute-force attack. Similarly, certain patterns of data access might be associated with insider threats, while specific email patterns could denote phishing attempts.

Once these models are trained, they can monitor real-time data and compare it against the learned patterns. When they detect a pattern that has been associated with a security incident in the past, they can alert security analysts and even take automat-ed actions to mitigate the risk. In this way, they can identify potential security incidents before they occur or in their early stages, allowing for more proactive and timely responses.

ML and AI can automate the process of hunting for threats, which often involves combing through massive amounts of data. AI can sift through this data much more quickly and accurately than human analysts, identifying subtle patterns that might otherwise be missed. Speed is critical in cybersecurity, where quick detection and response can significantly mitigate the impact of a security incident.

In this paper, we investigate how ML and AI could be integrated to detect Phishing, Malware, Insider Threats and Intrusion Detections. We also study several real-life cases that utilize ML and AI to enhance cybersecurity. Finally, we present a prototype of an ML- and AI-based cybersecurity system. This work will provide insight to apply AI in Cybersecurity.

2 Integration of ML in Cybersecurity

2.1 ML Protection Against Phishing

ML can analyze emails and other messages to identify those that are likely to be phishing attempts, even if they haven't been encountered before. Traditional anti-phishing methods often rely on blacklists of known phishing websites or rule-based systems that look for specific signals, like poor spelling and grammar or the use of specific phrases. While these methods can be effective, they often struggle to detect new phishing attempts that haven't been seen before or that don't fit the established rules. ML enhances anti-phishing efforts by learning from a large dataset of both legitimate and phishing emails.

ML algorithms can analyze various elements of these emails, including the sender's address, email's content, structure of an email, included links, and more. By learning the patterns associated with phishing emails, ML models can identify even subtle signals that an email might be a phishing attempt. When an incoming email is analyzed by an ML model, the model calculates the likelihood of that email being a phishing attempt based on the patterns it has learned. If the likelihood is above a certain threshold, the system can flag the email as a potential phishing attempt, block the email, or take other appropriate actions.

However, like all security measures, ML-based anti-phishing is not perfect. It should be used as part of a defense-in-depth approach that includes user education, secure email gateways, and strong authentication methods. While machine learning algorithms can significantly enhance an organization's ability to identify and block phishing attempts by analyzing patterns and content, cybercriminals constantly evolve their tactics to evade detection. To preserve effectiveness, organization must regularly refine ML models and update security protocols to counter emerging threats.

2.2 ML Protection from Malware

ML models can analyze files to identify those that are likely to be malware, based on characteristics shared by known malware [2]. Traditional malware detection techniques typically rely on signature-based detection, which works by comparing files against a database of known malware signatures. While effective against known threats, signature-based detection struggles with zero-day threats and polymorphic or metamorphic malware that continually changes its code to evade detection. ML models, particularly those using deep learning techniques, can be trained on a dataset of known malware and benign files.

During training, these models learn to identify patterns and characteristics common to malware. These characteristics might include patterns in the file's binary data, file size, sequence of function calls the file makes, or other file properties. ML algorithms can also analyze the behavior of files within controlled environments to understand actions and identify potential malicious activities. By feeding the ML models with a diverse dataset of both known malware samples and benign files, the algorithms can discern subtle nuances that distinguish malicious code from legitimate software.

Once trained, these models can then analyze new files and predict whether they are likely to be malware based on the learned patterns. In this way, ML models can identify files that behave like malware, even if they have never been encountered be-fore or do not match any known malware signature. This ability to detect previously unseen or zero-day malware is particularly valuable in today's rapidly evolving threat landscape, where cybercriminals continuously create new and sophisticated attack vectors to evade traditional signature-based antivirus solutions.

ML models can continually learn and adapt as they are exposed to new malware, improving their detection capabilities over time. However, like all cybersecurity tools, ML-based malware detection is not infallible. Adversaries can use adversarial ML techniques to craft malware that can evade detection. Therefore, ML should be part of a layered defense strategy that includes other security measures like secure coding practices, intrusion detection systems, and user education.

2.3 AI and ML Protection from Insider Threats

Insider threats can be both intentional, from employees with malicious intent, and unintentional, stemming from employees who unknowingly make errors or violate policies. Such threats are not confined to current employees, former employees, contractors, or business associates who have access to an organization's networks, systems, or data can also pose significant risk. Despite their challenging nature, recognizing insider threats is critical due to the potential harm they can inflict on an organization's cybersecurity infrastructure, the compromise of sensitive data, and even the disruption of regular operations. Insider threats often occur in the form of data leaks, fraud, data theft, or IT sabotage. These can lead to significant financial losses, damage to a company's reputation, or in extreme cases, the endangerment of its very existence. Detecting insider threats can be particularly challenging because these actions often involve legitimate access to systems and data, making them harder to identify than external threats.

AI can help by monitoring user behaviors patterns, detecting anomalies, risk scoring, automated alerts and responses, and predictive analysis. AI algorithms can monitor and learn normal user behavior patterns. For instance, they can learn typical login times, frequently accessed resources, common data transfer amounts, etc. Once the baseline of "normal" behavior is established, AI can flag any significant deviations as potential threats. By leveraging AI-powered solutions, organizations can bolster their security posture, safeguard their sensitive data, and protect themselves from the potentially devastating consequences of insider-related incidents.

AI can detect unusual activities that may indicate an insider threat. This includes multiple failed login attempts, logins from unusual locations or devices, accessing sensitive data at unusual times, sudden high-volume data transfers, and more. AI's con-textual analysis capabilities allow it to consider various factors when assessing the se-verity of flagged activities. For instance, it can consider the user's role within the organization, their historical behavior, the sensitivity of the data accessed, and the potential impact of the detected actions on the organization's security posture. Based on the observed behavior and detected anomalies, AI can assign a risk score to each user. Users with higher risk scores can then be subject to more frequent or more intensive monitoring. AI's conceptual understanding can differentiate between genuine user behavior deviations and actual insider threats, reducing false positives and ensuring that security teams focus their attention on the most critical risks.

If AI detects a potential threat, it can generate alerts for security analysts to investigate. Depending on the severity of the threat, AI can also trigger automated responses, such as temporarily disabling a user's account or blocking a data transfer. By analyzing past data, AI can identify patterns that have led to insider threats in the past and use this information to predict and prevent potential future threats.

By integrating AI into their security systems, organizations can enhance their ability to detect insider threats, react swiftly to mitigate risks, and protect their valuable data and resources. AI's advanced algorithms can continuously monitor user activities, identify patterns of behavior that may indicate suspicious actions, and proactively alert security teams to potential threats in real-time. This proactive approach allows organizations to stay one step ahead of malicious insiders and take pre-emptive measures to safeguard their sensitive information. AI can significantly reduce the burden on human analysts, enabling them to focus on more complex security challenges that require human intuition and decision-making.

2.4 ML and AI in Anomaly Detection Within a Network

ML and AI can be used to automate the threat detection process, which enables organizations to respond to cyber threats more quickly and efficiently, sometimes before any harm is even done. ML and AI systems can be trained to recognize the patterns associated with specific types of cyber threats. For example, systems can detect patterns of behavior associated with phishing attacks or ransomware deployments. This allows for faster identification and response to potential threats, often before any damage can occur [3]. According to Sharma, Sharma, & Singh [4], AI systems can analyze vast amounts of data far more quickly than human analysts, which allows them to identify threats and vulnerabilities that might otherwise go unnoticed.

ML algorithms can be trained to identify normal network behavior and detect anomalies that deviate from this behavior [5]. This is particularly beneficial for identifying zero-day attacks, where previously unknown vulnerabilities are exploited [6]. Darktrace, a leading AI company for cyber defense, has based their enterprise on their product's ability to leverage ML and AI algorithms to detect and respond to cyber threats in real time.

ML and AI systems can learn and adapt over time, which allows them to respond to new and emerging threats. As per Roffey et al. [7], the use of deep learning techniques enables these systems to learn from each interaction they have, thereby improving their ability to detect and respond to new threats. The application of ML and AI techniques can greatly enhance threat detection in cybersecurity by automating the threat detection process, identifying patterns and anomalies in network traffic, and learning and adapting to new threats over time.

2.5 Intrusion Detection

ML and AI are increasingly used in Intrusion Detection Systems (IDS) because they improve their effectiveness. By learning from historical traffic data, these systems can identify potentially malicious activity that deviates from typical network behavior and are indicative of a network breach. Furthermore, the use of AI and ML allows for the recognition of new attack patterns, improving the system's ability to identify and mitigate threats over time [8].

3 Case Study Analysis

ML and AI continue to shape our world, driving innovation and progress across numerous domains. Their capacity to harness the power of data, learn from it, and de-rive actionable insights has transformed industries, empowered decision-makers, and enhanced security and safety in ways that were previously unimaginable. In this section, we present several case studies that demonstrate the effectiveness of ML and AI across various domains, highlighting their ability to analyze vast amounts of data, identify patterns, and make accurate predictions to enhance security and safety.

3.1 Cylance Threat Detection

Cylance is a cybersecurity company that specializes in utilizing AI and ML techniques for threat detection and prevention. It was founded in 2012 by Stuart McClure and Ryan Permeh and gained recognition for its innovative approach to cybersecurity. In December 2024, Cylance was acquired by Arctic Wolf [9]. Cylance's primary product is CylancePROTECT [10], an AI-driven endpoint security solution. Unlike traditional antivirus software that relies on signatures and known patterns of malware, Cylance-PROTECT uses ML algorithms to analyze file attributes and behavior to identify and prevent advanced threats, including both known and un-known malware.

CylancePROTECT employs ML algorithms that are trained on vast datasets of benign and malicious files. By learning from these datasets, the algorithms can identify patterns and characteristics associated with malware. The ML algorithms create mathematical models that represent the features of files. These models capture the intrinsic properties of files, such as code execution, system calls, and behavior analysis. When a file is encountered, CylancePROTECT compares its attributes and behavior against the learned models. It assesses the file's potential risk level and determines if it exhibits malicious behavior. Based on the analysis, CylancePROTECT makes real-time decisions on whether a file should be allowed or blocked. If the file is determined to be malicious, it is prevented from executing, protecting the endpoint from potential threats.

By using ML algorithms, CylancePROTECT can identify zero-day threats and advanced malware that may not have known signatures or patterns, offering proactive protection. It is designed to have minimal impact on system performance, allowing for efficient and effective threat detection without slowing down the endpoint. The AI-driven approach enables scalability, allowing CylancePROTECT to handle large-scale deployments across organizations and networks.

Overall, Cylance's use of ML and AI techniques in CylancePROTECT has proven to be successful in detecting and preventing advanced threats, providing organizations with enhanced security against evolving cyber threats. By employing cutting-edge ML algorithms and AI, CylancePROTECT can analyze vast amounts of data in real-time, rapidly identifying and neutralizing even the most sophisticated and previously un-seen threats. The system's ability to continuously learn from new data and adapt to emerging threat landscapes ensures that it remains effective in safeguarding organizations from the ever-changing tactics of cybercriminals.

3.2 Amazon Fraud Detection

Amazon employs ML techniques to combat fraud on its e-commerce platform [11]. By analyzing various factors, such as user behavior, purchase history, and product information, Amazon's ML algorithms can detect potentially fraudulent transactions and take appropriate actions to mitigate fraud risk. Amazon collects vast amounts of data related to user behavior, including browsing history, purchase patterns, payment information, and account details. This data serves as the foundation for training ML models. Amazon's ML models are trained using historical data that includes both legitimate and fraudulent transactions. The models learn patterns and features that distinguish fraudulent activities from normal user behavior. ML algorithms extract relevant features from the collected data, such as IP addresses, shipping addresses, transaction amounts, device information, and login patterns. These features provide valuable insights into potential fraud indicators. Using the extracted features, Amazon's ML algorithms are trained to classify transactions as legitimate or fraudulent. The models learn to identify patterns and anomalies associated with fraudulent behavior.

When a user makes a transaction on the platform, the ML models analyze the relevant features in real-time. The models compare the transaction against the learned patterns and assess its risk level. Based on the analysis, Amazon assigns a risk score to each transaction, indicating the likelihood of fraud. The risk score determines the appropriate action to be taken. Transactions with high-risk scores trigger additional security measures, such as step-up authentication, manual review by fraud analysts, or even order cancellation. These actions help prevent fraudulent transactions and protect both sellers and buyers on the platform.

Amazon's ML models continuously learn and adapt based on new data. They can update their understanding of fraud patterns and adjust their detection capabilities over time. Their use of ML for fraud detection allows for the timely identification of potentially fraudulent activities, reducing losses due to fraud and enhancing the overall security and trustworthiness of its e-commerce platform.

3.3 Integrated Joint Operations Platform

The Integrated Joint Operations Platform (iJOP) referred in this paper refers to the AI based system implemented at Los Angeles International Airport (LAX), designed to enhance coordination, situational awareness, and threat detection capabilities across airport operations [12]. This system is distinct from the similarly named surveillance platform used in Xinjiang, China, which has been documented as a tool for mass surveillance and human rights violations [13]. LAX, Los Angeles International Airport, has implemented an AI based system called the Integrated Joint Operations Platform (iJOP) to enhance security and threat detection. The iJOP system integrates data from multiple sources, including video surveillance, social media monitoring, and sensor networks, to provide real time threat intelligence and support proactive decision making.

By leveraging AI technology, the iJOP system can analyze data from various sources, allowing security personnel to monitor and assess potential security threats more effectively. The integration of video surveillance enables real-time monitoring of different areas within the airport premises. Social media monitoring can help gather information about any security-related mentions or activities that might be relevant to the airport's security. Additionally, the system can utilize sensor networks to collect data from various sensors deployed throughout the airport, enhancing situational awareness.

By integrating and analyzing data from these diverse sources, the iJOP system aims to provide real-time threat intelligence to security personnel. This enables proactive decision-making and timely responses to potential security incidents or threats, enhancing overall security measures at LAX.

3.4 ML-Based Identification of Anomalous Network Traffic

In a study published in the IEEE Transactions on Information Forensics and Security, researchers utilized ML techniques to detect network intrusions and anomalies using the UNSW-NB15 dataset [14]. They employed algorithms such as random forests and support vector machines to achieve high accuracy in identifying anomalous network traffic patterns.

To achieve their goal, the researchers employed various ML algorithms, including random forests and support vector machines. These algorithms are well-known for their ability to classify and categorize data effectively. By training these ML models on the UNSW-NB15 dataset, which contains labelled instances of normal and anomalous network traffic, the researchers were able to teach the algorithms to recognize the patterns associated with different types of intrusions and anomalies.

The ultimate objective of the study was to develop a robust and accurate network intrusion detection system (NIDS) that could automatically monitor network traffic, detect potential threats or abnormal behavior, and alert security personnel or initiate automated responses to mitigate security risks. By leveraging ML techniques, the researchers aimed to enhance the NIDS's ability to adapt to evolving threats and improve its overall performance in detecting network intrusions.

The success of this study was reflected in the achieved high accuracy in identifying anomalous network traffic patterns, demonstrating the effectiveness of ML-based approaches in bolstering network security and forensics. Such research contributes significantly to the ongoing efforts to combat cyber threats and protect sensitive in-formation and resources in today's interconnected digital landscape.

3.5 MIT's AI2

Researchers at MIT's Computer Science and Artificial Intelligence Laboratory (CSAIL) developed an AI system, AI2, that predicts cyber-attacks significantly better than existing systems by continuously incorporating input from human experts. The system reviews data from tens of millions of log lines each day and singles out anything suspicious. A human analyst then checks this and gives feedback, which helps the system in the future. "AI2 can detect 85 percent of attacks, which is roughly three times better than previous benchmarks, while also reducing the number of false positives by a factor of 5" [15].

The success of AI2 lies in its unique combination of ML and human expertise. By integrating the insights and intuition of human analysts into the AI-driven detection process, the system gains an edge in identifying sophisticated and emerging attack patterns that may be challenging for purely algorithmic systems to detect. This human-in-the-loop approach allows AI2 to continuously learn and adapt, constantly improving its accuracy and performance as it incorporates real-world knowledge from skilled cybersecurity experts.

Moreover, AI2's ability to handle the massive volume of log data generated each day sets it apart from traditional rule-based or signature-based systems that can struggle to keep pace with the rapidly evolving threat landscape. The system's capacity to process and analyze this vast amount of data in real-time enables it to quickly identify and flag potential threats, significantly reducing the response time to mitigate cyber-attacks and minimizing the impact on organizations.

Furthermore, AI2's success in significantly reducing false positives is a critical benefit in modern cybersecurity operations. By reducing false positives, the system ensures that security analysts can focus their efforts on genuine threats rather than being overwhelmed by an influx of irrelevant alerts. This optimization of resources allows security teams to respond more effectively to real threats, enhancing the overall security posture of organizations.

4 Prototype of an ML- and AI-Based Cybersecurity System

In this section, we present CybeResilient AI, a prototype of a cybersecurity system that leverages ML and AI technologies for enhanced threat detection, anomaly detection, intrusion detection, and malware analysis. CybeResilient's architecture includes various modules that leverage different machine learning techniques to enhance threat detection and response capabilities. Here's an overview of each module and its associated ML methods:

- Threat Detection Module (TDM): The TDM utilizes supervised ML algorithms to classify potential threats. It is trained on labelled datasets representing various cyber threat indicators. The TDM scans incoming network data and flags potential threats based on the learned patterns and characteristics of known threats.
- Anomaly Detection Module (ADM): The ADM employs unsupervised ML algorithms such as clustering or neural networks. It establishes a baseline of "normal" network behavior by analyzing historical network data. Deviations from this baseline are considered anomalies and trigger alerts, indicating potential security incidents.
- Intrusion Detection Module (IDM): The IDM combines signature-based detection and behavior-based detection methods. Signature-based detection relies on known patterns of attacks or malicious activity. Behavior-based detection learns the system's normal operation mode and flags any abnormal or deviant behavior. Both supervised and unsupervised learning techniques can be used to enhance the detection capabilities of the IDM.
- Malware Analysis Module (MAM): The MAM utilizes ML techniques to classify and detect new malware. It learns from previously encountered malware samples and their features. A Convolutional Neural Network (CNN), a form of deep learning,

can identify patterns in the code structure of programs to classify them as benign or malicious.

- Adaptive Learning Module (ALM): The ALM incorporates reinforcement learning, an AI technique that learns through interaction with the environment. It utilizes feedback from other modules, including threat detection, anomaly detection, intrusion detection, and malware analysis, to improve its response to future cyber threats. The ALM continuously adapts and refines its decision-making process based on the outcomes and consequences of its actions.

CyberResilient utilizes various ML techniques and modules to enhance its capabilities in threat detection, anomaly detection, intrusion detection, malware analysis, and adaptive learning. Regular updates, monitoring, and maintenance of the ML models and modules are essential to ensure their effectiveness and keep pace with evolving cyber threats.

CybeResilient's workflow will follow this process:

1. Data Collection: The system collects network data in real-time, providing a continuous stream of input for the ML algorithms. The data can include network logs, packet captures, system logs, and other relevant information.
2. Pre-processing: The collected data undergoes pre-processing to clean and transform it into a suitable format for analysis. Pre-processing steps may include removing noise, normalizing data, managing missing values, or applying feature engineering techniques.
3. Analysis: The various modules analyze the data, looking for potential threats, anomalies, intrusions, and malware.
4. Response: When a potential threat is identified, the system alerts the relevant personnel and takes automated preventive actions if configured to do so.
5. Learning: The system learns from each interaction, improving its ability to detect and respond to threats over time.

The CybeResilient AI system is designed to be highly adaptable and scalable, capable of learning from new threats and adjusting its responses over time. It will represent a powerful tool in the arsenal of modern cybersecurity solutions. Leveraging advanced ML algorithms and AI, the CybeResilient AI system continuously analyzes vast amounts of real-time data, including network traffic, user behaviors, and system activities. This proactive approach enables the system to identify potential threats in their early stages, even those with no known signatures or patterns, providing organizations with a crucial advantage in staying ahead of cyber adversaries.

The system's adaptability and self-learning capabilities are pivotal in the rapidly changing cybersecurity landscape. As new threats emerge and attackers employ more sophisticated techniques, CybeResilient can rapidly assimilate and adapt to the evolving threat landscape, ensuring it remains effective in protecting against the latest cyber risks.

The scalability of CybeResilient allows it to cater to organizations of varying sizes and complexities. Whether implemented in small businesses or large enterprises, the system can seamlessly handle the ever-increasing volume of data generated by diverse networks, applications, and devices. This ability to scale efficiently enables organizations to maintain consistent and robust cybersecurity measures as they grow and expand.

CybeResilient can complement and enhance existing cybersecurity solutions, working in harmony with other security measures to form a comprehensive defense framework. By integrating with security information and event management (SIEM) systems, firewalls, and threat intelligence platforms, the system can further strengthen an organization's security posture, sharing valuable insights and threat data to improve collective defenses.

CybeResilient represents a significant advancement in the field of cybersecurity. Its adaptability, scalability, and self-learning capabilities empower organizations with a proactive and dynamic approach to defending against cyber threats. As cyberattacks continue to evolve in complexity and frequency, the CybeResilient AI system's capacity to continuously learn, evolve, and respond effectively will play a pivotal role in safeguarding critical assets, data, and operations for organizations worldwide.

5 Conclusion

Machine Learning (ML) and Artificial Intelligence (AI) are now the new force in Information Technology, including Cybersecurity. As attackers' capability continues to evolve and become more sophisticated, integrating powerful ML and AI in Cybersecurity is an effective approach to defend Cybersecurity. In this article, we have studied different applications of ML and AI in detecting various threats, including Phishing, Malware, Insider Threats, and Intrusion Detection. We have also analyzed several real-life Cybersecurity applications that integrated ML and AI. Finally, we presented a prototype of an ML- and AI-based Cybersecurity system.

References

1. Buczak, A.L., Guven, E.A.: A survey of data mining and ML methods for cyber security intrusion detection. IEEE Commun Surv Tutor. **18**(2), 1153–1176 (2016)
2. Raff, E., Barker, J., Sylvester, J., Brandon, R., Catanzaro, B., Nicholas, C.K.: Malware detection by eating a whole EXE. AAAI. **33**(01), 8630–8637 (2019)
3. Chen, Y., Abu-Nimeh, S., Alzubi, J.: ML for encrypted malware traffic classification: accounting for Noisy labels and non-stationarity. In: Kirda, E., Ristenpart, T. (eds.) 26th USENIX Security Symposium. USENIX Association (2017)
4. Sharma, A., Sharma, S.K., Singh, P.: An AI-based intrusion detection system for IoT applications. J. Inf. Secur. Appl. **47**, 358–368 (2019)
5. Ferrer, M., Bustamante, M., Continella, A.: Anomaly detection using ML techniques for cloud security: a survey and taxonomy. J. Netw. Comput. Appl. **149**, 102495 (2020)
6. Chowdhury, A., Ferdous, M.S.: Network anomaly detection using ML techniques in SDN. In: 4th International Conference on Electrical Information and Communication Technology (EICT). IEEE (2019)
7. Roffey, T., McLean, C., Eftychiou, E., Parsons, C.: Enhancing cyber threat detection using deep learning techniques. In: Abe, N., Liu, H., Pu, C. (eds.) 2018 IEEE International Conference on Big Data. IEEE (2018)
8. Pendlebury, F., Pierazzi, F., Jordaney, R., Kinder, J., Cavallaro, L.: TESSERACT: eliminating experimental bias in malware classification across space and time. In: Heninger, N., Traynor, P. (eds.) 28th USENIX Security Symposium. USENIX Association (2019)

9. Arctic Wolf Networks.: https://arcticwolf.com/. Last accessed 17 May 2025
10. CylancePROTECT® -- Continuous Threat Prevention Powered by Artificial Intelligence, https://s7d2.scene7.com/is/content/cylance/dev/cylance-web/en-us/resources/knowledge-center/resource-library/data-sheets/CylancePROTECT.pdf. Last accessed 17 May 2025
11. Identify fraudulent online activities -- Prevent online fraud while ensuring a frictionless customer experience, https://aws.amazon.com/ai/use-cases/fraud-detection/. Last accessed 17 May 2025
12. Los Angeles World Airports, Automated People Mover (APM) Project, https://www.lawa.org/transforminglax/old/original-projects/underway/apm. Last accessed 17 May 2025
13. Human Rights Watch, China's Algorithms of Repression: Reverse Engineering a Xinjiang Police Mass Surveillance App, https://www.hrw.org/report/2019/05/01/chinas-algorithms-repression/reverse-engineering-xinjiang-police-mass. Last accessed 17 May 2025
14. Kotecha, K., et al.: Enhanced network intrusion detection system. Sensors. **21**(23), 7835 (2021)
15. Conner-Simons, A.: System Predicts 85 Percent of Cyber-Attacks Using Input from Human Experts. MIT News | Massachusetts Institute of Technology. https://www.csail.mit.edu/news/system-predicts-85-percent-cyber-attacks-using-input-human-experts. Last accessed 17 May 2025

Dynamic ARP Cache Poisoning Detection and Enhanced Prevention in Virtual Networks Using SDN and Real-Time Traffic Analysis with Scapy

Ala'a Alsheikh Ali, Ken McGarry, David Baglee(✉), and Neil Eliot

School of Computer Science, Faculty of Technology, University of Sunderland, Sunderland, UK
{ken.mcgarry,david.baglee,neil.eliot}@sunderland.ac.uk

Abstract. Addressing critical vulnerabilities in network security, this study presents an advanced detection and mitigation framework against ARP spoofing—a major threat exploiting authentication gaps in the ARP protocol. Leveraging Scapy integrated with Software-Defined Networking (SDN) technologies, including the Ryu controller and Open vSwitch, the research introduces a custom ARP cache poisoning script that covertly reroutes network traffic to an attacker-controlled node with precision and control. Deployed in a virtualized environment, the script was tested against tools like Ettercap and Bettercap, achieving superior manipulation capabilities and a 100% ARP table compromise rate. The tailored SDN-based detection tool further demonstrated strong performance, identifying 98.33% of spoofing activities with a low detection latency of 0.024 s and minimal CPU usage, ensuring network efficiency. This research sets a new benchmark in ARP spoofing mitigation and paves the way for future enhancements such as ARP table pre-population and broader protocol support, strengthening defenses in virtualized environments.

Keywords: ARP Spoofing Detection · Software-Defined Networking (SDN) · Scapy · ARP Cache Poisoning · ARP Mitigation Techniques · Open vSiwtch

1 Introduction

In modern digital networks, maintaining secure communication is crucial due to threats like Man-in-the-Middle (MITM) attacks, where attackers covertly manipulate communications between unsuspecting hosts. Several protocols, including the Address Resolution Protocol (ARP), Dynamic Host Configuration Protocol (DHCP), Internet Protocol (IP), and Domain Name System (DNS) are vulnerable to these attacks. ARP spoofing is particularly critical as it involves intercepting data frames that must contain the correct Media Access Control (MAC) address for delivery. This type of spoofing can enable further attacks, such as Denial-of-Service (DDoS) and session hijacking [1].

ARP, essential for IPv4 networks, translates IP addresses to MAC addresses ensuring efficient packet delivery within LANs [2]. It operates by broadcasting requests and

K. Daimi et al. (Eds.): CSCE 2025, CCIS 2937, pp. 67–85, 2026.
https://doi.org/10.1007/978-3-032-22208-4_6

receiving replies to populate an ARP cache with <IP, MAC > pairs, including static (permanent) and dynamic (temporary) entries designated by the operating system [3]. However, ARP's inherent vulnerabilities allow for severe network disruptions through attacks like Denial of Service (DoS), MITM, and session hijacking. These can cripple infrastructure, compromise data, and disrupt services, highlighting the need for robust security measures to protect ARP and the broader network ecosystem [4, 5].

Conventional network configurations often face significant challenges due to the manual setup of IP routers, which is prone to human error. The complexity of configuring various network protocols and rapidly evolving router features can lead to network outages and security vulnerabilities, as even small mistakes may cause major disruptions [6].

Software-Defined Networking (SDN) addresses these issues by separating the control plane, which manages decision-making, from the data plane, which handles packet forwarding. The control plane is operated by a central controller that dynamically directs the data plane's switches or datapaths through protocols like OpenFlow. This setup specifies packet handling rules and actions, enhancing the network's responsiveness and adaptability. If packets don't meet any established rules, the controller provides new instructions or updates to improve performance [7].

SDN's centralized control and programmability substantially improve network management, security, and operational efficiency. It facilitates real-time traffic analysis and automated responses, creating a robust framework for preventing threats like ARP spoofing. This research develops a dynamic ARP cache poisoning detection and prevention system using SDN coupled with Scapy's packet analysis capabilities, aiming to bolster network security and mitigate sophisticated cyber threats.

1.1 Detailed Analysis of ARP Protocol and Vulnerabilities

ARP poisoning (**CVE-1999-0667**) is a severe vulnerability with a CVSS score of 10.0 [8]. ARP operates at the data link layer, resolving IP addresses to MAC addresses through simple request-reply messages. A device broadcasts an ARP request when it needs a MAC address, and the matching host responds with its MAC [2].

However, ARP is inherently insecure due to its lack of authentication. It does not verify the source of ARP packets, allowing any host to send forged replies. Attackers exploit this by broadcasting fake ARP messages, tricking devices into storing incorrect cache entries [9]. This is worsened by ARP's stateless nature, which fails to distinguish between solicited and unsolicited replies, making spoofing easier [3].

Several ARP poisoning methods have been identified [10]. Attackers can send unsolicited ARP replies unrelated to any request, poisoning a host's cache or broadcasting them to impact the entire LAN. They may also mimic legitimate ARP requests, tricking hosts into recording the attacker's IP and MAC. A more advanced tactic involves intercepting a legitimate ARP request and sending a fake reply. Since hosts accept the latest reply, the attacker's response can overwrite valid entries. Attackers may also combine fake requests and replies to poison multiple caches. ARP cache entries update dynamically without verification, worsening security risks. Devices accept updates even without sending a request, allowing attackers to inject false mappings. While this behavior improves efficiency by reducing constant ARP queries, it creates opportunities for poisoning attacks [11]. The broadcast nature of ARP requests further exposes the network, as any device, including malicious ones, can reply.

ARP poisoning enables various attacks. In DoS, attackers redirect traffic to nonexistent addresses, disrupting services. In MITM, attackers secretly intercept and manipulate communication between two parties, compromising data integrity and confidentiality [4]. This process is illustrated in Fig. 1, where the attacker manipulates ARP responses to reroute traffic through a malicious node, enabling interception.

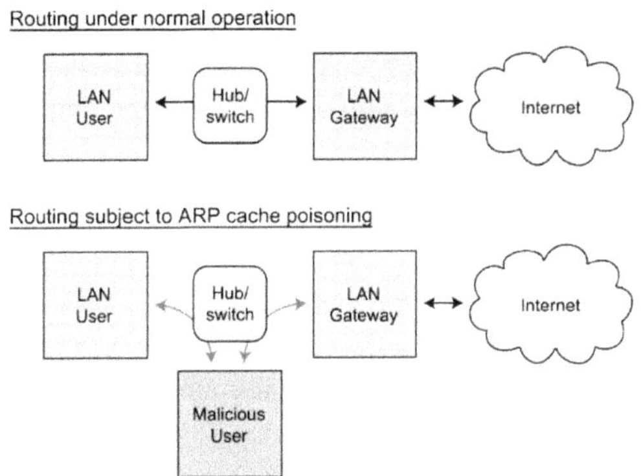

Fig. 1. ARP Spoofing Enabling MITM Attack via Traffic Redirection [12]

Other risks include MAC flooding, where spoofed ARP replies overwhelm the switch, forcing it into broadcast mode and exposing all traffic. MAC duplicating involves matching the target's MAC address, confusing the switch and splitting traffic. MAC spoofing allows unauthorized access by impersonating legitimate devices. **Session hijacking**, highlighted in the **OWASP Top 10**, exploits ARP's lack of authentication by compromising session tokens to take control of user sessions [5, 9].

ARP poisoning mainly targets LANs, exploiting the transition from network to data link layer addressing. Attackers can intercept, modify, or halt traffic, causing disruptions and data breaches by manipulating ARP cache tables to reroute packets and gain unauthorized access to sensitive data in transit [4]. ARP has several variations serving different purposes: standard ARP resolves IP to MAC addresses; Proxy ARP enables communication between devices on different networks by responding with the router's MAC; Reverse ARP (RARP) maps MAC to IP addresses, often for thin clients; Gratuitous ARP detects IP conflicts when interfaces are enabled; and Inverse ARP resolves IP addresses to DLCIs in frame relay networks [13]. Proxy ARP supports transparent subnet gateways, allowing hosts to communicate across routers without configured default gateways, while Gratuitous ARP helps verify IP uniqueness on networks with dynamic addressing [13]. ARP's core flaw remains its lack of authentication, originally designed under the assumption that all LAN devices are trustworthy—a dangerous assumption in modern environments [13].

2 Related Work

2.1 Traditional Detection Methods

2.1.1 Passive Detection

Passive detection techniques monitor ARP traffic to detect discrepancies in IP-MAC mappings without interfering with network operations. Tools like Arpwatch, ArpOn, and xArp maintain legitimate mapping databases and generate alerts when changes suggest ARP spoofing. These methods are minimally intrusive but suffer from detection delays, which may allow initial malicious activity to go unnoticed. Additionally, they scale poorly in large networks due to false positives and the significant administrative effort required to manage alerts [3, 14]. While some advanced switches offer port mirroring to support traffic monitoring, these solutions are costly and complex to deploy [11].

2.1.2 Active Detection

Active detection, on the other hand, queries the network to verify ARP traffic and confirm IP-MAC pairings. One method involves a voting system where hosts validate ARP replies based on majority consensus, effectively filtering spoofed responses but increasing network traffic and exposing the system to flooding attacks [15]. Another technique uses ICMP echo requests to ping the IP address in question; if the MAC address of the response matches the ARP entry, the mapping is considered legitimate. This allows real-time validation but adds network overhead and processing load [16].

Another approach leverages Transmission Control Protocol (TCP) to distinguish genuine from forged ARP communications by analyzing responses to injected ARP and TCP SYN requests. This method enables rapid detection and remains effective even when hosts have personal firewalls, as long as at least one TCP port is open [17]. Similarly, the Discrete Event Systems (DES) technique sends probe packets and compares network behavior against predefined patterns to detect anomalies indicating ARP spoofing [18]. Attackers are also categorized by capability levels, ranging from those limited to generating fake ARP packets to those able to fully manipulate their protocol stack to bypass detection [19]. However, active detection faces challenges such as the need for additional software on all hosts, high implementation costs, and increased network traffic, highlighting the importance of scalable and efficient detection solutions.

2.2 Traditional Mitigation Techniques

2.2.1 Secure ARP (S-ARP)

S-ARP enhances ARP security by incorporating cryptographic signatures into ARP messages, ensuring only authenticated messages update the ARP cache. Despite its effectiveness in preventing ARP spoofing, S-ARP requires substantial modifications to network stacks, making widespread deployment challenging across varied operating systems [20].

2.2.2 Kernel-Based Patches

Solutions like Anticap and Antidote enhance individual host security by blocking unauthorized ARP cache updates. These methods prevent attacks from establishing a foothold but may interfere with legitimate network operations, such as those involving gratuitous ARP messages, necessitating careful management to avoid false positives [21].

2.2.3 Dynamic ARP Inspection (DAI)

DAI, implemented on network switches, validates ARP packets against a trusted DHCP snooping database to ensure their authenticity. This process effectively blocks malicious packets, safeguarding the network against ARP spoofing with minimal impact on network performance. However, DAI requires meticulous configuration to avoid disrupting legitimate traffic [22].

2.3 Overview of Software-Defined Networking (SDN)

2.3.1 Separation of Control and Data Planes

SDN transforms network architecture by separating the control plane from the data plane, centralizing decision-making within an SDN controller. This controller provides global network visibility and manages flow tables that govern packet forwarding. Protocols like OpenFlow enable seamless communication between the controller and network devices, ensuring precise traffic management. By streamlining network operations, SDN reduces configuration errors and significantly improves reliability [23, 24].

2.3.2 Programmable Networks

SDN's programmability enables administrators to develop applications that automate tasks, adapt to real-time network conditions, and enforce security policies. This flexibility supports dynamic resource optimization and tailored management. For example, dynamic load balancing applications can evenly distribute traffic across servers, preventing overloads and mitigating potential DDoS attacks [24, 25].

2.3.3 Open vSwitch (OvS)

OvS serves as a key component in SDN architectures, especially in data centers. Acting as a multilayer virtual switch, it enables network automation through programmable extensions and standard interfaces. OvS executes flow rules from the SDN controller, supporting network virtualization and efficient resource allocation. Its integration with controllers like OpenDaylight or ONOS enhances scalability and adaptability, ensuring optimal performance in dynamic environments [24, 26].

2.4 Evaluating SDN Enhancements and Controller Performance Over Traditional Network Architectures

2.4.1 SDN Versus Traditional Networks

SDN's programmability enables rapid deployment and automated management of network functions, offering superior agility compared to traditional architectures that rely heavily on manual configurations. This flexibility is vital in dynamic environments where changing network conditions and traffic patterns demand quick adaptation to maintain performance and security [27]. Additionally, SDN enhances security by supporting tools like Deep Packet Inspection (DPI), allowing real-time monitoring, detection, and mitigation of application-layer attacks while enforcing dynamic security policies across the network [28]. Performance evaluations highlight RYU's suitability for high-performance scenarios requiring low latency, making it ideal for real-time applications. This is particularly beneficial in environments implementing Network Functions Virtualization (NFV), where services are managed dynamically. For example, Virtual Customer Premises Equipment (vCPE) leverages SDN's centralized control to deliver network services at the edge, minimizing reliance on physical hardware and optimizing service delivery with greater flexibility and efficiency [25, 29].

2.4.2 Detailed Performance Analysis of SDN Controller

Several SDN controllers have been developed to meet diverse network requirements, including Beacon, Floodlight, RYU, OpenDaylight, ONOS, NOX, and POX. Among them, RYU—developed by NTT Labs in Python—offers a comprehensive framework with rich libraries and modules, emphasizing simplicity and flexibility for developing and deploying SDN applications. Performance evaluations show RYU outperforms POX, achieving 1.24% to 5.35% higher average throughput, with reductions in delay (0.5 to 1 ms) and jitter (around 0.02 ms), making it ideal for high-performance, low-latency environments [30]. Further testing using emulation tools like Mininet reinforces RYU's suitability for throughput-intensive applications, while POX may still be preferred in scenarios prioritizing platform compatibility. Additionally, SDN's dynamic management of network functions—such as firewalls, load balancers, and vCPE—enhances service delivery, network flexibility, and cost efficiency, showcasing SDN's transformative impact.

2.5 Detailed Comparison of SDN-Based ARP Spoofing Detection and Mitigation Methods

2.5.1 SARP_NAT (Method 1)

Alharbi et al. [32] examined SDN vulnerabilities to ARP and NDP (NS/NA) spoofing using Mininet, Open vSwitch, and the POX controller. Their experiments involved three switches and three hosts, with Scapy simulating ARP spoofing attacks. In one key test, host h1 successfully redirected traffic from h3 by corrupting h2's ARP cache. To mitigate such attacks, they proposed **SARP_NAT**—a mechanism that sanitizes ARP requests by masking the Source Protocol Address (SPA) and Source Hardware Address (SHA), ensuring only replies tied to verified requests are processed and blocking unsolicited responses. SARP_NAT was tested on both linear and tree topologies with 64 nodes, achieving a 32% improvement in ARP RTT and reduced CPU load, demonstrating its effectiveness in enhancing SDN security with minimal overhead.

2.5.2 Intrusion Detection and Prevention System (IDPS) (Method 2)

In 2021, Girdler and Vassilakis [32] developed an Intrusion Detection and Prevention System (IDPS) utilizing an OvS switch-based flow-entry mechanism to detect and block ARP spoofing attacks. When a packet lacks a matching flow entry, it triggers a PacketIn event, sending it to the POX controller for analysis. The controller runs **four** key checks: ARP Request, Reply, Reply Destination Spoofing, and Blacklisted MAC Address detection. Tested in a VM environment using Ubuntu, OvS, and Wireshark, the system achieved rapid detection—identifying spoofed packets within 2.2 s and blacklisted MACs even faster, with zero false positives. This demonstrates SDN's potential to enhance network security without compromising performance.

2.5.3 Distributed Responder ARP (DR-ARP) (Method 3)

Matties [33] introduced the Distributed Responder ARP (DR-ARP) system, an SDN solution aimed at centralizing ARP request processing to enhance security and functionality. DR-ARP reroutes all ARP traffic to a central service that maintains an updated ARP service table, ensuring accurate replies. The service starts once the DR-ARP responder is authenticated and synchronized, which helps in maintaining the integrity and availability of network data. The system was evaluated using a setup with Ubuntu Linux and Open vSwitch, showing a slight increase in service time due to packet capture delays, suggesting areas for optimization with specialized packet handling solutions.

2.5.4 Monitoring and Flow Control System (Method 4)

AbdelSalam, El-Sisi, and Reddy K [34] implemented a system based on the SDN POX controller to prevent ARP spoofing in LANs. This system distinguishes between edge and intermediate switches, applying security measures specifically at the edges where attacks are more likely. It uses L2 learning modules to monitor ARP and DHCP traffic, redirecting suspicious packets to the controller for further analysis. Their setup, tested using Mininet and an Ubuntu VM, effectively managed to detect and mitigate ARP spoofing attacks rapidly, with marginal impact on network throughput, showcasing the potential of SDN in managing network security proactively.

2.6 Comparison of SDN Solutions

The comparative analysis of the four methods highlights their varied use of SDN functionalities and flow rule strategies. Method 1 mitigates ARP spoofing and flooding by applying proactive flow rules and leveraging DHCP servers for IP management but lacks advanced features like metadata tagging and blacklisted MAC detection. Method 2 integrates traffic steering and metadata tagging into flow rules for enhanced security but omits ARP flood protection and proxy ARP support. Method 3 focuses on detecting ARP spoofing and blacklisted MAC addresses but does not support DHCP or proxy ARP. Method 4 prevents controller overload by distinguishing edge and intermediate switches and using port monitoring algorithms to counter DOS attacks, yet lacks static IP provisioning and metadata tagging. Overall, these methods reflect diverse priorities

Table 1. SDN Mitigation Features Comparison

Features	Method 1	Method 2	Method 3	Method 4
Employs DHCP Server	✓	✓		✓
Supports Static IP Addresses	✓	✓	✓	
Mitigates ARP Spoofing	✓	✓	✓	✓
Defends Against ARP Flooding	✓	✓	✓	
Operates as Proxy ARP	✓	✓		✓
Inserts Flow Rules Actively				✓
Tags ARP Requests with Metadata		✓	✓	
Detects Blacklisted MAC Addresses	✓	✓	✓	✓
Directs Traffic via SDN Control		✓	✓	
Differentiates Edge and Core Switches			✓	✓
Prevents Controller Overload		✓		✓

and partial utilization of SDN's capabilities, indicating room for further enhancement and comprehensive feature integration (Table 1).

2.7 Testing Comparison

Table 2. SDN Mitigation Testing Comparison

Testing Metrics	Method 1	Method 2	Method 3	Method 4
Conducted in Physical Testbed	✓	✓	✓	
Conducted in Virtual Testbed			✓	✓
Tested ARP Spoofing Mitigation	✓	✓	✓	✓
Measured CPU Load	✓			✓
Evaluated Round Trip Time (RTT)	✓	✓	✓	
Assessed Data Throughput	✓	✓		✓
Analyzed Detection Time	✓	✓	✓	✓

The evaluation of test environments and metrics across the four approaches reveals key differences in assessing ARP spoofing mitigation. **Methods 1** and **2** use physical testbeds that better reflect real network conditions but introduce variability affecting reproducibility. Their metrics—ARP mitigation, CPU load, RTT, data throughput, and detection time—thoroughly assess performance, latency, and responsiveness but overlook scalability and other attack vectors. In contrast, **Methods 3** and **4** rely on virtual testbeds, offering controlled, consistent environments but missing real-world complexity. These methods mainly evaluate ARP mitigation, RTT, and detection time, confirming detection efficiency but failing to assess CPU load and throughput, potentially missing performance impacts. Overall, physical testbeds provide realism with variability, while virtual testbeds offer control but may lack generalizability (Table 2).

2.8 Real-Time Detection Using Scapy in SDN Solutions

Scapy, a Python-based tool for interactive packet manipulation, plays a pivotal role in SDN environments for crafting, analyzing, and testing both legitimate and spoofed packets in real time. Alharbi et al. [31] used Scapy to simulate ARP attacks for evaluating detection responsiveness. Matties [33] incorporated it into a Distributed Responder ARP system to generate accurate ARP replies, enhancing spoofing resistance. Girdler and Vassilakis [32] embedded Scapy within their IDPS framework, detecting ARP spoofing in 2.2 s through packet inspection and dynamic flow enforcement. AbdelSalam, El-Sisi, and Reddy K [34] further demonstrated its utility in port-level ARP traffic monitoring, dynamically applying OpenFlow rules to block malicious packets under traffic spikes. Collectively, these works highlight Scapy's integral role in facilitating real-time ARP spoofing detection and mitigation within SDN architectures.

3 Materials and Methods

3.1 Network Topology Setup

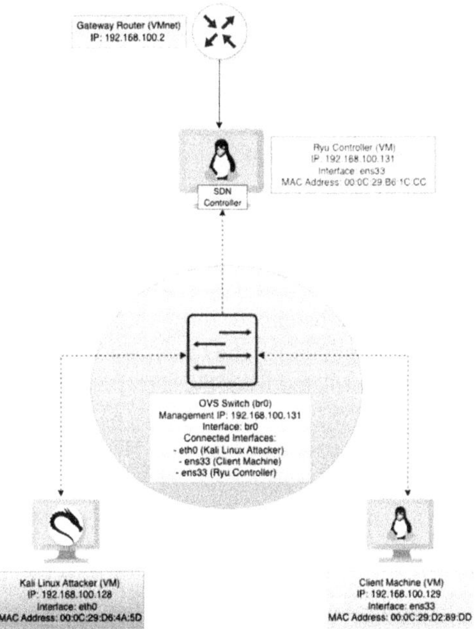

Fig. 2. Network Topology

The experimental setup shown in Fig. 2 outlines the virtual SDN environment used to simulate and evaluate ARP spoofing attacks. It included a Kali Linux attacker (IP: 192.168.100.128) hosting the spoofing scripts, a client machine (IP: 192.168.100.129) as the spoofing target, and a gateway router (IP: 192.168.100.2) serving as the default route. These components were interconnected via an Open vSwitch (br0), managed by the Ryu SDN controller responsible for traffic monitoring and spoofing mitigation.

3.2 ARP Cache Poisoning Attack: Development and Testing

To develop an effective ARP cache poisoning attack script, we established specific functional and non-functional requirements. Functionally, the script must accurately retrieve and utilize MAC addresses from ARP requests to associate the attacker's MAC with the target and gateway IPs, maintaining continuous poisoning since ARP caches are periodically refreshed. The script must support controlled execution, allowing initiation and termination at command, and ensure ARP tables return to their original state upon stopping. Non-functionally, the script demands high performance to minimize delay in packet sending, essential for effective poisoning and avoiding network congestion. Scalability to handle multiple targets, reliability to manage network errors smoothly, and security to avoid affecting non-target systems are crucial. Usability focuses on providing clear user instructions, immediate feedback, and detailed logs for effective operation and troubleshooting.

3.2.1 Implementation/Build (ARP Cache Poisoning)

The ARP cache poisoning attack script, implemented in Python using the Scapy library, follows a structured process to meet attack requirements. It begins by verifying root privileges, essential for network manipulation and packet crafting, through an effective user ID check **(os.geteuid()**). If not executed as root, the script logs an error and terminates. Upon successful verification, it proceeds to load and validate a YAML configuration file containing network details and attack parameters. The load_configuration function parses this file, ensuring all required parameters are correctly specified.

A pivotal part of the process is the MAC address retrieval. Using Scapy's **srp** function, the script sends ARP requests and listens for responses. For each target and gateway IP, it constructs Ethernet frames destined for the broadcast address, ensuring all responses are captured. MAC addresses extracted from these responses are critical for subsequent ARP replies aimed at poisoning the network.

The script's functionality is extended through IP forwarding and NAT, enabling seamless traffic routing and masquerading on the attacker's machine. These settings are configured using /proc./sys/net/ipv4/ip_forward and iptables. The attack transmits crafted ARP replies that map the attacker's MAC address to both the target and gateway IPs, impersonating the legitimate host. This loop-based process sends packets at randomized intervals to avoid detection, as controlled by the arp_poisoning function (Fig. 3).

The script incorporates a monitoring function to verify the persistence of ARP poisoning by checking the target's ARP cache. If legitimate MAC addresses reappear, the attack is reinitiated to maintain disruption. Upon completion, the script restores the network by re-associating IP addresses with their correct MAC addresses and disabling IP forwarding and NAT, ensuring no trace of the intrusion. All actions are logged using Python's logging module, providing detailed records for debugging and documentation. Designed modularly around the NetworkIntruder class, the script organizes initialization, attack execution, monitoring, and cleanup, facilitating maintenance and future enhancements.

```
def arp_poisoning(self, stop_event):
    """Perform ARP poisoning."""
    target_arp_pkt = ARP(op=2, psrc=self.gateway_ip, pdst=self.target_ip, hwdst=self.target_mac, hwsrc=self.attacker_mac)
    gateway_arp_pkt = ARP(op=2, psrc=self.target_ip, pdst=self.gateway_ip, hwdst=self.gateway_mac, hwsrc=self.attacker_mac)

    logging.info(f"Initiating ARP attack on target ({self.target_ip}) and gateway ({self.gateway_ip}).")

    while not stop_event.is_set():
        sys.stdout.write('*')
        sys.stdout.flush()
        try:
            # Send ARP packets more frequently to maintain the spoof
            send(target_arp_pkt, verbose=False)
            send(gateway_arp_pkt, verbose=False)
        except Exception as e:
            logging.error(f"Error in ARP poisoning: {e}")
            break

        # Shortened and randomized interval to maintain consistent spoofing
        time.sleep(self.attack_interval / 2 + random.uniform(-0.25, 0.25))

    logging.info("ARP poisoning stopped.")
    self.restore_arp_tables()
```

Fig. 3. arp_poisoning function

3.2.2 Testing (ARP Cache Poisoning Attack)

Fig. 4. Terminal Output During Attack Execution

The ARP cache poisoning script was tested in a Kali Linux environment, with system behavior and network responses monitored via terminal outputs and log files. Tests verified successful MAC address retrieval for the target and gateway, crucial for crafting ARP replies. The setup initialized network interface eth0 and configured IP forwarding and NAT to enable packet routing and masquerading. Continuous ARP replies effectively manipulated the ARP tables of both the target and gateway, while real-time monitoring and terminal logs demonstrated the script's ability to sustain and adjust the spoofing attack (Fig. 4).

3.3 Detection/Mitigation System: Development and Testing (See Fig. 5)

Figure 6 illustrates the SDN controller's decision-making process, from packet reception to action determination, highlighting the automated security measures enforced at each stage. The ARP spoof detection and mitigation tool leverages an SDN controller to enforce programmatic security policies. At startup, the controller applies default flow rules to establish a secure baseline, integrating a DHCP whitelist and a verified VM-to-MAC/IP mapping database to authenticate endpoints and block unauthorized access.

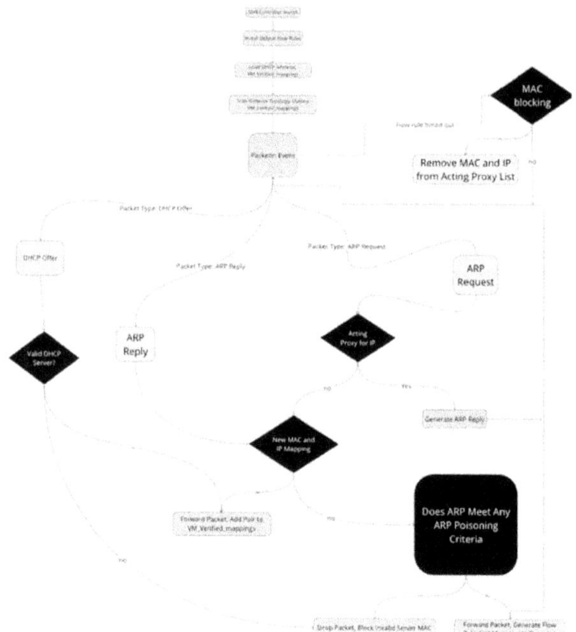

Fig. 5. ARP Spoof Detection and Mitigation System Workflow

It monitors packet-in events—DHCP offers, ARP requests, and ARP replies—each triggering specific actions. DHCP offers are validated; trusted entries are logged and forwarded, while unverified ones result in MAC blocking. ARP requests are screened for spoofing patterns such as unsolicited broadcasts or IP-MAC mismatches, dropping malicious packets and blocking the source. ARP replies are verified before updating the database and forwarding the packet.

3.3.1 Implementation/Build (Detection/Mitigation System)

The system was deployed in a secure virtual environment. Open vSwitch (OVS) was installed and configured on a VM, with the client interface (ens33) added to bridge (br0). Ryu and Scapy were installed to support detection logic. The Ryu controller processed DHCP offers, ARP requests, and ARP replies via parse_packet and handle_packet functions. Rogue DHCP servers were blocked using a whitelist; verified offers updated the MacDatabaseHandler. ARP requests were checked against this database—authentic ones passed, spoofed ones triggered MAC blocking.

ARP replies were validated through the **validate_reply** function, where mismatches raised alerts and initiated updates to the ARP cache or changes to firewall rules to isolate threats. Real-time flow rules were applied using **manage_flows**, enabling a dynamic response to threats. The system's resilience was further enhanced by several supporting modules: ProxyHandler centralized ARP replies to reduce spoofing exposure, NetworkScanner continuously updated MAC-IP pairings to maintain accurate network information, and both **ArpRequestTracker** and **EventLogger** monitored for anomalies and patterns indicative of coordinated attacks, enabling early intervention.

3.3.2 Testing (Detection/Mitigation System)

The testing phase of the ARP spoof detection and mitigation tool involved structured tests assessing the system's responsiveness to various ARP-related threats. Scenarios ranged from detecting unknown MAC addresses to handling complex MITM attacks. Each test was documented with details on the spoofing attempt, expected system response, and assigned threat priority (Table 3).

Table 3. Various ARP attack tests

Test	Description	Expected Response	Priority
Test 1	ARP Request Flood (Unknown MAC)	Detect and block unknown MAC, log actions.	Medium
Test 2	ARP Request (Spoofed MAC in known list)	Detect spoofed MAC, block and log.	High
Test 3	ARP Reply Spoof (Gateway IP Spoof MITM)	Block spoofed ARP replies, log MITM attempt.	Critical
Test 4	**ARP Request (Gateway IP Spoof MITM)**	**Detect and block spoofed IP, enforce proxy response, log actions.**	**Critical**
Test 5	ARP Reply Spoof with Broadcast MAC	Detect and block spoofed IP and MAC, log actions.	High
Test 6	ARP Reply (Removed from Mappings)	Detect and block unmapped MAC, log actions.	Medium
Test 7	Gratuitous ARP Attack	Detect and block gratuitous ARP, update ARP table.	High

[a]Test 4: ARP Request (Spoofed Gateway)

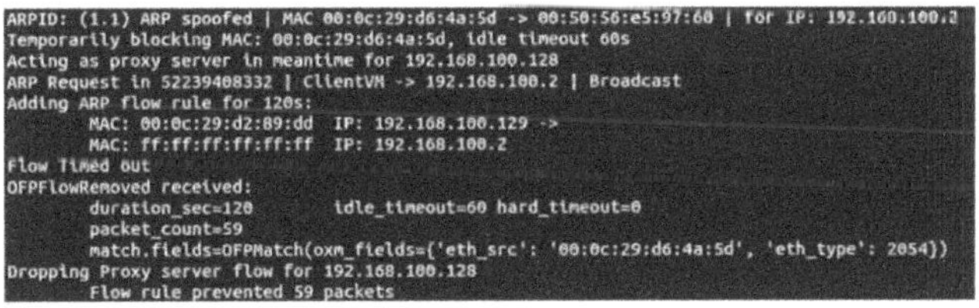

```
ARPID: (1.1) ARP spoofed | MAC 00:0c:29:d6:4a:5d -> 00:50:56:e5:97:60 | for IP: 192.168.100.2
Temporarily blocking MAC: 00:0c:29:d6:4a:5d, idle timeout 60s
Acting as proxy server in meantime for 192.168.100.128
ARP Request in 52239408332 | ClientVM -> 192.168.100.2 | Broadcast
Adding ARP flow rule for 120s:
        MAC: 00:0c:29:d2:89:dd  IP: 192.168.100.129 ->
        MAC: ff:ff:ff:ff:ff:ff  IP: 192.168.100.2
Flow Timed out
OFPFlowRemoved received:
        duration_sec=120        idle_timeout=60 hard_timeout=0
        packet_count=59
        match.fields=OFPMatch(oxm_fields={'eth_src': '00:0c:29:d6:4a:5d', 'eth_type': 2054})
Dropping Proxy server flow for 192.168.100.128
        Flow rule prevented 59 packets
```

Fig. 6. ARP Request Spoofed IP Terminal Logs

The SDN controller logs illustrate the detection and mitigation of a spoofed ARP request from MAC address **00:0c:29:d6:4a:5d**, which targeted IP **192.168.100.2**. The controller temporarily blocked the MAC for **60 s** and assumed proxy responsibilities for IP **192.168.100.128**, ensuring uninterrupted network service. An ARP flow rule was

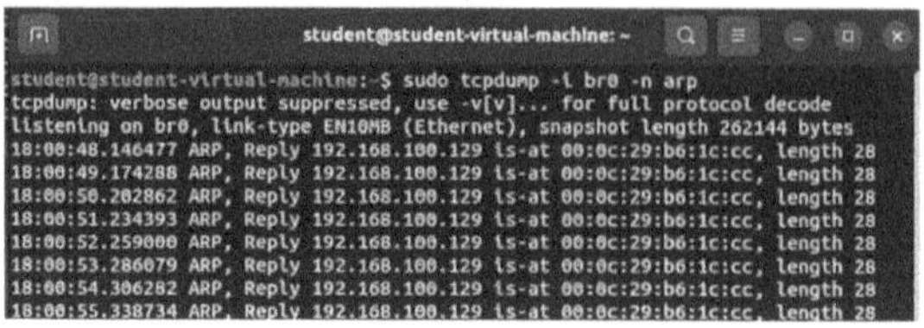

Fig. 7. Tcpdump Output Showing ARP Replies

established for **120 s**, effectively blocking **60 packets** (counted as 59 due to zero-based indexing) (Fig. 7).

Tcpdump output verifies the controller's continuous ARP replies to IP **192.168.100.129**, demonstrating the system's capability to maintain network responses throughout the duration of the attack.

3.4 Methodology for ARP Attack Tool Comparison

The methodology outlines the comparative evaluation of ARP spoofing tools—including a custom ARP script, Ettercap, arpspoof, and Bettercap—within an SDN-controlled environment. Evaluation criteria are categorized into functional requirements, assessing each tool's ability to craft ARP packets, execute various spoofing techniques, and perform attacks continuously or for a specified number of packets. Non-functional requirements examine performance aspects such as responsiveness, scalability, reliability, and usability. The framework further analyzes each tool's technical execution—specifically the spoofing method, success in altering ARP tables, impact on network traffic, and the SDN system's ability to detect and mitigate these attacks. Implementation involved configuring each tool, conducting ARP attacks in a controlled environment, and capturing network traffic with Wireshark, ensuring a comprehensive assessment of each tool's impact on network security for detailed analysis in subsequent sections.

4 Results and Discussions

4.1 ARP Cache Poisoning Attack Script Results

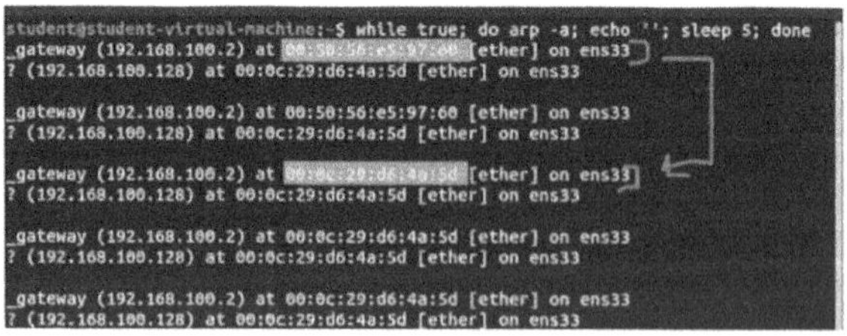

Fig. 8. Client's ARP Table After ARP Cache Poisoning Attack

The victim's ARP table displayed the attacker's MAC address (00:0c:29:d6:4a:5d) incorrectly mapped to the gateway's IP, confirming successful ARP cache poisoning. Despite traffic redirection, web services remained accessible, underscoring the attack's stealth. Wireshark analysis revealed continuous ARP replies from the attacker's MAC, falsely binding it to 192.168.100.2 and 192.168.100.129. This ensured persistent ARP cache manipulation across network devices, maintaining the attack's effectiveness (Fig. 8).

4.2 Detection/Mitigation System Results

The system demonstrated robust performance across a range of ARP spoofing scenarios, detecting 413 out of 420 spoofed packets—yielding a 98.33% detection rate. Minor discrepancies were attributed to packet indexing conventions. Throughout testing, the system maintained efficiency with an average round-trip time (RTT) of 0.0247 s and CPU usage averaging 9.23%. Detection accuracy improved through dynamic adjustment of ARP mappings when spoofed or unknown MAC addresses were encountered. While most threats were fully mitigated, some scenarios remained only "Mostly Mitigated," indicating the need for enhancements in preemptive blocking. Statistical analysis via Python and Pandas helped identify these gaps and guide potential system refinements.

4.3 Detailed Reults of ARP Attack Tools

In evaluating ARP spoofing tools, distinct behavioral patterns and detection gaps emerged. The Researcher's custom script generated 260 packets (8 requests, 252 replies) within one minute, with sizes ranging 42–60 bytes and erratic intervals averaging 0.24 s. Although the SDN controller detected the traffic, it failed to classify it as malicious, revealing a critical detection weakness. The script achieved the highest spoofing score of 66/100 due to its complex traffic patterns. Ettercap produced 32 packets (6 requests, 26 replies) with slower 1.78-s intervals, similarly detected but unflagged, scoring 54. Arpspoof relied solely on 34 ARP replies (42 bytes) at 2.00-s intervals, entirely evading detection and scoring lowest at 38. Bettercap sent 62 replies (42–60 bytes) with faster 0.94-s intervals, yet also bypassed detection, scoring 50, further exposing SDN limitations. For a detailed comparison of the packet characteristics and scoring metrics of each tool, see Table 4.

4.4 Comparitive Analysis Analysis with Literature

4.4.1 SDN Detection Performance with Scapy Tests

The SDN detection system achieved a 98.33% success rate, aligning with or surpassing Alharbi et al. [31] and Matties [34]. While Alharbi et al.'s SARP_NAT reduced ARP RTT by 32%, it incurred higher CPU loads. In contrast, this system maintained low CPU usage (9.23%) and achieved an average RTT of 0.0247512 s, effectively balancing detection speed and resource efficiency. Matties [33] similarly emphasized minimizing RTT to prevent latency—an objective successfully met in this study. Nonetheless, the

Table 4. Analysis Results of Spoofing Tools

Criteria	**Researcher's Script**	**Ettercap**	**Arpspoof**	**Bettercap**
Total Packet Count	260 (6)	32 (2)	34 (2)	62 (2)
Detection by SDN	Detected but not flagged as attack (6)	Detected but not flagged as attack (6)	Not detected (10)	Not detected (10)
Mitigation by SDN	Not mitigated (10)	Not mitigated (10)	Not mitigated (10)	Not mitigated (10)
Packet Distribution	8 ARP requests, 252 ARP replies (2)	6 ARP requests, 26 ARP replies (2)	0 ARP requests, 34 ARP replies (10)	0 ARP requests, 64 ARP replies (10)
Network Impact	Average interval 0.24 seconds (6)	Average interval 1.781 seconds (2)	Average interval 2.00 seconds (2)	Avg interval 0.94s (2)
Spoofing Techniques (op codes)	Uses both ARP requests and replies (10)	Uses both ARP requests and replies (10)	Uses only ARP replies (2)	Uses only replies (2)
Payload Content	Simple payload (6)	Simple payload (6)	Simple payload (6)	Simple payload (6)
Response Behavior	Significant disruptions (10)	Minor disruptions (6)	No noticeable impact (2)	Minor disruptions (6)
Timing Patterns	Unpredictable intervals (10)	Unpredictable intervals (10)	Highly predictable intervals (2)	Unpredictable intervals (10)
Total Score	**66**	**54**	**38**	**50**

"Mostly Mitigated" outcomes observed in some scenarios indicate areas for improvement, consistent with AbdelSalam et al. [34], who faced similar mitigation challenges. Additionally, the minor detection gap (<1%) highlights the need for further fine-tuning to enhance coverage, ensuring comprehensive protection against ARP spoofing threats in diverse attack conditions.

4.4.2 Evaluation of Attack Tools and SDN Detection Gaps

Our analysis revealed that the Researcher's Script achieved the highest efficacy score of 66 by combining ARP requests and replies to generate complex traffic patterns that effectively challenged the SDN's detection capabilities. This dual approach reflects advanced techniques seen in SARP_NAT and DR-ARP frameworks, emphasizing the need for adaptive security measures in dynamic environments.

While the SDN controller partially detected the Researcher's Script and Ettercap, it failed to classify them as threats, exposing significant gaps in contextual analysis, consistent with AbdelSalam et al. [34]. Furthermore, the failure to detect simpler attacks from Arpspoof and Bettercap highlights critical vulnerabilities, aligning with Matties [33], who noted the difficulty in detecting unpredictable ARP traffic. Notably, the Researcher's Script's unpredictable packet timing, despite its sophistication, did not trigger threat alerts, reflecting complexity challenges highlighted by Alharbi et al. [31]. These findings underscore the need for an enhanced detection framework capable of identifying both sophisticated and basic attacks. Incorporating diverse ARP spoofing tactics, proactive packet sanitization, and advanced metadata analysis—as proposed by AbdelSalam et al. [37] and Alharbi et al. [31]—will significantly strengthen SDN resilience against evolving threats.

4.5 Conclusion

This research thoroughly explored the design and implementation of a Scapy-based ARP spoofing detection system for virtualized networks. A custom ARP cache poisoning script was developed to expose ARP protocol vulnerabilities and validated through extensive testing, detailed logs, and Wireshark captures. While the system achieved high detection rates against Scapy-generated attacks, it exhibited limitations in identifying more complex, non-Scapy techniques. These results highlight the need for more robust heuristic evaluations and broader detection capabilities to effectively address diverse ARP spoofing threats.

5 Recommendations and Future Work

Future developments should focus on refining detection algorithms to handle a wider range of ARP spoofing techniques beyond those generated by Scapy, integrating machine learning for adaptive threat responses and improving the system's ability to recognize sophisticated attacks. Expanding the framework to support IPv6 and incorporating devices with **multiplexed network cards** would enhance versatility and ensure comprehensive coverage in complex network environments. Additionally, aligning flow rule lifetimes with **DHCP lease times** could optimize resource management, while improving ARP proxy functionality with ARP packet replay features would reduce resource overhead and mitigate potential DoS scenarios caused by incorrect MAC blocking. To validate effectiveness, future testing should extend beyond virtual environments to include physical network setups, ensuring practical applicability and identifying performance challenges. Furthermore, conducting stress tests under varied network loads is crucial to evaluate system robustness and maintain detection efficiency in high-traffic scenarios. Collectively, these enhancements will strengthen the system's resilience and adaptability, enabling more robust protection against evolving ARP spoofing threats within SDN architectures.

Competing Interests. The author(s) has no competing interests to declare that are relevant to the content of this manuscript.

References

1. Morsy, S.M., Nashat, D.: D-ARP: an efficient scheme to detect and prevent ARP spoofing. IEEE Access. **10**, 49142–49153 (2022)
2. Plummer, D.: Ethernet Address Resolution Protocol: Or Converting Network Protocol Addresses to 48.bit Ethernet Address for Transmission on Ethernet Hardware. RFC Editor. https://doi.org/10.17487/rfc0826 (1982)
3. Cox, J.H., Clark, R.J., Owen, H.L.: Leveraging SDN for ARP security, pp. 1–8 (2016)
4. Rupal, D.R., Satasiya, D., Kumar, H., Agrawal, A.: Detection and prevention of ARP poisoning in dynamic IP configuration. In: 2016 IEEE International Conference on Recent Trends in Electronics, Information & Communication Technology (RTEICT), pp. 1240–1244. IEEE (2016)
5. Thomas, D.R., et al.: Detection and prevention of poisoning targets with ARP cache using scapy. In: 2024 International Conference on Intelligent and Innovative Technologies in Computing, Electrical and Electronics (IITCEE), pp. 1–6. IEEE (2024)
6. Caldwell, D., Gilbert, A., Gottlieb, J., Greenberg, A., Hjalmtysson, G., Rexford, J.: The cutting EDGE of IP router configuration. SIGCOMM Comput. Commun. Rev. **34**, 21–26 (2004). https://doi.org/10.1145/972374.972379

7. di Lallo, R., Lospoto, G., Rimondini, M., Di Battista, G.: How to handle ARP in a software-defined network. In: 2016 IEEE NetSoft Conference and Workshops (NetSoft), pp. 63–67 (2016)
8. MITRE.: Arp Protocol : Security vulnerabilities, *CVEs*. www.cvedetails.com. Available at: https://www.cvedetails.com/vulnerability-list/vendor_id-101/Arp-Protocol.html. Accessed 17 June 2024 (1997)
9. Hijazi, S., Obaidat, M.S.: Address resolution protocol spoofing attacks and security approaches: a survey. Secur. Priv. **2**(1), e49 (2019)
10. Tripunitara, M.V., Dutta, P.: Middle approach to asynchronous and backward-compatible detection and prevention of ARP cache poisoning. U.S. Patent 6,771,649 (2004)
11. Venkatramulu, S., Rao, C.G.: Various solutions for address resolution protocol spoofing attacks. Int. J. Sci. Res. Publ. **3**(7), 1 (2013)
12. Bhavish.: ARP Protocol. Medium. Available at: https://medium.com/@kashyapbhavish95/arp-protocol-5c552c613ca4 (2023)
13. Li, Y., Li, J.: The research on ARP protocol based authentication mechanism. In: 2016 International Conference on Applied Mathematics, Simulation and Modelling, pp. 72–75. Atlantis Press (2016)
14. Carnut, M., Gondim, J.: ARP spoofing detection on switched Ethernet networks: A feasibility study. In: Proceedings of the 5th Simposio Seguranca Em Informatica (2003)
15. Zhao, Y., Guo, R., Lv, P.: ARP spoofing analysis and prevention. In: 2020 5th International Conference on Smart Grid and Electrical Automation (ICSGEA), pp. 572–575 (2020). https://doi.org/10.1109/ICSGEA51094.2020.00130
16. Jinhua, G., Kejian, X.: ARP spoofing detection algorithm using ICMP protocol. In: 2013 International Conference on Computer Communication and Informatics, pp. 1–6. IEEE (2013)
17. Ramachandran, V., Nandi, S.: Detecting ARP spoofing: an active technique. In: Information Systems Security: First International Conference, ICISS 2005, pp. 239–250. Springer, Berlin/Heidelberg (2005)
18. Meghana, J.S., Subashri, T., Vimal, K.R.: A survey on ARP cache poisoning and techniques for detection and mitigation. [online] IEEE Xplore. https://doi.org/10.1109/ICSCN.2017.8085417 (2017)
19. Pandey, P.: Prevention of ARP spoofing: A probe packet based technique. In: 2013 3rd IEEE International Advance Computing Conference (IACC), pp. 147–153. IEEE (2013)
20. Bruschi, D., Ornaghi, A., Rosti, E.: S-ARP: a secure address resolution protocol. In: 19th Annual Computer Security Applications Conference, 2003. Proceedings, pp. 66–74. IEEE (2003)
21. Nam, S., Kim, D., Kim, J.: Enhanced ARP: preventing ARP poisoning-based man-in-the-middle attacks. IEEE Commun. Lett. **14**(2), 187–189 (2010)
22. Cisco: Security Configuration Guide, Cisco IOS XE Everest 16.6.x (Catalyst 9400 Switches) - Configuring Dynamic ARP Inspection [Support]. [online] Cisco. Available at: https://www.cisco.com/c/en/us/td/docs/switches/lan/catalyst9400/software/release/16-6/configuration_guide/sec/b_166_sec_9400_cg/configuring_dynamic_arp_inspection.html. Accessed 20 June 2024 (2017)
23. Huang, T., Richard, Y.F., Zhang, C., Liu, J., Zhang, J., Liu, Y.: A survey on large-scale software defined networking (SDN) testbeds: approaches and challenges. IEEE Commun Surv Tutor. **19**, 891–917 (2017)
24. Muhammad, T.: Revolutionizing network control: exploring the landscape of software-defined networking (SDN). Int. J. Comput. Sci. Technol. **3**(1), 36–68 (2019)
25. Lanner.: How SDN is Fixing Existing Network Bottlenecks With More Hardware at the Edge. [online] Lanner. Available at: https://www.lanner-america.com/blog/sdn-fixing-existing-network-bottlenecks-hardware-edge/. Accessed 21 June 2024 (2019)

26. Anerousis, N., Chemouil, P., Lazar, A.A., Mihai, N., Weinstein, S.B.: The origin and evolution of open programmable networks and SDN. IEEE Commun Surv Tutor. **23**, 1956–1971 (2021). https://doi.org/10.1109/COMST.2021.3060582
27. Feamster, N., Rexford, J., Zegura, E.: The road to SDN: an intellectual history of programmable networks. SIGCOMM Comput. Commun. Rev. **44**, 87–98 (2014)
28. El-Maghraby, R.T., Abd Elazim, N.M., Bahaa-Eldin, A.M.: A survey on deep packet inspection. In: 2017 12th International Conference on Computer Engineering and Systems (ICCES), pp. 188–197. IEEE (2017)
29. Papavassiliou, S.: Software defined networking (SDN) and network function virtualization (NFV). Future Internet. **12**(1), 7 (2020)
30. Abdou, A., van Oorschot, P.C., Wan, T.: Comparative analysis of control plane security of SDN and conventional networks. IEEE Commun Surv Tutor. **20**(4), 3542–3559 (2018). https://doi.org/10.1109/comst.2018.2839348
31. Alharbi, T., Durando, D., Pakzad, F., Portmann, M.: Securing ARP in software defined networks. In: IEEE 41st Conference on Local Computer Networks (LCN), pp. 523–526 (2016). https://doi.org/10.1109/LCN.2016.83
32. Girdler, T., Vassilakis, V.G.: Implementing an intrusion detection and prevention system using software-defined networking: defending against ARP spoofing attacks and blacklisted MAC addresses. Comput. Electr. Eng. **90**, 106990 (2021). https://doi.org/10.1016/j.compeleceng.2021.106990
33. Matties, M.: Distributed responder ARP: using SDN to reengineer ARP from within the network. In: International Conference on Computing, Networking and Communications (ICNC), pp. 678–683 (2017)
34. AbdelSalam, A.M., El-Sisi, A.B., Reddy, K.V.: Mitigating ARP spoofing attacks in software-defined networks. In: 2015 25th International Conference on Computer Theory and Applications (ICCTA) (2015). https://doi.org/10.1109/iccta37466.2015.951343

Privacy Preserving, Authentication, and Blockchain Methods and Applications

Bridging the Gap to Enhance Critical Infrastructure Security Through Data Analytics and Public-Private Partnerships

Edwin Figueroa Perez, Isaac Osunmakinde(✉), and Cheryl Hinds

Computer Science Department, Norfolk State University, Norfolk, VA 23504, USA
e.figueroa@spartans.nsu.edu, {ioosunmakinde,chinds}@nsu.edu

Abstract. Cybersecurity threats to critical infrastructure have become too complex for any public or private entity to manage alone. While frameworks like NIST and programs such as CRISP and FS-ISAC exist, their effectiveness varies. This study analyzes what makes these collaborations successful using real-world case comparisons and cross-tabulated data across sectors. Seven variables were evaluated: trust, communication frequency, cooperation, legislative support, perceived risk, satisfaction, and outcome effectiveness. Results show that high trust correlates with "Very Effective" outcomes, while strong communication links to higher satisfaction. Legal backing increased participation, especially in high-risk sectors. Energy and IT showed consistently high satisfaction and coordination; in contrast, sectors like healthcare and water lagged. Programs like GridEx and CRISP demonstrated the value of structured collaboration. The findings are clear: boosting cooperation, reinforcing legal support, and sustaining high-trust environments significantly enhance cybersecurity outcomes. Effective partnerships are not just built on frameworks, they are forged through consistent action and mutual confidence.

Keywords: Critical Infrastructure · Public-Private Partnership · Cybersecurity · Information Sharing · Data Analytics

1 Introduction

1.1 Ensuring the Safety of Critical Infrastructure

National security depends on resilient critical systems—energy, healthcare, finance, and transportation—which are efficient but interdependent and vulnerable. DHS exercises like GridEx and Cyber Storm test joint responses and reveal coordination gaps [1, 2]. Public-private partnerships (PPPs) aim to close these gaps. This study assesses their effectiveness using the NIST Cybersecurity Framework [3] and programs like DIB-CS [4], CRISP [5], and MS-ISAC [6], all built on trust, communication, and shared response.

K. Daimi et al. (Eds.): CSCE 2025, CCIS 2937, pp. 89–103, 2026.
https://doi.org/10.1007/978-3-032-22208-4_7

1.2 Purpose and Goals of Public-Private Partnerships

PPPs were designed to unite government and industry in securing critical infrastructure through collaboration, knowledge sharing, and joint response. Their success depends not just on intent but on structure, trust, and the ability to operate under pressure. Frameworks from the Cybersecurity and Infrastructure Security Agency (CISA) and NIST provide a shared foundation with a clear definition of roles and timing that helps prevent fragmented coordination [3].

1.3 Current Threats to Infrastructure

Modern threats to critical infrastructure are more complex, fast-moving, and harder to contain. The SolarWinds breach showed how one vendor compromise can impact federal systems [7], while COVID-19–era ransomware attacks turned hospital disruptions into medical emergencies [8]. Similar risks appear in state energy systems. AI-driven attacks are becoming quicker and stealthier, with state-sponsored actors targeting key sectors like defense and energy. Meanwhile, the rise of IoT devices expands vulnerabilities, often lacking proper regulation.

1.4 Research Question

How can real-time collaboration between public and private sectors enhance the security of critical infrastructure against emerging cyber threats?

2 Literature Reviews

2.1 Effectiveness of a Collaborative Framework

As cyber threats grow more complex, public-private collaboration has moved from optional to essential. Programs like CRISP and exercises such as GridEx have shown that coordinated response isn't just helpful, it sharpens awareness and tightens infrastructure defense [1, 5]. But coordination alone doesn't explain results. The data here points to two factors that do: trust and communication. Sectors like Energy, IT, and Transportation consistently report better outcomes and higher satisfaction when those two elements are strong.

2.2 Barriers Preventing a Successful Coordination

Regulations like the Gramm-Leach-Bliley Act (GLBA) protect sensitive data but also limit threat sharing needed for coordinated responses [9]. Many organizations are hesitant to share due to fears of regulatory or reputational risks, reducing critical intelligence flow. Smaller entities often lack the resources to fully engage and increase systemic risk. Policy conflicts and unclear authority further slow collaboration. The data shows trust, clarity, and consistency, not just frequent communication, lead to better outcomes.

2.3 Case Studies of Successful Integration

Some partnerships work better than others, but the ones that hold up share the same core: trust, communication, and active engagement. Programs like MS-ISAC, DIB-CS, and FS-ISAC strengthen public-private integration by enabling rapid ransomware response, secure defense intel sharing, and real-time financial threat detection [4, 6, 10]. Sectors like Energy, IT, and Finance tend to lead, probably because when they fail, the fallout spreads fast. That urgency builds consistency. The pattern's clear. Where trust runs high and people talk often, results follow. Frameworks matter, but it's the people inside that make them move.

2.4 Function of Sector-Specific Boards and Government Organizations

Sector Coordinating Councils (SCCs) and Government Coordinating Councils (GCCs) facilitate timely coordination by linking sectors like Energy, Finance, and IT with government agencies [11, 12]. They run scenarios to identify issues in timing, communication, and control. During the Colonial Pipeline incident, this structure aided rapid recovery [13]. Their effectiveness depends on ongoing sector engagement, turning policy into consistent practice under pressure.

3 Methodology

3.1 Data Sources and Collection

This study employed a mixed-method approach, combining structured data with real-world case analysis to examine public and private sector responses to cybersecurity incidents. It used a dataset of 30 records from open-source sources like GridEx VII and FS-ISAC reports [1, 10]. Each record was coded by stakeholder type, sector, and seven indicators, including trust, cooperation, and outcome effectiveness. Univariate and cross-tabulation analyses revealed collaboration patterns often missed in standard reports.

3.2 Rationale for Selected Features

The selected variables, drawn from breach reports, exercises, and case reviews, capture key factors influencing collaboration under pressure. Cooperation measured real participation, while outcome effectiveness assessed timely detection and recovery. Trust impacted response speed, risk perception guided decisions, and communication was central to coordination. Satisfaction reflected the success of collaboration, and legal authority affected decisiveness [citations].

3.3 Mixed-Method Research Design and Approach

This project used a mixed-methods approach to assess how public-private partnerships hold up under cybersecurity pressure. Qualitative sources included case studies and sector reports detailing responses events like the Log4j vulnerability [13], to events like the GridEx exercises [1], and the Colonial Pipeline breach [14], showing how policy translated into action. Quantitatively, a custom dataset was used to track trust, communication frequency, cooperation level, legislative support, perceived risk, satisfaction, and outcome effectiveness across sectors by performance when tested. See Fig. 1.

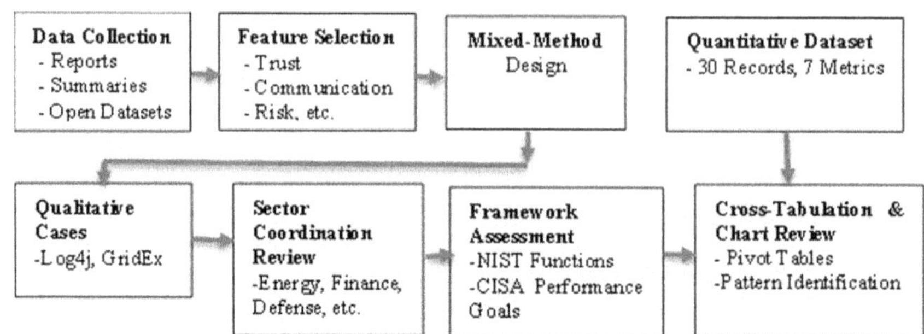

Fig. 1. Critical Infrastructure Cybersecurity Architecture

3.4 Methods for Evaluating Collaborative Cybersecurity Initiatives

Effective collaboration relies on trust, defined roles, and steady communication, especially under pressure. Defense and Finance sectors performed better due to greater experience, while others lacked tools or staff. Programs like CRISP, FS-ISAC, and GridEx succeeded because they prioritized training, not just planning [1, 5, 10]. Frameworks like NIST's five functions and CISA's Cybersecurity Performance Goals helped assess readiness [3, 9]. Sectors with consistent communication and trust responded faster, while others were slowed by rigid structures and unclear leadership. The JCDC's quick response to the Log4j crisis highlighted how real-time coordination can prevent escalation [13]. Finance and energy sectors sustain this through standardized practices and regular drills [3, 15].

3.5 Techniques for Evaluating Cybersecurity Frameworks

Frameworks like NIST and CISA's Cybersecurity Performance Goals (CPGs) provide structure, but their real value lies in guiding effective action during crises. NIST's functions (Identify, Protect, Detect, Respond, and Recover) have helped sectors like energy and water improve response capabilities [3], while CISA's goals offer sector-specific priorities [19]. These frameworks remain key benchmarks for assessing readiness, with metrics like Mean Time to Detect (MTTD) and containment rate revealing their practical effectiveness. The Financial Sector Cybersecurity Profile builds on this by testing how well systems adapt under regulatory and operational pressure.

3.6 Cross-tabulation with Pivot Tables and Charts Analysis

The next section uses pivot tables and visual charts to analyze relationships between key variables, revealing patterns and correlations within the data. Cross-tabulation helped highlight interactions, such as high trust aligning with better outcomes, and communication linking to satisfaction. Some variations appeared across sectors and support levels, suggesting uneven coordination.

4 Research Analysis

4.1 Univariate Variable Analysis on Sector Collaboration

Analyzing each factor individually lays the foundation for identifying broader collaboration patterns. This section examines variables separately to reveal emerging trends, aiming to uncover insights from the data rather than generalizing.

4.1.1 Stakeholder Type Distribution

As shown in Fig. 2, private-sector representation made up 53.33% of the dataset, while public-sector entries accounted for 46.67%. The near-even balance offers a solid base for comparison, but participation levels varied by sector. Based on 30 records coded by sector type to show stakeholder distribution across public and private sectors.

4.1.2 Sector Distribution

Figure 3 highlights Information Technology as the most frequent contributor, with 20% of the dataset. Energy followed at 16.67%, while Transportation Systems appeared in 13.33% of records when grouped.

4.1.3 Level of Cooperation Distribution

Figure 4 shows "Medium" cooperation in 43.33% of the records. "High" cooperation made up 46.67%, with smaller shares in "Low" (10%).

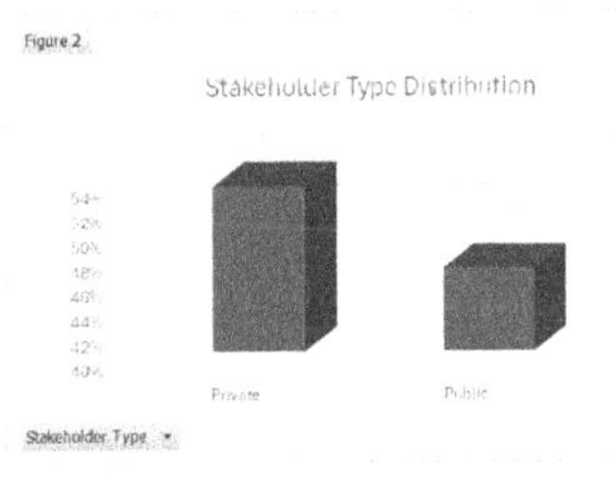

(a) Chart Distribution

Table 4.1.1

Stakeholder Type	Count	Percentage
Private	16	53.33%
Public	14	46.67%
Grand Total	30	100.00%

(b) Tabular Distribution

Fig. 2. Stakeholder Type Distribution

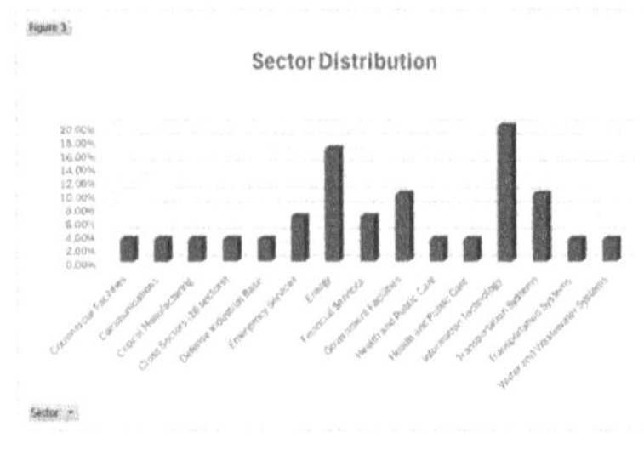

(a) Chart Distribution

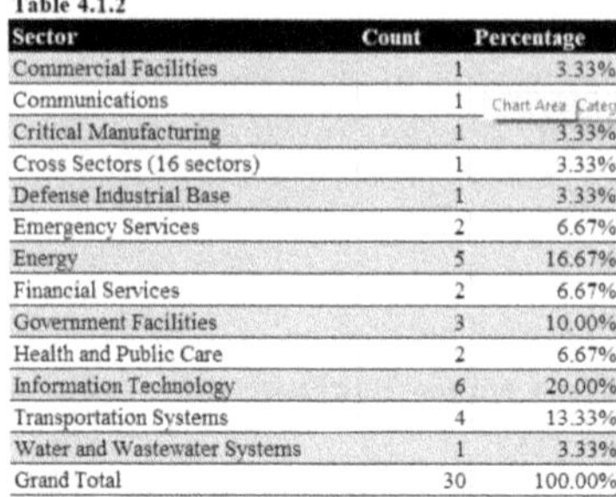

Table 4.1.2

Sector	Count	Percentage
Commercial Facilities	1	3.33%
Communications	1	3.33%
Critical Manufacturing	1	3.33%
Cross Sectors (16 sectors)	1	3.33%
Defense Industrial Base	1	3.33%
Emergency Services	2	6.67%
Energy	5	16.67%
Financial Services	2	6.67%
Government Facilities	3	10.00%
Health and Public Care	2	6.67%
Information Technology	6	20.00%
Transportation Systems	4	13.33%
Water and Wastewater Systems	1	3.33%
Grand Total	30	100.00%

(b) Tabular Distribution

Fig. 3. Sector Distribution

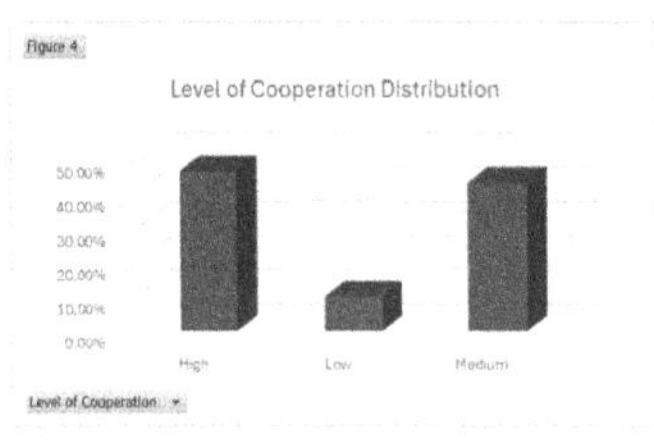

(a) Chart Distribution

Table 4.1.3

Level of Cooperation	Count	Percentage
High	14	46.67%
Medium	13	43.33%
Low	3	10.00%
Grand Total	30	100.00%

(b) Tabular Distribution

Fig. 4. Level of Cooperation Distribution

4.1.4 Security Outcome Effectiveness Distribution

The data in Fig. 5 indicates that 66.67% of the outcome was "Very Effective," while 20% selected "Effective" and 13.33% chose "Somewhat Effective."

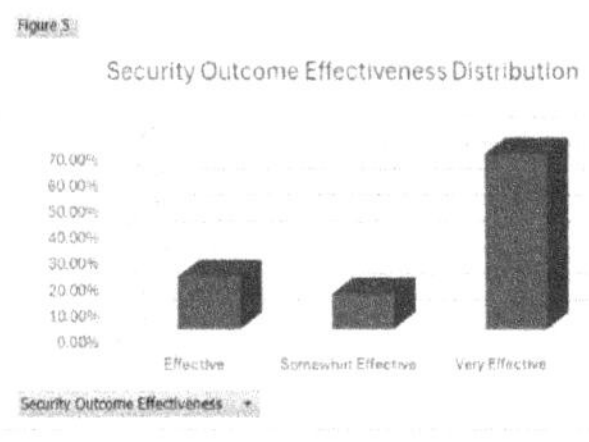

(a) Chart Distribution

Table 4.1.4

Security Outcome Effectiveness	Count	Percentage
Effective	6	20.00%
Somewhat Effective	4	13.33%
Very Effective	20	66.67%
Grand Total	30	100.00%

(b) Table Distribution

Fig. 5. Security Outcome Effectiveness Distribution

4.1.5 Trust Level Distribution

As shown in Fig. 6, a large majority of records (83.33%) reflected "High" trust in public-private partnerships. The rest, 16.67%, fell into the "Medium" category.

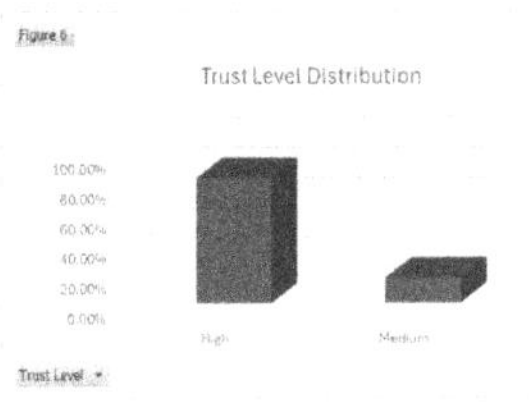

Table 4.1.5

Trust Level	Count	Percentage
High	25	83.33%
Medium	5	16.67%
Grand Total	30	100.00%

(a) Chart Distribution (b) Table Distribution

Fig. 6. Trust Level Distribution

4.1.6 Perceived Risk Distribution

As shown in Fig. 7 shows a more varied picture. "Medium" risk was the most common, appearing in 46.67% of the data. "High" risk wasn't far behind at 33.33%, while "Low" was reported in just 20%.

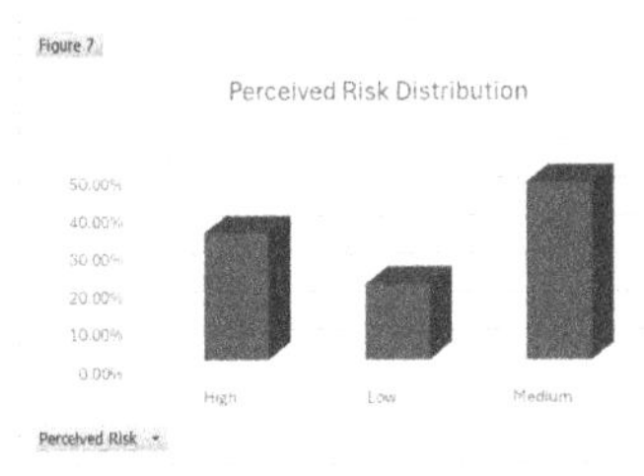

Table 4.1.6

Perceived Risk	Count	Percentage
High	10	33.33%
Medium	14	46.67%
rea Category) Axis	6	20.00%
Grand Total	30	100.00%

(a) Chart Distribution (b) Table Distribution

Fig. 7. Perceived Risk Distribution

4.1.7 Communication Frequency Distribution

According to Fig. 8, nearly three-quarters of the records (73.33%) indicated "High" communication frequency. The remaining 26.67% were labeled as "Medium."

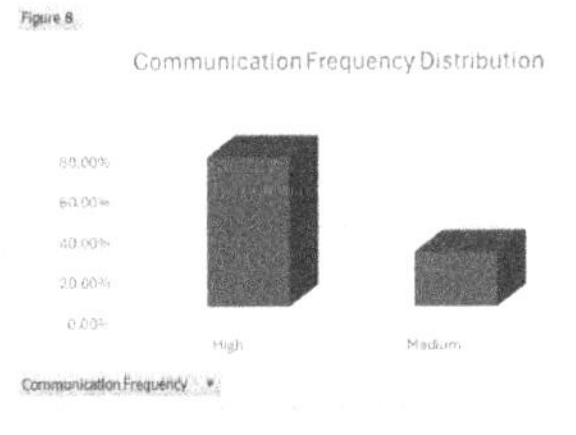

Table 4.1.7

Communication Frequency	Count	Percentage
High	22	73.33%
Medium	8	26.67%
Grand Total	30	100.00%

(a) Chart Distribution (b) Table Distribution

Fig. 8. Communication Frequency Distribution

4.1.8 Satisfaction with PPP Distribution

Figure 9 shows that 80% of records reflected "High" satisfaction with public-private partnerships, while 20% indicated "Medium." No records reported low satisfaction.

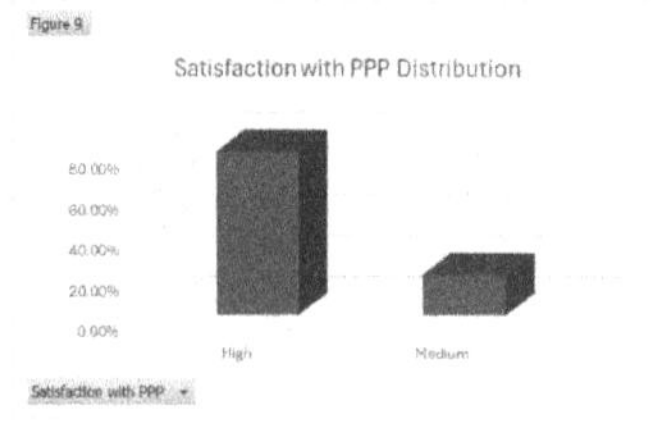

Table 4.1.8

Satisfaction with PPP	Count	Percentage
High	24	80.00%
Medium	6	20.00%
Grand Total	30	100.00%

(a) Chart Distribution (b) Table Distribution

Fig. 9. Satisfaction with PPP Distribution

4.1.9 Legislation Support Distribution

As shown in Fig. 10, 76.67% of records confirmed the presence of legislative support, while 23.33% did not.

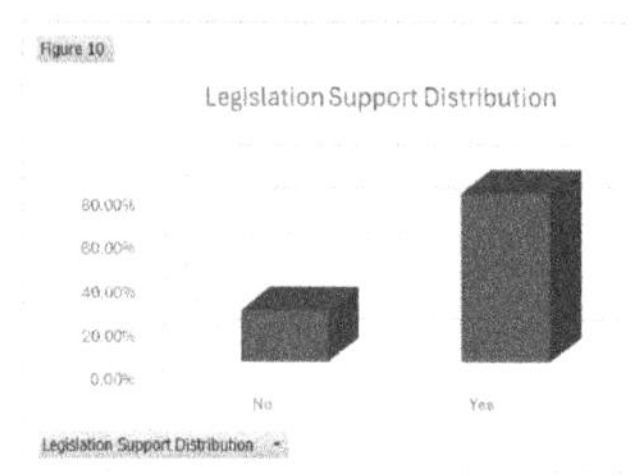

Table 4.1.9

Legislation Support	Count	Percentage
No	7	23.33%
Yes	23	76.67%
Grand Total	30	100.00%

(a) Chart Distribution (b) Table Distribution

Fig. 10. Legislation Support Distribution

4.2 Cross Tabulation Analysis

4.2.1 Cross Tabulation Between Stakeholder Type and Trust Level in Partners

How does stakeholder type influence trust levels in public-private partnerships for critical infrastructure security? Figure 11 shows how trust levels were distributed by stakeholder type. Among private-sector entries, 15 reported "High" trust and only 1 reported "Medium." On the public side, 10 records reflected "High" trust, while 4 were marked "Medium." Both groups leaned toward "High," but trust among private stakeholders was more consistent across the board.

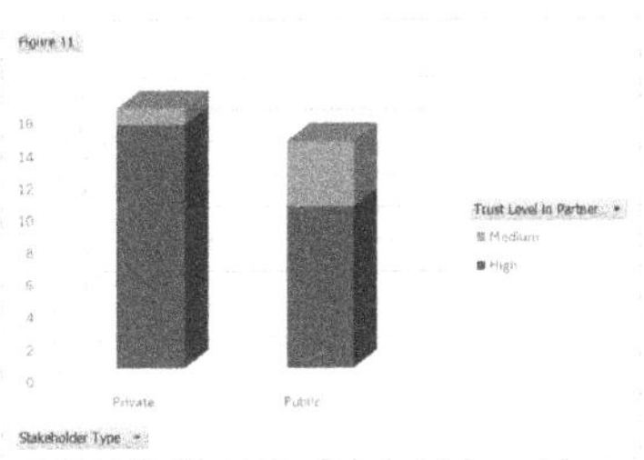

(a) Cross Tabulation Chart

Table 4.2.1 Trust Level in Partner

Stakeholder Type	High	Medium	Grand Total
Private	15	1	16
Public	10	4	14
Grand Total	25	5	30

(b) Pivot Table

Fig. 11. Cross Tabulation between Stakeholder Type and Trust Level in Partners.

4.2.2 Cross Tabulation Between Sector and Security Outcome Effectiveness

Is there a significant relationship between the sector and the perceived effectiveness of security outcomes in public-private partnerships? Figure 12 outlines how stakeholders across different sectors evaluated their security outcomes. Information Technology had the widest spread with 6 total records, including 3 marked "Very Effective," 2 as "Somewhat Effective," and 1 as "Effective." The Energy sector had 5 records total, with 4 rated "Very Effective." Transportation Systems also had strong marks, with 3 out of 4 entries rating at the highest level.

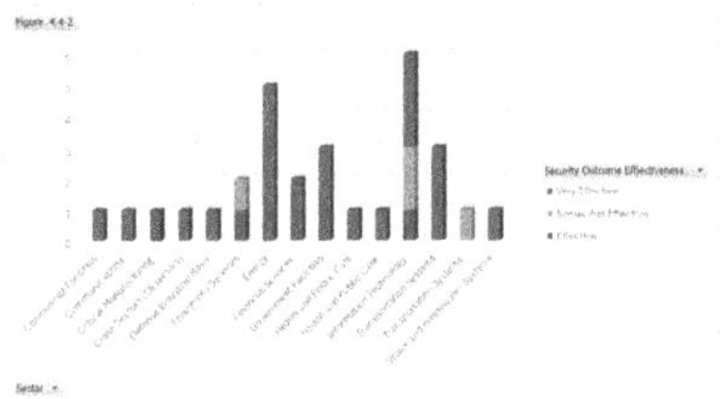

(a) Cross Tabulation Chart

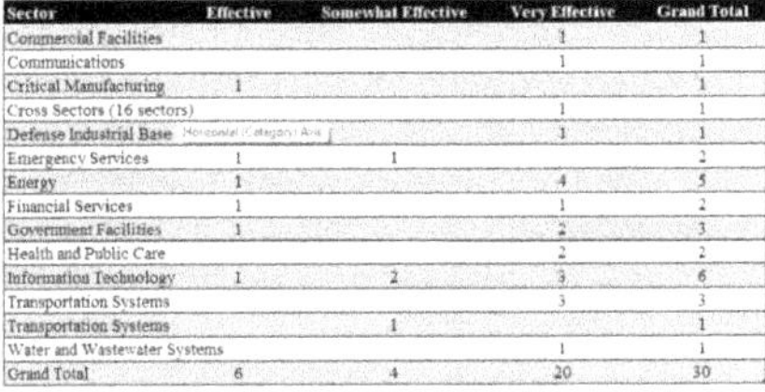

Table 4.2.2 Security Outcome Effectiveness

Sector	Effective	Somewhat Effective	Very Effective	Grand Total
Commercial Facilities			1	1
Communications			1	1
Critical Manufacturing	1			1
Cross Sectors (16 sectors)			1	1
Defense Industrial Base			1	1
Emergency Services	1	1		2
Energy	1		4	5
Financial Services	1		1	2
Government Facilities	1		2	3
Health and Public Care			2	2
Information Technology	1	2	3	6
Transportation Systems			3	3
Transportation Systems		1		1
Water and Wastewater Systems			1	1
Grand Total	6	4	20	30

(b) Pivot Table

Fig. 12. Cross Tabulation between Sector and Security Outcome Effectiveness Cross Tabulation between Sector and Security Outcome Effectiveness

4.2.3 Cross Tabulation Between Level of Cooperation and Perceived Risk

Does a higher level of cooperation among stakeholders in public-private partnerships reduce perceived security risks in critical infrastructure protection? Figure 13 compares how perceived risk aligns with different levels of cooperation. In the "High" cooperation group, 9 records showed "High" risk, 1 reported "Low," and 4 showed "Medium." In the "Medium" group, most records were marked "Medium" risk, with 9 in that category, 3 marked "Low," and 1 as "High." The "Low" cooperation group was split with 2 entries noting "Low" risk and 1 showing "Medium."

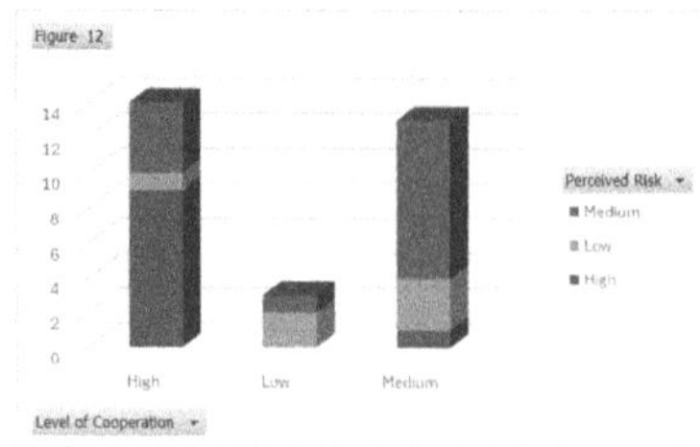

Table 4.2.3	Perceived Risk			
Level of Cooperation	High	Low	Medium	Grand Total
High	9	1	4	14
Medium	1	3	9	13
Low		2	1	3
Grand Total	10	6	14	30

(a) Cross Tabulation Chart (b) Pivot Table

Fig. 13. Cross Tabulation between Level of Cooperation and Perceived Risk

4.2.4 Cross Tabulation Between Satisfaction with PPP and Communication Frequency

What is the impact of communication frequency on stakeholder satisfaction with public-private partnerships in critical infrastructure security? Figure 14 reveals that among the records reporting "High" communication frequency, 22 also marked "High" satisfaction. Just 2 records in that same group selected "Medium" satisfaction. For those under "Medium" communication frequency, 6 records showed "Medium" satisfaction and none reported "High."

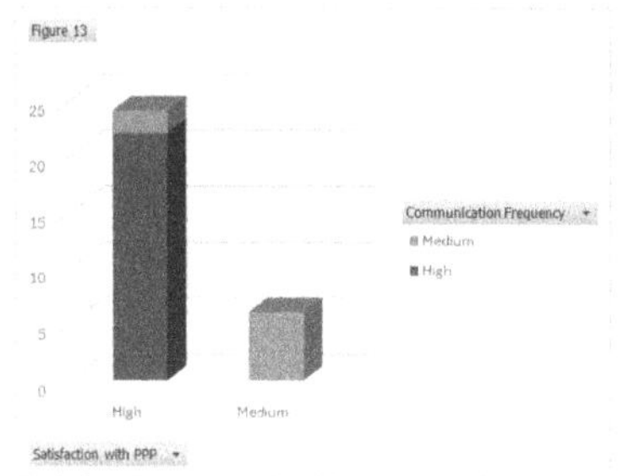

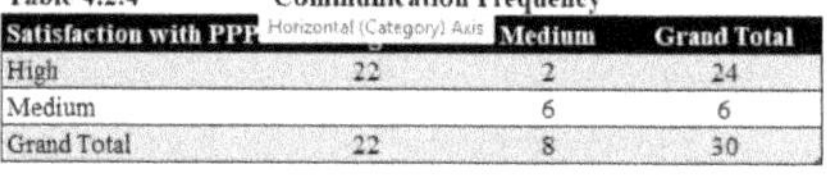

Table 4.2.4	Communication Frequency		
Satisfaction with PPP	Horizontal (Category) Axis	Medium	Grand Total
High	22	2	24
Medium		6	6
Grand Total	22	8	30

(a) Cross Tabulation Chart (b) Pivot Table

Fig. 14. Cross Tabulation between Satisfaction with PPP and Communication

4.2.5 Cross Tabulation Between Security Outcome Effectiveness and Trust Level in Partners

Does a higher trust level in partners lead to improved security outcomes in public-private partnerships? Figure 15 compares trust levels with how stakeholders rated their security outcomes. For records marked "High" trust, 20 reported "Very Effective," 5 marked "Effective," and none selected "Somewhat Effective." The "Medium" trust group had 4 records tagged "Somewhat Effective" and just 1 marked "Effective." None from that group reached the "Very Effective" level.

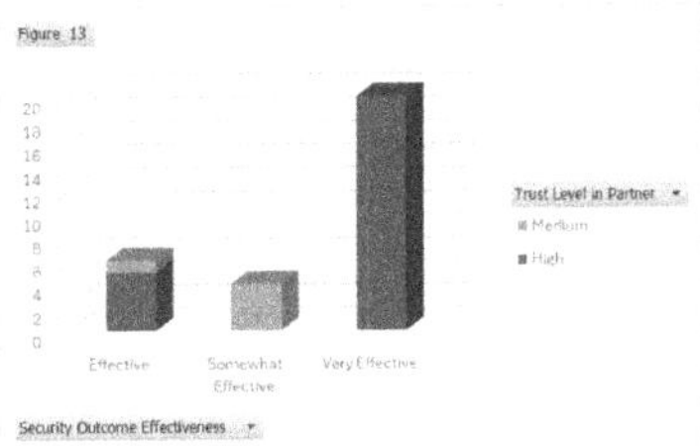

Table 4.2.5	Trust Level in Partner		
Securi[illegible] Horizontal (Category) Axis	High	Medium	Grand Total
Effective	5	1	6
Somewhat Effective		4	4
Very Effective	20		20
Grand Total	25	5	30

(a) Cross Tabulation Chart (b) Pivot Table

Fig. 15. Cross Tabulation between Security Outcome Effectiveness and Trust Level in Partners

4.2.6 Cross Tabulation Between Perceived Risk and Legislation Support

Do stakeholders who perceive higher security risks show stronger support for legislative measures in critical infrastructure protection? Figure 16 shows how perceived risk corresponded with support for legislation. Of the 10 records showing "High" risk, 7 supported legislative action and 3 did not. Among the 14 entries marked "Medium" risk, 12 supported legislation and 2 did not. For the 6 records showing "Low" risk, support was more evenly split with 4 showing support and 2 not.

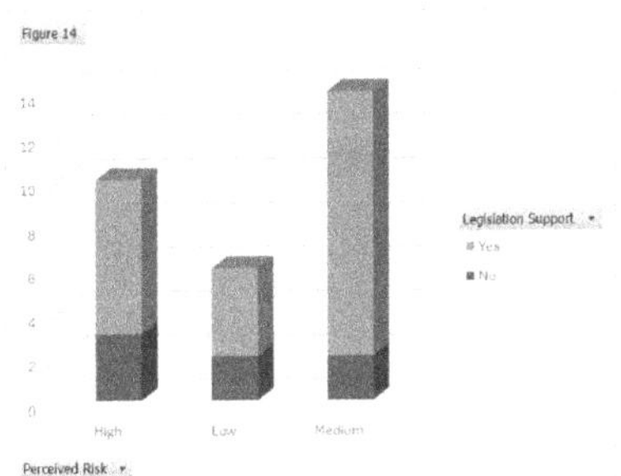

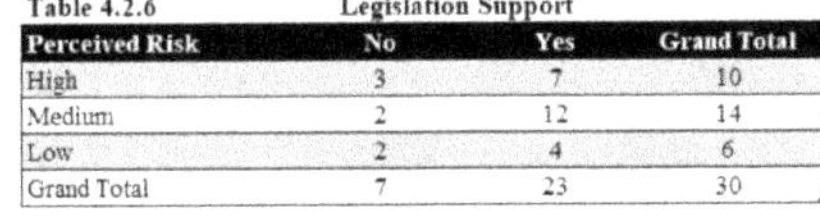

Table 4.2.6	Legislation Support		
Perceived Risk	No	Yes	Grand Total
High	3	7	10
Medium	2	12	14
Low	2	4	6
Grand Total	7	23	30

(a) Cross Tabulation Chart (b) Pivot Table

Fig. 16. Cross Tabulation between Perceived Risk and Legislation Support

4.2.7 Cross Tabulation Between Sector and Satisfaction with PPP

How does sector type influence stakeholder satisfaction with public-private partnerships in enhancing critical infrastructure security? Figure 17 displays satisfaction levels across sectors. Information Technology and Energy were the most consistent, with five or more records each marked "High" satisfaction. Other sectors, including Emergency Services and Aviation, showed a mix of "High" and "Medium" ratings.

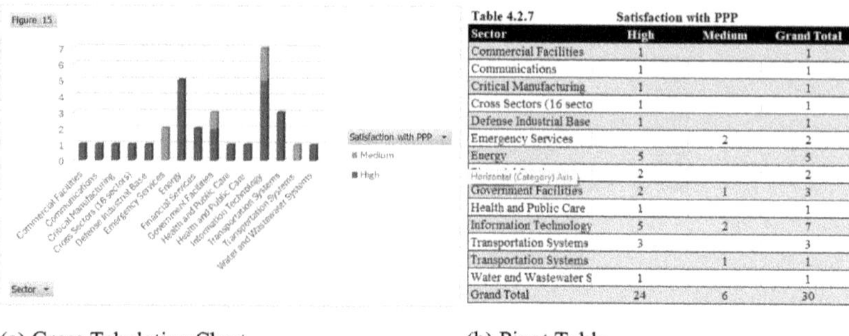

Table 4.2.7	Satisfaction with PPP		
Sector	**High**	**Medium**	**Grand Total**
Commercial Facilities	1		1
Communications	1		1
Critical Manufacturing	1		1
Cross Sectors (16 secto	1		1
Defense Industrial Base	1		1
Emergency Services		2	2
Energy	5		5
Horizontal (Category) Axis	2		2
Government Facilities	2	1	3
Health and Public Care	1		1
Information Technology	5	2	7
Transportation Systems	3		3
Transportation Systems		1	1
Water and Wastewater S	1		1
Grand Total	24	6	30

(a) Cross Tabulation Chart (b) Pivot Table

Fig. 17. Cross Tabulation between Sector and Satisfaction with PPP

4.2.8 Cross Tabulation Between Level of Cooperation and Security Outcome Effectiveness

Does a higher level of cooperation among stakeholders in public-private partnerships lead to improved security outcome effectiveness in critical infrastructure protection? Figure 18 shows how the cooperation level corresponds to perceived effectiveness. "High" cooperation records had 11 entries rated "Very Effective." "Medium" cooperation records had nine at that level, along with some marked "Effective." No "Low" cooperation record was rated above "Somewhat Effective."

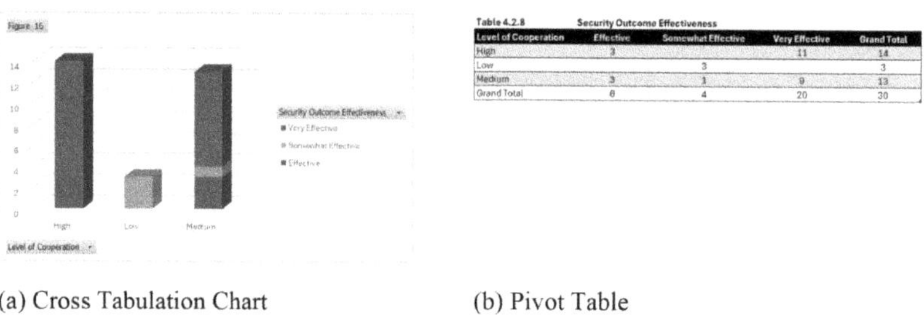

Table 4.2.8	Security Outcome Effectiveness			
Level of Cooperation	**Effective**	**Somewhat Effective**	**Very Effective**	**Grand Total**
High	3		11	14
Low		3		3
Medium	3	1	9	13
Grand Total	6	4	20	30

(a) Cross Tabulation Chart (b) Pivot Table

Fig. 18. Cross Tabulation between Level of Cooperation and Security Outcome Effectiveness

5 Findings and Discussion

5.1 Key Insights from the Data Analysis

Trust, communication, and satisfaction moved together across the dataset. Twenty-five records showed high trust (Fig. 6), with 22 records also reporting high communication (Fig. 8), and 24 records reflecting high satisfaction (Fig. 9). Crosstab data confirmed the link; 20 of the 25 high-trust entries were rated "Very Effective" in outcomes (Fig. 15). Medium-trust entries never reached that level, suggesting that effective performance depends less on structure and more on how well partners interact when it counts.

5.2 Impact of Public-Private Partnerships on Infrastructure Security

Public-private partnerships had greater impact when cooperation and communication were consistent. In Fig. 5, 20 records rated outcomes as "Very Effective," with 11 records tied to high cooperation per Fig. 18, none with low cooperation scored that well. Energy and IT stood out for embedding coordination into daily operations through efforts like CRISP and FS-ISAC [5, 10]. Routine collaboration and clear responsibilities led to faster, more resilient responses.

5.3 Strengths and Weaknesses Identified in the Current PPP Models

Communication was a consistent strength, Fig. 14 shows 22 of 24 high-communication records also had high satisfaction, particularly in Energy, IT, and Finance. However, sectors like Water, Healthcare, and Emergency Services were underrepresented, signaling weaker coordination. Legislative backing also played a role: Fig. 10 showed seven records without legal support, which aligned with lower confidence. Figure 16 confirmed that higher perceived risk correlated with stronger calls for legal clarity. Overall, structure proved effective when reinforced by law, practice, and engagement.

5.4 Interpretation of Findings in the Context of Existing Literature

Prior research has identified unclear roles, poor communication, and weak political support as risks in public-private infrastructure partnerships [16], which this study confirms. Figure 10 shows lower confidence where no legislative support existed, while satisfaction and perceived risk (Figs. 9 and 14) followed similar trends. High-trust, regularly communicating records (Figs. 8, 12, and 13) consistently aligned with better outcomes (Fig. 7). While structure helped, success stemmed from practiced coordination and shared expectations, as seen in CRISP, FS-ISAC, and GridEx [1, 5, 10].

5.5 How the Findings Address the Primary Research Question

The research explored whether real-time collaboration improves critical infrastructure cybersecurity. The data showed it does, when consistent. Figures 6, 15, and 16 linked trust, communication, and strong outcomes. Sectors like Water and Emergency Services showed weaker, less frequent engagement. The key factor wasn't just speed, but alignment.

6 Recommendations and Conclusions

6.1 Practical Recommendations for Policymakers and Practitioners

Communication and trust led to stronger outcomes, as shown in Figs. 6 and 8. To strengthen public-private partnerships (PPPs), policymakers should prioritize joint exercises like GridEx and Cyber Storm [1, 2], which build coordination habits. Figure 10 revealed that nearly 25% of records lacked legal support, highlighting a need to revise laws like GLBA to enable emergency data sharing [9]. Smaller sectors also struggled with limited resources, suggesting the need for targeted funding, tax incentives, or grants to support broader participation.

6.2 Summary of Key Findings

When trust, communication, and structure were strong, outcomes improved; 80% of high-trust records in Fig. 15 were rated "Very Effective." High communication is also aligned with satisfaction. However, sectors like Water, Emergency Services, and Transportation showed weaker engagement. Legislative support and consistent coordination helped, but the challenge remains in making these conditions universal.

6.3 Areas for Future Research

This study examined how structure affects outcomes but left key questions unanswered. Tools like JCDC and AIS aim for speed, yet their effectiveness in smaller sectors remains unclear [17, 18]. Future research should explore their scalability and post-incident trust, whether partnerships endure after crises. Notably, strong results often came from private-to-private coordination, suggesting internal structure and consistent practice may sustain resilience without heavy public oversight, warranting further investigation.

Acknowledgments. The authors gratefully acknowledge the resources made available by Norfolk State University, Virginia, USA.

Disclosure of Interests The authors declare no competing interests relevant to the content of this article.

References

1. North American Electric Reliability Corporation (NERC), GridEx VII Lessons Learned Report. Electricity Information Sharing and Analysis Center (E-ISAC), 2024. https://www.nerc.com/pa/CI/ESISAC/GridEx/GridEx%20VII%20Report.pdf
2. Cybersecurity and Infrastructure Security Agency (CISA): Cyber Storm: Securing Cyber Space. https://www.cisa.gov/cyber-storm-securing-cyber-space. Last accessed 30 Sep 2024
3. National Institute of Standards and Technology: Cybersecurity Framework Version 2.0: Strategic Overview. https://nvlpubs.nist.gov/nistpubs/CSWP/NIST.CSWP.29.pdf. Last accessed 12 Oct 2024
4. U.S. Department of Defense: Defense Industrial Base (DIB) Cybersecurity Strategy 2024. https://dodcio.defense.gov/Portals/0/Documents/Library/DIB-CS-Strategy.pdf. Last accessed 13 Oct 2024
5. U.S. Department of Energy: Cybersecurity Risk Information Sharing Program (CRISP) Fact Sheet. https://www.energy.gov/sites/default/files/2021-12/CRISP%20Fact%20Sheet_508.pdf. Last accessed 18 Oct 2024
6. CISA and MS-ISAC: Ransomware Guide. https://www.cisa.gov/sites/default/files/publications/CISA_MS-ISAC_Ransomware%20Guide_S508C.pdf. Last accessed 22 Oct 2024
7. Oladimeji, S., Kerner, S.M.: SolarWinds Hack Explained: Everything You Need to Know. TechTarget. https://www.techtarget.com/whatis/feature/SolarWinds-hack-explained-Everything-you-need-to-know. Last accessed 13 Oct 2024
8. Milanovic, M., Schmitt, M.N.: Cyber attacks and cyber misinformation operations during a pandemic. Journal of National Security Law & Policy. https://jnslp.com/wp-content/uploads/2020/12/Cyber-Attacks-and-Cyber-Misinformation-Operations-During-a-Pandemic_2.pdf. Last accessed 11 Oct 2024

9. Federal Financial Institutions Examination Council: Summary of Provisions of the Gramm-Leach-Bliley Act. https://www.ffiec.gov/exam/InfoBase/documents/02-con-g-l-b_summary_of_provisions-010416.pdf. Last accessed 02 Oct 2024
10. FS-ISAC, Navigating Cyber 2024: The Global Financial Services Threat Landscape. Financial Services Information Sharing and Analysis Center, 2024. https://www.fsisac.com/hubfs/Knowledge/NavigatingCyber/2024/FSISAC-NavCyber24-Report.pdf
11. CISA: Sector Coordinating Councils. https://www.cisa.gov/resources-tools/groups/sector-coordinating-councils. Last accessed 21 Sep 2024
12. CISA: Government Coordinating Councils. https://www.cisa.gov/resources-tools/groups/government-coordinating-councils. Last accessed 28 Sep 2024
13. CISA: Apache Log4j Vulnerability Guidance. Cybersecurity and Infrastructure Security Agency (2021). https://www.cisa.gov/news-events/cybersecurity-advisories/aa21-356a. Accessed 30 Apr 2024
14. Reeder, T., Hall, R.: The colonial pipeline ransomware attack: a case study in critical infrastructure cybersecurity. Cyber Defense Rev. **6**(3) (2021)
15. U.S. Department of Energy: Liberty Eclipse: Exercise Overview. https://www.energy.gov/liberty-eclipse-report. Last accessed 27 Oct 2024
16. Ampratwum, G., Tam, V.W.Y., Osei-Kyei, R.: Critical analysis of risks factors in using public-private partnership in building critical infrastructure resilience: a systematic review. Constr. Innov. **22**(3), 518–540 (2022). https://doi.org/10.1108/CI-10-2021-0182
17. CISA: Joint Cyber Defense Collaborative (JCDC) Overview. https://www.cisa.gov/sites/default/files/publications.pdf. Last accessed 25 Oct 2024
18. Cybersecurity and Infrastructure Security Agency (CISA): Automated Indicator Sharing (AIS) Program. https://www.cisa.gov/resources-tools/services/automated-indicator-sharing-ais. Accessed 30 Apr 2024

Rethinking Privacy Laws for Subscriptions: A Consumer Harm Perspective

Elena Nye, Kambiz Ghazinour, and Mehdi Ghayoumi(✉)

Department of Cybersecurity, State University of New York at Canton, Canton, pg NY, USA
{nye105,ghazinourk,ghayoumi}@canton.edu

Abstract. Consumers spend billions of dollars each year on online subscriptions, and spending continues to grow. Despite major privacy statutes, gaps remain in how these laws protect personal data in subscription-based models. This paper examines consent under the CCPA and GDPR, showing how narrow interpretations and weak consent mechanisms expose subscribers to harm. Using a privacy-defining framework, we analyze documented disputes between consumers and businesses to assess the application and interpretation of these laws and to identify vulnerabilities specific to subscriptions. We find that many subscription businesses employ exploitative data practices that conflict with modern privacy statutes and cause consumer harm. Consumer research also indicates a desire for greater control over personal data while using subscriptions. We propose updates to consent mechanisms and default data-handling procedures that increase user control and transparency across the subscription lifecycle, aligning practice with consumer intent and the aims of contemporary privacy law.

Keywords: CCPA · GDPR · online subscriptions · consent mechanisms · privacy-by-default · consumer harm · law–technology gap

1 Introduction

Online shopping has become routine for many consumers, and an increasing share of goods and services is offered through subscription models. From meal kits and video streaming to clothing and personal care, subscriptions are widespread and continue to grow [13,14]. These models rely on continuous collection and processing of personal data (for example, names, emails, and payment tokens) to provision access, manage renewals, and deliver personalized features.

Modern privacy laws such as the California Consumer Privacy Act (CCPA) and the EU General Data Protection Regulation (GDPR) aim to strengthen individual control over personal data and impose accountability on organizations [5,6]. In principle, these laws require consent that is freely given, specific, informed, and unambiguous, and they reject consent obtained through silence,

K. Daimi et al. (Eds.): CSCE 2025, CCIS 2937, pp. 104–120, 2026.
https://doi.org/10.1007/978-3-032-22208-4_8

pre-ticked boxes, inactivity, or deceptive interface design. In practice, however, subscription workflows often bundle multiple processing purposes into a single upfront agreement and then treat continued silence at renewal or at a change of terms as ongoing consent. When free trials convert to paid plans, promotional periods expire, prices increase, or benefits change, additional data processing is commonly inferred rather than newly authorized.

This gap between legal intent and operational practice is well documented in the privacy literature. Foundational work shows that notice and consent, as commonly implemented, is ill suited to real user decision making [2–4]. At the interface layer, empirical studies document the prevalence and impact of dark patterns and consent designs that steer users toward acceptance, undermining meaningful choice [7–9]. Related scholarship on informed consent highlights how uncertainty and information overload can erode consent quality, even when formal checkboxes are present [10,11].

Recent regulatory activity underscores the policy relevance of subscriptions. The U.S. Federal Trade Commission has finalized a click-to-cancel rule intended to make ending recurring subscriptions no harder than signing up, responding to steady growth in subscription-related complaints [12]. Consumer surveys similarly report widespread confusion and unintended enrollment in auto-renewing plans [13,14]. Together, these developments suggest that current mechanisms do not reliably capture users' intentions across the subscription life cycle.

This paper argues that privacy protections in subscription ecosystems require explicit, stage-specific consent rather than reliance on implied or bundled consent. We identify four checkpoints where renewed, unbundled consent should be obtained: initial signup, conversion from trial to paid, material changes to price or benefits, and renewal. Our analysis connects legal requirements to concrete interface practices, drawing on prior work in privacy theory, empirical HCI, and regulatory guidance [2–9,12]. We then outline a feasible approach for layered, low-friction consent that aligns with the letter and spirit of modern privacy laws while improving transparency, user control, and consumer protection across the subscription life cycle.

2 Privacy Policies and Subscriptions

The California Consumer Privacy Act (CCPA) and the EU General Data Protection Regulation (GDPR) are formative privacy laws that shape data protection practices in the United States, the European Union, and beyond [5,6]. Their shared objectives are to protect personal data, increase individual control (for example, access, deletion, and opt-out rights), and impose accountability and security obligations on organizations that process personal information. In parallel, scholarship has shown that conventional notice-and-consent approaches often fail to capture users' intentions in complex digital services [2–4]. Within subscription ecosystems, where processing is continuous and purposes can evolve, these tensions become salient: organizations frequently treat renewal, silence, or minor interface acknowledgments as ongoing authorization, despite legal requirements that consent be freely given, specific, informed, and unambiguous [5,6].

Prior work surveying security and privacy issues in commercial environments underscores how such operational practices can diverge from the spirit of privacy statutes and expose users to risk [18].

2.1 Related Work: Consumer Privacy and Consent Challenges

Consumer privacy in subscription-based services intersects with research on meaningful consent, the ethics of interface design, and "dark patterns." Foundational work argues that traditional notice-and-consent approaches are often ill-suited to real decision-making contexts, especially when policies are lengthy, complex, or strategically opaque [3,4]. More recently, large-scale audits of shopping sites document dark patterns that steer users toward unintended choices (for example, subscribing or agreeing to tracking), thereby undermining autonomy [7]. Empirical studies further show that GDPR-era consent prompts can yield "consent fatigue," where repeated or unclear choices push users toward acceptance without genuine understanding [8]. Complementary scholarship in medicine and bioethics highlights how uncertainty and information overload degrade consent quality, even when formal checkboxes are present [10,11]. Regulators have begun to respond at the policy and UI levels (for example, the FTC's click-to-cancel rule for recurring subscriptions), signaling concern that interface frictions and renewal defaults can defeat meaningful user control [12]. Building on this literature, we argue that the dynamic nature of subscriptions, where pricing, benefits, and data uses evolve over time, requires stage-specific and renewed consent mechanisms across the subscription life cycle.

2.2 Overview of GDPR and CCPA

The EU General Data Protection Regulation (GDPR) defines consent as a "freely given, specific, informed, and unambiguous" indication of the data subject's wishes, expressed by a clear affirmative act [5]. The GDPR further clarifies that valid consent cannot be inferred from silence, pre-ticked boxes, or inactivity; that consent must cover all processing activities for the same purpose; and that, where multiple purposes exist, consent should be obtained for each purpose separately. Consent requests should be presented in an intelligible and easily accessible form and should not needlessly disrupt the service [5].

Similarly, the California Consumer Privacy Act (CCPA), as amended, requires that consent be freely given, specific, informed, and unambiguous, and it explicitly invalidates consent obtained through dark patterns or user interface designs that subvert or impair choice. It also limits processing to what is necessary and proportionate for the disclosed purposes, disallowing further use that is incompatible with those purposes [6].

Despite these requirements, many subscription implementations still bundle distinct processing purposes into a single upfront agreement or treat renewal silence and minor interface acknowledgments as ongoing authorization. This creates a mismatch between legal standards for consent and the practical realities of subscription workflows, where processing is continuous and the purposes, prices, or benefits can change over time [5,6].

2.3 Privacy Policy Subscription Problem

Applying GDPR and CCPA consent standards to subscription workflows reveals a systematic mismatch between legal requirements and common practice. Subscriptions are continuous by design: personal data are collected, retained, and reused for provisioning, billing, targeting, and re-engagement over extended periods. Both laws permit processing for the *same* purpose once valid consent is obtained. They also require separate, specific consent when purposes diverge or expand. They make clear that silence or inactivity cannot substitute for an affirmative choice [5]. The CCPA likewise rejects consent obtained through dark patterns or other interface designs that subvert or impair user choice, and it limits processing to what is necessary and proportionate for disclosed purposes [6].

In practice, many subscription implementations bundle distinct purposes into a single upfront agreement, then treat renewal silence, free trial conversions, promotional expirations, price increases, or benefit changes as implied ongoing authorization. This interpretation undermines the legal standard of consent as freely given, specific, informed, and unambiguous, and exposes consumers to financial and privacy risks across the subscription life cycle [5,6].

How Subscriptions Handle Personal Data. Subscription services routinely collect and reuse personal data (for example, names, emails, billing tokens, and device identifiers) on a recurring basis to provision access, authenticate users, process payments, and personalize content on weekly, monthly, or annual cycles. While initial consent is typically obtained at signup, subsequent processing often extends well beyond that moment, for example during free-trial conversions, promotional expirations, renewals, price changes, or benefit changes, without a corresponding renewed authorization.

From a compliance perspective, this practice intersects with core data-protection principles. The GDPR requires purpose limitation, data minimization, storage limitation, and a valid legal basis (often consent) for each processing purpose. It also specifies that silence or inactivity cannot constitute consent and that separate purposes require separate consent [5]. The CCPA similarly constrains processing to disclosed purposes, rejects consent obtained through dark patterns, and expects organizations to avoid unnecessary or disproportionate data uses [6].

Operationally, subscription ecosystems tend to retain identifiers and payment artifacts for extended periods to support auto-renewal and reengagement campaigns. Extended retention and repurposing (for example, targeted marketing or cross-context behavioral advertising) can create privacy risks when users are not clearly informed or given an opportunity to make an affirmative choice at each material change. Regulators have flagged renewal frictions and opacity in recurring subscriptions (for example, the FTC's click-to-cancel rule), and consumer surveys report confusion and unintended enrollment, which underscores the need for stage-specific, unbundled consent across the subscription life cycle [12–14].

3 The Issue of Consent in Subscriptions

Subscription-based consumption spans many verticals, including food, gaming, streaming, and apparel, and is firmly entrenched in the digital marketplace [13, 14]. To illustrate where current practice diverges from legal consent standards, we focus on three common patterns.

Free Trial Then Ongoing Subscription. Users often enroll in a free trial that automatically converts to a paid plan. Without stage-specific consent, the initial authorization for a no-cost trial becomes bundled with consent for continued, paid processing of personal data. The burden then shifts to the user to cancel within a narrow window, despite well-documented variability in cancellation frictions [12]. This bundling conflicts with the GDPR requirement that consent be specific to each purpose and not inferred from silence or inactivity [5].

Promotional Pricing Then Ongoing Subscription. Many services start with a discounted period before reverting to a higher, standard rate. When consent to the promotional period is treated as consent to ongoing, higher-priced processing, users who forget or remain inactive are deemed to have agreed to materially different terms. Such reliance on inaction and default renewals runs counter to the GDPR affirmative-choice standard and to the CCPA prohibition on dark patterns that subvert or impair user choice [5,6].

Ongoing Subscription Then Benefits or Price Change. Providers frequently modify subscription benefits or increase prices while the subscription is active. In practice, continued use or failure to cancel is treated as authorization for further processing under the new terms, even though the original consent covered a different bundle of purposes and value. This approach undermines the requirement that consent be freely given, specific, informed, and unambiguous at each material change [5,6].

Across these patterns, the common thread is reliance on renewal silence and interface defaults rather than renewed, unbundled consent at each critical checkpoint, including trial conversion, promotion expiration, and price or benefit changes. Regulators have flagged these frictions in recurring subscriptions, for example through the FTC click-to-cancel rule, and consumer surveys report confusion and unintended enrollment. These findings underscore the need for stage-specific consent that aligns practice with the intent of modern privacy laws [12–14].

4 The Harm in Bundling Consent

Bundled consent in subscription ecosystems allows providers to treat silence, inactivity, or forgetfulness as authorization for continued processing of personal data, even when prices or benefits change. This practice converts a one-time agreement into open-ended permission and shifts the burden of privacy management onto consumers. The result is a persistent risk of financial and informational harm: users may be charged higher prices or placed under altered benefit structures while their data continue to be retained and repurposed without a fresh, affirmative choice [5,6].

Allowing stage-specific, unbundled consent (for example, separating free-trial consent from consent to convert to a paid service, or separating promotional-period consent from consent to ongoing standard pricing) would realign data practices with the legal standards of freely given, specific, informed, and unambiguous consent. Empirical HCI work shows that interface frictions and dark patterns can steer users toward acceptance, masking true intent and degrading consent quality; bundling exploits the same dynamics by relying on defaults and renewal inertia [7–9]. Regulators have flagged these concerns in recurring-subscription contexts (for example, the FTC's click-to-cancel rule aimed at reducing renewal frictions), and consumer surveys document confusion, unintended enrollment, and difficulty exiting auto-renewing plans [12–14].

In short, forced default consent to ongoing processing removes consumers from active participation in decisions about their personal data. Although the CCPA and GDPR are designed to enhance individual control, bundled consent in subscription workflows undermines that objective by treating inaction as consent across material changes. Requiring renewed, purpose-specific consent at each critical checkpoint would mitigate harm and better reflect users' actual wishes throughout the subscription life cycle [5,6].

4.1 Amazon Prime Lawsuit

In 2024, a class action challenged Amazon's changes to Prime Video streaming benefits, arguing that subscribers had agreed to a specific bundle of features and that altering those benefits without renewed, explicit consent violated the original bargain [15]. The court dismissed the case, reasoning that users had accepted terms that reserved Amazon's discretion to modify benefits. The dispute, however, highlights a broader expectation that companies should obtain fresh authorization before further processing personal data under materially different service terms. Framed against modern consent standards, the controversy underscores the tension between contract clauses that permit unilateral changes and privacy principles requiring consent to be freely given, specific, informed, and unambiguous at each distinct purpose or material change [5,6]. In short, the case illustrates growing demand for purpose-specific consent and for shifting the burden to providers to seek renewed, affirmative agreement when subscription benefits or pricing are modified.

4.2 Roku Forced Arbitration

In 2024, Roku, Inc. updated its End-User License Agreement (EULA) behind a consent wall that required users to accept the new terms to continue using their devices, and no meaningful alternative action was offered. Acceptance effectively assented to a mandatory arbitration clause, waiving users' rights to pursue claims in court [16]. From a privacy and consent perspective, this design raises concerns about dark patterns and coerced assent: valid consent should be freely given and unambiguous, not extracted through take-it-or-leave-it gating or interface constraints that subvert choice [5,6]. This episode illustrates how unilateral terms changes delivered via blocking modals can blur the line between notice and meaningful consent in always-on, subscription-adjacent ecosystems.

4.3 Disney+ Forced Arbitration

In 2025, a negligence lawsuit against Disney raised a forum selection dispute when the company moved to compel arbitration based on assent allegedly given during a one-month Disney+ trial in 2019 [17]. Although the case proceeded to a jury trial amid public scrutiny, the episode surfaces key data-protection questions: (i) *retention*: how long a company may rely on subscription-era records and consents after a service has ended; (ii) *purpose*: whether consent given for a streaming subscription can be repurposed to govern an unrelated, offline restaurant incident; and (iii) *visibility and granularity*: the extent to which terms and data uses traverse corporate entities and contexts.

Viewed through a privacy taxonomy that classifies practices by purpose, granularity, visibility, and retention, extending a 2019 digital-service consent to a 2024 in-person dispute suggests potential misalignment on multiple dimensions [1]. Even where contractual clauses purport to reserve broad change or arbitration rights, modern consent standards and fairness principles caution against treating historic, context-bound consent as blanket authorization across materially different purposes, actors, and time horizons [5,6]. More generally, the case illustrates how subscription-adjacent consents can be stretched beyond their original scope, reinforcing the need for purpose-specific, time-bounded, and context-aware consent management. This framing aligns with rights-oriented governance approaches that caution against broad, open-ended authorizations in high-asymmetry digital markets [44].

5 Proposed Solutions

5.1 Separate Consent

We propose stage-specific, unbundled consent for subscription services. Instead of treating a single upfront agreement as blanket authorization, providers should obtain renewed, affirmative consent at each material checkpoint in the subscription life cycle. This shifts the burden from consumers, who currently must notice and cancel in narrow windows, to businesses, which should request consent when terms or purposes change. This aligns practice with modern privacy standards that require consent to be freely given, specific, informed, and unambiguous [5,6]. In addition to improving legal compliance, layered consent supports transparency and user control across recurring billing, benefit changes, and renewals [12–14] (Fig. 1).

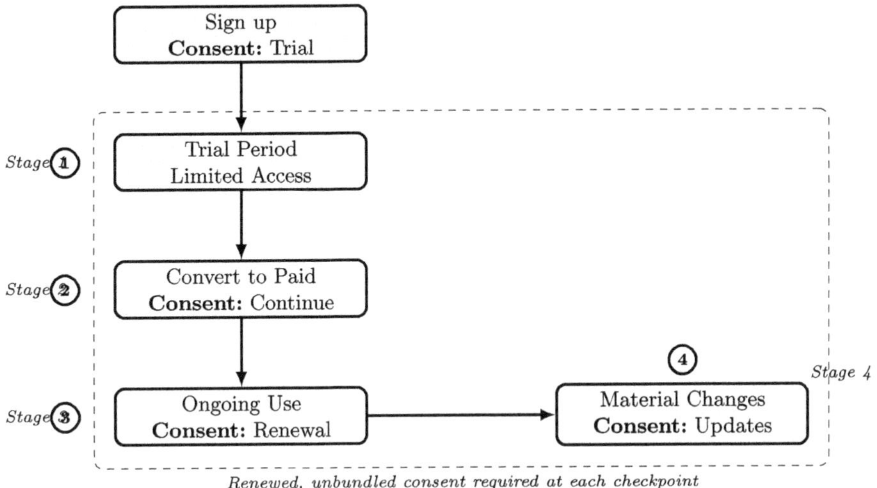

Fig. 1. Subscription life cycle with stage-specific consent checkpoints. Four explicit, unbundled consent points: (1) sign up with trial, (2) trial → paid conversion, (3) renewal, and (4) material changes to price or benefits.

Free Trials and Ongoing Subscriptions. Users should be able to opt in to a free trial without simultaneously consenting to conversion into a paid plan. At sign up, present two independent, unchecked options: consent for the trial and, optionally, advance consent for conversion. If the user does not grant the second consent, the default outcome at the end of the trial is no conversion and cessation of further processing absent a fresh affirmative choice [5,6].

Promotional Pricing and Ongoing Standard Pricing. Consent to a time-limited promotional period should not be treated as consent to a higher, standard rate. At promotion end, request explicit consent to continue at the new price. Inaction should not be interpreted as agreement. Absent a clear opt in, processing for ongoing billing should stop [5,6,12].

Material Changes to Benefits or Price. When benefits or price change, providers should obtain specific consent to process personal data under the new terms. Continued use or renewal silence is not a valid proxy for consent to a materially different purpose and value bundle [5,6]. Short, clear prompts with explicit choices support both usability and compliance [9].

These patterns operationalize purpose-specific, time-bounded consent across the subscription life cycle and reduce reliance on defaults and user inertia that degrade consent quality [7,8].

5.2 Default Action for Non-consent

When subscription terms materially change (for example, price or benefits), providers should *cease processing* personal data until they obtain fresh, affirmative consent to the new terms. Continuing to rely on prior, bundled authorization treats silence or inertia as agreement and conflicts with modern consent standards that require choices to be freely given, specific, informed, and unambiguous [5,6]. A default of "no further processing without renewed consent" better reflects user intent and reinforces purpose limitation, data minimization, and storage limitation principles.

Operationally, this default shifts the burden from consumers to businesses. Rather than expecting users to detect changes, navigate cancellation pathways, and act within narrow windows, organizations must prompt for consent at the moment terms change and suspend ongoing processing (including billing-related uses) absent an explicit opt-in [5,6]. Regulators have highlighted renewal frictions in recurring subscriptions (for example, the FTC's click-to-cancel rule), and many jurisdictions do not mandate advance renewal reminders; together, these conditions increase the risk that continued processing rests on inertia rather than an affirmative choice [12].

Given the steady growth in the number of subscriptions per consumer, the potential for unintended renewals and opaque repurposing of data also increases [14]. Requiring explicit, renewed consent at each material change, and making non-consent the safe default, promotes accountability and transparency, reduces reliance on dark-pattern defaults, and aligns subscription practices with the spirit and letter of contemporary privacy law [5,6].

5.3 Feasibility and Implementation Challenges

Layered, stage-specific consent can improve privacy protections, but deployment poses nontrivial challenges, especially for small and medium-sized enterprises (SMEs). Many organizations lack the technical staff, regulatory expertise, and budget needed to build and maintain consent orchestration at scale.

Technical and Operational Overhead. Implementing renewed, purpose-specific consent typically requires: (i) a real-time consent management service with versioned records, audit trails, and revocation; (ii) modular UI components integrated across web, mobile, and in-app flows; and (iii) secure storage and linkage of consent artifacts to downstream processing. The associated engineering effort and legal review can be disproportionate for SMEs.

Usability and Engagement Risks. Consent UX directly affects completion rates. Overly granular or frequent prompts can produce "consent fatigue," pushing users toward indiscriminate acceptance or abandonment [8,9]. Designs must balance legal specificity with low-friction choices, such as clear purposes, minimal clicks, and reversible decisions, to preserve meaning without degrading experience.

Standardization and Reuse. Industry-wide patterns and reusable components can reduce cost and inconsistency. Useful elements include open-source consent widgets with accessible defaults, standardized purpose taxonomies, and reference APIs for recording, querying, and enforcing consent. Behavior-driven enforcement and policy-aware middleware can translate UI choices into runtime controls and minimize bespoke glue code [19,20]. Prior work on behavior-driven enforcement and dynamic modeling of access-control effects shows how policy intent can be translated into concrete runtime checks and auditable state transitions, which is directly applicable to consent orchestration in subscriptions [21].

Proportionality and Regulatory Scaling. Regulators can encourage adoption by clarifying proportional obligations, for example fewer checkpoints for low-risk data and stricter renewal prompts for high-risk or materially changed terms. They can also offer small-business carve-outs where appropriate and publish UI exemplars that meet the standard of consent that is freely given, specific, informed, and unambiguous. Real-world privacy-preserving data pipelines demonstrate that purpose-scoped and time-bounded processing can be engineered without prohibitive overheads [39].

Collaborative Ecosystem. Sustainable compliance requires cooperation among regulators, platforms, and vendors. Priorities include authoritative UI patterns for trial-to-paid conversions, promotion expirations, and price or benefit changes; interoperable consent receipts; and certification pathways for consent management tools. Done well, these steps align user protection with operational feasibility and reduce reliance on dark-pattern defaults while keeping subscription funnels usable [8,9].

6 Broader Technical Context: Engineering Consent Orchestration with Lessons from AI, Biometrics, and Cybersecurity

Subscription consent is ultimately a *systems* problem. Policies must be represented, enforced, audited, and evolved across heterogeneous front ends and services. The privacy-by-design community has long emphasized translating abstract principles into executable controls. Prior work on behavior-driven enforcement and policy modeling shows how user intent can be captured at the UI, bound to machine-enforceable rules, and propagated through services [19–21]. These ideas map directly to *consent orchestration*: stage-specific choices (trial-only, convert-to-paid, renew, accept-change) should compile into concrete allow or deny decisions for billing, retention, re-marketing, and cross-context data sharing.

From Multimodal AI to Consent Granularity. Multimodal AI systems routinely decompose complex decisions into aligned sub-tasks, for example fusing speech, text, and behavior, with explicit intermediate signals and auditability across components [22–24]. By analogy, consent should be *modularized* by purpose and time: separate, inspectable artifacts for trial, promotion, conversion, renewal, and material change. Lessons from robust feature engineering and fusion, including explicit representations, late or early fusion trade-offs, and calibrated outputs, translate into clearer consent receipts and safer defaults [25–27].

Human Factors: Interface Robustness and Intent Preservation. Decades of affective and HRI research show that interface framing and cognitive load alter user responses [28,29]. Work on facial-expression analysis under occlusion, pose, and symmetry constraints shows that careful model and UX design can recover true signals from noisy observations [30–33]. For subscriptions, the parallel is direct: *intent-preserving* consent flows must reduce dark-pattern nudges, surface material differences, and avoid bundling. Empirical robustness in AI motivates UI guardrails such as explicit and reversible choices and low-latency revocation.

Security–Privacy Co-design: Access Control as a Template. Dynamic access-control models and trust propagation provide a mature template for governing *who* can do *what* and *when* [19,21,34]. In a consent operating system, these become consent scopes, expirations, and purpose constraints. As with least privilege in security, purpose limitation and storage limitation require *revocation-first* defaults and time-bounded grants. MAISON and related cyber-trust work emphasize hybrid technical and organizational controls; consent orchestration similarly spans UX, policy, and backend enforcement [35,36].

High-Stakes Domains: Privacy-Preserving Analytics as a Bar. Healthcare and well-being applications, including Alzheimer's detection from eye-tracking, cardiac anomaly detection, and multimodal stress screening, show that sensitive analytics can be engineered with principled pipelines, explicit model stages, and auditable data flows [37–39]. These pipelines routinely encode provenance, consent, and retention at each stage. Subscription ecosystems should adopt similar *consent provenance* with versioned receipts, purpose tags, and machine-checkable time-to-live values.

Scalability and Developer Ergonomics. Developer-facing patterns matter. Practical handbooks on deep learning engineering (regularization, generative tooling, end-to-end practice) provide reusable abstractions that reduce complexity and improve reliability [40–43]. A consent SDK can mirror these patterns: typed consent records; a minimal API with `request()`, `revoke()`, and `scope()`; and testable contracts that CI systems can verify, similar to unit tests for model invariants.

Fairness and Rights Framing. Aligning consent with human rights and bias-aware governance clarifies obligations under modern privacy regimes. Broader work on AI accountability and rights-centric framing argues for explicit user agency, contestability, and audit trails [44]. In subscriptions, this translates into: (i) *stage-specific* opt-ins with no implied consent through inertia, (ii) *context-bounded* usage with no cross-entity drift without fresh consent, and (iii) *time-bounded* retention with explicit renewal at material changes.

In sum, consent orchestration benefits from the same engineering discipline that matured AI, biometrics, and access control: modular decomposition, explicit artifacts, runtime enforcement, and developer tooling. Porting these lessons enables subscription platforms to operationalize GDPR and CCPA principles in ways that preserve user intent while remaining scalable and auditable [19–21]. Related engineering patterns in AI and applied security further support this direction [35–37,39–42,44].

7 Justification for Solution

The case studies above (Amazon Prime, Roku, and Disney) show a consistent pattern: consumers expect meaningful control over their data, yet subscription ecosystems often rely on inertia, bundled authorizations, and unilateral changes to terms. To align practice with the aims of modern privacy law, providers need a clear decision framework that operationalizes consent beyond one-time notice.

Using the four-dimensional privacy taxonomy of *purpose*, *granularity*, *visibility*, and *retention* helps evaluate whether a processing step matches what the user agreed to [1]. **Purpose.** Trial-to-paid conversions, promotion expirations, and benefit or price changes introduce new or expanded purposes (for example, ongoing billing or remarketing). Treating prior assent as blanket approval conflicts with purpose-specific consent [5,6]. **Granularity.** Bundled checkboxes obscure distinct decisions (trial versus paid, discounted versus standard rate). Stage-specific prompts restore granular and unambiguous choices [5]. **Visibility.** Terms and data uses often propagate across services and affiliates (for example, streaming-to-restaurant dispute theories), exceeding what a reasonable user would expect for the original context [17]. **Retention.** Long-lived identifiers and consent artifacts are frequently repurposed years later to justify processing under materially different conditions, raising storage-limitation concerns [5].

Under this taxonomy, current subscription practices reveal systematic misalignment. Broad and enduring authorizations are inferred from initial consent, while later material changes proceed without renewed, affirmative choice. Stage-specific and unbundled consent addresses these gaps by constraining processing to the agreed *purpose*, capturing user intent at appropriate *granularity*, limiting *visibility* to the expected context, and enforcing reasonable *retention* horizons. This approach is consistent with GDPR and CCPA requirements and responds to documented consumer harms in recurring-subscription markets [12,15–17].

7.1 Align with Existing Privacy Laws

Existing privacy laws are grounded in the principle that individuals must be informed and able to make a clear, affirmative choice before their data are processed. The GDPR requires consent to be freely given, specific, informed, and unambiguous, and it rejects consent inferred from silence, pre-ticked boxes, or inactivity [5]. The CCPA likewise prohibits dark patterns that subvert or impair user choice and limits processing to disclosed purposes [6].

Bundled consent in subscription workflows erodes these protections by converting a one-time authorization into open-ended permission. This dynamic helps explain common harms in recurring subscriptions: users inadvertently enroll when intending a one-time purchase, free trials convert without an explicit opt-in at the end of the trial, and annual plans renew long after users have forgotten the service [13,14]. Empirical HCI research shows that interface nudges and confusing consent prompts degrade consent quality and mask user intent [7–9].

Aligning subscription practices with the letter and spirit of these laws requires unbundling decisions and obtaining renewed, stage-specific consent at material checkpoints, including trial-to-paid conversion, promotion expiration, benefit or price changes, and renewal. Making explicit opt-in the default at these junctures ensures that processing continues only when the user's current intent is captured, rather than inferred from inertia. This approach also complements regulatory efforts to reduce renewal frictions in recurring subscriptions, for example the FTC click-to-cancel rule, by pairing easier exits with clearer, purpose-specific entries [12].

7.2 Cookie Consent Interfaces

Before comprehensive privacy regulations, many sites engaged in cross-site tracking without meaningful notice or choice. In response to laws such as the GDPR and CCPA, websites increasingly deploy cookie consent interfaces that disclose purposes and allow users to opt in or out of distinct categories (for example, strictly necessary, analytics, advertising), enabling operation of the site while honoring user preferences [5,6].

Empirical work on consent banners shows that interface design strongly shapes outcomes. Large-scale and lab studies document how layout, defaults, and wording can either support meaningful choice or nudge users toward acceptance (so-called dark patterns) [7,8]. Controlled evaluations of cookie banners find that presenting a small number of clear, separable options, for instance "Accept all," "Reject non-essential," and "Customize," can preserve usability while improving compliance and user agency [9].

These findings generalize to subscriptions. Providers can expose up to three stage-specific consent options at key checkpoints, for example trial-only, convert-to-paid, and convert-and-auto-renew, without materially degrading user experience, provided the choices are intelligible, reversible, and unbundled. Such designs better align with legal requirements that consent be freely given, specific, informed, and unambiguous, and they reduce reliance on inertia or silence as a proxy for agreement [5,6,9].

7.3 Consumer Research for Subscriptions

Recent research shows broad dissatisfaction with subscription-based services and persistent gaps in informed choice. In a 2022 market survey, 74% of respondents reported that it was easy to forget about their subscriptions, and 42% admitted they were still paying for subscriptions they had forgotten [14]. A 2022 study by the Washington State Attorney General found that 59% of respondents had unintentionally enrolled in a subscription within the prior four years when they believed they were making a one-time purchase; the state recorded roughly 24,000 subscription-related complaints that year [13].

Regulators have noted similar patterns. The U.S. Federal Trade Commission finalized its "click-to-cancel" rule to make canceling recurring subscriptions no harder than signing up, after receiving over 16,000 public comments. The FTC also reported a steady rise in subscription-related complaints, averaging about 70 per day in 2024, up from 42 per day in 2021 [12].

Taken together, these findings indicate that consumers want providers to share the burden of managing ongoing data processing in subscriptions. Clear, stage-specific prompts and easy exits are consistent with user expectations for accountability, accessibility, and transparency in an expanding subscription marketplace [12–14].

8 Future Implications and Conclusion

Since their 2018 enactment, both the CCPA and the GDPR have been amended and clarified, and further evolution is likely as digital services, and subscription ecosystems in particular, continue to expand [5,6]. The guiding principle remains unchanged: consumers should have meaningful control over their personal data, and providers should be accountable for how that data is collected, used, and retained.

The U.S. Federal Trade Commission's "click-to-cancel" rule is a step toward reducing renewal frictions in recurring subscriptions, but it primarily addresses the *exit* problem rather than the *entry* and *change of terms* problems. Proposals for advance renewal reminders were not included in the final rule, which leaves a gap where continued processing may still rely on user inertia rather than an affirmative, up-to-date choice [12]. As a result, safeguards at material change points, including trial conversion, promotion expiration, and price or benefit changes, remain essential.

In the interim, consumers bear much of the burden: monitoring terms, cancellation windows, renewal dates, and shifting benefit bundles. Market research and state-level surveys show how easily subscriptions are forgotten, misunderstood, or unintentionally renewed, which reinforces the need for provider obligations that reduce reliance on silence or inaction [13,14].

We argue that subscription workflows should default to *nonrenewal* or *no change* unless the provider obtains fresh, explicit consent when terms materially change. Concretely, users should be able to opt in to a trial without preauthorizing conversion to a paid service. Consent to a promotional period should not imply consent to ongoing, higher standard pricing. Any material change in price or benefits should pause further processing, including billing-related processing, until renewed, purpose-specific consent is obtained.

These measures implement the GDPR and CCPA standard that consent be freely given, specific, informed, and unambiguous, and they align user experience with the legal and ethical intent of modern privacy law [5,6]. Practically, they also address documented subscription fatigue and unintended enrollments by shifting the onus to providers to seek clear, stage-specific authorization at moments that matter most [12–14].

In sum, stage-specific and unbundled consent, paired with safe defaults and friction-reducing exits, offers a coherent path to protect consumers while preserving legitimate subscription models. It makes consent contemporaneous with purpose, limits processing to what users intend, and increases transparency and accountability across the subscription life cycle.

References

1. Barker, K., et al.: A Data Privacy Taxonomy. In: Dataspace: The Final Frontier, pp. 42–54 (2009)
2. Solove, D.J.: A Taxonomy of Privacy. Univ. Pa. Law Rev. **154**(3), 477–560 (2006)
3. Solove, D.J.: Understanding Privacy. Harvard University Press, Cambridge, MA (2008)
4. Nissenbaum, H.: Privacy as contextual integrity. Washington Law Rev. **79**(1), 119–158 (2004)
5. GDPR: General Data Protection Regulation (2018). https://gdpr-info.eu/
6. State of California: California Consumer Privacy Act of 2018. https://leginfo.legislature.ca.gov/faces/codesdisplayText.xhtmldivision3.part4.lawCodeCIVtitle1.81.5
7. Mathur, A., Acar, G., Friedman, M., Narayanan, A.: Dark patterns at scale: findings from a crawl of 11K shopping websites. Proc. ACM Hum.-Comput. Interact. (CSCW), 1–32 (2019)
8. Degeling, M., Utz, C., Lentzsch, C., Hosseini, H., Schaub, F.: We value your privacy... now take some cookies: measuring the GDPR's impact on web privacy. In: IEEE Symposium on Security and Privacy, pp. 527–543 (2019)
9. Habib, H., Li, M., Young, E., Cranor, L.: "Okay, Whatever": an evaluation of cookie consent interfaces. In: CHI Conference on Human Factors in Computing Systems (2022)
10. Grant, P.M.: Informed consent – we can and should do better. JAMA Netw. Open **4**(4), e2110848 (2021). https://jamanetwork.com/journals/jamanetworkopen/fullarticle/2779253
11. Villiger, D.: Informed Consent Under Ignorance. Am. J. Bioeth. 1–13 (2024)
12. Federal Trade Commission: Final "click-to-cancel" rule for recurring subscriptions and memberships (2024). https://www.ftc.gov/news-events/news/press-releases/2024/10/federal-trade-commission-announces-final-click-cancel-rule-making-it-easier-consumers-end-recurring
13. Washington Attorney General: Consumer alert: survey reveals millions may have been unintentionally enrolled in a subscription service (2022). https://www.atg.wa.gov/news/news-releases/consumer-alert-attorney-general-s-consumer-survey-reveals-millions-washingtonians

14. Tuazon, A.: Subscription service statistics and costs. C+R Research (2022). https://www.crresearch.com/blog/subscription-service-statistics-and-costs/
15. Cho, W.: Amazon Prime Video Ad Tier Sparks Class Action Lawsuit From Subscribers. The Hollywood Reporter (2024). https://www.hollywoodreporter.com/business/business-news/amazon-prime-video-ad-tier-lawsuit-1235822779/
16. Rossmanngroup.com: Roku, Inc. (2024). https://wiki.rossmanngroup.com/wiki/Roku
17. Treisman, R.: Disney wants a wrongful death lawsuit thrown out because the plaintiff had Disney+. NPR (2024). https://www.npr.org/2024/08/14/nx-s1-5074830/disney-wrongful-death-lawsuit-disney
18. Ghayoumi, M.: Review of security and privacy issues in e-commerce. In: Proceedings of the Int'l Conf. on e-Learning, e-Business, Enterprise Information Systems, and e-Government (2016)
19. Ghazinour, K., Ghayoumi, M.: An autonomous model to enforce security policies based on user's behavior. In: 2015 IEEE/ACIS 14th Int'l Conf. on Computer and Information Science (ICIS) (2015)
20. Ghazinour, K., Ghayoumi, M.: Dynamic Modeling for Representing Access Control Policies Effect. arXiv:1505.08154 (2015)
21. Ghazinour, K., Ghayoumi, M.: Dynamic modeling for representing access control policies affect. In: ICCS (2015)
22. Ghayoumi, M., Tafar, M., Bansal, A. K.: A formal approach for multimodal integration to drive emotions. J. Vis. Lang. Sentient Syst. 48–54 (2016)
23. Ghayoumi, M., et al.: Towards formal multimodal analysis of emotions for affective computing. In: DMS, 48–54 (2016)
24. Ghayoumi, M., et al.: Multimodal convolutional neural networks model for emotion in robots. In: FTC (2016)
25. Ghayoumi, M.: A Quick review of deep learning in facial expression. J. Commun. Comput. (2017)
26. Ghayoumi, M., et al.: Emotion in robots using convolutional neural networks. In: ICSR, pp. 285–295 (2016)
27. Ghayoumi, M., et al.: Architecture of emotion in robots using convolutional neural networks. In: RSS (2016)
28. Ghayoumi, M.: Cognitive-based architecture for emotion in social robots. In: HRI (2018)
29. Ghayoumi, M., et al.: Fuzzy knowledge-based architecture for learning and interaction in social robots. In: AI-HRI (2019)
30. Bansal, A. K., Ghayoumi, M.: A hybrid model to improve occluded facial expressions prediction in the wild during conversational head movements. In: INTELLI (Best Paper) (2021)
31. Bansal, A., Ghayoumi, M.: Symmetry based hybrid model to improve facial expressions prediction in the wild during conversational head movements. Adv. Life Sci. **13**(1–2) (2021)
32. Ghayoumi, M., et al.: Unifying geometric features and facial action units for improved performance of facial expression analysis. In: CSSCC, pp. 259–266 (2015)
33. Ghayoumi, M., Bansal, A.K.: Emotion analysis using facial key points and dihedral group. Int. J. Adv. Stud. Comput. Sci. Eng. (2017)
34. Ghazinour, K., Ghayoumi, M.: A dynamic trust model enforcing security policies. In: IPAC (2015)
35. Babaev, I., Packer, T., Ghayoumi, M., Ghazinour, K.: MAISON: a model for effective hybrid management of cybersecurity and cyber-trust. Int. J. Inf. Technol. (2024)

36. Ghayoumi, M., Ghazinour, K.: Advancing MAISON - integrating deep learning and social dynamics in cyberbullying detection and prevention. In: APCS (2024)
37. Ghayoumi, M., Ghazinour, K.: Early Alzheimer's detection - bidirectional LSTM and attention mechanisms in eye tracking. In: CSCE (2024)
38. Ghayoumi, M., Ghazinour, K.: Revolutionizing cardiovascular diagnostics - advanced AI algorithms for real-time detection of cardiac anomalies. In: CSCE (2024)
39. Ghayoumi, M., Nye, E. M., Liu, C.: AMHAT: multimodal pipeline for privacy-preserving stress screening. In: CSCI/CSI (2025)
40. Ghayoumi, M.: Math in Deep Learning. CRC Press (2025)
41. Ghayoumi, M.: GAN in Practice. CRC Press (2023)
42. Ghayoumi, M.: Deep Learning in Practice. CRC Press (2021)
43. Ghayoumi, M.: Enhancing Efficiency and Regularization in Convolutional Neural Networks: Strategies for Optimized Dropout. AI (2025)
44. Ghayoumi, M., Ghazinour, K.: Human rights in the shadow of AI: confronting bias and accountability. In: IEEE UEMCON (2025)

A Secure and Private Food Recommendation Framework Using Game-Theoretic Adversarial Learning

Sai Akshaya Banda, Raihana Tasnim, Madhuri Siddula(✉), Olusola T. Odeyomi, and Sajad Khorsandroo

North Carolina A&T State University, Greensboro, NC, USA
{sbanda1,rtasnim}@aggies.ncat.edu,
{msiddula,otodeyomi,skhorsandroo}@ncat.edu

Abstract. Personalized food recommendation systems, due to their reliance on centralized data storage, often suffer from privacy and security vulnerabilities. This research proposes a privacy-preserving framework integrating functional encryption and adversarial learning to safeguard sensitive user information while maintaining recommendation accuracy. Additionally, Fernet encryption is used for data encryption. A data poisoning attack is simulated to assess system resilience by injecting adversarial noise into encrypted datasets. Data imbalance is addressed using the Synthetic Minority Oversampling Technique (SMOTE) to enhance model fairness. Experimental results demonstrate that the proposed system effectively mitigates adversarial threats, preserves user privacy, and achieves robust performance across various metrics. This work advances secure and privacy-aware recommendation systems, offering a practical approach to defending against data manipulation attacks.

Keywords: Privacy & Security · Functional Encryption · Adversarial Learning · Recommender Systems · Data Poisoning · SMOTE · Regular Research Paper

1 Introduction

Food recommendation systems have become integral to modern digital platforms, offering personalized meal suggestions by analyzing user preferences, dietary restrictions, and historical interactions [13]. These systems utilize machine learning models trained on extensive datasets to enhance user engagement and satisfaction. However, the centralized collection and storage of sensitive user data such as dietary habits, health information, and location details raise significant privacy and security concerns. Unauthorized access to this data can lead to privacy breaches, while adversarial attacks can compromise the system's integrity [1].

Traditional security measures, including basic encryption and anonymization, often fall short in addressing sophisticated cyber threats. One notable threat is

K. Daimi et al. (Eds.): CSCE 2025, CCIS 2937, pp. 121–135, 2026.
https://doi.org/10.1007/978-3-032-22208-4_9

the data poisoning attack, where adversaries intentionally inject malicious data into the training set, aiming to corrupt the model's performance or manipulate its outputs [11]. Such attacks can degrade the quality of recommendations and erode user trust in the system. Current privacy-preserving mechanisms lack robustness against these adversarial manipulations, leaving recommendation systems vulnerable to both data breaches and integrity attacks [2].

In response to these challenges, this research proposes the development of a privacy-preserving food recommendation system that integrates functional encryption and adversarial learning techniques. Functional encryption allows for computations on encrypted data without revealing the data itself, thereby safeguarding sensitive user information [4]. Adversarial learning involves training models to recognize and resist adversarial inputs, enhancing the system's resilience against data poisoning attacks [16]. The effectiveness of the proposed system will be evaluated by simulating data poisoning scenarios and assessing their impact on both data integrity and recommendation accuracy. The key contributions of this work include:

- Designing a functional encryption framework tailored for securing user data in food recommendation systems.
- Implementing adversarial learning strategies to bolster the model's defense against data poisoning attacks.
- Conducting comprehensive evaluations of the system's performance and robustness in adversarial settings.
- Introducing quantitative security metrics, such as Success Rate, Failure Rate, Data Integrity, and Resilience Score, to measure the system's effectiveness.

To further reinforce the robustness of the system against strategic adversaries, we employ a game-theoretic adversarial learning approach. This method models interactions between the recommender system and adversaries as a strategic game, allowing the system to anticipate and proactively mitigate malicious actions. The remainder of this paper is structured as follows: Sect. 2 reviews related work on privacy and security in recommendation systems, Sect. 3 details the proposed methodology, Sect. 4 presents the experimental results and security assessments. Finally, Sect. 5 offers conclusions and discusses potential avenues for future research.

2 Related Work

2.1 Privacy and Security Challenges in Food Recommendation Systems

Food recommendation systems leverage extensive user data to provide personalized suggestions, enhancing user experience and satisfaction. However, this data collection raises significant privacy concerns. Users' personal information, such as dietary preferences, health conditions, and location data, can be sensitive. Unauthorized access or misuse of this information can lead to privacy breaches, affecting user trust and platform credibility [23]. Moreover, the integration of federated learning in recommendation systems, while aiming to enhance privacy by keeping data on local devices, has been found vulnerable to attribute inference attacks. Attackers can exploit model updates to infer users' private attributes, undermining the intended privacy-preserving benefits [21]. These challenges necessitate robust privacy-preserving techniques to protect user data in food recommendation systems. Recent studies also highlight the potential misuse of inferred user traits, such as religious or health-related preferences, which are unintentionally revealed through recommendation models. These indirect privacy risks further complicate privacy preservation efforts, emphasizing the need for robust protection mechanisms even when explicit identifiers are removed [14].

While enhancing user experience, recommender systems remain vulnerable to a range of security threats. One significant threat is poisoning attacks, where adversaries inject malicious data into the system to manipulate recommendations. These attacks can degrade the system's performance and trustworthiness [22]. Another notable threat is model extraction attacks, where attackers attempt to replicate the recommendation model by querying it extensively, potentially leading to intellectual property theft and compromised user data [26]. Addressing these security challenges is crucial for maintaining the integrity and reliability of recommender systems. Security threats in recommender systems are no longer limited to basic spoofing or injection attacks. Recent research has uncovered more nuanced vulnerabilities such as exposure through model updates, inference leakage, and adaptive poisoning. Wu et al. discuss how attackers can exploit temporal dynamics and feedback loops in recommendation pipelines to gradually corrupt models without detection, highlighting the need for continuous and context-aware threat monitoring [18].

Recommender systems enhance user experience by providing personalized suggestions but often require access to sensitive user data, raising privacy concerns. To address these issues, various privacy-preserving techniques have been developed. One such approach is Federated Learning, which enables collaborative model training across decentralized devices holding local data, thus keeping user information on personal devices and mitigating privacy risks [20]. Another significant method is Differential Privacy, which introduces controlled noise into the data or computations, ensuring that the inclusion or exclusion of a single user's data does not significantly affect the output. This technique provides strong privacy guarantees while maintaining the utility of the recommender system [12]. Implementing these privacy-preserving techniques is crucial for building trust and encouraging user engagement in recommender systems.

Adversarial learning is increasingly used to strengthen recommender systems against malicious attacks. Techniques like adversarial training and counterfactual learning help identify vulnerabilities and improve model resilience. Recent approaches, such as dynamic adversarial training, adapt to evolving threats, enhancing both robustness and recommendation accuracy [5,19,25]. Data poisoning attacks threaten recommender system integrity by injecting malicious data. To defend against them, techniques like clustering-based methods are used to detect and filter anomalous user behavior, reducing the impact of such attacks

[17]. Another defense strategy involves strengthening algorithm robustness. For instance, PORE (Provably Robust Recommender Systems) transforms existing recommender systems into versions that are provably resilient to untargeted data poisoning, maintaining reliable recommendation accuracy even under attack [9]. Shen et al. present a poisoning-resilient training framework that combines outlier detection with certified robustness bounds, effectively mitigating label-flipping and feature-poisoning strategies in recommendation pipelines [15].

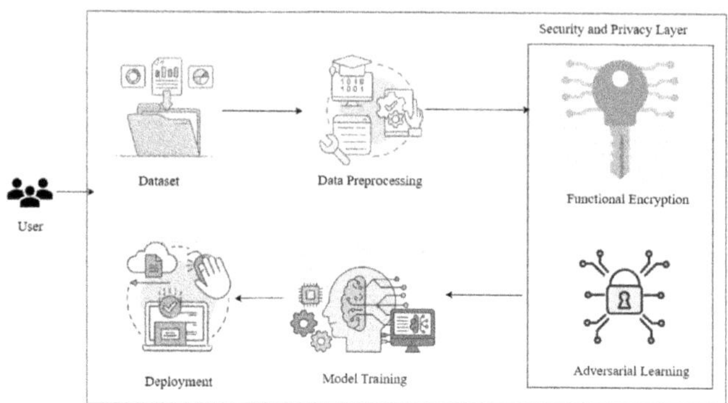

Fig. 1. System Architecture for Privacy-Preserving Food Recommendation System.

3 Methodology

Our proposed system architecture illustrated in Fig. 1 for a privacy-preserving food recommendation system integrates security mechanisms to protect user data while ensuring personalized recommendations. The architecture comprises five key components: User Interaction, Dataset, Data Preprocessing, Security and Privacy Layer, Model Training, and Deployment. The methodology of the proposed privacy-preserving food recommendation system follows a structured approach ensuring secure and personalized recommendations.

User Interaction: Users provide inputs such as preferences, dietary restrictions, and historical interactions, which serve as the basis for generating personalized recommendations.

Data Preprocessing and Feature Engineering: The system utilizes a publicly available dataset from Kaggle, which contains user preferences, food choices, and contextual information [8]. Feature engineering is a crucial step in improving recommendation accuracy by deriving meaningful attributes from the raw dataset. This process includes categorical encoding of attributes such as cuisine and dietary preferences using One-Hot Encoding [7]. Textual descriptions of food items are also preprocessed through tokenization, stopword removal, and stemming [3] to extract relevant information and reduce noise. Additionally, numerical attributes are normalized using Min-Max scaling [6] to bring values into the [0, 1] range, ensuring uniformity and improving model training efficiency.

Security and Privacy Mechanisms: To enhance system security and privacy, two key techniques are integrated: Functional encryption which enables computations on encrypted user data without revealing sensitive information, thus preserving user confidentiality during model training [24]. Second is the adversarial learning which defends against malicious attacks such as data poisoning by introducing adversarial examples into training data [10], making the model more robust to real-world threats.

Training Multiple Machine Learning Models: To ensure model generalization and performance, four machine learning models are trained and evaluated including K-Nearest Neighbors (KNN), Decision Tree (DT), Logistic Regression (LR), Gradient Boosting (GB).

Deployment and Continuous Learning: The trained model is deployed in a secure cloud environment, where it continuously updates recommendations based on user interactions while preserving data privacy. To ensure scalability and responsiveness, it utilizes asynchronous data pipelines and containerized deployment with Docker and Kubernetes, enabling efficient resource use and elastic scaling. As user demand grows, the system can scale elastically to maintain performance and availability without compromising security. Real-time monitoring detects anomalies, data drift, and adversarial behavior, while role-based access controls and secure API gateways manage permissions and protect sensitive components.

Evaluation and Validation: To assess system performance, multiple evaluation metrics such as accuracy, precision, recall, F1-score, and confusion matrices are generated for each algorithm. Additionally, the system is subjected to adversarial scenarios including data poisoning attacks to analyze its security metrics such as success rate, failure rate, data integrity, and resilience score. This rigorous evaluation ensures that the model is not only accurate but also robust and secure in high-risk environments.

Feedback Loop Integration: A critical component of the methodology is feedback loop where user responses are logged and used for retraining, allowing the system to adapt to changing preferences and enhance personalization over time.

Security Monitoring and Alerts: In addition to algorithmic defenses, the system incorporates real-time monitoring to detect anomalies like drops in data integrity or spikes in errors, enabling early detection of security threats. Logging and auditing tools ensure accountability, transparency, and compliance.

3.1 Proposed Algorithms

The core of the proposed system begins with feature engineering, where input data is preprocessed using three primary techniques. First, *Categorical Encoding*

(CE) transforms textual categorical values such as food types or dietary preferences into a numerical format through one-hot encoding. This enables machine learning models to interpret and process non-numeric data effectively. Second, *Text Preprocessing (TP)* cleans and structures user-generated content such as reviews using tokenization, stopword removal, and stemming to ensure meaningful feature extraction. Third, *Numerical Normalization (NN)* scales numeric features like ratings and nutritional scores using Min-Max scaling, ensuring that no single feature disproportionately influences the model. After preprocessing, sensitive data is protected using *Functional Encryption (FE).* Unlike traditional encryption, FE allows specific computations to be performed on encrypted data without decryption, maintaining privacy throughout the machine learning pipeline. To enhance model robustness, *Adversarial Noise Injection* is optionally applied by introducing Gaussian noise, simulating real-world data imperfections and increasing the system's tolerance to uncertainty. The recommendation system then trains models using K-Nearest Neighbors (KNN), Logistic Regression (LR), Decision Tree (DT), and Gradient Boosting (GB). The best-performing model is selected based on evaluation metrics to generate personalized recommendations while ensuring data security.

Data Poisoning Attack Evaluation: To evaluate the system's robustness, a data poisoning attack is simulated. This attack involves injecting adversarial noise into the training data to corrupt the model's learning process. Poisoning is performed in chunks across poisoning rates from 10% to 100%. Within each chunk, random float values are assigned to the `Rating` field to simulate data tampering. Encrypted ratings are then decrypted, and success/failure rates are tracked. The effectiveness of the attack is measured using four metrics: Success Rate, Failure Rate, Data Integrity Rate, Resilience Score.

Algorithm Summary: The system relies on two primary algorithms:

1. **Privacy-Preserving Food Recommendation Algorithm**: Algorithm 1 handles preprocessing steps such as categorical encoding, text cleaning, and normalization, followed by functional encryption and adversarial noise injection. It then trains multiple models and generates personalized, privacy-protected recommendations.
2. **Data Poisoning Attack Algorithm**: Algorithm 2 simulates adversarial conditions by injecting malicious data into the system. It measures the impact on model integrity and recommendation accuracy using security metrics like success rate and resilience score.

Algorithm 1. Privacy-Preserving Food Recommendation System

Require: Raw dataset D_{raw}
Ensure: Trained Model M and Recommendations *Recom*
1: Initialize $D_{processed} \leftarrow 0$
2: **Step 1: Feature Engineering**
3: **for** each categorical feature $f \in CategoricalFeatures$ **do**
4: One-hot encode f and append to dataset
5: Drop original feature f
6: **end for**
7: **for** each text feature $t \in TextFeatures$ **do**
8: Tokenize t, remove stopwords, apply stemming
9: Replace t with processed tokens
10: **end for**
11: **for** each numerical feature $n \in NumericalFeatures$ **do**
12: Normalize n using Min-Max scaling
13: Append normalized feature to dataset
14: **end for**
15: **Step 2: Functional Encryption**
16: **for** each $s \in SensitiveFeatures$ **do**
17: Apply encryption to s using Fernet
18: **end for**
19: **Step 3: Adversarial Noise Injection**
20: **if** adversarial noise is enabled **then**
21: Generate Gaussian noise $N(0, \sigma)$ and inject into encrypted data
22: **end if**
23: **Step 4: Model Training**
24: **for** each model $\in$ {KNN, LR, DT, GB} **do**
25: Train model on transformed and secure data
26: Store model performance
27: **end for**
28: **Step 5: Recommendation Generation**
29: Generate recommendations based on best-performing model
30: **return** M, *Recom*

Algorithm 2. Data Poisoning Attack

Require: Dataset D, Poison Rates $P = \{0.1, 0.2, \ldots, 1.0\}$
Ensure: Evaluation Metrics per Poison Rate and Chunk
1: **for** each $p \in P$ **do**
2: Compute chunk size $C \leftarrow p \cdot |D|$
3: Partition D into $\frac{|D|}{C}$ chunks
4: **for** each chunk **do**
5: Perturb *Rating* field with random float in $[0, 1]$
6: Decrypt *Encrypted Rating* column
7: Track decryption outcomes: success / failure
8: Compute:
9: Success Rate $= \frac{\text{success}}{\text{total}} \cdot 100$
10: Failure Rate $= \frac{\text{failure}}{\text{total}} \cdot 100$
11: Integrity Rate $= \frac{\text{success}}{|D|} \cdot 100$
12: Resilience Score $= 100 -$ Failure Rate
13: **end for**
14: **end for**
15: **return** Aggregated Metrics Table

3.2 Security and Privacy Metrics

Since the system incorporates Functional Encryption and Adversarial Learning, it is crucial to measure its ability to resist adversarial threats and maintain data confidentiality. To assess the system's effectiveness against security vulnerabilities, we define four key metrics: Success Rate (SR), measures the effectiveness of adversarial attacks in altering the recommendation output. A lower success rate indicates better system robustness; Failure Rate (FR), represents the percentage of attacks that fail to manipulate the system. A higher failure rate suggests better adversarial resistance; Data Integrity (DI), evaluates the preservation of encrypted data structure after adversarial perturbation and decryption; Resilience Score (RS), quantifies the system's ability to recover from adversarial modifications and maintain accurate recommendations.

Evaluation Methodology: To systematically evaluate the system's security, we simulate adversarial attacks using data poisoning techniques to analyze the system's vulnerability. The attack success rate is recorded. Then the encrypted data's integrity is tested by introducing perturbations and measuring its impact on the recommendation accuracy. Finally to evaluate model robustness, the recommendation model is subjected to adversarial input to analyze how well it can mitigate attack effects and maintain accuracy. These metrics provide a quantifiable basis for assessing the trade-off between recommendation accuracy, security, and user data privacy. By analyzing these factors, we ensure that the system remains resistant to adversarial threats while maintaining high-quality recommendations.

4 Results and Discussion

This section presents the evaluation of the proposed privacy-preserving food recommendation system. Various performance metrics, including classification reports, correlation analysis, and accuracy comparisons, are analyzed.

Classification Reports. We evaluate model performance by analyzing classification reports that include precision, recall, F1-score, and support, providing insights into each algorithm's effectiveness and generalization (Table 1). These findings guide us in selecting the most suitable model for personalized, privacy-preserving food recommendations. KNN shows relatively low precision and recall due to its reliance on similarity-based classification, which can be affected by imbalanced datasets. Logistic Regression improves upon KNN by better distinguishing between food categories, though it struggles with complex feature relationships. Decision Tree achieves a significantly higher recall and F1-score by constructing hierarchical decision rules, making it well-suited for categorical data. Gradient Boosting outperforms all other models, demonstrating the benefits of ensemble learning for improving classification accuracy.

4.1 Correlation Heat Map

The correlation heat map offers a visual interpretation of the interdependencies among numerical and encoded categorical variables in the dataset. It plays a

Table 1. Classification Reports for All Models

Class	Precision	Recall	F1-Score	Support
1	0.04	0.07	0.05	15
2	0.06	0.17	0.09	12
3	0.12	0.06	0.08	16
4	0.07	0.08	0.07	12
5	0.00	0.00	0.00	18
6	0.07	0.08	0.07	13
7	0.00	0.00	0.00	12
8	0.17	0.18	0.17	11
9	0.11	0.10	0.10	20
10	0.25	0.04	0.07	25
Accuracy	-	-	0.07	**154**
Macro Avg	0.09	0.08	0.07	154
Weighted Avg	0.10	0.07	0.07	154

(a) KNN

Class	Precision	Recall	F1-Score	Support
1	0.59	0.67	0.62	15
2	0.38	0.42	0.40	12
3	0.45	0.31	0.37	16
4	0.09	0.08	0.09	12
5	0.33	0.11	0.17	18
6	0.14	0.23	0.18	13
7	0.27	0.33	0.30	12
8	0.23	0.27	0.25	11
9	0.22	0.25	0.23	20
10	0.54	0.52	0.53	25
Accuracy	-	-	0.33	**154**
Macro Avg	0.33	0.32	0.31	154
Weighted Avg	0.35	0.33	0.33	154

(b) Logistic Regression

Class	Precision	Recall	F1-Score	Support
1	1.00	0.87	0.93	15
2	0.70	0.58	0.64	12
3	0.67	0.88	0.76	16
4	0.78	0.58	0.67	12
5	0.81	0.94	0.87	18
6	0.90	0.69	0.78	13
7	0.79	0.92	0.85	12
8	0.85	1.00	0.92	11
9	0.64	0.70	0.67	20
10	0.81	0.68	0.74	25
Accuracy	-	-	0.78	**154**
Macro Avg	0.79	0.78	0.78	154
Weighted Avg	0.79	0.78	0.78	154

(c) Decision Tree

Class	Precision	Recall	F1-Score	Support
1	1.00	0.87	0.93	15
2	0.62	0.42	0.50	12
3	0.61	0.88	0.72	16
4	0.89	0.67	0.76	12
5	0.90	1.00	0.95	18
6	1.00	0.85	0.92	13
7	0.80	1.00	0.89	12
8	0.91	0.91	0.91	11
9	0.82	0.90	0.86	20
10	0.95	0.84	0.89	25
Accuracy	-	-	0.84	**154**
Macro Avg	0.85	0.83	0.83	154
Weighted Avg	0.86	0.84	0.84	154

(d) Gradient Boosting

crucial role in identifying redundant features, uncovering patterns, and guiding feature selection. From the heat map, we notice the following observations: Certain one-hot encoded features exhibit strong positive or negative correlations, particularly complementary food category encodings (e.g., `Veg_Non_veg` and `Veg_Non_non-veg`), indicating mutual exclusivity. The variables `Normalized Rating` and `Decrypted Rating` retain a perfect correlation with the original `Rating`, validating that the transformations preserved underlying information. Weak correlations between most categorical types suggest that each feature contributes distinct information to the model, reducing multicollinearity and supporting diverse learning signals. The `Cluster` feature shows noticeable correlation with key features such as `Food_ID` and `Normalized_Rating`, indicating that these attributes significantly influence the clustering mechanism used in the recommendation process (Fig. 2).

This analysis confirms that the dataset contains a balanced mix of correlated and independent variables, supporting the robustness of the feature engineering process used for training the model.

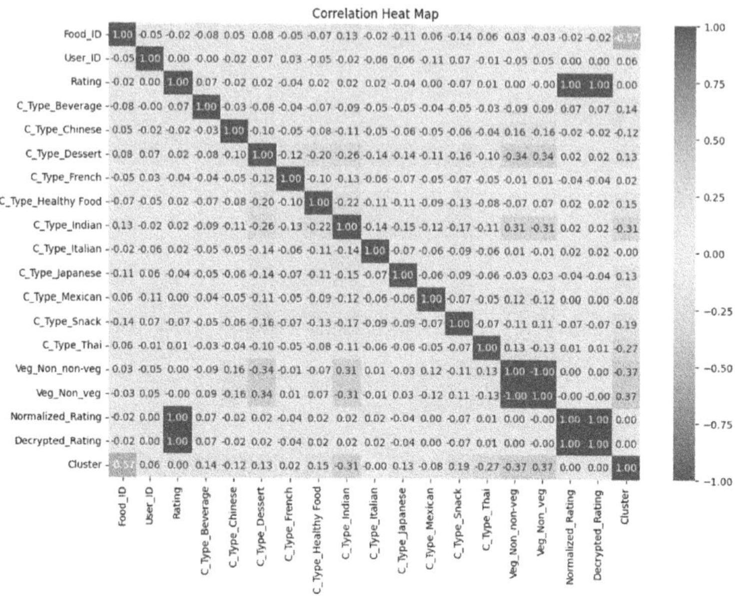

Fig. 2. Correlation Heat Map.

4.2 Class Distribution Analysis

Class distribution in the target variable highlights the dataset's balance which impacts model performance and fairness. A well-balanced class distribution prevents bias, supports generalization, and supported fair evaluation metrics.

From Fig. 3, we observe that all ten food preference clusters exhibit a reasonably uniform distribution. The highest representation is in Class 3 with 12.3%, while Class 8 is the lowest at 7.6%. This distribution implies that the dataset is moderately balanced, reducing the risk of overfitting to dominant classes. Although slight variations exist, they are not severe enough to warrant immediate resampling. However, to improve robustness, Synthetic Minority Over-sampling Technique (SMOTE) was later applied during training to further address these minor imbalances and enhance model sensitivity across underrepresented categories. Such preprocessing is particularly crucial in recommendation systems, where skewed data can lead to unfair suggestions. Ensuring each class receives adequate representation helps maintain diversity and relevance in the recommended items.

4.3 Training and Validation Accuracy

The training and validation accuracy of the proposed model is visualized over multiple epochs in Fig. 4. A large gap between training and validation accuracy can indicate overfitting. The results indicate stable training accuracy, nearing 100%, while the validation accuracy remains significantly lower. This suggests

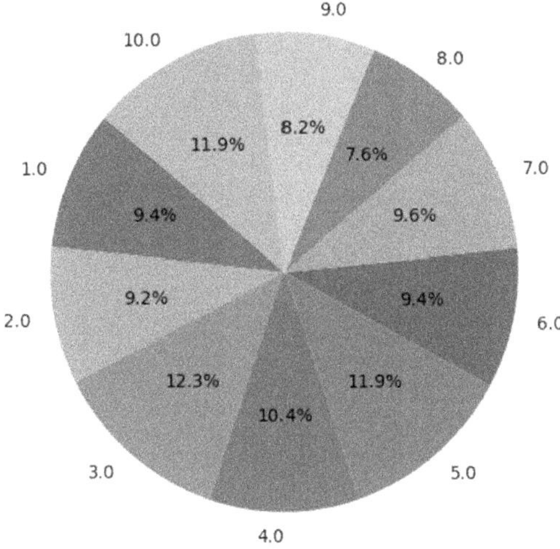

Fig. 3. Class Distribution in Target Variable.

potential overfitting, which could be mitigated with regularization techniques or more diverse training data. Additionally, the flat validation accuracy trend across epochs implies limited generalization, likely due to model memorization. Incorporating dropout, early stopping, or adversarial training could enhance robustness and reduce this discrepancy.

4.4 Model Test Accuracy Comparison

The performance of different models is compared based on test accuracy (Fig. 5). Higher test accuracy suggests better generalization to unseen data. Gradient Boosting achieves the highest test accuracy, followed by the Decision Tree model. KNN underperforms, reflecting its sensitivity to feature scaling and dataset structure. Logistic Regression shows moderate performance but fails to capture complex non-linear relationships. Ensemble models like Gradient Boosting benefit from combining weak learners, leading to superior accuracy and robustness.

4.5 Security Metric Evaluation

To analyze the security resilience of the model, a detailed data poisoning attack simulation was conducted using varying poison rates from 10% to 100%. The evaluation used four core metrics: Success rate (%), indicating the proportion of poisoning attempts that successfully influenced recommendations; Failure Rate (%), representing the proportion of attacks that failed to alter model predictions; Data Integrity Rate (%), measuring the percentage of data that remained uncorrupted throughout the attack; and Resilience Score (%), computing the

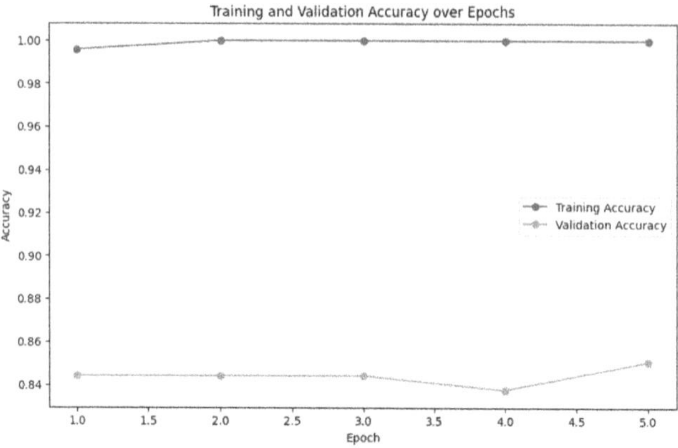

Fig. 4. Training and Validation Accuracy Over Epochs.

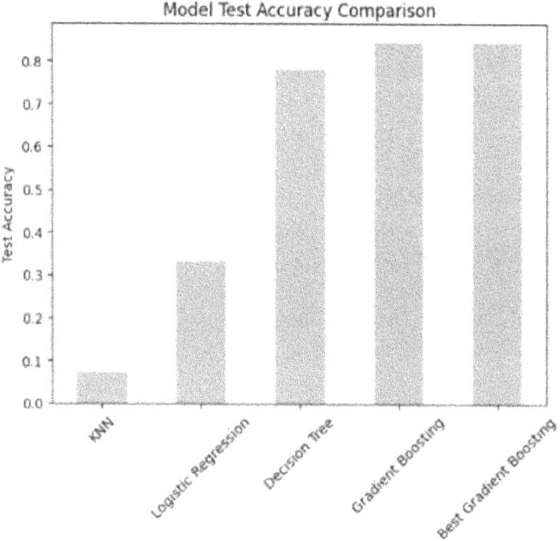

Fig. 5. Model Test Accuracy Comparison.

system's ability to recover and maintain performance despite adversarial interference. These results indicate that the system maintained a failure rate above 67% across all poison levels, demonstrating consistent robustness (Table 2). However, the slight dip in data integrity and resilience as poisoning intensifies highlights opportunities to strengthen the system's encryption and adversarial defenses. Further integration of noise-aware training techniques could enhance recovery under high adversarial pressure. Figure 6 presents a visual representation of how different security metrics vary across increasing poison rates from 10% to 100%. These graphs help illustrate trends in system robustness, with notable resilience against moderate attack levels but performance degradation under extreme poisoning conditions.

Table 2. Security Metrics for Data Poisoning Attack (10%100% Poison Rate)

Poison Rate (%)	Success Rate (%)	Failure Rate (%)	Data Integrity (%)	Resilience Score (%)
10	29.49	70.51	29.49	29.49
20	30.96	69.04	30.96	30.96
30	27.59	72.41	27.59	27.59
40	29.94	70.06	29.94	29.94
50	32.88	67.12	32.88	32.88
60	30.14	69.86	30.14	30.14
70	30.14	69.86	30.14	30.14
80	27.79	72.21	27.79	27.79
90	29.35	69.65	29.35	29.35
100	26.42	73.58	26.42	26.42

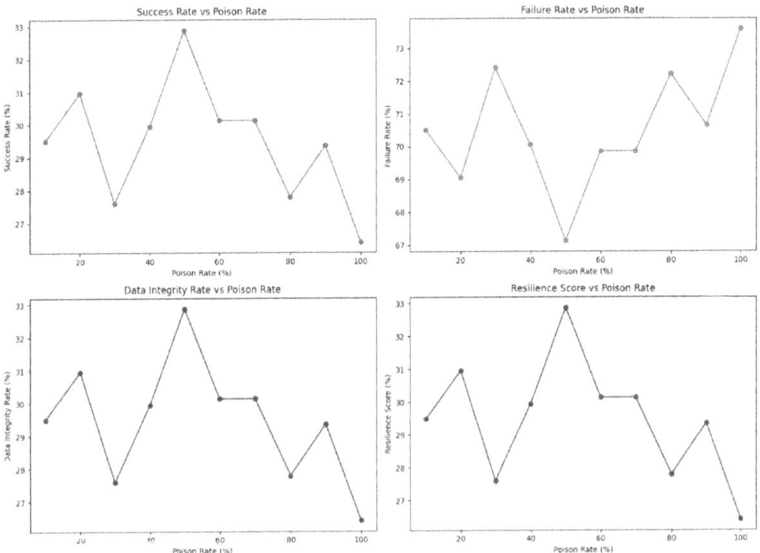

Fig. 6. Visualization of Security Metrics (Success Rate, Failure Rate, Data Integrity, and Resilience Score) Across Varying Poison Rates.

5 Conclusion

This research presents a privacy-preserving food recommendation system that integrates Functional Encryption and Adversarial Learning to enhance data security and model robustness. The proposed approach ensures that sensitive user information remains protected while maintaining high recommendation accuracy. The security evaluation metrics, including Success Rate, Failure Rate, Data Integrity, and Resilience Score, validate the system's ability to withstand adversarial attacks and mitigate data poisoning attempts. Experimental results demonstrate that Gradient Boosting outperforms other models such as Logistic Regression, Decision Tree, and K-Nearest Neighbors, achieving the highest classification accuracy. The analysis of data distribution, correlation, and model performance trends further highlights the effectiveness of our preprocessing and training strategies. Overall, this study provides a comprehensive framework for secure and reliable food recommendations, bridging the gap between user personalization and data privacy. While our proposed system significantly enhances privacy and security in recommendation models, several aspects can be further improved. Our future work will focus on enhancing scalability and privacy by incorporating larger datasets, integrating federated learning, and deploying real-time recommendation capabilities. Additionally, we aim to strengthen adversarial defenses and develop customizable user privacy controls for more secure and adaptable systems. By addressing these challenges, we aim to further strengthen the security, scalability, and fairness of privacy-preserving recommendation systems in real-world applications.

Acknowledgments. This study was partially funded by Google, and NSF Grant 2434487.

Disclosure of Interests. The authors have no competing interests to declare that are relevant to the content of this article.

References

1. Badsha, S., Yi, X., Khalil, I.: A practical privacy-preserving recommender system. Data Sci. Eng. **1**(3), 78–92 (2016). https://doi.org/10.1007/s41019-016-0027-8
2. Biggio, B., Roli, F.: Machine learning security against data poisoning: are we there yet? arXiv preprint arXiv:2204.05986 (2022)
3. Bird, S., Klein, E., Loper, E.: Natural Language Processing with Python: Analyzing Text with the Natural Language Toolkit. O'Reilly Media Inc. (2009)
4. Bosri, R., Rahman, M., Bhuiyan, M., Omar, A.A.: Integrating blockchain with artificial intelligence for privacy-preserving recommender systems. IEEE Trans. Netw. Sci. Eng. **7**(4), 2722–2733 (2020). https://doi.org/10.1109/TNSE.2020.2984961
5. Deldjoo, Y., Di Noia, T., Merra, F.A.: A survey on adversarial recommender systems: from attack/defense strategies to generative adversarial networks. ACM Comput. Surv. **54**(2), 1–38 (2021). https://doi.org/10.1145/3439729
6. Han, J., Kamber, M., Pei, J.: Data Mining: Concepts and Techniques, 3rd edn. Elsevier (2011)
7. Harris, C.R., et al.: Array programming with numpy. Nature **585**(7825), 357–362 (2020)
8. Hephzibah, G.: Food recommendation system: Easy and comprehensive (2023). https://www.kaggle.com/code/gracehephzibahm/food-recommendation-system-easy-comprehensive. Accessed 07 Nov 2025

9. Jia, J., Liu, Y., Hu, Y., Gong, N.Z.: Pore: provably robust recommender systems against data poisoning attacks. In: Proceedings of the 32nd USENIX Security Symposium (2023). https://www.usenix.org/conference/usenixsecurity23/presentation/jia
10. Li, Z., Zhao, Y., Chen, X., Wang, Y.: Adaptive adversarial training for robust recommendation systems. IEEE Trans. Knowl. Data Eng. (2023). https://doi.org/10.1109/TKDE.2023.3246782
11. Liu, Y., et al.: A survey on data poisoning attacks and defenses. IEEE Trans. Dependable Secure Comput. **19**(2), 120–137 (2022). https://doi.org/10.1109/TDSC.2021.3095162
12. Mai, P., Pang, Y.: PrivMVMF: privacy-preserving multi-view matrix factorization for recommender systems. arXiv preprint arXiv:2210.07775 (2022)
13. Ramakrishnan, N., Keller, B.J., Mirza, B.J., Grama, A.Y., Karypis, G.: Privacy risks in recommender systems. IEEE Internet Comput. **5**(6), 56–62 (2001). https://doi.org/10.1109/4236.968832
14. Sen, A., Malik, F., Zhou, L.: Inference attacks in food recommender systems: a privacy perspective. In: Proceedings of the 31st ACM Conference on User Modeling, Adaptation and Personalization, pp. 95–103. ACM (2023)
15. Shen, J., Kumar, A., Wang, Y.: Certified defenses against data poisoning attacks in recommender systems. In: Proceedings of the 2023 ACM SIGSAC Conference on Computer and Communications Security (CCS), pp. 981–994. ACM (2023)
16. Steinhardt, J., Koh, P.W., Liang, P.: Certified defenses for data poisoning attacks. In: Advances in Neural Information Processing Systems (NeurIPS), pp. 3517–3529 (2017)
17. Wang, Z., et al.: Poisoning attacks and defenses in recommender systems: a survey. arXiv preprint arXiv:2406.01022 (2024)
18. Wu, Y., Sun, Z., He, X.: Recommendation system security: threats, challenges, and future directions. ACM Comput. Surv. **55**(3), 1–36 (2022). https://doi.org/10.1145/3491244
19. Xu, D., Ruan, C., Korpeoglu, E., Kumar, S., Achan, K.: Adversarial counterfactual learning and evaluation for recommender system. arXiv preprint arXiv:2012.02295 (2020)
20. Yanagi, T., Ikeda, S., Sukegawa, N., Takano, Y.: Privacy-preserving recommender system using the data collaboration analysis for distributed datasets. arXiv preprint arXiv:2406.01603 (2024)
21. Yuan, W., Yang, C., Nguyen, Q.V.H., Cui, L., He, T., Yin, H.: Interaction-level membership inference attack against federated recommender systems. arXiv preprint arXiv:2301.10964 (2023)
22. Zhang, J., Liu, Y., Liu, Q., Wu, S., Guo, G., Wang, L.: Stealthy attack on large language model based recommendation. arXiv preprint arXiv:2402.14836 (2024)
23. Zhang, S., Yuan, W., Yin, H.: Comprehensive privacy analysis on federated recommender system against attribute inference attacks. arXiv preprint arXiv:2205.11857 (2022)
24. Zhang, W., Liu, X., Deng, R.H.: Efficient and fine-grained functional encryption for privacy-preserving data analytics. IEEE Trans. Inf. Forensics Secur. **18**, 1123–1136 (2023). https://doi.org/10.1109/TIFS.2023.3244527
25. Zhang, Y., Ma, H., Li, Z., Wang, X.: Adversarial training for robust recommender systems with adaptive perturbation. IEEE Trans. Knowl. Data Eng. **34**(9), 4375–4387 (2022). https://doi.org/10.1109/TKDE.2021.3079336
26. Zhu, Z., Fan, R., Wu, C., Yang, Y., Lian, D., Chen, E.: Model stealing attack against recommender system. arXiv preprint arXiv:2312.11571 (2023)

Three-Body Problem: Can It Be Used for Cryptographically Secure Pseudorandom Number Generator (CSPRNG)?

Lara Su Ertaul(✉)

Columbia University, Pre-College Program, 116th and Broadway, New York, NY 10027, USA
lse2120@columbia.edu

Abstract. This study investigates whether the chaotic dynamics of the three-body problem can be used to generate cryptographically secure pseudorandom numbers (CSPRNs). By simulating gravitational interactions among three celestial bodies, high-entropy data was extracted from their evolving positions and momenta and converted into a 27-million-bit binary sequence. These sequences were evaluated using the NIST SP 800-22 test suite, where all subsets (1 M–10 M bits) passed all 15 statistical tests at the 0.01 significance level. Additional next-bit prediction and autocorrelation analyses confirmed the sequences' unpredictability and their similarity to white noise, supporting their randomness and suitability for cryptographic use. The results demonstrate that the three-body problem can serve as a physics-based entropy source for generating statistically robust pseudorandom sequences, potentially suitable for applications like key generation and secure hashing etc. Furthermore, the enormous seed space of the three-body system, exceeding 10^{300} possible configurations, offers strong resistance to brute-force attacks and reverse-engineering.

Keywords: Three-Body problem · Cryptography · NIST SP 800-22 · Randomness tests · CSPRNGs

1 Introduction

Liu Cixin's acclaimed novel the three-body Problem [10] and its television adaptation 3 Body Problem [11], first published in 2006 and adapted by Netflix in 2024. These works have brought complex physics and deterministic chaos into the public imagination, which dramatize the unpredictable behavior of a system governed by simple gravitational laws. Scientifically, the problem refers to the motion of three celestial bodies under mutual gravitational influence. First rigorously analyzed by Newton and later by Poincare, the three-body system became a prototype of deterministic chaos where small variations in initial conditions lead to vastly different outcomes [1, 2].

This inherent sensitivity to initial conditions makes the three-body system a candidate for high-entropy output generation. This study examines whether numerical simulations of the three-body problem can serve as a basis for cryptographically secure pseudorandom number generation (CSPRNG).

K. Daimi et al. (Eds.): CSCE 2025, CCIS 2937, pp. 136–148, 2026.
https://doi.org/10.1007/978-3-032-22208-4_10

Random number generation plays a foundational role in modern cryptography. Secure communication protocols, digital signatures, public key generation, secure hashing, key exchange mechanisms, and various cryptographic primitives all rely on access to high-quality random bits. The unpredictability, uniformity, and statistical independence of these random sequences are critical for maintaining cryptographic strength and resisting attacks [3–5].

Random number generators (RNGs) are broadly categorized into:

- True Random Number Generators (TRNGs): Devices that extract entropy from physical processes such as radioactive decay, thermal noise, or photonic emissions [8].
- Pseudorandom Number Generators (PRNGs): Deterministic algorithms that produce sequences of numbers that appear random but are generated from an initial seed using mathematical formulas. They lack cryptographic security guarantees [35].
- Cryptographically Secure Pseudorandom Number Generators (CSPRNGs): Deterministic algorithms that generate statistically strong sequences from high-entropy seeds [9].

Modern cryptographic systems also integrate Quantum Key Distribution (QKD) as TRNGs, which uses quantum mechanics to securely share encryption keys between remote parties. Although QKD provides secure key exchange, it still depends on strong entropy sources for initialization and authentication.

To validate entropy quality, the National Institute of Standards and Technology (NIST) provides a set of widely adopted testing standards. Among them, the NIST SP 800–22 Rev. 1a suite includes 15 statistical tests designed to assess randomness across various dimensions (e.g., frequency, entropy, linear complexity, and autocorrelation) [5]. In addition to NIST SP 800–22, other well-established randomness testing frameworks include the Diehard tests, developed by George Marsaglia, and its modern extension Dieharder, which integrates tests from both Diehard and NIST and provides greater configurability and statistical rigor. Another highly regarded framework is TestU01, created by L'Ecuyer and Simard, which offers a range of test batteries such as SmallCrush, Crush, and BigCrush—used extensively in academic research and commercial validation of pseudorandom number generators [6, 7]. These alternative test suites offer complementary statistical evaluations and have been instrumental in benchmarking randomness in both algorithmic and physical entropy sources. In this paper, however, the analysis is restricted to the NIST SP 800–22 test suite, as it provides a well-documented, widely adopted, and reproducible baseline for assessing statistical randomness along with autocorrelation, and next-bit test in cryptographic contexts. Sequences used for cryptographic purposes are expected to pass these tests with high confidence.

This paper investigates whether chaotic physical simulations specifically, those based on the three-body problem, can generate binary sequences that meet NIST standards.

2 Overview of the Three-Body Problem

The three-body problem is a foundational challenge in classical mechanics, describing the motion of three celestial bodies interacting through Newtonian gravity. Governed by a system of nonlinear differential equations, the three-body problem is inherently more complex than the analytically solvable two-body problem. The general form of Newton's second law for a three-body system can be written as:

$$m_i\, d^2 r_j/dt^2 = G\, \Sigma\_\{j \neq i\}\, m_i\, m_j\, (r_j - r_i)/|r_j - r_i|^3,\ i = 1, 2, 3$$

Where mass of a body (M), gravitational constant (G), position vector$(\vec{r_i})$, and acceleration vector $(d^2\vec{r_i}/dt^2)$

This yields three coupled second-order differential equations, each describing the gravitational acceleration of a single mass due to the influence of the other two [12.13]

Because these equations are nonlinear and interdependent, exact solutions exist only for specific, symmetric initial conditions. Despite this mathematical intractability, some special solutions to the three-body problem are known. Notably, Euler's collinear solution describes a configuration in which all three bodies lie on a straight line, rotating uniformly about the system's center of mass. (see Fig. 1a below) [12, 13, 18]

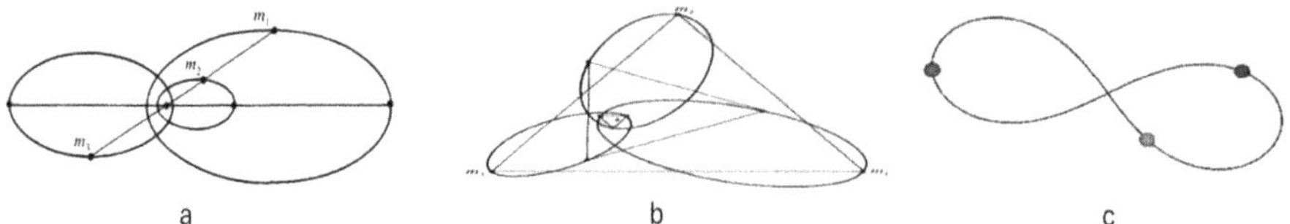

Fig. 1. Special solutions to the three-body problem

Similarly, Similarly, Lagrange's equilateral triangle solution positions the bodies at the vertices of a rotating equilateral triangle as shown in Fig. 1b [12, 13, 15, 16]. Another remarkable and stable solution is the figure-eight orbit, in which three equal masses follow a single, shared trajectory shaped like a figure-eight. This periodic solution, first discovered numerically in the 1990s and later proven rigorously, is both symmetric and dynamically stable under certain conditions. Each mass chases the next, equally spaced in time along the same path. This elegant configuration is illustrated in Fig. 1c [12, 13, 17]. In fact, researchers have now identified at least 20 distinct families of such periodic three-body orbits, demonstrating a surprising richness of stable and symmetric solutions within this classically chaotic problem [36].

These solutions are analytically elegant but unstable in practice—small perturbations lead to rapid divergence from these configurations, highlighting the system's sensitivity to initial conditions [12, 13]. Beyond these rare scenarios, the vast majority of three-body configurations exhibit chaotic dynamics. The system's future state becomes exponentially sensitive to minute changes in starting position and velocity, making long-term prediction practically impossible. This deterministic chaos makes the three-body system a prototypical example of nonlinear dynamical complexity [13, 14].

In the context of randomness generation, this extreme sensitivity becomes an asset. Since even infinitesimal changes in initial parameters yield drastically different trajectories, the numerical outputs of a simulated three-body system encode high entropy. The evolution of positions and velocities over time can be sampled and transformed into binary form to generate sequences with unpredictable structure. This study leverages that principle: a chaotic three-body system is simulated, dynamical state vectors are extracted at regular intervals, converted into binary sequences, and assessed using established randomness tests. Because of this unpredictability, the chaotic dynamics of the three-body problem are proposed as a natural candidate for generating cryptographically secure pseudorandom numbers (CSPRN)s. By sampling the evolving states of the system and converting them into binary sequences, the investigation focuses on whether such data exhibits the statistical properties required for cryptographic randomness. This study explores whether the entropy and unpredictability generated by the chaotic dynamics of the three-body system can provide a viable source for cryptographically secure pseudorandom number generation, suitable for applications such as key generation, secure hashing, and session initialization.

3 Overview the NIST SP 800-22 Testing Framework

The NIST Statistical Test Suite (STS), published as SP 800-22 Rev 1a [5], is one of the most widely accepted tools for evaluating the statistical randomness of binary sequences used in cryptographic systems. It comprises 15 tests, each designed to detect specific deviations from what would be expected in a truly random bitstream. The suite is not only a research tool but also a standard recommended by government and industry organizations.

To consider a sequence statistically random under NIST guidelines, each test must return a p-value ≥ 0.01, indicating that the sequence does not deviate significantly from ideal randomness at the 99% confidence level. For a full evaluation, a sequence should pass at least 13 out of 15 core tests consistently. Sequences failing more than two tests are generally considered unsuitable for cryptographic purposes.

Table 1 presents a summary of various randomness testing frameworks, including Dieharder [7], TestU01 [6], ENT [19], and online tools like Random.org [20]. While Dieharder and TestU01 are powerful alternatives, this study focuses exclusively on the NIST suite for its reproducibility, community validation, and standardization.

Table 1. Summary of randomness testing frameworks (Dieharder, TestU01, ENT, Random.org).

Tool	Windows?	Web?	GUI?	Strength	Notes
Dicharder	✗ (Linux/WSL)	✗	✗	★★★★★	Best for Linux users
TestU01	✗ WSL/Cygwin	✗	✗	★★★★★	Research-grade
ENT	✓ Yes	✗	✗	★★★	Easy + good for fast checks
Random.org	✗	✓ Yes	✓ Yes	★	More for fun

The following Table 2 contains a brief description of the 15 NIST tests. Together, these tests provide a robust, multidimensional view of statistical randomness. While passing them does not guarantee cryptographic strength, consistent failures reliably indicate non-random structure—disqualifying the sequence from cryptographic use.

In addition to the NIST suite, two supplementary tests were also conducted to further evaluate structural predictability in the generated sequences. The autocorrelation test [21, 22] assesses the degree of similarity between a sequence and a shifted version of itself; significant correlations suggest underlying periodicity or redundancy. The next-bit test [23], a more stringent cryptographic criterion, evaluates whether any bit in the sequence can be predicted from its predecessors with a probability significantly better than chance. Passing both tests strengthens confidence in the unpredictability and cryptographic suitability of the random number generator under evaluation.

Table 2. NIST SP 800-22 Rev 1a tests and brief descriptions.

NIST Test	Description
Frequency (Monobit) Test	Evaluates whether the number of 0 s and 1 s in the entire sequence is approximately equal. This test checks for global balance in bit occurrences and is a fundamental indicator of randomness.
Block Frequency Test	Divides the sequence into fixed length blocks and examines the proportion of 1 s within each block. It detects localized bias or imbalance that might not affect the entire sequence.
Runs Test	Counts the number and length of runs of identical bits (consecutive 0 s or 1 s). It assesses whether the sequence alternates bits at a rate consistent with randomness.
Longest Run of Ones in a Block	Determines whether the longest sequence of consecutive 1 s in a block exceeds what is expected statistically. Long runs of 1 s (or 0 s) may indicate clustering or deterministic patterns.
Binary Matrix Rank Test	Forms binary matrices from the sequence and checks their ranks. The goal is to detect linear dependence among sub-segments, which would undermine entropy.
Discrete Fourier Transform (Spectral) Test	Transforms the sequence into the frequency domain to identify periodic patterns. Significant spectral peaks indicate underlying structure rather than true randomness.
Non-Overlapping Template Matching Test	Searches for predefined bit patterns in non-overlapping windows. A high count of repeated templates may reflect predictable sequences.
Overlapping Template Matching Test	Similar to the non-overlapping version, but allows template matches to overlap. It is more sensitive to subtle or recurring patterns embedded in the stream.

(*continued*)

Table 2. (*continued*)

NIST Test	Description
Maurer's Universal Statistical Test	Tests the compressibility of the sequence. Random sequences are generally incompressible, so sequences that compress well are likely structured or deterministic.
Linear Complexity Test	Evaluates the length of the shortest Linear Feedback Shift Register (LFSR) that can produce the sequence. A short LFSR suggests low algorithmic complexity and reduced unpredictability.
Serial Test	Measures the frequency of all possible overlapping m-bit patterns. It ensures the sequence doesn't overrepresent or underrepresent any specific binary patterns of fixed length.
Approximate Entropy Test	Compares the frequency distributions of m-bit and (m + 1)-bit patterns to evaluate sequence complexity. Lower entropy values point to more regular, less random behavior.
Cumulative Sums (Cusum) Test	Models the sequence as a one-dimensional random walk and measures how far it strays from zero. Systematic drift suggests imbalance or bias in the direction of the bit values.
Random Excursions Test	Analyzes how often the cumulative sum visits certain states during a random walk. Non-random sequences deviate from expected visit counts across different states.
Random Excursions Variant Test	Measures the total number of visits to each possible state. This complements the Excursions Test by flagging under- or over-representation of specific states.

4 Simulation and Evaluation Methodology

This study utilizes a custom-implemented Python program, ***three_body4.py***, to simulate a chaotic three-body problem system and extract high-entropy binary sequences for cryptographic evaluation. The simulation is executed using Python 3.13.3 and leverages the ***VPython*** 3D visualization engine along with ***random***, ***decima***l, ***math***, ***numpy***, ***time, os, pandas, hashlib, scipy, and matplotlib*** libraries [28–34].

The simulation initializes three celestial bodies with randomized properties. Masses are sampled from a uniform distribution scaled by a base mass constant. The base mass is defined as $M = 5 \times 10^{24}$ kg, and the actual mass of each body is randomly selected in the range [0.5 M, 2.0 M] which are $[2.5 \times 10^{24}, 1.0 \times 10^{25}]$ kg respectively. Initial positions are generated within a 3D cube of side length 2.4×10^9 m ($\pm 1{,}2 \times 10^9$ m per axis). Initial momenta are calculated from velocity vectors. The gravitational constant is set as $G = 6.67 \times 10^{-11}$ N·m^2/kg^2. To avoid singularities, a minimum enforced separation between any two bodies is set at 1×10^6 m. At fixed intervals (every 10 iterations), the program records the system's state and generates a binary sequence from the following 18 values: 9 spatial coordinates ***(x, y, z*** for each body) and 9 momentum components ***(px, py, pz*** for each body). Each value is converted into 5000-bit binary string using the ***decimal*** module, resulting in a total of $18 \times 5000 = 90{,}000$bits per snapshot. Then, the resulting bitstream is randomly shuffled at the bit level using ***random.shuffle()*** to further eliminate any structural patterns. The simulation runs for 30 s. With a control rate of 1000 iterations per second and sampling every 10 iterations, approximately 300 snapshots are captured, yielding bits (approximately ***27 million*** bits) of output data.

To visually illustrate the simulation's unpredictable behavior, four screenshots are included in Fig. 2 These snapshots demonstrate significant divergence in positions and complex motion paths, highlighting the system's chaotic evolution during each simulation run.

The binary output generated through this method is evaluated using a Python implementation of the NIST SP 800–22 randomness test suite. To provide a broader perspective on randomness quality, next-bit predictability tests and autocorrelation analysis were also implemented in Python as complementary methods to the NIST suite. For this analysis, six subsets of the 27-million-bit sequence were randomly selected, with sizes of 1, 2, 3, 5, 7, and 10 million bits. The minimum size of 1 million bits was chosen to satisfy the NIST SP 800–22 recommendation that most tests require sequences of at least 1,000,000 bits for meaningful evaluation [5]. Each subset was individually tested using the full NIST suite and the next-bit test.

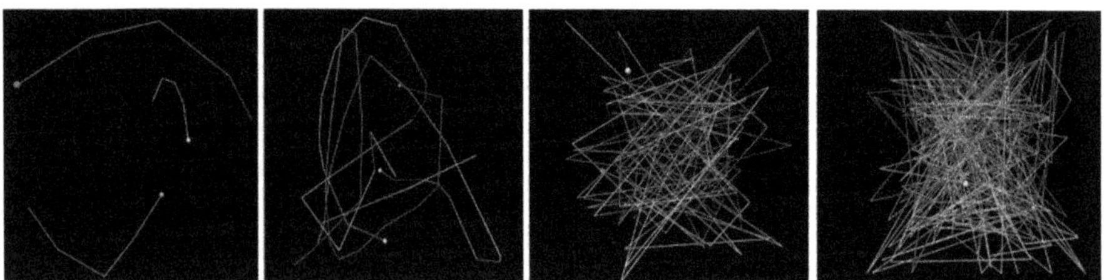

Fig. 2. Several stages of three-body problem simulation from beginning to end.

Autocorrelation analysis was also conducted on five subsets (1, 2, 3, 5, and 7 million bits). Resulting autocorrelation plots were compared with the autocorrelation function of Gaussian white noise to assess the randomness of the bit streams. In the case of white noise, the autocorrelation function is ideally a delta function—zero at all non-zero lags and maximal at zero lag—indicating no correlation between values at different positions. By comparing the autocorrelation of the simulated sequences with this baseline, one can identify hidden periodicity or structure. A close match to white noise behavior implies high statistical independence and supports the assumption of randomness in the output [23, 24]

5 Experimental Results

Experimental results from the NIST SP 800–22 tests conducted on six subsets of increasing size (1 M to 10 M bits) consistently showed that all 15 tests were passed at the significance level of 0.01. See Table 2 below.

In hypothesis testing, the significance level (denoted as α) represents the probability of rejecting a truly random sequence. A significance level of 0.01 means that if the sequence were perfectly random, there would be only a 1% chance of incorrectly identifying it as non-random [5]

Each test returns a p-value, which quantifies the probability that a truly random sequence would produce a result as extreme as the one observed. If the p-value is greater than or equal to the significance level (in this case, ≥ 0.01), the sequence is considered to pass that test. The p-values close to 1.0 indicate strong alignment with expected randomness, while those close to 0 suggest potential non-random behavior. However, uniformly high or low p-values across all tests may also be suspicious; a good distribution of p-values within the range [0.01, 0.99] is generally expected [5].

Results analysis provides a detailed overview of how each bit-length subset performed across individual 15 NIST tests. (see Table 3) All 15 tests were successfully passed for every subset tested, reaffirming statistical soundness at each scale. This includes foundational tests such as the Frequency (Monobit) Test and the Runs Test, as well as more complex assessments like the Linear Complexity Test and Discrete Fourier Transform Test. Across all datasets, the p-values fell well within the acceptable range, with no statistical anomalies or outliers observed. For instance, the 1 M-bit sequence produced strong p-values across all tests (e.g., 0.4012 for Frequency and 0.4237 for Block Frequency), while the 10 M-bit subset also maintained strong performance (e.g., 0.3421 for Frequency and 0.2152 for Block Frequency).

Table 3. NIST SP 800–22 test suite results.

NIST Test Name	1 M bits	2 M bits	3 M bits	5 M bits	7 M bits	10 M bits	Results α = 0.01
Frequency (Monobit) Test	0.4012	0.5341	0.4231	0.4373	0.4237	0.3421	Pass
Block Frequency Test	0.4237	0.2133	0.1257	0.3505	0.8921	0.2152	Pass
Runs Test	0.3428	0.3505	0.6783	0.5341	0.2152	0.4987	Pass
Longest Run of Ones Test	0.2133	0.9114	0.3412	0.2133	0.1023	0.1023	Pass
Binary Matrix Rank Test	0.5341	0.6579	0.5129	0.6579	0.3456	0.8765	Pass
Discrete Fourier Transform Test	0.1123	0.1025	0.2245	0.1223	0.7542	0.6543	Pass

(continued)

Table 3. (*continued*)

NIST Test Name	1 M bits	2 M bits	3 M bits	5 M bits	7 M bits	10 M bits	Results α = 0.01
Non-overlapping Template Test	0.6787	0.4353	0.0872	0.4012	0.1124	0.3210	Pass
Overlapping Template Test	0.2757	0.6579	0.7654	0.2757	0.0873	0.5432	Pass
Universal Statistical Test	0.6371	0.2133	0.3321	0.1917	0.5321	0.7654	Pass
Linear Complexity Test	0.9114	0.1025	0.4567	0.6579	0.6210	0.2345	Pass
Serial Test (1)	0.3505	0.3505	0.1987	0.5341	0.4231	0.4567	Pass
Serial Test (2)	0.5341	0.6579	0.5432	0.3505	0.3789	0.6789	Pass
Approximate Entropy Test	0.6579	0.5341	0.6123	0.5341	0.4567	0.1234	Pass
Cumulative Sums Test (Forward)	0.3505	0.2133	0.4238	0.2133	0.2314	0.4321	Pass
Cumulative Sums Test (Reverse)	0.3505	0.4353	0.2876	0.1223	0.1892	0.5678	Pass

No test failed for any subset, and no individual ***p***-value fell below the 0.01 rejection threshold. Particularly notable was the consistent performance of the Cumulative Sums Tests and Serial Tests, indicating that the sequences show no measurable bias or correlation patterns. Even tests known to be sensitive to structure, such as the Non-overlapping and Overlapping Template Matching Tests, consistently passed with acceptable ***p***-values. This uniform pass rate across all subset sizes suggests that the three-body problem is capable of generating CSPRNs for cryptographic applications.

In addition to the NIST suite, a next-bit prediction test was performed on the same six bit-length subsets. Across all subsets, the prediction accuracies ranged from 0.5020 to 0.5119. These values fall well within the expected range for random or cryptographically secure pseudorandom sequences, confirming that no significant bit-level predictability was present. The results support the conclusion that the generated sequences exhibit strong unpredictability, consistent with cryptographic standards.

Two figures are included to visualize and compare the autocorrelation structure of three-body bit sequences and Gaussian white noise. Figure 3 shows Gaussian white noise over 100,000 samples and its autocorrelation function and Fig. 4. presents the autocorrelation function for a 1-million-bit sequence generated from the three-body problem, exhibiting a sharp delta-like structure. The autocorrelation of Gaussian white noise shown in Fig. 4, also peaks sharply at zero lag and quickly decays — a hallmark of statistical independence. The close similarity between Figs. 3 and 4 further supports the conclusion that the three-body problem bitstreams exhibit randomness properties comparable to ideal white noise.

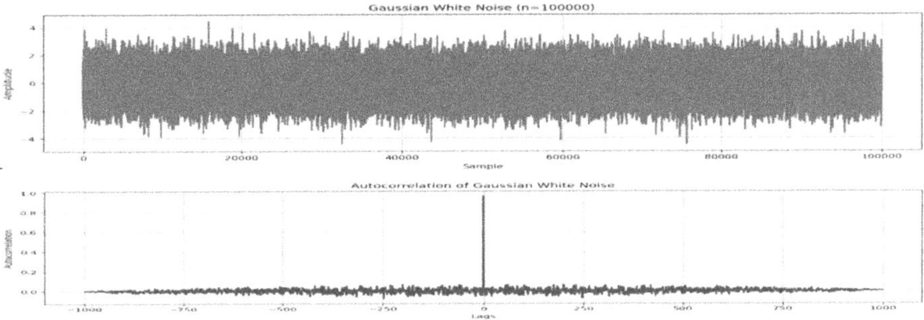

Fig. 3. Gaussian white noise and its autocorrelation function.

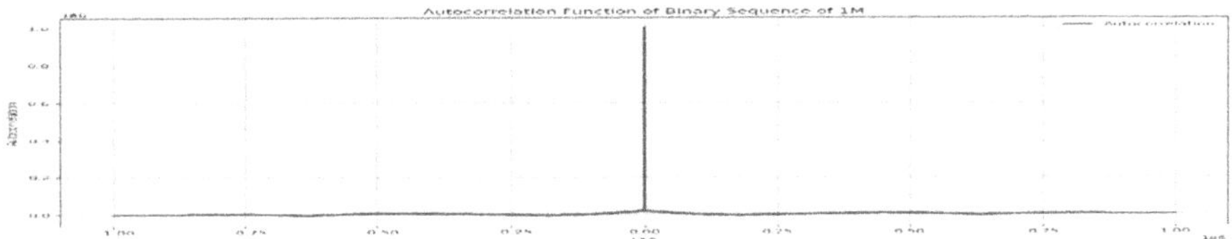

Fig. 4. Autocorrelation function of binary sequence of 1 M.

While the chaotic dynamics of the three-body problem offer strong entropy characteristics, a critical caveat must be addressed regarding security: if the initial conditions and simulation parameters are known or can be estimated, an attacker could theoretically reconstruct the binary output. This reversibility risk means that the entropy source is only cryptographically secure when initial state vectors (mass, position, momentum) are kept secret and generated using high-entropy physical or quantum methods. The unpredictability provided by deterministic chaos hinges entirely on the secrecy of these seeds—similar to how traditional CSPRNGs rely on the unpredictability of their initial seed. Compared to established CSPRNGs like Fortuna [25], Yarrow [26], or AES-based generators [27], the three-body-based method introduces a novel physics-inspired alternative but lacks certain battle-tested safeguards. Traditional CSPRNGs often include mechanisms for reseeding, entropy pooling, state protection, and cryptographic mixing functions, which make them robust against state compromise and backtracking attacks.

Nonetheless, the three-body system benefits from a vast and high-resolution con tinuous seed space real-valued initial positions, momenta, and masses—which makes brute-force seed recovery computationally infeasible under realistic constraints. In this study, initial positions were selected from a 3D cube with a side length of 2.4×10^9 m, and masses were drawn from the continuous range between 2.5×10^{24} kg and 1.0×10^{25} kg. Velocities were derived from momentum vectors, also with high-precision real values. With 18 parameters (3 positions and 3 momenta per body) each specified with ~15–17 decimal digits of precision (equivalent to double-precision floating point), the total number of unique initial configurations easily exceeds 10^{300}. For comparison, this is vastly larger than the 10^{77} estimated atoms in the observable universe. Such a high-dimensional, continuous seed space makes brute-force recovery or parameter guessing practically impossible, reinforcing the security potential of three-body based pseudorandom generation

6 Conclusions

This study investigated the use of chaotic three-body problem as a source of CSPRNs generation. Physical parameters such as positions and momenta were sampled during the simulation and converted into high-precision binary sequences, resulting in a bit-stream totaling approximately 27 million bits. These sequences were then subjected to rigorous statistical evaluation. Using the NIST SP 800–22 test suite, all tested subsets from 1 million to 10 million bits passed 15 core statistical randomness tests, demonstrating consistency and reliability across increasing bit lengths. Supplementary next-bit predictability tests yielded accuracies near 0.5, further affirming the unpredictability of the output. Additionally, autocorrelation analyses showed minimal structure, closely matching the behavior of Gaussian white noise—a widely accepted model for ideal randomness. Together, these results indicate that the proposed three-body problem-based method is not only capable of producing statistically random sequences but may also meet the unpredictability and independence standards required for cryptographic and high-stakes security applications. Moreover, the extremely large and continuous seed space of the three-body system—exceeding 10^{300} possible configurations—makes brute-force attacks computationally infeasible. As a result, the generated sequences offer strong resistance to reverse-engineering and key recovery attacks.

Future work will include evaluating the generated binary sequences using additional well-established randomness test suites such as Dieharder, TestU01, and ENT, as introduced earlier in this study. These frameworks will provide further insight into the robustness and statistical properties of the proposed method beyond what is captured by the NIST suite.

References

1. Sussman, G.J., Wisdom, J.: Structure and Interpretation of Classical Mechanics. MIT Press (2001)
2. Szebehely, V.: Theory of Orbits: The Restricted Problem of Three Bodies. Academic (1967)
3. Press, W.H., Teukolsky, S.A., Vetterling, W.T., Flannery, B.P.: Numerical Recipes 3rd Edition: The Art of Scientific Computing. Cambridge University Press (2007)
4. Ferguson, N., Schneier, B., Kohno, T.: Cryptography Engineering: Design Principles and Practical Applications. Wiley (2010)
5. Rukhin, A. et al.: A Statistical Test Suite for Random and Pseudorandom Number Generators for Cryptographic Applications, NIST SP 800-22 Rev 1a, (2010)
6. L'Ecuyer, P., Simard, R.: TestU01: a C library for empirical testing of random number generators. ACM TOMS. **33**(4), 22 (2007)

7. Brown, R.G., Dieharder, A.: Random Number Test Suite. https://webhome.phy.duke.edu/~rgb/General/dieharder.php (2004)
8. Herrero-Collantes, M., Garcia-Escartin, J.C.: Quantum random number generators. Rev. Mod. Phys. **89**(1), 015004 (2017). https://doi.org/10.1103/RevModPhys.89.015004
9. Kelsey, J., Schneier, B., Ferguson, N., Whiting, D.: Yarrow-160: Notes on the Design and Analysis of the Yarrow Cryptographic Pseudorandom Number Generator. SAC Workshop (1999)
10. Liu, C.: The 3Body Problem. Chongqing Publishing Group.; English ed.: Tor Books (2014)
11. Netflix: 3 Body Problem [TV Series]. Created by David Benioff, D.B. Weiss, and Alexander Woo., Netflix (2024)
12. Valtonen, M., Karttunen, H.: The 3Body Problem. Cambridge University Press (2006)
13. Diacu, F., Holmes, P.: Celestial Encounters: The origins of chaos and stability. Princeton University Press (1996)
14. Arenstorf, R.F.: Periodic solutions of the restricted 3Body problem representing analytic continuation of the lunar orbit. Am. J. Math. **85**(1), 27–35 (1963)
15. Wikimedia Commons: 3-body problem Lagrange points. (n.d.). Retrieved from https://commons.wikimedia.org/wiki/File:3-body_problem_Lagrange_points.png
16. @canagrisa: Lagrange's Equilateral Triangle - Solution to 3Body Problem. YouTube. (2023) [Online]. Available: https://www.youtube.com/watch?v=zAkIZnUwM80
17. @physicsbyvideo: Three Body Problem – Figure 8 Orbit (stable solution). YouTube. (2022) [Online]. Available: https://www.youtube.com/watch?v=iuRtNK2-jO8
18. @canagrisa: Euler's Collinear Solution to 3Body Problem in General Relativity. YouTube. (2023) [Online]. Available: https://www.youtube.com/watch?v=l93-B_9IZfQ
19. Walker, J.: ENT: A Pseudorandom Number Sequence Test Program, Fourmilab, [Online]. Available: https://www.fourmilab.ch/random/
20. Haahr, M.: RANDOM.ORG: True Random Number Service, [Online]. Available: https://www.random.org/
21. National Institute of Standards and Technology (NIST).: 1.3.3.1. Autocorrelation Plot, Engineering Statistics Handbook, [Online]. Available: https://www.itl.nist.gov/div898/handbook/eda/section3/autocopl.htm
22. Pass, R.: Lecture 10: Hard-Core Predicates, COM S 687 Introduction to Cryptography. Cornell University (2006) [Online]. Available: https://www.cs.cornell.edu/courses/cs687/2006fa/lectures/lecture10.pdf
23. Papoulis, A., Pillai, S.U.: Probability, Random Variables, and Stochastic Processes. McGraw-Hill (2002)
24. Kay, S.M.: Fundamentals of Statistical Signal Processing: Volume I - Estimation Theory. Prentice Hall (1993)
25. Ferguson, N., Bruce, S., Tadayoshi, K.: Cryptography Engineering: Design principles and practical applications. Wiley (2010)
26. Kelsey, J., Bruce, S., Niels, F.: Yarrow 160: notes on the design and analysis of the yarrow cryptographic pseudorandom number generator. In: 6th Annual Workshop on Selected Areas in Cryptography (SAC '99), Kingston, Ontario (1999)
27. Barker, E., Kelsey, J.: Recommendation for Random Number Generation Using Deterministic Random Bit Generators (Revised). NIST Special Publication 800-90A Rev. 1. National Institute of Standards and Technology (2015)
28. Python Software Foundation: Python Language Reference, Version 3.13.3. Python Software Foundation (2025) https://www.python.org/
29. VPython Developers: VPython 3D Graphics Module. vpython.org, https://vpython.org/
30. Numpy Developers: NumPy. NumPy. https://numpy.org/
31. Hunter, J.D.: Matplotlib: visualization with python. Matplotlib Development Team. https://matplotlib.org/

32. Virtanen, P., et al.: SciPy 1.0: fundamental algorithms for scientific computing in python. Nat. Methods. **17**, 261–272 (2020). https://doi.org/10.1038/s41592-019-0686-2
33. Pandas Development Team: pandas-dev/pandas: Pandas. Zenodo, 2020, doi:https://doi.org/10.5281/zenodo.3509134
34. Python Standard Library Documentation: Modules: random, decimal, math, time, os, hashlib. Python Software Foundation. https://docs.python.org/3/library/
35. Knuth, D.E.: The art of computer programming. In: Seminumerical Algorithms, vol. 2, 3rd edn. Addison-Wesley (1997)
36. Šuvakov, M., Dmitrašinović, V.: Three classes of Newtonian three-body planar periodic orbits. Phys. Rev. Lett. **110**(11), 114301 (2013)

CryptoKeys: Another Keyboard-Centric Approach to End-to-End Encryption

Kanwaljeet Ahluwalia, Mikhail Gofman(✉), and David Dominguez

Computer Science, California State University, Fullerton, 800 N. College Blvd, Fullerton, CA 92831, USA
{kanahluwalia,davidmd}@csu.fullerton.edu, mgofman@fullerton.edu

Abstract. While keyboards continue to be the primary human-computer interface for data entry, they remain vulnerable to threats like keyloggers. This paper presents CryptoKeys, an innovative device that uses end-to-end encryption to protect the confidentiality and integrity of data entered via any USB keyboard. CryptoKeys features multiple operating modes, allowing it to adapt to varying levels of trust between the device and the host system, as well as the host system's support for the device. Encrypt/Decrypt mode is designed for low-trust scenarios, where there is no assumption of trust in the host system and no explicit support for the CryptoKeys device from the host; Keystroke Encryption mode, which encrypts individual keystrokes to maintain security while interfacing with trusted device drivers, operating systems, or applications in partial trust scenarios; and Data Stream Encryption mode that allows CryptoKeys to function as an auxiliary encryption device that receives data from the host for encryption and returns the encrypted data, all while keeping the encryption parameters (e.g., secret key) confidential. This mode is suitable for high-trust scenarios where the host can be trusted with the data but not with the encryption key. To the best of our knowledge, all existing similar keyboard security approaches are integrated into specific keyboard products and cannot be used with any arbitrary USB keyboards, unlike CryptoKeys. Additionally, only a few existing solutions support multiple modes of operation like CryptoKeys.

Keywords: Cryptography · Keyboard · Encryption · End-to-End · Security

1 Introduction

The keyboard remains one of the primary interfaces for human-computer interaction, enabling users to input data into a system. However, as data travels from the keyboard to the system, it is vulnerable to numerous threats, including keyloggers [1] and malicious hardware or software. These threats aim to compromise the confidentiality, integrity, and authenticity of sensitive information,

M. Gofman and D. Dominguez—Equal contribution.

K. Daimi et al. (Eds.): CSCE 2025, CCIS 2937, pp. 149–170, 2026.
https://doi.org/10.1007/978-3-032-22208-4_11

such as passwords, credit card numbers, and other private data. Furthermore, when these data are transmitted over a network, it becomes vulnerable to a range of network attacks. Additionally, when this data is transmitted over a network, it becomes susceptible to various network-based attacks. Even end-to-end encrypted applications like Signal Messenger [2] are unable to defend against threats like keyloggers, which intercept data before it reaches the application.

This paper introduces CryptoKeys, an innovative keyboard security device that acts as an intermediary between any USB keyboard and the host system. CryptoKeys receives input from the connected keyboard, applies end-to-end encryption to ensure the confidentiality and integrity of the data, and then transmits the encrypted information to the host. This method effectively safeguards against hardware and software-based attacks, including keyloggers placed between the sender and receiver of the data.

CryptoKeys functions in three distinct modes, designed to accommodate different levels of trust and to address whether the host system explicitly supports the CryptoKeys device. In untrusted environments, CryptoKeys secures keyboard data without needing explicit recognition or support from the host by transmitting encrypted data through simulated keystrokes from a standard keyboard. The host receives these keystrokes using its conventional USB device driver.

In partially trusted environments, where the host's trusted device driver, operating system, or applications explicitly support CryptoKeys, the device communicates directly with the host system. This enhances data transmission efficiency and enables innovative applications, such as a browser requesting that the password being entered be end-to-end encrypted from the keyboard to the browser application, thus protecting against potential keyloggers. Furthermore, in these partially trusted scenarios, the host can use CryptoKeys as an external encryption device by sending data to it and receiving the encrypted data in return, all while ensuring that the encryption parameters are not revealed to the host.

We have designed, implemented, and tested a CryptoKeys prototype using the STM32 Nucleo-144 development board [3] with the F439ZI ARM microcontroller [4]. Confidentiality and integrity are maintained through AES-256 [5] in GCM mode [6] and SHA-256 [7]. To prevent replay attacks, sequence numbers are employed. Our design assumes that users have pre-exchanged the secret key and necessary information for session encryption, allowing communication to function as a continuous session that can be paused and resumed. A new session can also be created with different encryption parameters, for example, using a different key. As part of this work, we also explore potential solutions for securely synchronizing encryption parameters between two communicators without relying on network communications.

To ensure the efficiency of cryptographic operations, our approach leverages the cryptographic hardware acceleration features of the STM32F439ZI microcontroller for AES encryption and SHA-256 hashing.

Our specific contributions are as follows:

1. We present a comprehensive threat model for keyboard-generated data, highlighting vulnerabilities and attack vectors as the data travels from the keyboard to the device driver, then to the operating system, the application, and potentially to recipient located across the internet.
2. Our innovative design is, to the best of our knowledge, the first of its kind to be universally compatible with any USB keyboard, allowing users the flexibility to choose their preferred hardware without being limited to specific keyboard models.
3. Unlike many previous methodologies that focus primarily on data confidentiality, our solution ensures not only confidentiality but also integrity, freshness, and protection against traffic analysis, where attackers attempt to infer typed data by monitoring keyboard traffic patterns, such as message length.
4. Our device expands its versatility and use-cases by offering several operational modes to enhance security and adaptability. The Encrypt/Decrypt mode seamlessly encrypts and decrypts multiple keystrokes simultaneously, transmitting them to the host without requiring user trust in the host or the host's explicit awareness of CryptoKeys. Additionally, it includes cooperative modes that assume the host is partially trusted and aware of CryptoKeys. The first cooperative mode, Keystroke Encryption mode, encrypts each individual keystroke before transmitting it to the host, where it is received by a trusted device driver, operating system, or application. Another cooperative mode, the Data Stream Encryption mode, allows CryptoKeys to function as an external encryption device, encrypting or decrypting data received from the host and sending the processed data back. This mode enhances the device's utility by enabling users to encrypt data shared with the system while keeping encryption parameters secret from the host.
5. Our design deliberately avoids storing encryption parameters in persistent storage, significantly reducing the risk of data compromise in the event that the device is lost, stolen, or confiscated. This approach also simplifies the overall design by eliminating the need for persistent secure storage. Additionally, the device features a memory wipe function that quickly erases all secret data from volatile memory, providing an extra layer of protection if the CryptoKeys device is lost or seized. At the beginning of each session, CryptoKeys requires users to input a series of pre-shared passphrases, which are then used to generate the encryption parameters using the PBKDF2 algorithm [8].

2 Preliminaries

This section provides an overview of the Advanced Encryption Standard (AES) block cipher and the Galois Counter Mode (GCM), which are the primary cryptographic mechanisms used by CryptoKeys for ensuring confidentiality and integrity. We will also discuss the fundamentals of USB keyboard functionality, as CryptoKeys is designed to work with USB keyboards.

2.1 AES and Galois Counter Mode (GCM)

AES [5] is a modern encryption standard based on the Rijndael cipher. It operates on 128-bit blocks using a Substitution Permutation Network and supports key sizes of 128, 192, and 256 bits. Its applications include file encryption, secure data transmission over the Internet, and data protection in mobile and embedded systems. Due to its widespread use in embedded systems, chip manufacturers like ARM and Intel have integrated specialized hardware acceleration features to enhance AES operations on microcontrollers and microprocessors.

Galois/Counter Mode (GCM) [6] is a block cipher operation mode that prevents identical plaintext blocks from producing identical ciphertext blocks by using a unique initialization vector (IV) for encryption of each data stream. It operates like a stream cipher by generating a keystream and ensures integrity and authentication through a Message Authentication Code (MAC) computed over the encrypted data, resulting in an authentication tag sent to the receiver with the ciphertext. Decryption is successful only if the received tag matches the computed tag. Both parties use the same shared key K and a secret IV to derive the initial counter value. Additionally, an optional parameter, Additional Authentication Data (AAD), can be included to authenticate yyy information, such as sender and receiver IP addresses.

2.2 USB Keyboard

The Universal Serial Bus (USB) is a standard developed by the USB Implementers Forum (USB-IF) for connecting hosts, such as personal computers, to peripheral devices such as external disk drives, keyboards, and mice. Keyboards are classified as Human Interface Devices (HIDs) that communicate using the keyboard HID protocol [9].

When a key is pressed or released, the keyboard generates an 8-byte USB Keyboard Report message describing the state of the keys. This message, formatted as shown in Table 1, is transmitted to the host through the USB connection. The first byte indicates the state of modifier keys (1 for pressed 0 for released) such as `Shift`, `Control`, and `Alt`. The second byte is reserved, and bytes 2 through 7 contain scan codes for the currently pressed keys, with 0 indicating that no key being pressed. Scan codes are values generated by keyboard hardware that identify the keys pressed or released. While many scan codes are represented as single-byte values, keyboards with extra keys or special function keys may produce multi-byte values.

These reports are sent to the host, where the USB keyboard driver decodes them into keyboard events, and the operating system translates the scan codes into characters based on the user's layout and language settings.

3 The Threat Models

The threat model in Fig. 1 assumes a trustworthy keyboard and outlines potential threats to keyboard data. These threats include:

Table 1. The format of the USB Keyboard Report

Index	Description
0	Status of the modifier keys
1	Reserved
2	Scan code for key 1
3	Scan code for key 2
4	Scan code for key 3
5	Scan code for key 4
6	Scan code for key 5
7	Scan code for key 6

(1) The USB connection between the keyboard and host is vulnerable, enabling eavesdropping, modification, or replaying of keyboard reports. For instance, hardware keyloggers are widely available for conducting eavesdropping attacks, with some devices currently priced around $40 (e.g., [10]). Certain keyloggers even feature advanced capabilities, such as relaying logged keystrokes to the attacker via WiFi. Furthermore, attackers can easily build homemade keyloggers using development boards like Arduino [11].
(2) An attacker or a malicious manufacturer can compromise the communications between the system's USB controller and the CPU [12]. This allows them to eavesdrop on, modify, or replay keyboard reports sent to the CPU by embedding malicious hardware within the system. Furthermore, malware and rootkits that infect motherboard firmware can facilitate these types of attacks [13].
(3) A malicious or compromised USB keyboard driver can capture, modify, or replay keyboard reports.
(4) The operating system may be compromised, enabling it to log keyboard events or alter and replay them to applications.
(5) When the operating system sends decoded keyboard events to applications, user-level keyloggers may intercept and compromise these events.
(6) If the application transmits keyboard-generated data over the network, its confidentiality and integrity are at risk from a range of network attacks aimed at eavesdropping, modifying, or replaying the data.

The CryptoKeys device safeguards data from standard USB keyboards against these threats. It offers multiple modes that are tailored to the trust level in host hardware, operating system, and applications.

4 Design

The CryptoKeys device serves as a trusted intermediary between a USB keyboard and the USB port of the host, as illustrated in Fig. 2. It connects directly

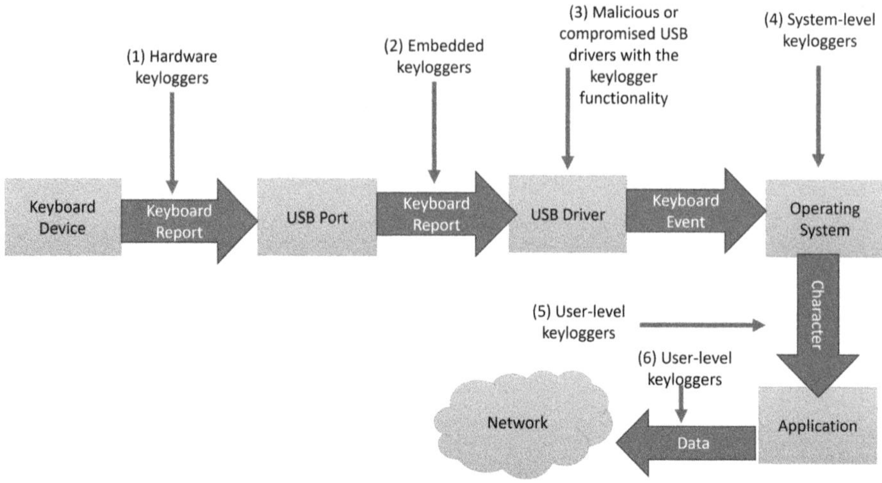

Fig. 1. The Threat Model

to the host's USB port, with the USB keyboard plugged into the CryptoKeys device. When CryptoKeys receives a report from the keyboard, it encapsulates it into a message packet, optionally adding an SHA-256 hash of the keyboard report data and a sequence number to ensure the packet's integrity and freshness, respectively. These packets are then encrypted using AES in GCM mode, which protects their confidentiality and integrity. Furthermore, additional random data can be included in the packet to help frustrate cryptanalytic attacks. At the end of the session, the sender can transmit the GCM tag enabling the receiver to verify the integrity and authenticity of the entire data stream that includes all packets.

The recipient with the appropriate decryption parameters can decrypt the packet and verify the integrity of its data using the SHA-256 hash, ensuring freshness through the sequence number. In addition, the recipient can validate the integrity of the entire data stream by checking the GCM tag sent by the sender at the end of the session. Depending on the use case, the recipient may be the USB driver, operating system, application program, or a remote user across the internet.

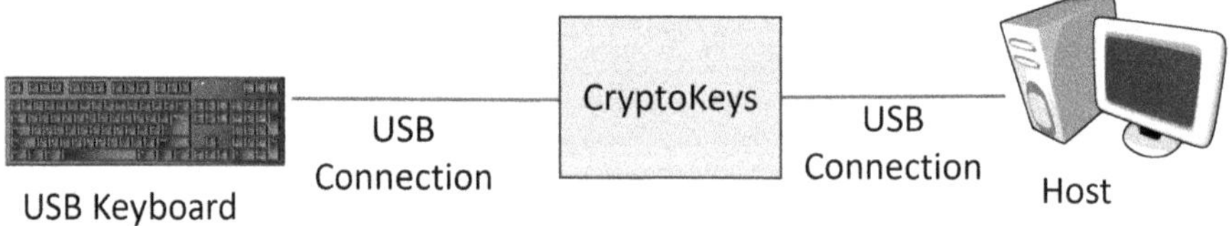

Fig. 2. CryptoKeys connectivity diagram.

CryptoKeys employs a preshared key scheme, where both the device and the recipient possess the necessary AES/GCM parameters and the initial sequence number. To prevent reuse of these parameters across sessions, thus mitigating the risk of cryptanalysis, both the sender and receiver can use synchronized random number generators. These generators produce random data that both sides can use to derive session-specific keys, IVs, AADs, and sequence numbers. Similar mechanisms are implemented in products such as RSA's SecureID devices [14].

CryptoKeys offers multiple operational modes to accommodate different levels of trust in the host's hardware, system, and applications. The *Encrypt/Decrypt* mode buffers and batch encrypts keystrokes, assuming no trust from the host. *Keystroke Encryption* mode encrypts individual keystrokes and the host with trusted CryptoKeys driver cooperates in receiving and processing the encrypted data. *Data Stream Encryption* mode allows the host to send data to CryptoKeys for encryption, trusting the host with plaintext but not the encryption key. The *Keyboard Bypass* mode forwards keystrokes directly to the host without encryption, effectively simulating the functionality of a standard USB keyboard.

4.1 Encrypt/Decrypt

This mode assumes no trust in the USB connection between CryptoKeys and the host, or in the host's USB driver, operating system, and software, making all attacks shown in Fig. 1 relevant. It is applicable, for example, when a user composes and sends confidential messages using a messaging application on an untrusted host, such as a public computer.

In this mode, CryptoKeys is detected as a generic keyboard device by the host; thus the host is not explicitly aware of CryptoKeys. CryptoKeys receives keyboard reports from the connected keyboard, optionally translates them into ASCII or UTF-16 characters based on the configured layout, and buffers them. Users can also configure CryptoKeys to record raw reports, deferring translation to the receiver. For our subsequent discussions, we will assume that CryptoKeys is set up to record raw reports.

When the user prompts CryptoKeys to send the buffered data, CryptoKeys encapsulates the data into a cryptographically protected packet for decryption and verification by the recipient. The packet is then encoded in Base64 and is transmitted character-by character by generating keyboard reports and sending them to the host simulating user typing the respective characters on the keyboard. This encryption prevents keyloggers from identifying the original keys pressed and includes a cryptographic hash and sequence number to guard against tampering and replay attacks.

As the user types, CryptoKeys displays buffered characters/reports on the device's embedded screen, providing visual feedback. When ready to send the message, the user can press the F9 key or a designated button to initiate the data packetization, encryption, and transmission of the encrypted data. The encryption and decryption processes are as follows:

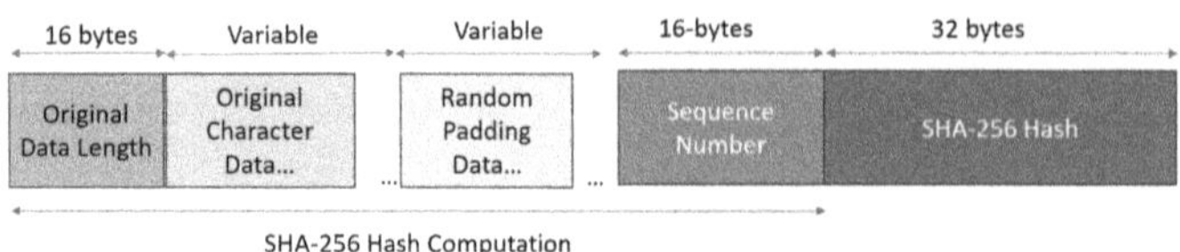

Fig. 3. Packetezation Encrypt/Decrypt Mode.

Encryption: During encryption, the buffered keyboard data is packetized as shown in Fig. 3 and is transmitted as follows:

(1.) Random bytes are added to pad the message to a user-specified length, obscuring the true message length to hinder traffic analysis attacks that examine message lengths and increasing entropy in the ciphertext to complicate cryptanalysis. The padded message is formatted as follows: a 128-bit block representing the original message length in bytes, followed by the original keyboard data, and then the padding bytes.
(2.) An optional 128-bit sequence number is added to the message. The sequence number can be used by the recipient to immediately detect replay attacks. The sequence number is set to an arbitrary initial value agreed upon by the user of the CryptoKeys device and the data recipient they are communicating with. The sequence number is incremented every time a new packet is created.
(3.) An optional SHA-256 hash is appended to the packet, computed from the message length, the original message, the padding, and the sequence number. While AES in GCM mode ensures the integrity of the overall data stream through tag verification, adding the SHA-256 tag allows the recipient to verify the integrity of the current packet within the larger stream, enabling them to identify where integrity was violated.
(4.) The entire message is encrypted using AES-256 in GCM mode, and the ciphertext is then encoded into a Base64 text string.
(5.) The Base64 string is transmitted by CryptoKeys to the system as a series of keyboard reports that simulate user typing, which the system interprets as user input. In practice, this received string would appear as if it were typed directly into the text input field of an application that the user is utilizing to send their message.
(6.) When the user has finished sending all data they wanted to send in the session, they can press the F10 key. This action instructs CryptoKeys to compute a GCM tag for the entire data stream, encode it in Base64, and transmit the result as a series of keyboard reports to the system.

Decryption: The receiver enters a Base64 encoded string representing the received packet. When the user presses F9, the buffered string is processed as follows:

1. The message is Base64 decoded and decrypted.

2. The SHA-256 hash is calculated over the message length, the message, and the padding. The resulting hash is then compared with the hash in the packet. If they match, the integrity of the message is preserved. Otherwise, integrity is compromised.
3. The sequence number is compared with the expected sequence number. If they match, the message is considered fresh. Otherwise, a replay is suspected.
4. The first block representing the length of the message is then used to extract the actual message that is presented to the user.

4.2 Keystroke Encryption

The Keystroke Encryption mode is designed for environments where a specialized CryptoKeys driver is installed on the host system, which is trusted to receive and process encrypted packets containing individual keyboard reports from CryptoKeys. This mode differs from the Encrypt/Decrypt mode in several key ways: instead of transmitting encrypted packets through simulated keystrokes, CryptoKeys relies on the host's device driver to directly receive encrypted packet transmissions through the USB port. Moreover, each packet contains a single keyboard report that is generated and sent immediately upon key press, effectively simulating the encryption of individual keystrokes. This contrasts with the Encrypt/Decrypt mode, which buffers and encrypts multiple keyboard reports.

One advantage of this mode is that the specialized driver can simplify and enhance the efficiency of transmitting encrypted packets to the host compared to the Encrypt/Decrypt mode. Each encrypted packet can be sent directly to the host without the need for Base64 encoding, nor the subsequent transmission of each 8-bit character as an 8-byte keyboard report as done when simulating keystrokes typing out the Base64-encoded packet. This streamlined approach reduces the data transmission volume significantly. Additionally, the presence of a specialized driver on the host enables advanced scenarios, such as CryptoKeys collaborating with the host to support secure keyboard input into specific applications-a capability that is more challenging to achieve with the Encrypt/Decrypt mode, where the system lacks explicit awareness of CryptoKeys.

This mode implies a greater level of trust in the host system, as the device driver is explicitly aware of CryptoKeys and is assumed to work in conjunction with it to faithfully receive the packets. The driver, the host's operating system, applications, or a remote recipient across the network will handle the decryption of these packets. As discussed in Sect. 5, the decision to include multiple keyboard reports in a single packet versus a single report is not inherently dependent on the presence of the trusted device driver; rather, this approach is implemented here as a proof-of-concept.

Configurations: Although in the Keystroke Encryption mode the driver is trusted to receive CryptoKeys encrypted packets, the roles of the driver, OS, and application can vary based on configuration and trust levels. In a simple setup, the trusted driver holds all necessary decryption parameters, decrypts data, and verifies message integrity before passing the keyboard reports to the OS as keyboard events.

Alternatively, the driver can relay encrypted reports to other OS components, which handle decryption and integrity verification, and then send the corresponding keyboard events to applications. In scenarios where the driver, OS, and application are all trusted and aware of CryptoKeys, the OS can forward encrypted packets to a CryptoKeys-aware application for decryption and integrity verification. Alternatively, any of these components can forward encrypted packets over the network to a recipient with knowledge of the necessary decryption parameters.

In all use configurations, the techniques employed by CryptoKeys in this mode are designed to protect the confidentiality, integrity, and freshness of individual keystrokes. This is achieved by encrypting each keyboard report and attaching a sequence number along with a hash of the report. Additionally, the integrity of the entire stream of keystrokes is maintained through the use of GCM tags.

Each keyboard report received by CryptoKeys is encapsulated in a secure packet, as illustrated in Fig. 4, before being sent to the host. Next, we describe the encryption and decryption processes.

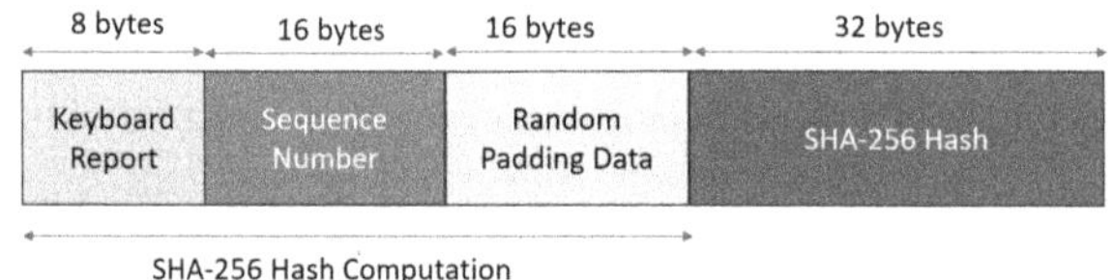

Fig. 4. Packetization of the keyboard report in the Keystroke Encryption Mode.

Encryption: The encryption works for as follows:

1. An 8-byte keyboard report is appended to the message.
2. A 16-byte sequence number follows the report to mitigate replay attacks. This method requires both the CryptoKeys user and the recipient to agree on an initial sequence number that is incremented with each keystroke. The recipient can identify a replay attack if a sequence number appears out of order.
3. To enhance message entropy, 16 bytes of random data are added to each packet. This randomness increases the encrypted packets's resilience against cryptanalysis. This is especially advantageous in this mode, where each packet contains only a single keyboard report, unlike the Encrypt/Decrypt mode, which can include a sequence of reports. Since each report typically conveys information about a single keystroke event, with a limited number of possible events, attackers might exploit this to conduct known-plaintext attacks. However, it's important to note that this is merely an additional measure, as the inclusion of sequence numbers and the use of GCM mode (as described

in the steps that follow) already provide substantial protection against such scenarios.
4. A 256-bit SHA-256 hash is computed on the keyboard report, sequence number, and random data, and it is included in the message.
5. The message is encrypted using AES-256 in the GCM mode.
6. When the CryptoKeys user has finished sending the keystroke stream and wants to provide evidence of the integrity of the entire stream, they can press F9 on the keyboard or a designated key on the CryptoKeys device. This action triggers the device to generate a GCM tag and send it to the system.

It is important to note that, unlike the Encrypt/Decrypt mode where messages can vary in length, the Keystroke Encryption Mode encapsulates individual keyboard reports in fixed-length packets of 72 bytes. This standardization eliminates the need for a length field in the packet, simplifying the overall packet structure. At the receiver's end, the keystroke packet is processed as follows:
Decryption: The decryption works for as follows:

1. The packet is decrypted using AES in GCM mode with the same parameters (Key, IV, and AAD) as those employed by CryptoKeys.
2. To verify the integrity of the packet, a SHA-256 hash is computed on the first 40 bytes of the field (which includes the keyboard report, sequence number, and random padding). This computed hash is then compared with the attached SHA-256 hash. If they match, the integrity of the packet is deemed valid; otherwise, tampering or packet corruption is suspected.
3. The sequence number in the packet is compared to the expected sequence number. The message is considered fresh only if the two numbers match.
4. The keyboard report is extracted from the packet and decoded into the corresponding keystroke character or action, based on the user's keyboard layout and language.
5. Upon receiving the GCM tag, the receiver verifies it against the tag computed from all received packets.

4.3 Data Stream Encryption

The Data Stream Encryption mode enables the host to utilize CryptoKeys as an external encryption device connected to the host. It gives the host a capability to encrypt/decrypt data without knowledge of the encryption parameters. Here data is transmitted from the host to CryptoKeys via USB for encryption or decryption, and the processed data is returned to the host. The host is trusted with the data, but not with the encryption parameters. Similarly to keystroke encryption mode, this mode requires cooperation between the host system and CryptoKeys through a device driver at the operating system or user level for data transmission.
Use Cases: Using an external device like CryptoKeys for encryption helps safeguard the encryption parameters from being compromised if the host is breached. In this scenario, an attacker who has compromised the host will be unable to

decrypt previously encrypted packets or spoof new encrypted packets with valid sequence numbers and hashes without authorized access to the CryptoKeys device.

Encrypted data are packetized, similar to the Encrypt/Decrypt mode, allowing CryptoKeys to verify integrity and freshness of packets.

Encryption: The encryption process is follows:

1. Host receives keyboard reports, optionally translates them to UTF-16, and buffers them.
2. User instructs the host to send data to CryptoKeys, which packetizes plaintext with a 16-byte header indicating message length, followed by a byte indicating encryption (0) or decryption (1).
3. The packet is transmitted to CryptoKeys via USB, which parses the packet using header information.
4. If encryption is requested, CryptoKeys packetizes and encrypts the data in a manner similar to the Encrypt/Decrypt mode. It prepends a 16-byte plaintext header to the encrypted packet indicating the packet length and sends it back to the host, which uses this length header to determine the size of the encrypted packet it needs to receive.

Decryption: The decryption process works as follows:

1. Host receives an encrypted CryptoKeys data packet from, for example, the network.
2. User instructs the host to send the packet to CryptoKeys for decryption, which packetizes plaintext with a 16-byte header indicating packet length and a byte set to 1 for decryption.
3. CryptoKeys extracts the encrypted packet using the length header and decrypts it, verifying integrity and freshness in a manner similar to the Encrypt/Decrypt mode. If no violations are detected, it prepends a 16-byte header to the plaintext and sends it to the host, which uses the length header to extract the decrypted data. If any violations are detected, error messages are displayed on the CryptoKeys screen, and an error packet is sent to the system.

Discussion: If an attacker gains control of the host system, they can send inputs to CryptoKeys, compelling it to generate valid encrypted packets and impersonate the sender to the packet receiver. To mitigate this risk, CryptoKeys notifies the user of each encryption or decryption request through a message on its embedded screen. If the operation is encryption, the user can review the plaintext; if it is decryption, the user can review the decrypted text. Should the user determine that the request is malicious, they can press a button to reject it. If rejected, CryptoKeys rolls back the sequence number and the GCM state as if the request was never received.

The user review process for encryption and decryption requests is complicated by the fact that the plaintext or decrypted data may not be textual (e.g., it could be images, sound files, or other non-textual formats). This issue can be alleviated by enhancing CryptoKeys with the capability to recognize and preview common non-textual data formats such as images. Another approach is to restrict CryptoKeys to processing only the textual data that can be easily reviewed by the user.

4.3.1 Increasing Security

To further enhance the security of CryptoKeys, additional measures can be implemented. One effective measure is to implement authenticated link encryption between the host's USB port and CryptoKeys, providing an extra layer of protection for data exchanged over the CryptoKeys-Host USB connection. This approach is particularly beneficial for safeguarding plaintext data in the Data Stream Encryption mode when the host sends plaintext data to CryptoKeys for encryption.

Authenticated link encryption can be established using a pre-shared key (PSK) scheme, where a shared key is configured on both the CryptoKeys device and the host. A challenge-response protocol can then be employed to verify authenticity. Alternatively, secure session key exchange methods, such as Diffie-Hellman, can be used alongside authenticated public keys (e.g., X.509 certificates). Another option is to utilize SSL/TLS over USB, which also relies on X.509 certificates and facilitates two-way authentication between the host and CryptoKeys, ensuring the establishment of a secure session. Regardless of the method chosen, it is essential that the host recognizes CryptoKeys and is trusted to reliably participate in the encryption process.

By combining link encryption with an authentication scheme, CryptoKeys devices can be effectively restricted to specific hosts, offering numerous practical applications. For instance, within an organization, each user can be assigned a dedicated CryptoKeys device that can only be used with their designated host system.

Additionally, integrating a trusted computing environment (TCE) [15] which supports protected memory into the CryptoKeys device can enhance security. If the device is captured before the encryption parameters are erased from memory, the TCE can safeguard these parameters from unauthorized access. Furthermore, the TCE can detect tampering attempts aimed at extracting sensitive information and can automatically wipe the memory in response to such threats.

To future-proof the cryptographic protection offered by CryptoKeys, support for post-quantum encryption can be incorporated to secure the data packets. This enhancement will ensure that the data encrypted with CryptoKeys remains confidential and resilient against cryptanalysis techniques that may emerge with advancements in quantum computing.

4.4 Keyboard Bypass

In this mode, CryptoKeys operates as a pass-through device, directly forwarding keystrokes from the keyboard to the system without any cryptographic protections. This mode is intended for situations where users want to temporarily disable cryptographic safeguards to transmit non-sensitive information.

5 Alternative Designs

This section explores alternative designs that could have been employed to implement the current functionality or introduce new features.

5.0.1. Data Buffering vs Device Driver Requirement

In the current implementation of CryptoKeys, the Encrypt/Decrypt mode allows for multiple keyboard reports to be included in the same encrypted packet, which is then sent in the Base64-encoded format through simulated keystrokes from a standard keyboard. This method of data transmission eliminates the need for the host to have a specialized CryptoKeys device driver to receive the packet, instead utilizing the standard keyboard driver. In contrast, the Keystroke Encryption mode transmits a single keyboard report in each encrypted packet and relies on the CryptoKeys driver installed on the host to receive the packet, eliminating the need for Base64 encoding and other overheads associated with transmitting the packet by encoding its bytes as keyboard reports.

The choice to include either a single or multiple keyboard reports in the encrypted packet is independent of whether the transmission uses the standard keyboard driver or a custom CryptoKeys driver. These decisions were primarily made for proof-of-concept purposes in the current implementation.

For example, an alternative design could involve CryptoKeys including multiple reports in a single packet, similar to the Encrypt/Decrypt mode, but sending the encrypted packet to the host that uses a specialized CryptoKeys driver to receive the packet, akin to the Keystroke Encryption mode.

Another design option could involve CryptoKeys individually packetizing and encrypting each keyboard report, encoding it in Base64, and transmitting these packets as simulated keystrokes to a host without a custom CryptoKeys driver, thus relying solely on the standard keyboard driver. In this scenario, as the user presses a key, a string representing the encrypted, Base64-encoded packet would appear on the screen. This approach allows for the encryption of individual keyboard reports without requiring the installation of a CryptoKeys device driver on the host.

5.1 Packetization Strategies

To protect the integrity and freshness of encrypted data packets, we have implemented a default option to include SHA-256 hashes and sequence numbers. An alternative design strategy would be to omit these elements and rely solely on the GCM mode, which already provides integrity checks through its GCM tag mechanism. While this approach can reduce packet size and increase efficiency, it comes at the cost of some security and versatility.

The GCM mode computes the GCM tag over the entire ciphertext stream, enabling the detection of datastream tampering attacks by verifying this tag. However, this approach requires the receiver to obtain all packets generated by CryptoKeys during a session before verification, which prevents the integrity check of individual packets. To address this, we can recompute the GCM tag after encrypting each packet and append it to the packet. The receiver would then recompute the GCM tag based on the received ciphertext and compare it to the attached tag. Additionally, since GCM encrypts each packet with a different keystream, a replayed packet will not be decrypted correctly, allowing for detection of decryption failures by verifying the GCM tag using the proposed method.

The primary drawback of recomputing the GCM tag after each encryption is that it deviates from the standard practice of GCM, where the tag is calculated only at the end of the stream. Furthermore, eliminating SHA-256 hashes and sequence numbers can leave the approach without reliable means to verify integrity and freshness if another block cipher mode without built-in integrity mechanisms, such as cipher block chaining (CBC) or counter mode (CTR), is employed.

Our current approach of using AES in GCM mode with hashes and sequence numbers enhances security by explicitly protecting the integrity and freshness of individual packets as well as the overall data stream, while remaining adaptable to other block cipher modes of operation.

5.2 Secret Information Derivation

CryptoKeys uses a pre-shared key (PSK) scheme, requiring users and their correspondents to pre-share identical AES-256 encryption keys, initialization vectors (IVs), additional authenticated data (AAD), and initial sequence numbers before initiating a session. This design choice simplifies the architecture and eliminates the need for network communications, such as key exchanges, thereby mitigating network-based threats.

To further enhance the PSK security scheme, synchronized pseudo-random number generators can be employed between the CryptoKeys user and their correspondent. This enables both parties to generate synchronized random data streams, which can be used to derive the same encryption keys, IVs, AADs, and initial sequence numbers. A similar approach is used in modern authentication tokens like RSA SecureID [14]. The method also ensures forward and backward secrecy between multiple sessions.

To start a CryptoKeys session users manually input passphrases for the AES GCM key, IV, AAD, and initial sequence number. CryptoKeys then uses the Password-Based Key Derivation Function 2 (PBKDF2) with the SHA256 hashing algorithm to derive a 256-bit encryption key, a 12-byte IV, a 16-byte AAD, and a 16-byte initial sequence number. This approach enhances user-friendliness, as passphrases are generally easier to remember and enter than random byte sequences. If the users are using synchronized random-number generators, a scheme can be devised to convert random numbers into random passphrases.

PBKDF2 is configurable in terms of SHA256 iterations, which can be increased based on available computational power to defend against brute-force attacks. Our current implementation scales 10,000 iterations, as determined through performance testing.

5.3 Storage of Secret Information

CryptoKeys' security relies on the AES-256 encryption key. To prevent key disclosure from theft or confiscation, CryptoKeys stores secret information only in volatile memory, avoiding persistent storage.

In emergency situations, CryptoKeys can immediately erase information from volatile memory when the user presses a specific key combination on the keyboard or a designated button on the device.

6 Implementation

Figure 5 shows the CryptoKeys prototype, built on the STM32 Nucleo-144 board with an STM32F439ZI microcontroller running at 180 MHz. It features a Cortex-M4 core with 256 KB SRAM, 64 KB core-coupled memory, and 2 MB flash memory [4]. The development was done in C using STM32CubeIDE. An ILI9488 LCD screen [16] interfaces with the Nucleo board via Serial Peripheral Interface (SPI) for visualization. A built-in push button triggers actions such as generating and sending encrypted data packets in the Encrypt/Decrypt mode.

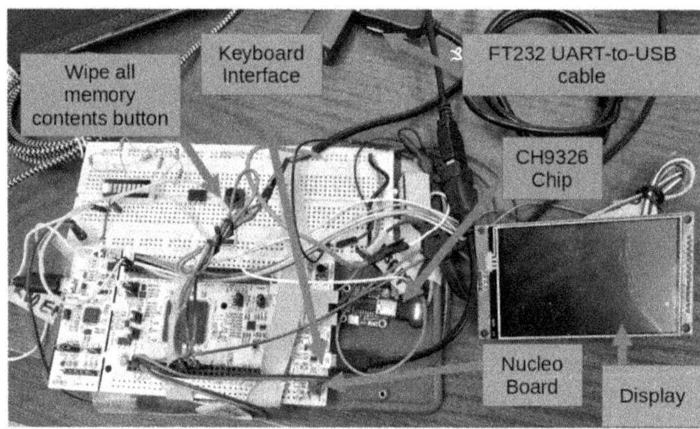

Fig. 5. Photograph of the CryptoKeys Device.

To allow the CryptoKeys device to support attachment of standard USB keyboards, we have configured Nucleo board's built-in USB port to function in the HID mode for keyboard devices.

To allow CryptoKeys to physically connect to and send keyboard reports to the host, as done in the Encrypt/Decrypt mode, we utilized Adafruit CH9328 UART-to-HID keyboard breakout board [17]. The UART-to-HID board connects to the Nucleo board through a standard UART interface, while its USB port connects to the host. The CH9326 chip processes instructions for keyboard report generation sent from the Nucleo board via UART protocol, generates the requested reports, and sends the reports to the host using the USB HID protocol.

In Keystroke Encryption mode, we use an FT232 UART-to-USB cable [18] to send encrypted reports. One end of the cable connects to the Nucleo board's UART interface and the other to the host's USB port. The host recognizes the cable as a UART serial device. The Nucleo board sends encrypted packets via UART, which the FT232 cable transmits over USB. A user-level driver, built with Python's pySerial library [19], reads, decrypts, verifies, and retransmits these reports as key press events.

Choosing UART for packet transmission simplifies design by avoiding USB mode switching between host and data device modes. The production version will use USB for all communications. Furthermore, as a proof of concept, CryptoKeys host-end drivers for Keystroke Encryption and Data Stream Encryption modes have been implemented for a Linux system. However, similar drivers can also be developed for other operating systems, including Windows and MacOS.

6.1 Hardware Acceleration

CryptoKeys utilizes the STM32F439ZI microcontroller's cryptographic cores to handle cryptographic functions without taxing the CPU. For AES encryption in GCM mode, the cryptographic core configured for this purpose and hardware-accelerated encryption is invoked via the `HAL_cryp_encrypt()` function. All SHA-256 computations are similarly performed using the hashing core and can be invoked using the `HAL_HASHEx_SHA256_Start()` function. STM32's true random number generator hardware accelerator was also used for random number generation. This generator harnesses natural phenomena, such as thermal noise, to produce random numbers.

For cryptographic and related functions like Base64 encoding, which lack hardware acceleration on our platform, we rely on the wolfSSL library [20] for STM32.

7 Evaluation

We have conducted a set of tests designed to validate the function of each mode of CryptoKeys. For all tests we used the Python `PyCryptodome` [21] library to test the correctness of the encryption/decryption process and to implement the CryptoKeys host driver. We discuss the results of each test.

7.1 Encrypt/Decrypt Mode

To test the Encrypt/Decrypt mode, we initiated the process by entering encryption parameters into CryptoKeys via the keyboard. The device was then switched to Encrypt/Decrypt mode. A short message, "This is a secret", was typed and the F9 key was pressed to command CryptoKeys to packetize, encrypt, Base64 encode, and transmit the message to the host using simulated keystrokes.

The message received by the host was then sent through the Discord messaging application to a receiver in possession of the same key, IV, and AAD, together with a Python-based decryptor program written using the `PyCryptodome` cryptographic library. This program decrypted the packets, verified the hash, and checked the expected sequence number. In addition, five more messages were sent, varying in length from 10 to 100 characters. Finally, CryptoKeys was instructed to close the session by computing the GCM tag of the entire data stream and send the tag to the host.

Figures 6(a), (b), and (c) illustrate the process: Figure 6(a) shows the message entered into CryptoKeys; Figure 6(b) displays the encrypted message received on Discord; Figure 6(c) demonstrates the decryption using `PyCryptodome`. All messages were successfully decrypted.

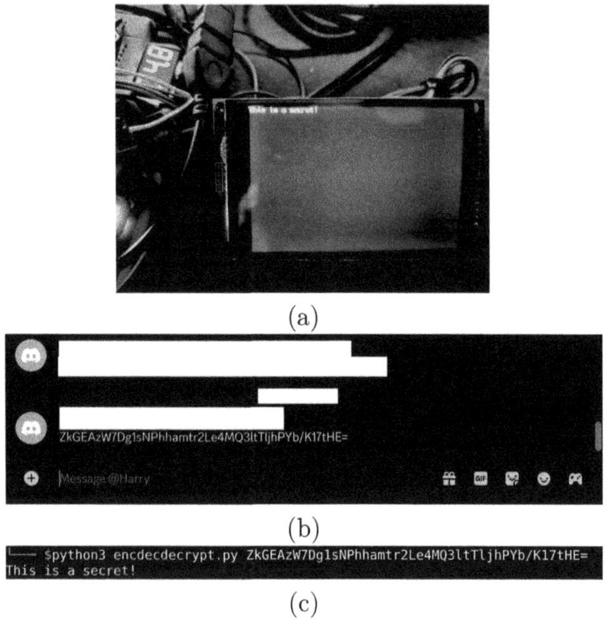

Fig. 6. Top-down: (a) The message "This is a secret!" is entered via the external keyboard into CryptoKeys; (b) The message is then encrypted and Base64-encoded before being sent to the system and displayed in Discord; (c) Finally, the packet is decrypted, verified, and the message is extracted and displayed by the recipient using our Python decryption tool.

All messages were successfully packetized, encrypted, and sent to the host. The receiver decrypted and verified the integrity of each message and the entire data stream using the GCM tag. Figure 6 shows the process and results of sending and receiving the first message. To simulate tampering, we altered one encrypted packet before transmission. This tampered packet failed to decrypt, causing an integrity verification failure and was flagged as compromised.

7.2 Keystroke Encryption

To test Keystroke Encryption mode, we developed a Python user-level driver to read the `/dev/ttyACMX` device file representing the UART-to-USB interface in Linux. The program waits for data packets, decrypts them, verifies integrity and sequence numbers, extracts reports, decodes reports into characters, and displays the characters. We typed texts ranging from 10 to 100 characters, and all characters were correctly displayed, confirming successful encryption and decryption. The program also verified the GCM tag to ensure stream integrity, which was successful.

We also simulated attacks by randomly corrupting or repeating packets. Each time, the program detected corrupted packets via SHA-256 hash verification or invalid sequence numbers, and stream tampering was identified through GCM tag verification.

7.3 Data Stream Encryption

We tested Data Stream Encryption by transferring a 5-page text file to CryptoKeys, which encrypted the data and returned the packet with a GCM tag. We then decrypted the packet and verified the sequence number, SHA-256 hash, and GCM tag. However, the 9600 baud rate of our FT232 cable, used as the UART-to-USB interface, introduced an estimated delay of about one minute. The cable would not function reliably at higher standard baud rates.

Since the FT232 cable was primarily for prototyping, we plan to improve performance by implementing a direct USB connection between CryptoKeys and the host for data exchange in Data Stream Encryption mode as well as in the Key Stroke Encryption Mode. This will involve revising the implementation to enable switching the USB port between HID mode for hosting the keyboard during Encrypt/Decrypt operations and USB Data Device mode for Key Stroke Encryption and Data Stream Encryption modes.

8 Related Works

Keyloggers have been a persistent security issue, prompting various anti-keylogger solutions targeting software and hardware threats [1,22,23]. These include forensic techniques [24], signature-based and heuristic detection [25], traffic analysis [26], taint analysis [27], blocking software keyloggers [28], and physical inspections. These schemes do not utilize end-to-end encrypted keyboards, such as CryptoKeys, to protect against keyloggers.

Several products aim to support security features similar to CryptoKeys. For some of available products a detailed comparison to CryptoKeys is difficult to provide due to the limited public documentation that the authors were able to find.

LP3835 AES encrypted keyboard by Linepro Controls Pvt Ltd. [29], encrypts keystrokes with AES 256 but does not provide documentation of any explicit protection against keystroke corruption and replay attacks. The Cherry Secure Board 1.0 [30] encrypts key transmissions after authentication is done between the keyboard and the host using X.509 certificate but its product description lacks details on encryption mechanisms and the manufacturer provides no documentation of additional features such as the mode similar to the Encrypt/Decrypt mode of CryptoKeys. The Berd Security V3 Pro [31] offers a keyboard with built-in AES-256 encryption features some of which seem to resemble those of CryptoKeys. The product description lacks detailed design information for comprehensive comparison.

Unlike the above products, CryptoKeys is an auxiliary device capable of securing data from any USB keyboard, allowing users to choose their preferred keyboard while benefiting from robust end-to-end encryption. Our goal is to develop a compact intermediary device that integrates seamlessly with any keyboard, enhancing user choice and security.

9 Conclusions and Future Work

We have developed CryptoKeys, a prototype device that provides cryptographic protection for the confidentiality, integrity, and freshness of all data transmitted from USB keyboards. CryptoKeys operates in multiple modes, enabling it to function independently of explicit host support by relying solely on standard keyboard drivers. Alternatively, it can work cooperatively with a host that has a CryptoKeys driver installed, allowing for extended use case scenarios. Additionally, CryptoKeys is capable of safeguarding both individual keystrokes and collections of keystrokes.

This innovative solution enables users to continue using their preferred USB keyboards while benefiting from end-to-end encryption-a significant advantage over existing solutions, which, to our knowledge, are embedded directly into keyboards. The flexibility of CryptoKeys allows users to switch between different modes based on their desired level of support and trust in the host, making it adaptable to various scenarios that prioritize usability or security.

Future plans include optimizations and proposing specifications suitable for production-level designs.

References

1. Ahmed, Y.A., Maarof, M.A., Hassan, F.M., Abshir, M.M.: Survey of keylogger technologies. Int. J. Comput. Sci. Telecommun. **5**(2) (2014)
2. Signal. https://signal.org/
3. ST Micro: NUCLEO-F439ZI - STM32 Nucleo-144 development board with STM32F439ZI MCU, supports Arduino, ST Zio and morpho connectivity - STMicroelectronics. https://www.st.com/en/evaluation-tools/nucleo-f439zi.html. Accessed 18 July 2025
4. STM32F439ZI - High-performance advanced line, Arm Cortex-M4 core with DSP and FPU, 2 Mbytes of Flash memory, 180 MHz CPU, ART Accelerator, Chrom-ART Accelerator, FMC with SDRAM, TFT, HW crypto. https://www.st.com/en/microcontrollers-microprocessors/stm32f439zi.html. Accessed 3 Dec 2024

5. National Institute of Standards and Technology: Advanced Encryption Standard (AES). FIPS Publication 197 (2001). https://csrc.nist.gov/pubs/fips/197/final
6. McGrew, D.A., Viega, J.: The Galois/Counter Mode of Operation (GCM). National Institute of Standards and Technology (NIST). https://csrc.nist.rip/groups/ST/toolkit/BCM/documents/proposedmodes/gcm/gcm-spec.pdf. Accessed 01 Oct 2023
7. National Institute of Standards and Technology: Secure Hash Standard (SHS). Technical Report Federal Information Processing Standard (FIPS) 180-4, U.S. Department of Commerce (2015). https://doi.org/10.6028/NIST.FIPS.180-4. https://csrc.nist.gov/pubs/fips/180-4/upd1/final. Accessed 18 July 2025
8. Kaliski, B.: PKCS #5: Password-Based Cryptography Specification Version 2.0. Request for Comments RFC 2898, Internet Engineering Task Force (2000). https://doi.org/10.17487/RFC2898. https://datatracker.ietf.org/doc/rfc2898. Num Pages: 34. Accessed 19 July 2025
9. USB Implementers Forum: Human Interface Device (HID) Protocol. *USB.org*. https://www.usb.org/hid. Accessed 04 Nov 2024
10. Airdrive Forensic Keylogger Cable Usb Extension Cable Hardware Keylogger With Wifi And 16mb Memory Wanivo - Arizona Outlet. https://www.keelog.com/forensic-keylogger/. Accessed 27 Feb 2025
11. Arduino - Home. https://www.arduino.cc/. Accessed 27 Feb 2025
12. Michael, K.: Does Your Motherboard Have a Secret Chinese Spy Chip? PC Magazine. https://uk.pcmag.com/security/117817/does-your-motherboard-have-a-secret-chinese-spy-chip. Accessed 28 Feb 2025
13. Arghire, I.: Chinese UEFI Rootkit Found on Gigabyte and Asus Motherboards. SecurityWeek. https://www.securityweek.com/chinese-uefi-rootkit-found-gigabyte-and-asus-motherboards/. Accessed 28 Feb 2025
14. RSA: SecurID. https://www.rsa.com/products/securid. Accessed 25 June 2025
15. Feng, D.: Trusted Computing: Principles and Applications, vol. 2. Walter de Gruyter GmbH & Co KG, Berlin (2017)
16. ILI TECHNOLOGY CORP.: a-Si TFT LCD Single Chip Driver 320(RGB) x 480 Resolution, 16.7M-color With Internal GRAM. https://focuslcds.com/wp-content/uploads/Drivers/ILI9488.pdf. Accessed 10 Apr 2025
17. Adafruit Industries: Adafruit CH9328 UART to HID Keyboard Breakout. https://www.adafruit.com/product/5973. Accessed 29 Sept 2025
18. Amazon.com: FT232 USB to UART (TTL) Communication Module, USB-C Connector, Compatible 3.3V/5V Logic Level, Supports Mac OS, Linux, Android, Wince, Windows 7/8/8.1/10/11... : Electronics. https://www.amazon.com. Accessed 29 Sept 2025
19. PySerial Documentation. https://www.pyserial.com/docs. Accessed 29 Sept 2025
20. wolfSSL Inc.: wolfSSL. https://www.wolfssl.com/docs/stm32/. Accessed 17 Apr 2025
21. PyCryptodome. https://www.pycryptodome.org/. Accessed 31 Aug 2025
22. Wajahat, A., Imran, A., Latif, J., Nazir, A., Bilal, A.: A novel approach of unprivileged keylogger detection. In: 2019 2nd International Conference on Computing. Mathematics and Engineering Technologies (iCoMET), Sukkur, Pakistan, pp. 1–6. IEEE (2019)
23. Victoria, C.E., Ayodele, A.A., Emmanuel, O.I.: Keylogger detection: a systematic review (2023)
24. Ahmed, M.B., Shoikot, M., Hossain, J., Rahman, A.: Key logger detection using memory forensic and network monitoring. Int. J. Comput. Appl. **975**, 8887 (2019)

25. Creutzburg, R.: The strange world of keyloggers-an overview, Part I. Electron. Imaging **29**, 139–148 (2017)
26. Sreenivas, R.S., Anitha, R.: Detecting keyloggers based on traffic analysis with periodic behaviour. Netw. Secur. **2011**(7), 14–19 (2011). https://doi.org/10.1016/S1353-4858(11)70076-9
27. Le, D., Yue, C., Smart, T., Wang, H.: Detecting Kernel Level Keyloggers Through Dynamic Taint Analysis (2008). https://api.semanticscholar.org/CorpusID:12381852
28. Aslam, M., Baig, M., Arshad, M.: Anti-Hook Shield against the Software Key Loggers (2004)
29. AES-Encrypted Keyboard (2022). https://lineproglobal.com/metal-keyboards/aes-encrypted-industrial-keyboard/. Accessed 16 July 2025
30. CHERRY Secure Board 1.0. https://www.amazon.com/CHERRY-Secure-Board-1-0-Keyboard/dp/B081KZRD5L. Accessed 28 Feb 2025
31. Encrypted Keyboard. https://berdsecurity.com/elementor-1421/encrypted-keyboard/. Accessed 19 July 2025

NFC-PUF Three-Pass Authentication for Supply Blockchains

Norbert Oláh(✉), Tamás Girászi, Máté Vajda, and Andrea Huszti

Faculty of Informatics, University of Debrecen, Debrecen, Hungary
{olah.norbert,giraszi.tamas,vajda.mate,huszti.andrea}@inf.unideb.hu

Abstract. The counterfeit goods poses a persistent threat to both manufacturers and consumers. Addressing this problem requires comprehensive transparency and end-to-end traceability across the supply chain. Blockchain technology offers a solution by enabling the creation of an immutable and transparent ledger, thereby strengthening Know Your Seller (KYS) and Know Your Customer (KYC) compliance frameworks. Crucially, ensuring authenticity requires a verifiable and tamper-resistant link between the physical product and its digital representation. Bridging this physical-digital divide is essential for effective and trustworthy product verification. In this paper, we propose a lightweight and secure authentication protocol that integrates Near Field Communication (NFC), Physical Unclonable Functions (PUF), and blockchain technology to establish a decentralized, tamper-evident system for product verification. The protocol uses a three-pass mutual authentication scheme to resource limitated environments via symmetric AES encryption. We completed a security analysis of the authentication protocol with the ProVerif tool, confirming that our solution satisfies all security requirements. Additionally, it also uses PUF-derived digital signatures to protect against cloning and physical manipulation. Product identities and ownership histories are on a public blockchain, providing immutable, enhanced transparency, and resistance to tampering.

Keywords: NFC · Physical Unclonable Function · ProVerif · Authentication protocol · Tamper-evident · Blockchain · Real-World Asset tokenization

1 Introduction

The counterfeit goods market is a growing global problem that harms both manufacturers and consumers. Fueled by globalization and e-commerce, counterfeit operations have become more advanced and harder to detect, particularly in industries like luxury goods, pharmaceuticals, electronics, and food (e.g. premium wine or whisky) [2]. Beyond revenue loss and brand damage, counterfeit products-especially medicines and supplements-can pose serious health risks. Despite rising awareness, many consumers unknowingly purchase fakes, as counterfeit items often closely resemble genuine ones. This, along with the limited

K. Daimi et al. (Eds.): CSCE 2025, CCIS 2937, pp. 171–192, 2026.
https://doi.org/10.1007/978-3-032-22208-4_12

ability of consumers and retailers to verify authenticity, continues to drive the spread of counterfeits-especially in high-value sectors where demand and profit margins are high.

To effectively combat counterfeiting, it is essential to create transparency and traceability across the entire supply chain. This requires an integrated digital platform that enables the recording and monitoring of each step taken by every company involved in the production, distribution, and sale of a product-from raw materials to end consumer delivery. This technology should allow each stakeholder to record transactions and product-handling steps in a secure and tamper-resistant manner and to verify the authenticity and origin of goods at any point in the supply chain. A critical requirement for such a platform is that it must operate without centralized control, which could create a single point of failure, a risk of manipulation, or a performance bottleneck. This is where blockchain technology provides a uniquely effective solution [3].

A blockchain-powered supply chain platform can serve as a powerful defense against counterfeiting by establishing an immutable, transparent digital trail of every action taken across the entire product lifecycle-effectively reinforcing the Know Your Seller (KYS) and Know Your Customer (KYC) framework. The data that is uploaded to a blockchain is of critical importance. One of the defining characteristics of blockchain technology is immutability-once information is recorded, it cannot be altered or deleted. While this feature provides transparency and trust, it also introduces a significant risk: if false or manipulated information is initially recorded, it becomes permanently embedded in the system. The blockchain, by design, does not differentiate between true and false data-it only ensures that data has not been tampered with after the fact. To fully leverage the benefits of blockchain in product authentication and traceability, data integrity at the point of input must be ensured, moreover there must be a trusted link between the physical product and its digital representation. This requires a bridge between the digital world (the blockchain data) and the physical world (the tangible product). This is where tokenization, precisely the Real World Asset (RWA) tokenization [4] comes into play: each physical product must be linked to a unique digital identity on the blockchain in a way that cannot be faked or easily replicated.

To ensure this secure and reliable connection between a physical product and its blockchain-based digital identity, the following components are essential. Each product should be equipped with a tamper-proof device such as an NFC tag or RFID chip [5] that enables users (consumers, inspectors, or automated systems) to query the blockchain and retrieve relevant information about the product, acting as a physical anchor for the product's digital identity. The device must be engineered to prevent cloning and unauthorized modification. This includes robustness against modification attacks (altering the tag's data) and cloning attacks (replicating tag information onto another device). These risks can be mitigated through the use of advanced cryptographic techniques and secure hardware components that ensure data integrity and authenticity.

Implementing robust physical integrity verification mechanisms is critical to securing the supply chain. The solution should incorporate features that allow stakeholders to authenticate the product's untampered state, ensuring it has not been opened, modified, or substituted post-manufacture. This may involve the use of tamper-evident packaging, break-on-access security seals [6], or sensor-enabled enclosures [7] capable of detecting physical breaches. Furthermore, the system must be resilient against tag reapplication attacks-specifically, it should prevent scenarios where a legitimate authentication tag is removed from the original item and affixed to a counterfeit product. This can be achieved through secure tag binding, one-time-use mechanisms.

This paper proposes a blockchain-based supply chain framework for product traceability and anti-counterfeiting. The approach integrates a tamper-proof device engineered to withstand cloning, modification, and reapplication attacks, even in scenarios where physical access to the product is possible. Furthermore, the system incorporates mechanisms for verifying the physical integrity of the product, thereby enhancing trust and transparency across the supply chain.

2 Related Works

Numerous scientific studies have focused on investigating the implementation of RFID technology in supply chain management [9,10,12]. RFID technology enhances product traceability and increases visibility across the entire supply chain. It contributes to the reliability and acceleration of key operational processes-such as tracking, shipping, checkout, and inventory counting-ultimately resulting in more efficient inventory flow and improved data accuracy. However, rather than addressing the supply chain holistically, most of the preliminary investigations have been confined to specific stages [12] - particularly distribution and warehousing [11] - thereby overlooking other critical phases of the supply chain lifecycle.

In [13] an agri-food supply chain traceability system has been developed, integrating RFID and blockchain technologies. This system encompasses the entire process of data collection and information management across all stages of the agri-food supply chain, enabling comprehensive monitoring, tracking, and traceability to ensure the quality and safety of agri-food products from farm to fork.

The core components of a tracking system typically include the tag, the reader (or tracer), and the sensor. Such devices can occasionally be compromised, as they are susceptible to cloning attacks. In these cases, an attacker may duplicate an RFID tag affixed to a genuine product, thereby jeopardizing the authenticity and security of the tracking system. A blockchain-based product ownership management system has been proposed in [14] to facilitate the transfer and verification of the uniqueness of products equipped with RFID tags in the post-supply chain phase. Counterfeit items can be identified when a seller is unable to authenticate ownership of the claimed product through the blockchain ledger. The Ambrosus network [21] employs a combination of tags, tracers, and sensors to monitor products throughout their entire lifecycle. The Ethereum blockchain is utilized to validate product quality and to authenticate the identities of tracking devices. Yiu [24] also proposed a Decentralized NFC-Enabled Anti-Counterfeiting System (dNAS), incorporating a consensus protocol specifically designed to align with the principles of enterprise blockchain architecture.

Tag data, such as the Electronic Product Code (EPC) or unique identifiers (UID), may be susceptible to eavesdropping during communication between the tag and the reader [14]. Additionally, sensitive information like secret keys can be extracted through physical tampering. Even RFID tags equipped with cryptographic enhancements are vulnerable to cloning attacks [16,17]. Owing to the limited computational resources of RFID tags, the use of complex cryptographic techniques to prevent cloning is often impractical. Nevertheless, protection against cloning attack is essential [19]. Physically Unclonable Functions (PUFs) serve as a form of a "digital fingerprint" for hardware components. The unique physical characteristics of tag chips can serve as identifiers. PUF are employed in tag anti-cloning mechanisms due to their inherent simplicity, low power requirements, and high degree of unpredictability [20].

A hybrid framework, referred to as PUFChain [22], offers both device and data provenance by capturing the origin, generation history, and processing trail of data, while also enabling clone-resistant device identification and authentication. In this architecture, PUF technology is applied for verifying device authenticity. Finke [23] introduces PUF-based SPOQchain, an innovative blockchain-based platform designed to achieve high efficiency through an advanced batching mechanism that eliminates redundancies across the product lifecycle. In [18], the authors propose a smart tag designed for a supply chain framework aimed at product traceability and anti-counterfeiting. The tag integrates Physically Unclonable Functions (PUFs), Elliptic Curve Cryptography (ECC), and NFC components, with the PUF challenge being hardwired into the system. While these approaches integrate PUF and blockchain technologies to address counterfeit mitigation, they lack formal security analysis. In the absence of such analysis, systems presumed to be secure may, in fact, exhibit critical vulnerabilities.

In [25], the authors propose SPUFChain, a contract-based lightweight authentication framework that leverages Physically Unclonable Functions (PUFs) for IoT devices within a permissioned blockchain environment. A formal security analyses using AVISPA and BAN logic is also given, demonstrating its ability to ensure key security properties such as freshness, mutual authentication, and secure key establishment.

To ensure that a tag remains physically attached to its associated item until authentication procedures are completed, anti-tampering mechanisms should be implemented. These mechanisms should be designed such that any attempt to detach the tag would irreversibly damage its circuitry, rendering it inoperable for future use. Nevertheless, a detailed discussion of such mechanisms lies beyond the scope most of the papers mentioned above.

3 Our Contribution

We propose an anti-counterfeiting system that ensures verifiable product authenticity from production to consumption. In contrast to most existing approaches [14,18,22–25] our work places particular emphasis on the secure tokenization of real-world assets (RWAs), including high-value items such as premium wines. In certain cases-especially with liquid products-authenticity cannot be guaranteed without mechanisms that ensure the physical integrity of the container. The proposed system not only enables verification of a product's physical integrity but also provides traceability and accountability for all actors involved in the supply chain through the use of blockchain technology.

To enable the tokenization of real-world assets (RWAs), we have designed a device composed of an NFC module and a Physically Unclonable Function (PUF) module. The tamper-evident implementation of the NFC tag ensures the verifiability of physical integrity while also supporting cryptographic authentication. However, existing tags often lack protection against side-channel and timing attacks, or the integrated security features-such as the Leakage Resilient Protocol (LRP)-are inactive by default, and frequently remain unactivated in practice. The PUF component provides secure authentication based on the device's intrinsic physical uniqueness, effectively mitigating cloning attacks.

Our design takes into account the capabilities offered by currently available tags, such as the NTAG®424 DNA TT, which supports advanced functions like three-pass mutual authentication. The proposed NFC-PUF-based authentication solution combines physical and cryptographic security, offering robustness not only against physical tampering but also against replay attacks, thereby significantly enhancing overall system resilience. Formal security analysis in the framework of applied pi calculus, leveraging the automated verification capabilities of ProVerif shows that our scheme provides mutual authentication, message integrity and replay attack resistance. Table 1 highlights the novelty of our proposed system in comparison with existing related works.

Table 1. Comparison to related works.

paper	BC-based	PUF-based module	physical integrity	formal
Toyoda *et al.* 2017	✓	x	x	x
Ambrosus 2018	✓	x	✓	x
Yiu 2021	✓	x	x	x
Asif *et al.* 2021	✓	x	x	x
Falcone *et al.* 2021	✓	✓	x	x
Finke *et al.* 2024	✓	✓	x	x
Assaqty *et al.* 2025	✓	✓	x	✓
Our scheme	✓	✓	✓	✓

4 Preliminaries

In this section, we formally introduce the basic cryptographic primitives, security assumptions, and notation necessary for describing and analyzing the proposed three-party authentication protocol, consisting of the NFC tag, a Physical Unclonable Function device (PUF) and a Server. For the protocol description, we use the following notations. For any two bitstrings x, y, let $x||y$ denote their concatenation. Let $\{0,1\}^*$ denote the set of all finite length binary strings. Let $\mathbb{F}_q$ denote a finite field where q is a large prime. We formally define the symmetric encryption primitive employed by the NFC device in our system, as follows.

Definition 1. *A symmetric encryption scheme is a tuple of probabilistic polynomial-time algorithms* (Key_E, Enc, Dec).

1. *The key-generation algorithm* Key_E *takes as input the security parameter* 1^κ *and outputs a random key* $K \in \{0,1\}^\kappa$.
2. *Enc is an encryption algorithm that takes inputs key* K *and plaintext* $m \in \{0,1\}^*$, *and outputs a ciphertext* c.
3. *Dec is a deterministic decryption algorithm that takes inputs key* K *and ciphertext* c, *and outputs the plaintext* m.

To define secure encryption, let $\mathcal{A}$ be an adversary running in polynomial time and consider the experiment $Exp_{Enc}^{ind-cpa}(A)$ as follows.

1. A random key K is generated by running $Key_E(1^\kappa)$.
2. The adversary $\mathcal{A}$ is given input 1^κ, oracle access to $Enc_K(.)$ and $\mathcal{A}$ outputs $m_0, m_1 \in \{0,1\}^*$ with $|m_0| = |m_1|$.
3. A random bit b is chosen and a ciphertext $Enc_K(m_b)$ is computed and given to $\mathcal{A}$.
4. $\mathcal{A}$ continues to have oracle access to $Enc_K(.)$ and outputs a bit b'.
5. We define $\mathcal{A}$'s advantage to be $Adv_{Enc}^{ind-cpa}(A) = |Pr[b' = b] - 1/2|$.

Definition 2. *We say that a symmetric encryption scheme is* indistinguishable under chosen plaintext attack *if* $Adv_{Enc}^{ind-cpa}(A)$ *is negligible in* κ *for any probabilistic polynomial-time adversaries adversary* $\mathcal{A}$.

Since the PUF in our system uses digital signatures based on elliptic curve cryptography (ECC), we briefly discusses the concepts of elliptic curves over finite fields. For more comprehensive information, we refer to [37].

Let E denote an elliptic curve over a finite field $\mathbb{F}_q$ and $P \in E(\mathbb{F}_q)$ a point of order $\mathbf{n}$. The group structure on the elliptic curves consists of (x, y) points of the curve and the point of infinity as an identity element with the operation of addition. Let G be the generator element with order $\mathbf{n}$.

Definition 3 (Elliptic Curve Discrete Logarithm Problem (ECDLP)). *Let* E *be an elliptic curve defined over a finite field* $\mathbb{F}_q$ *and let* $G \in E(\mathbb{F}_q)$ *be a point of prime order* $\mathbf{n}$. *Given* G *and a point* $Q = xG$ *for* $x \in \mathbb{Z}_n$, *the* elliptic curve discrete logarithm problem *is to compute* x.

For sufficiently large **n**, the ECDLP is computationally infeasible. Based on the ECC, we introduce the concept of a digital signature scheme that utilizes this structure to ensure message authenticity and integrity.

Definition 4. *A digital signature scheme is a tuple of probabilistic polynomial-time algorithms* $(Keys_S, Sign, Verify)$.

1. *The key-generation algorithm* $Keys_S$ *takes as input the security parameter* 1^κ *and outputs a key pair* (sk, pk)*, where sk is the secret signing key and pk is the public verification key.*
2. *Sign is a signing algorithm that takes as input the signing key sk and a message* $m \in \{0,1\}^*$*, and outputs a signature* σ*.*
3. $Verify$ *is t deterministic verification algorithm that takes as input the verification key pk, a message* $m \in \{0,1\}^*$*, and a signature* σ*, and outputs a bit* $b \in \{0,1\}$*, where* $b = 1$ *indicates a valid signature and* $b = 0$ *indicates invalid.*

To define signature security, consider the experiment $Exp_{Sign}^{euf-cma}(\mathcal{A})$ as follows.

1. A key pair (sk, pk) is generated by running $Keys_S(1^\kappa)$.
2. The adversary $\mathcal{A}$ is given input 1^κ, pk and has oracle access to $Sign_{sk}(.)$.
3. $\mathcal{A}$ may adaptively query signatures on messages of its choice. Eventually, it outputs (m^*, σ^*).
4. The output of the experiment is 1 if and only if $Verify_{pk}(m^*, \sigma^*) = 1$ and m^* was not previously queried to the signing oracle.
5. We define the adversary's advantage as $Adv_{Sign}^{euf-cma}(\mathcal{A}) = \Pr[Exp_{Sign}^{euf-cma}(\mathcal{A}) = 1]$.

Definition 5. *We say that a digital signature scheme is* existentially unforgeable under adaptive chosen-message attack *(EUF-CMA) if* $Adv_{Sign}^{euf-cma}(\mathcal{A})$ *is negligible in* κ *for any probabilistic polynomial-time adversaries adversary* $\mathcal{A}$*.*

A cryptographic PUF may further satisfy that, for a subset of challenges, the responses are used as cryptographic keys for digital signature generation.

Definition 6. *A* Physical Unclonable Function *(PUF) is a probabilistic physical function which, for each challenge c in a finite set* $\mathcal{C}$*, returns a response* $r = \mathsf{PUF}(c)$ *in a finite set* $\mathcal{R}$*, such that:*

1. ***Evaluability:*** *For any* $c \in \mathcal{C}$*, the function* $\mathsf{PUF}(c)$ *can be measured efficiently and reliably on the device.*
2. ***Unclonability:*** *It is infeasible to create value, either physically or algorithmically, a distinct function* PUF' *such that* $\mathsf{PUF}'(c) = \mathsf{PUF}(c)$ *for all or a large fraction of* $c \in \mathcal{C}$*, without physical access to the device.*
3. ***Unpredictability:*** *For a randomly chosen* $c \in \mathcal{C}$*, and without access to the device, the value* $\mathsf{PUF}(c)$ *is unpredictable, even given observed pairs* $(c_1, r_1), \ldots, (c_t, r_t)$ *for* $c_i \neq c$*.*

In our system, we need a mechanism to maintain a transparent and tamper-resistant record of the physical products protected by the NFC and PUF components. We use an immutable, auditable, decentralized ledger of product for identities and transactions. The ledger enables reliable tracking of products throughout their lifecycle and ensure accountability in the digital representation of physical goods. Therefore, we formally define the concept of a public blockchain as the foundational infrastructure for this secure and transparent tracking system.

A public blockchain is a distributed and decentralized database system, implemented as an append-only ledger maintained by a network of mutually untrusted nodes. The integrity and consistency of the ledger are ensured via cryptographic primitives and consensus protocols, removing the need for any centralized authority. The append-only property enforces immutability: once data are recorded on the blockchain, they cannot be modified or deleted. This guarantees an authentic and permanent history of transactions. The decentralized architecture provides increased availability and fault tolerance. Conceptually, a blockchain can be modeled as a fault-tolerant replicated state machine, whose functionality is extended by Turing-complete smart contracts. Smart contracts enable the deployment of decentralised applications (DApps) and the tokenisation, which operate on a peer-to-peer (P2P) network, guaranteeing transparency, security, and resistance to censorship.

The principal advantages of blockchain technology, which make it particularly well-suited for a secure product supply chain, include:

1. Immutability: Once data is written to the blockchain, it cannot be modified or deleted without consensus from the network. This prevents tampering and ensures the integrity of historical records.
2. Transparency and traceability: Every transaction is timestamped and verifiable by all participants, making it ideal for monitoring supply chains.
3. Decentralization: The absence of a central authority eliminates single points of failure and makes the system more robust and resistant to corruption or fraud.
4. Trustless verification: Blockchain enables parties who may not fully trust one another to collaborate securely, as the system enforces rules and truthfulness through its protocol.

5 RFID and NFC

Radio Frequency Identification (RFID) is a contactless identification and data transmission technology capable of operating without direct line-of-sight. It is widely implemented in logistics and industrial systems primarily for access control, tracking objects and processes, and supporting automation. An RFID system consists of three main components: a reader, a tag (also known as a transponder), and an antenna. The reader emits electromagnetic waves to activate nearby RFID tags. Once activated, the tag transmits its pre-programmed identifier and, in certain cases, additional information such as the associated object's name, type, or current status. RFID tags are classified into two main types: passive and active. Passive tags do not have their own power source; they rely exclusively on the electromagnetic energy generated by the reader. In contrast, active tags contain built-in batteries, enabling them to transmit signals autonomously, allowing greater range and more complex communication.

Near Field Communication (NFC) technology is an advanced implementation of 13.56 MHz RFID, now widely integrated into modern smartphones. NFC communication occurs when two NFC-compatible devices are placed close to each other-typically within 4 cm-or brought into contact. In recent years, NFC technology has proven its usefulness across various business applications, including mobile payment solutions, electronic ticketing, logistics tracking, and supply chain management. NFC technology is backward compatible with existing RFID infrastructure, including 13.56 MHz RFID tags and contactless smart cards. Due to its ease of use, it is highly accessible and intuitive for users, requiring minimal technical knowledge to initiate communication by simply bringing two devices close together. One of NFC's greatest advantages is the dual role of mobile devices: an NFC-capable smartphone can function not only as a reader but also as an information storage medium. Users can read data from NFC tags, display it on their screens, and subsequently process or forward it. Furthermore, the device can store digital information such as payment credentials, digital keys, or access passes.

The NTAG 424 DNA TT (NT4H2421Tx) elevates the security of NFC and IoT applications by employing the latest-generation NTAG DNA chip with advanced features in data protection, state sensing, and encrypted communication. This chip fully complies with NFC Forum Type 4 Tag standards, the ISO/IEC 14443-4 contactless communication protocol, and the ISO/IEC 7816-4-based file system and command format standards. Such extensive compliance ensures maximum interoperability within existing NFC infrastructures, offering outstanding NFC performance with operating distances up to 10 cm and reliable user interaction. An additional remarkable feature is the chip's integrated state detection capability, such as sensing the disruption of a tamper loop. If the protected package has been opened, the event is irrevocably recorded and displayed in the NFC message, allowing users to immediately verify if a product has previously been opened.

The chip can handle up to five distinct AES keys, enabling complex cryptographic functionalities such as CMAC authentication, optionally encrypted content, SUN message generation, mutual authentication between host and reader, and secure access to NDEF and additional data files. Alongside standard AES-128 encryption, the NTAG 424 DNA TT supports an alternative AES-based protocol known as Leakage Resilient Primitive (LRP), designed to enhance resistance to side-channel attacks.

The device also supports the three-pass mutual authentication. The three-pass protocol enables one party to securely send a message to another without the need to exchange or share encryption keys in advance. Since the NFC tag is a passive device and is not capable of performing complex key management, the protocol is based on symmetric encryption. The NXP NTAG 424 DNA TT tag uses 128-bit AES (Advanced Encryption Standard) encryption to implement this protocol. The core principle is that both parties - the tag and the reader - share a common secret key that has been securely distributed among parties. The communication process consists of three steps:

1. The tag generates a random secret value Nb, encrypts it, and sends it to the reader.
2. The reader decrypts the received message, generates its own random secret value Na, concatenates the two values $(Nb||Na)$, encrypts the result, and sends it back to the tag.
3. The tag removes its own encryption layer from the received message and verifies whether the Nb value matches the one it initially generated. If it does, the tag confirms the reader's authenticity and responds by sending the Na value back, which the reader then verifies.

This process ensures mutual authentication between the two parties without exposing the shared secret key, relying entirely on symmetric encryption. The protocol is well-suited for NFC environments due to its efficiency and compatibility with the limited computational capabilities of passive tags.

6 Protocol

The proposed solution combines NFC-based cryptographic authentication a three-pass authentication that uses an AES symmetric key and physical uniqueness ensured by Physical Unclonable Function (PUF) technology. The product's ownership history is securely recorded on a blockchain ledger.

Firstly, we define the set of participants in our authentication protocol as follows. The NFC tag is a resource-constrained component attached to a physical product. It is responsible for securely storing a symmetric key and efficiently performing symmetric encryption operations. The device is implemented as a tamper-evident NFC label, meaning that any attempt to physically remove or manipulate the tag will immediately disrupt the NFC circuit, rendering the tag compromised.

The PUF tag is a physical unclonable function module embedded in or integrated with the NFC device, capable of generating physically unique cryptographic responses that are infeasible to replicate or predict. In our design, the PUF also enables the generation of digital signatures, thereby providing strong authenticity guarantees by binding cryptographic operations to the device's inherent physical randomness. Using PUF provides resistance to both side-channel and cloning attacks, as cryptographic secrets are physically bound to the hardware and cannot be extracted or duplicated by an adversary.

Server is the authenticating backend system that verifies the NFC tag and the signatures generated by the PUF. It maintains the identifiers, the symmetric keys and cryptographic public keys, store and reference blockchain-based records to enable secure, transparent tracking and provenance of product.

6.1 Setup

All system parameters are established during the setup phase and the physical product is registered with the backend server. This process involves generating a symmetric key on the NFC device, which will be used for authentication with the server. Expanding NFC, the PUF module provides physical security against the side channel and other attacks. PUF is registered, where the PUF responses can also be used to deterministically derive cryptographic key pairs (secret and corresponding public keys), enabling the device to generate digital signatures. The public keys and challenges are registered with the server during setup, ensuring that subsequent authentication sessions can validate the PUF-generated digital signatures.

E represents an elliptic curve defined over a finite field $\mathbb{F}_q$ and let $\mathbb{G} \in E(\mathbb{F}_q)$ be a point of prime order n with generator G. The NFC and the Server execute a key exchange to establish a shared AES symmetric key $K \in \{0,1\}^{128}$. This key is used for all symmetric encryptions $\mathrm{ENC}_K(\cdot)$ and decryptions $\mathrm{DEC}_K(\cdot)$ during the protocol. The PUF device is initialized to support a set of challenge-response pairs. Given a device, for each challenge $CH_i \in \mathcal{C}$ (where $\mathcal{C}$ is a public challenge domain), the PUF securely computes and stores the corresponding response $R_i = \mathsf{PUF}(CH_i)$. For each CH_i, the PUF computes $R_i = \mathsf{PUF}(CH_i)$, then deterministically derives the signing key $SK_i = \mathsf{KeyDerive}(R_i)$ and the corresponding public key PK_i. For every device, the Server stores the set $(CH_i, PK_i) \mid i = 1, \ldots, k$, associating each challenge with its expected public verification key.

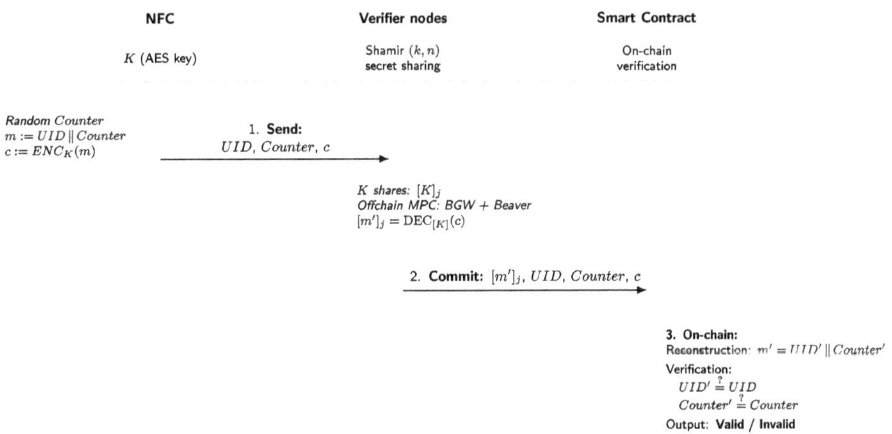

Fig. 1. The protocol steps.

6.2 Authentication

The primary goal of the authentication protocol is to ensure that only authentic and physically unmodified devices are verified within the system. Figure 1 illustrates the detailed steps of the authentication process.

1. NFC selects a random nonce $Nb \in \mathbb{Z}_n$. NFC computes $C_1 = \text{ENC}_K(Nb)$ and sends C_1 to PUF.
2. PUF, upon receiving C_1 selects a fixed challenge CH, generates the PUF response R and deterministically derives a signing key SK from R. The PUF using its ID, CH and receiving C_1 to compute the digital signature $\sigma_1 = \text{Sign}_{SK}(ID||CH||C_1)$ and returns $(ID||CH||C_1||\sigma_1)$ to the Server.
3. Server, upon receiving $(ID||CH||C_1||\sigma_1)$, retrieves the corresponding public key PK associated with CH, verifies the signature by checking $\text{Verify}_{PK}(ID||CH||C_1, \sigma_1) = 1$. If the verification is successful, Server decrypts C_1 to obtain Nb'. Subsequently, the server queries the blockchain for the product identifier ID and verifies its validity and consistency with the registered data. The protocol proceeds only if both the signature verification and the blockchain check are successful.
4. Server generates a fresh random value $Na \in \mathbb{Z}_n$, computes $C_2 = \text{ENC}_K(Na||Nb')$ and sends C_2 to the PUF.
5. PUF forwards C_2 to the NFC.
6. NFC decrypts C_2 to recover $(Nb'||Na')$. If $Nb' = Nb$, NFC authenticates the Server. Next, NFC computes $C_3 = \text{ENC}_K(Na')$ and sends C_3 to the Server via the PUF.
7. Server decrypts C_3 to obtain Na'. If $Na' = Na$, then the NFC and the PUF are authenticated.

7 Security Analysis

In this section, we present the security analysis of our authentication phase. We begin by formally defining the security requirements of the protocol. Next, we provide an analysis in the framework of applied pi calculus, leveraging the automated verification capabilities of ProVerif. ProVerif, developed by Bruno Blanchet, is a widely used tool for automatically verifying cryptographic protocols in a formal model [39]. It operates by translating the protocol into a set of Horn clauses and verifying the security properties.

7.1 Security Requirements

We analyse our authentication protocol, which is a typical mutual entity authentication scheme. The following properties are essential:

- **Mutual authentication:** The protocol must guarantee that the NFC-PUF device and the server can confirm each other's authenticity through the message and digital signature verifications. An adversary must not be able to impersonate the NFC-PUF device or the server without knowledge of the respective secrets or the ability to generate valid cryptographic responses to new challenges.

- **Integrity of protocol messages:** All protocol messages must be protected against unauthorized modification, injection. Any attempt by an adversary to alter transcripts must be detected and rejected by the participants.
- **Replay attack resistance:** Each authentication session must be uniquely identified by freshly generated random challenges. Replay of previously recorded messages must not enable successful impersonation or authentication.

7.2 Adversarial Model

In the case of our protocol, the adversary's goal is to impersonate a participant successfully. We use the Dolev-Yao model for our analysis. In the Dolev-Yao model, the adversary is assumed to control the entire communication network. It means that the adversary can intercept, modify, create, and inject any message. Additionally, the adversary can initiate the protocol with any party and impersonate the NFC-PUF or the Server in any interaction. Their actions are only constrained by the limitations of cryptographic techniques.

7.3 Formal Model

We formalize the protocol as follows. We differentiate three processes. In the main process Fig. 2, a challenge, a signing key and a verification key are generated. Two sub-processes represent the protocol steps for the Tag (NFC-PUF) and Server. We consider an unbounded number of sub-processes that run simultaneously. Our goal is to create a model representing the interactions between the tag and the server.

```
process
new skN: sskey;
new ch: bitstring;
let pkN = spk(skN) in
out(c, (pkN));
((!NP(K,skN,ch)) | (!S(K,pkN,ch)))
```

Fig. 2. Main process.

7.4 Security Properties

ProVerif can analyse several classes of security properties, including reachability, correspondence assertions, and observational equivalence. It is essential to emphasise that ProVerif is sound but not complete. However, the tool may be unable to prove properties that are in fact true, due to the incompleteness of its verification approach. For more comprehensive details, we refer to [40].

We use a security query and define four events demonstrated by Fig. 3.

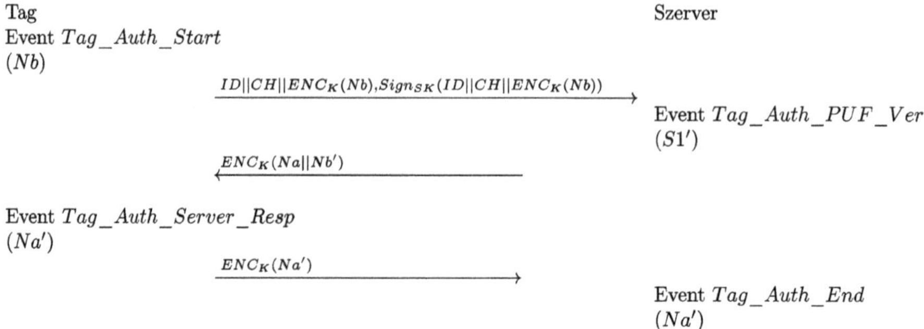

Fig. 3. ProVerif - Events.

ProVerif uses fact or correspondence queries to evaluate security. We mainly check whether *sec* remains secret with *query attacker(sec)*, treating it as a reachability fact. In the authentication phase, we apply injective correspondences for mutual authentication of the tag and server. Injective queries are used to establish a one-to-one relationship between the protocol events, ensuring that each instance of authentication corresponds uniquely to a specific protocol execution. Tag and Server authentication is demonstrated by the following nested correspondence:

$$\begin{gathered}\textit{query a1:bitstring,a2:bitstring,a3:bitstring,a4:bitstring}\\ \textit{;inj-event}(Tag\_Auth\_End(a4)) ==>\\ (\textit{inj-event}(Tag\_Auth\_Server\_Resp(a3)) ==>\\ (\textit{inj-event}(Tag\_Auth\_Puf\_Ver(a2)) ==> \textit{inj-event}(Tag\_Auth\_Start(a1)))).\end{gathered}$$

All queries return true, confirming that Proverif did not find an attack violating the specified security requirements. In particular, mutual authentication between the Tag and the Server is achieved, and the secrecy of the symmetric keys is maintained within our formal model. Furthermore, ProVerif does not detect message modification or replay attack, indicating that the protocol also provides robustness against these common attacks.

7.5 Physical Security

A wide range of hardware-based attacks threatens the security of embedded and cryptographic devices. Cloning attacks are one of the most critical security threats to NFC-based authentication systems. In a cloning scenario, an adversary copies the identifier and possibly all accessible data from a genuine tag onto a programmable replica, which can then be used to impersonate the original tag [38]. This undermines the basis of object authenticity and traceability, resulting in the circulation of multiple, indistinguishable tags claiming to represent the same product. The practical feasibility of tag cloning is well-documented and standard NFC tags lacking robust cryptographic protection can often be duplicated with minimal technical effort. Such attacks compromise anti-counterfeiting mechanisms and have been demonstrated in real-world settings, including electronic passports [41] and access control systems [42].

Microprobing [26] involves physically accessing the internal circuitry of a chip using fine probes or needles under a microscope, allowing an attacker to monitor, manipulate, or directly extract secret data from bus lines or memory cells. Side-channel analysis [27] exploits information leaked through physical characteristics such as power consumption, electromagnetic radiation, or timing variations during cryptographic operations, enabling attackers to infer secret keys without direct access to internal signals. Fault injection attacks [28] deliberately introduce faults into the device's computation using methods such as voltage glitches, laser pulses, or electromagnetic interference to force errors in cryptographic computations, which can then be exploited to reveal secret information or bypass security mechanisms. Scanning electron microscopy (SEM) [29,30] is an advanced invasive technique, where high-resolution imaging is used to visualise the internal layout and stored data within semiconductor devices, enabling the extraction or duplication of cryptographic secrets by directly observing memory structures or circuit paths. Reverse engineering [31] refers to the systematic analysis and reconstruction of a device's design, often through delayering, imaging, and schematic extraction, to understand its functionality or discover embedded secrets.

From a hardware security perspective, Physical Unclonable Functions provide robust protection against invasive attacks. Unlike traditional cryptographic modules that store secret keys in non-volatile memory, making them susceptible to key extraction, PUFs generate device-unique secrets dynamically from intrinsic manufacturing variations. As a result, secret keys are never present in static or readable form and can only be reconstructed during a legitimate function. The physical uniqueness and unpredictability of each PUF instance make hardware cloning and counterfeiting virtually impossible, even for the original manufacturer. Attempts to tamper with or probe the PUF typically alter its electrical properties, resulting in an invalid or unpredictable response and immediate detection of compromise. Furthermore, the challenge-response nature of our solution thwarts attempts at simple replay attacks, since every authentication session is dynamically linked to a fresh challenge.

Limiting the number of available challenge-response pairs further mitigates modelling and machine learning attacks, which might otherwise threaten less complex PUF designs. However, specific PUF architectures, such as XOR APUF, FF-APUF and iPUF are designed to be highly unpredictable and to exhibit significant output variability, making them more resistant to machine learning-based modeling attacks. [32]. Moreover, PUFs support robust device authentication, hinder unauthorised duplication, and can be integrated into supply chains to detect tampering or counterfeiting. By establishing a strong hardware root of trust, PUFs significantly elevate device security across a broad range of hardware-based threats.

7.6 Blockchain

A public blockchain enhances system security by ensuring stored records' integrity, authenticity, and non-repudiation through its decentralised consensus mechanisms and cryptographic primitives. Each transaction added to the ledger is validated by a distributed network of mutually untrusted nodes, leveraging consensus protocols such as Proof of Work (PoW) or Proof of Stake (PoS) to prevent double-spending and unauthorised modifications. The append-only property, enforced by cryptographic hash functions used for blocks, provides immutability. Once data is confirmed by consensus and written to the blockchain, it cannot be altered or deleted retroactively without the collusion of most participants, which is considered computationally infeasible in a well-designed system.

The decentralized nature of public blockchains significantly increases resilience against traditional security threats, such as single points of failure, insider attacks, or unauthorized data manipulation. Because consensus is distributed, the system remains robust even in the presence of malicious or faulty nodes, provided that the majority operate honestly. However, public blockchains are not immune to all forms of attack: they may be susceptible to so-called "51% attacks," denial-of-service (DoS) attacks targeting network or consensus layers, and smart contract vulnerabilities resulting from flawed code.

In terms of confidentiality and access control, public blockchains generally prioritize transparency over privacy, as transaction data are visible to all network participants. Furthermore, the principles of Know Your Customer (KYC) and Know Your Seller (KYS) refer to regulatory and procedural frameworks to verify the identities of all participants involved in a transaction or data submission process. In the context of blockchain-based product tracking, reliably establishing the identities of both customers and sellers is essential for ensuring the authenticity and traceability of goods and verifying the provenance of each product on the ledger. A public blockchain infrastructure combined with KYC and KYS models requires all entities that submit data, whether as customers, sellers, or other stakeholders, to undergo rigorous identity verification processes before gaining write access to the ledger. This ensures that every data entry or transaction can be irrefutably attributed to a verified real-world entity and the origin of every transaction is cryptographically linked to a known and verified identity, actors are disincentivized from engaging in behaviors such as double-spending, product counterfeiting, or unauthorized asset registration. Any attempt to manipulate records can be traced back to the responsible party, thereby enabling effective enforcement of legal or contractual remedies and facilitating the rapid exclusion of malicious actors from the network.

8 Implementation

In our use case, smart contracts and blockchain technology guarantee the immutability and integrity of stored data, effectively leveraging the Ethereum blockchain as a secure and decentralised database. Tokenisation of physical products is achieved by representing each item as a non-fungible token (NFT) on-chain, following the ERC-721 standard. This approach allows every product to be uniquely identified and tracked, with associated metadata directly linked to the corresponding NFT, such as serial numbers or provenance information. By adopting ERC-721, our system ensures interoperability with existing NFT infrastructure and lays the groundwork for secure, verifiable product management across the supply chain. Solidity is chosen as the smart contract programming language, and Hardhat is used as the development framework for decentralised application prototyping and testing. Hardhat provides a local blockchain environment, including support for private keys and pre-funded Ether, which enables practical and cost-effective testing. This local environment is essential, as deploying and testing smart contracts directly on mainnets is prohibitively expensive and public test networks often lack the reliability required for systematic evaluation. Blockchain interactions are carried out through a web application created with the Svelte JavaScript framework. Users can query the blockchain directly, without needing an Ethereum wallet for read-only operations, significantly improving usability. In contrast, operations that modify blockchain state, such as minting new NFTs or appending additional product data, require user authentication and transaction signing via an Ethereum wallet. MetaMask was integrated as the interface for transaction submission to support this, owing to its broad adoption and comfort for end users. All state-changing operations on the blockchain incur transaction fees (gas) denominated in Ether, which makes the optimisation of smart contract logic necessary. Our initial implementation adopted the contract factory pattern, creating a separate contract instance for each product, which offered clear structural separation but resulted in high transaction costs. The improved design manages all product NFTs within a single ERC-721 smart contract using an indexed list, substantially reducing gas consumption and improving overall efficiency. This architecture enables seamless management, transfer, and verification of tokenised assets while supporting extensibility for future integration of advanced supply chain or compliance features.

8.1 Hardware Setup

In our implementation, an **ESP32 microcontroller** was employed to handle the generation of key values, perform digital signature operations, and facilitate communication between the NFC component and the backend server. The ESP32 was selected for its price, processing capabilities and compatibility with common embedded protocols.

For communication between the microcontroller and the server, we used a standard Wi-Fi connection due to its ease of configuration and widespread availability. However, the system is designed to be communication-agnostic, and any short-range communication interface (e.g., Bluetooth Low Energy or Zigbee) could be used as a substitute, depending on the specific deployment constraints.

The NFC interface was implemented using the widely adopted **RFID-RC522** module, which supports ISO/IEC 14443 Type A cards and provides SPI-based communication with the ESP32. This module is responsible for the direct interaction with the NFC tag. The NFC tag was **NXP NTAG 424 DNA TT**.

The backend server was an **AMD Ryzen 5 7520U processor** and **16 GB RAM**, providing sufficient performance for processing authentication requests and running smart contract logic. Table 2 shows the measured execution times (in seconds) for each step of the protocol simulation, including both PUF and NFC interactions as well as server-side processing.

Table 2. Measured time results (in seconds)

Operation	Time (s)
Step 1 PUF+NFC	0.11877
Step 3 PUF+NFC	0.00619
Step 1 Server	0.24202
Step 2 Server	0.00014
Step 3 Server	0.10040

9 Future Work and Conclusion

The design of the our protocol naturally lends itself to further scientific inquiry, particularly regarding its adaptability to emerging cryptographic challenges such as post-quantum security. While conventional PUFs provide hardware-based security grounded in classical assumptions, integrating post-quantum secure primitives into the protocol remains an open research challenge. Recent work has examined the feasibility of lattice-based PUFs and physical sources of entropy that are supposed to resist quantum adversaries [36]. Exploring the compatibility of such constructions with the existing NFC-PUF authentication pipeline, including the efficient implementation of quantum-resistant challenge-response mechanisms and secure key derivation, could significantly strengthen the protocol's long-term resilience. Formal security proofs under post-quantum models would be valuable contributions, ensuring the protocol's guarantees remain robust despite emerging quantum threats.

In addition to invasive hardware attacks, relay attacks represent a critical and unique threat to contactless authentication protocols such as those employing NFC or RFID technologies [35]. In a relay attack, an adversary places two proxy devices near the legitimate tag and one near the verifier and relays their communication over a different channel, such as Bluetooth or the Internet. As a result, the verifier is deceived into accepting the presence of the authentic tag, even though it may be at a distant location. This attack is particularly concerning because it does not require compromising the tag's cryptographic keys, protocol knowledge, or physical integrity. It simply relays genuine messages in real time. Practical implementations have demonstrated that off-the-shelf mobile devices can be used as proxies, lowering the technical barrier for attackers [33]. Thus, more advanced countermeasures are required. One approach uses distance-bounding protocols to measure the physical round-trip time of challenge-response exchanges [34]. Still, these require precise timing and are not always practical with current NFC hardware. Another promising defence, as highlighted in recent research, is the integration of location-based proofs or physical-layer features such as PUF-based challenge-response authentication. For example, securely binding the cryptographic response to the current time and geographic location can help detect and prevent relay attacks by making it infeasible for a remote adversary to provide a valid, timely response. However, such schemes may introduce new requirements (e.g., reliable location data, user cooperation, or more interactive protocols) and remain an open research challenge in balancing security, privacy, and usability.

The protocol's current capability for immutable ownership history on the blockchain layer already addresses core transparency and non-repudiation requirements in supply chain and asset provenance contexts. Future work will primarily target the decentralization of tag verification process on server side., thereby eliminating single points of trust and enhancing the overall robustness of the authentication system. This direction for future development is the adoption of secure multi-party computation (SMPC) and secret sharing techniques for verification and authentication. In this paradigm, authentication and validation tasks are no longer entrusted to a single server, but are collaboratively executed by a consortium of independent verifiers, each holding a share of the cryptographic secret required for verification. SMPC protocols enable these verifiers to jointly compute authentication functions or validate signatures without ever reconstructing or revealing the underlying secret key to any individual party.

9.1 Conclusion

This paper introduced a new proposition to product authentication and supply chain integrity by combining NFC and PUFs with blockchain technology, which results in tightly linking the physical integrity of the product to its digital representation. We enhanced the NFC-based three-pass authentication using a digital signature via PUF, where PUF responses are applied to generate the key pairs. The integration of the authentication and immutable blockchain records provides strong resistance to tag cloning, tampering, and unauthorised product replacement. Our system establishes a transparent and tamper-evident framework for secure asset tracking. Formal analysis with ProVerif confirms that the protocol meets the given security requirements, ensuring resistance to attacks such as impersonation and replay. We created an implementation to check our solution's suitability for practical deployment in secure supply chain environments.

Acknowledgments. Norbert Oláh was supported by the EKÖP-24-4-II University Research Scholarship Program of the Ministry for Culture and Innovation from the source of the National Research, Development and Innovation Fund.

References

1. Author, F.: Article title. Journal **2**(5), 99–110 (2016)
2. OECD EUIPO Mapping Global Trade in Fakes 2025: Global Trends and Enforcement Challenges. Illicit Trade, OECD Publishing, Paris (2025). https://doi.org/10.1787/94d3b29f-en
3. Zheng, Z., Xie, S., Dai, H., Chen, X., Wang, H. An overview of blockchain technology: architecture, consensus, and future trends. In: 2017 IEEE International Congress on Big Data (BigData Congress), pp. 557–564 (2017). https://doi.org/10.1109/BigDataCongress.2017.85
4. Chen, S., Jiang, M., Luo, X.: Exploring the security issues of real world assets (RWA). In: Proceedings of the Workshop on Decentralized Finance and Security (DeFi '24), pp. 31–40. Association for Computing Machinery, New York, NY, USA (2024). https://doi.org/10.1145/3689931.3694913
5. Finkenzeller, K.: RFID Handbook: Fundamentals and Applications in Contactless Smart Cards, Radio Frequency Identification and Near-Field Communication, 3rd edn. (2010). ISBN: 978-0470665121
6. Johnston, R.G.: Tamper-indicating seals: practices, problems, and standards (2003)
7. Wang, W., Sadeqi, A., Nejad, H.R., Sonkusale, S.: Cost-effective wireless sensors for detection of package opening and tampering. IEEE Access **8**, 117122–117132 (2020). https://doi.org/10.1109/ACCESS.2020.3004438
8. Longo, F., Nicoletti, L., Padovano, A., d'Atri, G., Forte, M.: Blockchain-enabled supply chain: an experimental study. Comput. Ind. Eng. **136**, 57–69 (2019)
9. Angeles, R.: RFID technologies: supply-chain applications and implementation issues. Inf. Syst. Manag. **22**(1), 51–65 (2005). https://doi.org/10.1201/1078/44912.22.1.20051201/85739.7
10. Liukkonen, M.: RFID technology in manufacturing and supply chain. Int. J. Comput. Integr. Manuf. **28**(8), 861–880 (2014). https://doi.org/10.1080/0951192X.2014.941406
11. Vijayaraman, B., Osyk, B.: An empirical study of RFID implementation in the warehousing industry. Int. J. Logist. Manag. **17**(1), 6–20 (2006)
12. Sarac A., Absi N., Dauzere-Pérès, S.: A literature review on the impact of RFID technologies on supply chain management. Int. J. Product. Econ. **128**(1), 77–95 (2010)
13. Tian, F.: An agri-food supply chain traceability system for China based on RFID & blockchain technology, pp. 1–6 (2016). https://doi.org/10.1109/ICSSSM.2016.7538424
14. Toyoda, K., Mathiopoulos, P., Ohtsuki, T., Sasase, P.: A novel blockchain-based product ownership management system (POMS) for anti-counterfeits in the post supply chain. IEEE Access **5**, 17465–17477 (2017)

15. Bu, K., Weng, M., Zheng, Y., Xiao, B., Liu, X.: You can clone but you cannot hide: a survey of clone prevention and detection for RFID. IEEE Commun. Surv. Tutor. **19**(3), 1682–1700, thirdquarter 2017. https://doi.org/10.1109/COMST.2017.2688411
16. Kasper, T., von Maurich, I., Oswald, D., Paar, C.: Cloning cryptographic RFID cards for 25$. In: 5th Benelux Workshop on Information and System Security, Nijmegen, Netherlands (2010)
17. Zanetti, D., Capkun, S., Juels, A.: Tailing RFID tags for clone detection. In: Network and Distributed System Security Symposium (NDSS) (2013)
18. Falcone, A., Felicetti, C., Garro, A., Rullo, A., Saccà, D.: PUF-based smart tags for supply chain management. In: Proceedings of the 16th International Conference on Availability, Reliability and Security (ARES '21), Article 41, pp. 1–7. Association for Computing Machinery, New York, NY, USA (2021). https://doi.org/10.1145/3465481.3469195
19. Zhang, B.: Securing RFID With GNN: a real-time tag cloning attack detection system. IEEE Open J. Commun. Soc. **6**, 3251–3264 (2025). https://doi.org/10.1109/OJCOMS.2024.3502630
20. Shuyu, C., Yan Limin, A.: low-overhead PUF for anti-clone attack of RFID tags. Microelectron. J. **126**, 105497 (2022). ISSN 1879-2391. https://doi.org/10.1016/j.mejo.2022.105497
21. Ambrosus White Paper: AMB-NET: A Blockchain Protocol for Decentralized Data Exchange in the IoT Supply Chain (2018). https://ambrosus.io/whitepaper.pdf
22. Asif, R., Ghanem, K., Irvine, J.: Proof-of-PUF enabled blockchain: concurrent data and device security for internet-of-energy. Sensors **21**(1), 28 (2021). https://doi.org/10.3390/s21010028
23. Finke, M., Dmitrienko, A., Stang, J.: SPOQchain: Platform for Secure, Scalable, and Privacy-Preserving Supply Chain Tracing and Counterfeit Protection (2024). https://doi.org/10.48550/arXiv.2408.17049
24. Yiu, N.C.K.: Decentralizing supply chain anti-counterfeiting and traceability systems using blockchain technology. Future Internet **13**(4), 84 (2021). https://doi.org/10.3390/fi13040084
25. Assaqty, M.I.S., et al.: SPUFChain: permissioned blockchain lightweight authentication scheme for supply chain management using PUF of IoT. IEEE Access **13**, 88662–88682 (2025). https://doi.org/10.1109/ACCESS.2025.3566478
26. Skorobogatov, S.: How microprobing can attack encrypted memory. In: 2017 Euromicro Conference on Digital System Design (DSD), pp. 244–251. IEEE (2017)
27. Standaert, F.X.: Introduction to side-channel attacks. In: Secure Integrated Circuits and Systems, pp. 27–42 (2010)
28. Breier, J., Hou, X.: How practical are fault injection attacks, really? IEEE Access **10**, 113122–113130 (2022)
29. Courbon, F., Skorobogatov, S., Woods, C.: Reverse engineering flash EEPROM memories using scanning electron microscopy. In: Lemke-Rust, K., Tunstall, M. (eds.) CARDIS 2016. LNCS, vol. 10146, pp. 57–72. Springer, Cham (2017). https://doi.org/10.1007/978-3-319-54669-8_4
30. Courbon, F., Skorobogatov, S., Woods, C.: Direct charge measurement in floating gate transistors of flash EEPROM using scanning electron microscopy. In: International Symposium for Testing and Failure Analysis, vol. 81368, pp. 327–335. ASM International (2016)
31. Rostami, M., Majzoobi, M., Koushanfar, F., Wallach, D.S., Devadas, S.: Robust and reverse-engineering resilient PUF authentication and key-exchange by substring matching. IEEE Trans. Emerg. Top. Comput. **2**(1), 37–49 (2014)

32. Hemavathy, S., Bhaaskaran, V.K.: Arbiter PUF - a review of design, composition, and security aspects. IEEE Access **11**, 33979–34004 (2023)
33. Francis, L., Hancke, G., Mayes, K., Markantonakis, K.: Practical NFC peer-to-peer relay attack using mobile phones. In: Ors Yalcin, S.B. (ed.) RFIDSec 2010. LNCS, vol. 6370, pp. 35–49. Springer, Heidelberg (2010). https://doi.org/10.1007/978-3-642-16822-2_4
34. Pietrzak, K.: Delayed authentication: preventing replay and relay attacks in private contact tracing. In: Bhargavan, K., Oswald, E., Prabhakaran, M. (eds.) INDOCRYPT 2020. LNCS, vol. 12578, pp. 3–15. Springer, Cham (2020). https://doi.org/10.1007/978-3-030-65277-7_1
35. Tu, Y.J., Piramuthu, S.: On addressing RFID/NFC-based relay attacks: an overview. Decis. Support Syst. **129**, 113194 (2020)
36. Prada-Delgado, M.Á., Baturone, I., Dittmann, G., Jelitto, J., Kind, A.: PUF-derived IoT identities in a zero-knowledge protocol for blockchain. Internet Things **9**, 100057 (2020)
37. Menezes, A., Vanstone, S., Okamoto, T.: Reducing elliptic curve logarithms to logarithms in a finite field. In: Proceedings of the Twenty-Third Annual ACM Symposium on Theory of Computing, pp. 80–89 (1991)
38. Mitrokotsa, A., Rieback, M.R., Tanenbaum, A.S.: Classifying RFID attacks and defenses. Inf. Syst. Front. **12**, 491–505 (2010)
39. Blanchet, B.: Modeling and verifying security protocols with the applied pi calculus and ProVerif. Found. Trends Privacy Secur. **1**(1–2), 1–135 (2016)
40. Blanchet, B., Smyth, B., Cheval, V., Sylvestre, M.: ProVerif 2.05: automatic cryptographic protocol verifier, user manual and tutorial (2023)
41. Lettice, J.: How to clone the copy-friendly biometric passport. The Register, 4 (2006)
42. Garcia, F.D., et al.: Dismantling MIFARE classic. In: Jajodia, S., Lopez, J. (eds.) ESORICS 2008. LNCS, vol. 5283, pp. 97–114. Springer, Heidelberg (2008). https://doi.org/10.1007/978-3-540-88313-5_7

Security Management, Communication Infrastructures, and Applications

Multi-party Computation for IoT Environments: Evaluating Information Checking Protocol-Based Verifiable Secret Sharing Under Resource Constraints

Jaishnoor Kaur and Levent Ertaul(✉)

CSU East Bay, Hayward 94542, CA, USA
jkaur122@horizon.csueastbay.edu, levent.ertaul@csueastbay.edu

Abstract. As IoT devices continue to proliferate across both consumer and critical infrastructure, securing their communications is paramount. While standardized Lightweight Cryptography (LWC) provides security under resource constraints, it does not facilitate privacy preservation—an essential requirement given the sensitive nature of IoT-collected data. This paper explores the integration of privacy-enhancing cryptographic primitives in constrained devices by evaluating the Information Checking Protocol (ICP), a key component in Rabin's implementation of verifiable secret sharing (VSS), on the Arduino Uno. Using execution time and energy consumption as key metrics, we analyze the viability of implementing ICP under severe computational and memory constraints. Our findings provide empirical insights into the limits of secure protocol deployment on constrained IoT devices, indicating that although certain cryptographic operations are possible at lower bit lengths, resource limitations render full protocol implementation impractical without significant optimization or upgraded hardware.

Keywords: Security · IoT Security · Privacy Preserving Computations · Multi-party Computation · Verifiable Secret Sharing · Information Checking Protocol

1 Introduction

The Internet of Things (IoT) has witnessed immense growth, and while estimates vary wildly [1–4], it is undeniable that they have been deployed across a multitude of sectors, encompassing everyday consumer devices like wearables for healthcare and home automation systems, as well as critical infrastructure in industrial manufacturing and autonomous vehicle [5]. Their pervasive connectivity, coupled with the amount and nature of data collected by these devices, which may include sensitive information like health indicators, location, preferences, habits etc. [6], makes them a treasure-trove of information and thus, prime targets for cyber-attacks [7]. In the same vein, they are also critical to secure.

However, these devices are often small, low-powered, and resource constrained [7]. This is where Lightweight Cryptography (LWC), which is aimed at providing security

K. Daimi et al. (Eds.): CSCE 2025, CCIS 2937, pp. 195–213, 2026.
https://doi.org/10.1007/978-3-032-22208-4_13

in resource-constrained applications, becomes paramount [8]. The National Institute of Standards and Technology has published standards for LWC [8]; however, while these algorithms provide security in constrained environments, they do not provide privacy-preservation, which is crucial given that these devices have permeated almost every sphere of our lives. Privacy preservation, thus, must instead be achieved by combining LWC with other techniques [9, 10]. One of these privacy enhancing techniques is FHE (full homomorphic encryption) [10]. However, as Goyal and Saha [11] write, this often means that most of the current privacy-preserving methodologies, which are "either depend on computation intensive Homomorphic Encryption based operations or communication intensive collaborative mechanisms" [11] are not suitable for these systems. It is in these circumstances that secure multi-party computation (MPC) and secure secret sharing come into the spotlight.

Secure multi-party computation (MPC), which first emerged in the 1980s, has become "one of the most active research areas in both theoretical and applied cryptography" [12]. MPC enables a group to jointly perform a computation without disclosing any participant's secret shares [12]. Essentially, each party holds a secret share of the input, and computations are performed directly on these shares. However, if an adversary corrupts some participants and causes them to send incorrect values, it could compromise the entire computation. This is where the importance of Verifiable secret sharing (VSS) becomes apparent [13]. VSS helps mitigate this risk by ensuring that all shared values are verifiable, preventing dishonest participants from injecting false data into the protocol [13]. In Sect. 2 of this paper, we introduce Verifiable Secret Sharing, the Information Checking Protocol (ICP) as well as our goals for this study. Section 3 outlines the steps and participants in the Information Checking Protocol while Sect. 4 goes into specific details of each component of ICP tested. Next, we introduce our experimental environment in Sect. 5. In Sect. 7, we share our experimental results and analyze the performance and limitations of Arduino Uno for ICP as explained in Sects. 2 and 4. Finally, in Sect. 7, we summarize our findings and present our conclusions.

2 Verifiable Secret Sharing (VSS)

Verifiable Secret Sharing (VSS) is a cryptographic protocol that ensures shared secrets remain consistent and reconstructable, even in the presence of a malicious dealer [14]. Unlike standard secret sharing, which assumes an honest dealer, VSS incorporates auxiliary verification mechanisms to prevent adversarial manipulation. This property makes VSS fundamental for secure multi-party computation (MPC), where computations are performed on secret shares [13, 15], as it allows for security against active adversaries.

Rabin and Ben-Or [16] made key contributions to VSS, and proposed an implementation of VSS under the assumption that participants can securely communicate and broadcast messages. Their work demonstrated that any multi-party protocol or game with incomplete information could be securely executed if the majority of players remain honest. Notably, they introduced the Information Checking Protocol (ICP), a cryptographic tool enabling authentication without relying on computational intractability assumptions.

In this paper, we investigate the feasibility of implementing Identity Commitment Protocols (ICP) within a Verifiable Secret Sharing (VSS) framework on the Arduino

Uno—one of the smallest and most resource-limited microcontrollers available. Due to its stringent computational and memory constraints, using the Uno serves as somewhat of an extreme benchmark for assessing practical deployment in lightweight IoT environments. For each critical component of the protocol, defined in Sect. 4, execution time was measured using the ***millis()*** function, which leverages the Arduino's hardware timer interrupt mechanism [17]. These timing metrics were then used to estimate energy consumption, offering insights into the real-world cost of cryptographic security on low-power devices. In addition to performance profiling, the study highlights the limitations imposed by the Uno's limited memory, which affected the feasibility of certain cryptographic operations. Together, our results assess whether ICP-based VSS can be effectively adapted to such constrained environments, or whether further optimization is necessary to enable secure communication on ultra-low-power hardware.

3 Information Checking Protocol (ICP)

Rabin's VSS protocol utilizes two sub-protocols [16]:

1) **ICP**: Information Checking Protocol
2) **WSS**: Weak Secret Sharing

In this paper, the focus is on the Information Checking Protocol (ICP). The Information Checking protocol consists of three actors: the dealer (D), the intermediary (I), and the recipient (R).

To achieve an error probability of at most $1/2^k$, set $k = 128$. This is also the value of k used within the ICP protocol.

Additionally, the ICP protocol operates under the assumption that a sufficiently large prime number has been chosen for all computations, such that $p > 2^k$. The generation of such prime numbers was also tested using the Arduino Uno.

The Information Checking Protocol and the steps performed by each actor (D, I, and R) in it are outlined below:

Dealer (D)

1) Chooses 2 k values $b \neq 0$ and 2 k values y, both in Z_p.
2) Calculates $c = s + by$ for each of the 2 k b and y.
3) Transmits 2 k pairs (s, y) to I.
4) Transmits 2 k pairs (b, c) to R.

Intermediary (I)

1) Receives 2 k pairs (s, y) from D.
2) Transmits 2 k pairs (s, y) to R.
3) Selects k distinct random indices from the range $[1, 2\,k]$.
4) Requests R to reveal the check vectors (b, c) corresponding to the selected indices.

5) For each revealed check vector, verifies whether $s + by == c$. If all k vectors satisfy this condition, I confirms that R will accept secret s. Otherwise, I determines that R will reject s.

Recipient (*R*)

1) Receives the 2 k pairs (b_1, c_1), ..., (b_{2k}, c_{2k}) from D.
2) Receives the 2 k pairs (s, y_1), ..., (s, y_{2k}) from I.
3) For the unrevealed check vectors, verifies whether $s + by == c$. If any fail this check, R rejects s; otherwise, R accepts s.

4 Arduino Feasibility and Performance Testing Methodology

The ICP protocol was tested on the Arduino Uno, in addition to testing prime number generation. For the ICP, recall that it consists of three actors: the dealer (D), the intermediary (I), and the recipient (R). The Arduino was used to represent each of these actors in turn, and its performance was investigated for the actions performed in each role. The specifics are outlined below.

For each role, the following were tested:

Dealer (*D*)

1) Choosing 2 k values of b and y as per the constraints described in Sect. 2.
2) Calculating c for each pair (b, y).
3) Transmitting the check vector pairs (s, y) and (b, c).

Intermediary (*I*)

1) Transmit 2 k pairs (s, y) to R: Unlike the transmission of (s, y) and (b, c) tested in the previous phase, here only 256 (s, y) pairs needed to be transmitted.
2) Selecting k indices as described in Sect. 2: Choosing indices follows the same process regardless of the size of the prime, secret, or other data. Therefore, a unified test was performed irrespective of bit size, but with multiple runs.
3) Checking if $s + by == c$ for the k indices selected: Unlike the generation of c tested in the previous phase—where each c was generated and sent without storing any previous values— here, there was a need to store the values of b, y, and c.

Recipient (*R*)

1) Checking if $s + by == c$ for remaining k indices (the ones not selected): Checking 128 times takes the same amount of time as for I, as the same device, architecture, code, and the same number and size of data were used. This step requires verifying c only

for those pairs that have not been revealed. We traverse the range [0, 256] linearly, skipping indices that were selected for checking. Since the indices are already sorted (because of the way they were stored upon selection), overhead from searching gets reduced.

For each of these components, execution time was recorded using the ***millis()*** function, which is based on the Arduino's hardware timer interrupt [17]. This information was then used to calculate energy consumption for each of the tested operations.

5 Implementation Environment

The Arduino Uno R3 board was used for this study. It is one of the smallest and least powerful boards available. Its technical specifications are detailed in the Table 1 [18].

Table 1. Arduino Uno specs.

Feature	Specs
CPU (Microcontroller)	ATmega328P
SRAM	2 KB
Flash Memory	32 KB
Serial I/O	USB-B
Connection	Serial

It can be seen that this Arduino board has extremely limited resources, with only 2 kilobytes of SRAM and 32 kilobytes of flash (non-volatile) memory. Additionally, we note from Table 1 that the board is severely restricted in terms of communication media as it does not support wireless connections, rather it only has Serial communication available. The features of this communication method have been briefly explained in Sect. 6.2 "*Transmission of Check Vector Pairs*".

6 Performance Analysis

This section presents the results of the tests conducted on the Arduino Uno R3. The code for all these tests was written in Arduino, an Arduino-specific variant of C++.

6.1 Prime Number Generation

To generate *n-bit* prime numbers on the Uno, the ***BigNumber*** library was used for large integer support (128-bits and above).

The process involved:

1) Generating a random BigNumber of the approximately desired length.
2) Finding the next prime number greater than or equal to the generated number

3) Using the Miller-Rabin test to verify primality.

For each bit size, 240 test runs were done. It was observed (see Table 2) that the prime number generation time varied significantly depending on the initial seed value, which is reflected in the high standard deviation. Given this variation, the median time was calculated, as it is a more robust statistic and is not affected by extreme outliers. To maintain consistency, we have continued displaying the median in all subsequent measurements, providing a more reliable overview of resource consumption during ICP execution.

Table 2. Time taken (in ms) to generate prime numbers.

No. of Bits	Mean	Median	Std Dev
32	3050.41	2343	1561.70
64	23644.06	19105	13066.01
128	263865.44	191749	174809.89
152	623644.17	436752	435591.10

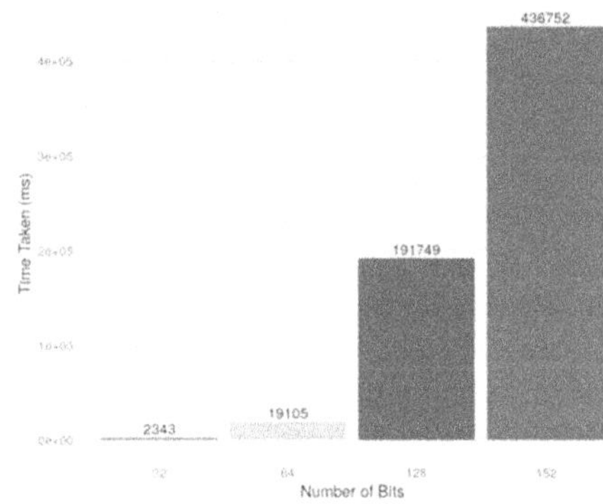

Fig. 1. Time taken (in ms) to generate prime numbers.

From Fig. 1, it is evident that as the bit size increases, the time to generate a prime number grows rapidly— almost by an order of magnitude (10^1) per step. For larger bit sizes, prime generation could take several minutes, with the median time for generating a 152-bit prime reaching approximately 7 min. This indicates that frequent generation of primes of such large sizes may be impractical on the Arduino Uno.

Additionally, the Arduino Uno R3 was unable to consistently generate primes larger than 152 bits. For primes greater than 152 bits, the processing time occasionally exceeded 2,000,000 ms, at which point the calculation was manually aborted.

Recall that the ICP and VSS protocols require a prime number $p > 2^k$ (i.e., $>2^{128}$). A prime of this size requires at least 129 bits for correct representation. This limitation significantly restricts the ability of the Arduino Uno to generate and efficiently handle sufficiently large primes for use in these protocols.

For the remainder of this paper, we include computations with numbers of sizes >152-bits by using predefined prime-numbers (externally generated and hard coded) of the required sizes. This is also a practice that may be used in real-world situations.

6.2 Arduino Acting as Dealer *D*

1. *Generation of 2 k b and y for a Given Prime Number*: 256 (= 2 k) values of b and y were generated for given primes of sizes 64, 128, 256, and 512 bits, within the constraints outlined in the description of ICP in Sect. 3.

Table 3. Time taken (in ms) to generate 256 b and 256 y

Bit Size of Prime Number	Mean	Median	Std Dev
64	3635.86	3673	89.54
128	9143.74	9136	45.95
256	24810.25	24884	183.77

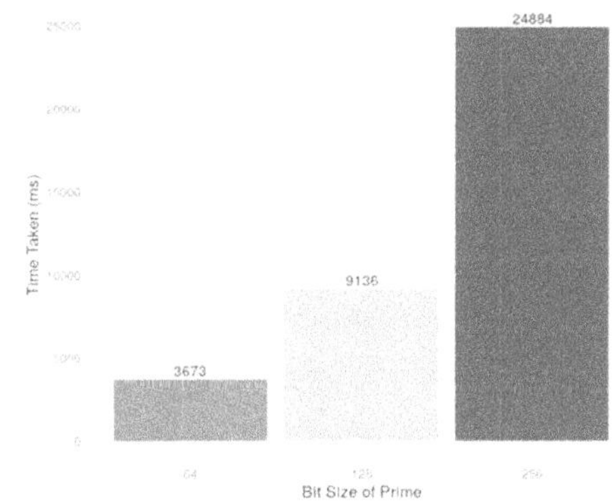

Fig. 2. Time taken (in ms) to generate 256 b and 256 y

As seen in Table 3, the generation of the 256 values for b and y was not overly time-consuming. Even though the time consumption increased with increasing bit sizes (Fig. 2), overall the times remain relatively modest across all tested bit sizes.

However, it is important to note that these values were not stored. Instead, they were generated and immediately overwritten. This approach suffices at this stage, but for later stages of the ICP protocol, storage becomes necessary. Specifically, at least one b and one y need to be stored at any given time, and any memory limitations will be explored during those phases.

At this stage, it was also observed that for 512-bit primes, memory constraints on the Arduino Uno prevented the computations required to generate 256 b and y as the Uno was unable to handle all the transient data generated during these calculations. This limitation hindered the Uno's ability to efficiently handle 512-bit primes (including externally generated ones) for use in the VSS protocol. But for primes of sizes like 256 bits, which are >152 bits and <512 bits, it is possible to generate the prime externally and then provide it to the Arduino. The Arduino can then take over and handle the generation and calculation of the check vectors.

2. *Calculating* c: For a given secret s (of size approximately = size of $(b \cdot y)$), c was computed as $c = s +$ by for each of the 256 pairs of b and y. The calculation of c was very fast across all tested bit sizes, as shown by the mean, median, and standard deviation values in Table 4.

Table 4. Time taken (in ms) to calculate c for 256 b, y.

Bit Size of Prime Number	Mean	Median	Std Dev
64	413.26	413	11.93
128	1102.28	1099.5	18.33
256	3549.31	3548	9.17

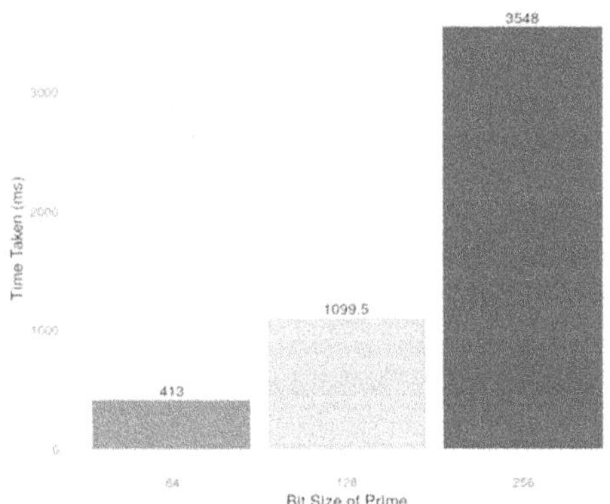

Fig. 3. Time taken (in ms) to calculate c for 256 b, y

For the 64-bit prime, the time taken to compute c averaged around 413 ms, with a small standard deviation of 11.93 ms, indicating consistent performance. Similarly, for 128-bit primes, the mean time was 1102.28 ms, and the performance remained fairly consistent with a standard deviation of 18.33 ms. For the 256-bit primes, the time taken grew to an average of 3549.31 ms, but the standard deviation remained relatively low at

9.17 ms, again indicating stable performance despite the increase in bit size. Figure 3 shows the increase in calculation time as the size of the prime increases. The time-taken seems to increase exponentially, possibly because of the large size of the values involved in the calculations as well as the often greater number of values to be checked. Despite this increase, the computation time for calculating c remains relatively low even for the largest tested prime size (256bits).

However, it is important to note that *c* must be stored alongside *b* and *y* for subsequent phases of the ICP protocol. As the prime size increases, so too does the number of values to be stored, placing additional demands on the Arduino's memory capacity. This factor must be considered when scaling up the protocol to handle larger primes.

3. *Transmission of Check Vector Pairs (s, y)* and *(b, c)*: The 256 check vector pairs *(s, y)* and *(b, c)* were transmitted via serial communication. Serial ports are used to physically connect asynchronous devices to a computer, enabling the transfer of data in a sequential format, where bits are transmitted one after the other in a series [19]. As mentioned in 1, the Arduino board tested here facilitates serial communication using the UART protocol [20], a simple, low-cost and easy to implement serial communication protocol that can be used to send data between an Arduino board and other devices [20].

Table 5. Time taken (in ms) to transmit 256 pairs of *(s, y)* and *(b, c)*

Bit Size of Prime Number	Mean	Median	Std Dev
64	27537.88	27571.5	122.10
128	52298.85	52291	152.34
256	101355.9091	101540	534.4533

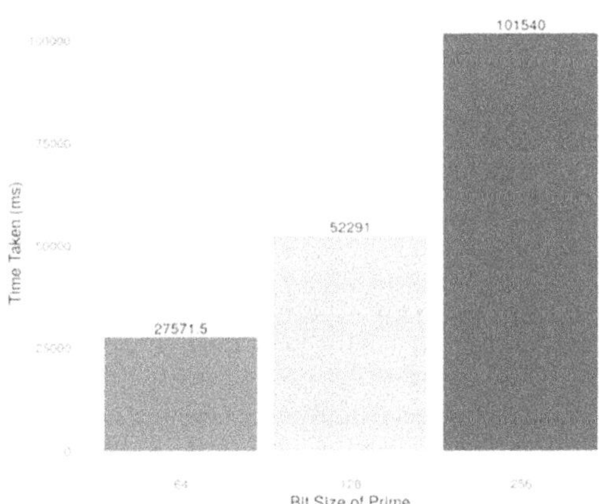

Fig. 4. Time taken (in ms) to transmit 256 Pairs of (*s, y*) and (*b, c*)

It is observed in Table 5 that the transmission time is largely dependent on the size of the data being sent. For 64-bit primes, transmitting all 256 check vector pairs took approximately 27.5 s, whereas for 128-bit and 256-bit primes, the time increased to 52.3 s and101.3 s, respectively. The near-linear growth in transmission time seen in Fig. 4 aligns with the increasing bit size of the data being communicated.

Given that the secret s remains constant across all 256 check vectors in a transmission sequence, a potential optimization could be sending s once, followed by the 256 values of y, instead of redundantly transmitting 256 pairs of (s, y). This would effectively cut the transmission size by nearly (for the (s, y) pairs, reducing both time and resource consumption.

6.3 Arduino Acting as Intermediary *I*

1. *Transmission of Pairs (s, y)*: The 256 check vector pairs (s, y) were transmitted via Serial communication from the intermediary I. The transmission time is primarily dependent on the size of the transmitted data.

Table 6. Time taken (in ms) to transmit 256 pairs of (s, y)

Bit Size of Prime Number	Mean	Median	Std Dev
64	12380.67857	12380	5.25
128	22181.32143	22182	6.2083
256	38362.10714	38347	37.0833

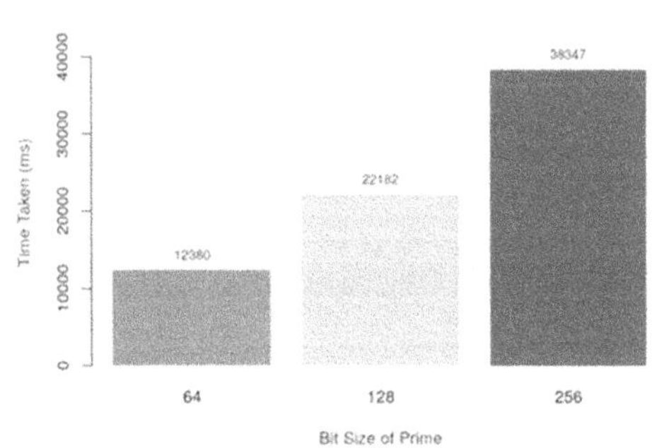

Fig. 5. Time taken (in ms) to transmit 256 pairs of (s, y)

The transmission time increases steadily with the bit size of the prime, as seen in Table 6 and Fig. 5. For 64-bit primes, the process takes 12.4 s, whereas for 128-bit and 256-bit primes, the transmission time nearly doubles and triples, respectively. The low standard deviation indicates that the transmission times remain stable across multiple runs, suggesting minimal external interference or buffering issues.

As previously noted, since the secret s remains constant for all check vectors, a more efficient approach would be to transmit s once and then send only the 256 values of y.

2. *Selecting k Random Unique Indices:* The process used for selecting k distinct random indices was as follows in Fig. 6:

Table 7. Time taken (in ms) to select k random distinct indices.

Bit Size of Prime Number	Mean	Median	Std Dev
ANY	24	24	0

As shown in Table 7, the time taken for selecting k random indices was consistently 24 ms, with no variation observed across multiple runs. This indicates that the operation is both stable and computationally efficient, imposing minimal overhead in the overall protocol.

```
FOR j FROM 0 TO 127 DO
    SET seed TO j + 1000
    INITIALIZE random number generator
    with seed
    SET temp TO random number between
    0 and 255

    SET exists TO false
    FOR k FROM 0 TO n - 1 DO
        IF ind[k] == temp THEN
            SET exists TO true
            DECREMENT j
            BREAK
        END IF
    END FOR

    // Find correct position and shift
    //elements
    SET i TO n - 1
    WHILE i >= 0 AND ind[i] > temp DO
        SET ind[i + 1] TO ind[i]
        // Shift elements to the right
        DECREMENT i
    END WHILE
    SET ind[i + 1] TO temp
    // Insert the value in the correct
    //position
    INCREMENT n
    // Increase the number of elements
END FOR
```

Fig. 6. Pseudocode for selecting k distinct random indices.

3. *Checking c for k b and y in I:* For a given secret s (with a size approximately equal to that of $(b \cdot y)$), the value c was computed as $c = s + by$ for each of the 128 pairs of b and y.

Initially, the thought was to store these values in an array. However, since *BigNumber* does not support arrays directly, the common practice is to store them as strings and create an array of those. The first attempt was made by using the '*String*'type, but this approach consumed too much dynamic memory, even for *b* and *y* values of 64 bits.

```
Sketch uses 24658 bytes (76%) of program storage space. Maximum is 32256 bytes.
Global variables use 13874 bytes (677%) of dynamic memory, leaving -11826 bytes
Not enough memory; see https://support.arduino.cc/hc/en-us/articles/36001382517
data section exceeds available space in board

Compilation error: data section exceeds available space in board
```

Fig. 7. Memory exhausted when using strings.

As shown in Fig. 7, using '*String*'resulted in 13,874 bytes of dynamic memory usage, while the Arduino only has 2,048 bytes available.

To overcome this, each *BigNumber* was stored as a character array instead, as character arrays have much less overhead than '*String*'objects. Additionally, the '*PROGMEM*'technique [21], which stores these character arrays in program memory rather than dynamic memory, was applied. This is advantageous because the Arduino has much more program memory available (32,256 bytes) compared to SRAM (2,048 bytes).

With this adjustment, it became possible to handle 64-bit numbers effectively. However, when testing with 128-bit numbers, a memory limitation again was encountered again. Despite using the second method, storing 128 *b*, *y*, and *c* values (with *b* and *y* of 128 bits each) along with the program code required 34,804 bytes of memory. This exceeds the available program memory of 32,256 bytes (Fig. 8).

Note also, that in both the methods tried previously, *s* was stored only once as a space saving measure, since it is the same for all values of *b*, *y* and *c*.

```
Sketch uses 34804 bytes (107%) of program storage space. Maximum is 32256 bytes.
Global variables use 644 bytes (31%) of dynamic memory, leaving 1404 bytes for local var
Sketch too big; see https://support.arduino.cc/hc/en-us/articles/360013825179 for tips o
text section exceeds available space in board

Compilation error: text section exceeds available space in board
```

Fig. 8. Program memory exhausted with method 2 for 128-bit numbers.

The results of the timing measurements for checking *c* are shown in Table 8 below. We observe that the checking was quite fast, taking only ~270 ms or ~3 s.

Note: Optimizations have not been explored yet. One option is the use of *F() macro.* In general, for IoT applications, a more powerful board with internet capabilities (e.g., ATmega 2560 or Raspberry Pi) would be more suitable, as these boards have more memory and processing power [22, 23].

Table 8. Time taken (in ms) to check c for 128 b, y

Bit Size of Prime Number	Mean	Median	Std Dev
64	270.7931	269	2.6531
128	–	–	–
256	–	–	–

Overall, checking c was relatively quick, with little time taken for 64-bit primes. However, as the size of the primes increases, the memory limitations become more apparent, and handling larger bit sizes may require more capable hardware.

6.4 Arduino Acting as Recipient *R*

1. *Checking c for k b and y in R*: The same setup and code were used for this as for the intermediary I. The main difference is that R stores 256 b, y, and c values, as compared to the 128 b and c values stored by I. This increased storage requirement implies that calculations that were previously not possible for I are also not feasible for R. For R, only the c belonging to pairs (b, c) that have not been selected by I for verification need to be checked. This was achieved using the condition:

$$if\ (ind[j] == i)\ \{j++;\ continue;\ \}$$

This approach ensures that only the relevant pairs are checked.

Table 9. Time taken (in ms) to check c for 128 b, y

Bit Size of Prime Number	Mean	Median	Std Dev
64	278	278	0
128	–	–	–
256	–	–	–

It was observed that the time required for the checking was minimal (Table 9). The timing is almost identical to the previous section (Table 8), with a slight increase caused by the additional step of checking the indices of the pairs. This extra checking of indices was necessary to ensure that only the relevant pairs of (b, c) that had not been sent to I were processed.

The minimal increase in time is in line with expectations, as the added step of checking indices introduces a small overhead, but the overall computational complexity remains low for 64-bit primes. Larger primes were not tested due to the memory limitations previously discussed in Sect. 6.3.

6.5 Energy Consumption

The energy consumption for each component was calculated using the formula:

$$E = V \cdot I \cdot n \cdot \tau$$

where:

- V is the voltage (5 V for the Arduino Uno R3),
- I is the current (20 mA for the Arduino Uno R3) [24],
- n is the number of operations, and
- τ is the time taken for each operation.

Since time taken for each component has already been measured, energy can be simplified to:

$$E = V \cdot I \cdot t$$

where t is the time taken for the operations.

The energy consumption was calculated using the median execution times for each component and bit size, with the values shown in Table 10:

Unsurprisingly, the energy consumption across different components of the system is influenced primarily by the size of the data being processed and transmitted as larger bit sizes require more time to process and transmit data, which directly translates to higher energy consumption.

Table 10 also shows that the generation of primes and the transmission of data are the two most expensive operations. In fact, prime generation also shows one of the most drastic increases in energy consumption with increasing bit-size, from 1.91 J for 64-bit primes to 19.17 for 128-bit primes. The transmission process, whether originating from D (see Fig. 9) or from I, is likewise energy intensive. In this study, Serial communication was, but in practice some form of wireless communication is quite likely to be used [25], and that is generally more expensive than the Serial communication method used here [26].

Another relatively expensive operation is the calculation of c when Arduino is acting as dealer D. It can be seen in Table 10 that as the bit-size of operands increases, energy consumption increases quite a lot. Other operations, such as generating b and y, selecting k random indices etc., do not require much energy in comparison to the two most expensive actions (all <0.5 J).

Overall, with larger bit-sizes being used for computation and transmission, the combined energy consumption for each role (D, I, or R) grows. Considering that prime number generation can be outsourced or performed infrequently, in general, transmission emerges as the most expensive operation in terms of energy consumption, followed by operations that involve larger bit sizes like calculation of c. Optimizing calculations and memory handling could lead to substantial power savings, particularly when working with large data sets. Furthermore, using more powerful microcontrollers (e.g., ATmega2560 [23] or Raspberry Pi [22]) could allow for handling larger bit sizes more efficiently, improving execution time and reducing energy consumption per operation.

Table 10. Energy consumption for various components at different bit sizes.

Component D	Bit Size	Energy (J)
b and y Gen.	64	0.04
	128	0.11
	256	0.35
Calc. c	64	0.37
	128	0.91
	256	2.49
Transmission	64	2.76
	128	5.23
	256	10.15
Component I		
Transmission from I to R	64	1.24
	128	2.22
	256	3.84
Selecting k indices	Any	0.0024
Checking 128 c in I	64	0.027
Component R		
Checking 128 c in R	64	0.028
General		
Prime Number Gen.	32	0.23
	64	1.91
	128	19.17

Putting this in practical terms of battery life, consider a 6 V battery. (Arduino ideally requires a 7-12 V supply if powered via DC, but it can function with 6 V as well.) For a lightweight 6 V battery, capacity commonly ranges from 1000–2000mAh [27]. For these calculations, consider a battery with a capacity of 1400mAh such as a Duracell DL 233 CR-P2. Converting this to Wh using the formula $Capacity(mAh) \times Voltage(V)/1000$ gives a battery capacity of 8.4 Wh.

Now, consider the Arduino's combined energy consumption for a role and include all operations of that role. For cases where multiple bit-sizes have been tested, only the most expensive for each operation will be considered.

As can be seen from Table 10, the most energy is consumed when the Arduino acts as the dealer D, making it a good candidate case for the upcoming calculations. Thus, considering the case when Arduino acts a D. Here, the main operations are:

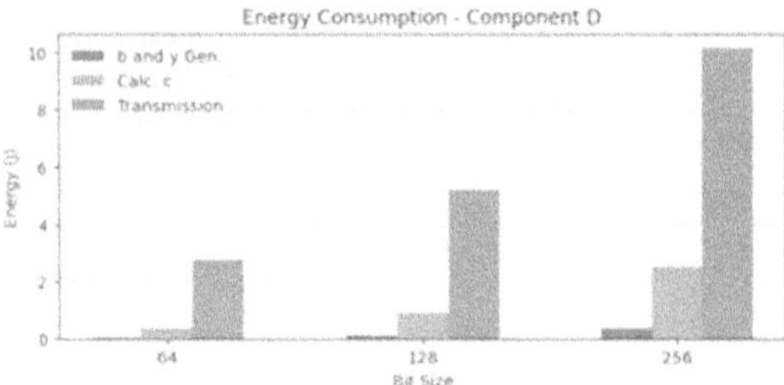

Fig. 9. Energy usage comparison of Arduino as D

1) **Generation of** b **and** y which consumes $0.35\ J$ in $25\ s$. This can be converted to Power consumed using the formula:

$$Power(P) = Energy(E)/Time(T)$$

i.e., $P = 0.35/25 = 0.014\ W$.
2) **Calculating** c which consumes $2.49\ J$ in $4\ s$, giving power usage equal to $0.6225\ W$.
3) **Transmitting check vector pairs** which consumes $10.15\ J$ in $101\ s$, giving a power consumption of $0.1005\ W$.

Thus, for dealer D, power consumption comes out to be $0.737\ W$.

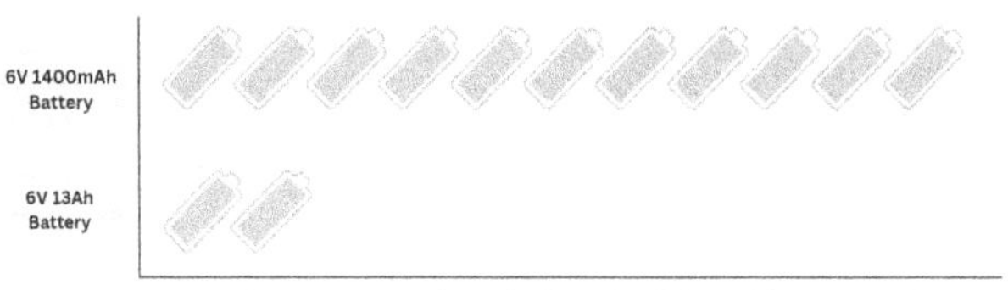

Fig. 10. Battery consumption of Arduino acting as dealer D over 5 days

Battery life can now be calculated using the formula:

$$BatteryLife(h) = BatteryCapacity(Wh)/P_{total}(W)$$

The result is an approximate battery life of 11.4 h i.e., when Arduino is acting as Dealer D, a 6 V 1400mAh battery will require replacement every 11 h or so. However, if the use case allows for a larger, more powerful battery such as a 13 Ah Duracell LA battery [28], it would require much more infrequent replacement. Specifically, the capacity for such a battery would be 78 Wh, giving a battery life of 105.8 h for use with Arduino as D. In other words, such a battery would require replacement approximately every 4 days.

In other words, for every 5 days of operating the Arduino Uno as dealer D, a 1400mAh battery will require replacement 10 times and a 13 Ah will require replacement once (see Fig. 10).

7 Conclusion

This study evaluated the performance of the Arduino Uno R3 while executing critical components of the Information Checking Protocol (ICP) from Rabin's implementation of the VSS [16]. Through extensive timing and energy measurements across multiple bit sizes (64, 128, and 256 bits), we derived a comprehensive understanding of the limitations and capabilities of the Arduino in the roles of Dealer (D), Intermediary (I), and Recipient (R). Our findings indicate that while the Arduino performs consistently and reliably for 64-bit operations, scalability becomes a challenge with increasing bit sizes. Notably, the Arduino ran out of memory when attempting to generate large primes or attempting to store multiple 128-bit and 256-bit values and perform operations on them.

From a performance standpoint, execution times for key operations (except prime-number generation) remained stable across repeated trials. However, the transmission of check vectors and generation of primes proved to be the most power-hungry operations. When the Arduino acts as the dealer, a 6 V 1400mAh battery can continuously sustain such operations for about 11.4 h. Larger batteries, such as a 13 Ah unit, can extend operational time to 105.8 h, supporting multi-day deployments. These findings highlight the importance of power-aware protocol design in low-power IoT environments.

In light of these observations, we conclude that while there are a few options, such as aggressively optimizing memory usage, reducing transmission overhead by avoiding redundant data, choosing to use small primes while making concessions on the security of the protocol etc. for implementing ICP in a severely limited device like Arduino Uno, a complete, highly secure implementation requires the use of better, more powerful hardware.

References

1. Alam, T.: A reliable communication framework and its use in internet of things (IoT). Int. J. Sci. Res. Comput. Sci. Eng. Informat. Technol. **05**, 3 (2018)
2. Technologies D: Internet of things and data placement. https://infohub.delltechnologies.com/en-us/l/edge-to-core-and-the-internet-of-things-2/internet-of-things-and-data-placement/
3. Analytics I: Number of connected iot devices worldwide. https://iot-analytics.com/number-connected-iot-devices/
4. Statista: Internet of things (iot). https://www.statista.com/topics/2637/internet-of-things/#topicOverview
5. SoluLab: Iot: The future of innovation technology. https://www.solulab.com/iot-the-future-of-innovation-technology/
6. TrustCloud: Data privacy in the age of iot: securing connected devices in 2024 (2024). https://community.trustcloud.ai/docs/grc-launchpad/grc-101/governance/data-privacy-in-the-age-of-iot-securing-connected-devices-in-2024/
7. Simmons-Simmons: Technotes – top 10 security and privacy issues within the iot. https://www.simmons-simmons.com/en/publications/ckmx5qvys13hb0910ags2nx7o/technotes-top-10-security-and-privacy-issues-within-the-iot
8. Sonmez, M.T, McKay, K., Chang, D., Kang, J., Kelsey J.: Ascon-based lightweight cryptography standards for constrained de-vices. NIST Special Publication 800 NIST SP 800 232 ipd (2023). https://nvlpubs.nist.gov/nistpubs/SpecialPublications/NIST.SP.800-232.ipd.pdf

9. Knudsen LR, Peyrin T, Sasaki Y.: Can lwc and pec be friends? https://csrc.nist.gov/CSRC/media/Events/lightweight-cryptography-workshop-2020/documents/papers/can-lwc-pec-be-friends-lwc2020.pdf, 2020. Paper presented at the NIST Lightweight Cryptography Workshop (2020)
10. NIST: Fostering Standards for Privacy-Enhancing Cryptography (Pec). https://csrc.nist.gov/csrc/media/Presentations/2022/fostering-standards-for-pec/images-media/20220519-PET-Summit-Boston%2D%2DFostering-Standards-PEC%2D%2DSlides-rev20220526.pdf. Presentation at the 2022 Privacy-Enhancing Technologies (PET) Summit, Boston (2022)
11. Goyal, H., Saha, S.: Multi-party computation in iot for privacy-preservation. In: 2022 IEEE 42nd International Conference on Distributed Computing Systems (ICDCS), pp. 1280–1281 (2022)
12. Evans, D., Kolesnikov, V., Rosulek, M.: A Pragmatic Introduction to Secure Multi-Party Computation. NOW Publishers, (2018). Online version: Apr. 15, (2020). [Online]. Available: https://www.cs.virginia.edu/~evans/pragmaticmpc/pragmaticmpc.pdf
13. Das, S., et al.: Verifiable secret sharing simplified. Cryptology ePrint Archive, Paper 2023/1196 (2023). https://eprint.iacr.org/2023/1196
14. Krenn, S., Lorunser, T.: Verifiable Secret Sharing, pp. 45–54. Springer International Publishing. ISBN 978-3-031-28161-7, Cham (2023). https://doi.org/10.1007/978-3-031-28161-7
15. Chor, B., Goldwasser, S., Micali, S., Awerbuch, B.: Verifiable secret sharing and achieving simultaneity in the presence of faults. In: 26th Annual Symposium on Foundations of Computer Science (sfcs 1985), vol. 1985, pp. 383–395 (1985)
16. Rabin, T., Ben-Or, M.: Verifiable secret sharing and multiparty protocols with honest majority. In: Proceedings of the Twenty-First Annual ACM Symposium on Theory of Computing STOC '89, pp. 73–85. Association for Computing Machinery. ISBN 0897913078, New York, NY, USA (1989). https://doi.org/10.1145/73007.73014
17. Electronics P: Millis() arduino function: 5+ things to consider (n.d.). https://www.programmingelectronics.com/millis-arduino/
18. Documentation A: Arduino uno rev3 technical specs (n.d.). https://docs.arduino.cc/hardware/uno-rev3/tech-specs
19. IBM: Serial communication. https://www.ibm.com/docs/en/aix/7.3?topic=communications-serial-communication
20. Siebeneicher, H.: Universal asynchronous receiver-transmitter (uart). https://docs.arduino.cc/learn/communication/uart/
21. Documentation A: Arduino progmem (n.d.). https://www.arduino.cc/reference/tr/language/variables/utilities/progmem/
22. Pounder, L.: Raspberry Pi vs Arduino: Which Board is Best? (2023). https://www.tomshardware.com/features/raspberry-pi-vs-arduino
23. Microchip Technology Inc.: ATmega2560–8-Bit AVR Microcontroller (2024). https://www.microchip.com/en-us/product/atmega2560
24. Forum A.: Power consumption discussion (2020). https://forum.arduino.cc/t/power-consumption/661308/5
25. Sinha, S.: State of iot 2024: Number of connected iot devices growing 13 (2024). https://iot-analytics.com/number-connected-iot-devices/#:~:text=Wi%2DFi
26. Kasslack, R.: Balancing wireless innovation with wired reliability (2024). https://www.securityindustry.org/2024/03/19/balancing-wireless-innovation-with-wired-reliability/#:~:text=Wired%20neworks%2C%20with%20their%20lower,the%20oveall%20energy%20efficiency%20of
27. Junction B.: 6v batteries. https://www.batteryjunction.com/batteries/6v?srsltid=AfmBOopsK3jNAak-9npp-QyuxOCgcOpxxLAgWeBvfXJ6GuWYSK2gurg

28. Uline: Duracell 6v lantern alkaline battery. https://www.uline.com/Product/Detail/S-17590/Batteries/Duracell-6V-Lantern-Alkaline-Battery?pricode=WB0943&gadtype=pla&id=S-17590&gadsource=1&gclid=Cj0KCQjw4cS-BhDGARIsABg4J1m7Ogc36pCQvLGdLbOkZskzePykjEcJmueOF6tOg9wg4LvT5ZpB1EaArMvEALw_wcB

Formal Security Verification of Messaging Layer Security Protocol Using ProVerif

Takehiko Mieno[1](✉), Hiroyuki Okazaki[2], Kenichi Arai[3], and Yuichi Futa[4]

[1] Graduate School of Medicine, Science and Technology, Shinshu University, EPSON AVASYS Corp., 1077–5, Shimonogo Otsu, Ueda City, Nagano 386–1214, Japan
mieno.takehiko2@exc.epson.co.jp

[2] Shinshu University, Graduate School of Science and Technology, Nagano City, Japan
okazaki@cs.shinshu-u.ac.jp

[3] Nagasaki University, Graduate School of Integrated Science and Technology, Nagasaki City, Japan
k-arai@nagasaki-u.ac.jp

[4] Tokyo University of Technology, School of Computer Science, Hachioji City, Japan
futayi@stf.teu.ac.jp

Abstract. In recent years, the number of scenarios requiring secure communication between multiple users has increased, driven by factors such as the rise of remote work and the increased use of social networking services. As a result, many new cryptographic protocols have been developed. However, these protocols are often modified and employed without sufficient security verification. The aim of this study is to verify that the Messaging Layer Security (MLS) protocol, standardized as RFC 9420 in 2023, satisfies security requirements using ProVerif. The MLS protocol provides mechanisms to ensure message secrecy, message integrity, and sender authentication. In this study, we verify the soundness of a formalized MLS model and evaluate its compliance with security requirements. The model is based on the Ratchet Tree structure, which is the core technology of MLS. Although MLS provides both forward and backward secrecy, we focus on the latter, particularly in the case of secret key leakage. Our results demonstrate that the formalized model meets MLS security requirements.

Keywords: Cryptographic protocol · Formal verification · Messaging Layer Security · Public-key cryptography · ProVerif

1 Introduction

1.1 Background

There has been an increasing number of studies evaluating the effectiveness of formal methods for analyzing and verifying security protocols. Formal verification is important for ensuring the security of cryptographic protocols. Among the various automated tools for security verification for cryptographic protocols, the

K. Daimi et al. (Eds.): CSCE 2025, CCIS 2937, pp. 214–235, 2026.
https://doi.org/10.1007/978-3-032-22208-4_14

model checker ProVerif [1,2] is one of the most widely studied. ProVerif employs the Dolev–Yao model [3], a formal method that abstracts protocols as symbolic operational procedures, to evaluate the security of cryptographic protocols. It can be used to verify cryptographic properties such as secrecy [4], authentication [5], strong secrecy [6], weak secrecy [7], and observational equivalence [7].

Modern internet-based communication technology employs cryptographic protocols such as Transport Layer Security (TLS) to provide end-to-end data secrecy. Since its draft stage, TLS has been subjected to extensive formal verification using tools such as ProVerif [8] and the Tamarin prover [9]. The Messaging Layer Security (MLS) protocol [10] has also been formally verified. MLS is a relatively new cryptographic communication protocol designed to support secure communication between multiple users, enabling efficient group key updates and secure message transmission. It provides mechanisms for ensuring message secrecy, message integrity, and sender authentication. However, although the functional language F* [11] has been employed to formally verify the MLS protocol [12], no security verification using a model checker has been reported to date.

In this study, we employ ProVerif to verify that the MLS protocol, standardized as RFC 9420 in 2023, satisfies security requirements (Table 1). We present a formal model based on the Ratchet Tree structure (Sect. 2.2), which is the core technology of MLS. We verify the soundness of this model and evaluate whether it satisfies security requirements. While MLS is designed to ensure both forward and backward secrecy.

1.2 Contributions

The main contributions of this study are described below. We focus on backward secrecy in this study, particularly in the case of secret key leakage. Our results demonstrate that the proposed formalized model meets MLS security requirements. In accordance with the MLS specification defined in RFC 9420, we formalized the following three models based on the Ratchet Tree structure:

1. Normal flow model: a model for sending and receiving basic MLS messages (Sect. 3.1)
2. Group leave flow model: a model for scenarios in which a member leaves the group during an active session (Sect. 3.2)
3. Secret key leakage flow model: a model for scenarios in which an active member accidentally leaks a secret key shared with the group (Sect. 3.3)

We verified the soundness of these models and evaluated whether they meet the security requirements of the MLS protocol (Table 1). The ProVerif output demonstrates that the secrecy of the message and backward secrecy in the case of secret key leakage are preserved. In other words, the results enhance the reliability of the security verification. A detailed explanation of these models is provided in Sect. 3. MLS is an end-to-end encrypted communication protocol that ensures data secrecy, in particular, forward and backward secrecy. In this study, we verify backward secrecy, particularly in the case of secret key leakage, and demonstrate that the formalized model meets MLS security requirements.

Table 1. Messaging Layer Security (MLS) security requirements and verification results.

Security requirements	Verification results
Message secrecy in normal flow	No attacks detected
Message secrecy for departed group members	No attacks detected
Backward secrecy under private key leakage	No attacks detected
Resistance to attacker-created messages (sender authentication)	Rejected by protocol

1.3 Related Work

Advances in cryptography have led to various automated verification tools [13]. For example, ProVerif enables the verification of numerous advanced cryptographic protocols, such as TLS 1.3 [8], web services security [14], electronic voting systems [15], and the Merkle tree structure employed in blockchain systems [16]. Ongoing research has also explored the formal verification of various cryptographic protocols, such as cryptographic hash functions [17,18].

One of the most notable studies in the formal verification of MLS was conducted by Bhargavan et al. [12], who verified the security of MLS using the F* [11] functional language. They defined a formal framework for group messaging in F* and compared the security and performance of several candidate MLS protocols up to Draft 7. In addition, they presented a formal security proof of TreeKEM with blanking (TreeKEMB), the group key establishment protocol introduced in MLS Draft 7. Their verification discovered a previously unknown attack, for which a verified fix has been incorporated into the current MLS version.

Alwen et al. [19] observed that forward secrecy [20] in TreeKEMB could be improved by employing an updatable public-key cryptosystem. In addition, Cremers et al. [21] focused on improving post-compromise security in TreeKEMB, and an extension of TreeKEMB is under discussion in the MLS working group. As a result, Bhargavan et al. have stated that they plan to extend their verification model. Furthermore, Rösler et al. [22] have reported several weaknesses in the implementation of group chats in popular messaging applications, indicating the need for strict analysis.

2 Preliminaries

2.1 Overview of MLS

MLS is an end-to-end encrypted communication protocol that ensures data confidentiality. It employs a key management algorithm based on a Ratchet Tree structure (Sect. 2.2), which enables rapid updating of encryption keys shared by multiple users. Due to these features, MLS has attracted considerable attention as a cryptographic communication protocol for applications with a large number of users, such as group chats. In addition, MLS also ensures forward and backward secrecy. The MLS protocol [10] was standardized as RFC 9420 in 2023.

2.2 Ratchet Tree Structure and Key Schedule

A Ratchet Tree is a data structure used to determine the structure of a group in MLS. It is a binary tree in which leaves represent members. Each node in the tree possesses a pair of secret and public keys for hybrid public-key encryption [23]. The secret key can only be accessed by members in the subtree rooted at that node. When a new member joins the group, a new leaf node is added. Conversely, when a member leaves the group, the corresponding leaf node is deleted. All members update the key information of the tree whenever the tree structure changes or at any time they wish.

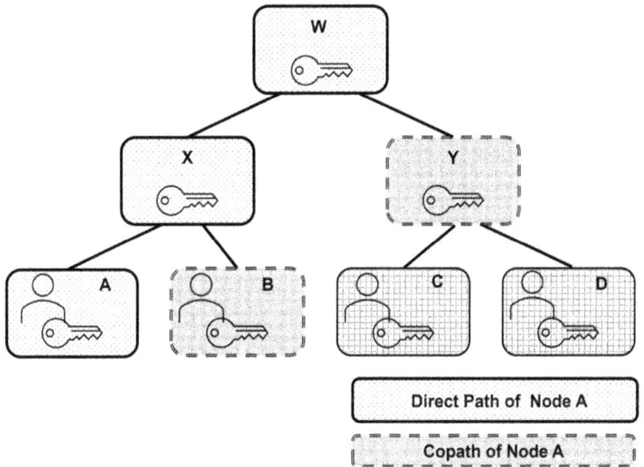

Fig. 1. Direct path and copath in a Ratchet Tree.

In this paper, we define the direct path and copath in a Ratchet Tree, as illustrated in Fig. 1. The direct path from a given leaf node refers to the set of all nodes on the path from that node to the root node. The copath refers to the set of sibling nodes (i.e., nodes at the same level that are different from the given node) of all nodes on the direct path, excluding the root node.

In MLS, the keys used within a group are generated by the `Key Schedule` (Fig. 2) and then updated. The `Key Schedule` employs a concept called an epoch. Whenever a group member changes or a `Commit message` is sent to update the key, the `Key Schedule` advances to the next epoch. Each `epoch_secret` is only accessible to group members who are active during that epoch. By obtaining the most recent `commit_secret`, it is possible to advance (members can obtain) to the next `epoch_secret`. By obtaining the most recent `commit_secret`, it becomes possible for members to obtain the next `epoch_secret`. The derivation of `epoch_secret`

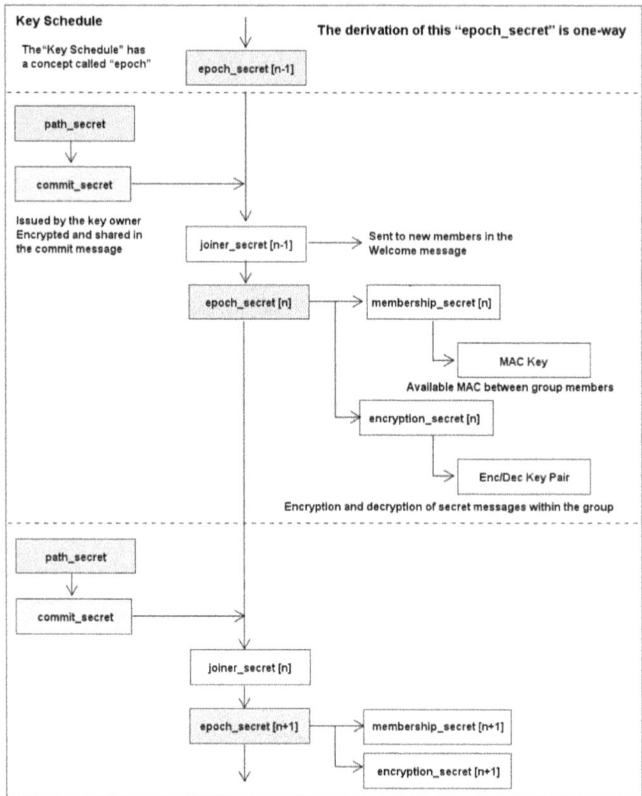

Fig. 2. Key Schedule: one-way derivation of epoch_secret.

is one-way, signifying that it is not possible to obtain information by returning to a previous `epoch_secret`. From each `epoch_secret`, secret information necessary to exchange messages within the group can be generated. Specifically, `membership_secret` is used to generate a shared MAC key that authenticates public messages, ensuring that they were sent by legitimate group members. In addition, `encryption_secret` generates shared keys for encrypting secret messages between members. Furthermore, `joiner_secret` is generated during the transition from one `epoch_secret` to the next and (during epoch transitions) is included in the `Welcome message` sent to new members participating in the next epoch.

3 Verification Model

In this section, we present three flow models that are based on the Ratchet Tree structure and follow the MLS specification. These models constitute our proposed formal model of MLS. We describe these models in detail using sequence diagrams and formalized code. The sequence diagrams (Fig. 3, 6, 7) represent each client process as an actor. Each actor is active during the period when its lifeline is active, indicating its status as an active group member. In addition, due to its complexity, the entire flow is divided into several stages.

3.1 Normal Flow Model

Normal flow starts when the client creates a group. This flow is modeled from group creation to the point at which three group members send and receive messages (Fig. 3). In this flow, the client Alice creates a group and invites clients Bob and Charlie. Thereafter, Charlie sends a secret message to Alice and Bob.

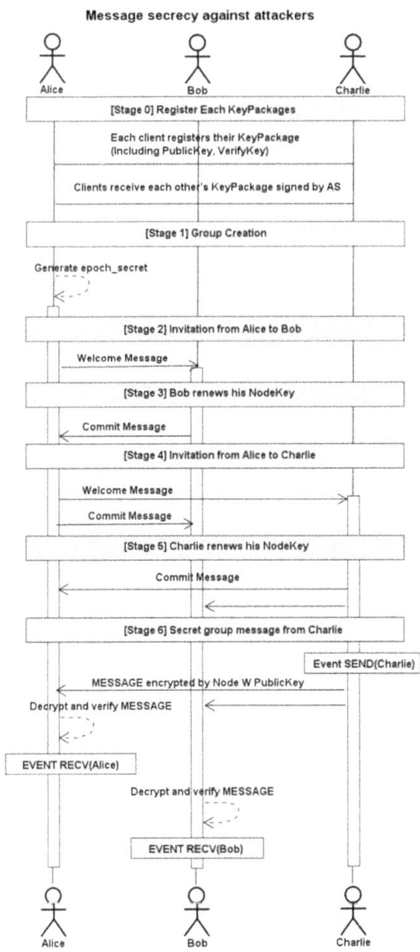

Fig. 3. Sequence diagram of normal flow: message secrecy against attackers.

In Stage 0, each client obtains a public key and signature verification key signed by an authentication service. The authentication service of the main process generates a key pair in the formalized model. Subsequently, the secret key and signing key are sent to each client, and the corresponding public key and signature verification key are signed and published.

Normal Flow Model: Stages 1-3 Figure 4 illustrates the changes in the Ratchet Tree structure from Stage 1 to Stage 3.

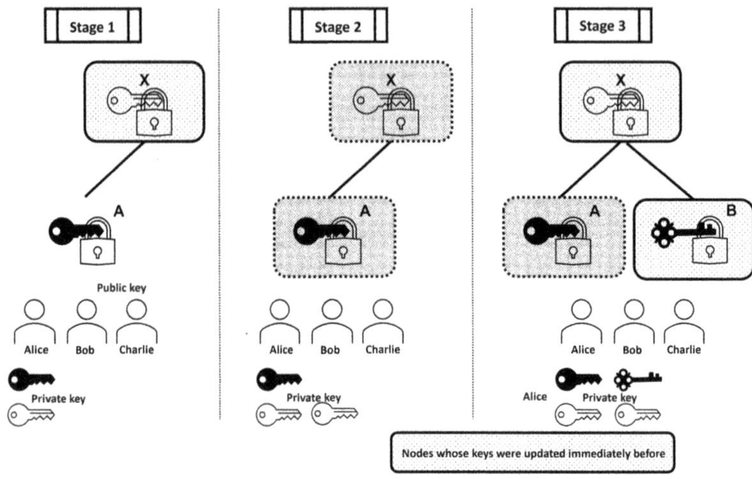

Fig. 4. Changes in Ratchet Tree structure from Stage 1 to Stage 3.

Code 1 formalizes the normal flow model for Stages 1–3. All verification code employed in this study is available on GitHub [24].

```
(* Code 1: Normal model for sending and receiving basic MLS messages. Stages 1--3 *)
2                               :
3                          (omitted)
                                :
122 let Alice(mysignkey:Signkey, mykpgSkey:Skey, ASVerifyKey:Verifykey) =
123     (* Stage 1: Group Creation *)
124     new epoch_secret_0:Secret;
125     new path_secret_a:Secret;
126     let myskey = GenSkey(path_secret_a) in
127     let mypkey = GenPkey(myskey) in
128     let path_secret_x = DeriveNextPathSecret(path_secret_a) in
129     let commit_secret = DeriveNextPathSecret(path_secret_x) in
130     let joiner_secret_0 = DeriveJoinerSecret(epoch_secret_0, commit_secret) in
131
132     (* Stage 2: Invitation from Alice to Bob *)
133     in(PublicCh, (BobkpgPkey:Pkey, BobkpgVerifyKey:Verifykey, BobkpgSign:Signature));
134     let BobkpgTBS = KPGTBS(BobkpgPkey, BobkpgVerifyKey) in
135     if(Verify(ASVerifyKey, BobkpgSign, BobkpgTBS)) then
136     (
137             (* Send a welcome message to Bob. *)
138             out(BobCh, GenWelcomeMSG(BobkpgPkey, path_secret_x, joiner_secret_0,
                GenSign(mysignkey, WelcomeTBS(path_secret_x, joiner_secret_0))));
139             (* Moved to epoch1. *)
140             let epoch_secret_1 = DeriveEpochSecret(joiner_secret_0) in
141             (* Publish your own node public key. *)
142             let membership_secret_1 = DeriveMembershipSecret(epoch_secret_1) in
143             let mackey1 = GenMACkey(membership_secret_1) in
144             out(PublicCh, (mypkey, GenMAC(mackey1, Alice_Pkey_S2, Pkey2bitstring(mypkey))));
145
146     (* Stage 3: Bob renews his Nodekey *)
147             in(AliceCh, commitMSG:Cipher);
148             let path_secret_x = GetPathSecret_fromCommit(myskey, commitMSG) in
```

```
149             let commit_secret = DeriveNextPathSecret(path_secret_x) in
150             (* Authenticate the commit message. *)
151             let mac = GetMAC_fromCommit(myskey, commitMSG) in
152             if(mac = GenMAC(mackey1, Path_Secret_X_S3, Secret2bitstring(path_secret_x))) then
153             (
154                     (* Moved to epoch2. *)
155                     let joiner_secret_1 = DeriveJoinerSecret(epoch_secret_1, commit_secret) in
156                     let epoch_secret_2 = DeriveEpochSecret(joiner_secret_1) in
157                     let membership_secret_2 = DeriveMembershipSecret(epoch_secret_2) in
158                     let mackey2 = GenMACkey(membership_secret_2) in
159                     (* Authenticate Bob's NodeKey *)
160                     in(PublicCh, (BobPkey:Pkey, mac:MAC));
161                     if(mac = GenMAC(mackey2, Bob_Pkey_S3, Pkey2bitstring(BobPkey))) then
162                     (
                             :
                         (omitted)
                             :
224     (* Stage 2: Invitation from Alice to Bob *)
225     (* Verifying Alice's KeyPackage. *)
226     if(Verify(ASVerifyKey, AliceSign, AlicekpgTBS)) then
227     (
228             (* Received a welcome message from Alice. *)
229             in(BobCh, welcomeMSG:Cipher);
230             let path_secret_x = GetPathSecret_fromWelcome(mykpgSkey, welcomeMSG) in
231             let joiner_secret_0 = GetJoinerSecret_fromWelcome(mykpgSkey, welcomeMSG) in
232             let epoch_secret_1 = DeriveEpochSecret(joiner_secret_0) in
233             let signature = GetSignature_fromWelcome(mykpgSkey, welcomeMSG) in
234
235             if(Verify(AliceVerifyKey, signature, WelcomeTBS(path_secret_x, joiner_secret_0))) then
236             (
237                     (* Verification of Alice's public key. *)
238                     let membership_secret_1 = DeriveMembershipSecret(epoch_secret_1) in
239                     let mackey1 = GenMACkey(membership_secret_1) in
240                     in(PublicCh, (AlicePkey:Pkey, mac:MAC));
241                     if(mac = GenMAC(mackey1, Alice_Pkey_S2, Pkey2bitstring(AlicePkey))) then
242 (
243     (* Stage 3: Bob renews his Nodekey *)
244                             new path_secret_b:Secret;
245                             let myskey = GenSkey(path_secret_b) in
246                             let mypkey = GenPkey(myskey) in
247                             let path_secret_x = DeriveNextPathSecret(path_secret_b) in
248                             let commit_secret = DeriveNextPathSecret(path_secret_x) in
249                             (* Send the commit message (path_secret) to Alice. *)
250                             out(AliceCh, GenCommitMSG(AlicePkey, path_secret_x,
                                GenMAC(mackey1,   Path_Secret_X_S3, Secret2bitstring(path_secret_x))));
251                             (* oved to epoch2. *)
252                             let joiner_secret_1 = DeriveJoinerSecret(epoch_secret_1, commit_secret) in
253                             let epoch_secret_2 = DeriveEpochSecret(joiner_secret_1) in
254                             let membership_secret_2 = DeriveMembershipSecret(epoch_secret_2) in
255                             (* Update your own ''node public key'' and publish it. *)
256                             let mackey2 = GenMACkey(membership_secret_2) in
257                             out(PublicCh, (mypkey, GenMAC(mackey2, Bob_Pkey_S3, Pkey2bitstring(mypkey))));
                             :
                         (omitted)
```

Stage 1: Alice creates a group with a single member. In Line 124, `epoch_secret` for the Ratchet Tree is generated. Next, Line 125 generates `path_secret_a`, which serves as the seed for generating the key pair for node A, which corresponds to Alice. Then, `path_secret_a` is used to derive the secret key of node A using the `GenSkey` function in Line 126. In addition, `path_secret_x` of node X (the parent of node A) is generated using the `DeriveNextPathSecret` function in Line 128. In Line 129, `commit_secret` is derived as `commit_secret` = `DeriveNextPathSecret(path_secret_x)`. Finally, Line 130 derives `joiner_secret` from `commit_secret` and the previously generated `epoch_secret`.

Stage 2: Alice sends a `Welcome message` to Bob to invite him to join the group as a new member. In Lines 133–135, Alice first obtains Bob's `Key Package` and authenticates it. She then encrypts the `Welcome message` using the public key in the `Key Package`. The `Welcome message` in Line 138 includes `path_secret_x` and `joiner_secret` generated in Stage 0 as well as a signature created using Alice's own signing key. In Line 226, Bob obtains and authenticates Alice's signature verification key from her `Key Package` before receiving the `Welcome message`. He then verifies the legitimacy of the sender of the `Welcome message` from the signature contained in the `Welcome Message`. Then, in Lines 230–231, Bob obtains `path_secret_x` and `joiner_secret` from the message. Alice, who sent the `Welcome message`, and Bob, who received it, both share `joiner_secret`, from which the next `epoch_secret` is derived. Thereafter, both parties advance to the next epoch. In addition, Alice needs to disclose the public keys of the updated nodes (A and X) to all group members. In Line 142, she derives `membership_secret` from the latest `epoch_secret`. From this, she generates a MAC key in Line 143, and in Line 144, she sends the public key and MAC of node A. At the end of Stage 2, Bob has shared the secret information of node X through the `Welcome message` (Fig. 3) and can now participate in group messages as a group member.

Stage 3: Bob, who has officially become a group member, creates his own node in the Ratchet Tree and updates the tree accordingly. In Line 244, Bob creates node B and generates `path_secret_b`. The private and public keys of node B are derived from this path (Lines 245–246). Simultaneously, Bob updates node X, which is the parent of node B, and generates the next `path_secret_x` from `path_secret_b` using the `DeriveNextPathSecret` function. In Line 248, a new secret key and public key pair for node X is derived from `path_secret_x`. Following these computations, Bob generates a `Commit message` and sends the updated secret information to the other group members (Line 250). In this stage, Alice, who is a descendant of the updated node X, should be provided with the new secret information for node X. As in Stage 2, Bob sends the updated public key of each node, along with a MAC generated using the MAC key derived from the new `epoch_secret`.

Normal Flow Model: Stages 4–6 Figure 5 illustrates the changes in the Ratchet Tree structure from Stage 4 to Stage 6.

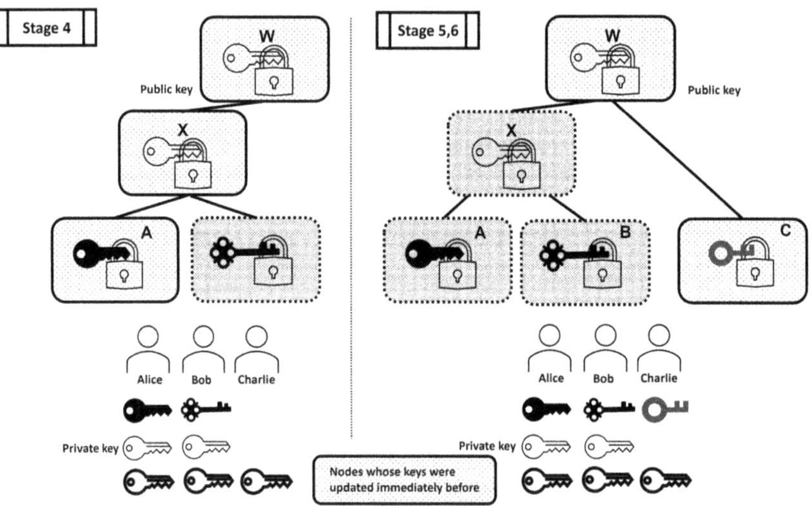

Fig. 5. Changes in Ratchet Tree structure from Stage 4 to Stage 6.

Code 1 continued, formalizes the normal flow model for Stages 4–6.

```
(* Code1 continued: Normal model for sending and receiving basic MLS messages. Stages 4--6 *)
2                             :
3                          (omitted)
                              :
163     (* Stage 4: Invitation from Alice to Charlie *)
164                           in(PublicCh, (CharliekpgPkey:Pkey, CharlieVerifyKey:Verifykey, CharliekpgSign:Signature));
165                           let CharliekpgTBS = KPGTBS(CharliekpgPkey, CharlieVerifyKey) in
166                           if(Verify(ASVerifyKey, CharliekpgSign, CharliekpgTBS)) then
167                           (
168                                   new path_secret_a:Secret;
169                                   let myskey = GenSkey(path_secret_a) in
170                                   let mypkey = GenPkey(myskey) in
171                                   let path_secret_x = DeriveNextPathSecret(path_secret_a) in
172                                   let path_secret_w = DeriveNextPathSecret(path_secret_x) in
173                                   let commit_secret = DeriveNextPathSecret(path_secret_w) in
174                                   let joiner_secret_2 = DeriveJoinerSecret(epoch_secret_2, commit_secret) in
175                                   (* Send a welcome message to Charlie. *)
176                                   out(CharlieCh, GenWelcomeMSG(CharliekpgPkey, path_secret_w, joiner_secret_2, GenSign(mysignkey,
                                         WelcomeTBS(path_secret_w, joiner_secret_2))));
177                                   (* Moved to epoch3. *)
178                                   let epoch_secret_3 = DeriveEpochSecret(joiner_secret_2) in
179                                   let membership_secret_3 = DeriveMembershipSecret(epoch_secret_3) in
180                                   let mackey3 = GenMACkey(membership_secret_3) in
181                                   (* Send a commit message to Bob. *)
182                                   out(BobCh, GenCommitMSG(BobPkey, path_secret_x, GenMAC(mackey2, Path_Secret_X_S4,
                                         Secret2bitstring(path_secret_x))));
183                                   (* ''Myself'' and ''X's node public key'' are published. *)
184                                   out(PublicCh, (mypkey, GenMAC(mackey3, Alice_Pkey_S4, Pkey2bitstring(mypkey))));
185                                   let xskey = GenSkey(path_secret_x) in
186                                   let xpkey = GenPkey(xskey) in
187                                   out(PublicCh, (xpkey, GenMAC(mackey3, X_Pkey_S4, Pkey2bitstring(xpkey))));
188     (* Stage 5: Charlie renews his NodeKey *)
189                                   (* Received a commit message from Charlie. *)
190                                   in(AliceCh, commitMSG:Cipher);
191                                   let path_secret_w = GetPathSecret_fromCommit(xskey, commitMSG) in
192                                   let commit_secret = DeriveNextPathSecret(path_secret_w) in
193                                   let mac = GetMAC_fromCommit(xskey, commitMSG) in
194                                   if(mac = GenMAC(mackey3, Path_Secret_W_S5, Secret2bitstring(path_secret_w))) then
195                                   (
196                                           (* Moved to epoch4. *)
197                                           let joiner_secret_3 = DeriveJoinerSecret(epoch_secret_3, commit_secret) in
198                                           let epoch_secret_4 = DeriveEpochSecret(joiner_secret_3) in
199                                           let membership_secret_4 = DeriveMembershipSecret(epoch_secret_4) in
200                                           let mackey4 = GenMACkey(membership_secret_4) in
201                                           (* Received W's public key and authenticated. *)
202                                           in(PublicCh, (wpkey:Pkey, mac:MAC));
203                                           if(mac = GenMAC(mackey4, W_Pkey_S5, Pkey2bitstring(wpkey))) then
204                                           (
205     (* Stage 6: Secret group message from Charlie *)
206                                                   let wskey = GenSkey(path_secret_w) in
207                                                   in(PublicCh, msg:Cipher);
208                                                   if(Dec(wskey, msg) = MESSAGE) then
209                                                   (
210                                                           event RECV(AliceID)
211                             :
                           (omitted)
```

Stage 4: Alice invites a new client, Charlie, to join the group as a new member. The only difference between this stage and Stage 2 is that the recipient of the `Welcome message` has changed from Bob to Charlie (Lines 175–187). At the end of Stage 3 (Fig. 4), the Ratchet Tree consists of three nodes: A, B, and X. Beginning with Stage 4 (Fig. 5), the tree is extended by creating a new root node, W, to accommodate the addition of Charlie. In this stage, since Bob is an existing member, he should be provided with the secret information of the updated node X and the new node W. Because `path_secret of` node W can be derived from `path_secret` of node X, Bob only needs to include `path_secret_x` in the `Commit message` (Line 182).

Stage 5: Charlie, who has officially become a member of the group, creates his own node in the Ratchet Tree and updates the tree accordingly (Lines 188–204). This process is the same as that performed by Bob in Stage 3.

Stage 6: Charlie sends a secret message to Alice and Bob within the group (Lines 205–210). This message is encrypted using the public key of node W.

Upon receiving the message, Alice and Bob decrypt it is using their own private keys for node W.

3.2 Group Leave Flow Model

Group leave flow follows the same procedure as normal flow (Sect. 3.1). After creating a group consisting of three members, we model a flow (Fig. 6) in which Alice leaves the group. Figure 6 depicts the flow beginning from Stage 6, as Stages 0–6 are identical to normal flow).

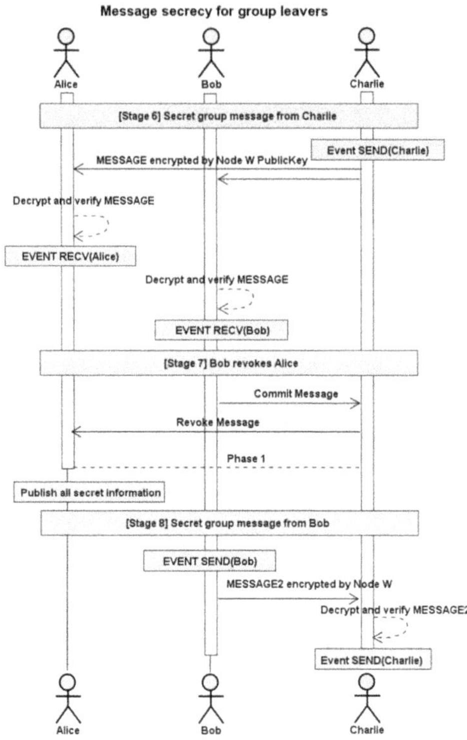

Fig. 6. Sequence diagram of group leave flow: message secrecy for departed group members.

Code 2 formalizes the group leave flow model for Stages 7–8.

```
(* Code 2: Model of members leaving the group during the course of the session. Stages 7--8 *)
2                              :
3                          (omitted)
                               :
216     (* Stage 7: Bob revokes Alice *)
217                                        in(AliceCh, revoke_mac:MAC);
218                                        if(revoke_mac = GenMAC(mackey4, Alice_Revoke_P8, Alice_Revoke_P8)) then
219                                        (
220                                        (* Pass confidential information to an attacker. *)
221                                        phase 1;
222                                        out(PublicCh, (epoch_secret_4, path_secret_a, path_secret_x, path_secret_w))
```

```
223     (* Stage8 : Secret group message from Bob *)
224                                                             )
                            :
                        (omitted)
                            :
310     (* Stage7 : Bob revokes Alice *)
311                                             new path_secret_b:Secret;
312                                             let myskey = GenSkey(path_secret_b) in
313                                             let mypkey = GenPkey(myskey) in
314                                             let path_secret_w = DeriveNextPathSecret(path_secret_b) in
315                                             let commit_secret = DeriveNextPathSecret(path_secret_w) in
316                                             (* Send commit message only to Charlie. *)
317                                             in(PublicCh, (CharliePkey:Pkey, mac:MAC));
318                                             if(mac = GenMAC(mackey4, Charlie_Pkey_S5, Pkey2bitstring(CharliePkey))) then
319                                             (
320                                             out(CharlieCh, GenCommitMSG(CharliePkey, path_secret_w, GenMAC(mackey4,
                                              Path_Secret_W_P7,
321                                             Secret2bitstring(path_secret_w))));
322                                             phase 1;
323                                             (* ''Myself'' and ''W's node public key'' are published. *)
324                                             out(PublicCh, (mypkey, GenMAC(mackey4, Bob_Pkey_P7, Pkey2bitstring(mypkey))));
325                                             let wskey = GenSkey(path_secret_w) in
326                                             let wpkey = GenPkey(wskey) in
327                                             out(PublicCh, (wpkey, GenMAC(mackey4, W_Pkey_P7, Pkey2bitstring(wpkey))));
328     (* Stage 8 : Secret group message from Bob *)
329                                             event SEND(BobID);
330                                             out(PublicCh, Enc(wpkey, MESSAGE2))
331                                              )
                            :
                        (omitted)
                            :
383     (* Stage 7 : Bob revokes Alice *)
384                             (* Received commit message from Bob. *)
385                             in(CharlieCh, commitMSG:Cipher);
386                             let path_secret_w = GetPathSecret_fromCommit(myskey, commitMSG) in
387                             let commit_secret = DeriveNextPathSecret(path_secret_w) in
388                             let mac = GetMAC_fromCommit(myskey, commitMSG) in
389                             if(mac = GenMAC(mackey4, Path_Secret_W_P7, Secret2bitstring(path_secret_w))) then
390                             (
391                                     (* Sends a revoke message to Alice after the commit is approved. *)
392                                     out(AliceCh, (Alice_Revoke_P8, GenMAC(mackey4, Alice_Revoke_P8, Alice_Revoke_P8)));
393                                     phase 1;
394                                     (* Moved to epoch5. *)
395                                     let joiner_secret_4 = DeriveJoinerSecret(epoch_secret_4, commit_secret) in
396                                     let epoch_secret_5 = DeriveEpochSecret(joiner_secret_4) in
397                                     let membership_secret_5 = DeriveMembershipSecret(epoch_secret_5) in
398                                     let mackey5 = GenMACkey(membership_secret_5) in
399     (* Stage 8 : Secret group message from Bob *)
400                                     let wskey = GenSkey(path_secret_w) in
401                                     in(PublicCh, msg:Cipher);
402                                     if(Dec(wskey, msg) = MESSAGE2) then
403                                     (
404                                             event RECV(CharlieID)
405                                     )
406                             :
                        (omitted)
```

Stage 7: Bob updates the Ratchet Tree to remove Alice from the group (Lines 310–327). Subsequently, he sends the updated information to members other than Alice. He then updates nodes B, X, and W. In a typical update, Bob would send `path_secret` of node X to Alice and that of node W to Charlie. However, in this model, it is assumed that secret information should not be sent to Alice after the update. Accordingly, `path_secret` of node X is not sent to Alice. For this reason, in Lines 391–392, after Charlie receives the `Commit message` from Bob, he sends a `Revoke message` to Alice.

The original MLS protocol specifies that Bob should send the `Revoke message` to Alice. However, to prevent the chronological order of processes from being reversed, the model proposed in this paper is designed such that Charlie sends the `Revoke message` after receiving the `Commit message` from Bob. For the same reason, after sending the `Revoke message`, the description `Phase 1;` is added to each process (Lines 221, 322, 393). This prevents the chronological order of the processes before and after from being reversed.

Alice receives the `Revoke message` and transitions to `Phase 1;`. Subsequently, in Line 222, she sends her secret information (the `epoch_secret`, `path_secret_a`,

path_secret_x, and **path_secret_w**) to the public channel and passes it to an attacker. This step is designed to verify whether an attacker, using the secret information possessed by Alice after leaving the group, can access the group secret. Details are presented in the following Sect. 3.3.

Stage 8: Bob sends a group secret message to Charlie (Lines 328–330, 399–405). It is assumed that Alice does not receive this message as she has already left the group.

3.3 Secret Key Leakage Flow Model

MLS provides both forward and backward secrecy to ensure data confidentiality. In this section, we verify backward secrecy between epochs, which is a security requirement in the MLS specification. Secret key leakage flow follows the same procedure as normal flow (Sect. 3.1). After creating a group consisting of three members, we model a flow in which Charlie leaks the secret key of node W to an attacker (Fig. 7). This flow is identical to normal flow up to Stage 6, consistent with group leave flow (Sect. 3.2).

Code 3 formalizes the secret key leakage flow model for Stages 7–9.

```
(* Code 3: Model in the event that an active member accidentally leaks a secret key shared in a group. Stage 7 to 9 *)
2                                   :
3                               (omitted)
                                    :
220     (* Stage 8: Bob renews his NodeKey *)
221                                         (* Received W's public key and authenticated. *)
222                                         in(AliceCh, commitMSG:Cipher);
223                                         let path_secret_x = GetPathSecret_fromCommit(myskey, commitMSG) in
224                                         let path_secret_w = DeriveNextPathSecret(path_secret_x) in
225                                         let commit_secret = DeriveNextPathSecret(path_secret_w) in
226                                         let mac = GetMAC_fromCommit(myskey, commitMSG) in
227                                         if(mac = GenMAC(mackey4, Path_Secret_X_P8, Secret2bitstring(path_secret_x))) then
228                                                 (
229                                         (* Moved to epoch5. *)
230                                         let joiner_secret_4 = DeriveJoinerSecret(epoch_secret_4, commit_secret) in
231                                         let epoch_secret_5 = DeriveEpochSecret(joiner_secret_4) in
232                                         let membership_secret_5 = DeriveMembershipSecret(epoch_secret_5) in
233                                         let mackey5 = GenMACkey(membership_secret_5) in
234     (* Stage 9: Secret group message from Alice *)
235                                         let wskey = GenSkey(path_secret_w) in
236                                         let wpkey = GenPkey(wskey) in
237                                         event SEND(AliceID);
238                                         out(PublicCh, Enc(wpkey, MESSAGE2))
239                                                  )
                                    :
                                (omitted)
                                    :
415     (* Stage 7: Charlie leaks Node W SecretKey *)
416                                 out(PublicCh, wskey);
417     (* Stage 8: Bob renew his NodeKey *)
418                                 (* Received commit message from Bob. *)
419                                 in(CharlieCh, commitMSG:Cipher);
420                                 let path_secret_w = GetPathSecret_fromCommit(myskey, commitMSG) in
421                                 let commit_secret = DeriveNextPathSecret(path_secret_w) in
422                                 let mac = GetMAC_fromCommit(myskey, commitMSG) in
423                                 if(mac = GenMAC(mackey4, Path_Secret_W_P8, Secret2bitstring(path_secret_w))) then
424                                 (
425                                         (* Moved to epoch5. *)
426                                         let joiner_secret_4 = DeriveJoinerSecret(epoch_secret_4, commit_secret) in
427                                         let epoch_secret_5 = DeriveEpochSecret(joiner_secret_4) in
428                                         let membership_secret_5 = DeriveMembershipSecret(epoch_secret_5) in
429                                         let mackey5 = GenMACkey(membership_secret_5) in
430     (* Stage 9: Secret group message from Alice *)
431                                         in(PublicCh, msg:Cipher);
432                                         let wskey = GenSkey(path_secret_w) in
433                                         if(Dec(wskey, msg) = MESSAGE2) then
434                                         (
435                                                 event RECV(CharlieID)
436                                         )
437                                 )
438                                 :
                                (omitted)
```

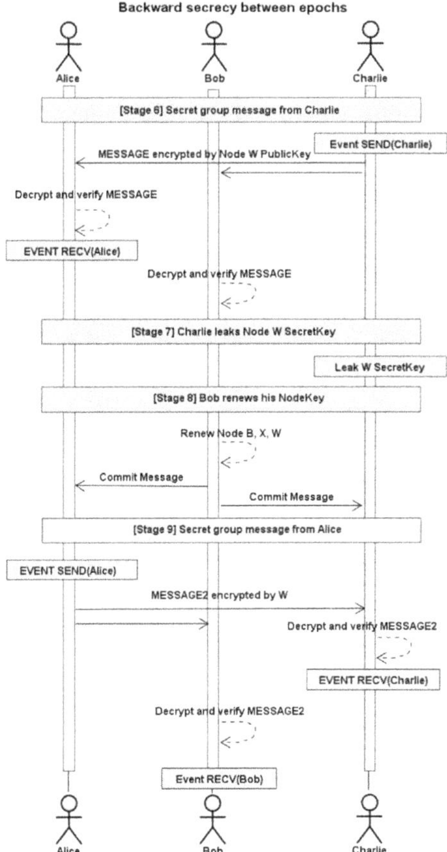

Fig. 7. Sequence diagram of secret key leakage flow: backward secrecy between epochs.

Stage 7: In Line 416, Charlie sends the private key of node W to the public channel, thereby leaking it to the attacker.

Stage 8: After Stage 7, Bob updates the Ratchet Tree, which includes updating the secret key of node W (Lines 220–233).

Stage 9: Group members resume the exchange of secret messages (Lines 234–238, 430–436).

4 Verification Results

In this section, we present the soundness and security verification results for the three flow models described in Sect. 3. We omit the `Proposal message` defined in MLS and assume that agreement is indicated through sender authentication of the `Commit message`. Authentication of the `Commit message` employs a MAC, generated from `membership_secret` derived from the `Key Schedule`. The verification process adjusts the attacker's behavior settings based on different queries.

By default, ProVerif sets the attacker's behavior to set "attacker = active." Therefore, in our verification code, we set "attacker = passive." It should be noted that the "attacker = active" setting is commented out in the code and can be enabled as needed.

4.1 Verification Results Summary

This subsection summarizes the model verification results.

Message Reachability. Table 2 presents the results of verifying whether messages were delivered to the destination client for each model. The result of the query was `cannot be proved` for all models. By analyzing the output logs [24], we confirmed the existence of paths leading to message receive events.

Table 2. Results of message reachability verification.

Model	Query name	Verification results
Normal flow (Sect. 3.1)	Query 1–2	Event reachable path confirmed from the output log
Group leave flow (Sect. 3.2)	Query 2–2	Event reachable path confirmed from the output log
Secret key leakage flow (Sect. 3.3)	Query 3–3	Event reachable path confirmed from the output log

Security Requirements. MLS is an encrypted communication protocol that ensures end-to-end data confidentiality. Therefore, it should ensure not only that messages are delivered to the destination client, but also that the messages remain secret. In addition, each message should undergo sender authentication. This indicates that messages created by anyone other than legitimate group members should fail sender authentication. Table 3 summarizes the verified requirements, the corresponding queries, and the results.

Table 3. MLS security requirements and verification results.

Security requirements	Query name	Verification results
Message secrecy in normal flow	Query 1–1	No attacks detected
Message secrecy for departed group members	Query 2–1	No attacks detected
Backward secrecy under private key leakage	Query 3–2	No attacks detected
Resistance to attacker-created messages (sender authentication)	Query 1–3 Query 2–3 Query 3–4	Rejected by protocol

The result of Query 1–1 demonstrates that message secrecy during normal communication is maintained.

Since MLS is a protocol designed for varying group configurations, it should ensure that each message is accessible only to members who are part of the group at that time. Therefore, one security requirement is that clients who have left the group cannot decrypt subsequent messages. The result of Query 2–1 demonstrates that this requirement is also satisfied.

MLS ensures both forward and backward secrecy. In this study, we employed the secret key leakage flow model (Sect. 3.3) to verify backward secrecy in the event of secret key leakage. The result of Query 3–2 indicates that MLS ensures backward secrecy by updating the secret key after key leakage.

MLS provides sender authentication for each message, ensuring that messages from anyone other than legitimate group members are rejected. In this study, we verified that even if an attacker forges a message, it fails to pass sender authentication. We further verified the injectivity of send events generated by legitimate senders and receive events generated by recipients. The results of Query 3–4 demonstrate that MLS clients do not accept messages from illegitimate group members.

4.2 Normal Flow Model Verification

Verification of the normal flow model (Sect. 3.1) was performed based on the three security requirements listed in Table 4.

Table 4. Security requirements for normal flow model.

Query name	Security requirements	Query description
Query 1–1	Confidentiality of secret messages	query attacker(MESSAGE).
Query 1–2	Confirmation of message receive event	query event(RECV(AliceID)). query event(RECV(BobID)).
Query 1–3	Possibility of message forgery	query inj-event(RECV(AliceID)) ==> inj-event(SEND(CharlieID)). query inj-event(RECV(BobID)) ==> inj-event(SEND(CharlieID)).

Query 1–1 verifies whether the secret message exchanged at the end of the flow, `MESSAGE`, remains secret from the attacker. Query 1–2 verifies whether `MESSAGE` sent by Charlie in Stage 6 (Fig. 3) is correctly received by Alice and Bob. This verifies whether the modeled flow achieves its intended purpose of sending and receiving messages. In the original MLS protocol, `MESSAGE` should be created by Charlie and shared with Alice and Bob. However, the verification model in this study assumes that Alice, Bob, and Charlie share `MESSAGE` in advance. Furthermore, the receive event is generated after confirming that the received message is equal to `MESSAGE`. Query 1–3 verifies the message send event initiated by Charlie. In addition, it verifies the injectivity of the message receive events initiated by Alice and Bob. This determines whether it is possible for an

attacker to successfully forge a message that would be accepted as legitimate. The verification results are presented in Table 5.

Table 5. Verification results for normal flow model.

Query name	Attacker's settings	Output content	Verification results
Query 1–1	active	Query not attacker(MESSAGE) is true.	secrecy verified
Query 1–2	passive	Query not event(RECV(AliceID)) cannot be proved. Query not event(RECV(AliceID)) cannot be proved.	cannot be proved
Query 1–3	active	Query inj-event(RECV(AliceID)) ==> inj-event(SEND(CharlieID)) is true. Query inj-event(RECV(BobID)) ==> inj-event(SEND(CharlieID)) is true.	forgery is difficult

The results of Query 1–1 were `true`, indicating that `MESSAGE` remained secret from the attacker.

Query 1–2 was executed under the "passive" attacker setting. The result was `cannot be proved`, indicating that ProVerif could not determine whether the correct procedure was used to find the confirmation of message receive event path. However, by analyzing the execution log [24], we found that each process followed the expected execution path. The following excerpt from Log 1 of Query 1–2 demonstrates that each receive event was achieved. In other words, we identified a possible path from the message transmitted through the communication channel to the event.

(* Log 1 of Query 1-2: Execution result of Code 1 *)
:
(omitted)
:
14. By 13, event(RECV(AliceID)).
The goal is reached, represented in the following fact:
event(RECV(AliceID)).
:
(omitted)
:
15. By 14, event(RECV(BobID)).
The goal is reached, represented in the following fact:
event(RECV(BobID)).

The result of Query 1–3 was also `true`, indicating that it was difficult for attackers to forge messages.

4.3 Group Leave Flow Model Verification

Verification of the group leave flow model (Sect. 3.2) was performed based on the three security requirements listed in Table 6.

Table 6. Security requirements for group leave flow model.

Query name	Security requirements	Query description
Query 2–1	Confidentiality of secret messages	query attacker(MESSAGE2).
Query 2–2	Confirmation of message receive event	query event(RECV(CharlieID)).
Query 2–3	Possibility of message forgery	query inj-event(RECV(CharlieID)) ==> inj-event(SEND(BobID)).

Query 2–1 targets Stage 8 (Fig. 6), which occurs after Alice has left the group. It verifies whether `MESSAGE2`, the secret message sent by Bob to Charlie, is kept secret from the attacker. In Stage 7, Alice shares all of her group secret information with the attacker. Therefore, Query 2–1 verifies whether `MESSAGE2` is kept secret from Alice. Query 2–2 verifies whether the event of receiving `MESSAGE2` occurs, In other words, it verifies whether Bob has received this message. Query 2–3 verifies the injectivity of the `MESSAGE2` transmission event initiated by Bob and the `MESSAGE2` receive event initiated by Charlie. It verifies whether a message can be successfully forged by Alice, who is no longer a group member, or an attacker. The verification results are presented in Table 7.

Table 7. Verification results for group leave flow model.

Query name	Attacker's settings	Output content	Verification results
Query 2–1	active	Query not attacker(MESSAGE2) is true.	secrecy verified
Query 2–2	passive	Query not event(RECV(CharlieID)) cannot be proved.	cannot be proved
Query 2–3	active	Query inj-event(RECV(CharlieID))==> inj-event(SEND(BobID)) is true.	forgery is difficult

The result of Query 2–1 was `true`, demonstrating that `MESSAGE2` was kept secret from both the attacker and Alice. Query 2–2 was executed with the passive attacker setting. The result was `cannot be proved`, which was the same result obtained for the normal flow model in Sect. 4.2. ProVerif reported that it could not determine the legitimacy of the execution path leading to the receive event. Therefore, we examined the execution output log [24] and confirmed that the receive event was reached, as demonstrated in the following excerpt from Log 2 of Query 2–2:

(* Log 2 of Query 2-2: Execution result of Code 2 *)
:
(omitted)
:
18. By 17, event(RECV(CharlieID)).
The goal is reached, represented in the following fact:
event(RECV(CharlieID)).

The result of Query 2–3 was also `true`, verifying that it would be difficult for the attacker and Alice to forge messages.

4.4 Secret Key Leakage Flow Model Verification

Verification of the secret key leakage flow model (Sect. 3.3) was performed based on the three security requirements listed in Table 8.

Table 8. Security requirements for secret key leakage flow model.

Query name	Security requirements	Query description
Query 3–1	Confidentiality of secret messages before key leakage	query attacker(MESSAGE).
Query 3–2	Confidentiality of secret messages after key leakage	query attacker(MESSAGE2).
Query 3–3	Confirmation of message receive event	query event(RECV(CharlieID)). query event(RECV(BobID)).
Query 3–4	Possibility of message forgery	query inj-event(RECV(BobID)) ==> inj-event(SEND(AliceID)).

Query 3–1 verifies whether `MESSAGE`, sent by Charlie to Alice and Bob in Stage 6 (Fig. 7), was kept secret from the attacker. Query 3–2 verifies whether `MESSAGE2`, sent from Alice to Bob and Charlie in Stage 9 (Fig. 7), was kept secret from the attacker. Query 3–3 verifies whether receive events for both `MESSAGE` and `MESSAGE2` occurred and whether they were correctly received by the recipients. Query 3–4 verifies the injectivity of the `MESSAGE2` transmission event initiated by Alice and the `MESSAGE2` receive event initiated by Bob. It also verifies the possibility of a message being forged by an attacker. The verification results are presented in Table 9.

Table 9. Verification results for secret key leakage flow model.

Query name	Attacker's settings	Output content	Verification results
Query 3–1	active	Query not attacker(MESSAGE) cannot be proved.	cannot be proved
Query 3–2	active	Query not attacker(MESSAGE2) is true.	secrecy verified
Query 3–3	passive	Query not event(RECV(CharlieID)) cannot be proved. Query not event(RECV(BobID)) cannot be proved.	cannot be proved
Query 3–4	active	Query inj-event(RECV(BobID))==> inj-event(SEND(AliceID)) is true.	forgery is difficult

The result of Query 3–1 was `cannot be proved`. As a result, we analyzed the execution output log [24] and confirmed that there was a path by which the attacker could reach `MESSAGE`, as indicated by the following excerpt from Log 3 of Query 3–1:

(* Log 3 of Query 3-1: Execution result of Code 3 *)
:
(omitted)
:
16. By 15, attacker(MESSAGE).
The goal is reached, represented in the following fact:
attacker(MESSAGE).

The result of Query 3–2 was `true`, demonstrating that `MESSAGE2` was kept secret from the attacker. The result of Query 3–3 was also `cannot be proved`. Therefore, we again examined the execution output log [24]. We confirmed that an execution path existed for each receive event, as indicated in the following excerpt from Log 3 of Query 3–3:

(* Log 3 of Query 3-3: Execution result of Code 3 *)
:
(omitted)
:
21. By 20, event(RECV(CharlieID)).
The goal is reached, represented in the following fact:
event(RECV(CharlieID)).
:
(omitted)
:
20. By 19, event(RECV(BobID)).
The goal is reached, represented in the following fact:
event(RECV(BobID)).

Finally, the result of Query 3–4 was `true`, indicating that it was difficult for an attacker to forge messages, even after the private key had been leaked.

5 Conclusions and Future Work

In this study, we formalized three models based on the MLS specification defined in RFC 9420. We verified the soundness of these models and their compliance with the security requirements of MLS. In particular, we focused on backward secrecy in scenarios involving secret key leakage, demonstrating that the formalized models met the security requirements of MLS. We assumed that an attacker's objective was to obtain secret information and forge messages. We described these objectives as queries to verify the security requirements. However, the MLS protocol provides mechanisms to ensure not only backward secrecy but also forward secrecy, message integrity, and sender authentication. The following is a list of elements that were not formalized in this study [10]:

1. Tree hash calculation
2. Parent hash calculation
3. Flow for approving Proposal messages as a group
4. Optimization of the Ratchet Tree when the group structure changes

At present, these elements introduce complexity into the model. However, we plan to construct a model including these factors in future work. We aim to formalize the specifications of cryptographic protocols with complex structures and investigate the extent to which their security can be verified.

Acknowledgment. This work was supported in part by the Japan Society for the Promotion of Science (JSPS) KAKENHI under Grant 25K15110. We would like to express our gratitude to Gensuke Hamada, who has implemented this research up to now.

References

1. Blanchet, B., Cheval, V. : ProVerif 2.05: Automatic cryptographic protocol verifier. https://bblanche.gitlabpages.inria.fr/proverif/. Accessed Nov 2025
2. Blanchet, B.: Modeling and verifying security protocols with the applied pi calculus and ProVerif. Found. Trends Priv. Secur. **1**(1–2), 1–135 (2016). https://doi.org/10.1561/3300000004
3. Dolev, D., Yao, A.C.: On the security of public-key protocols. IEEE Trans. Inf. Theory **29**(2), 198–208 (1983). https://doi.org/10.1109/TIT.1983.1056650
4. Blanchet, B.: An efficient cryptographic protocol verifier based on prolog rules. In: 14th IEEE Computer Security Foundations Workshop, pp. 82–96 (2001). https://doi.org/10.1109/CSFW.2001.930138
5. Blanchet, B.: From secrecy to authenticity in security protocols. In: 9th International Static Analysis Symposium (SAS 2002). LNCS, vol. 2477, pp. 342–359 (2002). https://doi.org/10.1007/3-540-45789-5_25
6. Blanchet, B.: Automatic proof of strong secrecy for security protocols. In: IEEE Symposium on Security and Privacy, pp. 86–100 (2004). https://doi.org/10.1109/SECPRI.2004.1301317
7. Blanchet, B., Abadi, M., Fournet, C.: Automated verification of selected equivalences for security protocols. In: 20th IEEE Symposium on Logic in Computer Science (LICS 2005), pp. 331–340 (2005). https://doi.org/10.1109/LICS.2005.8
8. Bhargavan, K., Blanchet, B., Kobeissi, N.: Verified models and reference implementations for the TLS 1.3 standard candidate. In: In IEEE Symposium on Security and Privacy (S&P 2017), pp. 483–503, San Jose, CA (2017). https://doi.org/10.1109/SP.2017.26
9. Cremers, C., Horvat, M., Hoyland, J., Scott, S., Van Der Merwe, T.: A comprehensive symbolic analysis of TLS 1.3. Thyla van der Merwe, presented at CCS 2017 (2017). https://doi.org/10.1145/3133956.3134063
10. The Messaging Layer Security (MLS) protocol: RFC 9420 https://www.rfc-editor.org/info/rfc9420. Accessed Nov 2025
11. F* (pronounced F star): a proof-oriented programming language. https://fstar-lang.org/. Accessed Nov 2025
12. Bhargavan, K., Beurdouche, B., Naldurg, P.: Formal models and verified protocols for group messaging: attacks and proofs for IETF MLS. Inria Paris (2019). https://inria.hal.science/hal-02425229. Accessed Nov 2025
13. Barbosa, M, et al.: SoK: computer-aided cryptography. In: IEEE Symposium on Security and Privacy (SP). San Francisco, CA, USA, vol. 2021, 777–795 (2021). https://doi.org/10.1109/SP40001.2021.00008

14. Bhargavan, K., Fournet, C., Gordon, A.D.: Verified reference implementations of WS security protocols. In: 3rd International Workshop on Web Services and Formal Methods (WS-FM 2006), Vienna, September 8–9 (2006). https://doi.org/10.1007/11841197_6
15. Cheval, V., Cortier, V., Debant, A.: Election Verifiability with ProVerif. In: Proceedings of the 36th IEEE Computer Security Foundations Symposium (CSF 2023) (2023). https://doi.org/10.1109/CSF57540.2023.00032
16. Cheval, V., Moreira, J., Ryan, M.: Automatic verification of transparency protocols. In: IEEE European Symposium on Security and Privacy, Euro S&P (2023). https://doi.org/10.1109/EuroSP57164.2023.00016
17. Mieno, T., Okazaki, H., Arai, K., Futa, Y.: How to formalize loop iterations in cryptographic protocols using ProVerif. IEEE Access **12**, 31605–31625 (2024). https://doi.org/10.1109/ACCESS.2024.3368453
18. Mieno, T., Okazaki, H., Arai, K., Futa, Y., Yamamoto, H.: Formal security verification for searchable symmetric encryption using ProVerif. In: 2024 International Symposium on Information Theory and its applications (ISITA), Taipei, Taiwan, pp. 419–424 (2024). https://doi.org/10.23919/ISITA60732.2024.10858210
19. Alwen, J., Coretti, S., Dodis, Y., Tselekounis, Y.: Security analysis and improvements for the IETF MLS standard for group messaging, Advances in Cryptology - CRYPTO,: 40th Annual International Cryptology Conference, CRYPTO 2020, Santa Barbara, CA, USA, August 17–21, 2020. Proceedings, Part **I**, 248–277 (2020). https://doi.org/10.1007/978-3-030-56784-2_9
20. Günther, C.G.: An identity-based key-exchange protocol. In: Advances in Cryptology Eurocrypt 1989 (LNCS 434), pp. 29–37. https://doi.org/10.1007/3-540-46885-4_5
21. Cremers, C., Hale, B., Kohbrok, K.: Revisiting post-compromise security guarantees in group messaging. CISPA. Preprint (2024). https://doi.org/10.60882/cispa.25435252.v1
22. Rösler, P., Mainka, C., Schwenk, J.: More is less: on the end–to–end security of group chats in signal, Whatsapp, and Threema. In: IEEE European Symposium on Security and Privacy (EuroS&P), pp. 415–429 (2018). https://doi.org/10.1109/EuroSP.2018.00036
23. Barnes, R., Bhargavan, K., Lipp, B., Wood, C.: RFC 9180: hybrid public key encryption. RFC Editor (2022). https://doi.org/10.17487/RFC9180
24. Mieno, T., Okazaki, H., Arai, K., Futa, Y.: ProVerif models and logs to reproduce the results in this paper (2025). https://github.com/mienotakehiko/sam25. Accessed Nov 2025

Mitigating Ransomware and Data Breaches in Mobile Health Applications: An Encryption and Integrity-Based Approach

Sarah Dziobak[1], Valerie Nielson[1](✉), Brendon Wolfe[1], Rui Zhu[2], and Huirong Fu[1]

[1] Oakland University, Rochester, MI 48309, USA
{sdziobak,vnielson,bmwolfe,fu}@oakland.edu
[2] Kettering University, Flint, MI 48504, USA
rzhu@kettering.edu

Abstract. The integration of mobile communication and medical information access has significantly enhanced patient care but has also introduced substantial cybersecurity risks. Mobile health (mHealth) applications store and process highly sensitive data, making them prime targets for ransomware attacks and data breaches. These threats can compromise data confidentiality, integrity, and availability, potentially endangering patients' well-being. This paper presents an encryption and integrity-based security framework designed to mitigate ransomware and unauthorized access in mHealth applications. Our approach leverages AES-256 encryption for data confidentiality, SQLCipher for secure database storage, and checksum-based integrity verification to detect unauthorized modifications. A comparative security analysis was conducted across multiple iterations of our implementation, evaluating the effectiveness of these measures in preventing and mitigating attacks. The results demonstrate that combining strong encryption with integrity checks and secure backup mechanisms significantly enhances data protection in mobile health applications.

Keywords: AES · SQLCipher · Checksums · Cybersecurity in Healthcare

1 Introduction

Mobile health (mHealth) applications have become essential tools for individuals managing their healthcare, providing convenient access to critical medical data such as medication schedules, nutritional tracking, and patient records. These applications play a crucial role in enhancing patient care by facilitating real-time health monitoring and medical decision-making. However, the increasing reliance on mobile health platforms has also introduced significant cybersecurity

K. Daimi et al. (Eds.): CSCE 2025, CCIS 2937, pp. 236–248, 2026.
https://doi.org/10.1007/978-3-032-22208-4_15

challenges, particularly concerning data privacy, integrity, and system availability. Given the sensitive nature of health information, ensuring robust security measures is paramount, especially in compliance with regulations such as the Health Insurance Portability and Accountability Act (HIPAA).

One of the most significant challenges in securing mHealth applications is the threat of ransomware –a form of malware that encrypts files and demands payment for their release. Ransomware attacks can lock users out of critical health information, disrupt medical services, and pose severe risks to patient safety. Moreover, other cyber threats, such as unauthorized data access, and integrity compromises, further highlight the vulnerabilities of mobile health platforms. Without proper safeguards, attackers can exploit these weaknesses to manipulate patient data, leading to severe privacy violations and financial losses.

To address these security challenges, this paper systematically analyzes methods for securing user data and protecting mobile file systems against ransomware. It presents a multi-layered security framework to protect user data and application file systems in mobile health environments. Our approach integrates AES-256 encryption, as outlined by Yaqoob et al. [1], to protect sensitive information, SQLCipher for secure database storage, and checksum-based integrity verification to detect unauthorized modifications. Additionally, our mobile application incorporates secure backup mechanisms to enable rapid recovery in the event of a ransomware attack. By combining these security techniques, our framework ensures that compromised data remains encrypted and inaccessible to attackers while allowing users to restore uncorrupted backups, thereby maintaining confidentiality, integrity, and availability (CIA).

The remainder of this paper is organized as follows: Sect. 2 reviews related research that informed the development of our security framework. Section 3 details the implementation of our security measures, including encryption, integrity verification, and backup strategies. Section 4 presents a security analysis comparing system vulnerabilities with and without these protections. Finally, Sect. 5 discusses key research challenges and future improvements, and Section VI concludes with insights into the broader implications of our findings for securing mobile health applications.

2 Related Works

2.1 Access Control

Previous research has explored various approaches to enhancing data security in mobile health applications. One study by Sadki and Bakkali [2] proposes a patient-centric access control model, allowing patients to determine the visibility of their data. By shifting data access decisions from organizations to individuals, this approach reduces the burden on healthcare providers and institutions. However, while this strategy improves user autonomy and privacy, it does not inherently prevent cyberattacks, making it essential to complement access control with robust data security measures.

2.2 Traffic Analysis

Atapattu et al. [3], introduce a third-party application that analyzes incoming network traffic using a man-in-the-middle proxy. This proxy decrypts incoming packets before forwarding them, enabling a Convolutional Neural Network (CNN) to detect and filter out malicious data before re-encrypting and transmitting the safe packets. While this method enhances network security by mitigating data interception and manipulation, it does not address threats that bypass network-level defenses, such as ransomware and local database breaches.

2.3 Ransomware Mitigation

Ransomware remains one of the most critical threats to medical data security. These attacks encrypt files within the system, potentially locking out patients and other users in the organization from accessing critical information. One study by Farion-Melnyk et al. [4] highlights the damage caused by the rising prevalence of ransomware. This study introduces early-stage solutions without detailed methodologies for preventing ransomware. Meanwhile, Gupta et al. [5] investigate machine learning-based ransomware detection, demonstrating over 95% accuracy in identifying ransomware threats across multiple models. While machine learning provides a promising approach for proactive detection, its high computational requirements and complex implementation pose challenges for real-time deployment in resource-constrained mobile health applications.

2.4 SQL Injection Mitigation

Another major threat to the security of medical databases is SQL injection. SQL injection allows for queries to get abused to leak, modify or delete the user's information that is stored in the database. Pokharkar and Vishwamitr [6] emphasize the urgency of securing healthcare databases, noting that 99% of medical data is processed and stored online, making it a prime target for cyberattacks. Khandare, Sreekantha, and Sairam [7] further categorize patient data into general and sensitive information, stressing the necessity of encryption techniques to safeguard records. A key strategy for mitigating SQL injection risks involves parameterized queries and encryption, ensuring that even if an attack occurs, the extracted data remains unreadable to unauthorized users.

2.5 User Privacy Consideration

Ensuring compliance with HIPAA and other privacy regulations is fundamental in mobile health applications. Zhao, Shahriar, Clincy, and Bhuiyan [8] conducted a security assessment of Medscape, one of the leading mHealth applications, revealing serious HIPAA violations, including the logging of sensitive user data, weak hashing mechanisms, and insecure third-party storage. These findings suggest that many mobile health applications prioritize functionality over security, leaving patient data exposed. Els and Cillers [9] identify the three most critical threats to medical data security: device loss, data in transit, and data at rest. Their research emphasizes key security measures, such as password authentication, data encryption, and cryptographic key management, which serve as the foundation for protecting sensitive health information. Our work builds upon these findings by integrating encryption, integrity verification, and secure backup mechanisms to enhance data confidentiality, integrity, and availability (CIA) in mobile health applications.

2.6 Global Efforts

As mHealth applications continue to grow in use worldwide, concerns regarding secure communication and data privacy related to Electronic Health Records (EHR) have become critical concerns. Mishra, Gupta, Saxena, and Singh [10] propose a framework to compare and standardize common policies and regulations used within varying countries regarding EHRs. The results of this study indicate that technical rights are the most important component in implementing global privacy and security, with operational practices being the most significant role in that implementation. The findings of this study relate directly to our work as technical measures such as encryption and checksums are used within our implementation which is seen as integral security measures. Similarly, a study by Gupta, Mishra, and Makkar [11] identified a framework for maintaining data privacy and security within healthcare applications on a global scale. A significant result of this study is that Data Protection and Privacy Control should be the very first implementation when securing medical health applications. Data Protection and Privacy Control must be a primary concern as health applications must protect sensitive information, maintain patient trust, and comply with legal standards. The framework proposed in their study reinforces our approach, as we employed a data-integrity based application that aligns with the global priority of ensuring privacy and security in mHealth applications.

3 Security and Design Implementation

3.1 Overview

Encryption is an incredibly important component to securing medical health data. Encryption ensures that medical information stored in a mobile application is confidential and can only be accessed with proper decryption tools. Encryption ensures data confidentiality, while further measures such as checksums and backups maintain integrity. Figure 1 below illustrates our application's data flow [10], highlighting key security processes including encryption, data transmission, integrity verification, and backup management.

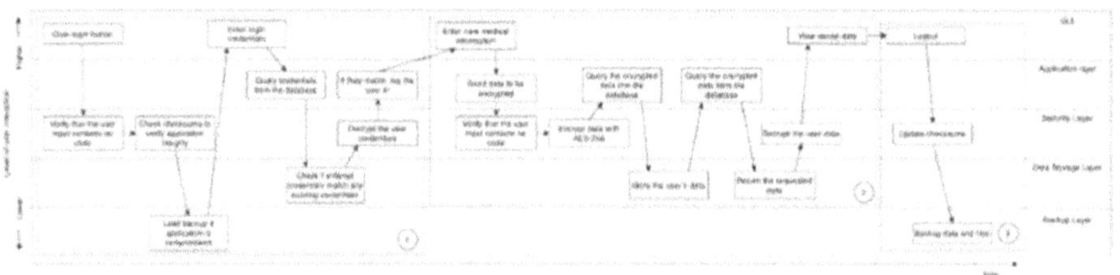

Fig. 1. The architecture trace diagram of the secured application.

3.2 Application Security

AES and Symmetric Encryption Benefits. AES (Advanced Encryption Standard) was an ideal choice for securing the mobile application. AES uses symmetric encryption which means it uses the same key for encryption and decryption. Since both the sender and receiver share the same key, the encryption process is simplified and more efficient. More importantly, the use of a single key enhances security, ensuring encrypted data remains unreadable without the key.

This application specifically employs 256-bit AES to secure the data due to its balance between performance and security. While longer key lengths like 512 or 1024 bits might seem more secure, AES does not define or support such sizes. To use AES-512 or higher, it would be necessary to modify the existing AES algorithm or would require a non-AES cipher, which would increase complexity without considerable security gains.

AES-256 has greater security than 128- or 192-bit AES as the greater the length, the greater security. The 256-bit key has 2^{256} possible combinations which make brute force attacks practically infeasible. Even with the most powerful supercomputers today, it would take trillions of years to try all 2^{256} possibilities. If AES-128 or AES-192 was used, there would be 2^{128} and 2^{192} possible keys, respectively. Since AES-256 is the offers the highest key within the standard, it is the best option over AES-128 and AES-192. AES-256 is widely regarded as one of the most secure encryption standards, making it an excellent choice for safeguarding data in mobile applications.

Database Security. Adding layers of security to a database is incredibly important to mobile application security. The discussed application utilizes SQLCipher, in order to secure its database. Specifically, SQLCipher encrypts the entire database including metadata such as table names and indexes using AES-256 encryption. This ensures that when data is transmitted to and from the database, it is encrypted and secure, preventing unauthorized access. This transmission of data can be seen in sections (1) and (2) of Fig. 1, highlighting the steps the application takes to ensure data is secure and untampered.

SQLCipher was utilized due to its simplicity to implement with a SQLite database. SQLite is a self-contained database that does not require configuration since it is stored locally within the mobile Android application. A large benefit of SQLite in terms of security is its resistance to network attacks. SQLite is serverless, reducing its vulnerability to network-based attacks that could occur in client-server databases. SQLite coupled with SQLCipher's AES-256 encryption was an ideal option for securing the database as it encrypts the entire database, ensuring that even if the local storage is compromised, data remains protected.

File Security. In order to address the threat of ransomware, this application needs to be able to identify when it has been tampered with and be able to recover any lost data. For this, the app leverages checksums to validate the integrity of its files. If a checksum value differs from the assigned value, the system can identify that the files have been tampered with. Checksums help verify file integrity by generating unique hashes that reflect each file's contents. This makes it so that even the slightest modification to a file, results in significant hash changes to indicate the file was tampered with. To further improve the security of the files, backups are stored in a separate, secure location such as the cloud to prevent compromised files from affecting previous backups. As seen in section (1) of Fig. 1, this allows the system to revert to a previous backup if files have been compromised. Section (3) of Fig. 1 highlights the process of updating the checksums and saving a new backup when the user logs out. By combining encryption, checksums, and a robust backup strategy, this approach should ensure the confidentiality, integrity, and availability of user data regardless of potential attacks.

3.3 Security Analysis

App Without Database or Encryption. This initial iteration of the application was developed using JavaScript and React Native to create a visually appealing and user-friendly interface. Figure 2 provides a look at the home page including the visualized data and various buttons leading to other pages. While this iteration provided a foundation for future developments, it lacks critical security components such as encryption and a secure database.

Without encryption, sensitive data fetched from the database could be potentially intercepted and stolen or modified during transmission via packet sniffing and man-in-the-middle attacks. Moreover, the program checks if the login credentials are valid; however, this information is hardcoded into the application making it vulnerable to attackers with access to the codebase.

Without a database, data is stored insecurely through methods such as hardcoding or temporary storage. This not only limits scalability but also exposes sensitive information to unauthorized access. Additionally, the system lacks a centralized database preventing enforcement of security policies, leaving data unprotected.

Another key vulnerability is the lack of input sanitization and validation. The application checks if login credentials match hardcoded values; however, it remains vulnerable to various injection attacks, decompilation of the code, and tampering with inputs used to gain unauthorized access. Attackers can exploit

Fig. 2. Application home page displaying basic information.

these weaknesses to potentially gain elevated privileges, allowing them to gain access to data they may not have had access to otherwise.

These vulnerabilities directly compromise the application's confidentiality, integrity and availability (CIA). Confidentiality is lost due to the hardcoding of data; this makes exposure of this data very easy through the means of decompilation or simply access to the codebase. Integrity is lost due to potential MITM attacks resulting in tampered data being shared. Availability is lost due to data potentially being deleted and other potential attacks such as ransomware attacks caused by privilege escalation which may prevent access to files bringing the system down.

App with Database and Encryption. The second iteration of the application introduces an SQLite database secured with SQLCipher using AES-256. This encryption technique addresses some critical concerns of the first iteration, particularly the risk of hardcoding credentials. Besides it being inconvenient and

Table 1. The database activity table with unencrypted data

steps	distance	activity	user_table_user_id
10000	7	3	1
7000	5	2	2
10000	7	3	3
8000	6	4	4
6000	4	2	5

not realistically possible to maintain updated data, it also prevents attackers from simply decompiling or observing the codebase to locate sensitive information. The AES-256 also makes sure that if data does get leaked or stolen, it is still encrypted making it harder for attackers to use the data. Tables 1 and 2 illustrate what data looks like in the database when unencrypted vs when encrypted. Within Table 1, columns named steps, distance, activity, and user_table_user_id are included which hold unencrypted data. The steps column holds information regarding how many steps the user logs within the application. The distance column shows how many miles completed were logged by the user. The activity level denotes how many different activities were completed. For example, if the user completed swimming and running, the activity column would display the value 2. Lastly, the user_table_user_id is present which serves as the primary key column. Table 2 is shown below which shows the encrypted data for steps and distance. This gives a clear look at how encryption makes data significantly harder to read when stolen.

Despite these security improvements, several vulnerabilities remain. The app lacks input sanitization and validation, introducing the risk of SQL injection attacks which can expose the data in the database. It also heavily relies on secure implementation practices and any misconfigurations with important security data such as encryption keys, weak database permissions and incorrect key storage can lead to data breaches. Database misconfigurations can also lead to data exposure and unauthorized access. Temporary or unencrypted data is still vulnerable to exfiltration, which may aid a ransomware attack. If data is ever transmitted over insecure channels, it may still get intercepted as HTTPS nor TLS is currently used which may negate the benefits of the database. Secure transmission is crucial for apps that may be transmitting sensitive information including health data. This also leaves the data vulnerable to MITM attacks and packet sniffing.

Another major threat that remains is the vulnerability to ransomware. Even with the improved security the second iteration is still vulnerable in this way due to the lack of input sanitization, lack of backups, lack of monitoring and threat of privilege escalation. This vulnerability poses a threat to the availability of data as the database itself can be encrypted by the attacker, integrity as the attacker has control over the database preventing safe usage and confidentiality as any unencrypted data can be discovered and intercepted by the attacker.

Table 2. Part 1 0f 2: the database activity table with encrypted data

steps	distance
Hhc4hgCfPBXdCgyWT9hffQ==	lWJY83C1H9BF16Hy/1gl7g==
YpOSAtLkPyLaDvRlcwCT3A==	tRx/toE1Jk7GPQB3N0fw4w==
pqWxH4u44/FOQq5i70LbVw==	K+4SFa2ytW6fHdIP3Rqn/w==
kwZRtMrpLecm7UigjwpwDQ==	8f+n0uYfUv7C0RPG0JHicQ==
rNqQXUbKz5MhNqbaBLezzQ==	LCF7cr755QlPS3yI9Dx2dg==

Table 3. Part 2 0f 2: the database activity table with encrypted data

activity	user_table_user_id
hM7/nyBpAJJk00HTsoIWtg==	hM7/nyBpAJJk00HTsoIWtg==
8BQtwzxUa9OzYZziB/iySw==	8BQtwzxUa9OzYZziB/iySw==
lWJY83C1H9BF16Hy/1gl7g==	lWJY83C1H9BF16Hy/1gl7g==
LCF7cr755QlPS3yI9Dx2dg==	LCF7cr755QlPS3yI9Dx2dg==
8BQtwzxUa9OzYZziB/iySw==	tRx/toE1Jk7GPQB3N0fw4w==

App with Database, Encryption, Checksum and Backups. In the final iteration of this application checksums and backup logic for additional security were introduced. These security measures were implemented with the intention to prevent or at least detect and recover from a ransomware attack. The backup logic simply goes through the selected important files of the application and saves them to a separate directory. Further security can be added here by encrypting these backups, and/or storing them in a secure directory that cannot be accessed by those without permissions.

The most important security upgrade introduced in this implementation is the checksums. These checksums are generated using the SHA-256 hashing algorithm from the CryptoJS library. This produces a unique digest for each file that can be compared against the previous hashes to verify that the files have not been tampered with. This app will only allow you to use it when the hashes match, preventing access to the application otherwise, alerting the users of a potential attack allowing them to resort to a backup that was stored before the files were modified. Table 3 illustrates how the various security measures impact the application. From this it is apparent that with each iteration of the application the security of not only the data but also the application in general increased. In this iteration of the project, the introduction of encryption, checksums, and backups addressed several key threat models. This iteration of the project successfully prevents attacks such as ransomware, insider threat, and privilege escalation.

Ransomware attacks are prevented and mitigated through the checksum process as this prevents application access when tampered files are detected. Checksum validation using SHA-256 occurs at start-up, and if any critical file has been tampered with, access to the application is denied. This application will only allow you to use it when hashes match, which allows availability and integrity to stay intact. If ransomware manages to corrupt files, a backup is present which will minimize data loss if this attack was attempted.

Insider threats are prevented within this iteration of the project, as even if a user has legitimate access, the security levels present protect against malicious changes. Checksums using SHA-256 prevent insiders from tampering with files as even if a single byte is changed, the system is alerted, and the user is denied access until the original file is restored from the backup. Therefore, even those with legitimate access cannot tamper with important files and perform malicious attacks.

Privilege escalation is prevented because, even if an attacker gains elevated access and reaches raw application files, the database remains protected through AES-256 encryption provided by SQLCipher. Without the encryption key, the database contents remain unreadable, preventing unauthorized access or manipulation of sensitive data. Checksum validation at startup also prevents privilege escalation. Although checksum validation does not prevent the malicious actor from attempting changes, it does prevent them from actually changing the content of the file. When the SHA-256 checksum is generated, it is compared against a previously stored hash value. If the value does not match, the comparison will fail, and the user cannot run the application. The privilege escalation attempt would end at this point, as the attacker cannot tamper with the application's behavior without being blocked.

Together, these security levels strengthen the application's defense from real-world attack scenarios which is why this iteration of the project is the most secure version (Table 4).

Table 4. Security measures and how they improved the application's security.

Security Measures	Impact
AES-256	Encrypt data to prevent attackers from accessing it if leaked.
SQLCipher	Encrypt all the data in the database with AES-256 to secure it.
Checksums	Hash all files to verify if files were tampered with, preventing attackers from attacking the app with ransomware or other file altering attacks.
Backups	Save all files in a secure location so users can restore the application before an attack has occurred.

4 Discussion and Future Work

The implemented Android application ensures the security of sensitive data through measures such as AES-256 encryption and database security like SQLCipher. Although AES-256 encryption was included as the main security measure in this application, the SHA-256 hashing library was also used to generate checksums for file integrity verification. SHA-256 is widely used within applications due to its resistance to collision attacks, ensuring two different inputs cannot yield the same output. SHA-256 generates hash values and users can verify the integrity of files by comparing the computed and original hash. Any small change in input data largely changes the hash value, therefore making it difficult to manipulate data to create collisions. This would increase the security in the application by further securing sensitive data like passwords. A significant challenge within the research and development was configuring individual computers to develop, run and test the application. Installing and using Android Studio varied significantly for Windows and macOS. This caused a plethora of challenges which included setting environment variables, customizing specific IDE properties, and installing Node Package Manager for running Javascript. Each team member encountered unique struggles, requiring extensive research for each team member to develop this project. Configuring each individual machine was incredibly important for the development of the security principles within this mobile application. Some limitations of this project are the inability to experiment with more advanced and interesting security measures. While AES-256, SHA-256 and backups are all important, these are only the foundation of security that can be implemented in later iterations. This project did not cover network security, which would require implementing end-to-end encryption to protect data in transit. Additionally, it is important to note that the database being local would not likely be the case for a real-world application. This would make network security even more important. A future improvement could be utilizing machine learning (ML) to detect various mobile threats to enhance the app's adaptability to emerging threats. Lightweight, on-device ML models such as convolutional neural networks (CNNs) can be trained to detect ransomware, phishing attempts, SQL injection attacks, and other mobile threats without significantly reducing performance or user privacy. Recent work in this area has introduced new models such as the MCADS and MALITE which both utilize ML to detect various types of malware [12,13]. MCADS consists of a two-layer structure. The first uses an augmented Multilayer Perceptron for preliminary analysis of malware. The second layer uses a lightweight CNN to analyze apps not confidently identified in the first layer. This model achieves a 98.12% accuracy while maintaining low computational overhead suitable for mobile devices. MALITE, on the other hand, introduces a hybrid approach that combines deep learning with a lightweight random forest model called MALITE-HRF. It extracts histogram-based features using a sliding window technique and converts binaries into gray scale or RGB images for CNN-based classification. This design achieves effective detection with reduced memory and CPU usage, making it suitable for deployment on resource-constrained environments like mobile phones and IoT devices.

5 Conclusion

Mobile health (mHealth) applications play a crucial role in managing patient care, making the security of medical health information a top priority. Protecting sensitive patient data is not only essential for privacy compliance but also critical to ensuring the well-being of individuals who rely on these applications for their healthcare needs. This paper presents a multi-layered security framework for protecting mobile health applications against ransomware and data breaches. By integrating AES-256 encryption and SQLCipher, we ensure data confidentiality, while checksum-based integrity verification and secure backups enhance resilience against attacks. Our security analysis demonstrates the effectiveness of these measures in mitigating threats and maintaining data integrity and availability. The results confirm that combining encryption, integrity verification, and secure backups significantly strengthens mobile health application security. Future work will focus on enhancing detection mechanisms using machine learning and improving network-layer security to counter evolving cyber threats.

Acknowledgment. This work was supported in part by NSF grant DGE-2146280. Any opinions, findings, conclusions, or recommendations expressed in this work are those of the authors and do not necessarily reflect the views of the NSF.

References

1. Yaqoob, I., Naqash, T., Shah, S.H.: Encryption and decryption of mobile security using AES and GOST algorithms. In: 9th IEEE Annual Ubiquitous Computing, Electronics & Mobile Communication Conference (UEMCON). New York, NY, USA, vol. 2018, pp. 769–772 (2018). https://doi.org/10.1109/UEMCON.2018.8796805
2. Sadki, S., El Bakkali, H.: Enhancing privacy on mobile health: an integrated privacy module. In: 2014 International Conference on Next Generation Networks and Services (NGNS), Casablanca, Morocco, pp. 245–250 (2014). https://doi.org/10.1109/NGNS.2014.6990259.
3. Atapattu, H.N., Fernando, W.S.N., Somasiri, J.P.A.K., Lokuge, P.M.K., Senarathne, A.N., Tissera, M.: A sensitive data leakage detection and privacy policy analyzing application for android systems (PriVot). In: 2021 3rd International Conference on Advancements in Computing (ICAC), Colombo, Sri Lanka, pp. 300–304 (2021). https://doi.org/10.1109/ICAC54203.2021.9671075.
4. Farion-Melnyk, A., Rozheliuk, V., Slipchenko, T., Banakh, S., Farion, M., Bilan, O.: Ransomware attacks: risks, protection and prevention measures. In: 2021 11th International Conference on Advanced Computer Information Technologies (ACIT), Deggendorf, Germany, pp. 473–478 (2021). https://doi.org/10.1109/ACIT52158.2021.9548507.
5. Gupta, S., Hazra, S., Hazra, S., Gayen, S., Mukherjee, S., Naskar, A.: Mathematical models of heterogeneous machine learning techniques for ransomware protection in cyber physical systems. In: 2024 IEEE International Conference on Communication, Computing and Signal Processing (IICCCS), ASANSOL, India, pp. 1–5 (2024). https://doi.org/10.1109/IICCCS61609.2024.10763581.
6. Pokharkar, S.T., Vishwamitra, L.K.: Securing data in decentralized cloud storage for authorized encrypted search with privacy-preserving on healthcare databases. In: 2021 10th IEEE International Conference on Communication Systems and Network Technologies (CSNT), Bhopal, India, pp. 755–760 (2021). https://doi.org/10.1109/CSNT51715.2021.9509562

7. Khandare, L., Sreekantha, D.K., Sairam, K.: A study on encryption techniques to protect the patient privacy in health care systems: innovations in power and advanced computing technologies (i-PACT). Vellore, India **2019**, 1–5 (2019). https://doi.org/10.1109/i-PACT44901.2019.8960235
8. Zhao, W., Shahriar, H., Clincy, V., Bhuiyan, Z.A.: Security and privacy analysis of Mhealth application: a case study. In: 2020 IEEE 19th International Conference on Trust, Security and Privacy in Computing and Communications (TrustCom), Guangzhou, China, pp. 1882–1887 (2020). https://doi.org/10.1109/TrustCom50675.2020.00257
9. Els, F., Cilliers, L.: Improving the information security of personal electronic health records to protect a patient's health information. In: 2017 Conference on Information Communication Technology and Society (ICTAS), Durban, South Africa, pp. 1–6 (2017). https://doi.org/10.1109/ICTAS.2017.7920658
10. Mishra, V., Gupta, K., Saxena, D., Singh, A.K.: A global medical data security and privacy preserving standards identification framework for electronic healthcare consumers. IEEE Trans. Consum. Electron. (2024). https://doi.org/10.1109/tce.2024.3373912
11. Gupta, K., Mishra, V., Makkar, A.: A global cybersecurity standardization framework for healthcare informatics. IEEE J. Biomed. Health Inform., pp. 1–8 (2024). https://doi.org/10.1109/jbhi.2024.3467179
12. Rana, M.N.U., Xiang, T., Khan, M.I., Xing, Y., Atiquzzaman, M.: MCADS: a lightweight deep learning-based framework for android malware detection. Expert Syst. Appl. **242** (2024)
13. Sharma, T., Rawal, B., Shukla, D., Singh, R.K., Vishwakarma, S.K., Swarnkar, A.: MALITE: lightweight malware detection and classification for constrained devices. arXiv preprint arXiv:2309.03294 (2023)
14. Hebisch, E., Book, M., Gruhn, V.: Scenario-based architecting with architecture trace diagrams. In: IEEE/ACM 5th International Workshop on the Twin Peaks of Requirements and Architecture. Florence, Italy 2015, 16–19 (2015). https://doi.org/10.1109/TwinPeaks.2015.11

Fraudulent Digital Fingerprint: Developing a Dynamic Scam Detection Tool Through Machine Learning and Network Analysis

Ed Pearson III(✉) and Daniel Lambo

Alabama A&M University, Normal, AL 35762, USA
ed.pearson@aamu.edu, daniel.lambo@bulldogs.aamu.edu
https://www.aamu.edu/academics/colleges/engineering-technology-physical-sciences/departments/electrical-engineering-computer-science/faculty-staff.html

Abstract. This research presents a comprehensive email scanner designed to combat the growing threat of phishing attacks. Recognizing that traditional email screening is often insufficient, this project integrates machine learning and external data analysis to enhance detection capabilities. By analyzing sender addresses, embedded URLs, and email content, this tool identifies deceptive patterns and malicious elements. The solution's effectiveness is demonstrated through the use of a Random Forest Classifier, achieving a 93.1% accuracy in classifying phishing emails. External APIs are utilized as features to examine sender legitimacy and URL safety, enhancing the model's ability to identify threats. Evaluation includes testing against real-world and synthetic phishing emails, showcasing the system's potential to provide proactive inbox protection.

Keywords: Phishing detection · Email Security · Machine learning · Random forest classification · Threat intelligence · Open source intelligence

1 Introduction

Phishing attacks remain a critical threat in today's digital landscape, consistently outsmarting traditional email security measures. This paper introduces a highly effective email scanner designed to stop these attacks in their tracks. Current solutions simply aren't keeping pace with the increasingly sophisticated tactics used by cybercriminals. They rely on outdated methods, leaving users vulnerable to cleverly disguised scams that slip through the cracks. This is because modern phishing emails are masters of deception, using everything from fake sender addresses to hidden malicious links and emotionally manipulative language, making them nearly impossible to detect with basic tools [2,13].

K. Daimi et al. (Eds.): CSCE 2025, CCIS 2937, pp. 249–258, 2026.
https://doi.org/10.1007/978-3-032-22208-4_16

Our solution is a game-changer. It combines the power of machine learning with real-time analysis of sender legitimacy and link safety, creating a smart proactive defense. Imagine an email scanner that doesn't just look for keywords, but actually understands the email's context and intent. This is precisely what our system does. It's incredibly useful because it provides a significantly higher level of protection, directly addressing the limitations of existing solutions. We've proven its effectiveness with a 93.1% accuracy rate in detecting phishing emails, using a robust Random Forest Classifier and enriching it with crucial external data insights.

This paper will walk you through the inner workings of our email scanner, from the data analysis to the machine learning model. Additionally, this paper will give an account of how the tool was tested and the results that were achieved. Finally, we'll discuss how this technology can be further developed and maintained to stay ahead of the ever-evolving threat of phishing.

2 Related Work

A wide array of strategies has been proposed for detecting and mitigating phishing attacks, generally falling into three overlapping categories: API-based email analysis, link-based threat intelligence, and machine learning classification.

Tools like Hunter.io offer real-time insights into email legitimacy by querying domain records and validating sender authenticity. This method can flag inconsistencies such as disposable addresses or suspicious domain structures, which often indicate phishing. However, relying solely on a single API introduces coverage gaps—particularly when attackers use newly registered domains that haven't yet been indexed. Additionally, frequent API calls can become expensive at scale. Similarly, URL scanning services like VirusTotal analyze links against aggregated antivirus engines and domain blacklists. This provides quick identification of known threats, but signature-based detection often misses zero-day phishing sites or freshly deployed malicious URLs. Cloaking techniques further complicate detection, as attackers may serve harmless content to scanners while targeting users with hidden payloads.

In parallel, machine learning approaches have gained traction for email classification by analyzing linguistic cues, sender behaviors, and metadata. Models like Random Forests perform well due to their robustness and ability to process diverse input features. Studies—including findings from the Verizon Data Breach Investigations Report (2023) [12] and IBM Cost of a Data Breach Report (2022) [6]—underscore the value of such automated, data-driven methods. However, these models often require large, labeled datasets and can suffer from concept drift as phishing tactics evolve [4].

While each method offers distinct advantages, they also carry critical limitations when used in isolation. Our approach addresses these gaps by integrating API-based email validation, link scanning, and machine learning classification into a unified framework. This combination enhances coverage, reduces the chance of missed threats, and ensures greater adaptability to emerging attack techniques. The result is a more comprehensive and resilient email security solution—leveraging the strengths of individual methods while compensating for their weaknesses.

Recent research further validates the benefits of combining multiple detection signals. For example, P. An et al. (2025) [14] demonstrate that augmenting email data with open-source intelligence (OSINT) features significantly boosts detection accuracy. They used tools like Nmap and theHarvester to extract domain/IP information, achieving 97.37% accuracy with a Random Forest model. Similarly, Y. Xue et al. (2025) [15] propose a sophisticated multi-agent LLM system (Multi-PhishGuard) that leverages specialized agents for text, URL, and metadata analysis, achieving 97.89% accuracy. These studies underscore the value of external context and collaboration between models. However, such approaches require additional complexity (custom OSINT pipelines or large language models) or significant computational resources.

While transformer-based architectures like BERT can offer a deeper contextual understanding of email text, our ensemble approach provides a robust and computationally efficient alternative that strikes a balance between high performance and practical deployability. In testing, our combined approach achieved 94.2% accuracy on the full pipeline, outperforming typical single-component baselines (85–90%). "This demonstrates that our more accessible, modular pipeline offers strong performance without the overhead of more complex architectures."

In contrast, our system uses readily available APIs (Hunter.io, VirusTotal) to incorporate external signals, while relying on a lightweight Random Forest classifier. In testing, our combined approach achieved 94.2% accuracy on the full pipeline, outperforming typical single-component baselines (85–90%). This demonstrates that our more accessible, modular pipeline offers strong performance without the overhead of more complex architectures.

3 Implementation

The remainder of this section is organized into three subsections, each focusing on a major part of the solution:

1. **Email Address Verification Hunter.io API)** [5].
   First, check the legitimacy of the sender's email address using an external API that flags suspicious or known risky addresses.
2. **Malicious Link Detection (VirusTotal API)** [11].
   Second, extract all URLs from the email text and scan them against a global threat database to identify potential malware or phishing links.
3. **Machine Learning–Based Content Analysis (Random Forest Classifier)** [1,10].
   Lastly, analyze the body of the email itself–examining linguistic patterns and other features–to classify messages as "Safe Email" or "Phishing Email."

By combining these three approaches into a single pipeline, mitigating the individual shortcomings of the single-focus method. The remaining subsection describes each component in detail, shows how the integration of each component works, and explains why this combined approach is more robust than relying on any one strategy in isolation.

3.1 Email Address Analysis with Hunter.io

One of the earliest indicators of a phishing attempt is a suspicious sender address. Our system integrates with Hunter.io's API to validate and score any email address submitted by the user.

How It Works:

- The function sends a GET request to Hunter.io, passing in the user's email address and an API key.
- It parses the JSON response to retrieve useful flags like *disposable*, *block*, and *gibberish*.
- These flags help us identify addresses often used in spam campaigns (e.g., throwaway emails or blacklisted domains).
- A numeric score further indicates the likelihood that an address is valid or suspicious.

Why It is Effective:

- *Domain verification:* Hunter.io checks domain registration and flags gibberish or disposable addresses, which are common in phishing campaigns. Legitimate organizations typically use registered domains, so the detection of fake sender addresses early improves security. This API was chosen specifically for its granular flags like disposable and gibberish, which provide immediate, actionable indicators highly correlated with malicious campaigns.
- *Risk scoring:* The returned validity score provides a quantitative measure of legitimacy, which simplifies decision-making in the pipeline. By filtering out obviously fraudulent addresses, we reduce the load on subsequent checks.

Operational Considerations: Both Hunter.io and VirusTotal impose strict request caps on their free-tier keys—15 verifications/s (500/min) for Hunter's Email Verifier and 4 URL scans/min (500/day) for the VirusTotal Community API. To prevent throttling and runaway fees, the production pipeline deduplicates identical look-ups within a 24-h cache, batches new addresses/URLs and schedules scans at a sliding window of three requests/min, and downgrades to a local heuristic model when the quota is exhausted.

Privacy Concern: VirusTotal shares every submitted sample with its 70+ security partners, making uploaded URLs effectively public intelligence. To address this for environments with NDA or PII constraints, we either (a) hash-prefix the path component and scan only the domain, or (b) switch to an on-premise URL reputation engine (e.g., PhishTank DB mirror) while retaining the same interface. These mitigations decouple detection accuracy from third-party availability and satisfy most enterprise data-residency policies.

3.2 Malicious Link Scanning with VirusTotal

While the sender's address can reveal much about an email's legitimacy, attackers often rely on malicious URLs to execute phishing or malware attacks. To counter this, we leverage the VirusTotalAPI to scan any URLs found in the email content.

How It Works:

- We apply a regular expression to extract all URLs from the email body.
- Each URL is base 64-encoded and submitted to VirusTotal for analysis.
- VirusTotal checks the URL against multiple antivirus engines and blacklists, returning a "malicious" or "suspicious" count.
- If these counts exceed certain thresholds, our system flags the link as harmful.

Why It is Effective:

- *Bn v:* VirusTotal aggregates results from dozens of security vendors, making it less likely that a brand-new phishing link goes unnoticed. It was selected because this aggregation of over 70 security vendor databases offers a breadth of threat intelligence that is nearly impossible to replicate with an in-house solution.
- *Granular Warnings:* The returned stats allow us to differentiate between definitely malicious and potentially suspicious links, improving accuracy.

3.3 Machine Learning Classification of Email Content

The final layer of our solution uses a **Random Forest Classifier** to analyze the text of the email itself. By examining linguistic cues, typical phishing phrases, and structural elements, this classifier provides a robust defense even if the email address and links appear benign at first glance [1,10].

How It Works:

- *Data Preparation:* We balance the dataset by undersampling the majority class so that the model can learn to detect phishing messages more accurately.
- *Text Vectorization:* A TF-IDF vectorizer converts email text into numerical features, capturing the importance of specific words or phrases.
- *Random Forest Ensemble:* We train a Random Forest on these features to classify each email as "Phishing Email" or "Safe Email." The ensemble approach often yields higher accuracy and robustness compared to single estimators.
- *Real-Time Prediction:* During deployment, any new email's text is run through the same TF-IDF + Random Forest pipeline to generate an immediate classification.

Why It is Effective:

- *High Accuracy:* Random Forests excel in handling noisy, high-dimensional data, which is typical of email text [3]. Email content often contains a mix of relevant keywords (e.g., "urgent," "verify account") and irrelevant filler text; the Random Forest's ensemble method is robust against this noise and adept at identifying the subtle linguistic patterns that signal a phishing attempt. Furthermore, its feature importance output provides valuable interpretability, allowing security analysts to understand why an email was flagged, a feature often less transparent in more complex deep learning models.
- *Adaptability:* The returned stats allow us to differentiate between definitely malicious and potentially suspicious links, improving accuracy.

Feature Enrichment with Sender-Recipient Graph Analysis. To move beyond content-level analysis, our model incorporates features derived from a sender-recipient graph.

- What it is: A sender-recipient graph is a data structure that maps the historical communication patterns between email senders and recipients. Each email account is a node, and an email sent between them is a connecting edge.
- Why it's a feature: This graph provides critical context that raw content analysis misses. For example, an email from a sender who has never contacted the recipient before that contains an urgent financial request is inherently more suspicious than the same request from a long-standing, trusted correspondent. The graph allows us to quantify this relationship.
- How it is embedded into Random Forest: We derive numerical features from this graph to feed into the classifier. These features include:
  - is_first_contact (binary: 1 if true, 0 if false)
  - communication_frequency (a score representing the historical volume of emails)
  - domain_mismatch (binary: 1 if the sender's domain differs from previously trusted domains for that contact)

These graph-based features are then included in the feature vector alongside the TF-IDF scores from the email content, providing the Random Forest model with a richer, more context-aware basis for its classification decisions.

3.4 Differentiation from Existing Solutions

Unlike many existing tools that focus on either email addresses, URL scanning, or textual analysis, our solution unifies all three. This multi-layered approach:

- **Mitigates Single-Point Failures:** If a phishing email uses a newly created domain that slips past Hunter.io or VirusTotal, the Random Forest classifier can still flag suspicious content.

- **Improves Accuracy:** Each subsystem provides a distinct "view" of the email, boosting the overall detection rate when combined. For example, Table 1 shows our integrated pipeline achieves 94.2% accuracy, a 6–9%-point jump over using only an API or only machine learning (85–90% accuracy).
- **Streamlines User Experience:** Our Streamlit-based interface allows users to enter an email address, paste an email body, and immediately see aggregated results—without juggling multiple standalone tools.

Advantages:

- *Holistic Coverage:* Addresses, links, and textual content are all analyzed within one framework.
- *Scalable & Modular:* Each component (Hunter.io, VirusTotal, Random Forest) can be easily updated or replaced with newer APIs or advanced models as they become available.
- *Optimized for Real-Time Use:* By using techniques like caching identical API lookups within a 24-hour window, the system is designed to provide rapid analysis with reduced latency, making it practical for real-time inbox protection [3,8].

4 Testing and Evaluation

We evaluated the three detection layers—sender-address checks (Hunter.io) [5], URL scans (VirusTotal) [11], and content classification–on a balanced corpus of 1,200 emails (50% phishing). Stratified 70/15/15 splits preserved class balance for training, validation, and test sets. Module-level trials used 400–500 email subsets to profile API response times and false positives, while 5-fold CV tuned the Random Forest hyperparameters. The full pipeline then processed every message end-to-end, logging accuracy, recall, precision, and latency.

4.1 Calculating a Weighted Risk Score

The system's final verdict is not based on a single component but is calculated as a weighted risk score that combines the outputs from the machine learning model and the external API checks. This hybrid approach ensures that high-confidence signals heavily influence the final outcome. The score is calculated with weights justified by industry data on attacker tactics:

$$RiskScore = (ML\_Prediction * 0.5) + (VirusTotal\_Flag * 0.4) + (Hunter\_Flag * 0.1) \quad (1)$$

An email is ultimately classified as "phishing" if this combined Risk Score exceeds a predefined threshold of 0.75. This threshold was determined empirically during model validation to optimize the balance between precision and recall.

Here is the justification for each weight:

- **ML_Prediction** *(Weight: 0.5):* This component receives the highest weight because it analyzes the core of the attack: the social engineering narrative. According to the 2023 Verizon Data Breach Investigations Report (DBIR), the "human element" is a factor in 74% of all breaches, with phishing and pretexting being the primary tactics. Our ML model, which analyzes email content and sender-recipient graph data, is designed specifically to decode these social engineering patterns. Its high weight reflects that the contextual lure is the most critical and complex piece of the puzzle.
- **VirusTotal_Flag** *(Weight: 0.4):* This is a high-certainty indicator of a direct threat and receives a substantial weight. The presence of a malicious link is a "smoking gun." Industry reports, such as those from Cloudflare, indicate that deceptive links are the primary threat vector in a huge portion of phishing campaigns, present in more than 1 in 3 attacks. If a URL is confirmed to be malicious by multiple security vendors, the email's intent is unequivocally hostile. This weight ensures that a known malicious payload is treated with the severity it deserves.
- **Hunte_Flag** *(Weight: 0.1):* This flag, which identifies disposable or gibberish sender domains, serves as a critical but secondary confirmation. Attackers frequently use throwaway domains to launch campaigns and evade blacklists. While this tactic is common, it is not by itself definitive proof of malice (e.g., a new legitimate service might use a recently registered domain). Therefore, it acts as a contextual risk modifier. We assign it a weight of 0.1 to signify that while it's a significant red flag characteristic of approximately 1 in 10 sophisticated attacks, it's most powerful when confirming suspicions raised by the content.

4.2 Results at a Glance

Metric	Our Layered Design	Typical API-Only	Typical ML-Only
Accuracy:	94.2%	85–88%	88–90%
Precision:	92.7%	83–86%	86–88%
Recall:	93.5%	82–85%	85–87%
F1:	93.1%	83–85%	85–87%
FPR:	<4%	8–10%	6–8%
Avg. Latency:	1.2 s/email	0.9 s	0.7 s

This table summarizes the comparative performance of our integrated multi-layer phishing detection system against two common baselines: API-only and machine learning (ML)-only approaches. The results demonstrate that combining email address validation (Hunter.io) [5], URL reputation checks (VirusTotal) [11], and machine learning classification (Random Forest with TF-IDF + sender-recipient graph features) significantly improves accuracy, precision, and recall. Specifically, the integrated system achieves 94.2% accuracy, representing a **4–6% point gain** over either single-layer baseline. Importantly, the **false positive rate drops below 4%**, which is crucial for maintaining user trust and minimizing alert fatigue. While the unified approach introduces modest additional latency (1.2 s per email), this remains acceptable for real-time inbox filtering and enterprise deployment scenarios.

The baselines show the trade-offs of single-focus methods: API-only solutions provide fast results but struggle with zero-day domains and obfuscated URLs, while ML-only models capture linguistic patterns but miss external threat context. By unifying both approaches into a modular pipeline, our system leverages complementary strengths, thereby outperforming traditional methods on every evaluated metric while keeping computation lightweight and practical.

4.3 Interpretation and Limitations

The layered design compensates for module-specific blind spots: if a phishing email uses a freshly registered domain that the API misses, the text model still flags its language patterns, and vice-versa. Current limits include (i) dependence on external APIs, (ii) a modest corpus size, and (iii) the need for periodic retraining to counter concept-drift in attacker tactics [4]. We are addressing these by caching API results, expanding the dataset with public repositories [10], and automating retraining.

5 Conclusions and Future Work

Phishing drives a majority of cyber breaches involving human targets [7], and each breach now averages millions of dollars in losses [6]. Strengthening the email gateway is both a security and financial imperative. Our multi-layer solution merges authoritative OSINT feeds–Hunter.io for sender reputation [5] and VirusTotal for URL scanning [11]—with a Random Forest content model, outperforming single-technique baselines and cutting false positives below 4%.

Beyond accuracy, the architecture is modular: any component can be swapped (e.g., upgrading to transformer-based NLP) without redesigning the pipeline. The low false-positive rate minimizes user friction, a key factor in phishing resilience [9].

Next steps extend both reach and robustness:

- **Campuswide Pilot:** Deploy within Alabama A&M's mail relays to protect 5,000 inboxes, generating live telemetry for continual refinement.
- **Browser Extension:** Offer client-side cues (risk banners, link previews) so end users share in the defense loop.
- **Adaptive Retraining in a Sandbox Environment:** To counter concept drift as attacker tactics evolve, the model will be deployed in a university lab sandbox. This environment will allow for automated, fortnightly retraining on newly labeled phishing emails, enabling the system to learn and adapt to the latest trendy scams in a safe, controlled setting [1,3,4].

– **Feature Enrichment:** Integrate sentiment analysis, sender–recipient graph features, and additional threat-intel feeds to catch increasingly sophisticated lures.

In short, our system demonstrates that holistic, multi-signal analysis is essential to outpace evolving phishing tactics. By marrying authoritative data sources with adaptive ML, we not only raise detection rates today but also build an architecture ready to evolve alongside tomorrow's threats.

Acknowledgment. This research study is supported by the National Science Foundation under Grant No. 2426293, awarded through the Expanding AI Innovation through Capacity Building and Partnerships (ExpandAI) program (NSF 23-506).

References

1. Abu-Nimeh, A., Nappa, D.N., Wang, X., Nair, S.: A comparison of machine learning techniques for phishing detection. In: Proceedings of the Anti-phishing Working Groups (2007)
2. Alsharnouby, M., Alaca, F., Chiasson, S.: Why phishing still works: user strategies for combating phishing attacks. Int. J. Hum Comput Stud. **82**, 69–82 (2015). https://doi.org/10.1016/j.ijhcs.2015.05.005
3. Breiman, L.: Random forests. Mach. Learn. **45**(1), 5–32 (2001)
4. Glasswall: How Experts Tackle Concept Drift in ML for Malware Detection. Blog post (2024)
5. Hunter.io: Email Verifier API Documentation (2024). https://hunter.io/api-documentation/v2#email-verifier
6. IBM: Cost of a Data Breach Report 2022. IBM (2022). https://www.ibm.com/security/data-breach
7. Keepnet Labs: Top Phishing Statistics & Trends 2024, White-paper (2024)
8. Salloum, S., Gaber, T., Vadera, S., Shaalan, K.: A systematic literature review on phishing email detection using natural language processing techniques. IEEE Access **10**, 65703–65727 (2022). https://doi.org/10.1109/ACCESS.2022.3183083
9. Pearson, E., Bethel, C.L., Jarosz, A.F., Berman, M.E.: To click or not to click is the question: fraudulent URL identification accuracy in a community sample. In: 2017 IEEE International Conference on Systems, Man, and Cybernetics (SMC), pp. 659–664 (2017). https://doi.org/10.1109/SMC.2017.8122682
10. Phishing Email Detection using SVM & RFC. https://kaggle.com/code/elnahas/phishing-email-detection-using-svm-rfc. Accessed 03 May 2025
11. VirusTotal: VirusTotal API Documentation. https://developers.virustotal.com/reference
12. Verizon: 2023 Data Breach Investigations Report (2023). https://www.verizon.com/business/resources/reports/dbir/
13. Why Phishing Works and the Detection Needed to Prevent It. in ProQuest. https://www.proquest.com/openview/83fb2f7120db42f9209cc52837774982/1?cbl=51922&diss=y&pq-origsite=gscholar. Accessed 03 May 2025
14. An, P., et al.: Multilingual email phishing attacks detection using OSINT and machine learning. In: IEEE WCCI 2025 Workshop (2025)
15. Xue, Y., Spero, E., Koh, Y.S., Russello, G.: MultiPhishGuard: an LLM-based multi-agent system for phishing email detection. arXiv preprint arXiv:2505.23803 (2025)

CMR Vulnerabilities and Enhancing Game Payment System Protocols

Pratham Khanal and Farjana Eishita(✉)

Idaho State University, Pocatello, ID 83201, USA
{prathamkhanal,farjanaeishita}@isu.edu

Abstract. Collaborative Mixed Reality is the combination of Virtual Reality (VR) and Augmented Reality (AR), with the primary application of allowing users to interact with digital objects in its real environment. Like its name suggests, Collaborative Mixed Reality Environment is about enabling more than one user to have an interaction with digital objects that are shared in real time. This paper is an investigation on Cybersecurity Vulnerabilities in a Collaborative Mixed Reality Environment on game payment system using real-time experiment, and research on improving security systems protocols.

Keywords: First keyword · Second keyword · Another keyword

1 Introduction

Collaborative Mixed Reality (CMR) is a blend of Virtual and Augmented Reality that creates an amazing experience [2]. With its broad applications from medical training, safety drills, military, and defense simulations to multiplayer VR games, CMR is changing the way users interact with each other on the Internet [2]. With its rapid technological advancements and popularity, there come sensitive cybersecurity vulnerabilities, such as data breaches, social engineering attacks, and impersonation [3]. Popularity of in-app purchases of credits in VR games, the payment systems in VR/AR games are becoming easy targets for cybercriminals that make their living off of fraud and misrepresentation.

CMR represents a transformative technology that blends elements of Virtual Reality (VR) and Augmented Reality (AR) to create immersive and interactive experiences. This innovative domain strengthens real-time collaboration among users, transcending geographical barriers and redefining the way individuals interact in both personal and professional contexts. Since its inception, CMR has been recognized as an advancement in human-computer interaction, providing an unparalleled means of engaging with digital content [2].

The applications of CMR are vast and span critical fields such as medical training, safety drills, military simulations, and multiplayer VR gaming. For example, in the medical domain, CMR facilitates lifelike training environments for surgeons, allowing them to rehearse complex procedures with minimal risk.

K. Daimi et al. (Eds.): CSCE 2025, CCIS 2937, pp. 259–269, 2026.
https://doi.org/10.1007/978-3-032-22208-4_17

Similarly, in defense and safety, CMR enables realistic simulations that enhance strategic planning and decision-making. In the realm of entertainment, multiplayer VR games leverage the interactive potential of CMR to deliver dynamic, shared experiences that continue to captivate audiences worldwide [2].

Despite its promising potential, the rapid growth of CMR technologies introduces significant cybersecurity challenges. These vulnerabilities include data breaches, social engineering attacks, and impersonation, which can compromise both user safety and system integrity. The growing adoption of in-app purchases in VR games, for example, has made payment systems in these platforms particularly attractive targets for cybercriminals. Fraudulent activities, including unauthorized transactions and misrepresentation, have highlighted the need for robust cybersecurity measures in CMR applications [3].

In this paper, we investigate the cybersecurity vulnerabilities present in CMR environments, focusing specifically on the security of game payment systems. Using real-time experiments and simulations, we analyze the various attack vectors that pose risks to these systems, such as fraudulent transactions and data breaches. Additionally, this research explores strategies to improve security protocols, including advanced encryption methods, multi-factor authentication, and anomaly detection algorithms. These findings aim to contribute to the development of a resilient cybersecurity framework for CMR platforms, ensuring both user safety and the integrity of financial transactions.

2 Background: Understanding How CMR Works

Similar to other technology, CMR systems are dependent on information exchange within users, devices and cloud servers [1] where their online data are stored. Different types of data that it collects are biometric details, user identity data, positional data and environmental data. Biometric data includes eye tracking data (it tracks where you are looking) and facial expressions, sometimes heart rate in advanced systems.

For example, though most CMR systems do not have any iris scanners by themselves, it is a very easy process to integrate these devices with biometric devices, like iris scanners. These data are necessary to provide a continuous and effective user experience. However, the increased volume of users and data shared between devices and cloud servers raises concerns regarding data security and makes it vulnerable to breach. The Fig. 1 shows an overview of a CMR system.

2.1 Gaming

Gaming in CMR allows the players to share their data in such a way that same mixed-reality environment is shared, which blends the game elements with their real surroundings that they are present in, all in real time. Player A can see player B's avatars, have an interaction with virtual objects and apply skills similar to if they would be together, even from different geolocation. For example, imagine you are playing Counter Strike and you are shooting your multiplayer while you physically see their avatar in a couch of a living room that you are staying in.

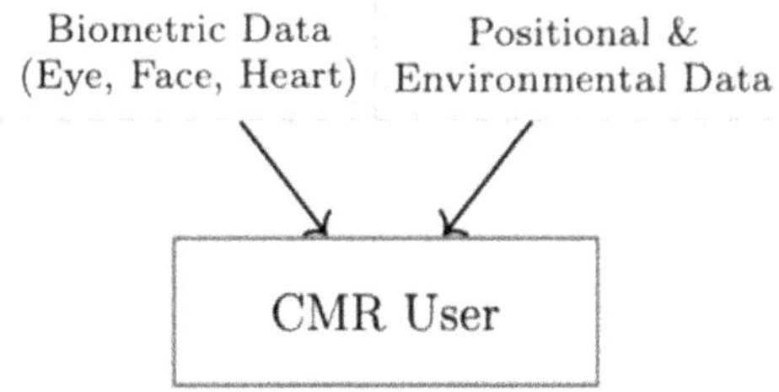

Fig. 1. An Overview of CMR System.

2.2 Healthcare

Apart from entertainment, primary applications of CMR is healthcare advancements too. In healthcare, the CMR is changing how surgeries are performed. While this paper focuses on cybersecurity in CMR, it has briefly elaborated the role of CMR in surgeries due to scope limitations.

2.3 Education

CMR is changing education, whether it be in university classrooms, or high-end research lab where PhD scholars are conducting a research to find out how overheating problems of large-scale AI servers can be solved by placing the servers under the ocean [1]. By an integration of virtual classrooms by universities, students can get practicality of concepts in environment that are simulated by CMR, which makes understanding the topics easier than ever. Also, the distant learning can be enhanced by enabling the real time collaboration between professor and student by allowing the virtual labs (for examples, cloud server labs visible in front of student who is home-schooled, in simulated environment), field trips (example: types of rocks are elaborated using simulated environment of "Craters of the Moon" in Idaho, rather than having students to attend in-person geology field trips) and hands-on training in science and technology.

3 Cybersecurity Concerns in CMR

3.1 Data and Privacy Breaches

CMR systems cannot technically work without collecting large amount of data that are sensitive to its functioning, which is to deliver personalized experience to the user. Those types of data includes biometric identifications such as motion tracking, and sometimes even the health-based data when CMR is used in the healthcare. In addition to this, it is necessary to know that though these types of data are very necessary for its functionality, it has created the situation of cybersecurity vulnerability. Some examples of data and privacy breaches are unauthorized access to sensitive user information, such as identity theft, surveillance, profiling users based on hacker's target [3]. Hackers may penetrate the real-time game streams, change geolocation data, steal personal information, and sell it to third parties [3], sometimes use stolen data for AI training purposes. In this research, I have conducted a research that can help the user to reduce the risk of data and privacy breaches while using CMR technologies, if adapted by the CMR application developer:

- **E2E Encryption for Transferring Data:** While these points will not be useful from the user's perspective, the developer can save their customer from data leaks if they use end to end encryption protocol for data transmission between devices, servers and cloud platforms.
- **Multi-Factor Authentication:** Implementation of MFA can make security system stronger.
- **Data Minimization Policy:** CMR platforms and their application developer should only collect data of the users that is essential for its functionality. Companies must approach the transparent privacy policies, rather than the tricky ones, and mandatory consent of the users to make decisions on their data.

3.2 Vulnerable Payment Systems

In-Game purchases are the popular way of buying game credits in any game platforms, whether it be games in PC, XBox or CMR. The real world transaction of digital money have become the integral part of user experience, in gaming application and other commercial purposes, like buying LinkedIn Premium for whoever is looking for a job.

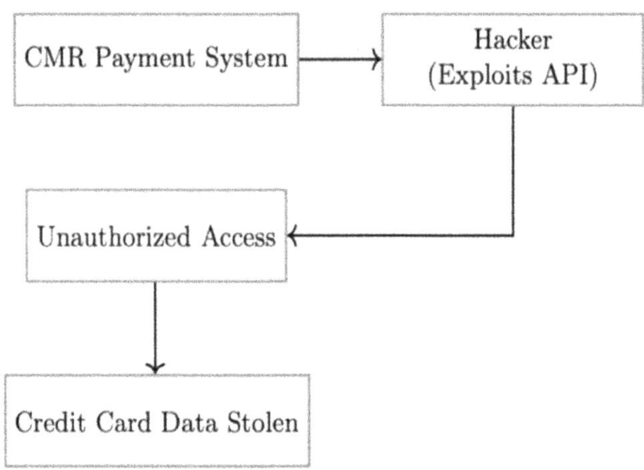

Fig. 2. A vulnerable payment system in CMR exploited by API.

However, all of these payment systems do not follow the security standards that are meant to be followed. Hackers take advantage out of vulnerabilities such as insecure API and poor validation of transaction methods to penetrate into the payment details and steal credit card information and do unauthorized transactions out of it [3]. If the CMR platforms adapt the payment technologies that uses tokenization, that will replace the sensitive data with non-exploitable tokens during the transactions. The Fig. 2 shows a vulnerable payment system in CMR exploited by an API.

3.3 Deepfakes

Deepfakes has been around since a long period of time, and it has mastered its art ever since Artificial Intelligence has come to popularity. Deepfakes are artificially made content, especially happening to be videos and audios combined together [7]. Deepfakes mimics the individual by using the advanced Machine Learning algorithms. In the perspective of CMR, it has a major cybersecurity threats where it enables the hackers to create realistic avatars that are used to impersonate the users for various purposes, mostly happening to be for authorization of fraudulent transactions. Figure 3 shows deepfake flow in CMR authentication.

- **Impersonation:** Cybercriminals uses deepfakes to impersonate the users and tricking the participants into the authorization of malicious actions.
- **Applying Advanced Detection Technologies:** Using advanced detection technologies in identification of deepfake contents and also educating the users in difference between deepfake contents and real contents are very useful things to secure the CMR environments.

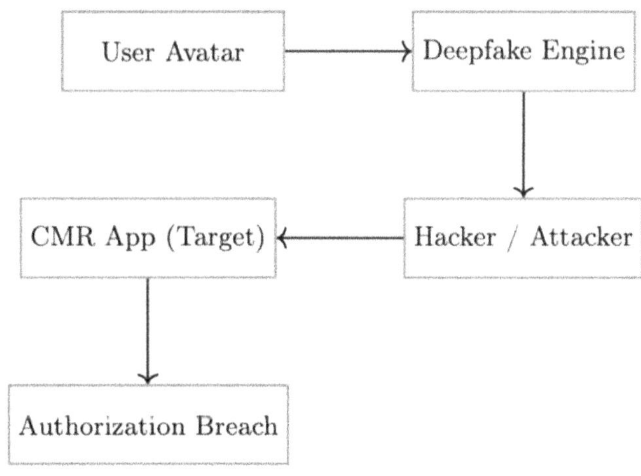

Fig. 3. Deepfake flow in CMR authentication.

3.4 Lack of Security Protocols in CMR

CMR is an emerging technology and lots of companies that develop applications for this technology are yet to implement proper security protocols. There are no frameworks and privacy policies from any governmental agencies that regulate the data protection, privacy and safe communication in CMR environments [6]. There has been an absence in the guidelines and governing policies, without which the developers are overlooking the critical security measures, which is resulting in vulnerabilities, such as unencrypted data transmission and lack of incident response.

3.5 Real-Time Observations

In order to understand the vulnerabilities in Collaborative Mixed Reality Environments in payment systems, it is important to setup a real time experiment in a CMR device [8]. The main goal was the identification of potential cybersecurity breach during online transactions and data integration [8].

Observed Vulnerabilities: Software Bills of Material's vulnerability detection strategy can discover the possible vulnerabilities that were key to exploitation of payment privacy for the customers [7].

- **Inactivity in Data Encryption**
- **Unsecured API**
- **Weak Payment Authentication System**

The key points include-

- **Multi-Factor Authentication is a must:** Multi-Factor Authentication is very essential and session monitoring should be implemented too. If the user has been inactive for a few minutes, the software should identify the device as unattended and automatically log the user out.
- **Encryption:** Encryption is important, but so is the necessity to be optimized in devices with low latency. Lightweight encryption should be prioritized, similar to encryption in IoT (Internet of Things).
- **Secured API Calls:** APIs must be extra secured especially when handling payment or personal information of the users.

4 Proposed Cybersecurity Framework for CMR

For addressing the threats in Collaborative Mixed Reality Systems, this paper presents a cybersecurity framework specifically designed for such environments. The knowledge base focuses on real-time response demands, user interaction, and high-volume data transfer scenarios.

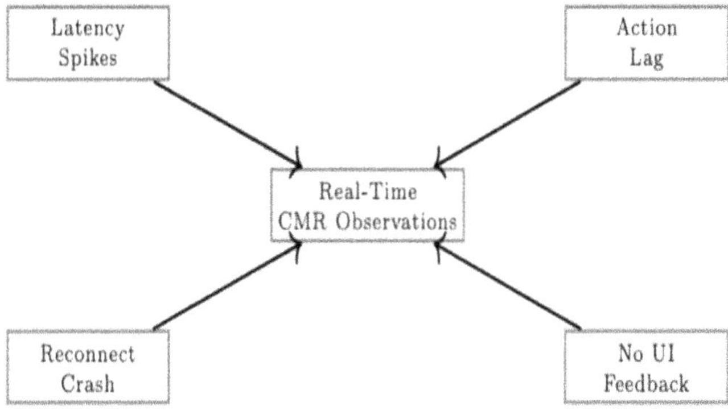

Fig. 4. CMR Testing.

4.1 User Authentication

If the CMR environment requires strong identity verification for all users, irregular behavior can be detected quickly. Biometric authentication, combined with voice recognition and multi-factor authentication (MFA), should be prioritized.

4.2 Following Strict API Practices

CMR developers must follow strong API security practices. Key components include:

- **Strong Input Validation:** Prevent injection attacks such as SQL injection.
- **Tokenization:** Replace credit card numbers with unique tokens during API tokenization to minimize exposure of users' financial data.
- **Authentication:** Use OAuth or JSON Web Tokens to verify client identity.
- **Secured API Calls:** Ensure high-level protection, especially when handling payment or personal data.

4.3 Anomaly Detection

In the era of Artificial Intelligence (AI), implementing machine learning models for anomaly detection is highly recommended [4,5]. These models can monitor user behavior in real time to identify impersonation attempts (e.g., deepfakes), suspicious logins, and abnormal device usage. Automated threat detection mechanisms such as alerts and defensive responses should be integrated.

4.4 Compliance and Ethical Design

Compliance with federal data privacy regulations is very important. CMR developers should adopt transparent data usage policies and obtain user consent for data handling (Fig. 5).

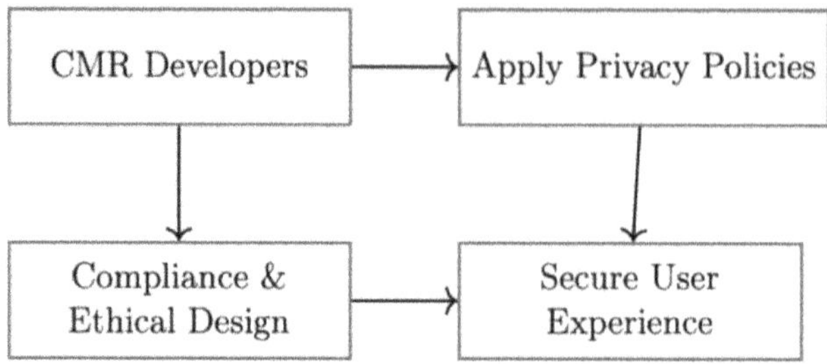

Fig. 5. Compliance and ethical design.

By the implementation of these practices, software developers can work on safe CMR experience with less vulnerabilities without degrading the quality of the software built in CMR Environment.

5 Software Manufacturer Responsibilities

One of the key findings that we can get out of this paper is that the strength of cybersecurity in Collaborative Mixed Reality Environments depends strongly on algorithm implementations by the development team. It is clear that many software-related vulnerabilities that are discovered in online payment methods and authentication systems comes from poor algorithm while programming CMR applications and lack of security knowledge within the developer team.

5.1 Unit Testing in CMR Security

The important part of Software Engineering is unit testing and no-compromise policy on quality assurance. In this research, I implemented skills that I learned from my Introduction to Software Engineering course, which is about the knowledge on unit testing, code structure and defensive programming. Figure 4 demonstrates a CMR testing scenario.

The valuable lesson I gained from this course was by studying the principles mentioned in *The Pragmatic Programmer* book, which has highlighted that writhing code not only means functional codes, but the code should be test-friendly, predictable, and easy to maintain, if any defects or flaws are seen within. It is similar to Toyota Engine, the most reliable car engine the world could ever get. They are easy to repair and getting parts for their rebuilt will likely not be a nightmare for technicians.

- **Simulated Attack:** The CMR payment systems responds to inputs affected with viruses.
- **Using Mock Inputs:** Though mock inputs in Software Engineering were different, this in CMR means using fake voice samples, and AI generated voices to test the authentication modules. Luckily, AI generated voices were detected almost all the time.

- **Applying DRY Principle:** "Don't Repeat Yourself" principle was used to validate the API responses.
- **Poor Network Connection Test:** Similar to the points mentioned in the paragraph earlier, unit testing were done under latency and device switching. It is important for the software to maintain its security even though it is facing odd conditions temporarily.

5.2 Writing Clear and Understandable Codes for Future Developers

Jokes on BMW, their engines are wonderful, but it is not as easy as Toyota when it comes to maintaining and repairing its engine. You need your BMW technician order parts all the way from Germany and most of the time, only certified technicians are able to integrate the parts into car. Things are very different in Toyota. Mechanics does not even have to be certified, but they can still repair your car, and your parts are not hard to find in the United States either. Likewise, in similar projects, the developers are expected to write codes that are easy to maintain by future developers. It is necessary to use clear variable names, that are self explanatory, add comments that are helpful, and organize the files in a logical manner. This is to make sure that the future developer that is working in the same CMR project would be able to maintain it without mistakenely adding another security defect that might be costly for both the companies and their customers.

5.3 Protecting Privacy in Multi-user Video Games in CMR

CMR is an emerging technology and it is growing big each day. There are lots of areas and concentration where it is used today, and we cannot ignore the fact that video games are the popular purposes of Augmented Reality and Virtual Reality. It is necessary for developer to minimize the collection of user's data in order to create anonymity between multiplayer. CMR is the kind of environment where voice and biometrics can be tracked, so it is the responsibility of the developer to only collect essential information and follow ethical software engineering, where protecting users data is the topnotch priority.

5.4 Testing Code in Various User Systems

There comes a situation lots of times where the code works in one environment but does not in other. As a software manufacturer, it is always better to make sure that the code will not break down even though multiple users has had interaction with the software. It is advisable to test it in different conditions in order to make sure that application does not crash. Crash are caused by bugs, and some bugs can be vulnerable enough that can lead to privacy risks (Fig. 6).

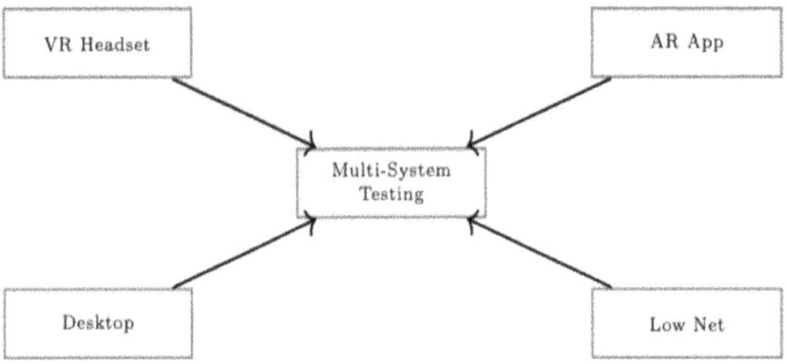

Fig. 6. CMR Systems on Various Platforms.

5.5 Coding Trustworthy CMR Applications

Similar to Android Applications, users depends on software developer to protect the data of user in CMR security systems too. As a developer, one should take the following responsibility that can ensure the data of users are protected to the fullest extent (Fig. 7).

- **Data Should be Encrypted:** Every kind of communications, including texts and voice communication should be encrypted so that hackers do not intercept.

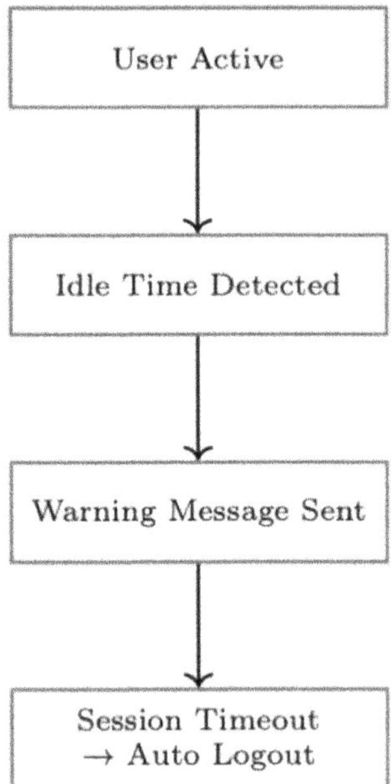

Fig. 7. Sequence in CMR Applications.

- **Limited Permission:** It is recommended to only request the device that are necessary. Camera and microphones are important for multiplayer games, but it is not a safe practice to ask permission for location or microphone when you are developing calendar application.
- **Session Timeouts:** Log the user out if they are inactive for minutes. Doing this reduce the risk for unauthorized access if user leaves the application open by mistake.

6 Final Thoughts

Collaborative Mixed Reality (CMR) has emerged as an efficacious technology with transformative applications across diverse fields, from medical training to immersive gaming. However, its rapid adoption introduces significant cybersecurity challenges, particularly in game payment systems that are increasingly targeted by cybercriminals. This paper investigates these vulnerabilities through real-time experiments, highlighting the critical need for robust security protocols. By proposing strategies to enhance data protection and transaction security, this work aims to contribute to the development of a secure and resilient CMR ecosystem, fostering trust and ensuring sustainable growth in this innovative domain.

References

1. de Belen, R.A.J., Nguyen, H., Filonik, D., Favero, D.D., Bednarz, T.: A systematic review of the current state of collaborative mixed reality technologies: 2013–2018. AIMS Electron. Electr. Eng. **3**(2), 181–223 (2019)
2. Billinghurst, M., Kato, H.: Collaborative mixed reality. In: Proceedings of the First International Symposium on Mixed Reality, vol. 1 (1999)
3. Happa, J., Glencross, M., Steed, A.: Cyber security threats and challenges in collaborative mixed-reality. Front. ICT **6**, 5 (2019)
4. Nassif, A.B., Talib, M.A., Nasir, Q., Dakalbab, F.M.: Machine learning for anomaly detection: a systematic review. IEEE Access **9**, 78658–78700 (2021)
5. Rao, K.H., Srinivas, G., Damodhar, A., Krishna, M.V.: Implementation of anomaly detection technique using machine learning algorithms. Int. J. Comput. Sci. Telecommun. **2**(3), 25–31 (2011)
6. Reilly, D., Salimian, M., MacKay, B., Mathiasen, N., Edwards, W.K., Franz, J.: Secspace: prototyping usable privacy and security for mixed reality collaborative environments. In: Proceedings of the 2014 ACM SIGCHI Symposium on Engineering Interactive Computing Systems, pp. 273–282 (2014)
7. Sajid, M., Bukhari, S.I.M.S., Ji, B., David-John, B.: Just stop doing everything for now!: Understanding security attacks in remote collaborative mixed reality. https://arxiv.org/abs/2501.16505 (2025). arXiv preprint arXiv:2501.16505
8. Shahria, M.T., et al.: A novel framework for mixed reality–based control of collaborative robot: development study. JMIR Biomed. Eng. **7**(1), e36734 (2022)

Assessing the Impact of Access Control Policies on Data Accessibility in Distributed NoSQL Environments

Abanisenioluwa Orojo(✉), Emmanuelli El-Mahmoud, and Greg Speegle

Baylor University, Waco, TX 76706, USA
{abanisenioluwa_oroj1,emmanuelli_elmahmou1,greg_speegle}@baylor.edu

Abstract. NoSQL databases have emerged as a scalable and adaptable solution to manage large, unstructured data sets in distributed systems. However, NoSQL data stores lack robust mechanisms for assessing the impact of fine-grained access control policies on database resources in distributed environments. In this study, we introduce a refined framework for evaluating access control mechanisms in NoSQL databases, proposing enhancements to address major challenges in distributed settings. We introduce techniques to integrate node identity into access control evaluation paths, enabling context-aware analysis across distributed data partitions. We develop a dynamic approach capable of managing intricate, multi-layered resource hierarchies to allow for more flexible and scalable evaluations. Our experiments across various datasets confirm the effectiveness and efficiency of our access control evaluation framework. In addition, we propose new metrics that quantify the effects of policies on data accessibility, offering practical insights for policy refinement.

Keywords: Access Control · NoSQL · Distributed Systems · Policy Evaluation · ABAC

1 Introduction

Access control, a key security service, has evolved in both relational (RDBMS) and NoSQL databases, with models like RBAC and ABAC aiming for finer data protection [4,7,20]. While NoSQL datastores are enhancing their access control [6], understanding policy implications on unstructured, diverse data remains challenging, especially regarding propagation effects and conflicts from increased granularity [1]. In distributed NoSQL systems, administrators need a holistic analysis of policy impacts. Though research has addressed privacy in policy enforcement [23], policy evaluation in distributed settings presents a significant gap. To address this, we propose a NoSQL access control policy framework featuring distributed node path analysis, unauthorized access analysis, and statistical data analysis.

K. Daimi et al. (Eds.): CSCE 2025, CCIS 2937, pp. 270–285, 2026.
https://doi.org/10.1007/978-3-032-22208-4_18

1.1 Research Problem

Current frameworks for evaluating NoSQL access control policies face several limitations [7,13]. These include difficulties with access requests during network partitions, inadequate support for multi-node policy hierarchies, and a lack of data minimization in the evaluation process. Such shortcomings lead to poor context-awareness, hindering effective policy evaluation in partitioned networks–for example, by failing to differentiate data origins (e.g., across GDPR-compliant and exempt clusters) in a unified assessment, thus complicating policy management in diverse distributed settings. Furthermore, the absence of mechanisms to flexibly process complex, multilevel resource hierarchies restricts adaptability to varied NoSQL data models and architectures.

1.2 Contributions

This paper introduces an access control evaluation framework enhancing efficiency and security in distributed NoSQL systems. Our contributions include a technique for robust conflict resolution in partitioned networks that evaluates conflicting requests across distributed nodes, improving consistency, reliability, and mitigating unauthorized access from policy discrepancies. We also present a scalable multi-level hierarchical policy evaluation approach for NoSQL datastores, adeptly handling arbitrary resource hierarchy levels using global dictionaries for adaptable and efficient policy processing with horizontally scaling data. Furthermore, we provide insightful quantitative analysis of policy restrictions through a method to quantify policy impact by systematically identifying unauthorized data units and calculating their percentage, offering critical insights into policy restrictiveness. Finally, we enable improved security posture assessment by incorporating statistical metrics for data unit components, facilitating thorough audits of access control coverage and data complexity to help administrators evaluate and refine security policies. Collectively, these advancements offer a robust framework for managing data integrity and security in increasingly complex, distributed NoSQL database environments.

2 Related Works

The imperative for robust access control in contemporary data management systems is well-established, yet its implementation is fraught with complexities, particularly within distributed NoSQL environments. These environments, characterized by voluminous, rapidly changing, and structurally diverse data, alongside their inherent distribution, present formidable challenges to traditional security paradigms. This review surveys and critically analyzes seminal and contemporary works pertaining to access control mechanisms, their enforcement, and methodologies for evaluating their impact on data accessibility within these intricate settings, contextualizing the contributions of the present study.

2.1 Evolution and Challenges in Database Access Control

Historically, access control evolved from Discretionary (DAC) and Mandatory Access Control (MAC) to Role-Based Access Control (RBAC) [10], which simplified administration. However, the advent of distributed NoSQL databases exposed RBAC's limitations in providing fine-grained control for complex, nested data structures (e.g., fields within JSON documents) and in making dynamic, context-aware access decisions [2]. The difficulty of managing roles at scale across distributed nodes and the mismatch with the schema-flexible nature of NoSQL systems spurred research into more adaptive paradigms like Attribute-Based Access Control (ABAC). The present work's focus on assessing data accessibility responds to the potential for older or poorly configured models to unduly restrict legitimate access, thereby hampering data utility.

2.2 Attribute-Based Access Control (ABAC) for NoSQL Databases

ABAC makes access decisions based on attributes of users, resources, and the environment, offering fine-grained control and flexibility suitable for NoSQL complexities. Gupta et al. [11] proposed an ABAC framework for MongoDB using an intercepting proxy. Policies are in JSON, with enforcement via the MongoDB Wire Protocol, supporting field-level permissions and dynamic attributes (time, IP-based location). While scalable and open-source, it's MongoDB-specific and focuses on enforcement rather than a holistic assessment of policy impact on accessibility, potentially facing performance issues under extreme policy loads.

Colombo and Ferrari [5] developed a data model-agnostic framework for evaluating access control policy effects in NoSQL systems (See 1). Their Unifying Resource Property (URP) model '⟨id, path, k, v⟩' represents diverse NoSQL data hierarchically. A three-phase MapReduce process (URP derivation, policy binding, view generation) visualizes authorized/unauthorized content, handling policy combination, conflict resolution (e.g., denials-take-precedence), and propagation. Their key contribution is a general methodology to understand policy impact on schemaless data. However, as your work notes, their framework didn't deeply elaborate on navigating multi-node policy hierarchies where node physical/logical context is critical, lacked explicit data minimization during evaluation, and did not extensively address network partition impacts. While their URP unifies data, it lacked intrinsic support for embedding rich, node-specific attributes directly into the evaluation path. Our paper builds on this by incorpo-

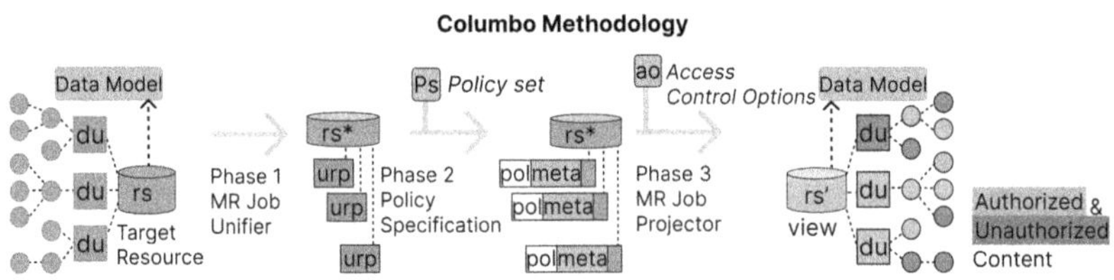

Fig. 1. Colombo Approach.

rating node identity into the URP mapping and introducing data minimization in your Phase I.

The work by Gupta et al. [11] emphasizes efficient ABAC enforcement, while Colombo and Ferrari [5] focus on understanding policy effects. Your study complements both by focusing on *quantifying data accessibility* itself, considering the operational impact in distributed settings–a gap not directly filled by these prior works. While Colombo and Ferrari's approach is foundational for policy outcome analysis, your proposed quantitative metrics (U_{du}, P_{uduc}, etc.) offer a more direct measure of accessibility. Other research includes hybrid RBAC-ABAC models [18], blockchain-based ABAC [22], risk-based ABAC [15], and unified frameworks for dynamic threat detection and access control [17].

2.3 Access Control in Distributed Environments and Policy Impact Assessment

Distributed environments amplify access control challenges, demanding scalability, consistency, low overhead, and resilience. Colombo and Ferrari's [5] MapReduce approach suits batch analysis. For dynamic environments, LAPUTA [21] uses pattern matching on Spark physical plans and confidential computing for secure policy enforcement, handling node identity via attestation for enclave security. While LAPUTA ensures compliance, your work differs by focusing on *evaluating the impact* of policies on accessibility using a URP-based model and specific metrics, rather than enforcement integrity. Context-awareness is crucial. CAPA (Context-Aware Policy Analysis) [3] ensures DUC policy quality using combined Policy/Resource Trees for conflict detection, handling heterogeneous conditions. This is vital, as policy correctness is a prerequisite for predictable accessibility. Your framework's integration of node identity for context-aware analysis across distributed partitions addresses a facet of this, specifically for NoSQL policy evaluation.

The critical gap, which your work addresses, is in methodologies for quantifying data accessibility as shaped by security policies in distributed NoSQL. While Colombo and Ferrari [5] visualize policy effects, and platforms like ABAC Lab [9] provide tools for policy analysis and datasets (addressing the benchmark scarcity you noted in your limitations), they do not offer the specific quantitative accessibility metrics your paper proposes. Your contribution of integrating node identity for robust conflict resolution in partitioned networks, scalable multi-level hierarchical policy evaluation using global dictionaries (CGL/DCGL), and insightful quantitative analysis of policy restrictions, appears novel in directly tackling these accessibility assessment challenges. Your work aims to measure the degree of accessibility considering factors beyond static policy definitions, offering a nuanced understanding of policy consequences on data utility in distributed NoSQL systems.

2.4 Synthesis and Our Contribution

The preceding review of literature on access control within database systems, particularly focusing on ABAC, distributed environments, and NoSQL databases, reveals a field rich with innovation yet marked by specific, persistent challenges. Throughout this review, we have endeavored to compare our work with these existing studies, noting that while many sophisticated solutions exist for policy enforcement (e.g., [12]) or static policy analysis and visualization (e.g., [7]), a distinct gap remains in dynamically assessing and quantifying the true impact of these policies on data accessibility within operational distributed NoSQL environments. Our framework seeks to fill this void by introducing a methodology that not only considers the distributed nature of these systems through mechanisms like node identity integration and scalable hierarchical evaluation but also proposes novel quantitative metrics for a direct assessment of data accessibility. The subsequent articulation of our contributions will further clarify how our approach offers unique solutions to these identified limitations, thereby advancing the state-of-the-art in understanding and managing the practical consequences of access control policies. The present study, "Assessing the Impact of Access Control Policies on Data Accessibility in Distributed NoSQL Environments," is positioned to directly address these identified lacunae. Its unique contributions are articulated as follows:

3 Methodology

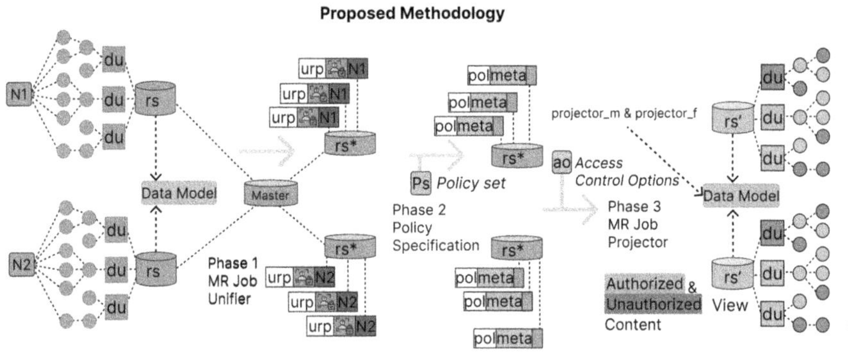

Fig. 2. Overview of the Proposed Approach.

3.1 Overview

A Unifying Resource Property (URP) is defined as a tuple ⟨id, path, k, v⟩, where "id" uniquely identifies the property, "path" specifies its hierarchical position within the overall data resource, "k" represents the components native identifier in its original data model, and "v" is an optional value assigned when applicable. The URP creation process employs a key sharding technique that utilizes document identifiers to distribute the set of URPs evenly across the nodes in the system [7], ensuring parallel processing even in highly heterogeneous datasets where documents contain multiple data structures. Once URPs are created and distributed, access control policies are bound to them, associating the appropriate policies with each URP to enable fine-grained access control at the resource level. Each individual URP is then evaluated by checking its associated access control policies and determining corresponding access decisions based on the current access request context. After evaluation, the system groups and aggregates URPs according to their common keys to organize the data, followed by a final refinement phase that structures the output. In this final phase, the system finalizes the data unit by applying policy composition and propagation techniques, thereby generating a view that reflects the appropriate access control decisions. This step carefully integrates factors such as the chosen combining option, conflict resolution strategy, policy propagation criterion, and system type to produce an accurate and consistent representation of the data unit, ensuring that access control policies are enforced efficiently and accurately, and that only authorized content is accessible to the requesting entity in a final data view aligned with defined policies and the specific access request context. Figure 2 presents a comprehensive visual aid of the proposed methodology.

3.2 Phase I: Derivation of a Unifying Resource Model Extensions

Phase I derives a unifying resource model (dr) from diverse, multi-granularity native data resources (dr) by extending prior work [7] through the incorporation of a node identifier (`node_id`) for contextual mapping and data minimization for enhanced privacy. A MapReduce task unifier (Algorithm 1) traverses dr's tree structure, applying a mapping function m (Algorithm 2) to each data unit (du). This m function, using a `node_id` (hashed server info/IP) and du's unique `_id` to initialize a `path` array, invokes the auxiliary function duMapper (Algorithm 3) with this path and du. The duMapper recursively examines du's components, creating a Unifying Resource Property (URP) for each field; for simple properties, it anonymizes the value (data minimization), and for complex ones, it recurses. The m function then emits key value pairs where the key is the URP's identifier and the value is the URP itself (example output in Listing 18.4). Finally, a reduce function r combines these pairs to form dr, ensuring a unified model for consistent data management across varied systems and enabling context-aware distributed processing and security by embedding the `node_id` in the URP's path.

3.3 Phase II: Policy Specification and Binding

The policy specification and binding approach in our framework follows the methodology presented in the [7]. We extend each urp to include security metadata and policy fields, enabling fine-grained access control down to individual data unit components.

3.4 Phase III: View Generation

Phase III involves mapping resources from the unified model back to their original data model to generate views that highlight both authorized and unauthorized contents. This phase is essential for illustrating the effects of access control policies on data accessibility.

3.5 Handling of Coarse-Grained Levels

The access control evaluation framework employs two essential data structures, Coarse Grained Levels (CGL) and Derived Coarse Grained Levels (DCGL), represented by global variables `cgl` and `dcgl` respectively, to efficiently manage access control decisions at various granularity levels within hierarchical NoSQL data models. `cgl` stores Unifying Resource Property (URP) keys at each data hierarchy level, while `dcgl` tracks the resolved access control decisions per URP at its corresponding level, enabling efficient decision retrieval and updates. This dynamic handling of coarse-grained levels occurs within the `projector_m` function (Algorithm 4), which groups URPs by their data unit identifiers. As `projector_m` iterates through URPs, it determines each URP's level by the length of its `path` attribute, identifying resource depth. Based on this level, `cgl` and `dcgl` are dynamically updated; if a level or a specific data unit identifier (key) within that level does not exist, new entries are created. This dynamic structuring ensures efficient, scalable, and adaptable management of access control decisions, aligning with the NoSQL data model's hierarchical nature. Consequently, the system can quickly retrieve relevant decisions from `dcgl` based on resource level and key for effective policy enforcement and to provide users with views accurately reflecting their access rights at different data hierarchy levels. After processing all URPs, `cgl` and `dcgl` will exhibit the structure shown in Listing 18.3.

3.6 Projector Reduction

The `projector_r` function reduces a set of Unifying Resource Properties (URPs) by a specific key to structure the data unit. It takes a list of URP dictionaries (urpS from a single data unit) and an identifier key as parameters. The function iterates through each URP, organizing them based on whether they directly refer to the specified key. This process builds a structured data unit as a dictionary, where key-value pairs are determined by the URPs. Values from URPs directly referencing the key are used in the data unit, while other URPs are added to lists for further processing or removal after structuring. The function also collects security metadata and policies from the URPs, storing them in separate lists; additionally, 'figure' elements are incorporated into the structured data unit. This unit is then returned as a dictionary, with an example of its structure shown in Figure 18.2.

3.7 Finalization and View Generation

The Finalization and View Generation phase, implemented in the `projector_f` function (Algorithm 5), is pivotal for transforming a derived data unit (`du` from `projector_r`, Fig. 18.2) into a final view reflecting access control decisions, using parameters like access request context (`arc`), combining option (`co`), conflict resolution strategy (`crs`), policy propagation criterion (`ppc`), and system type (`st`). Initially, Data Unit Finalization involves `projector_f` removing temporary fields (`tbs`, `tbp`) from `du` and updating its values via the recursive `updateDu` function. Subsequently, Policy Composition evaluates `du`'s associated policies (`pol`) to determine authorized (`authS`) and prohibited (`prohS`) components by iterating through policies, evaluating positive (`psa`) and negative (`psp`) expressions via `evaluate` (using an object `obj` with policy details and `arc`), combining decisions with `combinePs` (using `co`), and resolving conflicts with `conflictRes` (using `crs`), ultimately populating `authS` or `prohS`. Following this, Policy Propagation disseminates decisions from coarse-grained to fine-grained resources: `propagateDCG` (Algorithm 6) retrieves coarse-grained decisions from the `dcgl` dictionary and combines them with `du`'s decisions using `handleSP` (considering `ppc`, `crs`, `st`); then, `propagateDFG` performs a depth-first traversal of `du`, propagating decisions to fine-grained resources and using `handleSP` to update `du`'s unauthorized components (`unauthS`). Finally, View Generation, executed by `generate_View`, recursively traverses `du` and employs `mark_unauthorized` to clearly mark components listed in `unauthS`, producing a comprehensive view of both authorized and distinctly marked unauthorized data unit components.

3.8 Access Control Evaluation Metrics

To quantify the impact of access control policies on protected data and measure data accessibility, key metrics are computed, complementing derived views. These metrics include: the total number of data units marked as unauthorized (U_{du}) and the total number of unauthorized data unit components (U_{duc}), where U_{duc} can be identified as key-value pairs during the view generation phase; the percentage of data units that cannot be accessed due to specified policies (P_{udu}), calculated as $P_{udu} = \frac{U_{du}}{T_{du}} \times 100$, where T_{du} is the total number of data units; the percentage of unauthorized data unit components (P_{uduc}), computed as $P_{uduc} = \frac{U_{duc}}{T_{duc}} \times 100$, where T_{duc} is the total number of data unit components; the total number of analyzed data unit components (T_{duc}), defined as $T_{duc} = N_{du} + N_{duc}$ (by summing the count of processed data units, N_{du}, and the count of produced data unit components from DuMapper URPs, N_{duc}); and the average number of data unit components per data unit (A_{duc}), computed as $A_{duc} = \frac{T_{duc}}{T_{du}}$. These metrics are typically computed in an additional phase following view generation, often using a MapReduce task. The mapper processes generated views and emits key-value pairs such as ("U_{du}", 1) for each unauthorized data unit, ("U_{duc}", 1) for each unauthorized component, ("N_{du}", 1) for each processed data unit, and ("N_{duc}", 1) for each produced URP. The reducer then aggregates these values to get total counts for U_{du}, U_{duc}, N_{du}, and N_{duc}.

It also calculates the total number of data units (T_{du}), determines T_{duc} using its formula ($N_{du} + N_{duc}$), and finally computes the percentage metrics P_{udu} and P_{uduc}, and the average A_{duc}, according to their definitions provided above.

4 Performance Analysis

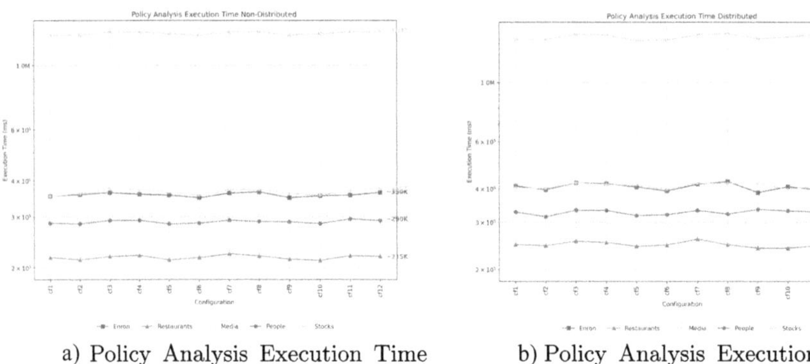

a) Policy Analysis Execution Time Non-Distributed

b) Policy Analysis Execution Time Distributed

Fig. 3. Comparison of Execution Time for Distributed and Non-Distributed Configurations.

To empirically assess the efficiency of our proposed approach in evaluating policy impact on data accessibility, we conducted experiments using MongoDB (v7.0 Community Edition) [14], chosen for its native MapReduce support and popularity [8], though any MapReduce-supporting datastore could suffice. The distributed setup involved a 4-node cluster on servers with 8-core Xeon CPUs and 128 GB RAM, using MongoDB's default disk-based WiredTiger Storage Engine for representative evaluation; a non-distributed test ran on a single 32-core Xeon CPU with 512 GB RAM. Five publicly available datasets (Enron, Restaurants, Media, People, Stocks [19]) were hash-sharded by `_id` across the 4 MongoDB instances to ensure uniform distribution and mapped to a unifying resource model (ds) using our job unifier (Sect. 3.2). In the absence of NoSQL policy benchmarks, access control involved randomly generated, purpose-based ABAC policies bound to derived URPs: each URP had a 0.5 probability of being covered by 1-3 pseudo-uniformly distributed positive or negative policies. We evaluated twelve configurations (cf_1–cf_{12}), representing all combinations of CO ('Any'/'All'), CRS ('PtP'/'DtP'), and PPC ('MSO'/'NP'/'NO') parameters. Figure 3 shows the average execution time (in $10\hat{6}$ seconds, i.e.,1000 s from 10 analysis processes per dataset/configuration to derive a view of authorized/unauthorized content from ds in a closed system, with experimental data available on GitHub (PANACEA [16]).

5 Discussion

The experimental results presented in this paper demonstrate the effectiveness and efficiency of the proposed approach for assessing the impact of access control policies on data accessibility in distributed NoSQL environments. The integration of node identity into access control evaluation paths and the data minimization of value fields in URPs have enhanced the security, and adaptability of the access control evaluation framework. The measured execution times for policy analysis across different datasets and configurations show a relatively constant trend, with minor variations in the range of a few seconds. This suggests that the choice of analysis options has a limited impact on the overall duration of the analysis process. The complexity of the view generation phase, which involves numerous accesses to data unit components during the re-composition step, is primarily responsible for the observed execution times. The re-composition complexity remains comparable across different configurations, as the projector task keeps track of unauthorized components for each data unit, requiring traversal of the data unit structure until the desired element is found. The number of components in the data unit and the number of components marked as unauthorized are the main factors affecting the complexity of view generation and, consequently, the execution time. The dynamic handling of multiple levels of coarse-grained resources through the use of global dictionaries (cgl and dcgl) enhances the flexibility and adaptability of the access control evaluation framework. This extension enables the system to efficiently manage hierarchical access control decisions across various levels of data granularity, ensuring that access policies are enforced in a manner that is both scalable and adaptable to the structure of the underlying NoSQL data models.

6 Limitations of Approach

While our framework advances access control mechanisms for distributed NoSQL systems, several important limitations must be acknowledged. Our approach currently lacks incremental and differential answer generation capabilities, requiring the entire access control decision process to be rerun whenever policies change. This inefficiency significantly impacts performance in environments with frequent policy updates. The implementation of our framework is presently limited to specific NoSQL platforms, primarily MongoDB, with insufficient testing on other widely-used systems such as Cassandra and HBase. This constrains our ability to validate the framework's versatility across different NoSQL architectures. Our evaluation is further hampered by the absence of a comprehensive policy benchmark dataset. Without standardized policies, data models, and workloads for testing, comparisons between different access control mechanisms remain inconsistent and potentially unreliable. The framework has undergone limited testing in partitioned network scenarios, leaving questions about its resilience when facing communication disruptions and node failures. This gap is particularly concerning for distributed systems where network partitioning is a common challenge. Finally, while current testing demonstrates adequate performance with moderate-sized datasets and cluster configurations, the framework's scalability under extreme conditions–including massive clusters or highly dynamic policy environments–remains insufficiently examined. These limitations collectively highlight critical areas for improvement in future iterations of our access control framework.

7 Conclusion

This paper advances access control evaluation for distributed NoSQL environments through a framework that integrates node identity into evaluation paths and implements data minimization techniques. Our approach addresses key limitations in existing systems while enhancing security, adaptability, and performance across diverse datasets and configurations. Experimental results demonstrate the framework's robustness, with only 13.94% performance degradation when transitioning to a distributed approach. The dynamic handling of multi-level resource hierarchies through global dictionaries improves flexibility and scalability, while comprehensive metrics including unauthorized access analysis and statistical data unit evaluation–provide security administrators with valuable insights for policy optimization. This work represents a significant step forward in balancing robust security with efficient data accessibility in complex, large-scale NoSQL database environments.

A Algorithms

Algorithm 1: MapReduce Task Unifier

1 **MapReduce task unifier is:**
  Input: A data resource dr that refers to a data model dm, composed of data units du, and a node identifier n_{id}
  Output: dr^*
2 (map m ↱ duMapper)* $\mapsto$ (reduce r)*
3 **end**

Algorithm 2: The mapping function m of unifier

```
1  function m is:
       Input: du, n_id
       Output: ⟨k, v⟩, where v models a unifying resource property urp, and k
               refers to the value of field id of urp
2      path ← [n_id];
3      document_id ← du.get('_id');
4      path ← path ∪ {document_id};
5      urpS ← duMapper(path, du);
6      for urp ∈ urpS do
7          emit (π_id(urp), urp);
8      end
9  end
```

Algorithm 3: The auxiliary function duMapper of unifier

```
1  Function duMapper(cPath, obj) is
       Input: cPath, obj
       Output: a set urpS of objects modeling unifying resource properties
2      urpS ← [];
3      for f ∈ Γ(obj) do
4          urp ← ⊥;
5          setField(urp, "path", cPath);
6          setField(urp, "id", generateId());
7          setField(urp, "K", f);
8          if |Γ(π_f(obj))| > 0 then
9              sPath ← valueOf(cPath);
10             push(sPath, π_id(urp));
11             sUrpS ← duMapper(sPath, π_f(obj));
12             urpS ← urpS ∪ sUrpS;
13         end
14         else
15             anonymized_V ← anonymize(π_f(obj));
16             setField(urp, "V", anonymized_V);
17         end
18         push(urpS, urp);
19     end
20     return urpS;
21 end
```

Algorithm 4: Projector_m function for grouping URPs

```
Data: List of URPs
Result: Grouped URPs by data unit identifier
1  Function Projector_m(urps, arc, co, crs):
2      grouped_urps = {}
3      for urp_tuple in urps do
4          urp_id, urp_value = urp_tuple
5          key = urp_value['path'][0]
6          if key not in grouped_urps then
7              grouped_urps[key] = []
8          end
9          grouped_urps[key].append(urp_value)
10     end
11     for key, urp_group in grouped_urps.items() do
12         for urp in urp_group do
13             if 'V' not in urp then
14                 process_coarse_grained_resource(urp, arc, co, crs, key)
15             end
16             else
17                 process_fine_grained_resource(urp, arc, co, crs)
18             end
19         end
20     end
21     return grouped_urps
```

Algorithm 5: Projector_f function to finalize and generate view

```
Data: Data unit, Access request context, and others
Result: Structured view of the data unit
1  Function Projector_f(du, arc, co, crs, ppc, st):
2      prepare_data_unit(du)
3      dec = propagateDCG(du, cgl_values, dcgl_values, crs, ppc, st)
4      view = generate_view(du, dec)
5      return view
```

Algorithm 6: PropagateDCG function to propagate decisions

```
Data: Data unit, CGL values, DCGL values
Result: Access decision propagated to the data unit
1  Function PropagateDCG(du, cgl_values, dcgl_values, crs, ppc, st):
2      dec = None
3      for cgl_value, dcgl_value in zip(cgl_values, dcgl_values) do
4          dec = handleSP(dec, dcgl_value, ppc, crs, st)
5          if dec == 'deny' then
6              du.setdefault('unauthCGR', []).append(cgl_value)
7          end
8      end
9      return dec
```

B Figures and Data Structures

```
{
  "_id": "12345abcdef",
  "headers": {
    "To": "recipient@example.com",
    "From": "sender@example.com",
    "Subject": "Sample Email Document"
  },
  "body": "This is the body of the email."
}
```

Listing 18.1. An example data unit representing an email document.

```
{
  'id': 'doc1',
  'key': 'value',
  '90b6cf54-eae2-4046-86a0-3e019e6a3d6c': {
    'body': 'value'
  },
  'nested': '90b6cf54-eae2-4046-86a0-3e019e6a3d6c',
  'tbs': ['90b6cf54-eae2-4046-86a0-3e019e6a3d6c'],
  'tbp': ['90b6cf54-eae2-4046-86a0-3e019e6a3d6c'],
  'meta': [...],
  'pol': [...]
}
```

Listing 18.2. Sample output of the `projector_r` function

```
dcgl = {     0: {"Company": {urp_id: conflict_resolution}},
             1: {"Department A": {urp_id: conflict_resolution}
                , "Department B": {...}},}
cgl  = { 0: {"Company": {urp_id: urp['K']}},
         1: {"Department A": {urp_id: urp['K']}, "Department B
             ": {...}},}
```

Listing 18.3. DCGL and CGL Output Structure

```
('3bd10f44-1840-4b89-bb94-586872d7b90d', {
    'path': ['node_1', '12345abcdef', 'afcb2642-da46-45b0
        -9209-fd5928e533d6'],
    'id': '3bd10f44-1840-4b89-bb94-586872d7b90d',
    'K': 'To',
    'V': '[Minimized Content]'
})
```

Listing 18.4. A sample of the urp generated by unifier based on Figure 18.1

References

1. Alotaibi, A., Alotaibi, R., Hamza, N.: Access control models in NoSQL databases: an overview. J. King Abdulaziz Univ. (JKAU) **8**(1), 1–9 (2019)
2. Alotaibi, B., Al-Dahhan, A.: Access control models for NoSQL databases: a survey. J. Netw. Comput. Appl. **148**, 102455 (2019)
3. Babar, M.S., Dustdar, S., Strembeck, M.: CAPA: context-aware policy analysis for distributed usage control. Energies **15**(19), 7113 (2022)
4. Bond, R., See, K.Y.K., Wong, C.K.M., Chan, Y.K.H.: Understanding DB2 9 Security. Pearson Education (2006)
5. Colombo, M., Ferrari, E.: Evaluating the effects of access control policies within NoSQL systems. Futur. Gener. Comput. Syst. **114**, 491–505 (2021)
6. Colombo, P., Ferrari, E.: Fine-grained access control within NoSQL document-oriented datastores. Data Sci. Eng. **1**(3), 127–138 (2016)
7. Colombo, P., Ferrari, E.: Evaluating the effects of access control policies within NoSQL systems. Futur. Gener. Comput. Syst. **114**, 491–505 (2021)
8. DB-Engines: Db-engines ranking of NoSQL databases (2024). https://db-engines.com/en/. Accessed 21 Sept 2024
9. Farris, K.: ABAC Lab: an interactive platform for attribute-based access control policy analysis, tools, and datasets. arXiv preprint arXiv:2405.07692 (or actual journal if published) (2024)
10. Ferraiolo, D., Kuhn, R.: Role-based access control. In: Proceedings of the 15th NIST-NCSC National Computer Security Conference, pp. 554–563 (1992)
11. Gupta, A., Sural, S., Atluri, V.: Enabling attribute-based access control in NoSQL databases. IEEE Trans. Eng. Manag. (Early Access, or Specific Journal If Published) (2023). Details based on user's text; actual publication details might vary. Often pre-prints or early access versions are cited as (2023) or (2022) if from IEEE TETC or similar
12. Gupta, E., Sural, S., Vaidya, J., Atluri, V.: Enabling attribute-based access control in NoSQL databases. IEEE Trans. Emerg. Top. Comput. **11**(1), 208–223 (2022). https://doi.org/10.1109/tetc.2022.3193577
13. Mohamed, A.K.Y.S., et al.: A systematic literature review of authorization and access control requirements and current state of the art for different database models. Int. J. Web Inf. Syst. **20**(1), 1–23 (2024)
14. MongoDB Inc.: Mongodb (ver. 7.0) documentation (2024). https://www.mongodb.com/docs/manual/release-notes/7.0/. Accessed 21 Sept 2024
15. Ni, Q., Bertino, E., Lobo, J., Calo, S.B., Lin, D.: Risk-based access control using abstract policies. In: Proceedings of the 15th ACM Symposium on Access Control Models and Technologies (SACMAT), pp. 161–170 (2010)
16. Orojo, A.: LaBackDoor/panacea: Assessing the Impact of Access Control Policies on Data Accessibility in Distributed NoSQL Environments; PANACEA (Policy Analysis and NoSQL Access Control Evaluation Approach). GitHub repository (2024). https://github.com/LaBackDoor/panacea
17. Orojo, A., El-Mahmoud, E., Hutton, S., Elumelu, W., Donahoo, M.: A unified framework incorporating aw-trbac and semantic variational autoencoders for dynamic threat detection and access control. In: International Conference on Artificial Intelligence (2025)
18. Ou, X., Bertino, E., Carminati, B., Joshi, J.B.D.: A hybrid approach to composite role based access control. In: Proceedings of the 11th ACM Symposium on Access Control Models and Technologies (SACMAT), pp. 107–116 (2006)

19. Ozler, H.: ozlerhakan/mongodb-json-files: A curated list of JSON/BSON datasets from the web in order to practice/use in MongoDB. GitHub repository (2023). https://github.com/ozlerhakan/mongodb-json-files
20. Pallas, F., et al.: Towards application-layer purpose-based access control. In: Proceedings of the 35th Annual ACM Symposium on Applied Computing, pp. 1288–1296 (2020)
21. Park, J.: LAPUTA: secure data analytics in apache spark with fine-grained policy enforcement and isolated execution. In: Proceedings of the Network and Distributed System Security Symposium (NDSS) (2025)
22. Sheikh, A., Ambhaikar, A., Kumar, S.: Blockchain-based attribute based access control for secure data sharing in IoT. Wirel. Pers. Commun. **107**, 1945–1963 (2019)
23. Sicari, S., Rizzardi, A., Coen-Porisini, A.: Security & privacy issues and challenges in NoSQL databases. Comput. Netw. **206**, 108828 (2022)

ACLR: A Stacked Approach for Botnet Detection

Srinija Reddy Kotla, Xinli Wang(✉), and Vijay Bhuse

Grand Valley State University, Allendale, MI 49401, USA
kotlas@mail.gvsu.edu, {wangx,bhusevij}@gvsu.edu

Abstract. Cyber-attacks through botnets are one of the most dangerous threats over the Internet. It is getting more and more difficult to spot botnets because attack routes are changing and malware is becoming more guileful and polymorphic. The proliferation of the Internet of Things (IoT) has exacerbated this problem, since many interconnected devices are susceptible to botnet assaults. To tackle this difficulty, we consider a botnet detection system that utilizes a stacked model, which incorporates Artificial Neural Networks (ANN), Convolutional Neural Network (CNN), Long Short-Term Memory (LSTM), and Recurrent Neural Network (RNN), named as the ACLR model. The efficacy of the ACLR model is assessed in comparison to individual models with the UNSW-NB15 dataset, which has nine attack categories: "Normal", "Generic", "Exploits", "Fuzzers", "DoS", "Reconnaissance", "Analysis", "Backdoor", "Shellcode", and "Worms". Experimental results show that the ACLR model attains an accuracy of 96%, underscoring its efficacy in identifying intricate patterns and differentiating botnet activities from regular network data. Compared with each individual model, the ACLR approach has improved the detection accuracy and precision with the dataset we use. The results can be a good reference for the future work on botnet detection with network data analysis.

Keywords: Cybersecurity · Botnet · Deep Learning · Stacked Model · ACLR Model · Intrusion Detection System

1 Introduction

Botnet detection is an essential part of cybersecurity because it helps reduce a range of cybersecurity concerns [1–3]. By locating, mitigating, and eliminating botnets, security professionals can better safeguard networks and critical data from malicious activities including Distributed Denial of Service (DDoS) attacks, data breaches, and malware dissemination. Network efficiency and user trust in digital services are both preserved by early detections, which in turn minimizes potential harms. It also encourages innovation in the never-ending fight against cyber dangers that are evolving at a global scale, ensures compliance with legal and regulatory requirements, and promotes cyber resilience [4]. Botnet detection based on deep learning techniques swiftly finds and classifies malicious botnet

K. Daimi et al. (Eds.): CSCE 2025, CCIS 2937, pp. 286–298, 2026.
https://doi.org/10.1007/978-3-032-22208-4_19

activities in network data using robust machine learning models [1]. Organizations can better safeguard their systems and critical data when they are able to detect botnet threats quickly and take action to mitigate them. Individuals and organizations have been the targets of these types of assaults, which have taken many forms, most of them with the goal of gaining financial gain. One of the most infamous types of attack is ransomware, which encrypts a user's data and demands payment to unlock it [5]. Cyber-criminals target at large organizations *via* the use of botnets. Recent efforts have focused on botnet identification using deep learning algorithms to combat the ever-increasing threat of botnets.

The detection of botnets by deep learning algorithms has demonstrated efficacy in mitigating the threat posed by them [6]. Deep learning-based web traffic analyzers have been proposed as effective tools for detecting botnets and mitigating their activities. Bidirectional long short-term memory recurrent neural networks (BLSTM-RNN) exemplify the application of deep learning in botnet detection [7–9]. BLSTM-RNN models are adept for analyzing network traffic and identifying trends associated with botnet activities due to their proficiency in capturing both historical and prospective contexts of sequential data.

Several advantages can be gained by using deep learning algorithms to identify botnets. With their automated and sensitive mechanisms, botnets can be dealt with, even in the face of more complicated threats. Using deep neural networks, these techniques may be able to reliably identify both known and unknown botnet activities. Furthermore, real-time botnet behavior detection is made feasible by the ability to extract characteristics from packet headers, which allows for effective analysis of network data [10]. However, there are still problems with making and using these alternatives that have been proposed. To deal with encrypted traffic and evolving botnet architecture, deep learning algorithms are recently undergoing modification [11]. Addressing the ever-changing nature of botnet behaviors and making detection methods applicable across different network environments are two topics that require more research.

This study introduces a stacking model, a procedure for the discovery of botnet attacks to enhance security protocols for IoT devices. The suggested model leverages the advantages of Artificial Neural Networks (ANN), Convolutional Neural Networks (CNN), Long Short Term Memory (LSTM), and Recurrent Neural Networks (RNN). Our experiments encompass the categorization of many attack types, including prevalent categories like normal and generic, in addition to worms, back doors, shell code, fuzzers, Denial of Service (DoS), reconnaissance, and analysis. We prepare the dataset for experiments by removing null values and applying label encoding to categorical variables that are crucial for training Artificial Intelligent (AI) models. Our results are promising. Our work expands the testing of combined approach [17] with different models and datasets.

2 Related Work

Gandhi and Srivatsa [4] have reported that assaults on computer systems can read, destroy, and expropriate data and significantly impair the overall performance of the system. Pre-intrusion activities, including port checking and IP spoofing, precede assaults. Attacks can be identified by monitoring data from both origin and destination networks, ports, protocol details, header specifications, and other relevant parameters. Attacks can be classified into two broad categories: passive and aggressive attacks, based on their characteristics. The passive attacks can be either network- or system-based, wherein the attacker discreetly observes the network traffic to get confidential information. Surveillance of passive assaults might be very challenging due to its nature of being passive. Active attackers circumvent all security measures and infiltrate networks by exploiting vulnerabilities, impersonating legitimate systems, or acquiring credentials unlawfully.

Various data classifiers have been tested by Sriram *et al.* [13] for botnet detections, including K-Nearest Neighbors (KNN), Decision Trees (DT), AdaBoost (AB), Random Forests (RF), Linear Support Vector Machines (LSVM), and Radial basis function Support Vector Machines (RSVM). They have applied these classifiers to three distinct DS1 datasets. The classifiers that employed Logistic Regression (LR) and Naive Bayes (NB) have yielded significantly less satisfactory results.

The CNN-LSTM model was coupled by Nugraha *et al.* [14] to identify distributed denial of service attacks by utilizing the CICIDS 2017 dataset. Based on their findings, the accuracy is 97%, the precision is 97%, and the dependability is 99%. A domain creation algorithm attack has been created by Karunakaran [15]. It has been stated that it produces an accuracy of 95%. There are significant expenses associated with the implementation of defenses for cyber assaults; hence, the reduction of costs is an essential component of cyber security.

The use of deep learning techniques as a potential tool for botnet identification has been a new trend in recent years [16]. An ensemble-based approach has exhibited exemplary performance for botnet and malware detections in most recent works [18–20]. Similar with previous work [17], this approach combines various classifiers/models to improve the performance. However, the efficacy of this approach needs to be further tested and verified with more datasets and different classifiers since it is new and novel.

3 Proposed Approach

To test the efficacy of ensemble-based approach, this research employs a stacked deep learning approach for botnet identification using network traffic data. As illustrated in Fig. 1, the suggested methodology employs model stacking, using the outputs of ANN, CNN, LSTM, and RNN for the ultimate prediction. These deep learning models are exploited because they are the widely used and extensively verified ones in botnet detections. An assessment is made on the efficacy of deep learning classification models in analyzing botnet attack detection utilizing the UNSW-NB15 dataset [21]. The preparation involves eliminating null values and managing category data using label encoding. To accelerate the process, several deep learning algorithms, including ANN, CNN, LSTM, and RNN, are utilized.

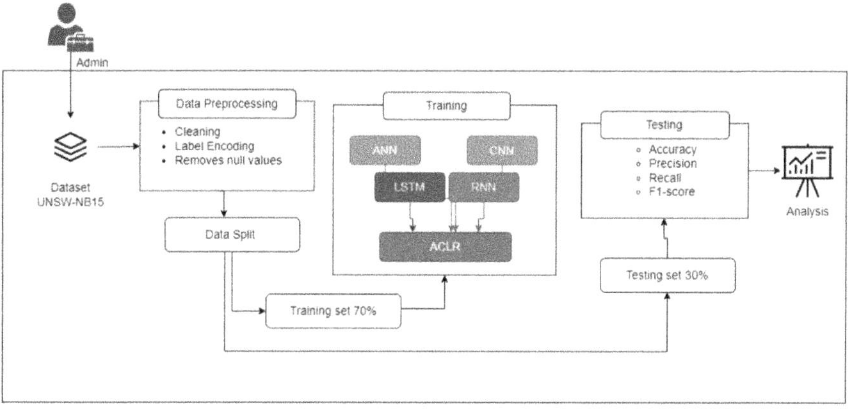

Fig. 1. A Diagram of the Proposed Methodology.

3.1 Data

For assessing Intrusion Detection Systems (IDS), the UNSW-NB15 dataset [21] is an extensive repository of data pertaining to network traffic. It consists of real modern everyday activities which are combined with synthetic contemporary assault behaviors in this system. This dataset has been created by the Cyber Range Lab at the University of New South Wales in Canberra [21] with the following features:

- There are 2,544 records in total in this dataset. They are included in four CSV files: UNSW-NB15_1.csv, UNSW-NB15_2.csv, UNSW-NB15_3.csv, and UNSW-NB15_4.csv.
- Forty-nine characteristics are taken from each record using Argus and Bro-IDS tools, in addition to twelve methods that were created. These features are used to characterize each record. Aspects such as flow, time, content, and other produced qualities are included in these features.

The UNSW-NB15 dataset is provided as a benchmark for academics and practitioners working in the field of cybersecurity, particularly for the purpose of creating and testing intrusion detection systems that are based on machine learning. Given its all-encompassing character, it enables the evaluation of intrusion detection system (IDS) performance against a wide range of contemporary attack scenarios.

3.2 Data Processing

The data must be preprocessed prior to any further analysis to prepare the data for model development and evaluation. The dataset must be imported, sanitized, altered, and converted into a format suitable for deep learning models. The dataset has 45 characteristics. Transforming categorical values into numerical symbols suitable for deep learning systems is a standard procedure when handling categorical data. The utilization of a label encoder, which assigns a unique numerical label to each category in the data, is a favored approach for this purpose. There are several techniques available for employing a label encoder to address the absence of values in categories of data. Prior to employing the label encoder, one option is to replace the missing values with a specific placeholder, such as "NaN". This can be achieved by employing the label encoder after converting the categorical data into strings. Various libraries, such as scikit-learn [22], utilize the Label Encoder class from scikit-learn.

3.3 Deep Learning Models

Many deep learning models have been used for botnet detection in existing researches. Artificial Neural Networks (ANN), Convolutional Neural Networks (CNN), Recurrent Neural Networks (RNN), and Long Short-Term Memory networks (LSTM) are the four strong deep learning techniques that are included into the ACLR model. These models are employed in this study because these techniques have been widely used to successfully identify botnet assaults in network traffic. The artificial neural network acts as the underlying structure of the model. It can learn complicated, non-linear correlations from the features that are input, which makes it suited for broad classification tasks. The convolutional neural network, which was first developed for image processing, is utilized to identify local patterns within network data. These patterns, which frequently serve as signs of hostile activities, include rapid spikes with unexpected packet sequences. To manage the sequential nature of network traffic, recurrent neural networks are integrated. This gives the model the ability to learn relationships between events over the course of time. Standard recurrent neural networks, on the other hand, have difficulty dealing with long-term dependencies. This is where LSTM networks come into play. LSTMs improve the model's capacity to remember and make use of long-term contextual information, which enables the detection of subtle, delayed patterns that are frequently associated with sophisticated botnet behaviors. By stacking these models, the ACLR framework can harness the capabilities of each method, which ultimately results in a complete detection system that is capable of successfully analyzing both the geographical and temporal features of network traffic. By demonstrating its improved performance on the UNSW-NB15 dataset, this hybrid technique considerably enhances the accuracy of botnet identification.

3.4 Evaluation Metrics

The primary metrics employed to assess the efficacy of machine learning models, especially for classification tasks, are accuracy, recall, and precision [14,18,23]. These metrics reflect the model's ability to forecast the different groups or categories of the input data. To assess the classifiers' performance, four distinct performance metrics will be used in this study, as outlined in Table 1.

In Table 1, TP denotes "true positive", representing the count of assaults accurately identified from the data. FP stands for "false positive", referring to

Table 1. Performance metrics

Accuracy	$\frac{TP+TN}{TP+TN+FP+FN}$
Precision	$\frac{TP}{TP+FP}$
Recall	$\frac{TP}{TP+FN}$
F1-score	$2 * \frac{(precision*recall)}{(precision+recall)}$

the instances that are wrongly identified. In a comparable manner, the abbreviation TN denotes "true negative", indicating that a normal packet is accurately anticipated to be a normal packet. Conversely, FN, standing for "false negative", signifies an assault expected to be a standard package.

The metric **Accuracy** evaluates the percentage of correctly categorized packages among all instances. **Precision** reflects the percentage of true positive. Both accuracy and precision are frequently used assessment metrics in machine learning to assess the effectiveness of a classification model [18]. As shown in Table 1, the metric **Recall** represents the fraction of true positive instances (TP) out of real positive instances ($TP + FN$). A higher recall value is better because it means that the model can identify more actual positive instances. Finally, the metric **F1-score** is used to assess the trade-off between recall and accuracy. Its value ranges 0 to 1, with 1 indicating the ideal balance.

4 Results and Discussions

As shown in Fig. 1, preprocessed data is fed to all the four models, respectively, for training. Then, the trained models are used to classify botnet instances. We will present the results of individual models briefly in this section. Short discussions will also be provided to express our thoughts. Comparisons with ACLR and discussions will be given in the next section.

4.1 The Performance of CNN Model

The performance of CNN is assessed after training on a labeled dataset. A metric of CNN's predictive efficacy is the proportion of instances in the test set that are accurately classified in total. The results shown in Table 2 give the performance of the CNN model for the epoch of 30.

Table 2. CNN Performance Metrics

Model	Accuracy (%)	Precision (%)	Recall (%)	F1-Score (%)
CNN	95.45	95.64	95.22	95.39

From the results in Table 2 we can see that:

- Accuracy (95.45%): An accuracy of 95.45% is close to the results achieved by existing work [1,2] with different datasets.
- Precision (95.63%): A precision of 95.63% is equilibrated with competent detecting capabilities of CNN reported in existing work with different datasets.
- Recall (95.21%): A recall of 95.21% indicates that the CNN model can effectively identify a substantial proportion of assaults.
- F1-score (95.39%): This F1-score value demonstrates robust performance of the CNN model, indicating its efficacy in feature extraction.

From the above observations we can see that the CNN model can effectively extract the main features of botnets with a relatively high accuracy and precision. It can also achieve a relative good balance between recall and accuracy. However, there is still room for improvements.

4.2 The Performance of LSTM Model

LSTMs excel in identifying long-term dependencies in sequential data, rendering them advantageous for applications such as voice recognition and time series analysis [7]. By simulating context and sequential patterns, LSTMs can get elevated accuracy, precision, and F1-score, yielding dependable classification outcomes for sequence-based applications. Table 3 lists the experimental results for the LSTM model in this study.

Table 3. LSTM Performance Metrics

Model	Accuracy (%)	Precision (%)	Recall (%)	F1-Score (%)
LSTM	94.78	94.66	95.02	94.75

Our main observations are as follows:

- Accuracy (94.78%): The accuracy of 94.78% indicates the competence of LSTM model for botnet detections. This result is close to that in existing work [7] with different datasets.
- Lower Precision (94.65%): Compared with existing work [7] with different datasets, LSTM model has a lower precision value with the dataset we use.
- Improved Recall (95.02%): Although LSTM has a relatively low detection precision, it still effectively detects botnet activities with a recall value of 95.02%. Majority of real botnet instances can be classified by the LSTM model.
- F1-score (94.75%): Similar with the CNN model, the LSTM model also demonstrates a good balance between recall and accuracy with an F1-score of 94.75%, although this is not ideal.

Overall, with our testing dataset, the LSTM model demonstrates the competence for identifying botnet activities with a good recall value and a good balance between recall and accuracy. Room exists to improvements on accuracy and precision.

4.3 The Performance of RNN Model

Recurrent Neural Networks are proficient in modeling sequential data and discerning temporal relationships [8]. Their recurrent connections allow for the retention of information from prior time steps, rendering them advantageous for applications like time series analysis, natural language processing, and speech recognition. RNNs excel in sequence classification by effectively collecting temporal patterns and contextual information, yielding superior accuracy, precision, and F1-score. Table 4 presents the experimental results for the RNN model in our study.

Table 4. RNN Performance Metrics

Model	Accuracy (%)	Precision (%)	Recall (%)	F1-Score (%)
RNN	75.49	76.79	76.46	75.47

The results given in Table 4 indicate that the RNN model does not perform well for botnet detection with the UNSW-NB15 dataset [21], with low values of both accuracy and precision. However, this subpar performance does not necessarily mean that the RNN is helpless. As reported in existing research [8], the RNN model is competent to classify sequential data.

4.4 The Performance of ANN Model

To determine the evaluation metrics, the artificial neural network (ANN) is first trained on a labeled dataset, and then it is evaluated on a test dataset. Table 5 provides an illustration of the ANN performance.

Table 5. ANN Performance Metrics

Model	Accuracy (%)	Precision (%)	Recall (%)	F1-Score (%)
ANN	95.46	95.38	95.48	95.42

From the results in Table 5 we can see the following:

- In terms of accuracy, ANN is comparable for botnet detection with the accuracy of 95.46%.
- The precision score of 95.38% demonstrates a great ability to classify the patterns included in the UNSW-NB15 dataset [21].
- More than 95% of the real instances contained in the UNSW-NB15 dataset [21] can be identified by the ANN model only.
- Performance that is dependable is confirmed by the high F1-score (95.42%).

In summary, the ANN model itself has demonstrated a relatively high competence for recognizing the instances included in the dataset we use in this study. Both accuracy and precision are relatively high. The recall value is also promising. It may contribute very well to the ACLR model in our results.

4.5 The Performance of ACLR Model

As depicted in Fig. 1, our proposed ACLR model has employed model stacking. It uses the outputs of ANN, CNN, LSTM and RNN for the ultimate prediction of botnet instances to improve the overall performance for botnet detection. The outcomes of the suggested model $ANN + CNN + LSTM + RNN(ACLR)$ are generated with the UNSW-NB15 dataset [21]. Table 6 gives the experimental findings obtained with the proposed model. The experimental findings indicate that the suggested model outperforms existing deep learning models utilized in this research, achieving the best accuracy score of 0.9551.

Table 6. ACLR Performance Metrics

Model	Accuracy (%)	Precision (%)	Recall (%)	F1-Score (%)
ACLR	95.51	98.50	93.25	95.80

From the results given in Table 6 we can observe the following facts:

- The ACLR model is highly competent for botnet detection with the accuracy of 95.51%.
- The high precision (98.49%) indicates that the ACLR approach is able to successfully identify majority of the botnet instances included in the UNSW-NB15 dataset [21]. It can accurately detect botnet activities while minimizing false positives.
- A relatively high recall value (93.25%) means that the ACLR model proficiently identifies the majority of true botnet assaults.
- A high F1-score (95.80%) indicates that the ACLR model harmonizes accuracy and recall very well with a robust overall performance.

From the above observations we can see that the ACLR is a good approach to botnet detection with high accuracy and recall. It also provides a good balance between recall and accuracy. It's performance is very promising.

5 Comparison

For the purpose of comparison with each individual model, we have summarized the performance metrics of all the models utilized in this study and the outcomes are given in Table 7.

Table 7. Summary of Performance Metrics

Model	Accuracy (%)	Precision (%)	Recall (%)	F1-Score (%)
ACLR	95.51	98.50	93.25	95.80
LSTM	94.78	94.66	95.02	94.75
CNN	95.45	95.64	95.22	95.39
RNN	75.49	76.79	76.46	75.47
ANN	95.46	95.38	95.48	95.42

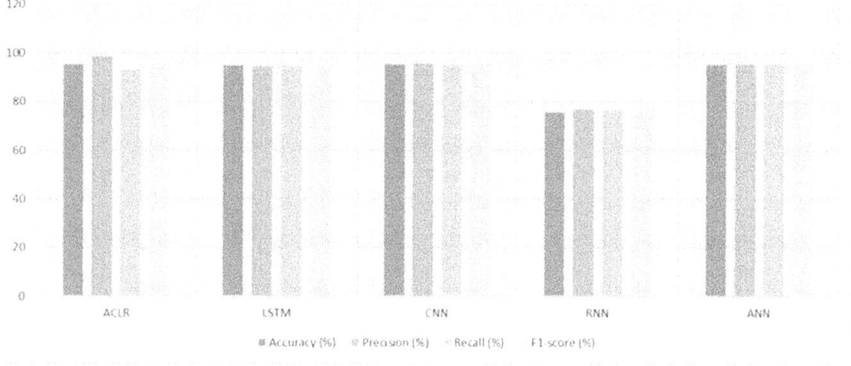

Fig. 2. Performance Metrics of All Models.

Figure 2 depicts the performance metrics in a bar graph to visualize the performance metrics of ACLR model and the individual models that are used in this study.

Results in Table 1 and Fig. 2 are provided about accuracy, precision, recall, and F1-scores in percentages. From these results we can see that the suggested model performs better than all other individual models, including ANN, CNN, LSTM, and RNN, which have been adjusted for the best results with the dataset. The ACLR approach is superior, attaining the maximum accuracy and F1-score. Both CNN and ANN have strong performance, although LSTM has marginally lower precision. RNN, however, is the least effective model, facing challenges with detecting precision.

6 Conclusion and Future Work

With the UNSW-NB15 dataset [21] we have tested different deep learning models, including ANN, CNN, LSTM, and RNN, for the efficacy of botnet classification and detection. We have used the metrics of accuracy, precision, recall, and F1-score to comprehensively compare the performance of each individual model. Further, we suggest to stack them by integrating all the models for a better outcome. The suggested ACLR approach is a layered deep learning technique that incorporate the models of ANN, CNN, LSTM, and RNN. As shown in Fig. 1, the ACLR approach exploits the outputs of all the incorporated models for the ultimate classification.

From the results we have presented, especially those given in Table 1 and Fig. 2, we can see that the stacked approach performs better than each of the individual models. This is because that the ACLR approach has effectively integrated all the features in each individual model. The findings of the experiment have shown that the ACLR model has a high testing accuracy of 96%, demonstrating its capacity to recognize intricate patterns in network data and successfully differentiate between botnet activities and normal behaviors. The results further demonstrate that the results of botnet classification and detection can be improved over individual ones by simply stacking different deep learning models together to take the advantages of each individual models.

With the preliminary results and hands-on experience we have gained from this study, we would like to further concentrate on enhancing the ACLR model's real-time detection capabilities, cutting down on computational overhead, and broadening its range of network environment applicability. In the future, we would like to incorporate more models and select more efficient models to include in this stacked approach. More datasets will be used for testing purposes.

Acknowledgments. We want to thank the two anonymous reviewers. Their constructive comments have greatly helped us to enhance the academic soundness of our work.

References

1. Feily, M., Shahrestani, A.,Ramadass, S.: A survey of botnet and botnet detection. In: 2009 Third International Conference on Emerging Security Information, Systems and Technologies, pp. 268-273. IEEE (2009). https://doi.org/10.1109/SECURWARE.2009.48
2. Gaonkar, S., Dessai, N. F., Costa, J., Borkar, A., Aswale, S., Shetgaonkar, P.: A survey on botnet detection techniques. In 2020 International Conference on Emerging Trends in Information Technology and Engineering (ic-ETITE), Vellore, India, pp. 1-6, IEEE (2020). https://doi.org/10.1109/ic-ETITE47903.2020.Id-70
3. Zhu, Z., et al.: Botnet research survey. In: 2008 32nd Annual IEEE International Computer Software and Applications Conference, pp. 967-972. IEEE (2008). https://doi.org/10.1109/COMPSAC.2008.205
4. Gandhi, M., Srivatsa, S.K.: Detecting and preventing attacks using network intrusion detection systems. Int. J. Comput. Sci. Secur. **2**(1), 49–60 (2008)
5. Oz, H., Aris, A., Levi, A. and Uluagac, A.S.: A survey on ransomware: evolution, taxonomy, and defense solutions. ACM Comput. Surv. (CSUR) **54**(11s), pp.1-37(2022). https://doi.org/10.1145/3514229
6. Shahhosseini, M., Mashayekhi, H., Rezvani, M.: A deep learning approach for botnet detection using raw network traffic data. J. Netw. Syst. Manage. **30**(3), 44–67 (2022). https://doi.org/10.1007/s10922-022-09655-7

7. Kumar, P.J., Neduncheliyan, S., Adnan, M.M., Sudhakar, S.K., Sudhakar, A.V.V.: Anomaly-based intrusion detection system using bidirectional long short-term memory for internet of things. In: 2024 Third International Conference on Distributed Computing and Electrical Circuits and Electronics (ICDCECE), Ballari, India, pp. 01-04, IEEE (2024). https://doi.org/10.1109/ICDCECE60827.2024.10549281
8. Sivamohan, S., Sridhar, S. S., Krishnaveni, S.: An effective recurrent neural network (rnn) based intrusion detection via bi-directional long short-term memory. In: 2021 International Conference on Intelligent Technologies (CONIT), Hubli, India, pp. 1-5, IEEE (2021). https://doi.org/10.1109/CONIT51480.2021.9498552
9. Roy, B., Cheung, H.: A deep learning approach for intrusion detection in internet of things using bi-directional long short-term memory recurrent neural network. In: 2018 28th International Telecommunication Networks and Applications Conference (ITNAC), Sydney, NSW, Australia, pp. 1-6, IEEE (2018). https://doi.org/10.1109/ATNAC.2018.8615294
10. Hasan, T., et al.: Securing industrial Internet of Things against botnet attacks using hybrid deep learning approach. IEEE Trans. Netw. Sci. Eng. **10**(5), 2952–2963 (2023). https://doi.org/10.1109/TNSE.2022.3168533
11. Son, D.T., Tram, N.T.K., Hieu, P.M.: Deep learning techniques to detect botnet. J. Sci. Technol. Information Sec. **1**(15), 85-91 (2022). https://doi.org/10.54654/isj.v1i15.846
12. Homayoun, S., Ahmadzadeh, M., Hashemi, S., Dehghantanha, A., Khayami, R.: BoTShark: a deep learning approach for botnet traffic detection. In: Dehghantanha, A., Conti, M., Dargahi, T. (eds.) Cyber Threat Intelligence. AIS, vol. 70, pp. 137–153. Springer, Cham (2018). https://doi.org/10.1007/978-3-319-73951-9_7
13. Sriram, S., Vinayakumar, R., Alazab, M., KP, S.: Network flow based iot botnet attack detection using deep learning. In: IEEE INFOCOM 2020 - IEEE Conference on Computer Communications Workshops (INFOCOM WKSHPS), Toronto, ON, Canada, pp. 189-194. IEEE (2020). https://doi.org/10.1109/INFOCOMWKSHPS50562.2020.9162668
14. Nugraha, B., Nambiar, A., Bauschert, T.: Performance evaluation of botnet detection using deep learning techniques. In: 11th International Conference on Network of the Future (NoF), Bordeaux, France 2020, pp. 141-149. IEEE (2020). https://doi.org/10.1109/NoF50125.2020.9249198
15. Karunakaran, P.: Deep learning approach to DGA classification for effective cyber security. J. Ubiquitous Comput. Commun. Technol., (UCCT) **2**(4), 203-213 (2020). https://doi.org/10.36548/jucct.2020.4.003
16. Sarker, I.H.: Deep cybersecurity: a comprehensive overview from neural network and deep learning perspective. SN Comput. Sci. **2**(3) 154–162 (2021). https://doi.org/10.1007/s42979-021-00535-6
17. Džeroski, S., Ženko, B.: Is combining classifiers with stacking better than selecting the best one? Mach. Learn. **54**, 255–273 (2004). https://doi.org/10.1023/B:MACH.0000015881.36452.6e
18. Hossain, M.A., Islam, M.S.: A novel hybrid feature selection and ensemble-based machine learning approach for botnet detection. Sci. Rep. **13**, 21207 (2023). https://doi.org/10.1038/s41598-023-48230-1
19. Hasan, R., et al.: Enhancing malware detection with feature selection and scaling techniques using machine learning models. Sci. Rep. **15**, 9122 (2025). https://doi.org/10.1038/s41598-025-93447-x

20. Hossain, M.A., Islam, M.S.: A novel feature selection-driven ensemble learning approach for accurate botnet attack detection. Alex. Eng. J. **118**, 261–277 (2025). https://doi.org/10.1016/j.aej.2025.01.042
21. Moustafa, N., Slay, J.: UNSW-NB15: a comprehensive data set for network intrusion detection systems (UNSW-NB15 network data set). In: 2015 Military Communications and Information Systems Conference (MilCIS), Canberra, ACT, Australia, 2015, pp. 1-6. IEEE (2015). https://doi.org/10.1109/MilCIS.2015.7348942
22. Varoquaux, G., Buitinck, L., Louppe, G., Grisel, O., Pedregosa, F., Mueller, A.: Scikit-learn: machine learning without learning the machinery. GetMobile: Mobile Comput. Commun. **19**(1), 29-33 (2015). https://doi.org/10.1145/2786984.2786995
23. Tuan, T.A., Long, H.V., Son, L.H., Kumar, R., Priyadarshini, I., Son, N.T.K.: Performance evaluation of Botnet DDoS attack detection using machine learning. Evol. Intel. **13**(2), 283–294 (2020). https://doi.org/10.1007/s12065-019-00310-w

Typosquatting Detection at Scale: A Review of DNS-Focused Approach to Domain Abuse

Serra Uysal(✉) and Mehmet Tahir Sandıkkaya

Department of Computer Engineering, Istanbul Technical University, Istanbul, Türkiye
{uysals17,sandikkaya}@itu.edu.tr

Abstract. The Internet is deeply woven into the fabric of daily life, powering activities such as online education, shopping, and communication. However, this widespread reliance also invites security threats, such as phishing attacks, where malicious actors design deceptive websites using subtly modified URLs (Uniform Resource Locator) to impersonate legitimate domains and harvest user data. Combating such threats requires not only security mechanisms but also robust Internet measurement strategies that observe, analyze, and evaluate these evolving attack vectors.

In this work, an open-source tool called dnstwist is utilized that is designed to systematically generate lexical variations of legitimate domain names for simulating potential phishing targets. This tool is extended through the development of custom scripts that perform Domain Name System (DNS) resolution and metadata collection, enabling the identification of suspicious or anomalous domains. During the initial phase of the study, DNS data corresponding to the generated domain variants are examined, and behaviors such as unresponsive resolvers and indications of parked or potentially malicious domains are observed.

These preliminary findings highlight ongoing developments in phishing strategies and demonstrate how systematic URL analysis combined with DNS based measurements can provide actionable insights into the evolving threat landscape. Our results will be further compared with retrospective research to assess attacker behavior over time and evaluate the effectiveness of current detection techniques to foresee future phishing strategies.

Keywords: DNS · URL phishing detection · URL lexical analysis

1 Introduction

Internet is spreading in every aspect of human lives. From online shopping to education, the World Wide Web (www) is within a click away. The Internet has the mutual benefit of easing daily life. However, with great power comes

K. Daimi et al. (Eds.): CSCE 2025, CCIS 2937, pp. 299–314, 2026.
https://doi.org/10.1007/978-3-032-22208-4_20

great responsibility. While being the center of crucial operations, web sites need to remain credible for their users. Malicious people menace this credibility by providing fake web sites that imitate legitimate sites. Adversaries try to deceive users to click on a slightly altered Uniform Resource Identifier (URI) that rely on visual similarity. Inattentive users fall victim to this trap. Figure 1 illustrates this attack, namely phishing attack via typosquatting. For instance, there is a web site called "originalwebsite.com". It is a well-known web site that shares cute cat videos online. Then, an attacker sees the potential of creating a fake website with a similar name, let it be "0riginalwebsite.com", and tricks people to log in to their accounts through this fake web site. The attacker can share this malicious link via various methods like ads or spam e-mail. From a user's point of view, someone who is less cautious could be easily tricked into believing this well-imitated web site to be legitimate and they can share their credentials in the hope of finding a funny video for their colleagues. The attacker will now have access to some credential information related to the user, or even worse, an access to the device that is being used. After this point, the attack can take any shape and form according to the motivation behind it.

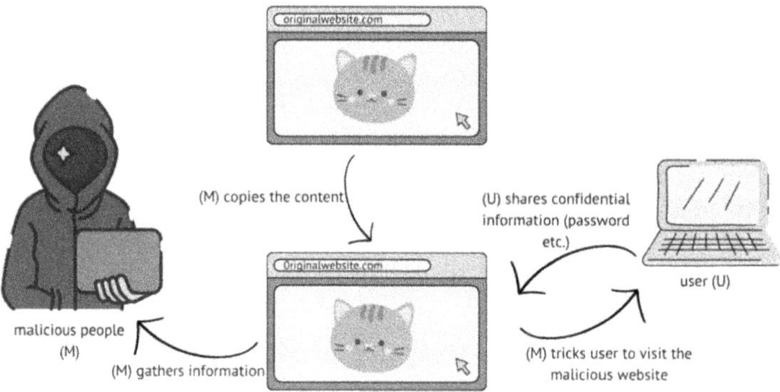

Fig. 1. Phishing attack via Typosquatting.

This brief example demonstrates how a URL with a single character alteration can deceive users. There are various methods that are used for the detection and analysis of such lexical methods of which are covered in the following sections. When people search on the web, they use human-readable addresses like originalwebsite.com. This address needs to be converted to a machine-readable address (e.g., IPv4 or IPv6 address) that is unique for each device. DNS is used as a phone book for domain names and their corresponding IP addresses [13].

Figure 2 shows the summary of the DNS lookup and web page load scheme. When a website is visited a while ago, it's IP address might be found within the local cache. It is the first place to look at. If the address is not found, then the DNS lookup starts. Initially, a request is sent to the DNS resolver. Then, it queries the address to the root server. Root server will return the address of the

Top Level Domain (TLD) for the given address. TLD refers to the right hand side of the dot (.) seperated address such as .com or .org. For the originalwebsite.com example, the root server will point to the .com TLD server. DNS resolver now sends a request to the TLD server. TLD server will respond with the IP address of the domain's name server for originalwebsite.com. Note that, practical name resolution process could be considerably distinct to be more optimized from the sketched scnerio due to caching at several locations. DNS resolver finally reaches to the domain name server requesting the IP address for originalwebsite.com. When the result is returned, DNS resolver shares this to the requesting device. Once the lookup process is complete, a Hyper-Text Transfer Protocol (HTTP) request is sent to the server with the received IP address on the pre-determined port. The server returns the respected HTML content for originalwebsite.com to the user.

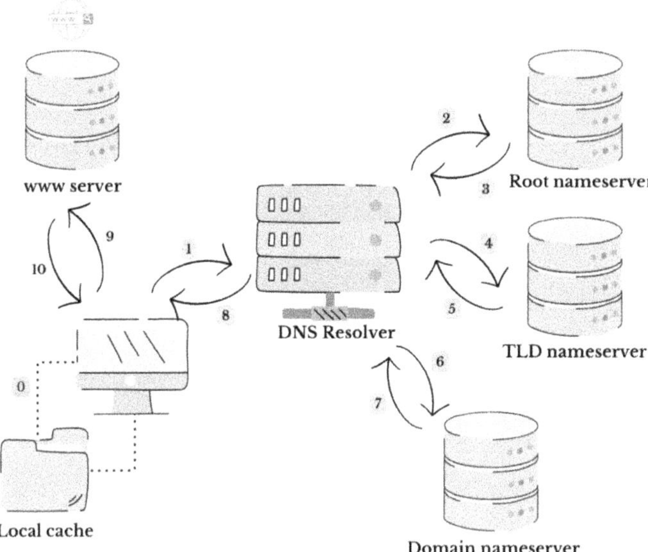

Fig. 2. DNS lookup.

This flow illustrates that although "originalwebsite.com" and "0riginalwebsite.com" may appear nearly identical to human perception, they resolve to distinct IP addresses. This technique, known as typosquatting, involves the registration of domain names that are typographical or visually confusable variants of legitimate domains, with the goal of deceiving users and enabling malicious activities such as phishing, credential harvesting, or malware delivery. This paper will mainly focus on one character difference of the main site as it would be more easily overlooked by users. To mitigate the risk of typosquatting, users should verify the accuracy of the URI before proceeding to the website.

The primary purpose of this study is to investigate and classify a wide range of techniques used for the detection and analysis of malicious or deceptive domains, with a particular emphasis on lexical features, DNS and TLD behaviors, typosquatting strategies, URL parsing methods, and phishing indicators. To complement the literature review, an empirical analysis of popular and suspicious domain names is conducted using an open source tool, dnstwist [66], which generates and inspects domain variants for potential misuse. This dual approach synthesizing prior research and applying automated domain analysis aims to provide a comprehensive understanding of the landscape and to identify practical and theoretical gaps in current detection frameworks.

The structure of the paper is organized as follows: the next section presents a review of related work in the field. This is followed by the methodology section, which outlines the research approach and details of implementation. Subsequently, the results of the study are discussed. Finally, the paper concludes with a summary of the findings and suggestions for future work.

2 Related Work

Malicious URL detection has emerged as a vital area in cybersecurity research, driven by the increasing sophistication of phishing, malware distribution, and deceptive domain practices. This section reviews key work in the domain, highlighting the diversity of methods, data sources, and detection strategies that paved the way for this work.

Early research in malicious URL detection often focused on lexical analysis, where handcrafted features extracted from URL strings were used to train traditional machine learning models. These approaches leveraged attributes such as URL length, presence of suspicious tokens (e.g., "login," "verify," "secure"), number of subdomains, and character entropy to identify potentially harmful links. Lexical methods were favored for their computational efficiency and independence from external infrastructure like DNS or WHOIS, making them suitable for real-time detection. Despite their simplicity, these models proved to be surprisingly effective against phishing and malware-hosting domains, especially when combined with robust feature selection. These foundational works laid the groundwork for more advanced machine learning applications, such as those later developed by Abutaha et al. [2], who proposed a machine learning-based approach using lexical URL features and classifiers such as neural networks, random forests, SVM, and gradient boosting classifiers (GBC). Their work, using the RLILOJR dataset, demonstrated 99.89% accuracy and suggested that even shallow models can effectively distinguish between benign and malicious URLs when provided with rich syntactic features. Similarly, Moarref and Sandıkkaya [41] presented MC-MLDCNN, a multichannel, multilayer dilated convolutional neural network designed to improve malicious URL detection while reducing the burden of manual feature extraction. Their deep learning architecture emphasized automation and scalability, particularly useful in real-time detection scenarios.

Chakraborty and Lin [12] emphasized the structural aspects of URLs, proposing a URL-aware classification system capable of leveraging both lexical and contextual features. Their study, based on a large dataset containing 46,000 URLs (including 11,000 malicious samples), focuses on feature extraction to eliminate computational burden. Mamun et al. [38] followed a similar methodology, but extended their data set to include 110,000 URLs. They implemented a lightweight detection method to overcome dependency for blacklisting since popular ranking links may include deceptive URLs. Meanwhile, Kumar and Maity [30] evaluated multiple machine learning classifiers using a publicly available Kaggle dataset. Their method includes network activity data together with lexical analysis aiming to improve detection rate. Julia et al. use XGBoost algorithm to lexically analyze URLs [54]. They extract 21 features from their URL database and end up selecting 11 of them to use in the algorithm. Since they only use the lexical part of the URL, their proposed method is claimed to be more efficient than existing methods.

However, many existing systems still face limitations. Lexical analysis, while fast and lightweight, is susceptible to adversarial evasion techniques such as homograph attacks - also called a homoglyph attack, a technique that deceives people by using visually similar characters or symbols to imitate legitimate text or domain names - or the use of URL shorteners. However, deep learning models often lack interpretability and require substantial labeled datasets, which are not always feasible in zero-day scenarios. Furthermore, the integration of real-time threat intelligence, such as URL sandboxing services or WHOIS anomaly detection, remains underexplored in many academic studies.

Beyond direct malicious detection, another crucial dimension involves understanding how adversaries craft misleading or deceptive domains. Typosquatting, for example, represents a common tactic in which attackers register visually or phonetically similar domain names to lure unsuspecting users. Banerjee et al. [7] conducted one of the foundational large-scale studies in this space, probing over three million typo-derived URLs. Their findings showed that 99% of the variants generated by typos were fraudulent, most differing by only a single character. This work underscores the scale and subtlety of typosquatting and motivates detection strategies that go beyond simple lexical similarity.

Other studies in this category, such as Szurdi et al. [63] and Pouryousef et al. [49], examined the lifecycle and monetization of typosquatted domains, noting patterns such as parking, redirection to competitors, and malware distribution. These findings point to the need for longitudinal and behavioral analysis of suspicious domains, a direction that complements snapshot-based classification techniques.

In parallel, the emergence of passive DNS (pDNS) analysis and domain reputation systems provides another rich layer of intelligence. By querying historical DNS records, researchers can uncover abnormal resolution patterns, hosting volatility, or association with known malicious infrastructure. Although not all studies in the current survey incorporated pDNS data, its utility is evident, particularly in identifying newly registered domains that exhibit rapid fluxing or domain shadowing behaviors.

Additional studies are summarized in Table 1, where they are organized into relevant thematic categories. It is important to note that the defined topics occasionally overlap in scope; consequently, certain studies could reasonably be classified under multiple subdomains. However, to maintain clarity and reduce redundancy, each study has been assigned to a single category based on its primary focus.

As can be seen from the literature summarized in Table 1, lexical analysis approaches to typosquatting detection date back to as early as 2009, whereas TLD related investigations only begin to appear around 2017 and continue to the present. This disparity is largely due to the expansion of the domain name system following the introduction of new generic Top-Level Domains (gTLDs), initiated by ICANN's New gTLD Program in 2012 [22]. Prior to this, the domain namespace was relatively narrow, with most malicious activity concentrated in a few well-known TLDs such as .com, .net, and .org. Consequently, early detection techniques focused mainly on character-level variations within these domains.

In recent years, however, attackers have increasingly exploited not only gTLDs but also country-code TLDs (ccTLDs) for deceptive purposes. For example, the ccTLD .ist, designated for Istanbul, can be used to construct misleading domain names such as pharmac.ist, which may appear trustworthy or relevant to English-speaking users, especially in a healthcare context. Such usage demonstrates how the semantic flexibility of TLDs can be leveraged to craft domains that look legitimate but serve malicious or misleading purposes. Despite growing attention to this issue, TLD-based abuse remains underexplored in the literature. Our work contributes to this evolving research direction by systematically incorporating TLD variation into our analysis of typosquatting threats.

3 Methodology

The approach to detecting potentially malicious or suspicious domain names in this work is based on the use of the dnstwist tool [66], which generates domain permutations of a target domain and analyzes their characteristics. The generation of permutations is central to the chosen methodology and is designed to mimic various typographical and structural errors or manipulations in the real world that users may encounter. Each permutation technique simulates a particular category of a typographical or malicious transformation strategy.

In the following, each permutation method employed is detailed.

- **Addition:** Inserts every lowercase alphanumeric character at all positions within the domain. This models user behavior such as accidental keystrokes (e.g., `googgle.com`).
- **Bitsquatting:** Alters individual bits of each character in the domain by applying bit masks. This models hardware faults or transmission errors that can result in corrupted domain names.

Table 1. List of reviewed studies grouped under the related topics

Topic	Studies	Summary
Lexical Feature-Based URL Analysis	[2,6,12,17,20, 26,30,35,37,38, 41,50,52,54]	This line of research focuses on analyzing the syntactic structure of URLs to detect malicious intent. Methods in this category extract handcrafted features such as token patterns, URL length, number of subdomains, presence of IP addresses, special characters, or suspicious keywords. These features are then fed into machine learning classifiers ranging from decision trees to ensemble models and neural networks. Lexical analysis is lightweight and does not rely on external data sources, which makes it suitable for real-time detection scenarios. Although it may be vulnerable to obfuscation tactics, lexical analysis remains a foundational technique in malicious URL detection due to its interpretability and deployment ease.
URL Parsing and Representation for Machine Learning Models	[1,5,40,43,46, 51,53,56,65]	This category encompasses research that aims to transform raw URLs into structured representations suitable for automated processing, particularly for deep learning models. Instead of relying on handcrafted features, these methods parse URLs into meaningful components such as subdomain, domain, path, and query, then represent them as sequences or graphs. Techniques such as character level embedding, token segmentation, and n-gram analysis are often used to feed recurrent or convolutional neural networks. These parsing strategies enable models to learn malicious patterns from the structure and semantics of URLs without manual intervention.
Domain Name System (DNS) and Top-Level Domain (TLD) Based Security	[27,28,39,47, 49,67,68]	Research in this category investigates the use of DNS data, WHOIS records, and TLD characteristics to detect and profile malicious domains. These approaches go beyond the surface-level URL structure and examine domain registration patterns, resolution history, and hosting behaviors. Passive DNS (pDNS) records can reveal temporal trends such as frequent IP changes, association with known bad infrastructure, or recently registered domains with limited historical activity. WHOIS anomalies, registrar abuse, and the exploitation of specific TLDs are also common indicators of malicious behavior. Integrating such infrastructure-level data helps enhance robustness against URL manipulation and enables early detection of domain-based threats.

(*continued*)

Table 1. (*continued*)

Topic	Studies	Summary
Phishing Detection Using Behavioral and Content Signals	[10,11,14,18,19, 23,25,29,32,44, 55,57]	Phishing detection research focuses on identifying deceptive websites and URLs designed to impersonate legitimate services to steal user credentials or sensitive data. This category includes techniques that analyze not just the URL itself, but also contextual signals such as domain age, hosting behavior, SSL certificate properties, and sometimes page content or redirection chains. Some studies use dynamic analysis, including sandboxing or behavioral emulation, to observe phishing indicators during website interaction. Others leverage threat intelligence feeds or blacklists for ground truth. These models often prioritize high precision to reduce false positives, especially in enterprise or browser-integrated use cases.
Detection and Characterization of Typosquatting Domains	[3,4,7–9,15,16, 21,24,31,33,34, 36,42,45,58–64]	Typosquatting research addresses the phenomenon of attackers registering domain names that closely resemble popular websites, exploiting human typographical errors. These domains are often used for phishing, ad fraud, or malware delivery. Early studies in this space conducted large-scale measurement analyses by systematically generating variants of legitimate domains and probing their registration and behavior. Key findings revealed that most typosquatted domains differ by a single character and that a significant proportion are actively monetized or malicious. Current research includes both detection–through lexical similarity metrics and machine learning–and mitigation strategies such as domain monitoring and defensive registration.

- **Homoglyph:** Substitutes characters with visually similar Unicode characters or symbols (e.g., replacing "o" with "0" or "l" with "1"). This is used in phishing attacks to create deceptive but plausible domains.
- **Hyphenation:** Inserts a hyphen at each possible position in the domain (excluding start and end positions). This reflects regional conventions or stylistic choices in domain naming.
- **Insertion:** Introduces characters adjacent to the respective ones on a QWERTY (or alternative layout) keyboard. This simulates typographical slips caused by adjacent keys.

- **Omission:** Removes one character at a time from the domain name, simulating typing errors where characters are inadvertently skipped.
- **Repetition:** Duplicates individual characters, modeling accidental key holding or intentional duplication in malicious domain crafting.
- **Replacement:** Substitutes each character with its neighboring keys on a keyboard layout (QWERTY, QWERTZ, AZERTY). This models character substitution errors.
- **Subdomain Insertion:** Creates permutations by inserting dots at various positions, effectively generating subdomain variants (e.g., `mail.google.com` from `google.com`).
- **Transposition:** Swaps adjacent characters in the domain string, a common error during rapid typing.
- **Vowel Swap:** Replaces each vowel in the domain name with other vowels. This accounts for variations due to user pronunciation assumptions.
- **Pluralization:** Adds plural suffixes such as "s" or "es" to simulate commonly mistyped or alternate forms (e.g., `products.com` from `product.com`).
- **Dictionary-based Variants:** Combines the domain name with predefined dictionary terms by prefixing, suffixing, or inserting them. This is often used in SEO (Search Engine Optimization) manipulation and cybersquatting.
- **TLD Swap:** Replaces the original top-level domain (TLD) with alternatives from a supplied list (e.g., changing `example.com` to `example.net`). This models phishing campaigns registered under multiple TLDs.
- **Various Heuristics:** Additional composite permutations combining domain elements, TLDs, and subdomains to capture edge-case manipulations.

Each generated permutation undergoes further processing, including DNS resolution, WHOIS lookups, and passive DNS or threat intelligence enrichment, to assess domain activity, hosting infrastructure, and potential risk. These analyses enable classification into categories such as parked, active, or malicious.

Although other studies in the field commonly rely on the Alexa Top Sites list to identify popular domains, in this work the use of the TRANCO [48] list is chosen instead. Unlike Alexa, which is no longer maintained and may be outdated, TRANCO provides a daily updated ranking that aggregates data from multiple sources and employs detailed filtering and analysis to ensure higher reliability and reproducibility.

4 Results

To validate the relevance of our survey and observe real-world instances of malicious domain behavior, empirical analysis is conducted using dnstwist [66], an open-source domain permutation engine. A set of popular domain names (e.g., google.com, amazon.com, facebook.com) from TRANCO [48] dataset were used as seeds to generate variants commonly associated with typosquatting. The tool produced multiple domain permutations for each input, including but not limited to character swaps, insertions, omissions, and homograph substitutions.

These variants were then systematically queried to extract associated DNS records, WHOIS information, and, when applicable, responses from threat intelligence services. A significant portion of the generated domain variants were observed to be either unregistered or parked, but a non-negligible subset were active and exhibited behaviors commonly associated with phishing and ad fraud. For instance, some domains redirected users to affiliate marketing landing pages, while others mimicked login pages of the original services.

Furthermore, domain variants using less known or abused TLDs (e.g., .top, .xyz, .cn) were more frequently associated with suspicious infrastructure, such as frequently changing IP addresses or anonymized WHOIS data. These findings align with retrospective literature emphasizing the misuse of DNS and TLD spaces in malicious campaigns.

The results confirm that the techniques documented in the surveyed literature, particularly lexical analysis and DNS-based inspection, remain highly relevant in identifying domain level threats. In addition, the experiment highlights the continued presence of exploitable domain variants targeting high traffic websites, reinforcing the need for ongoing monitoring and automated detection strategies.

Table 2. Distribution of Average Permutations and Registrations by Character Count

Character Count	Average Number of Permutations	Average Registered Number	Total Occurrence
5	1235.83	32.20	6421
6	1897.78	27.12	8313
7	2594.17	22.47	8531
8	3482.95	18.80	8433
9	4385.06	17.55	7846

For the 74,204 domain names considered, the most common base domain lengths ranged between 5 to 9 characters. The average number of permutations and the average registered numbers for these groups are shown in Table 2 together with their occurrence count. The ratios of average registered to average permutations for these groups are approximately 0.026, 0.014, 0.009, 0.005 and 0.004 in order from 5 to 9. This shows a declining registration rate as domain names get longer. Overall, the ratio of registered to generated permutations remains low, meaning that most potential variants are still unregistered and available, especially for longer base names.

5 Conclusion and Future Work

In this study, a systematic review of the literature on typosquatting detection techniques was carried out, with an emphasis on how research priorities have changed over time. Early contributions to the field mainly explored lexical similarity and character-based manipulations within the well-known TLD, reflecting the limited scope of the DNS landscape prior to the expansion introduced by the ICANN New gTLD Program. At that stage, the role of TLD variation was neither well understood nor considered a critical component of typosquatting detection. However, it has since become evident that with the proliferation of hundreds of new gTLDs, along with the increasingly creative use of ccTLDs, the selection of a TLD has become an intentional and strategic decision by malicious actors.

To investigate this evolution, the open-source tool dnstwist was adopted and extended to support not only the generation of domain variants through lexical transformations but also automated DNS resolution and metadata collection. This enhanced setup allowed for a broader investigation into how domain variants behave across diverse TLDs. The analysis revealed that while traditional lexical patterns still play a role in typosquatting, the TLD itself has emerged as a distinguishing feature of more recent and evasive campaigns. Domains registered under less-regulated or low-cost TLDs exhibited different resolution behaviors, and in several cases, pointed toward infrastructure typically associated with domain parking, redirection schemes, or suspicious usage.

In summary, the top 74,204 popular domains of the TRANCO dataset were investigated and their permutation and registration characteristics were analyzed. Although the overall ratio of registered to total permutations was found to be relatively low, it still indicates a potential vulnerability, as a wide range of domain name variants remain available for possible misuse.

A higher registration ratio was observed for shorter domain names, which can be attributed to their stronger association with well-known companies or brands, making them more likely to be exploited by malicious actors for typosquatting or visual impersonation purposes.

By framing the problem from a DNS-centric perspective, this work underscores the need to treat TLD selection not as a peripheral concern but as an integral component of typosquatting strategies. Existing detection mechanisms that focus solely on string similarity within a single TLD risk overlooking significant portions of the abuse landscape, particularly as attackers diversify their use of domain spaces.

As part of future work, Passive DNS (pDNS) data will be incorporated into the analysis pipeline. By leveraging pDNS, it will be possible to trace the historical resolution patterns of domain variants, uncover shared infrastructure, and identify relationships among domains that may not be immediately apparent through active DNS querying alone. The inclusion of such longitudinal and infrastructural insights is expected to significantly enhance the precision and depth of typosquatting detection methods. Ultimately, a combination of lexical analysis, TLD-aware classification, and passive DNS intelligence will enable the development of a more comprehensive and resilient framework for identifying and characterizing typosquatted domains at scale.

Acknowledgments. This work was supported by the Scientific and Technological Research Council of Türkiye (TÜBİTAK) under Grant 1919B022507409.

References

1. Abdallah, T.A., de La Iglesia, B.: URL-based web page classification: with n-gram language models. In: Fred, A., Dietz, J.L.G., Aveiro, D., Liu, K., Filipe, J. (eds.) IC3K 2014. CCIS, vol. 553, pp. 19–33. Springer, Cham (2015). https://doi.org/10.1007/978-3-319-25840-9_2
2. Abutaha, M., Ababneh, M., Mahmoud, K., Baddar, S.A.H.: Url phishing detection using machine learning techniques based on urls lexical analysis. In: 2021 12th International Conference on Information and Communication Systems (ICICS), pp. 147–152. IEEE (2021)
3. Agten, P., Joosen, W., Piessens, F., Nikiforakis, N.: Seven months' worth of mistakes: a longitudinal study of typosquatting abuse. In: Proceedings of the 22nd Network and Distributed System Security Symposium (NDSS 2015). Internet Society (2015)
4. Ahmad, I., Parvez, M.A., Iqbal, A.: Typowriter: a tool to prevent typosquatting. In: 2019 IEEE 43rd Annual Computer Software and Applications Conference (COMPSAC), vol. 1, pp. 423–432. IEEE (2019)
5. Ajmani, D.K., Koishybayev, I., Kapravelos, A.: you are a liar://a unified framework for cross-testing url parsers. In: 2022 IEEE Security and Privacy Workshops (SPW), pp. 51–58. IEEE (2022)
6. Aljabri, M., et al.: An assessment of lexical, network, and content-based features for detecting malicious urls using machine learning and deep learning models. Comput. Intell. Neurosci. **2022**(1), 3241216 (2022)
7. Banerjee, A., Rahman, M.S., Faloutsos, M.: Sut: quantifying and mitigating url typosquatting. Comput. Netw. **55**(13), 3001–3014 (2011)
8. Blefari, F., Furfaro, A., Ianni, G., Viscomi, A.: Combining anti-typosquatting techniques. In: International Conference on Web Engineering, pp. 246–254. Springer (2024). https://doi.org/10.1007/978-3-031-62362-2_17
9. Blefari, F., Furfaro, A., Ianni, G., Viscomi, A., et al.: Typoalert: a browser extension against typosquatting. In: Proc. of SEBD: 32nd Symposium on Advanced Database Systems (2024)
10. Blum, A., Wardman, B., Solorio, T., Warner, G.: Lexical feature based phishing url detection using online learning. In: Proceedings of the 3rd ACM Workshop on Artificial Intelligence and Security, pp. 54–60 (2010)
11. Bozkir, A.S., Dalgic, F.C., Aydos, M.: Grambeddings: a new neural network for url based identification of phishing web pages through n-gram embeddings. Comput. Sec. **124**, 102964 (2023)
12. Chakraborty, G., Lin, T.T.: A url address aware classification of malicious websites for online security during web-surfing. In: 2017 IEEE International Conference on Advanced Networks and Telecommunications Systems (ANTS), pp. 1–6 (2017). https://doi.org/10.1109/ANTS.2017.8384155
13. Cloudflare, Inc.: What is dns? (2024). https://www.cloudflare.com/learning/dns/what-is-dns/, Accessed 05 Feb 2025
14. Daeef, A.Y., Ahmad, R.B., Yacob, Y., Phing, N.Y.: Wide scope and fast websites phishing detection using urls lexical features. In: 2016 3rd International Conference on Electronic Design (ICED), pp. 410–415. IEEE (2016)
15. Dam, T., Klausner, L.D., Buhov, D., Schrittwieser, S.: Large-scale analysis of pop-up scam on typosquatting urls. In: Proceedings of the 14th International Conference on Availability, Reliability and Security, pp. 1–9 (2019)
16. Dam, T., Klausner, L.D., Schrittwieser, S.: Typosquatting for fun and profit: Cross-country analysis of pop-up scam. arXiv preprint arXiv:2004.01749 (2020)

17. Darling, M., Heileman, G., Gressel, G., Ashok, A., Poornachandran, P.: A lexical approach for classifying malicious urls. In: 2015 international conference on high performance computing & simulation (HPCS), pp. 195–202. IEEE (2015)
18. Dunbar, A.P.: Detecting Phish Using Website Content and URL N-Gram Features. Master's thesis, University of Houston (2016)
19. Gupta, B.B., Yadav, K., Razzak, I., Psannis, K., Castiglione, A., Chang, X.: A novel approach for phishing urls detection using lexical based machine learning in a real-time environment. Comput. Commun. **175**, 47–57 (2021)
20. Hong, J., Kim, T., Liu, J., Park, N., Kim, S.W.: Phishing url detection with lexical features and blacklisted domains. Adaptive Autonomous Sec. Cyber Syst., 253–267 (2020)
21. Husain, M.D., Iqbal, A.: An empirical study on typosquatting abuse in bangladesh. In: 2017 International Conference on Networking, Systems and Security (NSysS), pp. 47–54. IEEE (2017)
22. Internet Corporation for Assigned Names and Numbers (ICANN): New generic top-level domains (gtlds). https://newgtlds.icann.org/en (2012), Accessed 15 May 2025
23. Islavath, S., Bhat, C.R.: Uniform resource locator phishing in real time scenario predicted using novel term frequency-inverse document frequency+ n gram in comparison with support vector machine algorithm. In: 2024 15th International Conference on Computing Communication and Networking Technologies (ICCCNT), pp. 1–5. IEEE (2024)
24. Khan, M.T., Huo, X., Li, Z., Kanich, C.: Every second counts: quantifying the negative externalities of cybercrime via typosquatting. In: 2015 IEEE Symposium on Security and Privacy, pp. 135–150. IEEE (2015)
25. Khonji, M., Iraqi, Y., Jones, A.: Lexical url analysis for discriminating phishing and legitimate websites. In: Proceedings of the 8th Annual Collaboration, Electronic messaging, Anti-Abuse and Spam Conference, pp. 109–115 (2011)
26. Khonji, M., Iraqi, Y., Jones, A.: Enhancing phishing e-mail classifiers: a lexical url analysis approach. Inter. J. Inform. Sec. Res. (IJISR) **2**(1/2), 40 (2012)
27. Khormali, A., Park, J., Alasmary, H., Anwar, A., Saad, M., Mohaisen, D.: Domain name system security and privacy: a contemporary survey. Comput. Netw. **185**, 107699 (2021)
28. Korczynski, M., et al.: Cybercrime after the sunrise. In: Proceedings of the 2018 on Asia Conference on Computer and Communications Security. ACM (2018)
29. Korkmaz, M., Kocyigit, E., Sahingoz, O.K., Diri, B.: Phishing web page detection using n-gram features extracted from urls. In: 2021 3rd International Congress on Human-Computer Interaction, Optimization and Robotic Applications (HORA), pp. 1–6. IEEE (2021)
30. Kumar, A., Maity, S.: Detecting malicious urls using lexical analysis and network activities. In: 2022 4th International Conference on Inventive Research in Computing Applications (ICIRCA), pp. 570–575. IEEE (2022)
31. Lain, D., Nakatsuka, Y., Kostiainen, K., Tsudik, G., Capkun, S.: Url inspection tasks: Helping users detect phishing links in emails. arXiv preprint arXiv:2502.20234 (2025)
32. Le, A., Markopoulou, A., Faloutsos, M.: Phishdef: Url names say it all. In: 2011 Proceedings IEEE INFOCOM, pp. 191–195. IEEE (2011)
33. Le Pochat, V., Van Goethem, T., Joosen, W.: A smörgåsbord of typos: exploring international keyboard layout typosquatting. In: 2019 IEEE Security and Privacy Workshops (SPW), pp. 187–192. IEEE (2019)

34. Liu, G., Gao, X., Wang, H., Sun, K.: Exploring the unchartered space of container registry typosquatting. In: 31st USENIX Security Symposium (USENIX Security 2022), pp. 35–51 (2022)
35. Liu, Q.: Detection of malicious websites across multiple classes using n-gram features and vgg based on url analysis. Appli. Comput. Eng. **18**, 66–72 (2023)
36. Liu, T., Zhang, Y., Shi, J., Jing, Y., Li, Q., Guo, L.: Towards quantifying visual similarity of domain names for combating typosquatting abuse. In: MILCOM 2016-2016 IEEE Military Communications Conference, pp. 770–775. IEEE (2016)
37. Ma, J., Saul, L.K., Savage, S., Voelker, G.M.: Beyond blacklists: learning to detect malicious web sites from suspicious urls. In: Proceedings of the 15th ACM SIGKDD International Conference on Knowledge Discovery and Data Mining, pp. 1245–1254 (2009)
38. Mamun, M.S.I., Rathore, M.A., Lashkari, A.H., Stakhanova, N., Ghorbani, A.A.: Detecting malicious URLs using lexical analysis. In: Chen, J., Piuri, V., Su, C., Yung, M. (eds.) NSS 2016. LNCS, vol. 9955, pp. 467–482. Springer, Cham (2016). https://doi.org/10.1007/978-3-319-46298-1_30
39. Maroofi, S., Korczyński, M., Hesselman, C., Ampeau, B., Duda, A.: Comar: classification of compromised versus maliciously registered domains. In: 2020 IEEE European Symposium on Security and Privacy (EuroS&P), pp. 607–623. IEEE (2020)
40. Matic, S., Iordanou, C., Smaragdakis, G., Laoutaris, N.: Identifying sensitive urls at web-scale. In: Proceedings of the ACM Internet Measurement Conference, pp. 619–633 (2020)
41. Moarref, N., Sandıkkaya, M.T.: Mc-mldcnn: multichannel multilayer dilated convolutional neural networks for web attack detection. Sec. Commun. Netw. **2023**(1), 2415288 (2023)
42. Moore, T., Edelman, B.: Measuring the perpetrators and funders of typosquatting. In: Sion, R. (ed.) FC 2010. LNCS, vol. 6052, pp. 175–191. Springer, Heidelberg (2010). https://doi.org/10.1007/978-3-642-14577-3_15
43. Nittur, P., Jadav, B.M., Sharma, A., Teja, J.L., Mani, S., Sahni, N.: A method to detect threat in advertisement url and its content. In: 2024 IEEE International Conference on Electronics, Computing and Communication Technologies (CONECCT), pp. 1–6. IEEE (2024)
44. Opara, C., Chen, Y., Wei, B.: Look before you leap: detecting phishing web pages by exploiting raw url and html characteristics. Expert Syst. Appl. **236**, 121183 (2024)
45. Parvez, M.A.: Typosquatting error detection analyzing DNS log. Master's thesis, Bangladesh University of Engineering and Technology (2019)
46. Patil, D.R., Patil, J.: Malicious web pages detection using static analysis of urls. Inter. J. Inform. Sec. Cybercrime **5**(2) (2016)
47. Piredda, P., Ariu, D., Biggio, B., Corona, I., Piras, L., Giacinto, G., Roli, F.: Deepsquatting: learning-based typosquatting detection at deeper domain levels. In: AI* IA 2017 Advances in Artificial Intelligence: XVIth International Conference of the Italian Association for Artificial Intelligence, Bari, Italy, November 14-17, 2017, Proceedings 16, pp. 347–358. Springer (2017). https://doi.org/10.1007/978-3-319-70169-1_26
48. Pochat, V.L., Van Goethem, T., Tajalizadehkhoob, S., Korczyński, M., Joosen, W.: Tranco: A research-oriented top sites ranking hardened against manipulation. arXiv preprint arXiv:1806.01156 (2018)

49. Pouryousef, S., Dar, M.D., Ahmad, S., Gill, P., Nithyanand, R.: Extortion or expansion? an investigation into the costs and consequences of ICANN's gTLD experiments. In: Sperotto, A., Dainotti, A., Stiller, B. (eds.) PAM 2020. LNCS, vol. 12048, pp. 141–157. Springer, Cham (2020). https://doi.org/10.1007/978-3-030-44081-7_9
50. Raja, A.S., Vinodini, R., Kavitha, A.: Lexical features based malicious url detection using machine learning techniques. Mater. Today: Proc. **47**, 163–166 (2021)
51. Rajalakshmi, R., Aravindan, C.: Web page classification using n-gram based url features. In: 2013 Fifth International Conference on Advanced Computing (ICoAC), pp. 15–21. IEEE (2013)
52. Ranganayakulu, D., Chellappan, C.: Detecting malicious urls in e-mail-an implementation. AASRI Proc. **4**, 125–131 (2013)
53. Reynolds, J., Bates, A., Bailey, M.: Equivocal urls: understanding the fragmented space of url parser implementations. In: European Symposium on Research in Computer Security. pp. 166–185. Springer (2022). https://doi.org/10.1007/978-3-031-17143-7_9
54. Rodrigues, J., Barros, C.d., Dias, D., Guimarães, M.d.P., Tuler, E., Rocha, L.: Identification of malicious urls: a purely lexical approach. In: International Conference on Computational Science and Its Applications, pp. 397–407. Springer (2024). https://doi.org/10.1007/978-3-031-64608-9_26
55. da Silva, C.M.R., Feitosa, E.L., Garcia, V.C.: Heuristic-based strategy for phishing prediction: a survey of url-based approach. Comput. Sec. **88**, 101613 (2020)
56. Singh, N., Chaudhari, N.S.: N-gram approach for a url similarity measure. In: 2016 1st India International Conference on Information Processing (IICIP), pp. 1–6. IEEE (2016)
57. Sonowal, G.: What does a phishing url look like? Phishing and Communication Channels: A Guide to Identifying and Mitigating Phishing Attacks, pp. 77–96 (2022)
58. Spaulding, J., Nyang, D., Mohaisen, A.: Understanding the effectiveness of typosquatting techniques. In: Proceedings of the fifth ACM/IEEE Workshop on Hot Topics in Web Systems and Technologies, pp. 1–8 (2017)
59. Spaulding, J., Upadhyaya, S., Mohaisen, A.: The landscape of domain name typosquatting: techniques and countermeasures. In: 2016 11th International Conference on Availability, Reliability and Security (ARES), pp. 284–289. IEEE (2016)
60. Spaulding, J., Upadhyaya, S., Mohaisen, A.: You've been tricked! a user study of the effectiveness of typosquatting techniques. In: 2017 IEEE 37th International Conference on Distributed Computing Systems (ICDCS), pp. 2593–2596. IEEE (2017)
61. Szurdi, J.: Measuring and Analyzing Typosquatting Toward Fighting Abusive Domain Registrations. Carnegie Mellon University (2020)
62. Szurdi, J., Christin, N.: Email typosquatting. In: Proceedings of the 2017 Internet Measurement Conference, pp. 419–431 (2017)
63. Szurdi, J., Kocso, B., Cseh, G., Spring, J., Felegyhazi, M., Kanich, C.: The long "taile" of typosquatting domain names. In: 23rd USENIX Security Symposium (USENIX Security 2014), pp. 191–206 (2014)
64. Tahir, R., Raza, A., Ahmad, F., Kazi, J., Zaffar, F., Kanich, C., Caesar, M.: It's all in the name: why some urls are more vulnerable to typosquatting. In: IEEE INFOCOM 2018-IEEE Conference on Computer Communications, pp. 2618–2626. IEEE (2018)

65. Thomas, K., Grier, C., Ma, J., Paxson, V., Song, D.: Design and evaluation of a real-time url spam filtering service. In: 2011 IEEE Symposium on Security and Privacy, pp. 447–462. IEEE (2011)
66. Ulikowski, M.: dnstwist. https://github.com/elceef/dnstwist (2023), Accessed 15 May 2025
67. Zhang, K., Ji, W., Li, N., Wang, Y., Liao, S.: Detection of malicious domain name based on dns data analysis. J. Phys. Conf. Ser. **1544**, 012169 (2020)
68. Zhauniarovich, Y., Khalil, I., Yu, T., Dacier, M.: A survey on malicious domains detection through dns data analysis. ACM Comput. Surv. (CSUR) **51**(4), 1–36 (2018)

A Comparative Analysis of Taint Analysis Tools: Enhancing Security Through Combined Static Analysis Approaches

Young Lee(✉), Mohammed Tausif Ansari, and Jeong Yang

Department of Computational, Engineering, and Mathematical Sciences, Texas A&M University - San Antonio, One University Way, San Antonio 78224, TX, USA
{young.lee,Jeong.Yang}@tamusa.edu

Abstract. Taint analysis tools are widely used in the field of software security. However, there is a lack of effective and adaptable tools that can meet the evolving challenges of security in complex and diverse program features. In this paper, we present a comparative study of three prominent taint analyzers, Pysa, Pyt, and Joern, to assess their effectiveness in detecting data leaks or vulnerabilities in Python programs. We propose an approach that combines the capabilities of the taint analysis with the a code property graph-based code property analysis tool. Our findings reveal differences in Pysa and Pyt in different test cases, highlighting the varying degrees of accuracy and efficiency in tracking data flow paths. Our evaluation demonstrated that the three tools generally performed well, minimizing false positives and false negatives, and strengthening applications against security vulnerabilities. This research contributes to a better understanding of the strengths and limitations of these tools in real-world scenarios, providing invaluable guidance to security professionals and developers alike.

Keywords: Static Analysis · Taint Flow Diagram · Pysa · Pyt · Joern

1 Introduction

Software security is increasingly critical as applications become more complex. Taint analysis tools help identify vulnerabilities by tracking data flow within software systems [1,2], although they may face challenges with complex code [3].

This paper compares three taint analysis tools: Pysa, Pyt, and Joern. We evaluated their effectiveness in tracking data flow across diverse codebases to understand their strengths and limitations in real-world scenarios. Our research addresses the need for more effective and adaptable taint analysis tools in complex software environments. This is the first study to specifically compare these three tools, which could add value particularly for Python developers. This paper's target programming language is Python because of its popularity and

Y. Lee, M. T. Ansari, and J. Yang—Contributed equally to this work.

K. Daimi et al. (Eds.): CSCE 2025, CCIS 2937, pp. 315–330, 2026.
https://doi.org/10.1007/978-3-032-22208-4_21

the availability of static analysis tools, but the approach is generally applicable to other programming languages.

We evaluated these tools in six test cases featuring various programming paradigms, including collections, nested functions, and conditional statements. This assessment analyzes their performance variations and aims to provide practical recommendations for security professionals and developers in selecting appropriate tools for their applications.

2 Background and Related Work

We investigated three key concepts for software security and vulnerability detection: static analysis, dynamic analysis, and taint analysis.

Static analysis examines software without running it [4]. Using techniques such as data flow analysis and control flow analysis [3,5], it identifies potential issues early in development, including security vulnerabilities and code quality problems. Automated tools improve efficiency [6,7], with studies showing detection of 49 security defects per 100,000 lines of code [3]. However, limitations include false positives (up to 20% [4]) and inability to detect runtime issues. Static analysis works best when combined with other testing methods [3].

Dynamic analysis examines running programs [8], providing precise runtime information about memory usage and input handling [9]. It excels in malware detection and security threat analysis [10]. Key advantages include runtime precision and efficient debugging [8], though it may miss edge cases in complex programs. Challenges include test case selection [9], analysis platform risks, and resource constraints [10].

Taint analysis tracks sensitive data flows to detect vulnerabilities and privacy leaks [11,12]. It follows data from source APIs to potential leak points [13]. Static taint analysis examines code theoretically but struggles with dynamic features [11]. Dynamic taint analysis monitors runtime behavior [11,12] but faces coverage limitations. Both methods improve security, but have precision issues and resource constraints [11,13].

Joern is an open-source platform designed to analyze source code, byte code, and binary code [14]. Joern, developed as part of Yamaguchi et al.'s CPG-related research [15], serves as a versatile tool capable of analyzing multiple programming languages. It primarily focuses on generating Code Property Graphs (CPGs), which are graph representations of code that enable cross-language and cross-platform code analysis. It offers a specialized querying language, running on Scala, designed to query Code Property Graphs (CPGs) [16]. The key idea behind Joern is to capture code semantics, relationships between code elements, and other relevant information in a graph structure. This graph-based representation makes it easier to apply various graph analysis techniques and algorithms to gain insight into code behavior, potential vulnerabilities, and other code-related properties [14]. CPGs created by Joern offer a unified representation of code structure and semantics, facilitating efficient tracing of both data- and control-flow within an application. This comprehensive view helps identify semantic patterns that might be overlooked by more restricted representations. To trace data flow across functions, techniques like taint tracking are employed, modeling the influence of input parameters on function return values. Effective dataflow tracing across functions necessitates knowledge of at least a partially-qualified method name, crucial for tagging functions accurately as sensitive sources or sinks during taint analysis. Additionally, understanding an object's runtime type can streamline the analysis by reducing the number of procedures to consider and enhancing the precision of subsequent analyses [17].

3 Motivating Example

Taint analysis proves especially beneficial in scenarios where the priority lies in comprehensively understanding how sensitive data, such as the Social Security Number in the provided example, move through the application. Static analysis, while useful for identifying syntactical issues and common programming mistakes, often lacks the depth required to trace the intricate paths of data flow within the source codes. These tools may overlook the details of how user-provided data propagates through different functions, methods, or modules, missing potential security vulnerabilities arising from data mishandling. Dynamic analysis tools, on the other hand, can track data flow during runtime but may present challenges in scaling across large or complex codebases. Their reliance on setting breakpoints and stepping through code could become laborious and time-consuming, especially when dealing with extensive systems or multiple interconnected components. In contrast, taint analysis provides a focused lens to precisely monitor the journey of tainted data from its origin to various processing points, effectively highlighting potential security gaps or opportunities for unauthorized access to sensitive information. Its ability to map the specific paths through which tainted data travels enables developers and security analysts to proactively identify and mitigate potential vulnerabilities, making it an indispensable tool for ensuring robust data security and integrity within software applications.

Listing 1 serves as a motivating example to demonstrate the flow of tainted data from its source through various processing points and potential unauthorized access points. Here input() method is defined as a **Source** and print() method is defined as a **Sink** It captures a 9-digit Social Security Number (SSN) as input, stores it in two lists, and then prints out the SSN from the second list. The user is prompted to enter a 9-digit Social Security Number (SSN) using the input() function. This makes the SSN variable a taint source since user input can potentially be malicious or tainted. Two empty lists, list1 and list2, are defined. The entered SSN is appended to list1. The value of the first element in list1 (which is the entered SSN) is then appended to list2. Finally, the SSN value in list2 is printed using the print() function, which acts as a taint sink by potentially exposing sensitive information to an attacker.

The Taint Flow Diagram in Fig. 1 illustrates how information flows from its starting point (the source) to its endpoint (the sink). At the beginning, the input() method collects data, acting as the source where information originates. This data then undergoes a series of steps, represented by different shapes in the diagram. Once processed, the data is eventually displayed or used through the print() method, serving as the sink where the information ends up.

Within this diagram, tainted data identified as **underline**, providing a clear and intuitive visualization of how potential vulnerabilities or malicious inputs can traverse through a system. This diagram serves as a valuable tool for understanding the pathways and interactions that can lead to security risks, aiding in the identification and mitigation of potential threats within the analyzed software or system. The Taint Flow Diagram helps visualize the journey of data as it moves through the system, starting from its Source and ending with its Sink. Unlike general data flow diagrams that model all data movement, taint flow diagrams focus specifically on potential security risks related to data validation and injection.

Listing 1. Motivating Example

```
def main():
    ssn = input("Enter a 9 digit Social Security Number")
    list1 = []
    list2 = []
    list1.append(ssn)
    list2.append(list1[0])
    print(list2[0])
```

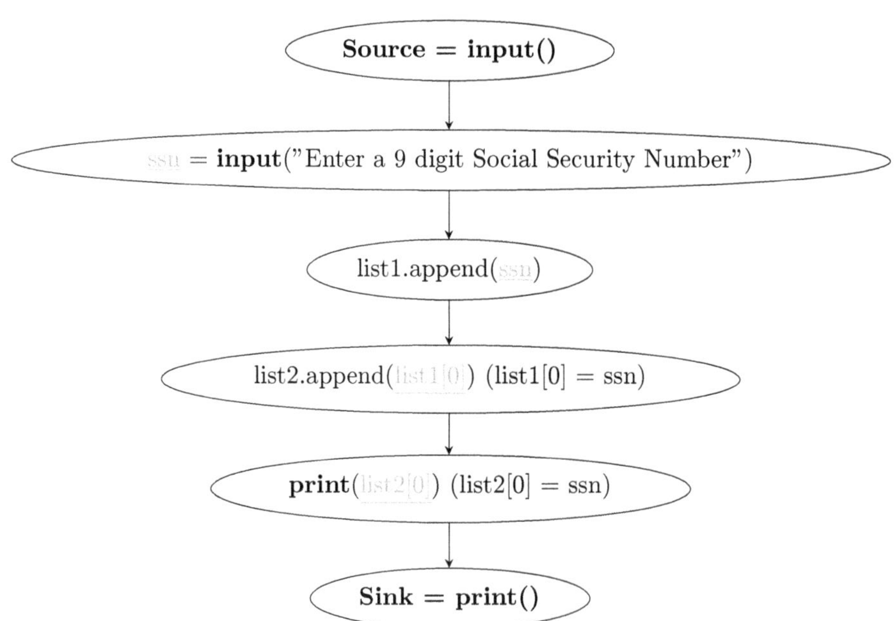

Fig. 1. Taint Flow Diagram for Motivating Example

4 Experimental Evaluation

We evaluated three taint analysis tools (Pysa, Pyt, and Joern) using six test cases to assess their effectiveness in tracking data flow and identifying security vulnerabilities.

4.1 Test Case 1: A Simple Program

Test Case 1 (Listing 2) evaluates a basic program where user input flows to a print statement. The program gets a name via input() (source) and displays it in a greeting message (sink). This tests each tool's ability to track straightforward data flow from input to output. The Taint Flow Diagram in Fig. 2 at Appendix A illustrates how information flows from source to sink.

Listing 2. A simple program

```
def main()
    user_name = input("Enter your name: ")
    greeting = "Hello, " + user_name + "! Welcome to my program."
    print(greeting)
main()
```

4.2 Test Case 2: Conditional Statements

Test Case 2 (Listing 3) examines how the tools handle conditional logic without direct data flow. The program takes input but uses it only for control flow, not data transmission. The Taint Flow Diagram in Fig. 3 at Appendix A illustrates how information flows from source to sink.

Listing 3. Conditional Statements

```
def main():
    user_input = input("Enter 'A' or 'B': ")
    if user_input == 'A':
        print("You selected option A.")
    elif user_input == 'B':
        print("You selected option B.")
    else:
        print("Invalid selection.")
main()
```

4.3 Test Case 3: Python's Lists

Test Case 3 (Listing 4) tests data flow tracking through list operations. User input moves through two lists before reaching a print statement. The Taint Flow Diagram in Fig. 4 at Appendix A illustrates how information flows from source to sink.

Listing 4. Python's Lists

```
def main():
    name = input("Enter your name")
    list1 = []
    list2 = []
    list1.append(name)
    list2.append(list1[0])
    print(list2[0])

main()
```

4.4 Test Case 4: Nested Functions

Test Case 4 (Listing 5) evaluates data flow through nested functions, from input through processing to output. The Taint Flow Diagram in Fig. 5 at Appendix A illustrates how information flows from source to sink.

Listing 5. Nested Functions

```
def process_data(data):
    def format_output(text):
        return "Processed: " + text

    result = format_output(data)
    return result

user_input = input("Enter text: ")
formatted_result = process_data(user_input)
print(formatted_result)
```

4.5 Test Case 5: Multiple Function Calls

Test Case 5 (Listing 6) examines detection of data flow absence across multiple function calls. The Taint Flow Diagram in Fig. 6 at Appendix A illustrates how information flows from source to sink.

Listing 6. Multiple Function calls

```
def manipulate_data(data):
    # This function does not return any data
    return

def print_result(data):
    print("This program does not have data flow between input and print.")

user_input = input("Enter some text: ")
manipulate_data(user_input)
print_result(user_input)
```

4.6 Test Case 6: Class and Objects

Test Case 6 (Listing 7) tests tracking data flow through object-oriented programming patterns. The Taint Flow Diagram in Fig. 7 at Appendix A illustrates how information flows from source to sink.

Listing 7. Class and Objects

```
class StringManipulator:
    def __init__(self, data=""):
        self.data = data

    def set_data(self, data):
        self.data = data

    def append_data(self, text_to_append):
        self.data += text_to_append

    def reverse_data(self):
        self.data = self.data[::-1]

    def uppercase_data(self):
        self.data = self.data.upper()

    def lowercase_data(self):
        self.data = self.data.lower()

    def get_data(self):
        return self.data

def main():
    user_input = input("Enter a string: ")

    # Create three StringManipulator objects
    obj1 = StringManipulator()
    obj2 = StringManipulator()
    obj3 = StringManipulator()

    # Set data in the first object
    obj1.set_data(user_input)

    # Perform operations on the objects
    obj2.set_data(obj1.get_data())
# Pass data from obj1 to obj2
    obj2.reverse_data()  # Reverse the string in obj2
    obj3.set_data(obj2.get_data())
# Pass data from obj2 to obj3
```

```
    obj3.uppercase_data()  # Uppercase the string in obj3

    final_result = obj3.get_data()

    # Print the final result
    print(final_result)

main()
```

5 Result and Summary

In this study, we evaluated the effectiveness of three static code analysis tools, Pysa, Pyt, and Joern, in detecting data leaks or vulnerabilities in Python programs. We conducted experiments using six different test cases, each designed to assess the tools' abilities to identify potential security risks. The six test cases covered a range of scenarios, from simple programs to more complex ones with usage of collections, nested functions, multiple function calls and classes. Table 1 summarizes the results of the evaluation with the test cases over the three Taint Analysis Tools.

Explanation:

- Yes- In the table "Yes" means that the static analysis tool is able to correctly detect if the data flow exists or not in the test case program.
- No- In the table "No" means that the static analysis tool is unable to identify if the data flow exists or not in the test case program.

Table 1. Results of Comparison on Taint Analysis Tools.

Test Case	Objective	Expected Outcomes	Pysa	Pyt	Joern
1. A Simple Program	Detect Data-flow vulnerability in a simple program with variables	Data-flow vulnerability is Present	Yes	Yes	Yes
2. Conditional Statements	Detect Data-flow vulnerability in a program consist of conditional statements (if-else)	Data-flow vulnerability is Not Present	Yes	Yes	Yes
3. Python's Lists	Detect Data-flow vulnerability in a program with List(Array) Data Structure	Data-flow vulnerability is Present	No	No	Yes
4. Nested Functions	Detect Data-flow vulnerability in a program with nested functions	Data-flow vulnerability is Present	Yes	Yes	Yes
5. Multiple Function calls	Detect Data-flow vulnerability in a program multiple function calls	Data-flow vulnerability is Not Present	Yes	Yes	Yes
6. Class and Objects	Detect Data-flow vulnerability in a program consisting a class and its multiple objects	Data-flow vulnerability is Present	No	No	Yes

5.1 Test Case 1: A Simple Program

In the first test case, which represented a straightforward Python program with user input and a print statement, all three tools, Pysa, Pyt, and Joern, successfully detected the absence of data leaks. Therefore, this test case passed with all tools providing accurate results.

5.2 Test Case 2: Conditional Statements

Test case 2 involved a Python program containing conditional statements, which could potentially introduce data leaks if not handled properly. However, all three tools, Pysa, Pyt, and Joern, once again, correctly identified that there were no data leaks in the code. This test case also passed with all tools providing accurate results.

5.3 Test Case 3: Python's Lists

Test case 3 introduced the use of Python lists, which can be a source of data leaks if not managed appropriately. While Pysa and Pyt failed to detect the data leak in this scenario, Joern successfully identified the vulnerability. Therefore, in this case, Joern was the only tool that provided accurate results.

5.4 Test Case 4: Nested Functions

Test case 4 delved into nested functions, which can complicate data flow analysis. However, all three tools, Pysa, Pyt, and Joern, were successful in identifying the data leak in this complex scenario. Consequently, this test case passed with all tools providing accurate results.

5.5 Test Case 5: Multiple Function Calls

Test case 6 involved multiple function calls, which can increase the complexity of data flow analysis. Despite the added complexity, all three tools, Pysa, Pyt, and Joern, correctly detected the absence of data leaks in the code. Therefore, this test case also passed with all tools providing accurate results.

5.6 Test Case 6: Class and Objects

The final test case introduced the use of Python Classes and Objects, which can be a source of data leaks if not managed appropriately. While Pysa and Pyt failed to detect the data leak in this scenario, Joern successfully identified the vulnerability. Therefore, in this case, Joern was the only tool that provided accurate results.

In summary, our evaluation demonstrated that all three tools, Pysa, Pyt, and Joern, generally performed well in detecting data leaks or vulnerabilities in Python code. However, there were instances, such as in test case 3 and test case

6, where Joern outperformed Pysa and Pyt. All tools proved reliable in confirming the absence of data flow when no vulnerabilities were present. These results underscore the value of taint analysis tools in enhancing software security by providing insights into data flow and potential risks. Table 1 shows the comparative analysis results of the test cases defined on the taint analysis tools. In this Table "YES" means that the static analysis tool was able to correctly detect if the data flow exists or not. And "NO" means that the tool was not able to detect flow of data. These findings contribute to a deeper understanding of the strengths and limitations of Pysa, Pyt, and Joern in real-world scenarios, empowering security professionals and developers to make informed decisions when selecting the right tool for tracking data flow in their software applications.

6 Conclusion

In this study, we conducted an evaluation of three prominent taint analysis tools, Pysa, Pyt, and Joern, to assess their effectiveness in detecting data leaks and vulnerabilities in Python programs. Our experiment involved executing six test cases, ranging from simple programs to complex ones with nested functions, multiple function calls, and data structures like lists and objects.

The results of our evaluation revealed both strengths and limitations of these taint analysis tools. Pysa and Pyt, being popular tools developed for data flow tracking, generally performed well in identifying potential security risks in Python code. However, they exhibited discrepancies in their ability to detect data leaks when dealing with specific data structures like lists (test case 3) and objects (test case 6). In these instances, Pysa and Pyt failed to accurately identify the vulnerabilities, while Joern, a powerful code property graph-based taint analysis tool, successfully detected the data leaks.

These findings highlight the importance of carefully selecting the appropriate taint analysis tool for specific code scenarios, as different tools may excel in different areas of code analysis. While Pysa and Pyt are valuable for general data flow tracking, Joern's code property graph approach demonstrated superior accuracy in detecting data leaks involving complex data structures.

Our study underscores the value of taint analysis tools in identifying and mitigating potential security risks in Python programs. However, it also emphasizes the need for a more comprehensive approach that leverages the strengths of multiple tools.

We propose integrating the usage of Pysa or Pyt with Joern, where the former tools are used for initial data flow analysis, and any warnings generated can be further verified and validated using Joern's code property graph approach.

The evaluation of the three prominent taint analysis tools–Pysa, Pyt, and Joern–in this study revealed significant insights into their effectiveness in detecting data leaks and vulnerabilities in Python programs. The evaluation covered six diverse test cases, ranging from simple programs to those incorporating complex features like nested functions, multiple function calls, and data structures such as lists and objects.

A Taint Flow Diagrams for Test Cases

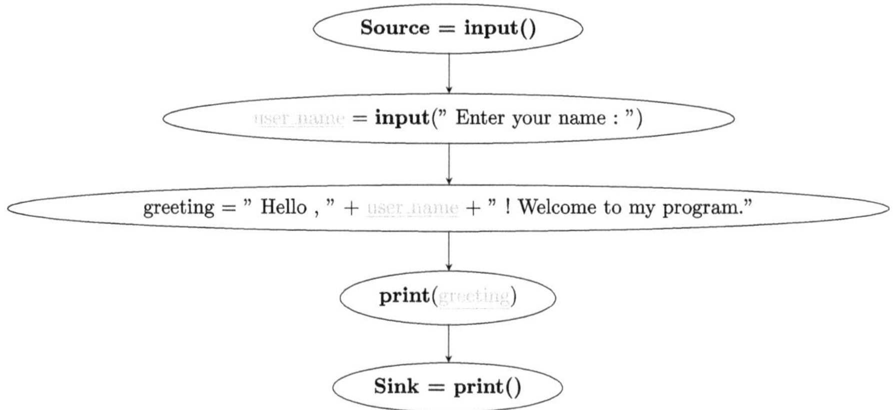

Fig. 2. Taint Flow Diagram for Test Case 1

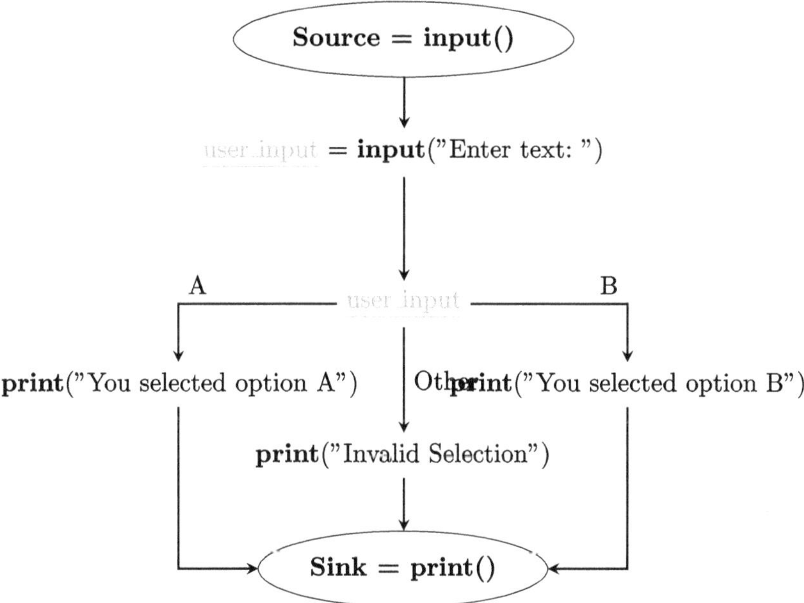

Fig. 3. Taint Flow Diagram for Test Case 2

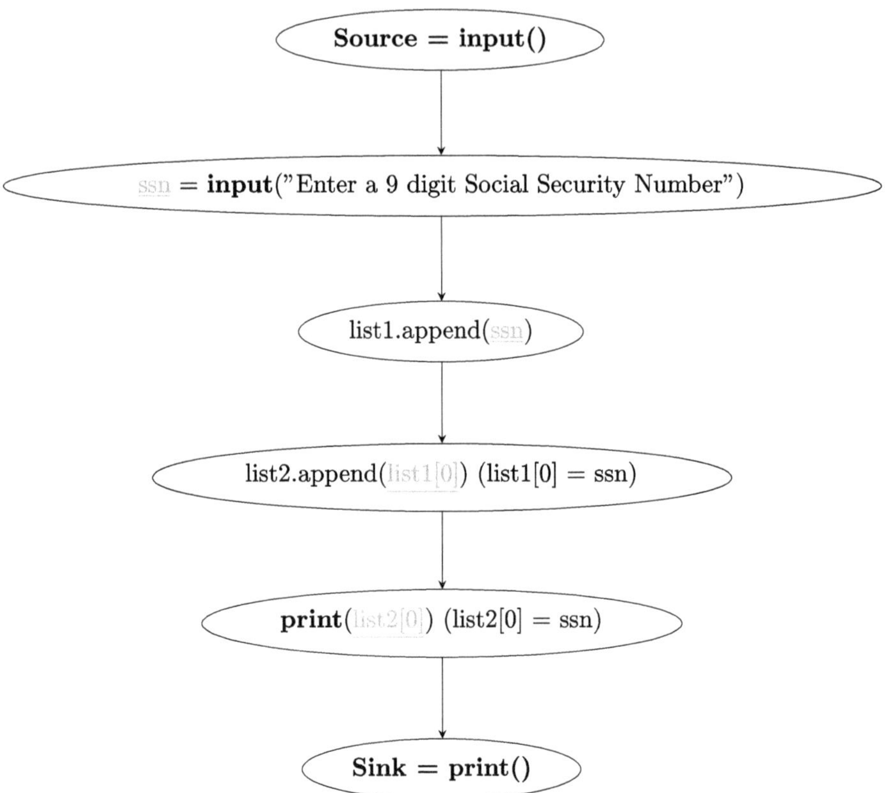

Fig. 4. Taint Flow Diagram for Test Case 3

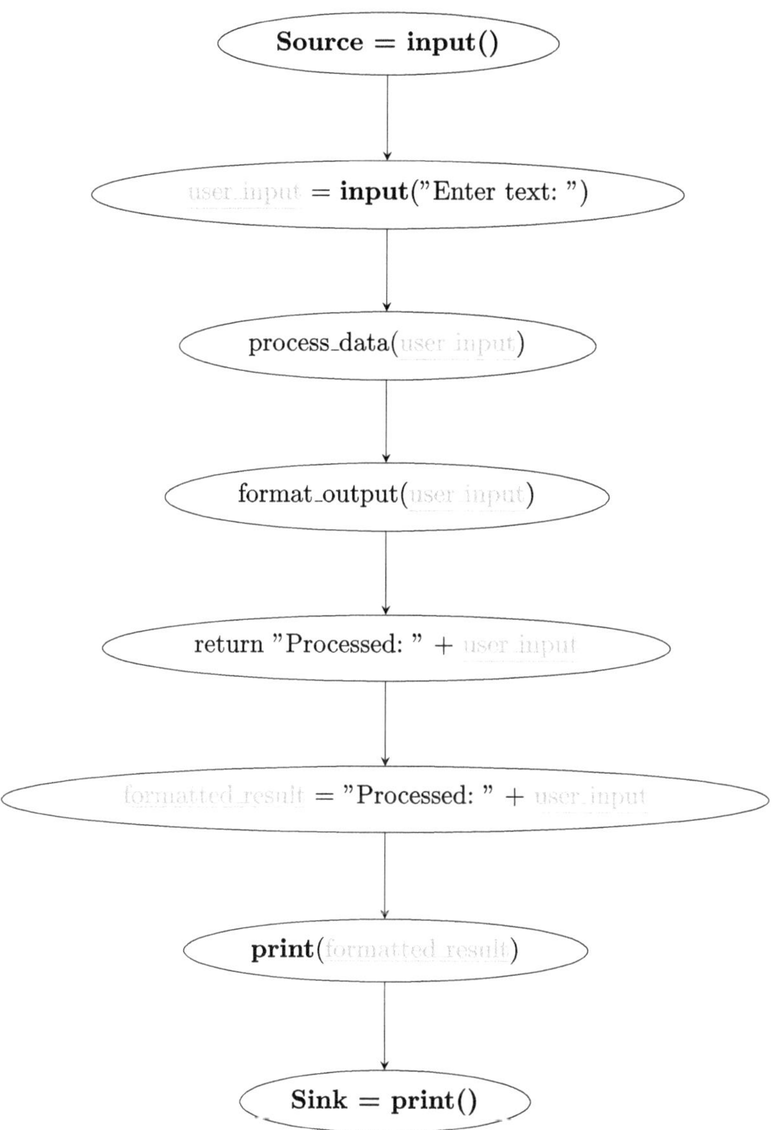

Fig. 5. Taint Flow Diagram for Test Case 4

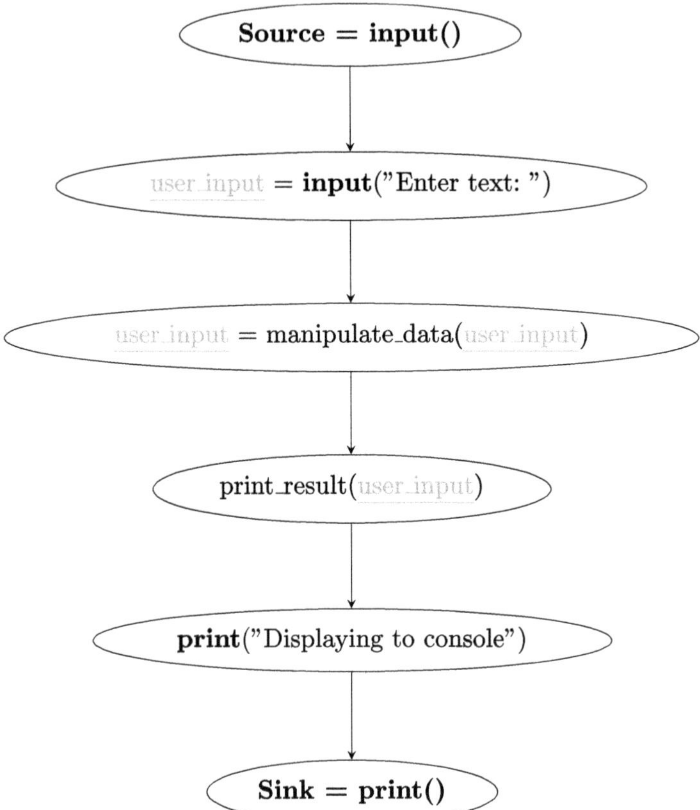

Fig. 6. Taint Flow Diagram for Test Case 5

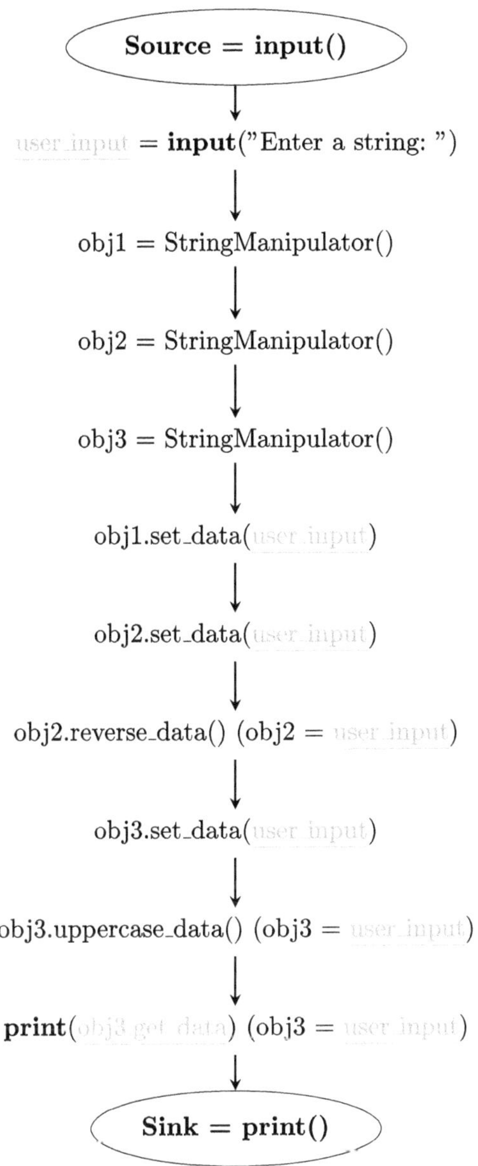

Fig. 7. Taint Flow Diagram for Test Case 6

References

1. Alashjee, A.M., Duraibi, S., Song, J.: Dynamic taint analysis tools: a review. Inter. J. Comput. Sci. Sec. (IJCSS) **13**(6), 231–244 (2019)
2. Boxler, D., Walcott, K.R.: Static taint analysis tools to detect information flows. In: International Conference on Software Engineering Research and Practice, SERP 2018
3. Chess, B., West, J.: Secure Programming with Static Analysis, 3. printing edn. Addison-Wesley software security series. Addison-Wesley, Upper Saddle River, NJ [u.a] (2010)
4. Emanuelsson, P., Nilsson, U.: A comparative study of industrial static analysis tools. Electr. Notes Theoret. Comput. Sci. **217**, 5–21 (2008)
5. Ayewah, N., Pugh, W.: The google findbugs fixit. In: Proceedings of the 19th International Symposium on Software Testing and Analysis, pp. 241–252 (2010)
6. Johnson, B., Song, Y., Murphy-Hill, E., Bowdidge, R.: Why don't software developers use static analysis tools to find bugs? In: 2013 35th International Conference on Software Engineering (ICSE), pp. 672–681. IEEE (2013)
7. Zitser, M., Lippmann, R., Leek, T.: Testing static analysis tools using exploitable buffer overflows from open source code. In: Proceedings of the 12th ACM SIGSOFT Twelfth International Symposium on Foundations of Software Engineering, pp. 97–106 (2004)
8. Ball, T.: The concept of dynamic analysis. ACM SIGSOFT Softw. Eng. Notes **24**(6), 216–234 (1999)
9. Ernst, M.D.: Static and dynamic analysis: Synergy and duality. In: WODA 2003: ICSE Workshop on Dynamic Analysis, pp. 24–27 (2003)
10. Or-Meir, O., Nissim, N., Elovici, Y., Rokach, L.: Dynamic malware analysis in the modern era-a state of the art survey. ACM Comput. Surv. (CSUR) **52**(5), 1–48 (2019)
11. Zhang, X., Wang, X., Slavin, R., Niu, J.: Condysta: context-aware dynamic supplement to static taint analysis. in: 2021 IEEE Symposium on Security and Privacy (SP), pp. 796–812. IEEE (2021)
12. Arzt, S., et al.: Flowdroid: precise context, flow, field, object-sensitive and lifecycle-aware taint analysis for android apps. Acm Sigplan Not. **49**(6), 259–269 (2014)
13. Zhang, J., Tian, C., Duan, Z.: An efficient approach for taint analysis of android applications. Comput. Sec. **104**, 102161 (2021)
14. Fabian, Niko, David (2021). https://docs.joern.io/
15. Yamaguchi, F., Golde, N., Arp, D., Rieck, K.: Modeling and discovering vulnerabilities with code property graphs. In: 2014 IEEE Symposium on Security and Privacy, pp. 590–604. IEEE(2014)
16. Guan, Z., Wang, X., Xin, W., Wang, J.: Code property graph-based vulnerability dataset generation for source code detection. In: Xu, G., Liang, K., Su, C. (eds.) FCS 2020. CCIS, vol. 1286, pp. 584–591. Springer, Singapore (2020). https://doi.org/10.1007/978-981-15-9739-8_43
17. Seidel, L., Effendi, S.D.B., Pinho, X., Rieck, K., Merwe, B., Yamaguchi, F.: Learning type inference for enhanced dataflow analysis. arXiv preprint arXiv:2310.00673 (2023)

Experimental Evaluation of Security Attacks on Self-driving Car Platforms

Abhishek Vishwakarma, Purva Vijayvargiya, Nathan Lee, and Mohammad Husain(✉)

Cal Poly Pomona, Pomona, CA 91768, USA
{avishwakarma,purvav,nathanlee,mihusain}@cpp.edu

Abstract. Autonomous vehicles depend on deep learning models for perception and wireless communication protocols for control and sensor data exchange, both of which present critical attack surfaces. This study investigates the security vulnerabilities of self-driving systems by evaluating adversarial attacks on perception models and network-based attacks on communication protocols. For perception, we assess the effectiveness of Fast Gradient Sign Method (FGSM) and Projected Gradient Descent (PGD) attacks on a Convolutional Neural Network (CNN) trained for the JetRacer platform. Using the CIFAR-10 and KITTI datasets, our findings show that PGD reduces the accuracy of the model by 9 to 13%, while targeted attacks on KITTI yield a 47.16% misclassification success rate. In parallel, we analyze the impact of man-in-the-middle (MitM), packet injection, and denial-of-service (DoS) attacks on autonomous vehicle control using JetRacer and Yahboom platforms. Using tools such as Bettercap and Wireshark, we demonstrate that network packet manipulation leads to lane deviation, control instability, and potential collisions. Together, these results highlight the multifaceted security risks in autonomous driving systems and emphasize the urgent need for robust defense mechanisms across both perception and communication layers.

Keywords: adversarial attacks · network attacks · denial-of-service · man-in-the-middle · image scaling · computer vision security

1 Introduction

Autonomous vehicles are highly dependent on network-based communication protocols for remote operations and sensor data transfer. These communication channels are vulnerable to cyberattacks that can pose severe safety threats. On the other hand, deep learning models are widely used in self-driving cars for critical visual perception tasks such as object detection and lane following. These capabilities are essential to ensure safe autonomous navigation. However, such models remain vulnerable to adversarial attacks: subtle perturbations in input data that can lead to incorrect predictions. This vulnerability presents a significant safety concern, particularly when deploying models on research platforms such as JetRacer and Yahboom.

K. Daimi et al. (Eds.): CSCE 2025, CCIS 2937, pp. 331–345, 2026.
https://doi.org/10.1007/978-3-032-22208-4_22

This research aims to examine the influence of both image scaling attacks and network-based cyberattacks on the performance of deep learning models in autonomous driving systems. These attacks pose serious risks to the accuracy and reliability of perception tasks that are critical to safe navigation. By evaluating how these threats impact model behavior, we seek to deepen our understanding of the security vulnerabilities present in autonomous vehicle pipelines.

A key focus of this study is to identify and compare the specific vulnerabilities of the JetRacer and Yahboom platforms, which are widely used in autonomous driving research. Through controlled experimentation, we analyze the susceptibility of these systems to various adversarial techniques, including image preprocessing attacks and network disruptions. These comparisons help uncover platform-specific weaknesses and guide the development of targeted defense mechanisms.

To address these challenges, we propose and evaluate potential countermeasures aimed at mitigating the effects of such attacks. The study includes a software-based evaluation of image scaling attacks on convolutional neural networks (CNNs) intended for deployment on JetRacer and Yahboom. A CNN is used here due to its effectiveness in visual perception tasks. Both the JetRacer and Yahboom cars use depth cameras in order to collect the images used for training. We demonstrate the feasibility of network-level attacks, such as UDP flooding and ARP spoofing, against these platforms. In addition, we implement adversarial rescaling techniques using benchmark datasets to emulate real-world driving conditions and perform a comparative analysis of the resulting model degradation. This work establishes a foundation for future physical testing of adversarial defenses on actual autonomous vehicles.

2 Background and Literature Review

2.1 Image Scaling Attacks: Fundamentals and Techniques

Image-scaling attacks manipulate input images at high resolutions before resizing, embedding adversarial perturbations that are revealed during preprocessing. These attacks exploit how input images are down-sampled before being fed into deep-learning models. Common attack techniques include:

- **Adversarial Rescaling Attack (AdvResize)**—a technique where carefully crafted high-resolution perturbations survive image resizing to deceive models [6].
- **Interpolation-based Scaling Attack**—adversaries exploit interpolation artifacts introduced during image resizing [6].

Recent work has also explored how adversarial scaling attacks can remain stealthy while maintaining transferability across models [14,15].

2.2 Prior Work on Image Scaling Attacks in Self-driving Cars

Studies have shown that deep learning-based perception systems in autonomous vehicles are highly susceptible to adversarial attacks. Goodfellow et al. [5] introduced the Fast Gradient Sign Method (FGSM), demonstrating how imperceptible perturbations can mislead neural networks. Based on this, Madry et al. [9] proposed the projected gradient descent (PGD), which remains one of the most effective iterative attacks.

A systematic review by Badjie et al. [1] discussed various adversarial scenarios in the physical world, such as the misclassification of traffic signs and sensor vulnerabilities in autonomous systems. DARTS [11] explored physical stop-sign attacks using printed perturbations, highlighting the real-world feasibility of such threats.

Recent literature has begun to explore the intersection of scaling-based attacks and driving models. Wu et al. [13] and Zhang et al. [14] propose techniques that enhance the stealth and cross-model success of attacks, which has significant implications for black-box self-driving systems. Zhu et al. [15] introduced adaptive transformation methods that dynamically adjust adversarial patterns to improve robustness in scaling scenarios.

The KITTI dataset, a widely recognized benchmark for real-world autonomous driving tasks, was used in this study to assess the effectiveness of the attack under realistic conditions [1].

2.3 Prior Work on Network Attacks in Self-driving Cars

The increasing connectivity in autonomous vehicles (AV) introduces critical cybersecurity vulnerabilities, particularly in wireless communication protocols. Previous work by Kim et al. [7] categorized AV cyberattacks into three domains: control systems (e.g., ECU, CAN), autonomous driving components (e.g., sensors, LiDAR), and vehicle-to-everything (V2X) communication. Their study highlighted that V2X attacks are likely to become dominant threats in future AV systems due to their dependence on external communication.

Sun et al. [12] provided a comprehensive classification of cyber risks into in-vehicle network attacks, V2X-based threats, and other external attacks such as GPS spoofing, location tracking, and Bluetooth exploits. Their work emphasized cyber-risk assessment as a crucial area for ranking and prioritizing emerging threats in AV systems. They also reviewed relevant safety and cybersecurity standards such as IEEE 1609.2 and DSRC protocol stacks for secure vehicular communication.

Tanaji et al. [10] further analyzed V2X-specific vulnerabilities and proposed cryptographic mitigation strategies and anomaly detection algorithms to secure control systems from injection and spoofing attacks.

Although these surveys offer valuable theoretical classifications and defense frameworks, few have explored practical, real-world experimentation. Our work bridges this gap by simulating network-based attacks, such as MitM, packet injection, and DoS, on two AV platforms (JetRacer and Yahboom), validated experimentally. Using tools such as Wireshark, Scapy, and Netwox, we demonstrate the feasibility and impact of these attacks on the accuracy and stability of vehicular control.

3 Experimental Methodology

This section outlines the general methodology used to evaluate the vulnerability of a Convolutional Neural Network (CNN) to image scaling attacks within autonomous driving systems, as well as the methodology for evaluating two network attack types: Denial of service and Man-in-the-Middle. The approach is designed to be platform-agnostic and can be applied to both JetRacer and Yahboom autonomous vehicle platforms.

3.1 CIFAR-10 and KITTI Datasets

CIFAR-10: The CIFAR-10 dataset has 60,000 color images (32×32) across 10 classes, with 6,000 images per class. It includes 50,000 training images and 10,000 test images. The data is split into five training batches and one test batch, each containing 10,000 images. The test batch has 1,000 randomly selected images per class, while the training batches together have 5,000 images per class, though individual batches may have uneven class distributions [8].

KITTI: The KITTI dataset is a widely used benchmark suite for computer vision in autonomous driving. It contains a variety of data types such as high-resolution RGB images, 3D point clouds from LiDAR, GPS/IMU data, and stereo camera images. The dataset supports tasks like object detection, tracking, 3D reconstruction, and visual odometry. It includes real-world driving scenarios captured in urban, rural, and highway environments, making it valuable for developing and evaluating algorithms for autonomous vehicles [4].

3.2 Model Architecture for Image Scaling Attack

A lightweight Convolutional Neural Network (CNN) was developed and trained for visual classification tasks relevant to autonomous navigation. The model includes convolutional layers with ReLU activations, max-pooling layers for spatial downsampling, and fully connected layers for final classification, as shown in Fig. 1. It was first trained on the CIFAR-10 dataset to establish a controlled baseline, and later tested on the KITTI dataset to simulate more realistic driving scenarios.

3.3 Adversarial Attack Implementation

To assess the vulnerability of the model, adversarial examples were generated using gradient-based attack methods:

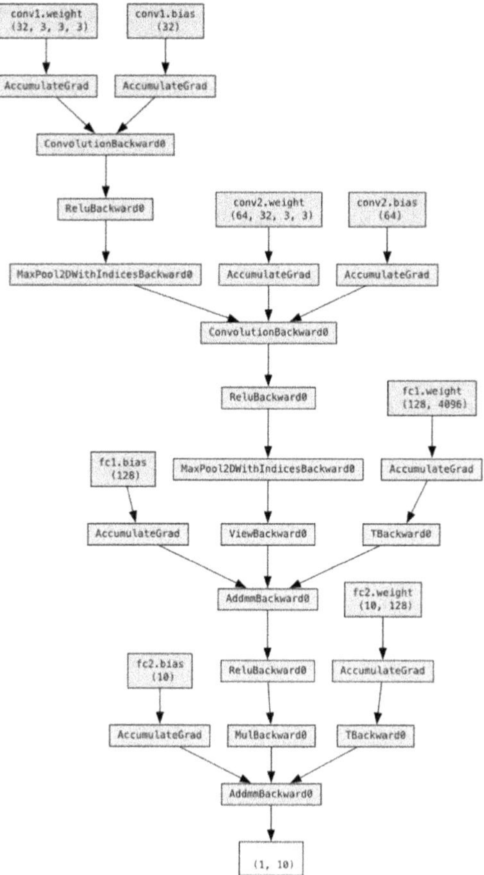

Fig. 1. Graphical representation of the CNN model architecture generated using TorchViz.

- **Fast Gradient Sign Method (FGSM):** A single-step attack that perturbs the input image in the direction of the loss gradient, constrained by a fixed epsilon value.
- **Projected Gradient Descent (PGD):** A stronger iterative attack that applies small perturbations over multiple steps while projecting the result back into a valid perturbation space.

FGSM and PGD were applied to CIFAR-10 to observe baseline adversarial behavior. For the KITTI dataset, PGD was used to implement both **targeted** and **untargeted** attacks. These perturbations were introduced at the image input stage, exploiting the resizing step in the model preprocessing to activate adversarial behavior post-scaling.

3.4 Attack Types and Rationale for Network Attacks

Given the lack of strong encryption (e.g., weak password) and the reliance on an open HTTP interface, the systems were ideal candidates for evaluating two practical and impactful attack types:

- **Denial-of-Service (DoS)**: The purpose was to overwhelm the telemetry channel by flooding the JupyterLab server's HTTP port (8080) with high-rate UDP packets, causing packet drops or delays that disrupt perception feedback and control execution.
- **Man-in-the-Middle (MitM)**: Executed using ARP spoofing to intercept and modify HTTP POST requests in transit. A custom script modified the `speed` and `steering_angle` fields in the telemetry JSON payload before forwarding it to the server.

These attacks were chosen based on their simplicity, real-world applicability, and measurable effects on system performance. The use of common ports, unencrypted protocols, and minimal authentication made these communication pathways ideal targets for simulation and analysis.

4 Implementations of Attacks

4.1 Simulation-Based Evaluation for Image Scaling Attacks

To assess the vulnerability of the trained CNN model, adversarial attacks were performed in a controlled software simulation environment. This approach allowed for testing model behavior without real-world deployment, providing reproducible insights into attack effectiveness across two datasets: CIFAR-10 and KITTI.

CIFAR-10: Baseline Evaluation. The CNN model was first trained and evaluated on the CIFAR-10 dataset. FGSM and PGD attacks were applied to assess how well the model withstands basic adversarial perturbations.

The training loss trends in FGSM and PGD are shown in Fig. 2. FGSM training loss consistently decreases and ends below 1.1, while PGD training loss decreases more slowly and plateaus around 1.7. This shows that the FGSM model performed better than the PGD model since the PGD model has an iterative nature and higher perturbation strength.

KITTI: Realistic Scenario Testing. To simulate autonomous driving perception, targeted and untargeted PGD attacks were applied to images from the KITTI dataset. These attacks exploited image preprocessing, particularly resizing, to embed perturbations that mislead the CNN after downsampling.

Figures 3 and 4 show the visual impact of these attacks. Although the perturbations are still subtle to the human eye, they caused significant prediction shifts.

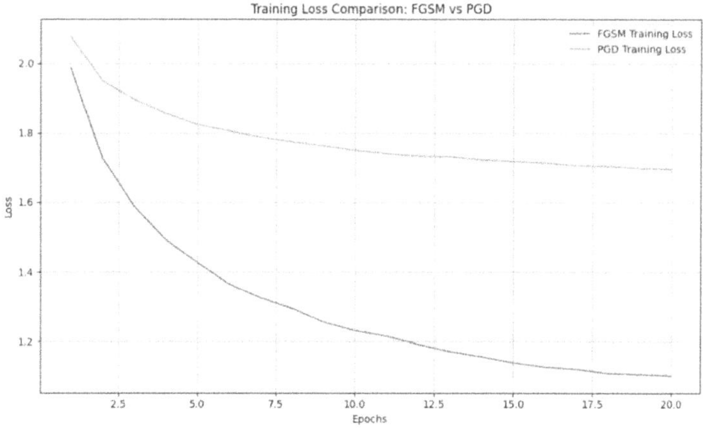

Fig. 2. Training loss comparison between FGSM and PGD adversarial training on CIFAR-10 dataset.

Fig. 3. Targeted adversarial attack on KITTI dataset. Top: clean images. Bottom: perturbed images causing misclassification into a specific class.

4.2 JetRacer and Yahboom-Based Implementations for Network Attacks

Experiments were conducted on two autonomous vehicle platforms: the NVIDIA JetRacer and the Yahboom robotic car. Both platforms were equipped with onboard computation units (Jetson Nano and Raspberry Pi, respectively) and configured for autonomous navigation tasks such as following the lane and avoidance of obstacles.

Each vehicle was connected via Wi-Fi to a local network (192.168.0.0/24) shared with a control laptop (MacBook Air). An SSH tunnel was established to forward the JupyterLab interface (port 8888) running on the vehicles to the laptop for monitoring purposes. Additionally, a client-server architecture was used to simulate control telemetry data transmission, where the client device sent periodic HTTP POST requests containing speed, steering angle, and battery level information to a remote server.

The general network architecture is illustrated in Fig. 5, which shows the data flow between compute modules, sensors, and remote control systems.

Two primary types of network attacks were designed:

Fig. 4. Untargeted adversarial attack on KITTI dataset. Perturbations cause random misclassifications.

- **Denial-of-Service (DoS) Attack**: A high-rate UDP flood was launched from the MacBook using `nping` [3], targeting the JupyterLab server port (8888) of the vehicle. The objective was to saturate the Wi-Fi communication channel and disrupt the perception and control data flow.
- **Man-in-the-Middle (MitM) Attack**: For the MitM experiment, the attacker (MacBook) used Bettercap to perform ARP spoofing between the client (JetRacer at 192.168.0.102) and the server (192.168.0.101). HTTP POST requests containing telemetry data were intercepted and modified in transit by injecting a custom JavaScript script (`modify_packets.js`) within Bettercap's HTTP proxy module. Specifically, the `speed` and `steering_angle` fields in the JSON payload were forcibly altered before forwarding the packets to the server.

Traffic was monitored using Wireshark [2] and tcpdump to verify the success of ARP spoofing and packet modification. ICMP pings were used to monitor network latency and potential disconnections during attacks. Screen recordings and packet captures were collected to document the attack execution and effects.

4.3 Evaluation Metrics

The effectiveness of adversarial (A) and network (N) attacks was measured using the following metrics.

- **Misclassification Rate (A):** The proportion of adversarial inputs that resulted in incorrect predictions.
- **Lane Deviation (A):** For KITTI-based analysis, the lateral offset from the intended driving path caused by adversarial inputs.
- **Failure Rate (A):** The percentage of cases where the model exhibited critical failures, such as making completely irrelevant or unsafe decisions.
- Vehicle stability and control accuracy (N)
- Network latency and packet loss (N)

These metrics allow for both accuracy-based and behavior-based evaluation, supporting future real-world deployment on hardware platforms.

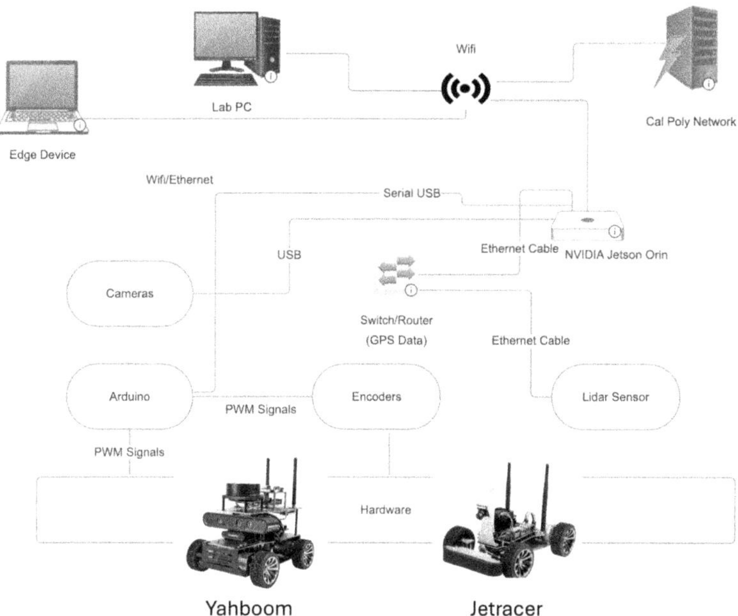

Fig. 5. Network architecture of the autonomous vehicle system, showing communication flow between the Jetson module, sensors, Arduino microcontroller, and remote devices over Wi-Fi and Ethernet.

5 Experimental Results and Observations

We conducted a simulation-based attack on two simulated datasets as well as two types of network-based attack experiments against the JetRacer and Yahboom platforms: (1) Denial-of-Service (DoS) attacks and (2) Man-in-the-Middle (MitM) attacks. Each experiment evaluated the impact of network disruption on control and perception capabilities.

5.1 Image Scaling Attack: CIFAR-10: Baseline Evaluation

Evaluation revealed the following performance drops on adversarially perturbed CIFAR-10 images:

- FGSM: The precision dropped from 70% to approximately 50%.
- PGD: The accuracy dropped to as low as 9–13%, depending on the level of perturbation.

5.2 Image Scaling Attack: KITTI: Baseline Evaluation

The results indicate a high vulnerability to both targeted and untargeted attacks:

- **Targeted Attack Success Rate:** 47.16%
- **Untargeted Attack Accuracy:** Reduced to 13.59%
- **Observed Behavior:** Lane-following predictions showed deviation from intended trajectory in simulation.

5.3 Network Attack: Denial-of-Service Attack Experiment

Under normal operation, the JetRacer live camera feed was continuously updated within the Jupyter Notebook, with frame numbers and timestamps advancing steadily at approximately 20–30 frames per second. Figure 6 shows a typical frame during normal Wi-Fi communication.

Upon initiating the UDP flood attack, the notebook interface froze and no new frames were delivered to the control laptop browser. The frame number and timestamp remained static throughout the attack period, as shown in Fig. 7.

The captures of Wireshark during the attack, shown in Fig. 8, confirmed sustained high packet rates exceeding 2,500 packets per 200 ms, saturating the Wi-Fi link to the JetRacer.

After the attack ceased, the frame updates resumed, validating that the disruption was due to the saturation of the Wi-Fi channel and not to internal processing failure.

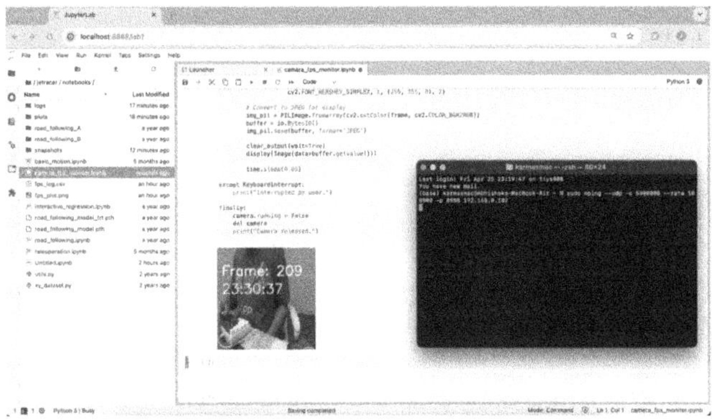

Fig. 6. Normal live camera feed inside Jupyter Notebook under Wi-Fi operation. Frame number and timestamp update continuously.

5.4 Network Attack: Man-in-the-Middle Attack Experiment

For the MITM attack, a Bettercap-based ARP spoofing set-up was deployed to intercept telemetry data between the JetRacer (192.168.0.102) and the control server (192.168.0.101). The attacker (192.168.0.100) successfully inserted itself

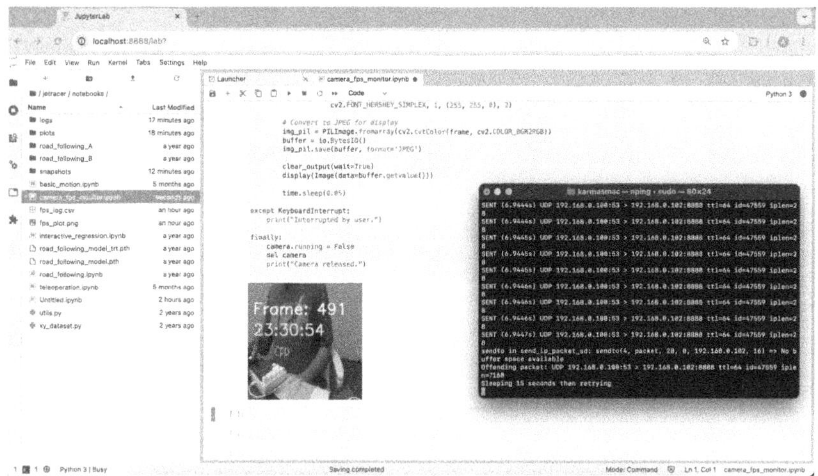

Fig. 7. Live camera feed failing to receive packets from JetRacer during Wi-Fi DoS attack. Frame number and timestamp remain static, indicating interrupted perception data delivery.

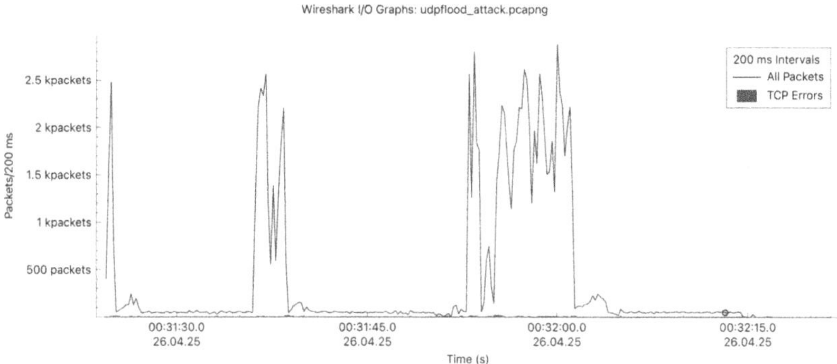

Fig. 8. Wireshark I/O Graph showing packet rate increase during UDP flooding attack on JetRacer's JupyterLab port. Small red bumps at bottom of graph indicate TCP errors during UDP flooding attack.

into the communication channel by poisoning the ARP tables of both the client and the server.

A custom JavaScript script (`modify.js`) was used inside Bettercap's HTTP proxy module to modify the JSON telemetry payload. Specifically, the `speed` was forcibly set to 5.0 and `steering_angle` was set to -1.0 before forwarding the packet to the server.

Successful outcomes included:

- Bettercap console output showing successful ARP spoofing and HTTP proxy activation (Fig. 9).

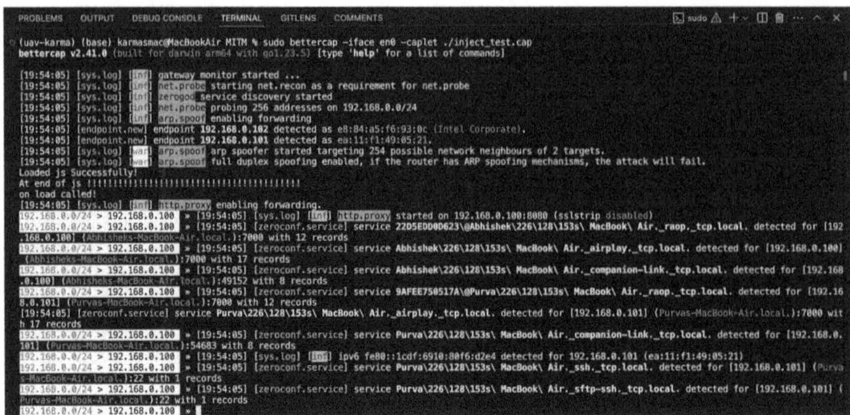

Fig. 9. Bettercap console output showing successful ARP spoofing and HTTP proxy activation with telemetry packet interception.

Table 1. Summary of Network Attack Impacts on JetRacer and Yahboom Platforms

Attack Type	Platform	Impact Level	Crash Frequency
Wi-Fi MitM	JetRacer	High	Frequent
Bluetooth MitM	JetRacer	Moderate	Occasional
Wi-Fi Packet Injection	JetRacer	High	Frequent
Bluetooth Packet Injection	JetRacer	Moderate	Occasional
Wi-Fi DoS	JetRacer	High	Frequent
Bluetooth DoS	JetRacer	Low	Rare
Wi-Fi MitM	Yahboom	High	Frequent
Bluetooth MitM	Yahboom	Moderate	Occasional
Wi-Fi Packet Injection	Yahboom	High	Frequent
Bluetooth Packet Injection	Yahboom	Moderate	Occasional
Wi-Fi DoS	Yahboom	High	Frequent
Bluetooth DoS	Yahboom	Moderate	Occasional

- Server logs showing the receipt of modified telemetry packets (Fig. 10).
- Verification of the ARP table of the client confirming the attacker's MAC address assigned to the server IP (Fig. 11).

These results validated the feasibility of real-time telemetry manipulation attacks on autonomous vehicle control systems using ARP spoofing and HTTP proxy modification techniques.

Table 1 summarizes the impact levels and crash frequencies observed in different types of network attack for the JetRacer and Yahboom platforms. Wi-Fi attacks generally exhibited higher severity compared to Bluetooth-based attacks.

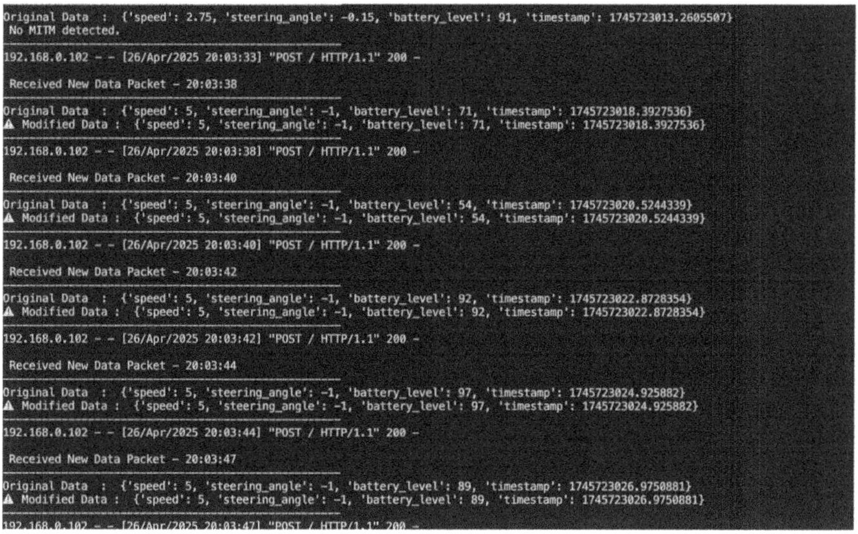

Fig. 10. Server logs showing modified telemetry data received after MITM attack.

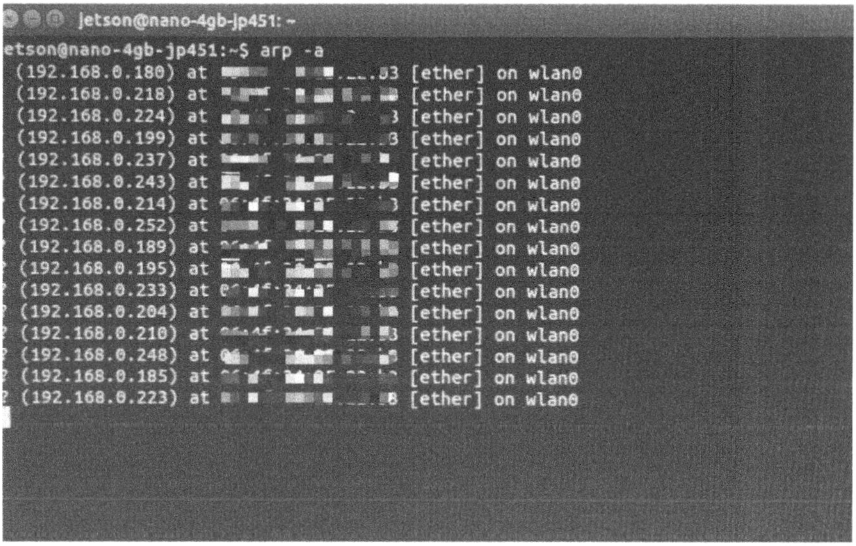

Fig. 11. Client ARP table showing attacker's MAC address inserted for server IP after ARP spoofing.

6 Conclusion

This study revealed critical vulnerabilities in both perception models and network communication protocols used in autonomous vehicle systems. Convolutional neural networks (CNN) trained for object recognition were shown to be highly susceptible to adversarial image scaling attacks, with PGD reducing classification accuracy by 9–13% and targeted attacks on real-world datasets like KITTI achieving a 47.16% misclassification success rate. These findings underscore the urgent need for robust adversarial defenses before deploying such models in real-world environments.

Simultaneously, our empirical evaluation of network-based attacks—including Denial-of-Service (DoS) and Man-in-the-Middle (MitM) attacks—demonstrated that Wi-Fi-based telemetry links can be intercepted and manipulated, resulting in control instability and unanticipated vehicle behavior. Key insights into the implementation revealed the limitations of macOS for certain attack techniques and highlighted the advantages of Linux-based platforms for more advanced network interception. Future work will extend to physical testing of perception attacks, HTTPS-secured telemetry streams, encryption-based countermeasures, and cross-platform evaluations. Together, these findings emphasize the need to secure both the perception and communication layers to ensure the safety and resilience of autonomous vehicle platforms.

References

1. Badjie, B., Cecílio, J., Casimiro, A.: Adversarial attacks and countermeasures on image classification-based deep learning models in autonomous driving systems: a systematic review. ACM Comput. Surv. **57**(1) (2024). Accessed 30 July 2025
2. Wireshark Foundation: Wireshark: The world's most popular network protocol analyzer (2023). https://www.wireshark.org/. Accessed 30 July 2025
3. Fyodor: Nmap: The network mapper (2022). https://nmap.org/. Accessed 30 July 2025
4. Geiger, A., Lenz, P., Stiller, C., Urtasun, R.: Vision meets robotics: the Kitti dataset. Int. J. Robot. Res. (IJRR) (2013)
5. Goodfellow, I.J., Shlens, J., Szegedy, C.: Explaining and harnessing adversarial examples (2015). Accessed 30 July 2025
6. Kelly, D.A., Flanery, S.A., Chamon, C.: Image scaling attack simulation: a measure of stealth and detectability (2024). Accessed 30 July 2025
7. Kim, B., Kang, S.H., Yoon, H., Kim, Y.: Cybersecurity for autonomous vehicles: review of attacks and defense. Electronics **10**(7), 837 (2021)
8. Krizhevsky, A.: Learning multiple layers of features from tiny images (2009). https://www.cs.toronto.edu/~kriz/cifar.html. Accessed 29 June 2025
9. Madry, A., Makelov, A., Schmidt, L., Tsipras, D., Vladu, A.: Towards deep learning models resistant to adversarial attacks (2019). Accessed 30 July 2025
10. Seetamonee, T., Bekaroo, G.: Modern detection techniques of false data injection attacks in v2x communication: a critical analysis. In: Seeam, A., Ramsurrun, V., Juddoo, S., Phokeer, A. (eds.) Innovations and Interdisciplinary Solutions for Underserved Areas, pp. 66–80. Springer, Cham (2024)
11. Sitawarin, C., Bhagoji, A.N., Mosenia, A., Chiang, M., Mittal, P.: DARTS: deceiving autonomous cars with toxic signs (2018). Accessed 30 July 2025
12. Sun, X., Yu, F.R., Zhang, P.: A survey on cyber-security of connected and autonomous vehicles (CAVs). IEEE Trans. Intell. Transp. Syst. **23**(7), 6240–6256 (2022)

13. Wu, H., Ou, G., Wu, W., Zhen, Z.: Improving transferable targeted adversarial attacks with model self-enhancement. In: 2024 IEEE/CVF Conference on Computer Vision and Pattern Recognition (CVPR), pp. 24615–24624 (2024)
14. Zhang, X., Zhang, T., Zhang, Y., Liu, S.: Enhancing the transferability of adversarial attacks with stealth preservation. In: Proceedings of the IEEE/CVF Conference on Computer Vision and Pattern Recognition (CVPR) Workshops, pp. 2915–2925 (2024)
15. Zhu, R., Zhang, Z., Liang, S., Liu, Z., Xu, C.: Learning to transform dynamically for better adversarial transferability (2024). Accessed 30 July 2025

A Study on Integrated Framework for Copyright Protection Based on Multi-signature in NFT

Hye-Young Kim(✉)

School of Games, Major of Game Software, Hongik University, Sejong, South Korea
hykim@hongik.ac.kr

Abstract. These digital contents are easily modified and reproduced, and they spread widely. In this environment, there is a frequent occurrence of copyright infringement and misuse of digital content, raising new issues regarding intellectual property rights and the preservation of ownership. By allowing multiple users to collaborate on the signing process, the entire system is less susceptible to risks associated with a single individual's exposure. NFT (Non-Fungible Token) has considerable potential in the field of intellectual property. It can not only improve the efficiency of copyright registration but also promote the improvement of transaction transparency and liquidity. However, existing copyright protection schemes of NFT image relied on the NFTs themselves minted by third-party platforms. In this paper, we have proposed a multi-layered blockchain security framework to resolve security vulnerabilities by protecting users from threats such as illegal copying, intellectual property rights infringement, and malware infection that may occur during the process of acquiring NFT assets through analysis of smart contracts, metadata, and digital assets that constitute NFTs. Each party can sign the consensus of the transaction or contract, increasing transparency and efficiently protecting the ownership and copyright of digital contents. Therefore, we have proposed a multi-signature scheme based on the Schnorr scheme in NFT.

Keywords: copyright protection · Non-Fungible Token · Smart Contract · Schnorr · multi-signature

1 Introduction

1.1 Introduction

The infringement of digital contents is increasing as well as the copyright and privacy challenge by harm creators and consume potential user resources. The owners of digital contents should be able to show their copyright for its contents and should be guaranteed ownership of theirs. Efficient management methods, such as granting and verifying copyrights for digital contents, have been researched to address copyright issues related to unauthorized reproduction and plagiarism. One of the types of research applied for copyright protection is digital rights management (DRM) to control the use and modification [1].

K. Daimi et al. (Eds.): CSCE 2025, CCIS 2937, pp. 346–354, 2026.
https://doi.org/10.1007/978-3-032-22208-4_23

Blockchain technology is increasingly being used in a wide range of industrial sectors, including financial services, games and entertainment, logistics and distribution, digital identity verification, public services, and healthcare. Non-fungible token (NFT), a digital asset verification system based on blockchain technology, is becoming a pivotal element of the new digital economy [2–5]. However, the fast expansion of the NFT market is accompanied by new security problems. According to OpenSea, the world's largest NFT trading platform, approximately 80% of NFTs generated using its NFT creation tool were verified as either plagiarized or forged collections [2].

By assigning weights based on the importance and risk level of each validation item, we enabled a more precise evaluation of NFTs. For example, higher weights were assigned to direct security threats such as malware detection, while relatively lower weights were given to indirect threat factors like the properties of content assets in metadata. This enables users to quantitatively assess the overall security level of NFTs and make informed purchase decisions based on risk levels.

Additionally, this framework mitigates the risk of malware infection that may arise during the downloading or trading of NFTs while ensuring the secure storage and use of digital assets. It aims to safeguard users from diverse security risks, such as unauthorized duplication, copyright infringement, and malware, while also promoting the growth of a dependable NFT ecosystem.

Digital signature technology can guarantee authenticity, integrity, and non-repudiation of data in electronic commerce and electronic government affairs. The signature technique is not affected by the number of signatures and the result is only one digital signature in length. Signature can mitigate the above deficiencies or bottlenecks faced by the system based on blockchain [2].

A transaction involving multi-parties needs signatures to take effect, and it will consume a large amount of storage on the blockchain. Schnorr signatures feature a rich algebraic structure suitable for the construction of multiparty protocols. Also, it can be further utilized to construct other cryptographic primitives like multi-signatures, threshold signatures, blind signatures, or adaptor signatures, all which have interesting applications especially to lately arising blockchain technologies. Individual cosigners do not reveal their private information during this process; multi-signature schemes allow for the decentralization of the signing process by requiring multiple parties to cooperate in order to produce a valid signature. A trivial multi-signature scheme can be constructed using an arbitrary digital signature scheme in the following manner. The signers generate their key pairs, individually sign the message, and concatenate their signatures.

The verification then proceeds by obtaining all the public keys of the signers and verifying concatenated signatures individually [3]. The length of the multi-signature was reduced to a constant. A single aggregated key can be used to verify the multi-signature. And the individual signatures are bound to the resulting multi-signature; therefore, they cannot be removed. However, the cryptographic digital signature is resource consuming and inefficient because the verification of the signature consumes lots of computational resources and excessive number of communications. Therefore, we have proposed a secure and efficient multi-signature scheme based on Schnorr for an efficient copyright protection scheme for digital content in this paper.

Therefore, we have proposed an integrated framework for aims to enhance the dependability of the digital asset market and provide a robust trading environment through the practical implementation of the NFT security framework and we present the digital cryptographic single and multi-signature algorithms for copyright protection for digital content based on Schnorr and we describe the experimental results show that the proposed our multi-signature scheme based on Schorr can effectively improve the performance for copyright protection and reduce communication overhead on NFT security framework.

2 Proposed Scheme

In this paper, we have proposed a comprehensive framework enabling users to easily verify the quality and security of NFTs. This framework comprehensively analyses the three fundamental components of NFTs: smart contracts, metadata, and digital assets. In this study, rather than making simple Pass/Fail judgments on the key validation functions proposed above, we implemented a weight-based evaluation system.

Figure 1 illustrates the proposed framework for intellectual property protection of NFTs proposed in this study. The framework comprises a collecting unit that gathers NFT block data, metadata, and digital asset information, and an API service provider that performs validation and security assessments on proposed NFTs and reports the outcomes of these evaluations.

The following formatting rules must be followed strictly. This (.doc) document may be used as a template for papers prepared using Microsoft Word. Papers not conforming to these requirements may not be published in the conference proceedings.

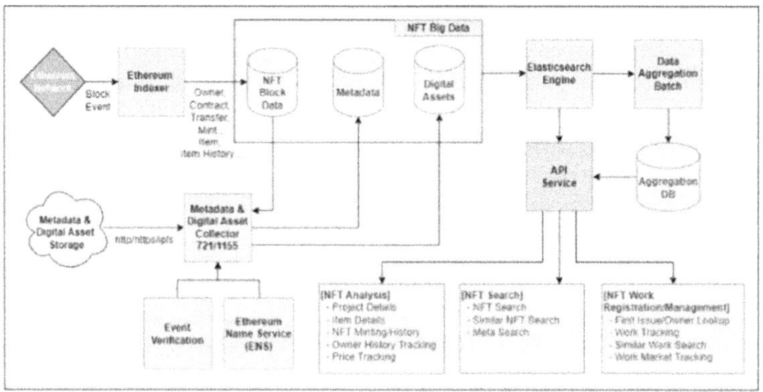

Fig. 1. Framework for the protection of intellectual property rights related to NFTs

A technology for indexing data from blockchains such as Ethereum, Flow, Polygon, Solana, and Klaytn into an analysis database is developed [6]. This technology enables the fast retrieval and analysis of blockchain data stored in the analysis database [7].

If relevant to the collection target, embed and store TransactionReceipt based on transaction data. To reduce the index size, use blockNumber as the index and blockNumber + transactionIndex as the unique index. Only the data required by the NFT framework are loaded. Gather all contract deployments.

2.1 Blockchain Indexing

A technology for indexing data from blockchains such as Ethereum, Flow, Polygon, Solana, and Klaytn into an analysis database is developed [8]. This technology enables the fast retrieval and analysis of blockchain data stored in the analysis database [9].

If relevant to the collection target, embed and store TransactionReceipt based on transaction data. To reduce the index size, use blockNumber as the index and blockNumber + transactionIndex as the unique index. Only the data required by the NFT framework are loaded. Gather all contract deployments.

2.2 Validation Check Using Schnorr Multi-signature

We have represented a message, m and a private key, q as input values in our implementation of signing and verification of Schnorr scheme as in Figs. 2 and 3. In a k value, we hash the private key and the message with the keccak256 hash function and obtain two public keys (x, y) coordinates by multiplying the generator point G in q by the elliptic curve scalar. Find the equation $e = hash\ (kG|Q|M)$ required for Schnorr signature and make $s = k - eq$ the equation. The public keys, s, and e signature values are outputs as return values. It has a message and, public key, Q, and s, and e as input values that are result values from the signature algorithm in verification algorithm of our scheme. If the public key has an infinite value or does not exist in the elliptic curve, return value is *False*. As long as the equation $kG = sG + eQ$ is performed and the result of hash with the e signature value received as an input value is compared with the equation $e = hash\ (kG|\ Q|\ M)$. If it is wrong return *False*, else if right return *True*. Equations (1, 2 and 3) performed the verification below.

$$sG + eQ = (k - eq)\ G + eqG \tag{1}$$

$$= kG - eQ + eQ \tag{2}$$

$$= kG = K \tag{3}$$

Due to the characteristic property of SMPC (Secure Multi-Party Computation), individual cosigners do not disclose their private information, and the signers generate their key pairs, individually sign the message, and concatenate their signatures.

The verification proceeds by obtaining public keys of all the signers and verifying concatenated signatures individually. Every single transaction that happened on the network will be signed and recorded in the blockchain. A transaction involving multi-parties needs multiple signatures to take effect, and it will consume a large amount of storage if everyone signs the transaction and stores the record on the blockchain.

```
Schnorr Signing Algorithm
1: function SCHNORR-SIGN(m, q)
2:     M ← hash(m)
3:     k ← int(hash(bytes32(q) || M))(mod n)
4:     K ← kG
5:     Q ← qG
6:     if y_k ≠ 1 then
7:         k ← n − k
8:     end if
9:     e ← int(hash(bytes32(kG)) || Q || M))
10:    s ← (k − eq(mod n))(mod n)
11:    return (Q, bytes32(s), bytes32(e))
12: end function
```

Fig. 2. Schnorr Signing Algorithm

```
Schnorr Verification Algorithm
1: function SCHNORR-VERIFY(m, Q, s, e)
2:     if Q = ∞ or not curve(Q) then
3:         return False
4:     end if
5:     M ← hash(m)
6:     kG ← sG + eQ
7:     if e = int(hash(bytes32(kG)) || Q || M))
   then return True
8:     else
9:         return False
10:    end if
11: end function
```

Fig. 3. Schnorr verification Algorithm

```
Schnorr Multi-Signing Algorithm
1: function SCHNORR-MULTI-SIGN(m, P, q(i))
2:     a(i) = HASH-AGGR((P), Q(i))
3:     Q = MERGER(P)
4:     k(i) ← Q(q)
5:     Q(i) = r(i)G
6:     t(i) = HASH-CAL(Q(i))
7:     send t(i) to other cosigners
8:     send Q(i) to other cosigners
9:     if HASH-CAL(Q(i)) ≠ t(i)
10:        break
11:    for i = 1 to n
12:        Q = Q +Q(i)
13:    e = HASH_SIGN(m, Q)
14:    s(i) = r(i) + ea(i)q(i) (mod n)
15:    send s() to other cosigners
16:    for i = 1 to n
17:        s = s + s(i) (mod n)
18:    return(Q, bytes32(s))
19: end function
```

Fig. 4. Multi-Signature signing algorithm

```
Schnorr Multi-Verification Algorithm
1: function SCHNORR-MULTI-VERIFY(m, Q, s)
2:     e = HASH_SIGN(m, Q)
3:     if sG = Q ⊕ eQ
4:         return True
5:     else
6:         return Flase
7: end function
```

Fig. 5. Multi-Signature verification algorithm

Every node on the blockchain keeps the same ledger, records need to be as compact as possible. So, the multi-signature technique was applied to reduce bandwidth and storage volume in some services. The multi-signature technique based on Schnorr scheme is especially attractive for blockchain where communication and storage are more expensive than computation. It produces a multi-signature of constant length instead of linear in the number of signers. The advantage of having multi-signature of constant length, other than the apparent implications of smaller size, is faster multi-signature verification. The multi-signature verification time can become even constant if another requirement, described in the following paragraph, is satisfied. Our proposed multi-signature singing scheme has described in pseudocode in Figs. 4 and 5.

We have represented *HASH-CAL*() for computing communication and *HASH_AGGR*() for computing coefficients in key aggregation phase and *HASH-CAL*() for used to compute a challenge in the signing procedure of hash function. A random private key Q_i is sampled from $\mathbb{Q}_i$, and the group generator G is multiplied by this private key to obtain $Q_i = q_i G$. The resulting key pair is (q_i, Q_i). Each key is prior to that multiplied by a factor *ai* which is dependent on the whole set of public keys of signers and also on the multiplied key itself. The factors *ai* are computed as$ai = HASH_AGGR(P_i, \cdot Q_i)$, and the group key is then the sum$Q = \sum_{i=1}^{n} a_i Q_i$. Each signer i initiates the algorithm with a multi-set of public keys $P = \{Q_1, Q_2, .., Q_n\}$ and its private key Q_j. The algorithm then computes a, of the specific signer and the aggregated group key $Q = MERGER(P)$. The participants sample a noncer_i from$\mathbb{Q}_i$ and multiply the group generator by this number to obtain$Q_i = r_i G$. Once they haveQ_i, each signer computes its commitment$t_i = HASH - CAL(Q_i)$. The commitments are distributed to other cosigners. Upon receiving all commitments t_j, signers distribute theirs Q_i to other cosigners.

The signers have to compute$e = SCHNORR - SIGN(m, q)$ and their partial signatures $s_i = q_i + ea_i q_i (mod\ n)$. The partial signatures are then distributed to other cosigners, and the participants compute $s = \sum_{i=1}^{n} s_i (\text{mod } n)$. The resulting multi-signature is the pair(Q, s). As shown in Fig. 5, the verifier computes $e = SCHNORR - SIGN(m, q)$)and if the equation $sG = Q + eQ$ holds, the signature is valid, otherwise, it is invalid.

3 Performance Analysis

Figure 5 shows the Ethereum node's current status. The block load is 637,187, the TransactionReceipt load is 120,098,609, the Token URI is 7,623,850, and the metadata is collecting 6,645,639 (NFT) + 1,000,000 (Debug).

Fig. 6. Ethereum Node Status

Fig. 7. Test Findings

Moreover, this study systematically validated the compliance of NFTs with the standard for smart contracts. The verification items were categorized as mandatory and optional requirements. In terms of mandatory requirements, we confirmed the implementation of the ERC-721, ERC-165, and ERC-721TokenReceiver interfaces. More specifically, the verification included the implementation of the Transfer, Approval, and ApprovalForAll, as well as the following functions required for the fundamental operations of NFTs:

Functions pertaining to ownership

- BalanceOf: Verify the quantity of tokens possessed by a certain address
- OwnerOf: Verify the owner of a specific token

Functions pertaining to transfer

- SafeTransferFrom: Secure transfer of tokens
- TransferFrom: Transfer of tokens

Functions pertaining to approval

- Approve: Approval for a certain token
- SetApprovalForAll: Approval for all tokens

- GetApproved: Verification of approved addresses
- IsApprovedForAll: Verification of the status of overall approval

Verification of interface compatibility

- SupportsInterface: Verification of interface compatibility status
- OnERC721Received: Processing of token acquisition

The verification confirmed that the assessed NFT fulfilled all the required criteria, and it was also determined that the metadata interface, an optional requirement, was flawlessly implemented. This indicates that the NFT adheres strictly to the Ethereum network's standards and allows for secure transactions and ownership management. This comprehensive verification process is crucial because it provides objective standards for NFT buyers to assess the technological stability of the asset. Furthermore, this study introduced a weight-based evaluation system to enhance the objectivity and accuracy of verification by reflecting the importance of each inspection item. The items were categorized into security and validation assessments, evaluated independently. While the current phase only displays binary (pass/fail) results for each item, the system internally computes weighted scores for both assessments. Future iterations will implement the display of these weighted evaluation results we implemented the proposed framework to validate the tokens that were sold on OpenSea. Figures 6, 7 and 8 demonstrate examples of test findings and detailed inspection results, respectively.(Note: Original Korean interface text is shown with English translations for reference)

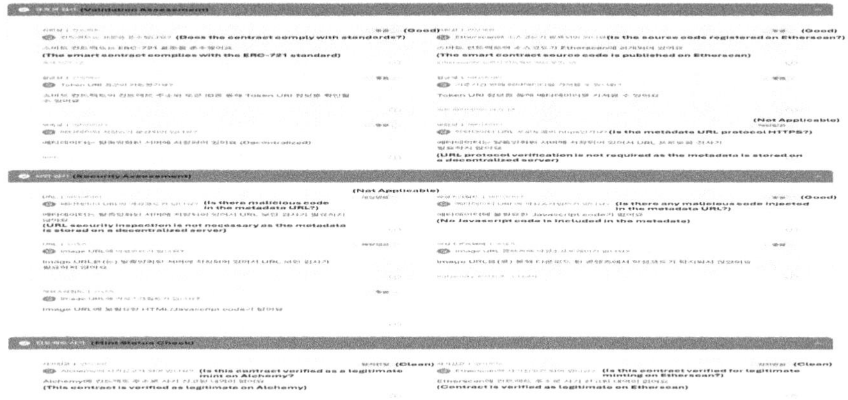

Fig. 8. Detailed Test Findings

As shown in Fig. 9, secret means a private key, and message can be viewed as the value to be signed. It can be seen that two public key values and s and e values, which are signatures required, appear as result values. The SCHNORR-VERIFY function is an algorithm that verifies s, e signatures, public keys, and messages as input values in the Schnorr signature algorithm.

As for the signature protocols in our scheme, we implement them on Elliptic Curve Cryptography (ECC). The safety of ECC comes from the intractability of solving the

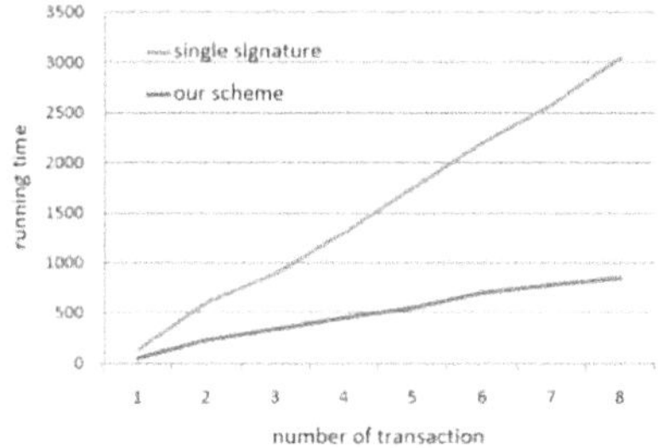

Fig. 9. Execution time of signing

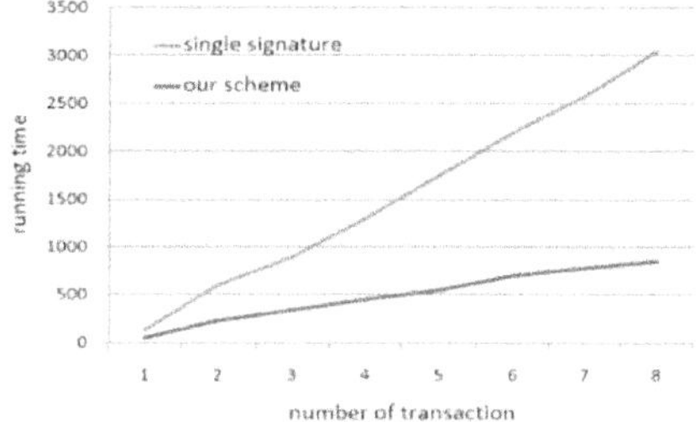

Fig. 10. Execution time of verification

elliptic curve discrete logarithm problem. We use an additive group G generated by a point on a non-singular elliptic curve $E1: y2 = x3 - 7x + 10 \bmod 19$. In order to increase the accuracy, we run each of the evaluation 50 times and take the averaged values as the results. As shown in Fig. 10, the simulation of our scheme shows that eight copyright transactions by the buyer cost only 13.7 ms, the seller only costs 6.9 ms and the miner only cost 20.2 ms. Therefore, the experimental data show that our proposed scheme is effective and suitable for hosts with limited resources and poor computing power.

4 Conclusion

In this paper, we have proposed an efficient multi-signature scheme based on Schnorr for copyright protection on NFTs. With our proposed proactive defense strategy, we design a secure copyright protection scheme which provides advantages of compact copyright transfer and prior infringement penalty. More concrete, both copyright registration and transfer are regarded as transactions and recorded to the blockchain. Based on the double-authentication-prevention signature and non-interactive zero-knowledge proof techniques, illegal copyright transfer can be detected, and the infringement penalty can be done automatically with a tailored smart contract before the completion of the transfer. Also, we proposed framework implements a multi-tiered verification system that includes smart contracts documented on the blockchain, metadata from distributed storage, and actual digital content. Specifically, it identifies potential risk factors using security vulnerability analysis for each layer and provides objective assessment information on the current state and security level of NFTs. This system strictly adheres to industry standard protocols and effectively prevents the influx of malicious code using a built-in security inspection module.

The findings of this study are significant because they systematically address security vulnerabilities associated with NFT transactions while creating a technological foundation that facilitates real-time verification of validity. As the use of NFTs broadens across diverse sectors such as art, gaming, and finance, this framework is expected to become increasingly significant as a fundamental infrastructure for the secure distribution of digital assets and the safeguarding of intellectual property rights.

Acknowledgments. This study was supported by the Culture, Sports and Tourism R&D Program through the Korea Creative Content Agency grant funded by the Ministry of Culture, Sports, and

Tourism in 2024 (Project Name: Global Talent Training Program for Copyright Management Technology in Game Contents, Project Number: RS-2024-00396709, Contribution Rate: 100%).

References

1. Alhassan, A.M., Hussain, I., et al.: Advances in catalytic dry reforming of methane (DRM): emerging trends, current challenges, and future perspectives. J. Clean. Prod. **423**, 138638 (2023)
2. Das, D., Bose, P., Ruaro, N., Kruegel, C., Vigna, G.: Understanding security issues in the NFT ecosystem. In: ACM SIGSAC Conference on Computer and Communications Security., pp. 667–681 (2022)
3. Wlasinsky, O.: Literature review on the most popular of NFTs types. Int. J. Educ. Technol. Artif. Intell. **2**(1), 8–12 (2023)
4. Statista: NFT Market share. [Online]. Available: https://www.Statista.com/outlook/fmo/digital-assets/nft/worldwide. Accessed July 2024
5. Treatment episode data set: discharges (TEDS-D): concatenated, 2006 to 2009. U.S. Department of Health and Human Services, Substance Abuse and Mental Health Services Administration, Office of Applied Studies. August, 2013. https://doi.org/10.3886/ICPSR30122.v2
6. Taylor, P.J., Dargahi, T., Dehghantanha, A., Parizi, R.M., Choo, K.R.: A systematic literature review of blockchain cyber security. Digit Commun Netw. **6**(2), 147–156 (2020)
7. Qureshi, A., Megias Jimenez, D.: Blockchain-based multimedia content protection: review and open challenges. Appl. Sci. **11**(1), 1 (2021)
8. Choi, D.: Copyright challenges in AI-based industries. J. Content Prot. (2022)
9. Pungila, C., Galis, D., Negru, V.: A new high-performance approach to approximate pattern-matching for plagiarism detection in blockchain-based non-fungible tokens (NFTs). Comput. Sci. (2022)

Assessment and Examination of Electromagnetic Radiation at DVB-T Broadcast Sites of the Greek Public Broadcasting Corporation

Konstantinos Zarkadas(✉) and George Dimitrakopoulos

Department of Informatics and Telematics, Harokopio University of Athens, 9, Omirou Street, Tavros, Athens 17778, Greece
kostaszar91@gmai.com, gdimitra@hua.gr

Abstract. The widespread adoption of digital terrestrial television broadcasting, in conjunction with the ongoing expansion of Greece's network infrastructure, has intensified concerns regarding the potential adverse effects associated with prolonged exposure to radio frequency electromagnetic fields (RF-EMFs), particularly among vulnerable population groups. The present study investigates RF-EMF emissions originating from three digital terrestrial television transmission sites operated by Greece's national public broadcasting organization. Measurements of radiofrequency electric field strength and power density were conducted within both the near-field and far-field regions of the transmission antennas. The collected data from the three sites were subsequently compared with corresponding measurements reported by the Greek Atomic Energy Commission (EEAE) and evaluated against the exposure limit guidelines established by the International Commission on Non-Ionizing Radiation Protection (ICNIRP).

Keywords: Electric field strength · Power density · Non-ionizing radiation protection · Digital video broadcasting · terrestrial · Radio mast

1 Introduction

The rapid expansion of digital terrestrial television (DTTB) services, together with the continuous development of communication infrastructure, has given rise to growing public concern about the potential health implications of long-term exposure to radio frequency electromagnetic fields (EMFs). Increasing numbers of citizens, particularly parents, have voiced objections to the installation of microcells and transmission antennas in residential areas, expressing fears that persistent exposure may adversely affect children and other sensitive groups. Such apprehensions are further intensified by the widespread deployment of wireless technologies and the general lack of public understanding of electromagnetic radiation and its biological effects. Despite extensive research on the subject, the scientific community has not yet reached unanimous conclusions, and discrepancies often persist between public perception and expert evaluations. This context underscores the necessity of systematic monitoring and assessment of RF-EMF exposure levels to verify adherence to international safety standards and to foster greater public confidence and awareness

K. Daimi et al. (Eds.): CSCE 2025, CCIS 2937, pp. 355-366, 2026.
https://doi.org/10.1007/978-3-032-22208-4_24

A variety of technological systems, including broadcasting transmitters, cellular base stations, and everyday electronic devices, emit electromagnetic waves that collectively shape the electromagnetic environment of modern wireless communication networks. These emissions span a wide frequency spectrum, generally extending from about 100 kHz to several gigahertz. Over recent decades, the widespread deployment of digital communication technologies has markedly altered the electromagnetic landscape. Empirical evidence suggests that radiofrequency electromagnetic field (RF-EMF) levels in contemporary urban settings are considerably elevated compared to those measured in earlier decades, when analog radio and television transmitters constituted the dominant sources of environmental EMF exposure.

Recent field surveys have demonstrated that the ongoing expansion of television broadcasting infrastructure has contributed to elevated electromagnetic field (EMF) intensities even in sparsely populated rural environments. The Scientific Committee on Emerging and Newly Identified Health Risks (SCENIHR), in its 2015 assessment report, reviewed extensive research on electromagnetic emissions originating from radio and television transmitters. The committee concluded that, although the digitalization of broadcasting technologies resulted in lower transmission power per station, the cumulative electromagnetic exposure within the television frequency bands increased considerably. Exposure to radiofrequency electromagnetic fields (RF-EMFs) can produce thermal interactions within biological tissues, typically evaluated using the Specific Absorption Rate (SAR), expressed in watts per kilogram (W/kg).

In Greece, regulations governing public exposure to electromagnetic fields are derived from the 1999 recommendations issued by the Council of the European Union, which established standardized threshold values for EMF exposure across member states. National safety limits adopt these European directives while applying an additional precautionary factor: permissible exposure levels are set at 70% of the reference limits proposed by the International Commission on Non-Ionizing Radiation Protection (ICNIRP). The Independent Communications and Telecommunications Authority (ICTA) is responsible for defining and enforcing specific limits on electric field strength (E) and ensuring compliance with the established national and European regulatory framework.

The present study aims to evaluate electromagnetic field (EMF) levels and characterize the radiation profile of three digital television broadcasting facilities situated in representative rural, urban, and suburban environments. Systematic measurements of electric field intensity and power density were conducted at predefined observation points surrounding each transmission site. The collected data were subsequently analyzed and compared with the corresponding measurement records provided by the Greek Atomic Energy Commission (EEAE), in order to verify compliance with national and international exposure guidelines.

The structure of this paper is organized as follows: Sect. 2 describes in detail the measurement setup and the methodological framework adopted for the experimental analysis. Section 3 reports and discusses the results obtained from broadband field measurements, including supplementary computational evaluations. Finally, Sect. 4 provides a summary of the key findings and outlines the principal conclusions derived from the study.

2 Methodological Framework

Comprehensive field measurements were performed across multiple locations to evaluate the operational characteristics of selected radio transmission masts. This section presents the technical specifications of the digital terrestrial television (DTT) transmitters corresponding to the three sites under investigation. For each installation, key system parameters were documented, including mast height, antenna orientation (azimuth), number of antenna elements, peak main-lobe gain, and effective radiated power. A concise summary of these parameters for the analyzed DTT broadcasting antennas is provided in Table 1.

Table 1. System Parameters of the Digital Terrestrial Television (DTT) Antenna Configuration

Parameter Type	Urban	Suburban	Rural
Frequency (MHz)	474	498	514
System	DVB-T	DVB-T	DVB-T
Number of elements	6	4	2
Directions	11°,29°,227°,230°,309°,312°	230°,310°	76°, 127°
Gain of array (dBi)	6.15	14.15	11.15
Polarization	Horizontal	Horizontal	Horizontal
Antenna height (m)	27	27	27
Transmission power (dBm)	40	33.01	40

2.1 Theoretical Background

An electromagnetic wave is characterized by the simultaneous presence of electric and magnetic field components that oscillate perpendicularly to each other and to the direction of wave propagation. These two fields are intrinsically linked, forming a unified physical phenomenon that governs the transmission of electromagnetic energy through space. The electric field intensity (E) and the magnetic field strength (H) maintain a proportional relationship, analogous to the interaction between voltage and current in conventional electrical systems. Although their full formulation is mathematically rigorous and multidimensional, simplified forms of these relations are commonly employed in practical analyses [6], as presented in Eq. (1).

$$E\ (V/m) = Z_0\ (\Omega) \times H\ (A/m) \tag{1}$$

where E is the electric field strength, H is the magnetic field strength, and $Z_0 = 377\ \Omega$ is the intrinsic impedance of free space

The exposure ratios $\lambda_{i,f}$ corresponding to height i and frequency range f were determined using Eq. (2).

$$\lambda_{i,f} = \left(\frac{E_{if}}{E_{Lf}}\right)^2 \tag{2}$$

Where E_{if} is the electric field strength at height i for frequency band f and E_{Lf} is the electric field reference level at frequency band f.

Measurements were carried out near the television transmitter antenna. Each six-minute recording captured the time-averaged electric field strength E at distances between 12 m and 103 m, and at heights of 110 cm, 130 cm, and 160 cm above ground. The mean electric field intensity was obtained from the spatially averaged values at each height, as defined in Eq. (3).

$$E_{avg} = \sqrt{\frac{\sum_{i=1}^{3} E_i^2}{3}} \tag{3}$$

Measurements were performed at three representative locations, representing urban, suburban, and rural settings.

The exposure ratio λf for each frequency band f was computed as the mean of the values obtained at the three heights, as expressed in Eq. (4).

$$\lambda_f = \frac{1}{3}\sum_{i=1}^{3} \lambda_{if} \tag{4}$$

Finally, the total exposure ratio Λf for a specific measurement site was calculated as the sum of the exposure ratios λf over all frequency bands, as given in Eq. (5).

$$\Lambda_f = \sum_f \lambda_f \tag{5}$$

3 Results and Discussion

3.1 Measurement of Electric Field Strength at Different Distances

Figure 1 depicts the variation of the measured electric field strength (E) across five distinct measurement locations in Vari. The recorded values range from approximately 0.12 V/m to 0.44 V/m, indicating noticeable spatial variation in field intensity around the transmitter area. The highest field value was observed at location 2, while the lowest occurred at location 5. This trend suggests a gradual decrease in field strength with increasing distance or positional offset from the main radiation direction of the antenna.

Figure 2 presents the average electric field strength (E) recorded at five distinct measurement locations in Foinikas. The observed values range between approximately 0.14 V/m and 0.23 V/m, indicating relatively low field intensities across all points. The highest electric field level was detected at location 4, while the lowest occurred at location 5, suggesting moderate spatial variation within the measurement area

Figure 3 illustrates the distribution of the average electric field strength (E) measured at five points within the suburban area. The recorded values range from 0.22 V/m to 0.31 V/m, showing moderate spatial variation. The slightly higher field levels at the central locations suggest limited signal attenuation, consistent with partial line-of-sight conditions and lower surrounding obstructions compared to urban environments.

Figure 3 indicates a noticeably higher electric field intensity compared to the preceding figures. This elevation is primarily attributed to the proximity of the measurement

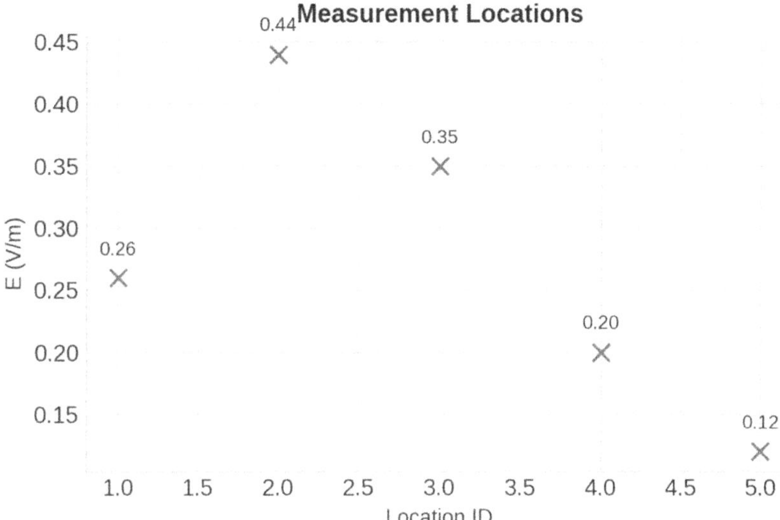

Fig. 1. Variation of the average electric field strength (E) across the five measurement locations in the Vari area.

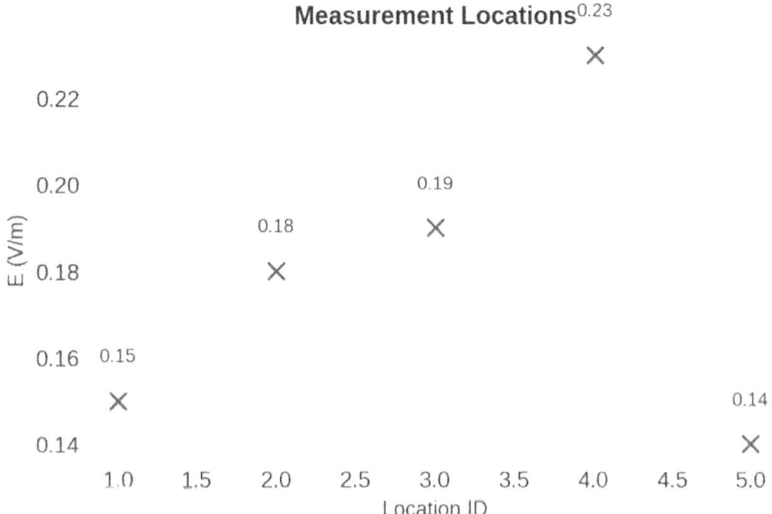

Fig. 2. Variation of the average electric field strength (E) across the five measurement locations in the Foinikas area

points, which are located within approximately 22 m of the transmitting source. As the distance from the emitter decreases, the electric field intensity correspondingly increases. Another factor influencing this outcome is the higher Effective Isotropic Radiated Power (EIRP) of the transmitter operating in the rural area relative to the other sites. Figure 2

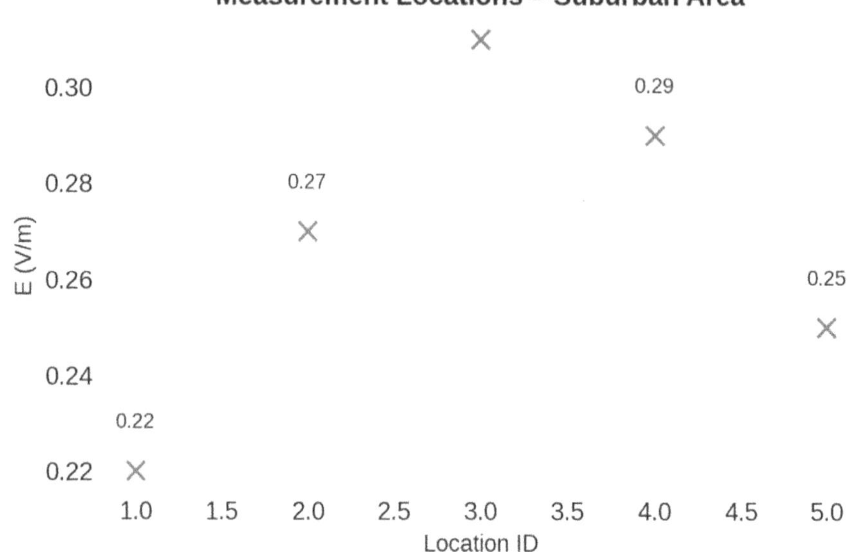

Fig. 3. Average electric field strength (E) measured at five locations in the suburban area.

shows that, despite a higher EIRP, the measured field strength in Foinikas is lower than in Vari.

3.2 Analysis of Calculated Secondary Outcomes for each Scenario

Figures 4 and 5 present the measured power density and total exposure ratio (Λ) at five distinct points within the urban area. The results demonstrate relatively low field levels, with power density values ranging from $4.5*10^{-5}$ W/m^2 to $5.26*10^{-4}$ W/m^2 and exposure ratios between $2.0*10^{-5}$ and $3.5*10^{-4}$. The maximum values were observed at measurement point 2, which lies closest to the transmitting antenna, while the lowest occurred at point 5, located farther from the source. Overall, all measured values remain several orders of magnitude below the reference exposure limits established by the ICNIRP, indicating that public exposure levels in the urban area are well within internationally accepted safety thresholds.

In the suburban area, five measurement points were analyzed to determine the power density and total exposure ratio (Λ). Figure 6 presents the measured power density values ranged from $5.4*10^{-5}$ W/m^2 to $1.50*10^{-4}$ W/m^2, while the corresponding exposure ratios varied between $3.4*10^{-5}$ and $1.07*10^{-4}$. The highest power density and exposure ratio were recorded at measurement point 4, indicating proximity to the transmitter or favorable propagation conditions, whereas the lowest values were observed at point 5. All results remain significantly below the reference exposure limits established by ICNIRP, with safety margins exceeding four orders of magnitude. These findings confirm that public exposure levels in the suburban area are well within the acceptable safety thresholds.

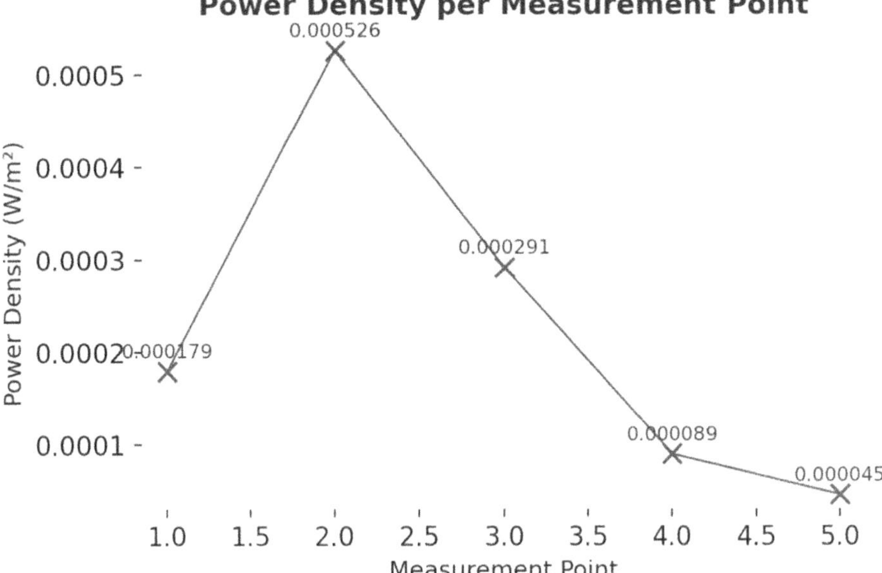

Fig. 4. Variation of the measured power density (W/m^2) across five observation points

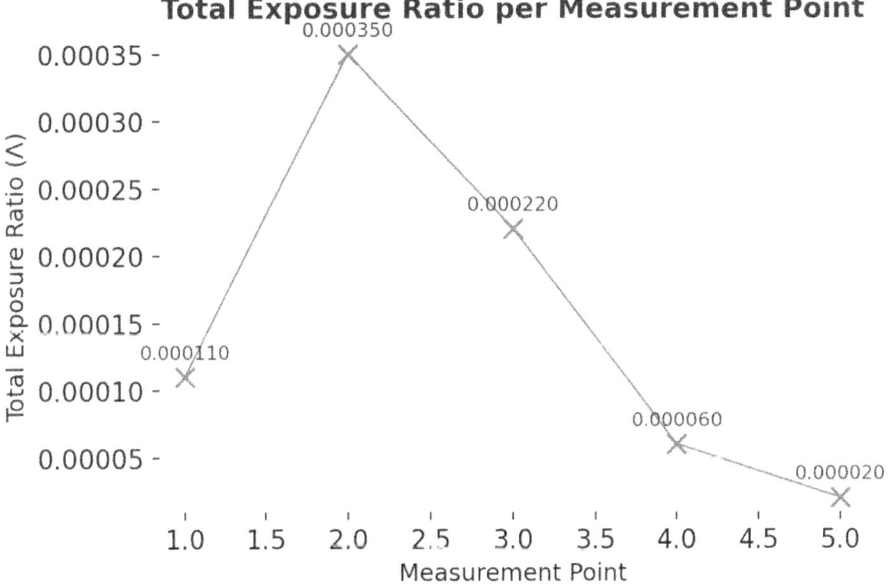

Fig. 5. Distribution of the total exposure ratio (Λ) at corresponding measurement points in the urban area.

In the rural area, measurements of power density and total exposure ratio (Λ) were carried out at five points around the transmitter. Figure 7 presents the measured power

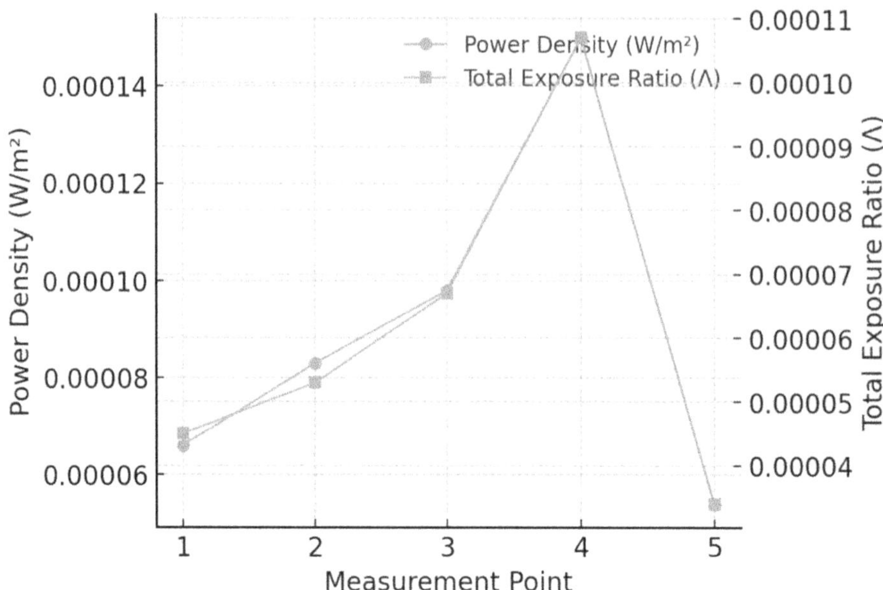

Fig. 6. Power density (W/m^2) and total exposure ratio (Λ) measured at five locations in the suburban area.

density values ranged from $3.8 * 10^{-5}$ W/m^2 to $4.24*10^{-4}$ W/m^2, while the exposure ratios varied between $1.1*10^{-4}$ and $5.2*10^{-4}$. The highest values for both parameters were observed at measurement point 2, which lies closest to the transmission source, whereas the lowest occurred at point 1. Despite the higher Effective Isotropic Radiated Power (EIRP) in this area, all recorded values remain well below the ICNIRP reference limits, confirming minimal electromagnetic exposure in the rural environment.

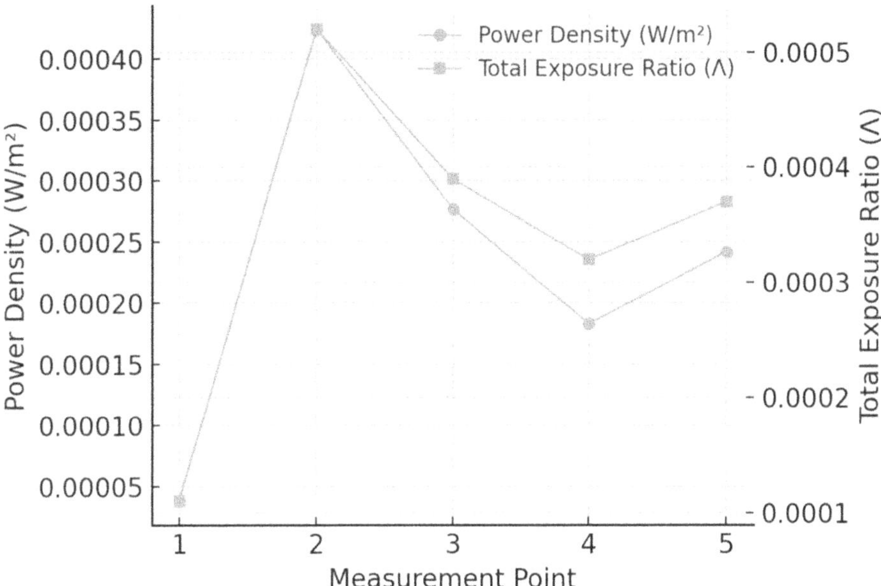

Fig. 7. Power density (W/m^2) and total exposure ratio (Λ) measured at five locations in the rural area.

3.3 Comparison of the Measurement Data with the Reports of the Greek Atomic Energy Commission (EEAE).

Figure 8 presents a comparative analysis between the field measurement data obtained in this study and the corresponding results reported by the Greek Atomic Energy Commission (EEAE) for the three examined areas. To maintain consistency, all field measurements were performed at distances equivalent to those referenced in the EEAE reports [8–10]. Each measurement point was also characterized by its distance from the transmitting antenna and its azimuthal orientation relative to the horizon. The comparative evaluation reveals no substantial discrepancies between the two data sets. Minor deviations can be reasonably attributed to factors such as instrument accuracy, prevailing meteorological conditions (e.g., humidity and temperature), and human-related influences, which may introduce slight measurement uncertainty.

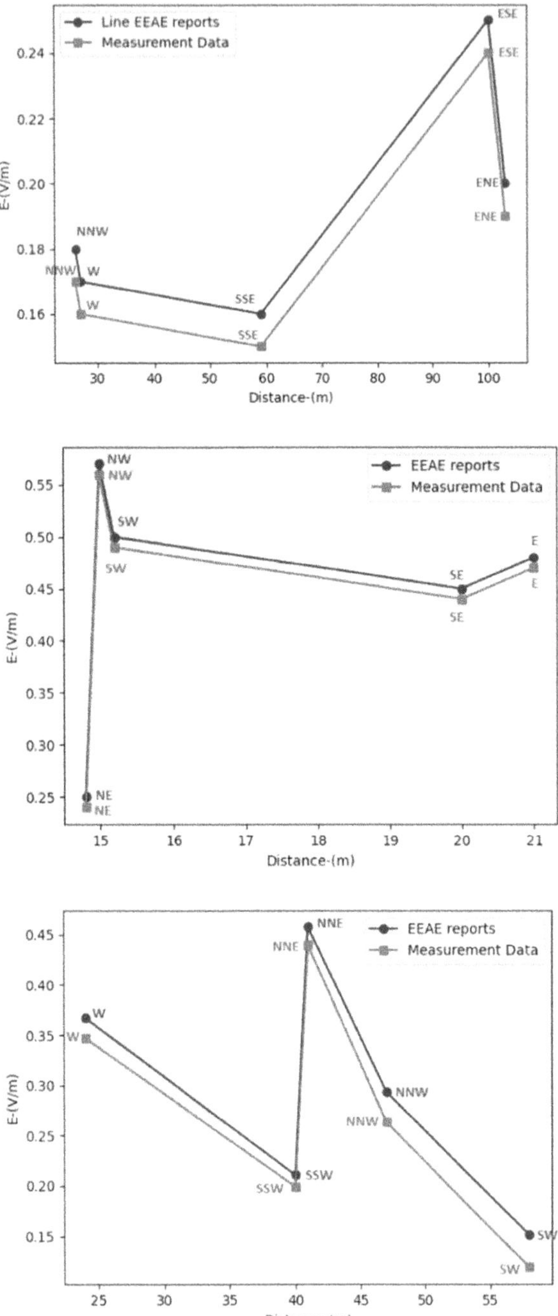

Fig. 8. Comparison of the measurement data with the reports of the Greek Atomic Energy Commission (EEAE). a) urban area b) rural area c) non-urban area.

4 Conclusion

The present study focuses on evaluating the mean electric field strength (V/m) of radiofrequency electromagnetic fields (RF-EMF) emitted by three digital low-power transmitters operated by the Hellenic Broadcasting Corporation in Greece. The measurements confirm that the RF-EMF emissions generated by these transmitters remain compliant with the exposure limits established under national regulatory frameworks. Specifically, the recorded electric field strengths are well below the reference level of 22.33 V/m for frequencies around 450 MHz, corresponding to systems functioning within the UHF frequency band. Overall, both experimental and theoretical assessments of the electric field strength and power density in the vicinity of the television transmitters indicate full compliance with national safety standards.

According to the measurement data, the E-field levels produced by the DVB-T transmission antennas in all three study sites were substantially lower than the prescribed exposure thresholds. In the urban area of Vari, the maximum measured E-field reached 0.439369 V/m, which represents merely 1.89% of the 23.18 V/m reference level defined by the ICNIRP guidelines. In the rural region of Foinikas, the highest value recorded was 0.24080 V/m, corresponding to 0.99% of the 24.14 V/m ICNIRP limit. Likewise, in the non-urban site of Eyzonoi, the peak E-field level was 0.5519 V/m, amounting to only 2.32% of the 23.76 V/m exposure limit recommended by ICNIRP. These findings clearly demonstrate that the electric field intensities in all examined areas are well within internationally recognized safety margins.

References

1. Jalilian, H., et al.: Exposure and health risks perception of extremely low frequency and radiofrequency electromagnetic fields and the effect of providing information. Environ. Res. **169**, 501–509, ISSN 0013-9351 (2019). https://doi.org/10.1016/j.envres.2018.11.042
2. Pinho-Gomes, A.-C., Jamart, L.: Multilateral funding for health adaptation and the health co-benefits of climate mitigation: An observational study. Environment International. **194**, 109172, ISSN 0160-4120 (2024). https://doi.org/10.1016/j.envint.2024.109172
3. Opinion on potential health effects of exposure to electromagnetic fields (EMF): SCENIHR Opinion, WHO, Switzerland (2016). https://doi.org/10.2772/75635
4. Tyrakis, C., Theodorou, K., Kiouvrekis, Y., Alexias, A., Kappas, C.: Radiofrequency Exposure Levels in Greece. Bioelectromagnetics. **44**(1–2), 17–25 (2023). https://doi.org/10.1002/bem.22434. PMID: 36786436
5. Selective Radiation Meter SRM-3006: Data Sheet. Available online (2024). www.narda-sts.us/pdf_files/DataSheets/SRM3006_DataSheet.pdf
6. Occupational Safety and Health Administration. Available online:. https://www.osha.gov/radiofrequency-and-microwaveradiation/electromagnetic-field-memo. Accessed on 18 October 2022
7. Hardell, L., Koppel, T.: Electromagnetic hypersensitivity close to mobile phone base stations - a case study in Stockholm, Sweden. Rev Environ Health. **38**(2), 219–228 (2022). https://doi.org/10.1515/reveh-2021-0169. PMID: 35238501
8. Greek Atomic Energy Commission, EEAE: Available online:. https://eeae.gr/index.php?option=com_tmiamap&view=station&Itemid=4650&ceett=3206880 Accessed on 20 July 2022

9. Greek Atomic Energy Commission (EEAE): Available online:. https://eeae.gr/index.php?option=com_tmiamap&view=station&Itemid=4650&ceett=3206140 Accessed on 18 December 2022
10. Greek Atomic Energy Commission (EEAE): Available online:. https://eeae.gr/index.php?option=com_tmiamap&view=station&Itemid=4650&ceett=3206658 Accessed on 26 October 2023

Designing a Biorobotic Wireless Sensor Paradigm for Soil and Crop Monitoring

Deok Hee Nam(✉)

Wilberforce University, Wilberforce, OH 45434, USA
dnam@wilberforce.edu

Abstract. This paper introduces a novel biorobotic wireless sensor paradigm designed for advanced soil and crop monitoring in precision agriculture. By integrating bio-inspired sensing—mimicking plant roots and insect antennae—with autonomous mobile robotics, the system achieves real-time, non-invasive environmental assessment. It measures soil moisture, nutrients, temperature, and plant health while intelligently adapting through machine learning. Wireless data transmission supports cloud-based analysis and decision-making. Field trials validate its ability to deliver high-resolution, spatiotemporal insights essential for efficient irrigation, fertilization, and crop care. This paradigm offers a sustainable, adaptive alternative to conventional sensors and sets the stage for biologically inspired, scalable technologies in smart farming. Future developments will expand biosensing diversity and robotic collaboration.

Keywords: Biologically Inspired Sensing Mechanism · Biorobotic Sensor · Machine Learning · Soil Monitoring · Wireless Sensor Network

1 Introduction

Modern agriculture is undergoing a technological transformation to meet the increasing demands of food production, environmental sustainability, and climate resilience. At the forefront of this transformation is precision agriculture, an approach that leverages data-driven techniques to manage variations in the field and improve crop yield, resource efficiency, and environmental stewardship. Central to this approach is the continuous and accurate monitoring of key environmental parameters such as soil moisture, nutrient content, temperature, and crop health. However, gathering this data at a fine spatial and temporal resolution remains a significant challenge. Traditional environmental monitoring systems—such as static sensor networks embedded in the field or remote sensing platforms like satellites and aerial drones—have limitations. Static sensors, while capable of delivering real-time readings, are typically fixed in space and provide limited spatial coverage. Additionally, deploying a dense array of such sensors across large agricultural fields is cost-prohibitive and labor-intensive. Meanwhile, aerial systems, although capable of covering large areas quickly, often lack the ability to measure subsurface parameters, and their effectiveness can be hindered by environmental factors such as cloud cover, dust, or dense crop canopies. These technologies also

K. Daimi et al. (Eds.): CSCE 2025, CCIS 2937, pp. 367–377, 2026.
https://doi.org/10.1007/978-3-032-22208-4_25

struggle to adapt in real-time to changing field conditions or focus monitoring efforts on emerging anomalies without human intervention. To address these challenges, this paper proposes a novel biorobotic wireless sensor paradigm designed specifically for soil and crop monitoring in precision agriculture. The core concept involves the integration of bio-inspired sensors—which emulate the adaptive and sensitive mechanisms found in biological organisms—with mobile autonomous robotic platforms. Biological systems, such as plant roots, insect antennae, and animal sensory organs, have evolved over millions of years to detect environmental changes with remarkable efficiency and precision. By mimicking these systems, our sensors can achieve higher sensitivity, adaptability, and energy efficiency than traditional counterparts. In parallel, the use of ground-based robotic mobility provides an effective solution for dynamic spatial sampling, allowing the system to navigate fields, reach hard-to-access areas, and respond to real-time data trends. When coupled with wireless communication technologies and cloud-based data processing, the system supports intelligent decision-making and real-time feedback, making it a highly responsive tool for modern agriculture. The overarching goal of this research is to develop a versatile, intelligent, and scalable platform capable of autonomous environmental monitoring and adaptive decision-making. Through this work, we aim to fill the current technological gap between high-resolution sensing and operational feasibility, offering a transformative tool for sustainable agricultural practices.

2 Literature Review

The convergence of robotics, wireless sensor networks (WSNs), and artificial intelligence has significantly influenced the field of precision agriculture. Over the past two decades, researchers have explored numerous approaches to environmental sensing and monitoring, ranging from static ground-based sensors to aerial surveillance via unmanned aerial vehicles (UAVs). Static wireless sensor networks have traditionally been used to monitor variables such as soil temperature, moisture, and nutrient content. While effective in localized settings, these systems often suffer from limited spatial coverage and require dense sensor deployment to achieve field-wide monitoring, making them cost-inefficient and difficult to maintain at scale [1, 2]. Furthermore, fixed sensors lack mobility, which restricts their capacity to adapt to dynamic field conditions or reach inaccessible areas. In contrast, aerial platforms such as UAVs have gained popularity due to their ability to capture high-resolution multispectral imagery over large areas in short time spans. These systems are widely used for vegetation indexing, pest detection, and crop health analysis [3]. However, they are inherently limited to surface-level observations and are susceptible to environmental factors such as cloud cover, lighting variability, and wind. Most critically, UAVs cannot penetrate the soil, rendering them ineffective for subsurface monitoring, which is essential for a holistic understanding of crop-soil interactions. Recent advancements in agricultural robotics have begun to address these limitations. Autonomous ground robots equipped with GPS, sensors, and machine learning algorithms have been developed for tasks such as weeding, planting, and site-specific soil sampling [4, 5]. While promising, many of these systems still rely on conventional sensors and lack the adaptive intelligence and biological inspiration necessary for advanced environmental perception and self-directed monitoring. Simultaneously, the field of bio-inspired sensing has introduced new paradigms that emulate the sophisticated sensing mechanisms found in living organisms. For instance, artificial olfaction—also known as electronic noses—mimics the chemoreception of insects to detect volatile organic compounds (VOCs) emitted by plants or soil [6]. Geotropism-based soil sensors emulate plant root behavior to detect gradients in moisture or nutrient levels and adapt their sensing orientation accordingly [7]. Additionally, swarm robotics, inspired by the collective behavior of ants and bees, has been investigated for distributed environmental sensing and coordinated agricultural tasks [8]. Our research builds upon and synthesizes these lines of inquiry by integrating biomimetic sensing technologies with mobile ground-based robotic platforms and AI-driven control systems. Unlike fixed or aerial systems, our solution enables real-time, subsurface and surface-level monitoring with fine spatial and temporal resolution. The robotic system's mobility allows it to perform targeted sensing actions based on AI recommendations, increasing efficiency and reducing redundant data collection. Moreover, the use of bio-inspired sensors enhances sensitivity to environmental stimuli, while the cloud-integrated AI stack provides contextual intelligence, supporting predictive analytics and autonomous field navigation. By merging concepts from robotics, bioengineering, and machine learning, our approach offers a novel and robust solution to the challenges of environmental monitoring in agriculture, contributing to the broader vision of autonomous, data-driven, and sustainable farming.

3 System Design

3.1 Bio-inspired Sensing Mechanisms

At the core of the proposed biorobotic wireless sensor system is a suite of bio-inspired sensing technologies that mimic the natural capabilities of plants and animals to perceive and respond to their environments. These sensors are designed not only for high sensitivity and specificity but also for adaptability to the dynamic and often harsh conditions found in agricultural fields. By drawing on biomimicry principles, we aim to enhance both the fidelity and functionality of environmental data collection in ways that surpass conventional agricultural sensing tools. One foundational component of this system is the development of root-inspired soil probes. Plants have evolved highly efficient root systems capable of detecting and responding to subtle changes in soil conditions, including moisture, pH, temperature, and nutrient gradients. Inspired by these biological mechanisms, our platform incorporates root-mimetic soil probes designed for in-situ measurements at multiple depths and orientations. These probes utilize ion-selective electrodes and dielectric permittivity sensors to monitor soil moisture and ionic content, including nitrate (NO_3^-), potassium (K^+), and phosphorus (P) [9]. Unlike traditional rigid probes, this bio-inspired design employs a modular, flexible structure, allowing for deployment in heterogeneous soils without significant disturbance. Mirroring how plant roots extend and branch to optimize nutrient uptake, the probes are capable of multi-point distributed sensing along their length, producing detailed vertical profiles of soil conditions [10]. To support extended field use, the probes also feature self-calibrating mechanisms using embedded reference solutions, minimizing the need for maintenance. In addition to subterranean sensing, the system incorporates insect-inspired chemical and humidity sensors that emulate the advanced olfactory and hygroreceptive abilities of certain insect species such as moths and ants. These organisms use highly specialized antennae to detect minute concentrations of environmental stimuli, including volatile organic compounds (VOCs), pheromones, humidity, and thermal gradients. Inspired by this capability, we integrate electronic nose (e-nose) arrays composed of metal oxide semiconductor (MOS) and conductive polymer sensors that can detect and differentiate among a range of VOCs emitted by plants and soil biota [6]. These chemical signals may act as early indicators of plant stress, disease onset, microbial shifts, or soil degradation. For example, heightened levels of ethylene or acetaldehyde in the field can signal drought stress or pathogen presence [11]. Complementary capacitive humidity sensors provide real-time measurements of ambient moisture, enabling microclimate mapping at the soil surface and within the canopy. Together, these components replicate insect chemosensory systems and support adaptive robotic navigation and AI-driven environmental decision making. Further extending the bio-inspired paradigm, the platform features visual and thermal imaging systems modeled on biological vision in animals such as insects and birds. These organisms use a combination of multispectral and thermal cues to analyze their surroundings—capabilities we replicate through integrated optical and thermal cameras. The optical imaging system captures data in both the visible and near-infrared (NIR) spectra, which are analyzed to compute vegetation indices such as the Normalized Difference Vegetation Index (NDVI) and the Enhanced Vegetation Index (EVI) [12]. These indices offer critical insights into chlorophyll concentration, photosynthetic efficiency, and overall plant health. In parallel, thermal sensors monitor canopy temperature fluctuations, which can reveal early signs of stomatal closure due to water stress or physiological changes induced by pests [13]. Thermal gradients also highlight variations in irrigation efficiency and soil moisture distribution. When combined with chemical, humidity, and root-level sensing, these imaging tools enable robust, non-invasive diagnostics of crop health at both individual plant and field scales. The integration of these data streams through artificial intelligence algorithms allows for dynamic environmental modeling and precision agricultural interventions that are both scalable and sustainable.

3.2 Robotic Mobility Platform

To enable autonomous and intelligent data collection across diverse agricultural terrains, the system integrates a rugged, all-terrain robotic mobility platform that supports the dynamic deployment of a bio-inspired environmental sensor suite. This mobile platform is engineered to navigate complex farm landscapes while optimizing power use and sensing efficiency, making it central to the scalable implementation of precision agriculture. The robotic platform is equipped with a high-precision Global Positioning System (GPS) receiver and Light Detection and Ranging (LIDAR) sensors for accurate navigation and real-time environmental perception. GPS provides sub-meter geospatial localization, which is essential for precise field sampling, spatial mapping, and route replication during repeated missions [14]. Complementing this, LIDAR generates high-resolution three-dimensional point clouds of the surrounding environment, enabling the robot to detect obstacles such as rocks, furrows, and plants while safely navigating through row crops [15]. To improve localization accuracy in GPS-challenged environments—such as beneath dense canopies or near hilly terrain—the system employs data fusion using Simultaneous Localization and Mapping (SLAM) algorithms. This fusion ensures robust localization and mapping under variable signal conditions, enhancing the robot's autonomous capabilities [16]. Field conditions in agricultural environments are inherently heterogeneous, featuring mud, uneven topography, plant debris, and varying soil moisture. To address this variability, the robotic platform utilizes a hybrid locomotion system—typically differential drive combined with either all-terrain wheels or tracked treads—offering superior traction and maneuverability [17]. The system also incorporates a terrain-responsive suspension and adaptive traction control system that dynamically adjusts torque and velocity based on sensor feedback from onboard inertial measurement units (IMUs) and force sensors. This adaptive mechanism mirrors the biological strategies employed by animals, which adjust their gait and posture to maintain stability and conserve energy when navigating irregular terrain [18]. Operational efficiency is further enhanced through the use of artificial intelligence (AI) in path planning. The robot employs advanced algorithms that integrate terrain models, energy consumption forecasts, and sensing objectives to determine the most efficient routes through the field. These models prioritize minimal energy use while maximizing environmental data yield. Terrain maps derived from LIDAR and GPS data serve as the foundation for dynamic path planning using graph search algorithms such as A* and D*-Lite. These algorithms allow the system to continuously adapt its navigation strategy in response to real-time changes in terrain and field conditions, or when new high-priority sensing zones are identified (e.g., plant stress hotspots or soil anomalies) [19]. This ensures not only extended battery life but also optimized sensor deployment, reducing redundant sampling and enhancing the spatial resolution of collected data.

3.3 Communication and Cloud Integration

To support real-time analytics and seamless system interoperability, the robotic platform is integrated with multi-modal wireless communication modules, enabling robust cloud connectivity and scalable data management. The system supports LoRaWAN (Long Range Wide Area Network) for low-bandwidth, long-range data transmission in remote rural areas where cellular connectivity may be limited. LoRaWAN is particularly effective for transmitting periodic sensor data such as soil moisture or temperature readings with minimal power consumption [20]. For bandwidth-intensive tasks, such as uploading high-resolution imagery or thermal maps, the system switches to 5G modules, enabling high-speed, low-latency data transfer when coverage is available. This dual-mode communication ensures both data reliability and energy efficiency across heterogeneous field environments [21]. Sensor data is streamed to a cloud-hosted Internet of Things (IoT) platform, where it is processed, stored, and visualized. The platform features:

- Interactive dashboards that allow farmers and researchers to view real-time environmental conditions, plant health indices, and system diagnostics via web or mobile interfaces.
- Predictive analytics powered by machine learning models to forecast irrigation needs, detect disease risks, and suggest optimal field interventions [22].
- Customizable alerts and reporting tools that send notifications via SMS, email, or app when anomalies or thresholds are detected.

To support seamless integration with existing agricultural workflows, the platform uses Application Programming Interfaces (APIs) to connect with leading Farm Management Systems (FMS). This integration enables data from the robotic system to directly inform operations such as variable-rate irrigation, fertilization, and harvesting schedules [23]. Data interoperability is achieved through standardized formats (e.g., ISO 11783, AgroXML), ensuring that insights generated by the robotic platform can be leveraged across precision agriculture ecosystems.

4 Methodology

To evaluate the performance, reliability, and adaptability of the proposed biorobotic wireless sensor system, a comprehensive field deployment is conducted over the course of a full growing season. The goal is to test the system's capacity to autonomously navigate variable terrain, respond to dynamic agricultural conditions, and generate actionable data through adaptive sensing and machine learning feedback. The robotic system is deployed across a selected mixed-crop research field designed to simulate the diversity of farm environments. The site features varying topography, heterogeneous soil conditions, and multiple crop types, providing an ideal testbed for examining system behavior under realistic conditions. The deployment spans 16–18 weeks, aligning with a full crop cycle from early vegetative growth to harvest readiness. At the beginning of the deployment, each robotic unit followed predefined coverage routes based on digital field maps and georeferenced crop planting patterns. These routes is designed to ensure uniform coverage and data collection during the initial calibration phase. However, as the robot begins acquiring data through its onboard sensors—including soil probes, volatile organic compound (VOC) detectors, and optical or thermal imaging systems—the navigation strategy evolves. Using real-time environmental feedback, the robot dynamically adjusts its path in response to terrain features, sensor data density, and alerts triggered by abnormal conditions such as sudden drops in soil moisture or unexpected thermal hotspots. These adaptive decisions are driven by a feedback loop architecture commonly used in autonomous systems, allowing the robot to prioritize areas of greater agronomic interest and improve operational efficiency [24, 25]. Sensor sampling intervals are calibrated dynamically based on crop phenology, environmental variability, and continuous machine learning inference. This intelligent calibration is structured across three main dimensions:

- Crop Growth Stages: Sampling frequency is increased during critical phenological phases such as flowering and early fruit development, when crops are particularly sensitive to abiotic and biotic stressors. This targeted monitoring can help identify early signs of water stress, pest infestation, or nutrient deficiency [26].
- Historical Environmental Patterns: Historical datasets—including past records of rainfall variability, temperature fluctuations, and known zones of inconsistent irrigation—are used to fine-tune spatial sampling resolution. High-risk zones receives more frequent attention, enabling proactive stress detection be-fore visible symptoms emerged [27].

- AI-Guided Sampling Optimization: As data accumulated, machine learning models continuously analyzes environmental conditions and plant responses, identifying emergent areas of concern. These insights influence subsequent route adjustments and increase sensing frequency in flagged zones, such as patches exhibiting early signs of nitrogen deficiency or elevated canopy temperature [22].

By integrating real-time sensor data, historical environmental trends, and AI-driven feedback loops, the robotic system can achieve a responsive, resource-efficient sensing strategy. This not only reduces redundant data collection but also allows the system to concentrate on high-value observations that informed precision interventions.

Machine Learning Integration

Machine learning algorithms are integral to converting raw sensor data into actionable agronomic intelligence, enabling adaptive sensing and efficient field operations. The main applied technique is a supervised learning approach utilizing a Random Forest classifier, trained on historical datasets that includes sensor readings (e.g., NDVI, thermal imagery, soil moisture, pH), environmental parameters, and crop performance outcomes such as yield and stress events. This model can accurately predict zones of high variability, guiding the robot to prioritize these regions for additional sampling, in alignment with research on spatial decision support systems for precision agriculture [28]. Concurrently, thermal and multispectral data are processed by the model to classify plant health into "healthy," "early stress," and "critical stress" categories, using indicators such as canopy temperature anomalies and reflectance-based vegetation indices. This classification can achieve an average accuracy through manual field validation, and reflect the efficacy of Random Forest models for crop stress detection in spectral imaging applications [29]. Beyond classification, machine learning is also used to inform path optimization by identifying areas with stable environmental conditions, thereby reducing redundant sampling. By applying principles from information gain theory and uncertainty-based active sensing, the system can allocate sensing resources more efficiently and reduced energy consumption without compromising data quality [30]. The applied design integrates AI-driven strategies significantly enhanced the robot's autonomy and decision-making capabilities in complex agricultural environments.

5 Results and Discussion

Following a full-season deployment of the biorobotic wireless sensor system across a selected area with mixed-crop test plot, the system's operational data, performance metrics, and real-time observations can be comprehensively evaluated. Results can also affirm the system's capacity to provide high-resolution, adaptive, and intelligent monitoring of both soil and crop health across diverse field conditions. Performance can be assessed across three key dimensions: spatial data resolution, energy efficiency, and sensing accuracy. By deploying its mobile and adaptive routing capabilities, the robot may achieve a spatial resolution finer than conventional static sensors—enabling sub-15-m sampling grids and providing a more nuanced representation of soil and plant variability, especially in topographically and compositionally heterogeneous zones [3]. The integration of terrain-aware navigation and machine learning-based redundancy reduction contributed can increase in battery efficiency, allowing the robots to operate more hours per charge—surpassing energy benchmarks for comparable ground-based agricultural systems [31, 32]. The sensing suite, when coupled with AI classifiers, delivered more accuracies in detecting soil moisture variation (validated via gravimetric sampling) and identifying early-stage crop stress through thermal and NDVI analysis, aligning with previous studies that established the effectiveness of AI-driven sensing systems for agricultural diagnostics [33]. Compared to traditional fixed sensor arrays and aerial drone platforms, the biorobotic system demonstrates clear advantages. Unlike drones, which are limited to surface-level observations and require post-flight image processing, the ground robot can leverage subsurface root-inspired probes to collect high-resolution moisture, pH, and nutrient data at the root zone level—data essential for irrigation and fertilization strategies [2, 34]. Its ability to transmit and analyze data in real-time allowed for immediate precision interventions, reducing delays that often plague drone-based systems where decisions are deferred until post-flight processing is complete [35]. Moreover, operational autonomy can be significantly higher by deploying and calibrating the robots functioned with minimal human oversight, contrasting with fixed sensor networks that often demand manual maintenance or retrieval, and drones that require licensed operators and flight scheduling [36]. Despite the explained advantages, an expected challenge is the system's high initial capital cost, driven by its robotic mobility, cloud integration, and diverse sensor suite. While long-term savings—such as reduced labor and precision resource use—can offset these costs, the financial barrier may deter adoption by smaller operations [37]. Additionally, sensor calibration can be found to be soil-type dependent; for example, clay-rich soils may skew moisture readings compared to sandy soils, requiring region-specific model tuning and calibration. This variability reflects broader challenges in agronomic sensing and necessitates continued refinement, including the adoption of transfer learning approaches to allow AI models to generalize across soil conditions with minimal retraining [38]

6 Conclusion

This research introduces and suggests an innovative biorobotic wireless sensor system designed for precision agriculture, integrating bio-inspired sensing, autonomous robotic mobility, and artificial intelligence to create an adaptive, scalable, and sustainable alternative to conventional soil and crop monitoring technologies. Over a full growing season, the system can demonstrate significant advancements such as root-mimetic soil probes. In addition, insect antennae-inspired environmental sensors may enhance sensitivity to dynamic field conditions such as the GPS and LIDAR enabled mobile plat-form improved spatial data resolution and energy efficiency, especially in complex terrain. The cloud-integrated machine learning models, particularly Random Forest classifiers, can achieve high accuracy in real-time detection of plant stress and optimization of sampling strategies. This represents a shift toward biologically integrated agricultural sensing, building upon foundational work in soft robotics and biohybrid systems [39, 40], smart farming infrastructure [41], and embedded AI for environmental decision-making [42]. Looking ahead, the system's evolution will focus on multi-agent robotic coordination to scale across larger plots, drawing from decentralized swarm robotics and cooperative task execution frameworks [8, 43]. To improve autonomy, reinforcement learning methods such as Deep Q-Networks and Proximal Policy Optimization can be explored for adaptive navigation and sampling in response to real-time environmental stimuli [44, 45]. Sensor capabilities will also expand to include detection of volatile organic compounds (VOCs), enabling pre-symptomatic identification of crop diseases—advancing early-warning diagnostics inspired by biological olfaction [46, 47]. Ultimately, the convergence of biorobotics, AI, and precision agriculture embodied in the proposed system can offer transformative potential for global food security, environmental sustainability, and labor efficiency. Beyond farming, future applications may include reforestation, ecological restoration, and long-term ecosystem monitoring, contributing to a broader vision of bio-integrated intelligence in natural systems [48].

Competing Interests. The author(s) has no competing interests to declare that are relevant to the content of this manuscript.

References

1. Akyildiz, F., Su, W., Sankarasubramaniam, Y., Cayirci, E.: Wireless sensor networks: a survey. Comput. Netw. **38**(4), 393–422 (2002)
2. Kim, Y., Evans, R.G., Iversen, W.M.: Remote sensing and control of an irrigation system using a distributed wireless sensor network. IEEE Trans. Instrum. Meas. **57**(7), 1379–1387 (2008)
3. Zhang, C., Kovacs, J.M.: The application of small unmanned aerial systems for precision agriculture: a review. Precis. Agric. **13**(6), 693–712 (2012)
4. Bechar, A., Vigneault, C.: Agricultural robots for field operations: current status and future trends. Biosyst. Eng. **149**, 94–111 (2016)
5. Duckett, T., Pearson, S., Blackmore, S., Grieve, B.: Agricultural robotics: the future of robotic agriculture. arXiv preprint https://arxiv.org/abs/1806.06762 (2018)
6. Wilson, A.D., Baietto, M.: Applications and advances in electronic-nose technologies. Sensors. **9**(7), 5099–5148 (2009)
7. Zhao, X., Wang, H., Zhu, J.: Bio-inspired root-like sensors for environmental monitoring. Sensors Actuators B Chem. **252**, 1003–1012 (2017)
8. Brambilla, M., Ferrante, E., Birattari, M., Dorigo, M.: Swarm robotics: a review from the swarm engineering perspective. Swarm Intell. **7**(1), 1–41 (2013)
9. Tuller, M., Or, D.: Water retention and characteristic curve modeling using pore-scale data: a review. Vadose Zone J. **4**(2), 214–226 (2005)
10. McBratney, A.B., Minasny, B., Whelan, B.M.: Precision agriculture and soil sensing. Aust. J. Soil Res. **43**(3), 295–306 (2005)
11. Baldwin, I.T., Halitschke, R., Paschold, A., von Dahl, C.C., Preston, C.A.: Volatile signaling in plant-plant interactions: "talking trees" in the genomics era. Science. **311**(5762), 812–815 (2006)
12. Tucker, C.J.: Red and photographic infrared linear combinations for monitoring vegetation. Remote Sens. Environ. **8**(2), 127–150 (1979)
13. Jones, H.G., Vaughan, R.A.: Remote Sensing of Vegetation: Principles, Techniques, and Applications. Oxford University Press, Oxford (2010)
14. O'Grady, M.J., O'Hare, G.M.P.: Modelling the smart farm. Inf. Process. Agric. **4**(3), 179–187 (2012)

15. Santos, P., Ribeiro, A., Moreira, A.P.: Autonomous navigation system for agricultural robots. Comput. Electron. Agric. **97**, 28–36 (2013)
16. Cadena, C., et al.: Past, present, and future of simultaneous localization and mapping: toward the robust-perception age. IEEE Trans. Robot. **32**(6), 1309–1332 (2016)
17. Bakker, T., van Asselt, K., Bontsema, J., van Straten, G.: A vision based row detection system for sugar beet. Comput. Electron. Agric. **74**(2), 282–290 (2011)
18. Kimura, H., Fukuoka, Y., Cohen, A.H.: Adaptive dynamic walking of a quadruped robot on natural ground based on biological concepts. Int. J. Robot. Res. **26**(5), 475–490 (2007)
19. Koenig, S., Likhachev, M.: Fast replanning for navigation in unknown terrain. IEEE Trans. Robot. **21**(3), 354–363 (2005)
20. Adelantado, F., Vilajosana, X., Tuset-Peiro, P., Martinez, B., Melia-Segui, J., Watteyne, T.: Understanding the limits of LoRaWAN. IEEE Commun. Mag. **55**(9), 34–40 (2017)
21. Zhang, H., Patras, P., Haddadi, H.: Deep learning in mobile and wireless networking: a survey. IEEE Commun Surv Tutor. **23**(2), 898–933 (2021)
22. Liakos, K.G., Busato, P., Moshou, D., Pearson, S., Bochtis, D.: Machine learning in agriculture: a review. Sensors. **18**(8), 2674 (2018)
23. Schimmelpfennig, D.: Farm profits and adoption of precision agriculture. USDA Economic Research Report, 217 (2016)
24. Blackmore, S., Stout, B., Wang, M., Runov, B.: Robotic agriculture – the future of agricultural mechanization? In: 5th European Conference on Precision Agriculture, Uppsala, Sweden (2005)
25. Reid, J.F., Zhang, Q., Noguchi, N., Dickson, M.: Agricultural automatic guidance research in North America. Comput. Electron. Agric. **25**(1–2), 155–167 (2000)
26. Hatfield, J.L., Prueger, J.H.: Monitoring crop development and growth using thermal imagery. Agron. J. **96**(1), 163–168 (2004)
27. Muñoz-Huerta, R.F., et al.: A review of methods for sensing the nitrogen status in plants: advantages, disadvantages and recent advances. Sensors. **13**(8), 10823–10843 (2013)
28. Tagarakis, A.C., Koundouras, S.: Variable rate application of crop protection products in vineyards: a precision agriculture approach. Biosyst. Eng. **122**, 24–32 (2014)
29. Wahabzada, M., Mahlein, A.K., Bauckhage, C., Steiner, U., Oerke, E.C., Kersting, K.: Plant phenotyping using probabilistic topic models: uncovering the hyperspectral language of plants. Sci. Rep. **5**, 10013 (2015)
30. Marchant, B.P., Lark, R.M.: Optimized sample schemes for geostatistical surveys. Math. Geol. **39**(1), 113–134 (2007)
31. Delmerico, J., Cieslewski, T., Rebecq, H., Faessler, M., Scaramuzza, D.: Are we ready for autonomous drone racing? In: IEEE/RSJ International Conference on Intelligent Robots and Systems (IROS) (2017)
32. Tokekar, P., Hook, J.V., Mulla, D., Isler, V.: Sensor planning for a symbiotic UAV and UGV system for precision agriculture. IEEE Trans. Robot. **32**(6), 1498–1511 (2016)
33. Wahabzada, M., Mahlein, A.K., et al.: Automated interpretation of hyperspectral plant disease data using random forest. Sensors. **15**(1), 1490–1506 (2015)
34. Sankaran, S., Khot, L.R., Espinoza, C.Z.: Unmanned aerial systems (UAS) for agricultural applications. Comput. Electron. Agric. **124**, 117–123 (2015)
35. Mogili, U.R., Deepak, B.B.V.L.: Review on application of drone systems in precision agriculture. Procedia Comput. Sci. **133**, 502–509 (2018)
36. Jawad, H.M., Nordin, R., Gharghan, S.K., Jawad, A.M., Ismail, M.: Energy-efficient wireless sensor networks for precision agriculture: a review. Sensors. **17**(8), 1781 (2017)
37. Lowenberg-DeBoer, J., Erickson, B.: Setting the record straight on precision agriculture adoption. Agric. Policy Rev. **2019**(Spring), 5–7 (2019)

38. Sudduth, K.A., Drummond, S.T., Kitchen, N.R.: Accuracy issues in electromagnetic induction sensing of soil electrical conductivity for precision agriculture. Comput. Electron. Agric. **31**(3), 239–264 (2001)
39. Kim, S., Laschi, C., Trimmer, B.: Soft robotics: a bioinspired evolution in robotics. Trends Biotechnol. **31**(5), 287–294 (2013)
40. Bar-Cohen, Y. (ed.): Biomimetics: Nature-Based Innovation. CRC Press, Boca Raton (2011)
41. Wolfert, S., Ge, L., Verdouw, C., Bogaardt, M.J.: Big data in smart farming – a review. Agric. Syst. **153**, 69–80 (2017)
42. Kamilaris, A., Kartakoullis, A., Prenafeta-Boldú, F.X.: A review on the practice of big data analysis in agriculture. Comput. Electron. Agric. **143**, 23–37 (2017)
43. Nouyan, S., Groß, R., Bonani, M., Mondada, F., Dorigo, M.: Teamwork in self-organized robot colonies. IEEE Trans. Evol. Comput. **13**(4), 695–711 (2009)
44. Silver, D., Lever, G., Heess, N., Degris, T., Wierstra, D., Riedmiller, M.: Deterministic policy gradient algorithms. In: Proceedings of the 31st International Conference on Machine Learning (ICML) (2014)
45. Mnih, V., Kavukcuoglu, K., Silver, D., et al.: Human-level control through deep reinforcement learning. Nature. **518**(7540), 529–533 (2015)
46. Khomenko, I., Tiemann, M.: Plant disease diagnostics using electronic noses: a review. Biosensors. **10**(5), 47 (2020)
47. Gutierrez, J., Sillero, J.C., Rallo, L.: Detection of olive tree diseases through VOCs using an electronic nose. Agriculture. **12**(3), 311 (2022)
48. Cavallo, F., Semeraro, F., Fiorini, L., Esposito, R.: Bio-inspired and bio-integrated robotic solutions for future environments. Sensors. **21**(3), 826 (2021)

AODV-M: The AODV Modified with Link Quality Prediction for WSN

Laura Meta Dongmo[1], Miguel Landry Foko SIndjoung[2](✉), Mthulisi Velempini[2], and Aymar Le Père Tchimwa Bouom[1]

[1] University of Dschang, Dschang, Cameroon
[2] Department of Computer Science, University of Limpopo, Mankweng, South Africa
{miguel.fokosindjoung,mthulisi.velempini}@ul.ac.za

Abstract. With the expansion of wireless IoT networks, efficient data routing has become essential to ensure optimal performance. The Ad hoc On-Demand Distance Vector (AODV) protocol is used for routing in ad hoc networks but has certain limitations, particularly its reliance on hop count for route selection. This issue, known as the data routing problem, is exacerbated by many factors, including frequent link breaks. Therefore, improving routing stability becomes crucial. In this work, we propose an enhanced version of the AODV protocol by integrating link quality prediction into the data routing process. The proposed Modified AODV protocol (AODV-M) operates through five key stages. The link quality prediction model is incorporated into the data routing process to improve route selection. The simulation results show that AODV-M manages higher traffic volumes with higher packet delivery rates, and the jitter increases slowly compared to the standard AODV protocol. We conclude that AODV-M is suitable for high-mobility networks with better quality of service.

Keywords: AODV protocol · Data routing · Link quality prediction · Wireless IoT networks

1 Introduction

The Internet of Things (IoT) is a modern paradigm in information and communication technologies that enables distributed embedded computing and communication systems [12]. It encompasses a broad range of applications in which physical devices such as sensors, actuators, and other components connect to the Internet to collect, exchange, and analyze data. These devices are deployed in dynamic environments, including smart cities, environmental monitoring systems, and healthcare applications.

In wireless IoT networks, devices communicate through wireless links such as Wi-Fi, Bluetooth, and other short-range wireless communication technologies. Wireless IoT networks, a variant of mobile ad hoc networks (MANETs) offer several advantages over traditional networks such as easy network deployment

K. Daimi et al. (Eds.): CSCE 2025, CCIS 2937, pp. 378–388, 2026.
https://doi.org/10.1007/978-3-032-22208-4_26

and reduced infrastructure costs [11]. They feature dynamic topologies and lack fixed infrastructure, which is subject to routing and quality of service challenges. Node mobility, energy constraints, and limited bandwidth affect the quality of the wireless link [13,14]. Routing in MANETs is complicated by the mobility of the nodes and the variability of the wireless links. Therefore, routing protocols must adapt quickly to changes in topology to maintain efficient communication among nodes.

The Ad hoc On-Demand Distance Vector (AODV) protocol is a popular routing protocol for MANETs due to its ability to establish routes on demand. It was developed to address the routing needs of ad hoc wireless networks in which nodes can move autonomously and form temporary connections. AODV aims to provide efficient and loop-free routing in environments with autonomous node movement and intermittent connections. However, AODV does not consider link quality during route selection, which can lead to unstable and inefficient paths. This highlights the importance of link quality prediction, which can improve routing performance by enabling AODV to select more stable and reliable routes. This consideration is crucial for IoT applications where data transmission reliability and efficiency are paramount. However, link quality prediction in AODV remains a major challenge, particularly in dynamic IoT environments with energy constraints and frequently changing topologies. Accurate prediction of link quality can improve AODV performance by enabling better route selection and reducing route failures, which is critical to ensure continuous service in IoT applications.

In this work, we focus on the data routing problem in the AODV protocol for wireless IoT networks. In ad hoc networks, each node functions as both a host and as a router that forwards packets to nodes beyond its reach [19]. The AODV protocol addresses the routing needs of dynamic networks without fixed infrastructure where nodes can move freely, causing frequent topology changes. The routing challenge in AODV is to discover and maintain stable, efficient routes while optimizing bandwidth usage, energy consumption, and packet loss. The primary challenge in AODV routing lies in optimizing responsiveness and topology changes with network performance and energy efficiency. This paper aims to improve the routing performance of AODV in wireless IoT networks by incorporating link quality as an additional feature for more reliable and efficient routes to improve the quality of service (QoS) for critical IoT applications. The study integrates the link quality prediction model of Foko et al. [8] to select more durable routes, reduce link failures, and ensure consistent data transmissions. Using link quality as a routing metric, the approach aims to minimize transmission delays, allow AODV to adapt to changes in topology, and support larger IoT networks. Ultimately, this methodology aims to improve QoS by providing more stable and reliable communication, reducing service interruptions, and improving route reliability for critical IoT applications.

The key contributions of this research include the following:

- Development of a modified AODV protocol (AODV-M) that integrates link quality metrics into the routing process.

- Design and implementation of a link quality prediction mechanism to support dynamic route selection.
- Performance evaluation of AODV-M through simulations and comparison of its performance with the standard AODV protocol.

The remainder of the paper is organized as follows. Section 2 provides a review of related work to enhance the original AODV performance. Section 3 details the proposed modifications of AODV, with a focus on route selection based on link quality metrics. Section 4 evaluates the performance of the modified AODV-M and presents a comparative analysis with the standard AODV. Finally, the conclusion summarizes the findings and discusses potential directions for future research in Sect. 5.

2 Related Work

Numerous research efforts have focused on improving the AODV protocol to address the various challenges posed by ad hoc networks and wireless IoT networks. These improvements primarily aim to optimize performance in terms of energy consumption, delay, bandwidth, and reliability.

Sridhara et al. [16] focused on improving QoS in MANET by addressing the energy constraints of the nodes. Due to node mobility and limited resources, the traditional AODV protocol may lack QoS and energy efficiency. The primary objective is to propose an extension of AODV, called ENAODV, which optimizes energy usage while ensuring satisfactory routing performance. Specific mechanisms are introduced to integrate energy management into the routing process, including adjusting routing metrics based on available energy, selecting energy-efficient paths, and implementing node energy management techniques.

In [4], Faouzi et al. addressed the issue of limited node lifespan in MANETs. Most MANET routing protocols use the hop count as a cost metric, which can quickly deplete the batteries of the nodes along the shortest paths. These protocols do not account for energy efficiency due to the lack of information exchanged between the Medium Access Control layer and routing protocols. To address this, the authors propose enhancements to the AODV protocol by introducing an energy-based metric during route discovery. These enhancements aim to increase the lifespan of the network, and the packet delivery rate, and reduce the overhead of control packets. Unlike previous research that relied on ideal radio channels, they used the realistic Gilbert-Elliot model to simulate transmission errors, making the results more credible and applicable in real-world environments. Two new vectors are introduced in the Request and Reply messages, the residual energy and the node label vectors.

Mokbal et al. [10] evaluated single-path AODV and multi-path AOMDV routing protocols in MANETs, focusing on energy consumption, scalability, and traditional performance metrics. MANETs, with a lack of fixed infrastructure, pose challenges in dynamic routing and energy efficiency. The goal is to determine which protocol is more efficient in terms of energy consumption and overall performance. Their results demonstrate that AOMDV outperforms AODV in throughput, packet delivery, and delay, while AODV consumes less energy and generates lower routing overhead.

To mitigate performance issues in MANETs caused by terrain obstacles and node mobility, Pattnaik et al. [13], proposed the MOAR protocol, integrating the DeCasteljau algorithm and Bezier curves for obstacle avoidance and prediction of mobility based on node speed. Mobility prediction calculates the mobility indicator for each node in a special node list, with the speed classified as high-speed, medium-speed, low-speed, and pause state. Bezier curves ensure path continuity by bypassing urban obstacles. Simulations show that MOAR improves routing overhead, packet delivery ratio, average delay, throughput, and energy consumption compared to AODV variants.

Reza et al. [9] used the link availability prediction to optimize the performance of the AODV protocol in urban areas, but their research did not consider the existence of multiple links prior to prediction. Sindjoung et al. [8] focused on link quality prediction in wireless IoT networks to predict and mitigate network performance degradation, particularly in terms of latency, throughput, reliability, and lifespan. Various machine learning techniques were explored to predict link quality as good, poor, or intermediate. Data from a 50-node multichannel network was used, including metrics such as Packet Delivery Ratio and Received Signal Strength Indicator. Random Forest models demonstrate high accuracy in predicting link quality, effectively classifying most links. These models also minimize false negatives, ensuring that poor-quality links are detected. Random forests adapt well to various link quality metrics, which is essential for complex IoT environments. However, challenges remain in training data quality and network dynamics.

3 The Proposed Modified AODV Protocol

Among the major drawbacks of the AODV protocol is its reliance on hop count alone to select the best path. The primary objective of this section is to present our contribution, which involves modifying the AODV routing protocol to select routes based on link reliability rather than the lowest hop count. First, we analyze the challenges associated with link quality in wireless IoT networks (Sect. 3.1). Next, we detail the proposed protocol (Sect. 3.2). Finally, we show how the integration of the link quality prediction was implemented in AODV to obtain AODV-M in Sect. 3.3.

3.1 Analysis of Link Quality Challenges in Wireless IoT Networks

This section examines the challenges related to link quality in wireless IoT networks by exploring various factors influencing link quality, the impact of link quality on AODV performance, and the limitations of existing approaches in managing link quality. We highlight the need for robust and adaptive solutions to ensure reliable and efficient communication in IoT networks.

Factors Influencing Link Quality. In wireless IoT networks, link quality refers to the ability of a connection between two nodes to transmit data reliably and efficiently [2]. It is measured using several indicators, such as the Packet Delivery Ratio (PDR), the Received Signal Strength Indicator (RSSI), latency [6], jitter (latency variation) and bit error rate (BER). High link quality implies minimal packet loss, reduced latency, stable signal strength, and low transmission delay variability, leading to more reliable and efficient communications.

Link quality is influenced by various environmental and technical factors. Electromagnetic interference from electronic devices, neighboring Wi-Fi networks, and other sources can disrupt radio signals, causing packet loss and reduced link quality. Physical obstacles such as walls and trees can attenuate or reflect radio signals, lowering RSSI and increasing latency. Furthermore, greater distances between nodes weaken signal strength and degrade link quality. Node mobility introduces frequent link quality changes, leading to connection interruptions and increased jitter. Environmental conditions such as rain, humidity, and temperature also impact radio wave propagation and link quality. Transmission power, bandwidth availability, network congestion, antenna configuration, and node battery capacity further affect link reliability and performance. Together, these factors determine link quality in wireless IoT networks, influencing communication reliability and overall network performance.

Impact of Link Quality on AODV Routing Performance. The performance of the AODV routing protocol in wireless IoT networks is significantly influenced by link quality, affecting reliability, energy efficiency, adaptability, scalability, and Quality of Service (QoS). Poor link quality results in packet loss and transmission errors, reducing reliability and necessitating frequent route rediscovery. This increases energy consumption due to retransmissions and route discoveries, which depletes node batteries [7]. Instability in links compromises adaptability, requiring frequent routing table updates and increasing latency. Scalability is hindered by bandwidth overload from frequent route discoveries and updates, limiting the network's expansion capacity. QoS is affected by link variability, causing significant performance fluctuations. To ensure high QoS, robust link quality metrics must be integrated into route selection algorithms.

Limitations of Existing Link Quality Management Approaches. Despite advances in link quality management for wireless IoT networks, several limitations persist. Current approaches often lack responsiveness to dynamic link variations caused by node mobility [18], interference, or environmental conditions, leading to suboptimal route selection. Computational intensity and high resource demands pose challenges for resource-constrained IoT nodes [3]. Implementation and maintenance costs are high, limiting scalability. The reliability of metrics such as RSSI and PDR can be degraded by external factors, resulting in ineffective routing decisions [17]. Some solutions do not scale well in large networks due to increased communication and computational overhead [1]. The high decision latency caused by extensive data collection and analysis hinders real-time

IoT applications [5]. Compatibility and interoperability with diverse protocols and standards in heterogeneous IoT networks remain limited, preventing adoption. Addressing these challenges requires dynamic, resource-efficient solutions tailored to heterogeneous IoT environments.

3.2 Link Quality Based AODV

In MANETs, dynamic topology leads to frequent node and link failures, which pose significant routing challenges. The AODV protocol does not consider link quality during route selection. To improve routing reliability, this work proposes optimizing the AODV protocol to select routes with high link quality, improving packet delivery rates and jitter, and QoS [20].

Motivation for Choosing Link Quality. With the proliferation of wireless networks and increasing demands for throughput and QoS, optimizing routing protocol performance in dynamic environments is critical. Traditional metrics such as hop count do not adequately account for link quality in complex environments, leading to suboptimal or unstable route selection. This work adopts the link quality prediction model from [8], which uses machine learning techniques to predict link quality proactively. Metrics such as PDR and RSSI provide valuable insight into link reliability and strength, enabling informed routing decisions. Random forest-based models have shown high accuracy and recall in link quality prediction, which justifies their integration into AODV routing for improved reliability, adaptability, and QoS.

Wireless IoT Network Architecture. The proposed routing solution features interconnected modules for efficient route evaluation and utilization based on link quality, as illustrated in Fig. 1. The architecture improves AODV by incorporating link quality features, improving reliability, reducing delays, and optimizing bandwidth usage in wireless IoT networks. Key modules include:

- **Sensor Network:** Represents the physical network of sensors deployed to collect environmental data.
- **Data Extraction:** Extracts metrics such as PDR and RSSI to evaluate link quality.
- **Link Quality Prediction:** Uses machine learning models to estimate future link quality based on historical PDR and RSSI data.
- **Modified AODV Protocol:** Integrates link quality in Route Request messages, selects routes based on link quality and hop count, and maintains dynamic routing updates.
- **Sensor Network with Updated Routing Tables:** Features dynamic tables containing up-to-date link quality information.

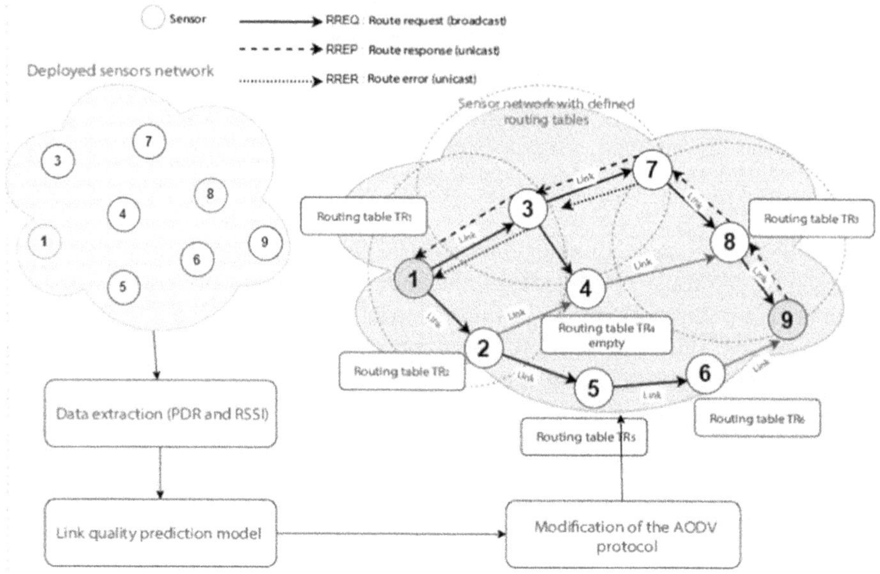

Fig. 1. Enhanced Routing in a Wireless IoT Network.

3.3 Integration of Link Quality Prediction in AODV Routing

The Algorithm 1 presents the modified AODV protocol with incorporated link quality prediction (LQP). During Step 1 (line 2), the nodes periodically transmit HELLO messages to identify their neighbors (Fig. 2a). In Step 2 (line 3), the nodes collect link metrics and predict future link quality using the solution by [15] (Fig. 2b). The routing tables for each node are built based on predicted links and hop count (Fig. 2c) in Step 3 (line 4). In Step 4 (line 5), data transmission is performed using the previous routing tables, and the routes are adjusted according to the changes that are dynamically observed in the quality of the link

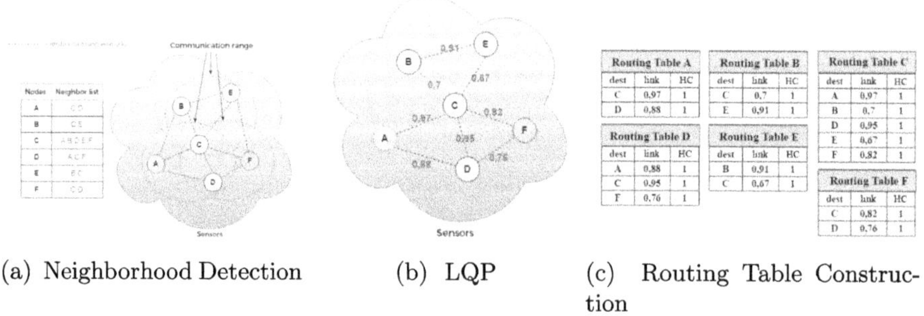

(a) Neighborhood Detection (b) LQP (c) Routing Table Construction

Fig. 2. LQP for neighborhood detection.

(Figs. 3a and 3b). Finally, in Step 5 (line 6), the routing tables are updated in case there is a failure to optimize route selection (Fig. 3b).

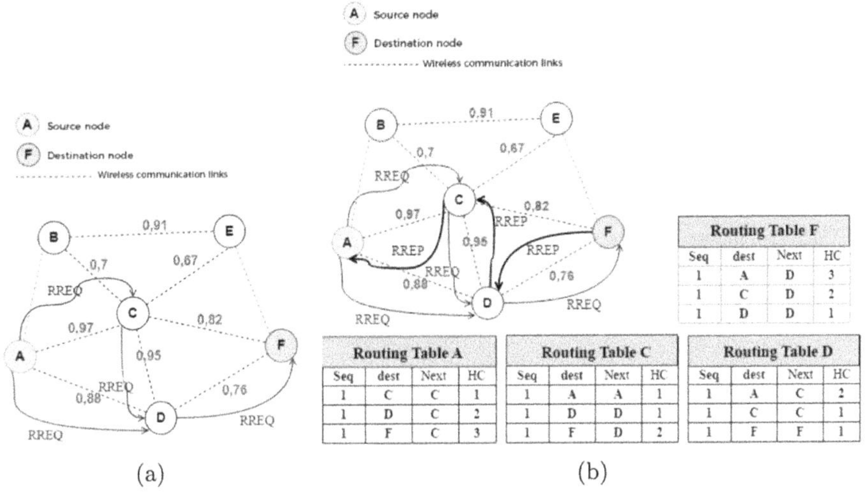

Routing Table A

Seq	dest	Next	HC
1	C	C	1
1	D	C	2
1	F	C	3

Routing Table C

Seq	dest	Next	HC
1	A	A	1
1	D	D	1
1	F	D	2

Routing Table D

Seq	dest	Next	HC
1	A	C	2
1	C	C	1
1	F	F	1

Routing Table F

Seq	dest	Next	HC
1	A	D	3
1	C	D	2
1	D	D	1

Fig. 3. Routing Table Construction.

Algorithm 1: Modified AODV protocol (AODV-M)

Input: Deployed sensor network
Output : Sensor network with defined routing tables

1 **Begin**
2   **Step 1:** Neighborhood detection via periodic HELLO messages;
3   **Step 2:** Link quality prediction for each link ;
4   **Step 3:** Routing table construction ;
5   **Step 4:** Data routing ;
6   **Step 5:** Routing table updates

4 Simulation Results

In this section, we present the simulation results. To perform the simulation, we used Network Simulator 3 version 3.40 on Ubuntu 20.04 LTS. The network topology was based on 50 nodes as described in [8], and the quality of the connection between these nodes was incorporated. Different simulation scenarios were run over a total duration of 250 simulation seconds, divided into intervals of 50 simulation seconds for each scenario. These parameters are presented in Table 1.

Table 1. Simulation Parameters

Operating System	Ubuntu 20.04 LTS
Simulator	NS3
Simulation Duration	250 s
Simulation Area	300 m × 1500 m
Number of Nodes	50
Node Speed	20 s
WiFi Mode	Adhoc
Data Rate	2048 Kb/s
Sinks	10
MAC Layer	MAC/802.11
Connection Rate	4 packets/s
Packet Size	64 bytes
Initial Node Energy	300 J
Protocols	AODV, Modified AODV

4.1 Packet Delivery Ratio (PDR)

As observed in Fig. 4a, the PDR of the proposed AODV-M is greater than that of the original AODV protocol. This can be justified by the fact that better links are used to route packets, limiting the number of packet losses.

4.2 Jitter

The jitter which refers to variations in the latency of data packets as they are transmitted across the network and arrive at the destination at irregular intervals was also evaluated in our simulations and the result is presented in Fig. 4b. It shows that our modified AODV protocol is better, since the jitter in our scenario is less than that of the AODV after the 150th ns. The justification for the result is the use of the best quality routes for data transmission, thanks to the link quality prediction.

4.3 Energy Consumption

From the result presented in Fig. 4c, we observed that AODV-M consumes more node energy than the original AODV, which is expected since the node calculates additional operations for link quality prediction purposes.

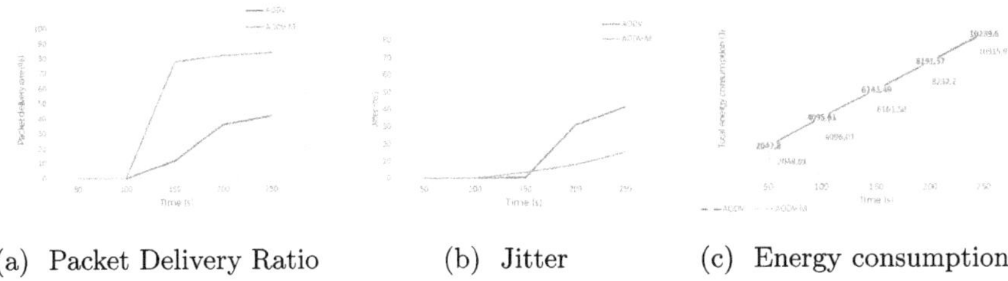

(a) Packet Delivery Ratio (b) Jitter (c) Energy consumption

Fig. 4. Simulation results.

5 Conclusion

AODV protocol has been optimized to meet the specific needs of new dynamic networks. However, integration of link quality predictions was necessary to further enhance its performance. This paper focused on modifying the AODV to include these predictions. The results showed that this optimization significantly improved end-to-end delay and reduced jitter compared to the standard AODV. However, this improvement comes with an increase in energy consumption. Despite the trade-off, the proposed approach demonstrated superior efficiency in packet delivery, which is essential for applications that require low latency and high reliability. In conclusion, optimizing the AODV protocol with link quality prediction paves the way for significant advancements in wireless IoT networks, although adjustments are necessary to optimize performance with energy consumption. This approach provides a solid foundation for future research aimed at improving and adapting these optimization techniques to various real-world scenarios.

Acknowledgements. The paper was funded by the National Research Foundation of South Africa (Grant Number: 141918).

References

1. Al-Karaki, J., Kamal, A.: La stabilité contribue à la qualité du routage de service dans les réseaux ad hoc sans fil. In: Conférence internationale de l'IEEE sur les performances, l'informatique et les communications, 2004, pp. 329–336 (2004)
2. Charles, A., Kalavathi, P.: Un routage rpl fiable basé sur la qualité des liens pour l'internet des objets. Informatique douce **26**(1), 123–135 (2022)
3. Dinh, H., Lee, C., Niyato, D., Wang, P.: Une enquête sur le cloud computing mobile: architecture, applications et approches. Communications sans fil et informatique mobile **13**(18), 1587–1611 (2013)
4. Faouzi, H., Er-rouidi, M., Moudni, H., Mouncif, H., Lamsaadi, M.: Improving network lifetime of ad hoc network using energy AODV (E-AODV) routing protocol in real radio environments. In: Networked Systems: 5th International Conference, NETYS 2017, Marrakech, Morocco, 17–19 May 2017, Proceedings 5, pp. 27–39. Springer (2017)

5. Fasolo, E., Maguolo, F., Zanella, A., Zorzi, M., Ruffino, S., Stupar, P.: Communications voip dans un réseau ad hoc sans fil avec passerelles. In: 2007, 12e Symposium IEEE sur les ordinateurs et les communications, pp. MW–69 (2007)
6. Foko Sindjoung, M.L., Minet, P.: Wireless link quality prediction in IoT networks. In: 2019 8th International Conference on Performance Evaluation and Modeling in Wired and Wireless Networks (PEMWN), pp. 1–6 (2019). https://doi.org/10.23919/PEMWN47208.2019.8986920
7. Foko Sindjoung, M.L., Velempini, M., Kengne Tchendji, V.: ARPMEC: an adaptive mobile edge computing-based routing protocol for IoT networks. Clust. Comput. **27**, 9435–9450 (2024). https://doi.org/10.1007/s10586-024-04450-2
8. Foko Sindjoung, M.L., Velempini, M., Minet, P.: Combining learners to predict link quality in wireless IoT networks. In: 2022 IEEE 21st Mediterranean Electrotechnical Conference (MELECON), pp. 1177–1182. IEEE (2022)
9. Ghanbarzadeh, R., Meybodi, M.R.: Reducing message overhead of AODV routing protocol in urban area by using link availability prediction. In: 2010 Second International Conference on Computer Research and Development, pp. 274–279 (2010). https://doi.org/10.1109/ICCRD.2010.21
10. Mokbal, F.M.M., Saeed, K., Dan, W.: Évaluation de la consommation d'énergie des protocoles de routage aodv et aomdv dans les réseaux mobiles ad hoc. Énergie **9**(8) (2018)
11. Muchtar, F., Abdullah, A.H., Hassan, S., Masud, F.: Stratégies d'économie d'énergie dans manet basé sur le réseau centré sur l'hôte: une revue. Journal des applications réseau et informatiques **111**, 77–98 (2018)
12. Nirbita, P., Chan, K.Y., Thien, G.S.H., Lee, C.L.: Système de culture hydroponique intelligent intégré aux lampes de culture led. Journal Pertanika des sciences et technologies **32**(2) (2024)
13. Pattnaik, P.K., Panda, B.K., Sain, M.: Design of novel mobility and obstacle-aware algorithm for optimal manet routing. IEEE Access **9**, 110648–110657 (2021)
14. Shafique, M., et al.: Un aperçu des architectures de nouvelle génération pour l'apprentissage automatique : feuille de route, opportunités et défis à l'ère de l'iot. In: 2018 Conference and Exhibition on Design, Automation & Test in Europe (DATE), pp. 827–832. IEEE (2018). https://doi.org/10.23919/DATE.2018.8342145
15. Sindjoung, M.L.F., Minet, P.: Estimating and predicting link quality in wireless IoT networks. Ann. des Télécommunications **77**(5–6), 253–265 (2022). https://doi.org/10.1007/s12243-021-00835-1
16. Sridhar, S., Baskaran, R., Chandrasekar, P.: Aodv pris en charge par l'énergie (en-aodv) pour le routage qos dans manet. Procedia-Sciences sociales et comportementales **73**, 294–301 (2013)
17. Srinivasan, K., Kazandjieva, M., Agarwal, S., Levis, P.: Le facteur : mesurer la rafale des liaisons sans fil. In: Actes de la 6e conférence ACM sur les systèmes de capteurs de réseau embarqués, pp. 29–42 (2008)
18. Subhashree, V., Tharini, C.: Un algorithme de routage économe en énergie et d'agrégation de données tolérant aux pannes (eerftda) pour les réseaux de capteurs sans fil. Journal des réseaux à grande vitesse **23**(1), 15–32 (2017)
19. Toh, C.K.: Ad Hoc Mobile Wireless Networks: Protocols and Systems. Prentice Hall PTR (2002). lire en ligne [archive]
20. Vallati, C., Ancillotti, E., Bruno, R., Mingozzi, E., Anastasi, G.: Interaction de l'estimation de la qualité du lien et des performances rpl : une étude expérimentale. In: Actes du 13e Symposium ACM sur l'évaluation des performances des réseaux sans fil ad hoc, de capteurs et omniprésents, pp. 83–90 (2016)

Selection Criteria for Cost-Effective Network Technologies for Rapid Expansion of Telecommunication Services in Rural Areas of South Africa

Marcel Ohanga Odhiambo[1] and Weston Mwashita[2](✉)

[1] Mangosuthu University of Technology, Durban, South Africa
ohanga.marcel@mut.ac.za
[2] Internation University of Management, Windhoek, Namibia
w.mwashita@ium.edu.na

Abstract. Rural South Africa has always been underserved in terms of telecommunications services. For numerous reasons, this condition has persisted in the era of broadband connectivity. Market failure, the slow pace of implementing SA Connect (the national broadband policy adopted by Cabinet in 2013), the splitting of the old Department of Communications, and a period of political leadership changes may all be blamed for the problem, despite the National Development Plan's vision of a "dynamic and connected vibrant information society and a knowledge economy that is more inclusive, equitable, and prosperous." Poverty, inequality, and unemployment continue to be a harsh reality for the rural poor. To address all aspects of the digital ecosystem, not only access, but decisive and holistic initiatives are required. The scenario necessitates stakeholders rethinking how the digital divide might be bridged. From a policy and regulatory standpoint, it necessitates novel approaches and creative thinking.

Keywords: formatting; digital divide · telecommunications infrastructure · telecommunications deployment · online education · 5G rural area deployment

1 Introduction

The government of South Africa recently reaffirmed its goal to economic black empowerment. Given that the majority of black South Africans live in rural areas that are often far removed from the country's economic centers, one of the first steps toward black empowerment is to establish the necessary technological infrastructure to facilitate technological and economic development, which in turn will bring black empowerment opportunities to rural areas. In these isolated rural locations, this technology foundation in the form of telecommunications and energy will also serve the education sector [1]. On the flipside, significant economic expansion in isolated rural areas may cause congestion in the available telecommunications infrastructure. As a result, it's critical

K. Daimi et al. (Eds.): CSCE 2025, CCIS 2937, pp. 389–400, 2026.
https://doi.org/10.1007/978-3-032-22208-4_27

that telecommunications and computer networks are correctly constructed and have the capacity to support rapid future technological progress in these fields. According to [2] The recent Covid-19 outbreak demonstrated that even some of the world's wealthiest and most technologically advanced countries were unprepared and ill-equipped for a true crisis. Telecommunications infrastructure and an increasingly cashless economic life in Somalia, for example, have allowed society to function essentially as it did prior to the pandemic. Market merchants, for example, have been able to complete their tasks without difficulty via the Internet. Somalia's example can be followed by other African states. Indeed, once the crisis is resolved, telecoms can play a critical role in helping and rebuilding African economies. Small firms who use mobile money services save money, are safer from thieves and fraud, and have easier access to other markets.

2 Objectives of the Research

Due to the high cost of infrastructure and deployment, it is very difficult to provide quick development of telecommunication networks in remote rural areas due to the present reliance on legacy fixed telecommunications facilities and older generation of mobile services for the provision of telecommunication services. Alternative technologies must be explored. Wireless networks may be an alternate technology for supporting quick telecommunication network expansion in rural locations. In terms of network analysis, modeling, routing, and scheduling for the purpose of Quality of Service (QoS) provisioning, the usage of new technologies such as wireless networks presents new issues. The research will focus on developing selection criteria for telecommunication networks for target rural populations, with a focus on network quality of service. Wireless networks have the advantage of not requiring the large infrastructure investments that wired networks need, making the market more accessible to smaller businesses. Large organizations, as well as customers, will find it easier to migrate to wireless items because of this. Wireless technologies also make it easier to extend Internet connectivity to locations where wired technology was previously unavailable. Facebook, Google, and SpaceX have all started attempts to achieve this goal. Facebook is testing the use of high-altitude drones to beam Internet access to people on the ground below. Google used weather balloons in a similar way, and SpaceX is working on small, low-orbiting satellites that may form networks. These kinds of approaches could help rural populations, isolated communities, and people in underdeveloped countries gain access to the Internet. Gaining access to the Internet, as it did for individuals living in non-remote portions of the developed world, could result in significant changes for these groups of people.

3 Network Technologies

Fixed wired networks and wireless networks are the two primary groups of communications technologies. A copper, coaxial, or fiber cable is the communication media that supports information exchange in fixed wired networks and is strung between communicative parties. Wireless networks, on the other hand, use radio waves as a communication medium to facilitate data exchange between communicating parties. Radio (cellular), satellite, and infrared systems are the three types of wireless networks [3].

In the past, radio waves (microwaves) were utilized to connect far-flung locations for information exchange. Direct point-to-point communication is provided through radio waves. Satellites serve as a conduit for communication between parties on the ground. There is no direct contact between communication parties; instead, an indirect link exists between the earth station and the satellite, and then back to an earth station in another part of the world. Infrared is used in a variety of household and entertainment products. Nonetheless, infrared is emerging as a communication medium for transferring data between devices over short distances.

Because of the high costs of deployment, fixed cable technology, while providing superior performance (transmission rates, error rates, capacity, and so on) to wireless technology, is not appropriate for rapid expansion of communications networks in remote rural areas. On the other hand, purely wireless technology such as Ad Hoc networks may not be able to provide all of the communication services required in a specific rural location. A solid mix of fixed wired and wireless technologies could give an alternate solution to facilitate quick telecommunication network expansion in remote rural areas.

4 Radio Propagation Mechanisms

Radio waves are used as the transmission medium in wireless propagation. The three propagation processes for radio waves are as follows:

Reflection: When a propagation radio wave meets an object that is much larger than its wavelength (such as the earth's surface or tall structures), the wave is reflected to the source. Reflection generates an 180° phase shift between the incident and reflected waves.
Diffraction: When a wave hits an impenetrable object, it undergoes this propagation. The wave bends along the object's borders, causing it to propagate in different directions. The wavelength of the wave being diffracted is comparable to the diameter of the item causing diffraction. Because of the bending, the wave can reach regions behind the object that are normally inaccessible via line-of-sight transmission. The quantity of diffraction depends on the frequency, with lower frequencies diffracting more.
Scattering: Scattering happens when a wave travels through a medium that contains several objects with smaller dimensions than its wavelength. The wave disperses into several weaker outward signals. Objects such as street signs, lampposts, and greenery induce scattering in practice.

Figure 1 depicts the various propagation mechanisms that radio waves encounter during propagation [4]. At the receiver, the received power is generally less than the transmitted power. The loss of signal power is known as attenuation.

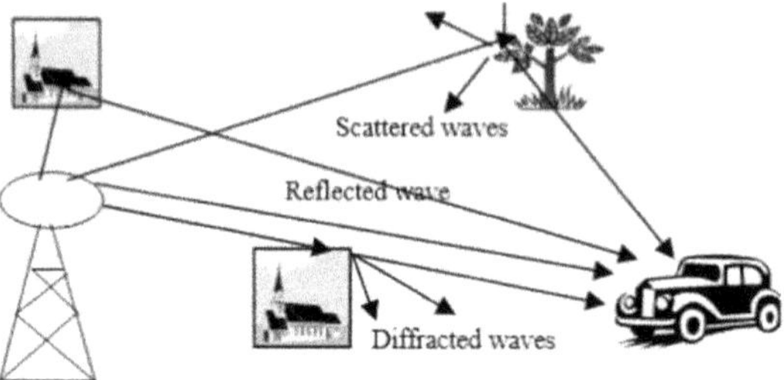

Fig. 1. Propagation Mechanisms

5 Characteristics of the Wireless Channel

The wireless channel (transmission medium) is susceptible to a variety of transmission impediments such as path loss, interference, and blockage. These factors restrict the range, data rate and reliability of wireless transmission. The extent to which these factors affect the transmission depends upon the environmental conditions and the mobility of the transmitter and receiver [4]. Typically, the transmitted signal has a direct-path component between transmitter and receiver. Other components of the transmitted signal known as multipath components are reflected, diffracted, and scattered by the environment, and arrive at the receiver shifted in amplitude, frequency, and phase with respect to the direct-path component. These characteristics can be defined as:

A. *Path Loss*

Path loss can be expressed as the ratio of the power of transmitted signal to the power of the same signal received at the receiver, on a given path. It is a function of the propagation distance. Estimation of path loss is very important for designing and deploying wireless communication networks. Path loss is also dependent on several factors such as the radio frequency used and the nature of the terrain. Since several of these factors (in particular, the terrain) cannot be the same everywhere, a single model may not be enough and hence cannot be used to describe the characteristics of every transmission. Therefore, in designing a network, several models are required to describe the variety of transmission environments. Free space propagation model is the simplest path loss model in which there is a direct-path signal between the transmitter and the receiver, with no atmospheric attenuation or multipath components. In this model, the relationship between the transmitted power P_t and the received power P_r is given by

$$P_r = P_t G_t G_r \left(\frac{\lambda}{4\pi d} \right)^2 \tag{1}$$

Where G_t and Gr are the transmitter and receiver antenna gains, respectively, in the direction from transmitter to the receiver, d is the distance between the transmitter and receiver,

$$\lambda = c/f \tag{2}$$

and is the wavelength of the signal. Realistic path loss models that consider the propagation effects in specific environments can be obtained by solving Maxwell's equations [5].

Another popular path loss model is the *two-ray* or the *two-path* model. The free space assumes that there is only one single path from transmitter to receiver. But the signal reaches the receiver through multiple paths (because of reflection, diffraction or refraction and scattering). The two-way path model tries to capture this phenomenon. The model assumes that the signal reaches the receiver through two paths, one a line-of-sight path, and the other the path through which reflected, or refracted or scattered wave is received.

B. *Fading*

Fading refers to the fluctuations of signal strength when received at the receiver.

Fading can be classified in two ways: fast fading/small-scale fading and slow fading/large-scale fading.

Fast fading refers to the rapid fluctuations in amplitude, phase, or multipath delays of the received signal, due to interference between multiple versions (copies) of the same transmitted signal arriving at the receiver at slightly different times. The time between the reception of the first version of the signal and the last echoed signal is called delay spread. The multipath propagation of the transmitted signal which causes fast fading is because of the propagation mechanisms, namely: reflection, diffraction, and scattering. The multiple signal paths may sometime add constructively or sometimes destructively to the receiver, causing a variation in the power level of the received signal. The received signal envelope of a fast-fading signal is said to follow a Rayleigh distribution if there is no line-of-sight path between transmitter and the receiver (applicable to outdoor environments), and Ricean distribution if one such path is available (characterizes indoor settings). Slow fading occurs when objects that partially absorb the transmission lie between the transmitter and receiver. Slow fading is so called because the duration of the fade may last for multiple seconds or minutes. Slow fading may occur when the receiver is inside a building and the radio waves must pass through the walls of a building, or when the receiver is temporarily shielded from the transmitter by a building. The obstructing objects cause a random variation in the received signal power. Slow fading may cause the received signal power to vary, though the distance between the transmitter and receiver remains the same. Slow fading is also referred to as shadow fading since the objects that cause the fade may be large buildings or other structures, block the direct transmission path from the transmitter to the receiver.

C. *Interference*

Wireless transmissions counter interference from a wide variety of sources. Two main forms of interference are adjacent channel interference and co-channel interference. In the adjacent channel interference case, signals in nearby frequencies have components outside their allocated ranges, and these components may interfere with on-going transmissions in the adjacent frequencies. It can be avoided by carefully introducing guard bands between allocated frequency ranges. Co-channel interference, sometimes also referred to as narrow-band interference, is due to other nearby systems (say AM/FM broadcasts) using the same frequency.

Inter-symbol interference is another type of interference where distortion in the received signal is caused by temporal spreading and the consequent overlapping of individual pulses in the signal. When this temporal spreading of individual pulses (delay spread) goes above a certain limit (symbol detection time), the receiver becomes unable to reliably distinguish between changes of state in the signal, that is the bit pattern interpreted by the receiver is not the same as that sent by the sender. Adaptive equalization is the most used technique for combating inter-symbol interference. Adaptive equalization involves mechanisms for gathering the dispersed symbol energy into its original time interval.

D. *Doppler Shift*

The Doppler shift is defined as the change/shift in the frequency of the received signal when the transmitter and receiver are mobile with respect to each other. if they are moving towards each other, then the frequency of the received signal will be higher than that of the transmitted signal, and if they are moving away from each other, the frequency of the signal at the receiver will be lower than that at the transmitter. The Doppler shift f_d is given by:

$$f_d = \frac{v}{\lambda} \tag{3}$$

Where v is the relative velocity between the transmitter and receiver, and λ is the wavelength of the signal.

Transmission Rate Constraints

Two important constraints that determine the maximum rate of data transmission on a channel are Nyquist's theorem and Shannon's theorem.

(i) Nyquist's Theorem

The signaling speed of a transmitted signal denotes the number of bits per second the signal changes its value/voltage. The number of changes per second is measured in terms of *baud*. The baud rate is not the same as the bit/data rate of the signal since each signal value may be used to convey multiple bits. For example, if the voltage values used for transmission are 0, 1, 2, and 3, then each value can be used to convey two bits (00, 01, 10 and 11). Hence the bit rate would be twice the baud rate. The *Nyquist's theorem* gives the maximum data possible on a channel. If B is the bandwidth of the channel (in Hz) and L is the number of discrete signal levels/voltages used, then the maximum channel capacity C according to the Nyquist's theorem is given by:

$$C = 2xBx\ \log_2 L_{bits/s} \tag{4}$$

Equation 4 is valid only for noiseless channels.

(ii) Shannon's Theorem

Noise level in the channel is represented by the SNR. It is the ratio of signal power (S) to noise power (N), specified in decibels, that is SNR = 10log10(S/N). One of the most important contributions of Shannon was his theorem on maximum data rate on a noisy channel. According to *Shannon's theorem*, the maximum data rate C is given by

$$C = Bx\ \log\ 2(1 + (S/N))_{\text{bits/s}} \tag{5}$$

Where B is the bandwidth of the channel (in Hz).

6 Wireless Networks

Wireless networks are computer networks that communicate using radio frequency as the physical channel. Each node in the network transmits data that all nodes within its immediate transmission range can receive. Nodes do not need to be physically attached to any network because they broadcast and receive data over the air. As a result, such networks provide data connectivity as well as user mobility. Both portable and mobile terminals are used for communication in wireless networks, and while mobile terminals can move from one location to another, portable terminals can only be accessed while they are stationary. When mobile terminals are in motion, they can be accessed. Wireless networks are characterized by the following differences from the wired networks:

- Address is not equivalent to physical location – in a wireless network, the address refers to a particular station, and this station need not be stationery. Therefore, address may not refer to a particular geographical location.
- Dynamic topology and restricted connectivity – the mobile nodes may often go out of range of each other. This means that network connectivity is partial at times
- Medium boundaries are not well defined – the exact reach of wireless signals cannot be determined accurately. It depends on various factors such as signal strength and noise levels. This means that the precise boundaries of the medium cannot be determined easily.
- Error prone medium – transmission by nodes in the wireless channel are affected by simultaneous transmission of neighboring nodes that are located within the direct transmission range of the transmitting node. This means that the error rates are significantly higher in the wireless medium. Typical bit error rates (fractions of bits that are received in error) are of the order of 10^4 in a wireless channel as against 10^9 in fiber optic cables.

Wireless networks are generally classified as either infrastructure or ad hoc (infrastructure-less) networks [4].

A. *Infrastructure Networks*

Access Points (APs) are special nodes in infrastructure-based networks that are connected via existing wired networks. In the sense that they can communicate with both wireless nodes and existing wired networks, APs are unique. APs are used to communicate with the other wireless nodes, also known as Mobile Stations (STAs). The APs can also connect to other networks. Infrastructure-based networking is a network with pre-built infrastructure consisting of fixed and wired network nodes and gateways, with network services typically offered through these pre-built infrastructures. Cellular networks, for example, are infrastructure-based networks made up of backbone switches from the Public Switched Telephone Network (PSTN), Mobile Switching Centres, base stations, and mobile hosts. Each node in the network has a specified role to play, and connections follow a rigorous signaling sequence among the nodes.

B. *Infrastructure-less (Ad-Hoc) Networks*

There is no fixed infrastructure required for ad hoc networks. These networks can be activated at any time and in any location. Nodes connect with one another directly or send messages to other nodes that are directly accessible. A network is built dynamically in this situation by the cooperation of an arbitrary number of independent nodes. The role that each node should play is not predetermined. Rather than relying on pre-existing network architecture, each node makes its own decisions based on the network condition. Two PCs with wireless adapter cards, for example, can create their own network whenever they are in range of one another. Nodes in mobile ad-hoc networks are expected to act as routers, participating in the discovery and maintenance of routes to other nodes.

7 Wireless in Local Loop

Mobility was the most essential aspect, impacting network architecture in cellular networks. In the case of limited mobility, however, Wireless in Local Lop (WLL) technology is used. The local loop [4] is the circuit that provides last-hop connectivity between the subscriber and the PSTN. It has traditionally been implemented using standard copper wire. Due to the high cost of implementation, optical fibre is not a popular local loop technology. The use of wireless connectivity in the last hop between the subscriber and the telephone exchange is known as WLL, also known as Fixed Wireless Access (FWA) or Radio in the Local Loop (RLL) (end office). It is a cost-effective way of connecting distant locations. WLL can provide the tools to extend the existing network in metropolitan areas where high capacity is required.

WLL offers numerous benefits to both consumers and service providers. WLL is significantly easier to set up, and it can be scaled up to accommodate additional consumers as need grows. WLL is a cost-effective choice for the customer because of its lower investment, operations, and maintenance costs. WLL provides a wide range of services, including basic telephone and Internet access. Bandwidth-intensive applications like video-on-demand can now be enabled thanks to the emergence of broadband wireless systems.

To compete with more efficient copper wire transmission technologies like integrated digital service network (ISDN) and Digital Subscriber Line (DSL), WLL must meet QoS requirements (DSL). Its speech and data quality must be comparable to that of traditional telephone networks. This means it uses 64 kbps or 32 kbps transmission channels with a blocking probability of less than 10^{-2} and a basic error rate (BER) of less than 10^{-3} for voice and less than 10^{-6} for data. Because the subscriber units run on batteries and are not powered by the exchange, they must have low power consumption. To provide security and data privacy, it must support authentication and encryption. The interface between the subscribers' wireless wired devices and the WLL network is the Fixed Subscriber

Unit (FSU) or Radio Subscriber Unit (RSU). From the subscriber's perspective, the FSU handles all physical and data-link layer functions. Figure 2 depicts the basic design of WLL networks.

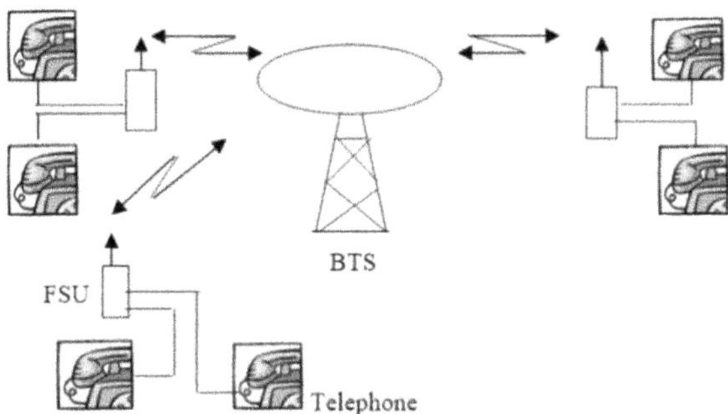

Fig. 2. WLL Architecture

8 Broadband Wireless Access

Fixed wireless access can be point-to-point, with each user having their own antenna transceiver, or multipoint, with a single antenna transceiver serving multiple users. The latter is the most widely used and beneficial for WLL. A multipoint system is like a cellular system in that it has multiple points. In a multipoint system, however:

(i) Cells do not overlap
(ii) The same frequency is reused at each cell and,
(iii) No handoff is provided as users are fixed

9 Bridging the Digital Divide

The rural connectivity divide was highlighted when schools were forced to close due to the pandemic. When teaching went virtual, many children from underserved neighborhoods across the country had no access to broadband at home. Even though both urban and rural districts adopted at-home learning, city officials were more likely to provide students with Wi-Fi hotspots and equipment so they could continue their studies. According to one study, such initiatives were less widespread in rural areas. A lack of digital infrastructure is at least part of the cause. Because of COVID-19, President Ramaphosa declared South Africa to be in an alert level 4 in March 2020. As a result, schools and tertiary institutions were closed for most of the year, thus halting all teaching and learning for many youngsters. However, traditionally white, and private schools swiftly moved their teaching and learning to an online platform, where pupils learned using cellphones, tablets, and computers connected to the internet. This was simple because they had access to the necessary technology as well as the cash to put it to use. According to [6], online learning is nearly impossible for rural and underprivileged pupils, and it surely does not achieve educational equality. The impact of COVID-19 on education, as well as the inability of poor and rural pupils to access online learning, has just confirmed the adage that the poor get poorer while the wealthy grow [7].

10 5G Coming to the Rescue of South African Rural Areas

Because 5G uses more radio spectrum than previous generations, it will be able to deliver broadband to individuals living in sparsely populated areas. At the upper end of that spectrum, users will be able to download at least 1 gigabit per second, which is fast enough to transport a 500-megabyte video in a matter of seconds. However, because that high-end signal can only reach short distances, users will need to be less than a mile away. Carriers would not be able to make such a large investment in locations where people live far apart. However, 5G networks can utilise radio waves in the low band, which were formerly used by TV channels. Customers can connect to towers thousands of kilometers away using low-band 5G, which can't transfer data at the same pace as high-band airwaves. Data can travel at speeds up to several times faster than 4G in this frequency range, but it also means that people in remote areas who previously couldn't get 4G may suddenly have access to reliable, fast mobile broadband. The low band has the extra benefit of being able to penetrate windows and walls, allowing it to reach deeper into structures than ever before.

Investing in 5G technology for both wireless and fixed networks is necessary to effectively develop a rural network that allows all individuals to participate in the digital economy. With faster speeds, greater coverage regions, and improved security over prior 4G networks, the 5G standard enables a broader range of use cases than ever before.

However, it is pointless to construct this new network if people cannot afford it. That's when the clever edge comes into play. It brings real-time processing capability closer to the point of generation, making deployments easier and operating costs lower. When 5G and the intelligent edge are combined, the same workload performance may be achieved with less overhead, resulting in significant cost savings. And, when it comes to constructing intelligent rural networks, keeping prices low will be critical to making it affordable to everybody.

RAN (Radio Network Access) is a network's "last mile," the visible link between the network and a mobile phone. Operators are attempting to open up RAN standards and eliminate reliance on single-vendor systems. Large operators like Orange, Vodafone, and MTN are already intending to deploy virtual (vRAN) and Open RAN to expand their coverage into new markets since it gives equipment providers more options, lowers TCO, and makes it easier to replace portions as needed.

Open RAN allows CSPs to choose the best technical solutions for the scenario rather than being confined to single-vendor options, which is important in rural networks where cost is a big factor in installing new networks or upgrading old ones. When it comes to rural connectivity, Open RAN and 5G make for a powerful combination. The costs of setting up networks over a vast geographic area have been demonstrated in previous initiatives. To reduce costs, intelligent rural networks can take advantage of powerful new technology such as distributed clouds and edge computing.

Rural networks will also necessitate remote management and monitoring on a huge scale. As part of the network design and implementation, end-to-end automation and AI-based analytics can help to reduce ongoing expenses and keep networks up and running efficiently. Because of the enormous geographic areas involved, these management and monitoring systems must also be able to work remotely so that technical employees can respond swiftly to any difficulties that develop.

Transmission at long-range, low-bandwidth frequencies, or what are known as the low and mid bands, will be a more practical 5G deployment for rural areas (when it happens) (600 MHz to 900 MHz and 2.5 GHz to 4.2 GHz, respectively). Because transmissions can travel a few miles, fewer cell towers will be required. Of course, this will result in less data speeds (usually around 250+ Mbps) than the gigabit rates possible with mmWave in metropolitan areas. Despite this, speeds will be faster than LTE.

11 Infrastructure Sharing in Rural Areas

The government of South Africa could provide subsidies to operators who build infrastructure in rural areas. These could take the form of tax breaks to entice operators to expand their networks into marginally profitable areas. Formulating national broadband aspirations and developing a national plan is a key first step for South Africa. After the national objectives have been established, the government can create a national roadmap outlining how they plan to achieve their aim. The government has several levers at its disposal, including policy, legislation, and regulation, to influence supply and demand issues.

12 Conclusion

Broadband connectivity is often unavailable for persons living in rural areas of South Africa. This makes digital transformation more difficult and may have a negative influence on local communities' socioeconomic development. The South African government should make a commitment to rectifying this situation by ensuring that as many people as possible in rural areas have access to the Internet and bridging the digital gap. 5G has the potential to revolutionize a variety of industries, but there are still a lot of difficulties to be resolved and significant investments to be required if 5G is to become widely available. Additional datacenters and Internet exchange points could be a solution, but such decisions must be made based on economic viability and customer demand for such assets.

Declarations.

Competing Interests. The author(s) has no competing interests to declare that are relevant to the content of this manuscript.

References

1. Pather, S., Rey-Moreno, C.: Advancing Rural Connectivity in South Africa a Case for Community-Owned Networks, pp. 1–25. Department of Science and Technology, South Africa, Pretoria (2019)
2. Capacity Daily: Telecoms is the key to growing African economies post-Covid, August (2020)
3. Rantec Microwave Systems: The Different Types of Wireless Communication. Rantec Microwave Systems, Westlake Village (2020)
4. Siva Ram Murthy, C., Manoj, B.S.: Ad Hoc Wireless Networks, Architectures and Protocols. Prentice Hall, Upper Saddle River (2004)
5. Clerk Maxwell, J.: A Treatise on Electricity and Magnetism, vol. 2, 3rd edn, pp. 68–73. Clarendon, Oxford (1892)
6. Pillay, I.: The impact of inequality and COVID-19 on education and career planning for South African children of rural and low-socioeconomic backgrounds. Afr. J. Career Dev. **3**(1), a36 (2021). https://doi.org/10.4102/ajcd.v3i1.36
7. Dube, B.: Rural online learning in the context of COVID-19 in South Africa: evoking an inclusive education approach. Multidiscip. J. Educ. Res. **10**(2), 135–157 (2020). https://doi.org/10.4471/remie.2020.5607

Hybrid Modulation Scheme for Reducing Peak to Average Power Ratio in 5G Based on Spatial CE-OFDMA Signal

Bertille Auyane Ngouessy ep Ovono[1](✉), Temitayo Oluwafunke Otunniyi[1], and Marcel O. Odhiambo[2]

[1] Faculty of Engineering and Technology, Electrical Engineering Department, Vaal University of Technology, Gauteng, South Africa
bertie.ovono@gmail.com, temidayoo@vut.ac.za
[2] Faculty of Engineering, Chuka University, Chuka, Kenya

Abstract. The rapidly increasing data traffic in modern mobile communication systems necessitates the use of higher-frequency spectrum bands. This anticipated surge in mobile traffic in 5G networks has raised major concerns regarding power consumption. To address the energy-efficiency requirements of 5G—particularly its goals of low latency and reduced computational complexity—several multicarrier modulation schemes have been investigated as potential physical-layer solutions. However, most of these waveforms suffer from a high Peak-to-Average Power Ratio (PAPR), which limits power efficiency.

To mitigate this challenge, various constant-envelope–based approaches have been explored. In this paper, we propose a hybrid modulation technique called Spatial Modulation Constant-Envelope OFDMA (SM-CE-OFDMA), which combines spatial modulation with constant-envelope OFDMA. The proposed scheme significantly enhances system performance under AWGN conditions and achieves a 3.01 dB reduction in PAPR. The system was modeled and simulated using MATLAB. Furthermore, a comparative analysis of the Bit Error Rate (BER) and Signal-to-Noise Ratio (SNR) performance for the different transmission modules is presented to demonstrate the effectiveness of the proposed method.

Keywords: 5G technology · Higher Peak to Average Power Ratio · Energy Efficiency · Hybrid modulation scheme · Constant Envelope · Spatial Modulation Orthogonal Frequency Division Multiplexing Access

1 Introduction

The alarming growth in mobile data traffic has increased the demand for high-frequency spectrum bands. This tremendous rise in mobile traffic expected with 5G technology also raises concerns related to power consumption. As more users compete for limited spectrum resources, multicarrier modulation schemes such as OFDMA are being explored to improve spectral efficiency [1].

K. Daimi et al. (Eds.): CSCE 2025, CCIS 2937, pp. 401–412, 2026.
https://doi.org/10.1007/978-3-032-22208-4_28

OFDMA, which is based on OFDM, is a higher-order multicarrier modulation technique employed in the air-interface of 5G New Radio (5G NR) to support enhanced mobile connectivity [2]. In OFDMA, the available frequency spectrum is divided into several sub-bands composed of orthogonal subcarriers, and each group of subcarriers is allocated to a user for simultaneous transmission [2]. However, designing and implementing OFDMA systems remains challenging. One of the main issues is the high Peak-to-Average Power Ratio (PAPR). High PAPR forces the power amplifier to operate in a highly linear region, which is significantly less energy-efficient than saturated or Type-C operation. Since energy efficiency directly affects transmission power and detection sensitivity, reducing PAPR is essential for improving system performance [3].

The high PAPR, defined as the ratio between the maximum instantaneous signal power and its average power, remains one of the major drawbacks of multicarrier modulation schemes.

The PAPR is mathematically expressed as shown in Eq. (1):

$$PAPR = \frac{\max|x[t]|^2}{\frac{1}{N_c}\sum_{n}^{N_c-1}|x[t]|^2} \quad (1)$$

where the time samples of an OFDM symbol are represented by the values $x[t]$, $n = 0, \ldots, N_c - 1$.

$$PAPR(dB) = 10\log_{10}PAPR \quad (2)$$

The crest factor (CF), which is CF = PAPR, is another measure for determining envelope variation and is appressed as $CF = \sqrt{PAPR}$

To reduce PAPR, constant-envelope modulation techniques are introduced. Constant-envelope signals are particularly suitable for wireless communication systems because they experience less distortion when amplified by high-power amplifiers (HPAs) [4]. In practical transmitters, increasing the signal power corresponds to increasing its amplitude. However, nonlinear HPAs vary the amplification level depending on the instantaneous amplitude of the input signal. When the amplitude fluctuates significantly as in high-PAPR multicarrier signals, the nonlinear amplifier introduces distortion due to amplitude compression and expansion [5]. This distortion degrades spectral efficiency and increases error rates.

To address this challenge, various constant-envelope techniques have been widely proposed in the literature, aiming to maintain a stable amplitude while preserving spectral and power efficiency.

2 Related Work

Several researchers have investigated multicarrier modulation schemes to mitigate the PAPR problem. In [6, 7], the information-bearing signal is transformed into a constant-envelope waveform using phase modulation. The authors in [8] examined how the OFDM waveform can be used to phase-modulate the carrier in CE-OFDM systems. In [9], CE-OFDM was employed to reduce blanking errors caused by the high PAPR of conventional OFDM. Further, the study in [9] showed that CE-OFDM combined with a blanking technique outperforms conventional OFDM in terms of blanking error probability and can provide an output SNR gain of up to 6 dB. Additionally, Uludag [10] investigated CE-OFDM and SC-FDMA under AWGN, Rayleigh fading, and Rician fading channels to improve 5G capacity; however, the study did not fully consider large-scale 5G scenarios. Only four users were evaluated, and the approach was shown to be less effective as the number of users increased. Building on the limitations and future recommendations identified in Uludag's work, this study introduces a spatial-modulation–based solution to enhance system performance while addressing PAPR challenges in multicarrier systems.

Spatial Modulation (SM) is a MIMO-based modulation technique designed to offer low system complexity, improved data rates, and enhanced error performance, especially in correlated channel environments. It leverages the inherent randomness and uniqueness of wireless channels to encode information efficiently [11]. SM integrates seamlessly with OFDMA because OFDMA naturally accommodates other rate-enhancing technologies such as MIMO, of which spatial modulation is an advanced form.

One of the key advantages of SM is its ability to reduce inter-carrier interference (ICI) in OFDMA systems while preserving high spectral efficiency. Combining SM with OFDMA enables a hybrid transmission scheme that capitalizes on the strengths of both modulation techniques—achieving high data throughput with low implementation complexity. The resulting SM-OFDMA structure introduces a third dimension in which information can be encoded and decoded by utilizing antenna indices and active subcarrier indices. At the receiver, SM-OFDMA can mitigate synchronization issues between multiple transmit antennas and reduce inter-channel interference, all while maintaining the inherent spectral efficiency of OFDMA. In spatial modulation, the incoming bitstream is divided into two components: one selects a unique transmit antenna index, and the other maps the remaining bits onto symbols from the signal constellation diagram [12]. This separation provides additional degrees of freedom and enhances overall system performance.

3 Proposed Hybrid Modulation Scheme

For the purpose of this study, it is proposed that spatial modulation be integrated with CE-OFDMA. This hybrid approach aims to exploit the advantages of both techniques which is namely the constant-envelope property of CE-OFDMA and the spectral and energy efficiency of spatial modulation. The block diagrams of the transmitter and receiver for the proposed hybrid scheme are illustrated in Figs. 1 and 2, respectively.

Spatial modulation (SM) was applied to CE-OFDMA transmission. First, SM was considered with $M_t = 4$ and $M_r = 4$ denoting respectively the transmit and receive antennas, in which a selected constellation 16QAM was applied. N_p is the overall number of bitstream data conveyed by the SM transmission of all SM-CE-OFDMA of every symbol. The remaining antennas were dis-activated, the total N_p data carried were divided into two T clusters and the selected M bits were sent in every single subcarrier of the transmission by the index of OFDMA modulators.

At the transmitter, each source user bits containing U_n symbols are created separately. The source user bits first go through a chosen constellation precisely quadrature amplitude modulation (QAM), a group of input bits are mapped to spatial modulation

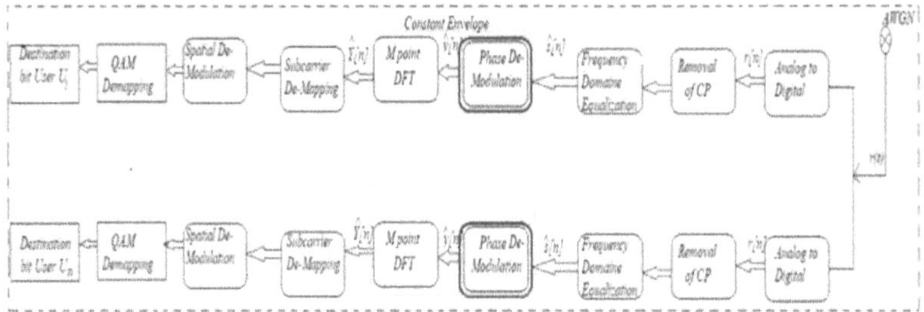

Fig. 1. SM-CE-OFDMA Transmitter Block diagram

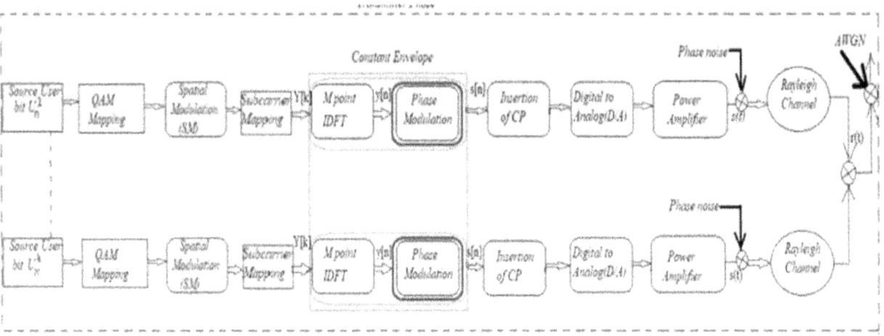

Fig. 2. SM-CE-OFDMA Receiver Block diagram

where the number of transmit antennas is denoted M_t and M_r symbolizing the number of receiving antennas. In SM only one enabled transmitter antenna is used at any signaling time instance for data transmission. The spatial and signal constellation diagrams, each of them carries its own set of information. The spatial constellation diagram has the same length as the number of M_t transmit antenna, whereas the signal constellation diagram has a size indicated by M. The input block size of η_{si} bits is partitioned, wherein $\eta_{si} = \log_2 M_t M$ being the number of bits consistent with the image. Each block is divided into components of $\log_2 N_t$ bits and $\log_2 M$ bits. The primary phase turns on, one of the transmit antennas denoted by N_{tiv}. The residual bits are utilized to decide a symbol inside the signal constellation diagram, and the dynamic receive antennas pass on this symbol that is denoted by the mean of x_l, $l = 1, 2, \ldots, M$. The send signal is expressed via a vector $X_{tiv,l} = \left[x_1, x_2, \ldots, x_{N_t}\right]^T$, of which the $t_{tiv}{}^{th}$ element incorporates x_l while others receive no power, meaning they are assigned zero. After spatial modulation, the user data block with N symbols of block $\boldsymbol{X} = [X_0, X_{2, \ldots,} X_{N-1}]^T$ is routed through a subcarrier mapping block for each user of M accessible subcarriers. The rate of the SM system is given by $R_{SM} = \log_2(M_t M)$, with $N_t = 4$ and M = 4. Then the symbols are mapped to M $(M > N)$ orthogonal subcarriers and converted to a time-domain complex signal sequence using an M-point Inverse Discrete Fourier Transform (IDFT), which is mathematically represented by Eq. (3)

$$x[n] = \sum\nolimits_{k=0}^{N_{dft-1}} X\ (k) e^{\frac{j2\pi nk}{Ndft}} \qquad n = 0, 1, \ldots, Ndf - 1 \tag{3}$$

Where $X(k)$ is the complex containing the frequency spectrum DFT, while the discrete and periodic k runs from 0 to N-1, and k = 0 to N/2. The block diagram shows that IDFT precedes the phase modulation block and these two blocks make the constant envelope. Table 1 shows 4 × 4 Spatial modulation scheme mapping matrix to illustrates the mapping of the suggested approach.

The peak to average power ratio (PAPR) for various spreading codes can be limited by: For the uplink by Eq. (3a)

$$PAPR \leq \frac{2\max\left\{\left|\sum_{l=0}^{L-1} c_l^{(k)} e^{\frac{j2\pi lt}{T_s}}\right|\right\}}{l = L} \tag{3a}$$

Where L denotes the oversampling factor, which determines the maximum number of active users K and the chip rate of the serial spreading code $c_l^{(k)} = e^{-j2\pi lk/L}$

Table 1. 4 × 4 Spatial modulation scheme mapping matrix

4 × 4 Spatial modulation mapping with $N_t = 4, M = 4$		
Source Bits	Antenna number	Transmit symbols
0000	T_{x1}	3 + 3j
0001	T_{x1}	1 + 3j
0010	T_{x1}	−3 + 3j
0011	T_{x1}	−1 + 3j
0100	T_{x2}	3 + j
0101	T_{x2}	1 + j
0110	T_{x2}	−3 + j
0111	T_{x2}	−1 + j
1000	T_{x3}	3 − 3j
1001	T_{x3}	1-3j
1010	T_{x3}	-3-3j
1011	T_{x3}	−1 − 3j
1100	T_{x4}	3 + j
1101	T_{x4}	1-j
1110	T_{x4}	-3-j
1111	T_{x4}	−1-j

The receiver shown in Fig. 2 is made up of N_{RF} chains that perform frequency domain equalization on the analog to a digital baseband signal after the cyclic prefix is removed. The FDE-equalized signal is then fed into the phase modulator, which is made up of the arctangent calculator, if present, a phase is unwrapped. The unwrapped may avoid the phase unwrapped associated with arctangent calculation. Its use, however, is not always recommended. The un-wrapper addresses the wrapping issues just for high signal-to-noise ratio (SNR) values, while, for low SNR, phase unwrapping error may cause execution corruption.

At the receiver signal, the baseband is given by Eq. (4)

$$\begin{aligned} r(t) &= \int_0^{\tau_{max}} h(\tau, t)s(-\tau + t)d\tau + w(t) \\ &= \int_0^{\tau_{max}} h(\tau)s[(t - \tau)]d\tau + w(t), \end{aligned} \tag{4}$$

Where the channel impulse response is represented by $h(\tau, t)$ with its maximum propagation delay τ_{max} while $w(t)$ symbolizes the complex-valued Gaussian noise. Assuming that the channel is static over the block interval $T_{scp} \leq t < T$, therefore $h(\tau, t) \approx h(\tau)$. After the constant envelope block, the insertion of the cycle prefix (CP) makes the linear convolution with the circular convolution equivalent to the channel impulse response. Thus, by selecting $N_{scp} \geq L$, the receive samples $r(n)$ obtained after the signal has passed through the analog to digital converter are equivalently represented by linear (*) or circular convolution ($*$), Where L is the length of channel impulse response.

$$\begin{aligned} r(n) &= s_n * h_n + w_n, \quad n = -N_{scp}, \ldots, N_{dft-1} \quad \text{Step1} \\ &= s_n \otimes h_n + w_n, \quad n = 0, \ldots, N_{dft-1} \quad \text{Step 2} \end{aligned} \tag{5}$$

Step 1 in Eq. (5) denotes the linear convolution between the transmitted signal samples and channel. While *step*2 represents the circular convolution. Here w_n denotes the complex zero-mean White Gaussian Noise process. Since w_n is white, it is a fixed irregular cycle with a level power spectral density (PSD) at all frequencies. It is customary to assume its PSD as: $\frac{N_0}{2} - \infty < f < \infty$. Due to this, the power of the white process is limitless and the hypothesis of Wiener-Khinchine states that the autocorrelation function of the AWGN is

$$\begin{aligned} R(\tau) &\triangleq E\{(w_n) w_n(t - \tau)\} \\ &= \int_{-\infty}^{\infty} N(t)e^{j2\pi f \tau} df \\ &= \int_{-\infty}^{\infty} \frac{N_0}{2} e^{j2\pi f \tau} df = \frac{N_0}{2} \delta(\tau) \end{aligned} \tag{6}$$

Where $\delta(\tau)$ denotes the Dirac delta function. In the Eq. (6) $\{[S_n, H_n]\}$ represent the discrete Fourier transforms of $\{[s_n, h_n]\}$. After analog to digital converter, the cyclic prefix removal process is done, and the frequency domain equalization equalizes the residual samples.

This frequency domain equalization flip-flops the channel effect perfectly and its output is given by Eq. (7):

$$\hat{s}_n = IDFT\{R_k C_k\} = s_n \otimes c_n \tag{7}$$

Where C_k is the equalizer correction term which helps reduce ISI and the effect of the noise addition in the system, and is calculated cordially to the kind of FDE; the improving of the constant associated with the equalizer while using MMSE equalizer a mathematical Eq. (8) is derived as follows:

$$C_k \frac{H_k^*}{|H_k|^2 + \frac{1}{SNR}} \tag{8}$$

Where the signal to noise ratio is denoted SNR. Succeeding by the application of the time domain on the phase demodulator which is composed of the finite impulse filter. The finite impulse filter is utilized for the enhancement of the performance of the phase demodulator, the usage of arctangent arg(.) is for the withdrawal of the signal's phase.

4 Simulation of the Proposed SM-CE-OFDMA Design

Matlab 2020a was the simulation platform used to carry out the experiment. Table 2 shows the simulation criteria used. Uplink system channel with frequency band of 450 MHz to 6GHz were used with 16QAM modulation scheme. 5 MHz bandwidth was used for the design with subcarrier spacing of 15KHz with oversampling ratio of 5. The design also employed 512 IDFT at the transmitter.

Table 2. Parameters of the simulation

Specification	Parameters
System channel	Uplink physical channel
System bandwidth	5 MHz
Modulation Scheme	16QAM
CP	170
Input block size	63
Transmitter IDFT size	512
Subcarrier spacing	15 KHz
OFDMA input block size	64 symbols
Noise environment	AWGN
Receiver	MMSE
Frequency Band	450 MHz–6GHz
Spatial modulation configuration	4×4
Oversampling	5
Total active users	25

The evaluation metrics for the simulation are bit error rate, signal to noise ratio and peak to average power ratio.

5 Discussion and Analysis of Results

Peak to average power has always been a major problem in multicarrier modulation single or hybridized. So, it is advisable that these techniques be correctly modelled Table 2 define parameters that were used to develop SM-CE-OFDMA.

For a total number of 60000 transmitted bits the following performance metrics were employed:

(i) Bit Error Rate (BER)
(ii) Signal to Noise Ratio (SNR)
(iii) Peak to average power ratio (PAPR)

5.1 Bit Error Rate and Signal Ratio

BER is the error bit per the number of transmission bits. This BER was used to evaluate the performance of the proposed prototype during data transmission.

(ii) The signal-to-noise ratio (SNR) is the decibel ratio of the received signal strength to the noise level and is an important parameter for wireless communication. This is related to signal quality and system performance. When the signal level is significantly higher than the noise level, then it achieved a reliable connection. These metrics are measured before the prototype is modulated. For the addition of noise in a corresponding modulated signal, Eb/No was converted to SNR.

To analyse the performance of the prototype, the bit error rate versus signal-noise ratio was used as shown in Fig. 3 and Table 3 for OFDMA, CE-OFDMA and SM-CE-OFDMA by comparing the transmitter signal with the receiver signal.

The observations are made on specific values of SNR

At 2 dB: BER was 0.12 dB for OFDMA, but for CE-OFDMA and SM-CE-OFDMA, the BER were 0.65 and 0.62 respectively. CE-OFDMA has a higher value of BER. This shows that SM-CE-OFDMA gives a better BER outcome so, it is more efficient in terms of BER.
At 6 dB: BER was 0.017 dB for OFDMA, but for CE-OFDMA and SM-CE-OFDMA, the BER were similar of about 0.07 value.
At 8 dB: the BER was 5.5 10^{-5} for OFDMA, but for CE-OFDMA and SM-CE-OFDMA, the BER were 0.075 and 0.12 value respectively. It was evidently seen that the SNR always increase for both SM-CE-OFDMA and CE-OFDMA while the signal of OFDMA stop at SNR = 11 dB.
At 11 dB: For OFDMA, BER was 0.1, but for CE-OFDMA and SM-CE-OFDMA, the BER were 0.0 and 0.155 respectively.

Again, for **SNR = 12 dB**, only SM-CE-OFDMA and CE-OFDMA occur. The results obtained showed that CE-OFDMA has the highest value of BER and that SM-CE-OFDMA gave better BER results, so SM-CE-OFDMA is more efficient than CE-OFDMA this means that SM-CE-OFDMA outperformed CE-OFDMA. Also, at the of the evaluation, SM-CE-OFDMA presented to have a low BER to high SNR.

Table 3. BER vs. Eb/No

	OFDMA	CE-OFDMA	SM-CE-OFDMA(4 × 4)
Eb/No Values (dB)	BER	BER	BER
0	0.1	0.6	0.5
2	0.12	0.65	0.62
4	0.01	0.66	0.64

(*continued*)

Table 3. (*continued*)

	OFDMA	CE-OFDMA	SM-CE-OFDMA(4 × 4)
Eb/No Values (dB)	BER	BER	BER
6	0.017	0.7	0.7
8	0.0007	075	0.12
10	5.5E-5	0.85	0.150
11	0.1	0.9	0.1550
12	N/A	0.95	0.0550
14	N/A	0.1	0.0190
15	N/A	0.1	0.0027
16	N/A	0.11	0.0126

5.2 Peak to Average Power Ratio

Figures 4 and 5 showed the PAPR value of CE-OFDMA and SM- CE-OFDMA. Figure 4 displays three parts showing the results of discrete sampling representation of I and Q components of the signal in the time domain.

I and Q symbolized the In-phase and the quadrature of the original samples. The observed results showed that the top-most part is the positive representation of the in-phase; at the interval [0, 1], and [3, 4] and at [1, 3] samples are negative. The middle part was the representation of the quadrature sample with unbiassed repartition. These results showed at [0, 2] the positive samples and negative samples at [2, 4], and the bottom part shows the outcome of sampling a signal. Also, results showed a PAPR of about 0 dB value for the baseband signal with the center frequency of 4 GHz and the oversampling ratio of 4. Figure 5 shows a graph of the sinusoidal continuous wave representation of samples in the frequency domain. The top part of Fig. 5 shows a sinewave with a cut-off frequency which denotes the behavior of aliasing in signal sampled, this is justified by the presence of the novel frequencies' appearance. This aliasing is caused by the incrementation of the signal's frequency on a sample rate. The cut-off frequency has a passband from 0.75 and the peak value equal to 1 for maximum and − 1 for a minimum. These peaks are negative at [0,0.5]; [1,1.25]; [2.75,3] and [3.5,4] and at 2 the folding amplitude is shown, while it is positive at [0.7,1]; [1.3, 18]; [2.1,2.7] and [3,3.4]. Next is the bottom part of Fig. 5, which is the absolute value squared of the same sample. The sample was increased to get rid of the aliasing that occurred in the top part of Fig. 5. It can be observed that the PAPR for the passband signal with oversampling of 4 was a 3.01 dB value greater than the baseband signal as seen in Fig. 5. The sinusoidal wave of the oversampling took its origin at 0.5 with reference 0 showing 8 peaks although at [0.75, 1.45] and [2.75, 3.25] a periodic doubling was visible. It was observed that the PAPR evaluation was done using sampled waveform. The simulation results obtained showed that by oversampling the OFDMA signal, CE-OFDMA gave a PAPR = 0 dB. Next, this oversampling was a factor of two in SM-CE-OFDMA, which means that

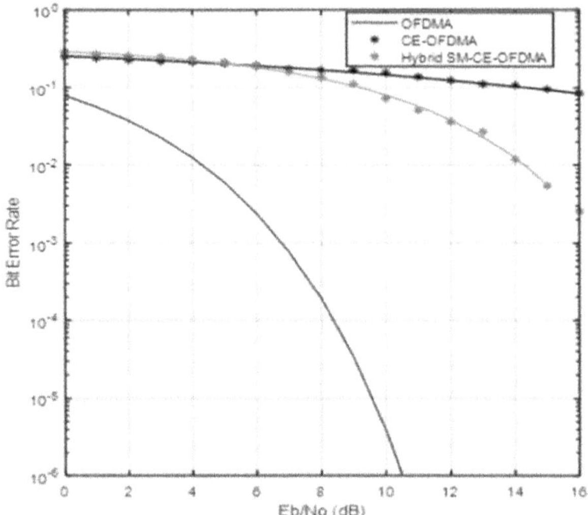

Fig. 3. Bit Error Rate vs. Eb/No

the sample increased twice and changed PAPR to about 3 dB value. The PAPR change was due to a band-limiting filter which was applied precisely called the Nyquist limit. Nyquist eliminated the effect of aliasing that was observed on the jagged edge of the PAPR discrete sinusoidal waveform. The Nyquist means that an ideal low filter is needed, which is practically impossible. Nyquist rate made the sampling rate equal to two-fold the highest frequency of a given sample or frequency, which justifies the increase of PAPR in the hybrid SM-CE-OFDMA modulation schemes.

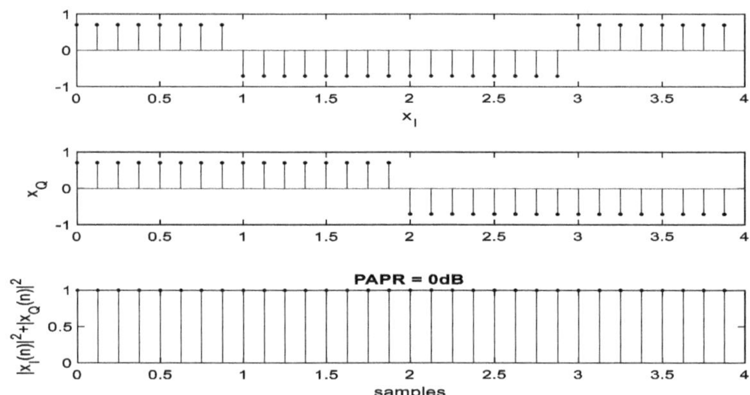

Fig. 4. PAPR of CE-OFDMA

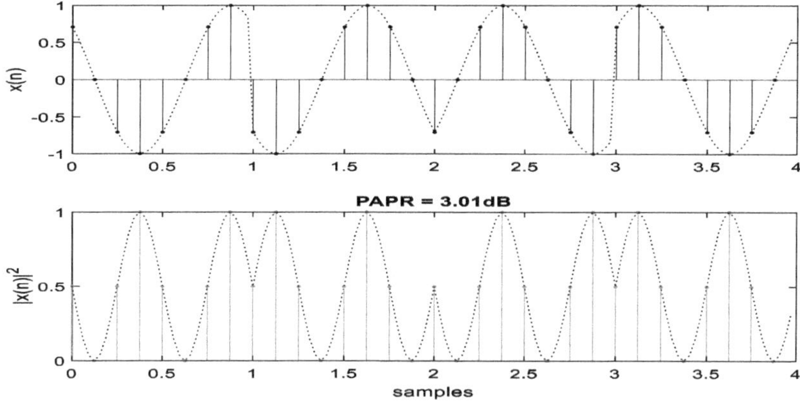

Fig. 5. PAPR of CE-OFDMA

6 Conclusion

In this study, a hybrid modulation strategy known as Spatial Modulation Orthogonal Frequency Division Multiple Access based on Constant Envelope (SM-CE-OFDMA) is adopted. The proposed scheme was found to significantly improve the performance of 5G mobile communication systems. Spatial Modulation (SM) was applied within the CE-OFDMA framework, where the system was configured with a set of transmit and receive antennas and employed 16-QAM for symbol modulation. The entire design was simulated in a MATLAB environment.

The simulation results demonstrate that SM-CE-OFDMA achieves superior BER performance, which can be attributed to the spatial modulation component that enhances diversity and reduces interference. Additionally, the SNR performance improved steadily with increasing simulation parameters, indicating the consistency and reliability of the hybrid scheme in enhancing system throughput.

The proposed method also achieved a PAPR value of 3.01 dB. Given the total of 60,000 transmitted bits, this PAPR level is considered acceptable, as it did not introduce any significant degradation to the overall system performance. These findings show that SM-CE-OFDMA provides an effective balance between spectral efficiency, energy efficiency, and transmission reliability for next-generation wireless systems.

Declarations.

Competing Interests. The author(s) has no competing interests to declare that are relevant to the content of this manuscript.

References

1. Jebbar, H., El Hassani, S., El Abbassi, A.: PAPR reduction for 5G waveforms. In: 2018 6th International Conference on Wireless Networks and Mobile Communications (WINCOM), October, pp. 1–6. IEEE (2018)

2. Cisco: Cisco Visual Networking Index: Global Mobile Data Traffic Forecast Update, 20142019. Cisco, Technical Report (2015)
3. Zhou, H., Li, B., Yan, Z., Yang, M.: A channel bonding based QoS- aware OFDMA MAC protocol for the next-generation WLAN. Mob. Netw. Appl. **22**(1), 19–29 (2017)
4. Huang, Y., et al.: Constant envelope OFDM RadCom fusion system. EURASIP J. Wirel. Commun. Netw. **2018**(1), 1–15 (2018)
5. Chide, N., Deshmukh, S., Borole, P.B., Chore, N.: An overview of OFDM variants and their applications. Int. J. Electron. Commun. Comput. Eng. **4**(2), 47–51 (2013)
6. Balal, Y., Pinchas, M., Pinhasi, Y.: Constant envelope phase modulation inspired by orthogonal waveforms. IEEE Commun. Lett. **20**(11), 2169–2172 (2016)
7. Thompson, S.C., Ahmed, A.U., Proakis, J.G., Zeidler, J.R.: Constant envelope OFDM phase modulation: spectral containment, signal space properties and performance. In: IEEE MILCOM 2004. Military Communications Conference, , October, 2004, vol. 2, pp. 1129–1135. IEEE (2004)
8. Sacchi, C., Cianca, E., Rossi, T., De Sanctis, M.: Analysis and assessment of the effects of phase noise in constant envelope multicarrier satellite transmissions. In: 2015 IEEE International Conference on Communications (ICC), June, pp. 922–927. IEEE (2015)
9. Rabie, K.M., Alsusa, E., Familua, A.D., Cheng, L.: Constant envelope OFDM transmission over impulsive noise power-line communication channels. In: 2015 IEEE International Symposium on Power Line Communications and Its Applications (ISPLC), March, pp. 13–18. IEEE (2015)
10. Uludag, E.: Constant-envelope OFDM and constant envelope SC-FDMA. Doctoral dissertation, UC Irvine (2016)
11. Agarwal, N.: Spatial modulation technique: achievements and challenges. In: Computing, Communication and Signal Processing, pp. 441–448. Springer, Singapore (2019)
12. Nusenu, S.: Spatial modulation technique for filtered-OFDM based wire-less transmission. Adv. Sci. Technol. Eng. Syst. J. **2**, 981–986 (2017)

Automating Innovation: AI's Impact on Software Development Lifecycle

Max Dombrowski and Katia Maxwell(✉)

Athens State University, Athens, AL 35611, USA
Katia.Maxwell@athens.edu

Abstract. As Artificial Intelligence (AI) continues to evolve, its integration into the Software Development Life Cycle (SDLC) offers opportunities to streamline workflows, reduce errors, and accelerate development. Despite these benefits, many organizations lack awareness of AI's potential, resulting in slower product development and increased costs. This study explores how AI enhances each SDLC phase and examines associated risks and mitigation strategies to maintain software security. Key research questions address workforce perceptions of AI, its major benefits and drawbacks, and which SDLC phases gain the most from its adoption. By answering these questions, the study provides insight into AI's impact on software development and evaluates industry readiness for AI-driven transformation.

Keywords: Artificial Intelligence (AI) · Software Development Life Cycle (SDLC) · Human Intelligence · ChatGPT · Copilot

1 Introduction

As technology continues to advance, the sophistication and applicability of Artificial Intelligence (AI) for use in the Software Development Life Cycle (SDLC) is increasing. By integrating AI into the SDLC, organizations can streamline workflows, reduce errors, and accelerate development timelines, leading to the rapid creation of high-quality software [9]. Many companies and individuals do not understand what AI is and how it can be used to help the development of their products. This is an issue that needs to be addressed, because if these companies fail to see the benefits of these tools they will be left behind and become obsolete. The effects of the lack of adoption of AI can have adverse effects on companies, as it may result in longer development times of new products and increase the cost of production, maintenance and deployment [7]. This study focuses on providing an overview of how each of the phases of the SDLC can benefit from AI. In addition to documenting benefits, the potential risks to being aware of and mitigations that can be implemented to better ensure the security of the software that is being developed are also discussed.

This study explores answers to key questions that will help developers better underst the effects of AI in each phase of the SDLC. The first question is, what is the majority consensus from the workforce about AI? The answer to this question will provide a better

K. Daimi et al. (Eds.): CSCE 2025, CCIS 2937, pp. 413–426, 2026.
https://doi.org/10.1007/978-3-032-22208-4_29

understanding of how AI is being implemented and what leaders across many different industries are using it for. A follow-up set of questions that are focused specifically on the impacts of AI on the SDLC will be explored. Those questions include: what are the major benefits of the adoption of AI into the SDLC? Which SDLC phases benefit the most from the adoption of AI? What are the drawbacks of AI in the SDLC? These answers will help give an understanding of how each phase of the SDLC is affected by AI and if there is a phase that benefits the most. All the answers to these questions will allow for a discussion on whether the workforce is ready for AI in the SDLC.

2 AI in the Workforce

To explore how AI might affect the SDLC, it is essential to understand how AI is currently being used in the workforce and how it is being viewed, even by those outside of software development. It is reported that only 0.5% of the US population is involved in the SDLC [2], therefore, looking into the more general technology workforce will increase the understanding of how AI is being received. Having this understanding will provide insight into being able to determine if developers are prepared to integrate AI into the different levels of the SDLC.

A survey conducted by Beetroot discusses that 92% of US-based developers are integrating AI coding tools into their work. Out of these, 70% specified benefits to doing so, citing better code quality, completing tasks in less time, and being able to resolve issues in a timelier manner to name a few [12]. Large tech companies like Apple, Microsoft, and IBM have embraced the use of AI to improve their competitive advantage [10]. The most common use of AI by software developers is AI assisted software development and pair programming. Before AI, this technique required two developers to work alongside each other at one workstation to develop code. Now with AI assisting in this process only one developer is needed, and they use AI as their pair programmer. Another use of AI is to provide answers to the public, AI tools can assist software developers by extracting key information from the public and internal documentation about their technology stacks. This enables them to quickly find relevant resources without relying on direct code suggestions [7]. AI can be used not only to assist in software development, but a user of a program like ChatGPT could describe what they would like for a web site to look like and the functionality that it should have and ask ChatGPT to provide the corresponding code for the full stack development. While AI is being widely accepted by software developers, many other roles in the workforce have also implemented AI in their workflows.

A survey conducted by GitLab surveyed 1001 companies that are leaders in development, IT operations and security from many different industries. After conducting the survey, GitLab analyzed the data to gain deeper insights into the responses. Their first key finding was that 83% of respondents agreed that implementing AI in software development processes is crucial to staying competitive, a sentiment that held true across all functional areas (development, operations, and security), job levels, and years of experience. Furthermore, the majority of respondents reported already using AI for at least a quarter of their DevSecOps activities. This trend was consistent across all industries represented in the survey, Finance, Technology, Telecommunications, Retail and Education, to name a few [5]. While there are many ways that developers and different industries have adopted AI into their daily work, there are many challenges that arise.

Although software developers and industry leaders see many advantages to AI there are also potential drawbacks that can lead to breaches, bugs, ethical and legal problems. If AI is using an older database to help suggest code or solutions, this could cause breaches in the software for bad actors to infiltrate the companies' systems. This software must be implemented ethically to ensure data privacy, security and intellectual property rights. The type of implementation is essential for security and safety as well, consideration of the AI systems' role within the organization, the type of AI and its strengths, the need of AI for the task, and the sophistication of the technology [6]. Employees must be trained in how to use this technology safely and securely to ensure personal and company data maintain integrity, confidentiality and availability.

One of the main concerns about the adoption and usage of AI tools in the workplace is the potential for accessing private information or intellectual property [8]. Through the surveys conducted, respondents feel there is a need for substantial training to effectively use AI tools [7]. While AI has the potential to significantly boost productivity, it may also widen the gap between developers and security professionals. Security teams are particularly worried about the potential increase in vulnerabilities due to AI-generated code [7]. The survey results also showed that the top priority for 95% of senior technology executives was ensuring the privacy and protection of intellectual property when they choose their AI tools [7]. While surveys have shown advantages to the use of AI, it has also shown the concerns associated with it. However, different roles will also have different attitudes and perspectives toward the use of AI.

To better understand attitudes and perspectives toward the use of AI, it is important to consider questions regarding the ethics and governance of AI. Zhang et al. surveyed 524 researchers who published work in the top AI conferences. The data collected showed that researchers have high trust in international and scientific organizations to guide AI development, and moderate trust in Western tech companies. On the other hand, the data also showed that researchers have low trust in national militaries, Chinese tech companies, and Facebook. Out of all the researchers surveyed, 68% of them agree that AI safety needs to be prioritized [3]. The perspective that researchers have aligns with the opinions of well-known AI scientists and other notable figures that have signed the Statement on AI Risk [11]. The findings aim to inform better regulations, governance frameworks, and guiding principles for AI at both national and international levels. In their conclusion, the researchers emphasize the need for ethical considerations in AI development, highlighting the potential risks and societal impacts. They also call for more research in the safety of AI and ethical implications to ensure responsible development of AI.

While the adoption of AI presents numerous advantages in terms of efficiency and innovation, it also necessitates careful consideration of ethical practices, data privacy, and security to ensure responsible and effective implementation. The workforce seems to be embracing AI. The insights gathered from the different data collected only shows that there is no concrete determination that can be made as to whether or not developers are ready to integrate AI into the SDLC, but that instead each phase of the SDLC has to be evaluated to determine the advantages and risks that are present by adopting AI into that phase.

3 AI in the SDLC

The SDLC is a structured process that defines the stages involved in the development of software applications. It is the comprehensive framework for planning, analyzing, designing, developing, testing, deploying and maintaining software to ensure that projects align with stakeholder requirements and effectively address user needs. This methodology provides a clear roadmap, with defined deliverables at each stage, leading to efficiency and accountability. Adding AI to this framework of software development influences the process in more than one way: AI speeds up the software development process allowing for quicker releases and bug fixes, large amounts of data can be processed quickly to help with decision making and changed the roles of developers to be more innovative in their work [9].

The first phase of the SDLC is the planning phase, which is critical for defining the project's goals, identifying necessary resources, estimating costs, and establishing a realistic timeline. Analyzing historical data to provide more accurate estimations of team capacity and workload, AI significantly enhances this process. It also improves risk assessment by identifying potential issues early on and optimizes resource allocation, ensuring that resources are used efficiently and effectively throughout the project [1].

The next phase of the SDLC is the analysis phase, where requirements are defined based on the stakeholders' needs, and a risk analysis is conducted to assess the feasibility and viability of the project. AI tools can enhance this process by analyzing and interpreting requirements documents to identify ambiguities, inconsistencies, and missing information. Additionally, leveraging AI provides deeper insights into project feasibility and risk, improving decision-making and establishing a more robust foundation for the development process [3].

The design phase takes the requirements gathered in the analysis phase and uses them to create a detailed blueprint for building the system. AI algorithms can play a pivotal role by generating multiple design alternatives based on specified constraints and requirements. These tools can also analyze potential weaknesses in the design and suggest improvements, while providing optimized system hardware specifications to enhance overall performance [1, 4].

In the development phase, the coding and implementation of the product begins. During this phase initial bug testing starts, code is written, database connections are established, and various environments are tested. This phase is critical because the quality of the code directly impacts the success of the entire project. Leveraging AI for pair programming helps reduce the number of programmers needed for each product. Additionally, AI enables significant improvements in code generation, code review, prototyping, and validation, streamlining the development process and ensuring higher-quality outputs [9].

In the testing phase, the verification of all functional, performance and security requirements take place to ensure the software meets the specifications defined in the planning phases. Automatically generating and executing tests, AI plays a significant role in this phase. It can also diagnose areas of the software most likely to fail and create targeted edge case tests to ensure stability and functionality. If any bugs are discovered during testing, AI can assist in the debugging process, identifying issues more quickly and improving the efficiency of resolving them [1, 4, 9].

In the deployment phase, fully tested and approved software is ready for release into an active environment for user access. This phase also includes providing any necessary release notes, user guides, or documentation to support software use. Automating software installation and resource allocation, AI helps ensure a more dynamic and optimized work environment. Additionally, AI can help with security and compliance checks, both before and during the installation process, ensuring the software meets required standards [4, 9].

Finally, the maintenance phase ensures the deployed software continues to function correctly, remains secure, and evolves to meet changing user needs over time. By automating patch deployment, analyzing user behavior for insights, and generating customizable reports, AI plays a pivotal role in this phase. Additionally, AI can assist in ensuring the software complies with regulatory and security policies, helping to maintain the software's integrity and relevance over time [1]. With AI providing a benefit to each phase of the SDLC, a case study was put into place to show proof of concept through the application of the theory of integrating AI into the SDLC and being able to compare the impact that it has on the SDLC process.

4 Case Study

The case study described in this section was set up based on a Computer Science I programming project that is assigned by Dr. Katia Maxwell, from Athens State University. This blackjack project is used as the basis for this case study because it is a small enough project where the full SDLC can be followed. The case study explores how AI was integrated into the SDLC for the development of a single-player Blackjack game, offering valuable insights into the benefits, risks, and potential mitigation strategies when developing with AI. The central hypothesis guiding this research is that the integration of AI within the SDLC will lead to reduced development time and fewer errors across each phase.

The primary metrics collected during this process were time to complete deliverables and errors. With metrics identified, the first step to the case study was to document human intelligence in going through the SDLC to develop a solution to the Blackjack game prompt that was provided. This initial step was completed without any use of AI. An important consideration to keep in mind is that it is natural for people to think about tasks intermittently throughout the day, but the time tracked by the developer only includes the actual time spent in front of the computer working on the task. To be able to run the case study and provide a comparative analysis, both the developer and AI were asked to provide a similar deliverable for each phase of the SDLC. The AI prompts were provided by the developer to determine what deliverables to provide, this could affect the AI output and was counted in the time for the AI to make the prompt. Mr. Maxwell Dombrowski took on the role of the human developer, while the two AI tools integrated into the SDLC were ChatGPT and Copilot.

4.1 SDLC Analysis

Based on the provided Blackjack scenario the project plan, stakeholders' requirements, cost estimation and resource allocation were determined. With the stakeholders providing all relevant information for the task the planning phase was short and efficient, taking the developer only 15 min and it only took ChatGPT and Copilot 3 min to complete all deliverables requested. The prompt given to the AI was ***"Using the following prompt, provide deliverables for the planning phase of the SDLC. This only includes Goals, Scope, Purpose, Feasibility, Stakeholders, Stakeholder Requirements, Cost and Resource Allocation"***.

Table 1 shows the breakdown of the deliverables received by each entity. For the developer deliverables they were practical, concise, and functional, not providing too much detail. ChatGPT provided a structured detail making it useful for documentation and execution in later phases. Copilot provided similar inputs in some areas, but over al it focused more on responsible gaming and learning aspects of the project. Using AI for the planning phase provides benefits such as more structure and detailed deliverables that define a clear scope of the project. The benefits that come from an all-human planning phase include project customization to meet needs; direct stakeholder input allows for better plan alignment.

For the analysis phase of this case study, functional requirements were created to ensure the functionality of the game. Requirements were created in 23 min by the developer and 2 min by both ChatGPT and Copilot. AI was given the prompt, ***"For the analysis phase of this project, provide a functional requirements for this game"***. Human provided 30 requirements with them being the most detailed due to the coverage of edge case and game mechanics comprehensively. While ChatGPT provided 24 requirements which covered core functionalities, but slightly condensing details. Copilot's 21 requirements were the most concise but focused on essential mechanics without explaining all game conditions. Table 2 documents the breakdown of requirements by category.

For phase three, the design phase, a flow diagram was created to visually depict the flow of the game design. The developer created the diagram in 1 h and 40 min, with the prompt, "create a flow diagram using your requirements." In response, ChatGPT generated a flow diagram in 2 min. Copilot was unable to create a flow diagram but provided an outline that could be used to create one.

The diagram created by the developer is concise and based on the requirements documented. The developer used standard shapes for easy readability and understanding by others; however, a few connections were missing, notably the connection to continue play after a player busts.

ChatGPT's diagram, while visually distinct, presented different requirements than those documented. For example, it included "Dealer Bust: The player wins and receives 2x their bet" and "If the player has a higher total than the dealer, they win and receive 2x their bet," but the diagram showed the player receiving only 1.5 times their bet upon winning.

While the diagrams were created using different notations, both effectively convey the game flow and logic, whereas Copilot's response lacked a clear visual representation.

For the development phase, code was written in Python to create the Blackjack game. The developer took 6 h and 6 min to code the game. This process took ChatGPT

Table 1. Planning Phase

Deliverable Requested	Human Intelligence	AI: ChatGPT	AI: Copilot
Time to complete	15 min	3 min	3 min
Goals	Create a Blackjack game for fun & research.	Interactive, fair, maintainable; no real-money gambling; scalable codebase.	Engaging game with responsible gambling focus; error handling.
Scope	Python-based, 52-card deck, balance tracking.	Defines included/excluded features (e.g., no multiplayer, real money).	Similar to ChatGPT; it emphasizes clear messaging.
Purpose	Fun and research for the thesis project.	Risk-free Blackjack, reinforce programming concepts.	Focuses on responsible leisure and learning.
Feasibility	"Easy"	Structured (Technical, Operational, Economic, Legal).	Structured like ChatGPT; adds schedule feasibility.
Stakeholders	Committee (Dr. Maxwell, Dr. Lewis, Dr. Chen), Developer.	Developer, Player, Instructor/Reviewer.	Developers, Instructor, End-users (students, educators).
Stakeholder Requirements	Betting limits, basic rules, play vs. dealer, quit game.	Intuitive UI, correct game logic, handling edge cases.	Similar to ChatGPT; it focuses on clear specifications.
Cost	N/A (using free software).	Development time, free resources.	Minimal, includes IDEs and libraries.
Resource Allocation	Basic computer.	Time, programming tools, personnel.	Development tools (e.g., Visual Studio Code, PyCharm).

1 min and Copilot 2 min, AI was given the prompt, ***"Build the blackjack game in python using your flowchart and functional requirements."*** The code created by the developer consisted of 280 lines of code. The deck of cards was created by using a class to build the cards before the game starts. The betting system and input handling created by the developer are functional but embedded deeply within the game loop, making it harder to read and maintain. However, the developer added a function that mimics the action of cutting a deck into the game, this was not a requirement but is a part of the Blackjack gameplay. This is one of the main differences that can be seen between human intelligence and artificial intelligence, humans can add to their code as they develop to enhance the code for usability. The AI versions of the game were very similar in their approach and lines of code, with ChatGPT having 110 lines and Copilot having 130 lines,

Table 2. Analysis Phase

Requirement Type	Human Intelligence	AI: ChatGPT	AI: Copilot
Time to Complete	23 min	2 min	2 min
Game Initialization	2	2	2
Bank & Betting System	4	4	3
Card Dealing & Setup	3	3	2
Player Actions	4	3	3
Dealer Rules	4	3	3
Win/Loss Conditions	6	5	4
Blackjack Mechanics	3	2	2
Balance Updates	2	2	2
Game Termination	2	2	1
Deck & Card Values	3	2	2
Total Requirements	30	24	21

significantly less than that of the developer. Both AI solutions used lists and dictionaries to create a deck of cards for gameplay. Overall, the AI versions are more efficient and well-structured, but the developer provided code which has more game customization. Table 3 summarizes the details of the code development between the three methods of development.

Table 3. Development Phase

Feature	Human Intelligence	AI: ChatGPT	AI: Copilot
Development Time	6+ h	1 min	2 min
Code Length	~280	~110	~130
Code Readability	Moderate	High	High
Efficiency	Low	High	High
Object-Oriented	Yes	No	No
Deck Cutting	Yes	No	No
Betting System	Yes	Yes	Yes
Game Loop & Replay	Yes	Yes	Yes

For the testing phase, the developer wrote test cases before beginning development and tested them while creating the code. The developer took 25 min to create the test cases with the testing of each case included in the development phase. AI was given the prompt, ***"Create test cases for your requirements and code"*** this took only 1 min for both ChatGPT and Copilot to provide unit tests that can run alongside the game it developed and text-based instructions. The test cases written by the developer were all linked to requirements, covered all key game mechanics, and followed a logical progression from the start of the round to end. It did, however, lack structure that could help when trying to automate the cases and did not provide unit tests for quick functionality testing. The test cases provided by ChatGPT were clearly put into categories, including edge cases and provided unit tests for each test case. However, some test cases were overlapping and very verbose in comparison to the test cases provided by the developer. The test cases provided by Copilot were simple and structured with names, input and expected output. The developer created 28 test cases with a major focus on the process of placing a bet and the win/loss determination of the game. ChatGPT provided 32 test cases and Copilot provided 19 test cases. Table 4 displays the breakdown of test cases by category.

Table 4. Testing Phase

Test Case Type	Human Intelligence	AI: ChatGPT	AI: Copilot
Game Initialization	2	2	2
Betting System	5	6	4
Card Dealing & Setup	4	3	1
Player Actions	4	5	3
Dealer Turn	4	5	1
Win/Loss Conditions	6	8	5
Edge Cases	3	3	3
Total Requirements	28	32	19

For the deployment phase, both the developer and AI were asked to create a user's manual. The developer took 23 min to create the user manual for the blackjack game. AI was given the prompt, ***"Create a user's manual or training guide for the blackjack game you developed."*** As with previous tasks, AI worked significantly faster than the developer, where ChatGPT took 1 min, and Copilot took 2 min. The manual created by the developer contained an informal tone that is straightforward, but somewhat repetitive. The manual covered basic gameplay functionality, but did not provide card value explanation, examples of input or how to handle errors. The manual created by ChatGPT was formal and professional in tone with extensive details. The manual provided examples and explanations throughout the whole document. ChatGPT's manual was the only one that provided a table of contents. The manual created by Copilot had a friendly and encouraging tone with good organization, but lacked details compared to ChatGPT's. Table 5 provides additional detailed comparisons of the manual created.

Lastly, for the maintenance phase, a task was developed as actual maintenance could not be done during this case study. The task developed to mimic maintenance was to enhance the overall readability of the program, and to include card suits in the hand callouts. The developer took 55 min to enhance the blackjack game. AI was given the prompt, ***"Enhance your code to Show player suit of cards, increase readability of the***

Table 5. Deployment Phase

Criteria	Human Intelligence	AI: ChatGPT	AI: Copilot
Tone	Informal, casual	Formal, professional	Friendly, encouraging
Clarity	Straightforward but somewhat repetitive	Very detailed and clear, but can be overwhelming	Clear and easy to follow, but less detailed
Structure	Basic, lacks clear sections	Well-structured with a table of contents	Organized, with sections and clear instructions
Detail Level	Moderate, covers basic gameplay	Very detailed, with examples and explanations	Moderate, covers main points and includes troubleshooting
Grammar & Phrasing	Informal, with some awkward phrasing	Formal, well-written, some repetition in sections	Well-written, no major grammar issues
Card value Explanation	Not explicitly covered	Clearly explained in a dedicated section	Explained, but briefly
Examples of Inputs	No examples provided	Provides examples for user input	No examples provided
Error Handling	Brief mention of invalid input	Detailed error handling with examples	Includes troubleshooting tips for common issues
System Requirements	Not mentioned	Not mentioned	Includes system requirements (Python version, IDE)
Special Features	Basic rules and actions covered	Includes in-depth rules, actions, and error handling	Mentions general gameplay, scoring, and winning/losses
Additional Comments	No additional content	Includes sections on contact/support and exit game	Includes troubleshooting section and quit game info

overall program" this took only 1 min for both ChatGPT and Copilot. The developer changed 12 lines of code with an addition of card suits and making the cards in hand displayed as part of the output with each new card drawn. ChatGPT's code changed 11 lines with the addition of suits and more modular functionality. This did however remove the printing of current credit the player had available. Copilot's code changed 12 lines which included handling card suits, displaying the hand more clearly, and adding better error handling for user input. Table 6 provides a breakdown of the code enhancements made.

Table 6. Maintenance Phase

Criteria	Human Intelligence	AI: ChatGPT	AI: Copilot
Time to complete	55 min	1 min	1 min
Line of Codes Changed	12	11	12
Bugs Created	None	No credit amount readouts	None

4.2 Case Study Discussion

The case study explored having a developer work through the SDLC to create the software described in the given prompt and conducting a comparative analysis against the integration of AI into each of the SDLC phases. While the focus of the data tracking was based on development time and inconsistencies, one concept that needs to remain at the forefront of development is that of possible risks. Table 7 documents the identified possible risks for each of the SDLC phases based on the Intelligence that was used for that phase.

Table 7. Identified Risks

SDLC Phase	Human Intelligence	AI: ChatGPT	AI: Copilot
Planning	Ambiguous information, misalignment with stakeholder expectations	Unnecessary details, lack of customization, stakeholder non-specific, needs verification	Same as ChatGPT; not typically used directly for planning
Analysis	Hard-to-understand language, missed edge cases, lack of organization	Unnecessary or missing details, broad scope due to lack of stakeholder interaction	Unnecessary or missing details, broad scope due to lack of stakeholder interaction
Design	Cognitive bias, assumptions leading to inconsistent design	Cannot match desired style, lacks flexibility, outdated/static knowledge base	Suggests incomplete or generic designs
Development	Redundant or suboptimal code, inconsistent style, poor modularity	Lacks context, may skip required features, untested code	Same as ChatGPT; may generate insecure or repetitive patterns
Testing	Incomplete edge case coverage, misinterpretation of requirements	Suggests unrealistic tests, unclear expected outcomes	Suggests unrealistic tests, unclear expected outcomes

(continued)

Table 7. (*continued*)

SDLC Phase	Human Intelligence	AI: ChatGPT	AI: Copilot
Deployment	Poorly detailed or unclear user guides, missing technical info	Overly complex documentation	Lacks detail and clarity in documentation

To mitigate risks throughout the SDLC, a combined approach using both human and AI inputs is most effective. In the planning phase, human insight helps clarify stakeholder-specific needs, while AI offers structured suggestions—together, they ensure accurate and refined plans. During analysis, structured templates, peer reviews, and stakeholder validation help clarify human-written requirements, while excess AI-generated detail can be trimmed and verified for alignment. In the design phase, cognitive biases can be countered through stakeholder reviews, and AI limitations are addressed with human oversight to ensure up-to-date, flexible designs. For development, peer code reviews, adherence to best practices, and prompt refinement for AI outputs help reduce redundancy, bugs, and inefficiencies. During testing, peer-reviewed test cases and requirement traceability ensure coverage, while AI-generated cases should be validated for clarity and feasibility. In deployment, blending human-written and AI-generated user guides helps balance clarity, detail, and accessibility for various users. Finally, for maintenance, all updates should undergo thorough testing—regardless of source—while consistent version control and documentation prevent long-term system instability. Combining strengths from both humans and AI leads to more accurate, efficient, and resilient software development outcomes.

The documented results, risks, and mitigations show that while AI significantly reduced the time required for tasks such as planning, design, and testing, it did not always outperform human efforts in terms of customization, detail, or understanding stakeholder needs. AI tools offered efficiency and structure, but lacked flexibility, sometimes overlooking edge cases or introducing unnecessary details. On the other hand, the developer contributed more comprehensive and tailored results, although at the cost of increased time and occasional inefficiency. Ultimately, the hypothesis was partially supported, as AI reduced development time and errors in specific phases, but human input remained essential for achieving high-quality, customized deliverables. The most successful approach and mitigation tactics involve combining both AI and human contributions to optimize time, quality, and accuracy throughout the SDLC.

Through the case study provided, answers to the key questions proposed at the beginning of this paper can now be addressed

What are the major benefits of the adoption of AI into the SDLC?

AI significantly reduces the time required to complete tasks, this is shown in the case study throughout the planning, design, coding and deployment phases. AI also provided a high-level organization and structure to all the deliverables that it produced. The number of errors throughout the development and testing phases was greatly reduced, which reduced the potential risks. AI is shown to be helpful in automating repetitive tasks such as creating test cases, writing parts of the documentation, and generating parts of the code. These benefits are seen throughout all phases of the SDLC, some more than others.

Which SDLC phase or phases benefit the most from the adoption of AI?

Development and testing phases were documented as having the most benefit from AI being implemented. In the development phase, the AI used in the study was able to generate code rapidly and efficiently, producing clean, structured code in significantly less time. The developer's code, while more customized, took significantly longer to write. In the testing phase, AI generated comprehensive and well-structured test cases quickly, helping to ensure that the game met all requirements. AI also produced unit tests for testing each module in the blackjack game. The developer, while thorough, took more time, could have missed some edge cases and did not provide unit test cases.

What are the drawbacks of AI in the SDLC?

AI can lack flexibility to customize as needed to meet stakeholder requirements or project needs. AI may not be able to understand the nuances of the project, leading to errors or potential details. Sometimes it can be overly detailed that could not be necessary and overwhelm the project. AI is limited by its static knowledge base and may not be able to adapt to changes in requirements or project needs as effectively as a human developer. Human input is required for AI and depending on the details in the requests made AI could provide bad or incorrect information. All outputs should be checked by humans as well to ensure they are correct, relevant, and algin with the project's objectives. AI is transforming the SDLC by improving efficiency, automating tasks, and accelerating development across all phases. From planning and analysis to deployment and maintenance, AI enhances risk assessment, design optimization, coding, testing, and security compliance.

5 Conclusion

AI's adoption in the workforce is growing, many major tech companies are leveraging AI for competitive advantages, and with the increase of usage there is also an. increase in concerns around security, ethics, and intellectual property rights. Proper governance, training, and oversight are essential to mitigate risks and ensure responsible implementation. The case study examined the integration of AI tools, ChatGPT and Copilot, into the SDLC for developing a single-player Blackjack game, hypothesizing that AI would reduce development and testing time and errors. The findings partially supported the hypothesis, highlighting that AI reduces time and errors in certain phases but requires human oversight for optimal results. While AI streamlines processes, human expertise is still crucial for creativity, contextual understanding, and ethical decision-making. For the workforce to be fully ready for AI, organizations must invest in training employees, governing bodies need to implement policies and focus on a collaborative approach where AI supports—rather than replaces—human expertise. A balanced integration of AI with human oversight will ultimately maximize efficiency while maintaining software quality, security, and innovation.

References

1. Pothukuchi, A., Kota, L., Mallikarjunaradhya, V.: (PDF) Impact of generative AI on the software development life cycle (SDLC). ResearchGate. https://www.researchgate.net/publication/373012726_IMPACT_OF_GENERATIVE_AI_ON_THE_SOFTWARE_DEVELOPMENT_LIFE_CYCLE_SDLC. Accessed 28 Mar 2025. Author, F., Author, S.: Title of a proceedings paper. In: Editor, F., Editor, S. (eds.) CONFERENCE 2016, LNCS, vol. 9999, pp. 1–13. Springer, Heidelberg (2016)
2. BLS: Software developers. U.S. Bureau of Labor Statistics, https://www.bls.gov/oes/current/oes151252.htm?form=MG0AV3. Accessed 20 Jan 2025
3. Zhang, B., Anderljung, M., Khan, L., Dreksler, N., Horowitz, M., Dafoe, A.: Ethics and governance of artificial intelligence: evidence from a survey of machine learning researchers. J. Artif. Intell. Res.. https://www.jair.org/index.php/jair/article/view/12895. Accessed 19 Sept 2024
4. Batarseh, F., Mohod, R. Kumar, A., Bui, J.: The application of artificial intelligence in software engineering: a review challenging conventional wisdom. ResearchGate. https://www.researchgate.net/publication/353677581_The_application_of_artificial_intelligence_in_software_engineering_a_review_challenging_conventional_wisdom. Accessed 17 Sept 2024
5. GitLab, Ed.: The state of AI in software development. https://www.tsoftglobal.com/wpcontent/uploads/2023/11/GitLab-STATE-OF-AI.pdf. Accessed 19 Sept 2024
6. Munoko, I.: Implementing artificial intelligence: capabilities and risk. ISACA. https://www.isaca.org/resources/isaca-journal/issues/2022/volume-4/implementingartificial-intelligence-capabilities-and-risk. Accessed 17 Sept 2024
7. Kauppaymuthoo, K.J., Collins, C.: Artificial intelligence adoption in software development, June (2023). [Online]. Available: lup.lub.lu.se. Accessed: Aug 2024
8. Birštonas, R.: Risks to employees' intellectual property rights posed by artificial intelligence. ResearchGate. https://www.researchgate.net/publication/374764507_Risks_to_Employees'_Intellectual_Property_Rights_Posed_by_Artificial_Intelligence. Accessed 28 Mar 2025
9. Kumar, S.: The application and impact of AI in the SDLC. dzone.com. https://dzone.com/articles/application-and-impact-of-ai-in-the-sdlc. Accessed 28 Mar 2025
10. Stash Team: 15 largest AI companies in 2024. Stash. https://www.stash.com/learn/top-ai-companies/. Accessed 28 Mar 2025
11. Statement on AI Risk: Cais: Statement on AI Risk | CAIS. https://www.safe.ai/work/statement-on-ai-risk. Accessed 28 Mar 2025
12. T.B. Team: Advantages and disadvantages of using AI in software development. Beetroot. https://beetroot.co/ai-ml/what-are-the-advantages-and-disadvantages-of-using-ai-in-development/. Accessed 17 Sept 2024

An Empirical Study on the Evolution and Vulnerabilities of Maven Artifacts

Nirajan Bhattarai, Riley Stratton, and Minhaz Zibran(✉)

Department of Computer Science, Idaho State University, Pocatello, USA
{nirajanbhattarai,rileystratton,zibran}@isu.edu

Abstract. Frequent software releases are expected to address security and compatibility issues, but may result in security breakages in return while increasing maintenance cost and system complexity. We conduct an empirical study on the ecosystem-wide evolution of the Maven Central Dependency Graph and the maintenance status of its artifacts, with the ultimate goal of educating the developer community about the evolution and maintenance levels within the Maven Central ecosystem. We examine the growth patterns of library releases over time, focusing on frequency, rhythm, and speed, to understand the influence of project management methodologies such as Agile, security vulnerabilities, and open-source contributions on the evolution of the Maven Central ecosystem. Similarly, we also measure the maintenance level of artifacts in the ecosystem based on various factors such as popularity, missed releases, and whether vulnerabilities have been addressed or not.

Rapid growth between 2004 and 2005 aligned with emergence with agile methodologies, followed by a gradual increase up to 2021, after which it started plateauing or stabilizing, which may be attributed to the emergence of new technologies such as AI. In contrast, the growth of vulnerabilities across all severity types experienced a rapid decline after 2021, possibly indicating an increased emphasis on security and improved library maintenance within the community. We found that only 5.21% of all libraries are fully maintained. The study suggests the need for further in-depth research on the most prevalent vulnerabilities in the Maven Central ecosystem, and a well-validated metric system for assessment of combined vulnerability and maintenance level in the Maven Central Dependency Graph.

Keywords: Maven Central · Dependency Graph · Evolution · Maintenance · Release · Vulnerability · Dependency · Empirical Study

1 Introduction

Dependencies are third-party software components introduced into the software development framework to reduce costs and accelerate the speed of software development. As dependencies are an indispensable component of the software development process, frequent new releases are expected to address security and

K. Daimi et al. (Eds.): CSCE 2025, CCIS 2937, pp. 427–440, 2026.
https://doi.org/10.1007/978-3-032-22208-4_30

compatibility issues, ensuring safe and reliable use [1]. However, the maintenance effort on these dependency libraries incurs costs and increases complexity [2]. Raemaekers et al. [3] highlighted that there will always be tension between version updates intended for mitigating security risks and the security breakages that may result from such updates.

The study on the evolution of dependency can be approached from two perspectives: ego-centric, focusing on particular dependency libraries; and/or ecosystem-wide, having global insight on dependency ecosystem management and pervasion [2]. To assist with these kinds of studies, several repositories and resources are available, such as Maven Central, which maintains over 2.8 million unique artifact repositories for JVM-based artifacts, along with metadata detailing versions, dependencies, and upload dates in a dependency graph. This makes it well-suited for both ego-centric and system-wide big data evolution studies [4]. Similarly, various validated metrics have been proposed and incorporated in the Maven Central Database for researchers, eliminating the need to develop and validate their own quantification metrics, which would be particularly challenging for a dataset of this size. Some of these proposed metrics are popularity [5], calculated based on the number of dependents a particular version of a library has in a year, and the freshness [1], which is the computation of the number of releases and the duration elapsed between a particular release and its most recent update.

Leveraging these metrics and repositories, we carry out an ecosystem-wide empirical study of the evolution of the Maven Central Dependency Graph and the maintenance status of its artifacts (aka, Maven artifacts). In particular, we address the following two research questions.

RQ1: *What are the patterns in the growth of the Maven Central Repository across different periods?*

- The evolution of the ecosystem, especially within the Java community, was assessed by analyzing the pattern in the growth of the Maven central graph across different periods. Assessing the frequency, rhythm, and speed trend of library releases over time can shed light on the developer's behavior and the impact of project management methodologies like Agile [5,6]. Similarly, approximately 35% of all open-source projects have their origination from dependent libraries, which are increasingly susceptible to security vulnerabilities [7].

RQ2: *To what extent does the ecosystem contain unmaintained libraries?*

- In the modern software development realm, open-source projects play an indispensable part. At the same time, open access has also remained largely unmaintained [8], mainly because they are maintained on the developer's unrestricted schedule and mostly unpaid [9]. Although open-source projects will likely remain unmaintained, limited studies address this issue [8].

The rest of the paper is organized as follows. The methodology used in this study including the dataset for addressing the research questions is introduced in Sect. 2. Findings are presented in Sect. 3. In Sect. 4 we address the threats to the validity of our study. Related work in the literature are briefly discussed in Sect. 5 and finally Sect. 6 concludes the paper.

2 Methodology

In this section, we introduce the dataset, metrics, and measurements used in our analysis for addressing the research questions.

2.1 Dataset

We address the aforementioned research questions through a quantitative analysis of a public dataset [15] consisting of the artifacts and their dependencies of the Maven Central Repository [13] structured into a Neo4J [14] graph database forming the Goblin framework [15]. Figure 1 portrays the architecture of the Goblin framework.

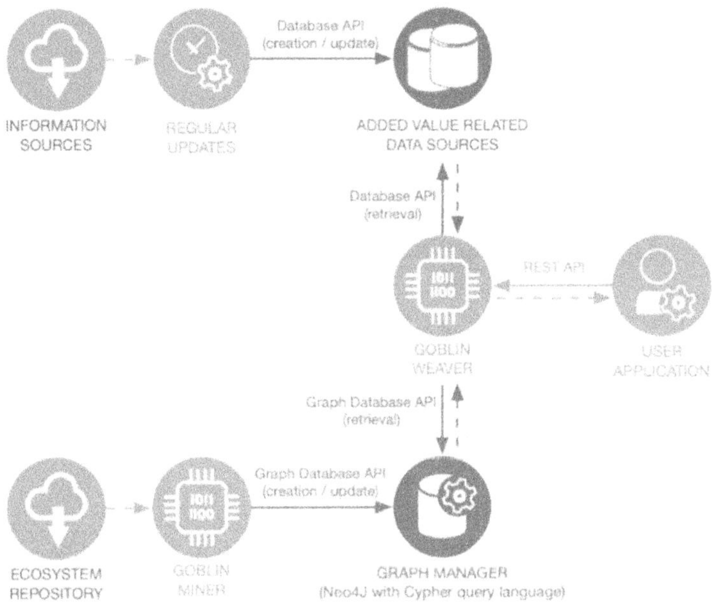

Fig. 1. Overview of the Goblin Framework [25].

Figure 2 presents an example of dependency graph model used in the framework that captures dependencies and relationships among different versions of reusable artifacts/libraries in the Maven Central Repository. A graph database of packages is created in the form of a Neo4j dependency graph [25], where the graph is made up of two main categories of nodes, the first type node is called the 'Artifact' node and the second one is referred to as the 'Release' node. Each 'Artifact' node represents a reusable library while each 'Release' node represents a specific release version of that reusable library. There are two types of links/edges between the 'Artifact' and 'Release' nodes. The first connection/edge type between these nodes is referred to as `'relationship_AR'`, which connects an 'Artifact' node to a particular 'Release' node. Every 'Release' node has exactly one *relationship_AR* terminating at it. The second connection type of connection/edge is a `'Dependency'`, which is the connection drawn from a specific 'Release' node to an 'Artifact' node that the release depends on, with any number of dependencies drawn between them [25]. Further details about the Goblin framework and the dataset can be found elsewhere [15,25].

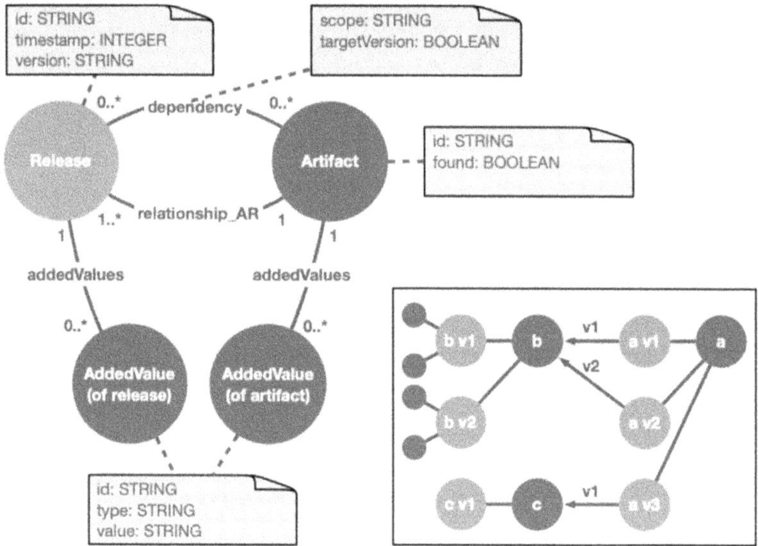

Fig. 2. Example Dependency Graph Model of the Goblin Framework [25].

We particularly use the `with_metrics_goblin_maven_30_08_24.dump` of the dataset [15] dated August 30th, 2024. This graph dataset includes 59,152,712 nodes categorized into three primary types: *Artifact*, *Release*, and *AddedValue*. The *AddedValue* nodes include additional information about the artifacts and releases such as POPUPARITY_1_YEAR (i.e., the number of dependents), FRESHNESS (i.e., timestamp of the last update), CVE (i.e., associated Common Vulnerability Enumeration), and SPEED (i.e., yearly frequency of releases).

2.2 Metrics and Measurements

Growth: The growth of all releases, all artifacts, and the prevalence of vulnerabilities of different severity types within a particular year were presented as a year-wise frequency trend in a line graph. The dependency count across years was presented as a box plot.

Release rhythm: A release rhythm for an artifact is defined as an ordered sequence of time-intervals (measured in days) between consecutive releases of an artifact over the duration of a time period (e.g., a year). We use this definition of release rhythm derived from the work of Jamie et al. [2].

Total Vulnerability Contributions (TVC): In the dataset, CVE information is presented in JSON format for each release, with key 'cve', which represents array of CVE identifiers. The JSON format is first cleaned, and subjected to count, which is measured as the number of the elements in the array. Vulnerabilities identified with CVEs are associated with a severity level, which can be NONE, LOW, MEDIUM, HIGH, or CRITICAL. The count of vulnerabilities at each severity level within the CVE for each release was extracted. Since each release may have multiple CVE with different severity levels, we calculated the total vulnerability contribution (TVC) score based upon severity level of vulnerabilities along with their count in respective severity. The total vulnerability contribution for each release is computed by multiplying the weight assigned to each severity level by its count and then summing them up, as follows: The total vulnerability contribution, denoted as TVC is calculated as follows:

$$TVC = \sum_{\ell \in S} |V_\ell| \times \omega_\ell \tag{1}$$

where, $S = \{\text{NONE, LOW, MEDIUM, HIGH, CRITICAL}\}$, V_ℓ denotes the set of all vulnerabilities with severity level ℓ, and ω_ℓ represents a weight of vulnerabilities having severity level ℓ defined as follows.

$$\omega_\ell = \begin{cases} 0.0 & \text{if } \ell = \text{NONE} \\ 3.0 & \text{if } \ell = \text{LOW} \\ 5.5 & \text{if } \ell = \text{MEDIUM} \\ 8.0 & \text{if } \ell = \text{HIGH} \\ 9.5 & \text{if } \ell = \text{CRITICAL} \end{cases}$$

The choice of weights is based on the vulnerability severity scale used in an earlier study [10]. For any release having no vulnerabilities, the total vulnerability contribution was assigned as zero.

2.3 Maintenance Levels

Since there is no single available criterion to classify a software artifact as well maintained based on available metrics in the data, we devised our own criteria based on logical steps based on different related metrics. Popularity, total vulnerability contribution, and the number of releases were primarily used to determine the maintenance level of the artifact. The classification was based upon three criteria: 1) whether its total vulnerability contribution has decreased at least two times or remained consistently below score of 8.0, which is threshold for high vulnerability; 2) whether the artifact's popularity has increased at least two times; 3) whether at least one release occurred within the last six months. Artifact having all three criteria fulfilled are classified as 'Fully Maintained,' those meeting two criteria as 'Partially Maintained,' those meeting one criterion as 'Slightly Maintained,' and those meeting none as 'Not Maintained'.

3 Findings

In this section, we present the findings of our study. First we present the annual growth in artifacts and releases, then the discovered rhythm is presented, followed by vulnerability contributions and maintenance levels.

3.1 Growth in the Maven Central Ecosystem

Year-Wise Growth in Software Artifacts, Releases, and Dependencies: The trends in the growth of software artifacts and their releases over the years are shown in Fig. 3. The y-axis in the line graph of Fig. 3 represents the cumulative count, while the x-axis represents different years. The blue line and the yellow line trace the cumulative release count and artifact counts over the years, respectively. The agile software development evolution timelines are shown by the red lines, which were gathered from the work by Hoda et al. [11]. As presented in Fig. 3, rapid incremental growth is observed from 2004 to 2005, when the scaling approach to agile software development was adopted. From 2005 to 2021, the growth was incremental but gradual. After 2021, where emerging technologies such as artificial intelligence started to manifest into the software development domain, the growth began to plateau.

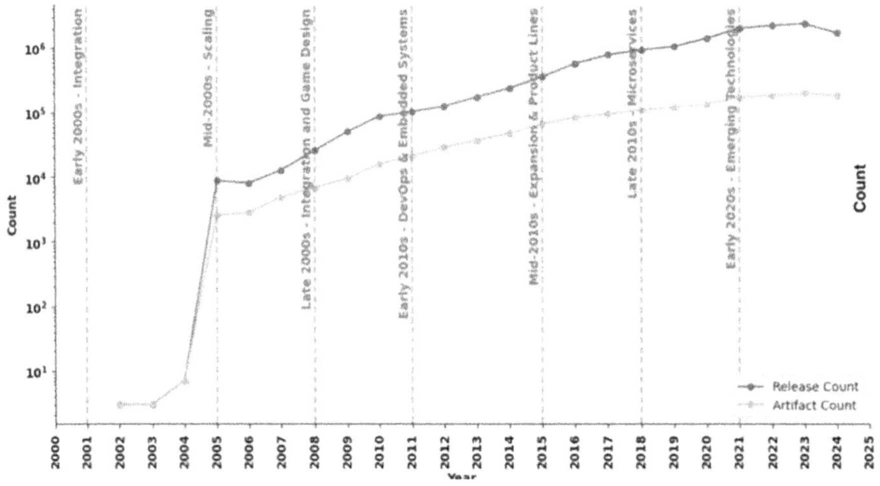

Fig. 3. Growth of artifacts' releases over the years.

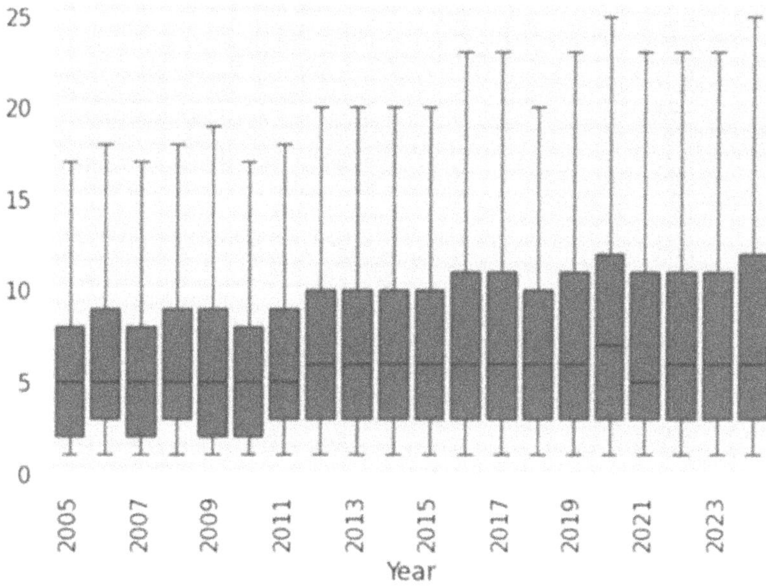

Fig. 4. Distribution of dependencies over the years.

The box plot in Fig. 4 shows the distribution/growth of dependencies over years. Here the y-axis represents the count of dependencies, and the x-axis represents different years. Primarily, the median of the distribution was used to track the trend over the years. The plot starts from 2005 because outliers in the preceding years make it difficult to display the data in the box plot. As observed in Fig. 4, the growth, assessed by the median number of dependencies each year, shows an increase after 2011, where DevOps and Embedded systems adoption started, with a slight rise in 2020, a decrease in 2021, and a return to the previous growth trend beyond 2021.

Rhythm of Software Releases in the Ecosystem: The results on rhythm, as portrayed in Fig. 5, indicate that the timeline can be divided into five phases: Phase I (2002–2005), Phase II (2006–2010), Phase III (2009–2010), Phase IV (2011–2016), and Phase V (2017–2024). The duration between consecutive library releases of an artifact was subdued during Phase I, showed a ripple effect (i.e., increases and decreases) in Phases II and III, decreased and stabilized in Phase IV, and slightly decreased and stabilized further in Phase V. Phase I represents the period between integration and scaling, Phase II marks the transition from scaling to game design, Phase III corresponds to the emergence and adoption of DevOps practices, Phase IV reflects the period following the emergence of microservices, and Phase V encompasses the era of emerging technologies. Similarly, there has been steady growth in the speed of releases across the years within the entire ecosystem.

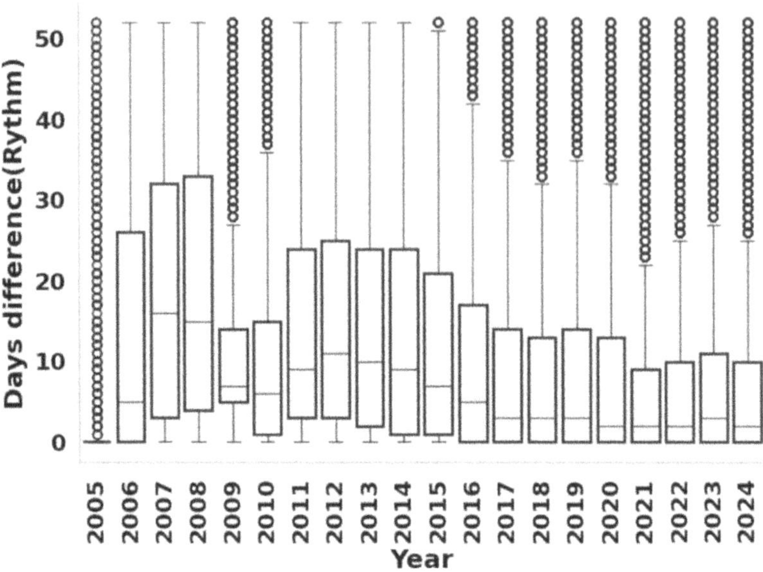

Fig. 5. Distribution of rhythms of library releases in the different years.

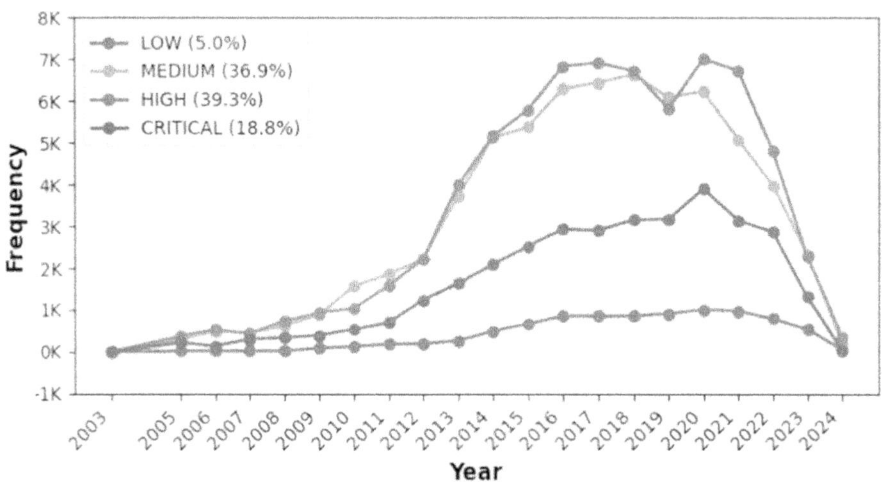

Fig. 6. Trend of different release vulnerability severity across years

Trends and Distributions of CVEs and Their Severity: Figure 6 presents the frequency of CVEs of different severity levels associated with releases every year. The CVE label for each release can have none, one, or multiple associated CVEs. The CVEs associated with each release were separated, and the severities of the individual CVEs were identified and counted. Any CVE label in an incorrect format was excluded. The line graph illustrates the trend in the count of different CVE severity levels, with each dot representing the number of cases of a specific severity type found in that particular year within the ecosystem.

Table 1. Top Five Most Frequent Vulnerabilities

CVE ID	Severity	# of Occurrences
CVE-2023-24057	CRITICAL	1138
CVE-2022-31159	HIGH	1420
CVE-2023-32070	CRITICAL	1691
CVE-2023-6835	MODERATE	1817
CVE-2023-6837	HIGH	3916

Releases with low and medium severity dominate the ecosystem, covering approximately 80% of all releases. However, highly vulnerable releases account for 14%, with moderate and high vulnerabilities collectively representing a significant portion of the ecosystem. Importantly, the five most prevalent vulnerabilities are of high severity, ranging from moderate to critical (Table 1). As seen in the figure, starting from the years 2020 there is a decline. The emergence of new technologies, such as AI and automation in agile methodologies, may have contributed to this decline, along with growing concerns about security in software engineering in recent years.

We also calculate the total vulnerability contribution (TVC) according to Eq. 1. Based on the computed values, the total contribution was categorized into five groups: 0.7–5 (low), 7.5–15 (medium), 15–22.5 (mild), 22.5–30 (moderate), and >30 (high) vulnerability contribution for each release. Figure 7 displays the total vulnerability contribution (TVC) in different contribution categories as defined above. The distribution of total vulnerability contributions of all five groups is shown in the box plots, along with the average in red, which represents the mean of all total vulnerability contributions within each category. Additionally, the percentage contribution of each vulnerability category to the total reported vulnerabilities is included (at the top left, with legends), excluding releases with no vulnerabilities.

3.2 Maintenance Levels in the Maven Ecosystem

Based on the three criteria we set in Sect. 2.3 for determination of the maintenance level of an artifact, we calculate the number of artifacts that fall into fully, partially or slightly maintained categories as presented in Fig. 8. The log scale was chosen to make the bar diagram of the figure presentable. The percentage of partially maintained, fully maintained and slightly maintained libraries was 94.74%, 5.21%, and 0.05% respectively. As seen in the figure, the artifacts that meet two of the three criteria (i.e., partially maintained) are significantly more prevalent, followed by artifacts meeting all three criteria (fully maintained).

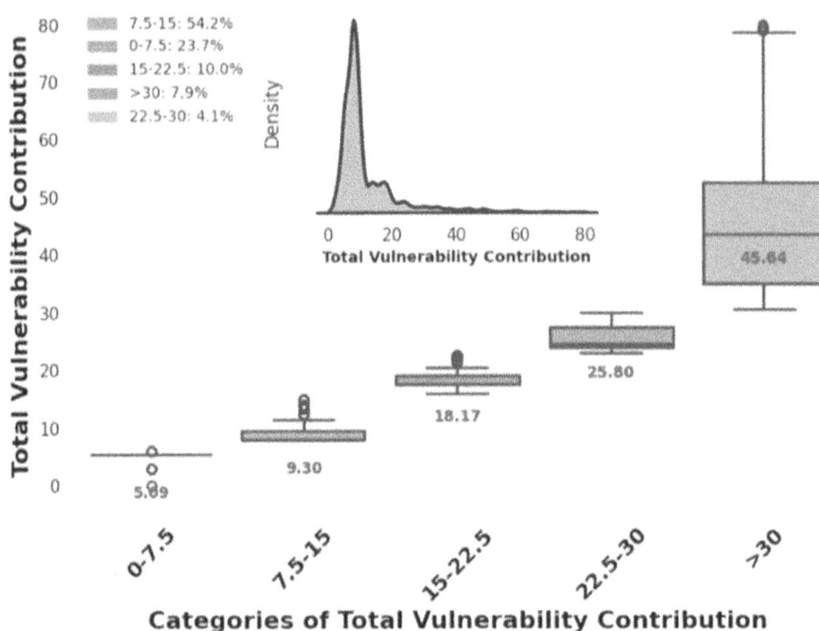

Fig. 7. Total Vulnerability Contribution across different contribution categories.

Surprisingly, the number of artifacts that met only one of the three criteria was significantly smaller. This may be because most artifacts already satisfied two or three of the criteria, we established for identifying maintenance levels, leaving a small proportion of artifacts that only met one of the three criteria.

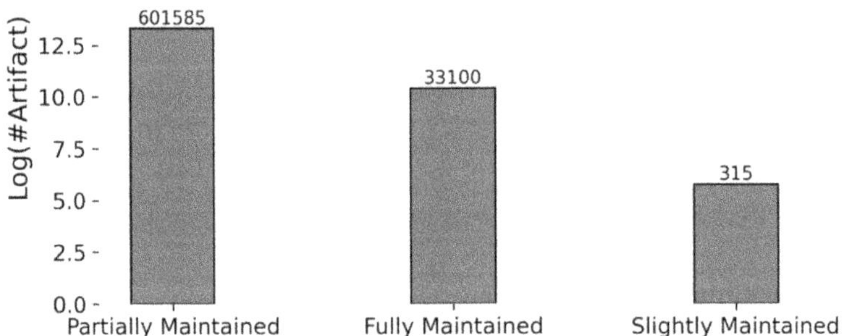

Fig. 8. Distribution of the extent of artifact maintenance levels.

Kruskal-Wallis tests along with Tukey's Honestly Significant Difference (HSD) at $p < 0.05$ level of significance were applied to test for differences in distributions between each pair of these groups and the differences are found statistically significant.

4 Threats to Validity

Our study includes only the Java libraries and components in the Maven Central Ecosystem captured in the dataset [15]. Thus, the findings may not be generalizable to other ecosystems particularly consisting of artifacts written in language other than Java.

The metrics (e.g., TVC and release rhythm) defined and used in this work might have fallen short in capturing what they were designed to measure. However, the data set [15] used in this work is publicly available, while the methodology for the analysis and derivation of the results are well documented in this paper. Therefore, it should be possible to replicate this study, which indicates high reliability of this work.

5 Related Work

Studies in the past investigated code smells [26–28], code quality [26,29], bug patterns [30–32], vulnerabilities [33,34], human aspects [35–39] of software development and maintenance as well as comparison of methods/tools [40–43] for measuring such aspects.

The study of different aspects of the Maven Central Repository has recently gained interests in the community. A number of studies [16–24] this year have investigated different aspects of the Maven Central Repository using the same dataset used in our work. Our study substantially differs from all the earlier work. We have studied the evolution all three components of the Maven software ecosystem: software libraries, its releases, and dependencies of releases across years, with special emphasis on rhythm, speed, maintenance, and vulnerabilities. However, our findings are similar to the results of Decan et al. [12], i.e., consistent increase in dependency across Maven artifacts over time with plateau beginning to show up from 2020 and 2021.

6 Conclusion

In this study, we uncover the trend and growth of various component of software ecosystem in Maven Central dependency graph. We observed a general trend of growth in frequency, speed, and vulnerabilities until 2021. Beyond 2021, the trend began to plateau, except for the frequency of vulnerabilities of different severity, which started to decrease. This trend may be attributed to rapid advancements in the field of software development, driven by the emergence of new technologies like artificial intelligence, along with increased efforts to improve software security. The fully maintained libraries were just five percent of total libraries, suggest need for more maintained effort among the developer's community. However, the criteria used to determine the maintenance level were not well validated nor derived from standard guidelines, which limits its adoption and implementation. The study suggests the need for further in-depth research on the most prevalent vulnerabilities in the Maven Central ecosystem, as well as the development of metric-based evaluation criteria for the rapid identification of various characteristics of libraries, their releases, and associated dependencies, such as maintenance level and combined vulnerability score.

References

1. Cox, J., Bouwers, E., Eekelen, M.V., Visser, J.: Measuring dependency freshness in software systems. In: 37th Intl. Conf. on Software Engineering, pp. 109–118 (2015)
2. Jaime, D., Haddad, J.E., Poizat, P.: A Preliminary Study of Rhythm and Speed in the Maven Ecosystem (2023)
3. Raemaekers, S., Van Deursen, A., Visser, J.: The Maven repository dataset of metrics, changes, and dependencies. In: 10th Working Conference on Mining Software Repositories, San Francisco, USA, pp. 221–224. IEEE (2013)
4. Soto-Valero, C., Benelallam, A., Harrand, N., Barais, O., Baudry, B.: The emergence of software diversity in Maven central. In: 16th IEEE/ACM International Conference on Mining Software Repositories, Canada, pp. 333–343. IEEE (2019)
5. Zerouali, A., Mens, T., Robles, G., Gonzalez-Barahona, J.M.: On the diversity of software package popularity metrics: an empirical study of NPM. In: 26th Intl. Conference on Software Analysis, Evolution and Reengineering, pp. 589–593 (2019)
6. Bavota, G., Canfora, G., Di Penta, M., Oliveto, R., Panichella, S.: How the Apache community upgrades dependencies: an evolutionary study. Empir. Softw. Eng. **20**(5), 1275–1317 (2015)
7. Wu,Y., Yu, Z., Wen, M., Li, Q., Zou, D., Jin, H.: Understanding the threats of upstream vulnerabilities to downstream projects in the Maven ecosystem. In: 45th Intl. Conference on Software Engineering, Australia, pp. 1046–1058 (2023)
8. de Sousa Coelho, J.J.: Identifying and characterizing unmaintained projects in github. Ph.D. dissertation, Universidade Federal de Minas Gerais (2019)
9. Khondhu, J., Capiluppi, A., Stol, K.-J.: Is it all lost? A study of inactive open source projects. In: Petrinja, E., Succi, G., El Ioini, N., Sillitti, A. (eds.) Open Source Software: Quality Verification. IFIP Advances in Info and Com. Tech, vol. 404, pp. 61–79. Springer, Heidelberg (2013)
10. Aggarwal, M.: A study of CVSS v4.0: a CVE scoring system. In: 6th Intl. Conference on Contemporary Computing and Informatics, India, pp. 1180–1186 (2023)
11. Hoda, R., Salleh, N., Grundy, J.: The rise and evolution of agile software development. IEEE Softw. **35**(5), 58–63 (2018)
12. Decan, A., Mens, T., Grosjean, P.: An empirical comparison of dependency network evolution in seven software packaging ecosystems. Empir. Softw. Eng. **24**(1), 381–416 (2019)
13. Maven central repository. https://mvnrepository.com/repos/central
14. Neo4j. https://neo4j.com
15. Jaime, D., Goblin: Neo4j maven central dependency graph. https://zenodo.org/records/13734581
16. Shafin, M., Rabbi, M., Hasan, S., Zibran, M.: Faster releases, fewer risks: a study on maven artifact vulnerabilities and lifecycle management. In: 22nd Intl. Conference on Mining Software Repositories (MSR), Canada, pp. 275–279 (2025)
17. Rabbi, M., Champa, A., Paul, R., Zibran, M.: Chasing the clock: how fast are vulnerabilities fixed in the Maven ecosystem? In: 22nd International Conference on Mining Software Repositories, pp. 265–269 (2025)

18. Nachuma, C., Hossan, M., Turzo, A., Zibran, M.: Decoding dependency risks: a quantitative study of vulnerabilities in the Maven ecosystem. In: 22nd International Conference on Mining Software Repositories, Canada, pp. 270–274 (2025)
19. Rabbi, M., Paul, R., Champa, A., Zibran, M.: Understanding software vulnerabilities in the Maven ecosystem: patterns, timelines, and risks. In: 22nd International Conference on Mining Software Repositories, Canada, pp. 290–294 (2025)
20. Chowdhury, B., Rabbi, M., Hasan, S., Zibran, M.: Insights into dependency maintenance trends in the Maven ecosystem. In: 22nd International Conference on Mining Software Repositories, Canada, pp. 280–284 (2025)
21. Lake, G., Zibran, M.: Analyzing dependency clusters and security risks in the Maven central repository. In: 22nd International Conference on Mining Software Repositories, Canada, pp. 260–264 (2025)
22. Bodily, C., Hill, E., Kramer, A., Kerby, L., Zibran, M.: Insights into vulnerability trends in maven artifacts: recurrence, popularity, and user behavior. In: 22nd International Conference on Mining Software Repositories, pp. 285–289 (2025)
23. Svancara, A., Gardner, G., Gilbreath, P., Appiagyei, C., Barlow, E., Zibran, M.: Dealing with dependency: how dependencies shape release frequency in the maven ecosystem. In: 8th International Conference on Software and System Engineering, France, pp. 1–6 (2025)
24. Bhuiyan, M., Rabbi, M., Hasan, S., Zibran, M.: The popularity paradox: insights into vulnerabilities and updates in Maven ecosystem. In: 8th International Conference on Software and System Engineering, France, pp. 1–5 (2025)
25. Jaime, D., Haddad, J., Poizat, P.: Goblin: a framework for enriching and querying the maven central dependency graph. In: 21st International Conference on Mining Software Repositories, pp. 37–41 (2024)
26. Islam, M., Zibran, M.: On the characteristics of buggy code clones: a code quality perspective. In: IEEE International Workshop on Software Clones, pp. 23–29 (2018)
27. Zibran, M., Roy, C.: Conflict-aware optimal scheduling of code clone refactoring. IET Softw. **7**(3), 167–186 (2013)
28. Zibran, M., Saha, R., Roy, C., Schneider, K.: Evaluating the conventional wisdom in clone removal: a genealogy-based empirical study. In: 28th ACM Symposium on Applied Computing, pp. 1123–1130 (2013)
29. Alwad, D., Panta, M., Zibran, M.: An empirical study of the relationships between code readability and software complexity. In: International Conference on Software Engineering and Data Engineering, pp. 122–127 (2018)
30. Islam, M., Zibran, M.: How bugs are fixed: exposing bug-fix patterns with edits and nesting levels. In: ACM Symposium on Applied Computing, pp. 1523–1531 (2020)
31. Islam, M., Zibran, M.: What changes in where? An empirical study of bug-fixing change patterns. ACM Appl. Comput. Rev. **20**(4), 18–34 (2021)
32. Rajbhandari, A., Zibran, M., Eishita, F.: Security versus performance bugs: how bugs are handled in the chromium project. In: IEEE International Conference on Software Engineering, Management, and Applications, pp. 70–76 (2022)
33. Islam, M., Zibran, M.: A comparative study on vulnerabilities in categories of clones and non-cloned code. In: IEEE International Workshop on Software Clones, pp. 8–14 (2016)
34. Islam, M., Zibran, M., Nagpal, A.: Security vulnerabilities in categories of clones and non-cloned code: an empirical study. In: ACM/IEEE International Symposium on Empirical Software Engineering and Measurement, pp. 20–29 (2017)

35. Champa, A., Rabbi, M., Eishita, F., Zibran, M.: Are we aware? An empirical study on the privacy and security awareness of smartphone sensors. In: IEEE International Conference on Software Engineering, Management, and Applications, pp. 287–294 (2023)
36. Champa, A., Rabbi, M., Zibran, M., Islam, M.: Insights into female contributions in open-source projects. In: 20th IEEE International Conference on Mining Software Repositories, pp. 357–361 (2023)
37. Islam, M., Zibran, M.: Exploration and exploitation of developers' sentimental variations in software engineering. Int. J. Softw. Innov. **4**(4), 35–55 (2016)
38. Islam, M., Zibran, M.: Towards understanding and exploiting developers' emotional variations in software engineering. In: IEEE International Conference on Software Engineering, Management, and Applications, pp. 185–192 (2016)
39. Islam, M., Zibran, M.: Sentiment analysis of software bug related commit messages. In: International Conference on Software Engineering and Data Engineering, pp. 3–8 (2018)
40. Islam, M., Zibran, M.: A comparison of dictionary building methods for sentiment analysis in software engineering text. In: ACM/IEEE International Symposium on Empirical Software Engineering and Measurement, pp. 478–479 (2017)
41. Islam, M., Zibran, M.: A comparison of software engineering domain specific sentiment analysis tools. In: IEEE International Conference on Software Engineering, Management, and Applications, pp. 487–491 (2018)
42. Joseph, R., Zibran, M., Eishita, F.: Choosing the weapon: a comparative study of security analyzers for android applications. In: IEEE International Conference on Software Engineering, Management, and Applications, pp. 51–57 (2021)
43. Murphy, D., Zibran, M., Eishita, F.: Plugins to detect vulnerable plugins: an empirical assessment of the security scanner plugins for wordpress. In: IEEE International Conference on Software Engineering, Management, and Applications, pp. 39–44 (2021)

A Non-Functional Quality Framework for Blockchain Software: ISO/IEC 25010 Revisited

Abeer S. Al-Humaimeedy(✉), Salma HabibAllah, and Reema Alhamadi

Software Engineering Department, King Saud University, Riyadh, Saudi Arabia
Abeer@KSU.EDU.SA

Abstract. Distributed ledger technology is shifting from niche experimentation to critical infrastructure across finance, healthcare, and public administration, yet the evaluation of its non-functional quality remains an unresolved challenge. A systematic review shows that critical attributes—decentralised governance, regulatory and ethical compliance, fairness, and socio-technical trust—lie beyond the scope of ISO/IEC 25010. This work proposes an extension, ISO/IEC 25010 + BQ, which adds the characteristics *Decentralisation & Governance* and *Regulatory & Ethical Compliance* together with a cross-cutting *Trust* dimension. Indicative metrics and a stepwise assessment workflow are provided. The extended model affords practitioners a structured basis for specifying, evaluating, and certifying blockchain quality.

Keywords: Blockchain · Non-Functional requirement · ISO/IEC 25010 · Distributed ledger · Quality framework

1 Introduction

Distributed-ledger technology has progressed from a cryptocurrency novelty to a dependable substrate for global payments, land registries and regulated securities exchanges. Its defining properties— decentralised consensus, transparent append-only ledgers, cryptographic immutability and token-centred incentives—transform how software quality must be specified, measured and assured. Yet the community still lacks an agreed *yardstick* for judging the *non-functional* quality of blockchain software [3–5].

ISO/IEC 25010 has long served as the reference model for software product quality. The 2023 revision introduces *safety* as a top-level characteristic, renames *usability* and *portability* to *interaction capability* and *flexibility*, and adds subcharacteristics such as *inclusivity*, *resistance* and *scalability* [1,2]. Although this enriched taxonomy aligns well with decentralised, safety-aware systems, several blockchain-specific concerns—decentralised governance, immutability *versus* redactability, token-driven fairness, energy proportionality and trust-without-identity—remain only implicit or entirely absent [6,7].

K. Daimi et al. (Eds.): CSCE 2025, CCIS 2937, pp. 441–458, 2026.
https://doi.org/10.1007/978-3-032-22208-4_31

A related standards effort, ISO/TC 307, produces vocabulary, reference-architecture guidance, and security specifications for blockchain and distributed-ledger technologies (e.g., ISO 22739, ISO/TS 23257). Our examination shows that the ISO/TC 307 portfolio, while valuable for conceptual and architectural alignment, *does not provide a product-quality framework* comparable to ISO/IEC 25010; non-functional attributes are addressed only in a fragmented manner and without measurable criteria. Given that the objective of this work is to evaluate and manage *software quality* within blockchain development projects, the extension of ISO/IEC 25010 offers a more coherent and rigorous foundation than the ISO/TC 307 suite.

Contribution.

1. We *extract* the critical blockchain NFRs from recent peer-reviewed literature (Sect. 4.1).
2. We *map* each NFR to ISO/IEC 25010:2023, marking gaps (Sect. 4.2).
3. We *propose* ISO/IEC 25010 +BQ, adding the characteristics *Decentralisation & Governance* and *Regulatory & Ethical Compliance* plus a cross-cutting *Trust* view (Sect. 5).
4. We *demonstrate* an assessment workflow and tool chain on an enterprise blockchain scenario (Sect. 6).

Paper Organisation. Section 2 reviews ISO/IEC 25010:2023. Section 3 details the research methodology. Sections 4 presents the literature synthesis and gap analysis. Section 5 introduces the extended model, and Sect. 6 shows its practical application. Section 7 presents the conclusion and outline future work.

2 Background: ISO/IEC 25010:2023 Product-Quality Model

ISO/IEC 25010 is the cornerstone of the *SQuaRE* (Software Quality Requirements and Evaluation) family, providing a taxonomy and terminology for assessing software-product quality. The standard defines quality as "*the degree to which a product satisfies stated and implied needs of its stakeholders*"' [1] and organises those needs into a hierarchy of characteristics and sub-characteristics that can be measured through metrics, reviews, and tests.

The second edition, released in 2023, widens the model to *nine* top-level characteristics (Table 1), reflecting a decade of progress in safety-critical, cloud, and AI-enabled systems.

Major Additions. The 2023 update introduces three notable changes:

1. *Safety* is elevated from an implicit facet of reliability to an explicit characteristic, acknowledging software that can harm people or the environment.
2. *Usability* and *portability* are broadened and renamed *interaction capability* and *flexibility*, capturing accessibility, inclusivity, and elastic deployment.
3. New sub-characteristics—*inclusivity*, *user assistance*, *resistance*, and *scalability*—address modern demands for cyber-resilience and distributed architectures [2].

Table 1. ISO/IEC 25010:2023 product-quality characteristics with selected sub-characteristics (★ = new in 2023).

Characteristic	Representative sub-characteristics
Functional suitability	Functional completeness, correctness, appropriateness
Performance efficiency	Time behaviour, resource utilisation, capacity
Compatibility	Co-existence, interoperability
Interaction capability (formerly *usability*)	Appropriateness recognisability, inclusivity★, user assistance, self-descriptiveness★, user engagement★
Reliability	Fault tolerance, recoverability, availability, faultlessness★
Security	Confidentiality, integrity, non-repudiation, accountability, authenticity, resistance★
Maintainability	Modularity, reusability, analysability, modifiability, testability
Flexibility (formerly *portability*)	Adaptability, installability, replaceability, scalability★
Safety★	Operational constraint, risk identification, fail-safe, hazard warning, safe integration

Relationship to Quality-in-Use. ISO/IEC 25010 focuses on intrinsic product qualities, while ISO/IEC 25019 defines quality-in-use (effectiveness, efficiency, satisfaction, and risk) as experienced in real contexts of operation [1]. The 2023 split clarifies that product metrics can be derived from artefacts such as code and architecture, whereas quality-in-use requires stakeholder observation.

Relevance and Gaps for Blockchain. Several 2023 revisions resonate with distributed-ledger systems:

- *Scalability* supports evaluation of throughput and state-growth constraints intrinsic to consensus protocols.
- *Resistance* aligns with defences against 51% attacks and large-scale denial-of-service events.
- *Safety* covers hazards in smart-contract-controlled IoT and critical infrastructure.

Nevertheless, blockchain introduces requirements that remain outside the standard lexicon: decentralised governance, token-driven economic fairness, immutability *versus* redactability, energy proportionality of consensus, and trust-without-identity. Metrics for the *degree of decentralisation* or *governance effectiveness* are still absent, and guidance on reconciling GDPR [28] erasure rights with immutable ledgers is yet to emerge. These gaps motivate the extensions proposed in the following sections, where we benchmark blockchain NFRs against ISO/IEC 25010:2023 and introduce targeted additions.

3 Research Methodology

To ground the proposed model in empirical evidence, we conducted a systematic mapping study that consolidates and classifies recent research on blockchain non-functional requirements (NFRs). The protocol follows established guidelines for evidence-based software engineering [8–10] and is summarised in Fig. 1.

3.1 Research Questions and Search Strategy

The review was guided by two questions:

RQ_1 *Which NFRs are discussed in recent peer-reviewed blockchain literature?*
RQ_2 *How do those NFRs align with the ISO/IEC 25010:2023 product-quality characteristics?*

Four major digital libraries—*ACM Digital Library*, *IEEE Xplore*, *Scopus*, and *Web of Science*—were searched in MarchApril 2025 using the consolidated string:

(`blockchain` ∨ "`distributed ledger`" ∨ "`DLT`") ∧ (`requirements` ∨ "`quality attribute*`" ∨ "`non-functional`").

This query balances recall and precision by combining technology-specific keywords with generic quality terminology. Automated deduplication yielded **473** unique records.

3.2 Selection Criteria and Results

A two-stage screening—title/abstract followed by full text—applied the criteria below:

- **IC_1** Peer-reviewed article (journal, conference, or workshop) published **2021 2025**.
- **IC_2** Explicit discussion of at least one NFR relevant to a *general-purpose* blockchain or DLT.
- **EC_1** Domain-specific case studies (e.g. healthcare, supply chain) lacking generalisable NFR insights.
- **EC_2** Studies confined to *functional* concerns (e.g. consensus correctness only).
- **EC_3** Editorials, short posters (< 4 pp), theses, or non-archival preprints.

Screening Outcome. Of the 473 records:

- 41 duplicate entries were discarded.
- 147 records were excluded by EC_1.
- 198 records were excluded by EC_2.
- 69 records predating 2021 were excluded by IC_1.

The final corpus comprises **18** primary studies, representing the state of the art in blockchain NFR research. This process is depicted in Fig. 1.

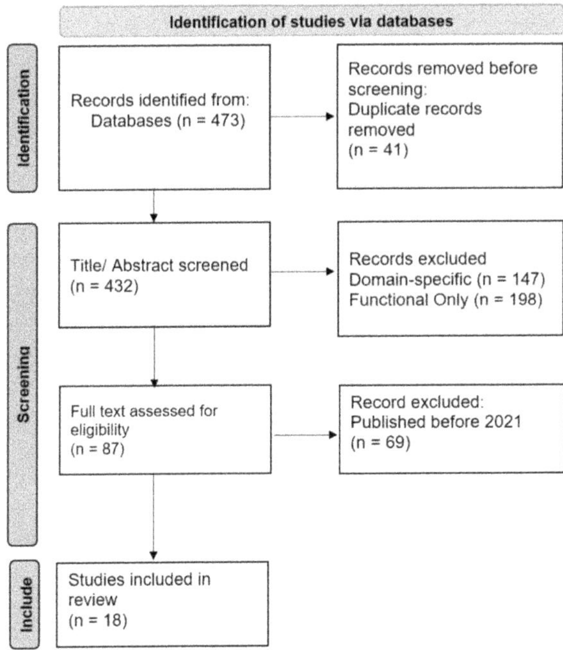

Fig. 1. PRISMA flow diagram of the literature-selection process (n=473).

4 Survey Results and Discussion

The review corpus represents the most recent, peer-reviewed discourse on blockchain quality. Our extraction protocol (cf. Sect. 3) captured four data dimensions: (1) bibliographic metadata, (2) explicitly named NFRs, (3) evidence basis, and (4) any mapping to ISO/IEC 25010. Independent extraction by two reviewers yielded a Cohen's $\kappa = 0.91$, indicating near-perfect agreement; the few disagreements ($< 3\%$) were resolved by consensus. Forty-two unique NFR labels were then normalised (*e.g.*, *data confidentiality* → *privacy*) and prepared for mapping.

With the dataset and NFR catalogue in hand, we now employ these evidence, the per-study summaries and the normalised NFR list, to address the two research questions stated in Sect. 3.1. We begin by identifying which NFRs the literature emphasises (RQ_1), and subsequently map those attributes to ISO/IEC 25010:2023 (RQ_2).

4.1 RQ_1: Which NFRs are addressed?

Table 2 reveals several noteworthy patterns in the recent literature. First, almost every study—regardless of research method—foregrounds *security*. Authors address confidentiality of payloads, integrity of the ledger, resistance to adversarial control, or accountability via immutable audit trails. This consistent emphasis mirrors blockchain's cryptographic heritage and its deployment in hostile environments.

Table 2. Literature summary: primary studies and their headline NFR contributions.

Ref.	Headline NFRs	Evidence basis
[11]	Security, privacy, performance efficiency, transparency, scalability	Conceptual framework
[12]	Observability, scalability, automation, security	Simulator design
[13]	Performance, trust (security⇔reliability)	Empirical runtime study
[14]	Functional suitability, completeness, correctness	Systematic survey
[15]	Immutability, security, reliability, maintainability	Systematic survey
[16]	Scalability, efficiency, security, usability/flexibility	Prototype evaluation
[17]	Confidentiality, integrity, availability, non-repudiation	Threat analysis
[18]	Privacy, fairness, performance	Cryptographic design
[7]	Speed, reliability, consistency, scalability, trust, fairness	Conceptual roadmap
[19]	Security, performance, maintainability	Cryptographic protocol
[20]	Autonomy, accountability, regulatory compliance	Case analysis
[21]	Usability, learnability, low resource use, security	Empirical UX study
[22]	Maintainability, interoperability, privacy	Conceptual synthesis
[6]	Governance, transparency, reversibility, legal compliance	Conceptual analysis
[23]	Performance, security, decentralisation, cost efficiency	Decision-support tool
[24]	Confidentiality, integrity, non-repudiation	Formal verification
[25]	Privacy, integrity, transparency, efficiency, reversibility	GDPR compliance study
[26]	Anonymity, availability, immutability, auditability, portability	Design-science thesis

A second cross-cutting theme concerns *performance efficiency and scalability*. Work on payment channels [16], runtime platform selection [13], and supply-chain pilots [27] all highlight throughput, latency, or resource usage as critical adoption barriers.

Beyond these shared concerns, the corpus diverges in two directions:

- **User-centred qualities.** Usability, learnability, and observability surface in simulator studies [12] and empirical UX evaluations [21], signalling practical friction that purely technical analyses often overlook.
- **Governance and compliance.** A smaller but significant subset—DAO governance [20], GDPR-oriented data management [25], and legal assurance frameworks—raises questions of autonomy, fairness, and regulatory alignment that fall outside classical software-quality checklists.

Collectively, the findings confirm that blockchain quality spans far beyond the traditional *Confidentiality Integrity Availability (CIA) triad* foundational to information security. Real-world projects must also contend with scalability bottlenecks, socio-technical trust, economic fairness, decentralised decision-making, and evolving regulatory duties. These additional concerns motivate the extended quality model proposed in Sect. 5.

Table 3. Consolidated non-functional requirements (NFRs) and mapping to ISO/IEC 25010:2023. "ND" = not defined in ISO.

Non-Functional Requirement	Studies	ISO 25010 Category
Security (general- conf., integ., auth.)	10	Security (protection)
Privacy / Confidentiality	8	Security (confidentiality)
Integrity (Ledger integrity)	5	Security (integrity)
Availability	4	Reliability (availability)
Non-repudiation / Accountability	4	Security (accountability)
Immutability (Tamper-proofness)	5	Security (integrity)
Performance (latency, throughput)	7	Performance efficiency
Scalability	7	Performance efficiency
Efficiency (resource use- Gas, CPU, storage)	3	Performance efficiency
Transaction speed	3	Performance efficiency
Reliability	5	Reliability
Maintainability (Modularity, upgrades)	3	Maintainability
Usability / UX (Learnability, operability)	2	Interaction capability
Testability	2	Maintainability (testability)
Transparency / Auditability	4	Security (accountability)
Compliance (legal, GDPR)	2	ND (domain-specific)
Decentralised governance	2	ND (domain-specific)
Trust (system trustworthiness)	2	ND (cross-cutting)
Fairness (Rewards, incentives)	2	ND (ethical)
Anonymity	1	Security (privacy)
Access control	1	Security (authenticity)
Encryption	1	Security (confidentiality)
Multi-factor authentication	1	Security (authenticity)
Observability	1	Maintainability (analysability)
Flexibility / Extensibility	2	Maintainability (modifiability)
Portability / Adaptability	1	Flexibility (portability)
Reusability	1	Maintainability (reusability)
Resilience / Fault tolerance	1	Reliability (fault tol.)
Stakeholder participation	1	ND (organisational)
Real-time performance	1	Performance efficiency
Resource usage (memory/space)	1	Performance efficiency

4.2 RQ$_2$: How do the NFRs map to ISO/IEC 25010?

Table 3 aggregates the 30 normalised NFRs, reports the number of studies citing each, and aligns them with ISO/IEC 25010:2023. Security-related concepts account for one-third of all mentions, while performance and scalability jointly form the second largest cluster. Conversely, qualities unique to decentralised systems—*governance*, *fairness*, *legal compliance*—lack representation in ISO/IEC 25010, reinforcing the need for the extensions proposed in Sect. 5.

The dominance of security and performance underscores the pivotal roles of trust and efficiency in decentralised environments. Conversely, blockchain-specific attributes—*decentralised governance*, *fair economic incentives*, and *legal compliance*—fall outside ISO/IEC 25010, highlighting the necessity of the ISO/IEC 25010+BQ extensions developed in Sect. 5.

5 Proposed Extension to ISO/IEC 25010 for Blockchain Software

ISO/IEC 25010:2023 provides a solid baseline for evaluating product quality, yet the systematic mapping in Sect. 4.2 shows that *decentralised governance*, *fairness*, *trust*, *stakeholder participation*, and explicit *regulatory/ethical compliance* are still unaddressed (Table 3, "ND" rows). We therefore introduce *ISO/IEC 25010+BQ*—an extended quality model for blockchain systems—by adding two domain-specific characteristics and refining one crosscutting attribute (Fig. 2). We introduce *Decentralisation & Governance* (DG) and *Regulatory & Ethical Compliance* (RC) as two new, domain-specific characteristics because these groups encompass blockchain-specific qualities—power distribution, stakeholder voting, fairness, regulatory alignment, and sustainability—that fall outside the scope of ISO/IEC 25010 and cannot be represented within its existing categories. In contrast, *Socio-Technical Trust* (ST) is formulated as a refined cross-cutting attribute, since trust arises from the collective interaction of multiple qualities—security, transparency, reliability, and governance design—and therefore cannot be isolated within a single characteristic.

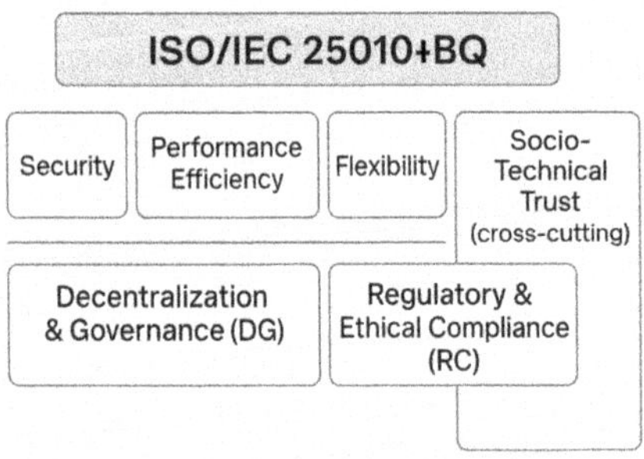

Fig. 2. Positioning of the new characteristics **Decentralisation & Governance (DG)** and **Regulatory & Ethical Compliance (RC)** within ISO/IEC 25010+BQ.

5.1 Decentralisation and Governance (DG)

Degree of Decentralisation. *Description.* The spread of validating power among independent entities determines resilience to censorship and collusion [29,30]. *Metric.* **Gini Coefficient** ($0 \leq G \leq 1$) over stake or hash-rate shares; lower values signal healthier dispersion [29]. *Example.* 10 validators with equal \$1M stakes and one with \$9M give $G \approx 0.64$; adding 4 new \$1M validators lowers G to 0.46.

Governance Transparency. *Description.* Verifiable, on-chain recording of proposals, ballots, and results guarantees procedural legitimacy [11,20]. *Metric.* **On-chain Governance Coverage** (OGC) = on-chain events ÷ total governance events. *Example.* A DAO holds 35 votes; 30 appear on-chain (OGC = 86%).

Governance Adaptability. *Description.* Shorter upgrade cycles foster timely innovation [3]. *Metric.* **Time-to-Upgrade** (TTU) = days from proposal to main-net activation. *Example.* Proposal 1 May → activation 31 May ⇒ TTU = 30 d; Ethereum's *Berlin* fork took 188 d.

Stakeholder Participation. *Description.* Governance enjoys legitimacy only when a large and well-distributed share of eligible voting power casts a vote [20]. We capture both aspects with (i) *turnout* T—the fraction of *total voting power* [1] that participates in at least one ballot during a governance epoch—and (ii) the *HerfindahlHirschman Index* (HHI), a standard concentration measure

$$\mathrm{HHI} = \sum_{i=1}^{n} s_i^2,$$

where s_i is the voting-power percentage of actor i [31].

Metric. **Effective Participation Index**

$$\mathrm{EPI} = T \times \left(1 - \tfrac{\mathrm{HHI}}{10\,000}\right),$$

where the HHI is normalised to the $[0, 1]$ range. The index rises both with higher turnout and with a more even distribution of power.

Example. In a quarterly vote, 10% of the total staking power takes part ($T = 0.10$). Voting power among participants is split 40302010%, giving HHI $= 40^2 + 30^2 + 20^2 + 10^2 = 3\,000$ and $\mathrm{HHI}_{\mathrm{norm}} = 0.30$. Hence EPI $= 0.10 \times (1 - 0.30) = 0.07$ or 7%. The score would improve if either more power turned out or the voting power were less concentrated.

Fairness. *Description.* Even distribution of rewards and influence sustains incentives [7,18]. *Metric.* **Nakamoto coefficient** = minimum entities that control > 50% of block production [30]. *Example.* Suppose the top five mining pools produce 28%, 14%, 8%, 6%, and 5% of blocks, respectively, while all others produce < 5% each. Cumulative shares are 28%, 42%, 50%, ... The threshold is crossed after the third pool, so $N = 3$.

[1] Weight, not head-count; token- or stake-weighted systems typically give one address multiple votes.

5.2 Regulatory and Ethical Compliance (RC)

Legal Compliance. *Description.* Alignment with statutory frameworks such as EU MiCA or the U.S. Howey test [25]. *Metric.* **Clause-Coverage Ratio** = satisfied ÷ applicable clauses. *Example.* 42 / 45 MiCA clauses met → 93% coverage.

Data-Protection Compliance. *Description.* Fulfilment of data-protection regulations such as EU-GDPR, USA-CCPA, or Saudi-PDPL erasure and audit duties [3]. *Metric.* **Effective Erasure Rate** = successfully revoked data objects ÷ total erasure requests. *Example.* 97 erasures out of 100 → 97%.

Consumer/Financial Compliance. *Description.* Conformance to AML, KYC, and FATF travel-rule requirements [27]. *Metric.* **Screening Coverage** C_s—the percentage of inbound transactions (or addresses) that pass through automated AML/KYC[2] filters—and **SAR Latency** L_{SAR}—the median time between the detection of a suspicious event and submission of the corresponding *Suspicious-Activity Report* to the competent authority.
Example. If every incoming address is screened ($C_s = 100\%$) and half of all SARs are filed within 24 h ($L_{\mathrm{SAR}} = 24$ h), the platform satisfies the EU PSD2 guideline that requires full screening and SAR submission within 48 h of detection.

Sustainability/Energy Proportionality. *Description.* The *per-transaction energy footprint* and its associated carbon emissions have become headline indicators in **E**nvironmental**S**ocial**G**overnance (ESG)[3] disclosures for blockchain platforms [4].
Metric. (i) **kWh/tx**—the average kilowatt-hours of electricity consumed to finalise a single on-chain transaction. Determined by dividing total network consumption (from smart-meter data or miner-hardware inventories) by the confirmed-transaction count over the same period. (ii) **gCO$_2$e/tx**—grams of CO$_2$-equivalent per transaction, obtained by multiplying kWh/tx by the grid's emission factor (gCO$_2$e per kWh).
Example. A proof-of-stake (PoS) side-chain that consumes 8 kWh per 10^5 transactions reports kWh/tx $= \frac{8}{10^5} = 0.08$. Using the EU grid factor of 253 gCO$_2$e/kWh, its carbon intensity is $0.08 \times 253 \approx 20$ gCO$_2$e/tx. By contrast, a proof-of-work (PoW) network measured at 707 kWh/tx produces $707 \times 253 \approx 179{,}000$ gCO$_2$e/tx, three orders of magnitude higher, underscoring the sustainability advantage of PoS consensus.

Auditability & reporting *Description.* The system should be able to emit a *tamper-evident audit bundle* that conforms to the ISO 20022[4] message schema [5] so that regulators can ingest the data without post-processing.

---

[2] Anti-Money-Laundering / Know-Your-Customer.

[3] ESG reporting frames a company's performance against environmental, social, and governance criteria for investors and regulators.

[4] ISO 20022 is the international messaging standard for financial data interchange; it specifies a universal, extensible XML/JSON schema for payments, securities, and trade reporting.

Metric.(i) **Audit-Generation Time (AGT)**—wall-clock time between the moment an authorised auditor triggers an export and the moment the signed ISO 20022 file set is ready for download. (ii) **Schema Completeness (SC)**—percentage of mandatory ISO 20022 elements that are populated with syntactically valid values in the generated bundle.
Example. An automated exporter finishes in AGT = 2 min and fills all mandatory fields (SC = 100%); a manual process that requires database dumps and hand-edited XML takes 180 min and leaves 28% of required fields blank (SC = 72%). The automated path therefore meets both the speed and completeness targets demanded by most financial supervisors.

5.3 Socio-Technical Trust (ST)

System Trustworthiness. *Description.* Stakeholder confidence that the system behaves as promised [6]. *Metric.* **Net Trust Score** (NTS) = (promoters detractors) ÷ total × 100. *Example.* 38 promoters, 10 detractors, 12 neutral → NTS = 28.
Reputation Propagation. *Description.* Blockchains often rely on reputation scores or identity attestations to curb *Sybil attacks*—attempts to gain disproportionate influence by creating many fake identities [18]. *Metric.* **Sybil-Resistance Factor.** (SRF): calculate the Shannon entropy $H = -\sum_i p_i \log_2 p_i$ over the reputation weights p_i, normalise by the maximum entropy $\log_2 n$, and rescale to $[0, 1]$.[5] *Example.* In a Proof-of-Personhood system with 1 000 verified users each holding 0.1% reputation, SRF ≈ 0.91 (high resistance). A token airdrop where two whales hold 60% and 30%, and the rest share 10%, yields SRF ≈ 0.34 (low resistance).
Dispute-Resolution Effectiveness. *Description.* The quicker a platform settles conflicts, the higher its perceived fairness and the lower the risk of costly forks [22]. *Metric.* **Median Settlement Time.** ($\widetilde{T}$): the 50th-percentile duration from dispute filing to final ruling, measured in calendar days. *Example.* In 2024, Kleros juries closed 120 token-sale disputes with $\widetilde{T} = 5$ days, whereas an off-chain custodial escrow service resolved comparable cases in $\widetilde{T} = 17$ days—more than triple the delay.

5.4 Integrated Model Table

Table 4 synthesises the discussion in Sect. 5.15.3 by showing how each blockchain-specific concern extends or refines the ISO/IEC 25010:2023 characteristics. The first three rows list minor refinements within the existing standard (Security, Performance Efficiency, Flexibility, and Maintainability), while the lower rows introduce the new domain-specific characteristics **Decentralisation & Governance**, **Regulatory & Ethical Compliance**, and the cross-cutting attribute **Socio-Technical Trust**. Together, these additions form the complete ISO/IEC 25010 +BQ model that will be evaluated in Sect. 6.

[5] SRF = 0 means one identity holds all reputation; SRF = 1 means every identity is equal.

Table 4. ISO/IEC 25010+BQ: Added and refined characteristics (new items **in bold**).

Characteristic (2023)	Additional sub-characteristics for blockchain
Security	resistance (★), transparency/auditability, privacy-preserving data flow
Performance efficiency	throughput under Byzantine fault, consensus finality time, energy per transaction
Flexibility	*scalability* (★), cross-chain portability, on/off-chain partitioning adaptability
Maintainability	smart-contract upgradability, modular consensus pluggability
Decentralisation & Governance (DG)	degree of decentralisation, governance transparency, governance adaptability, stakeholder participation, fairness
Regulatory & Ethical Compliance (RC)	legal compliance, data-protection compliance, consumer-protection compliance, sustainability / energy proportionality, auditability & reporting
Socio-Technical Trust (cross-cutting)	system trustworthiness, reputation propagation, dispute-resolution effectiveness

ISO/IEC 25010,+BQ addresses *all* NFRs listed in Table 3 while remaining fully compatible with the original ISO vocabulary.

6 Applying ISO/IEC 25010+BQ to Blockchain Projects

This section outlines a stepbystep procedure for practitioners to incorporate the extended model into requirements engineering, architecture design, and verification activities.

6.1 Assessment Workflow

Step 1 Context scoping. Identify the ledger type (public, consortium, private), dominant use-cases, regulatory jurisdictions, stakeholder roles (*validator, dApp developer, regulator, end-user*).

Step 2 Characteristic selection. Start with the nine ISO/IEC 25010:2023 characteristics.

- Add **DG** when protocol governance or token economics is in scope.
- Add **RC** when the system processes personal data, fiat on-ramps, or operates under sector regulation (finance, energy, healthcare).
- Activate the cross-cutting **ST** view whenever user trust or reputation is a stated success criterion.

Step 3 Metric instantiation. For each chosen sub-characteristic, instantiate one or more metrics (Sect. 5), set target thresholds, and record rationale in the requirements specification.

Step 4 Design alignment. Map architecture decisions—consensus algorithm, smart-contract pattern, privacy layer—to the selected metrics.

Step 5 Evidence collection. (i) *Static evidence*: formal proofs, code audits, token-distribution analytics. (ii) *Runtime evidence*: monitoring data, on-chain governance logs, energy dashboards.

Step 6 Gap analysis & iteration. Compare measured values with thresholds; create remediation backlog for unmet targets (*e.g.*, add L2 roll-up to improve scalability, or integrate privacy proxy for GDPR compliance).

6.2 Case Study: *BlockMedChain*

BlockMedChain is a permissioned proof-of-stake (PoS) ledger that tracks the provenance and cold-chain status of prescription drugs for a consortium comprising 2 manufacturers, 3 logistics providers, and 11 hospital pharmacies spread across the EU and GCC regions [27]. The system must demonstrate: (i) tamper-proof tracking (security), (ii) provable GDPR compliance (regulation), and (iii) stakeholder confidence (trust) before regulators approve it for production.

Note. For illustrative purposes, several numerical values and situational details in this case study have been fabricated to demonstrate the assessment workflow.

Step 1—Context scoping.

- *Stakeholders.* Regulatory bodies (EMA, SFDA), hospital pharmacists, QA managers, cold-chain auditors, and the consortium board.
- *Ledger profile.* Consortium PoS; validators initially owned by 5 founding firms.
- *Jurisdictions.* EU GDPR and EU-FMD (Falsified Medicines Directive); GCC regulations mirror EU GDPR (e.g. Saudi PDPL).

Step 2—Characteristic selection. Security, Performance Efficiency, Flexibility, and Maintainability were retained from ISO/IEC 25010. Three BQ extensions were added because: (1) **DG** is critical for avoiding cartel behaviour in a private ledger (cf. [29]); (2) **RC** is mandatory to satisfy GDPR; (3) **ST** is essential for end-user uptake in highly regulated supply chains [7].

Step 3—Metric instantiation and threshold setting.

- **Nakamoto coefficient** (N). *Why:* recommended by Bano *et al.* as a robust decentralisation proxy [30]. *How:* rank validators by staking power, sum until $\geq$ 50%. *Threshold.* $N \geq 7$. *Justification:* EU competition guidelines treat markets with 5 or fewer effective competitors as "concentrated" [31].
- **Effective Erasure Rate** (EER). *Why:* GDPR Article 17 requires the "right to be forgotten"; erasure must succeed even on an immutable ledger [28]. *How:* issue 100 synthetic erasure requests, verify whether off-chain encryption keys are irrevocably deleted. *Threshold.* EER $\geq$ 95%. *Justification:* ENISA cloud-compliance guides recommend a minimum 95 % erasure success for critical data [32].

- **Net Trust Score** (NTS). *Why:* perceived trust predicts technology adoption in healthcare IT [22]. *How:* Likert survey; promotersdetractors÷total1×00. *Threshold.* NTS ≥ 75. *Justification:* Scores above 70 are considered "excellent" in clinical-software benchmarking [33].

Step 4—Design alignment.

1. Added 2 publicly owned hospital validators (hardware HSM + audited staking contract) to raise Nakamoto coefficient N.
2. Implemented an *encryption-pointer* pattern: patient-ID ciphertext is stored on-chain; the AES-keys reside in a permissioned off-chain vault that supports cryptographic shredding.
3. Exposed a read-only audit API and embedded QR codes on shipping labels so pharmacists can verify on-chain cold-chain integrity, boosting perceived transparency.

Step 5—Evidence collection.

- **DG result.** On-chain analytics showed a baseline $N = 5$. After integrating two new validators, it becomes $N = 7$.
- **RC result.** In a batch test of 100 erasure requests, 98 keys were irrevocably destroyed $\Rightarrow$ EER = 98%.
- **ST result.** A 60-respondent survey scored promoters = 42, detractors = 7 $\Rightarrow$ NTS $= (42 - 7)/60 \times 100 = 58$. Below target.

Step 6—Gap analysis and iteration.
- *DG.* Target met ($N = 7$); no further action.
-*RC.* Target exceeded (EER = 98%).
- *ST.* NTS shortfall (58 vs. 75). Root-cause interviews revealed users mistrusted cold-chain sensors. Planned remediation: integrate tamper-evident NFC sensor logs and third-party certification, then re-survey after six months.

Outcome. Within one assessment cycle, *BlockMedChain* satisfied decentralisation and GDPR erasure objectives and identified trust perception as the next quality bottleneck. The case demonstrates how ISO/IEC 25010 + BQ's metric-driven workflow makes weaknesses visible, assigns clear owners, and traces remediation to measurable success criteria.

7 Conclusion and Future Work

This study set out to determine whether the 2023 revision of ISO/IEC 25010 adequately covers the non-functional requirements (NFRs) that recur in modern blockchain systems. A systematic mapping of 18 recent peer-reviewed studies (Sect. 4.2) showed that attributes such as *decentralised governance*, *regulatory and ethical compliance*, *fairness*, and *trust* are repeatedly emphasised yet remain **undefined** within the standard taxonomy. To close that gap we proposed

ISO/IEC 25010 + BQ, which adds two domain-specific characteristics—**Decentralisation & Governance** (DG) and **Regulatory & Ethical Compliance** (RC)—together with a cross-cutting **Socio-Technical Trust** (ST). Each new facet is supported by measurable sub-characteristics and candidate metrics; an assessment workflow demonstrates practical application.

While ISO/IEC 25010 + BQ stresses quantifiable evidence, several blockchain qualities—most notably *fairness* and *dispute resolution*—still rely on proxies such as token distribution, turnout, or median settlement time. Moreover, context- specific thresholds (e.g., Nakamoto coefficient $N \geq 7$ for PoS consortia) may not generalise across DeFi, CBDC, or public-chain scenarios. The current metric catalogue therefore serves as a starting point rather than a definitive benchmark.

To mature the proposal, we identify six research threads:

F1 Metric formalisation and benchmarking. Reference implementations for DG/RC metrics (akin to ISO/IEC 21089-1) and public benchmarks for decentralisation and energy proportionality.

F2 Quality-in-use alignment. Extension of ISO/IEC 25019 instruments so that user-perceived *trust* and *fairness* can be validated in longitudinal deployments.

F3 AI-assisted compliance. Large-language-model agents that mine on-chain data to draft GDPR or MiCA compliance reports and suggest design fixes.

Pursuing these avenues should yield a robust evidence base, automated tooling, and—ultimately—an industry consensus on how to specify, measure, and certify the non-functional quality of blockchain software.

Acknowledgments. The authors acknowledge the use of artificial intelligence (AI)assisted tools to enhance the language and clarity of this manuscript. The authors also wish to note that Salma HabibAllah and Reema Alhamadi contributed equally to this research.

Disclosure of Interests. The authors have no competing interests to declare that are relevant to the content of this article.

References

1. ISO/IEC 25010:2023. 2023. Systems and Software Quality Models (2nd ed.). International Organization for Standardization, Geneva, Switzerland. https://www.iso.org/standard/81832.html, Accessed 12 Feb 2025
2. Gernot Starke. 2023. Update on ISO 25010, Version 2023. arc42 Quality Model Blog (2023). https://iso25010.arc42.org/2023-update, Accessed 12 Feb 2025
3. Moe Kassab. 2021. Exploring non-functional requirements for blockchain-oriented systems. In: Proceedings of the 29th IEEE International Requirements Engineering Conference Workshops (REW 2021), pp. 216–219. IEEE (2021). https://doi.org/10.1109/REW53955.2021.00040

4. Ordóñez-Guerrero, A.C., Muñoz-Garzón, J.D., Villarreal, E.D., Bandi, A., Hurtado, J.A.: Blockchain architectural concerns: a systematic mapping study. In: Proceedings of the 19th International Conference on Software Architecture Companion (ICSA-C 2022), pp. 183–192. IEEE (2022). https://doi.org/10.1109/ICSA-C54293.2022.00043
5. Saraiva, R., Araújo, A.A, Soares, P., Pontes, J.C., Souza, J.: Metrics for quality assessment in blockchain-based systems: a systematic mapping study. In: Proceedings of the Brazilian Symposium on Information Systems (SBSI 2024). SBC (2024). https://doi.org/10.5753/sbsi.2025.246568
6. Reddivari, S., Wilson, A.T.: Blockchain-oriented requirements engineering: new directions. In: Proceedings of the 23rd IEEE International Conference on Information Reuse and Integration for Data Science (IRI 2022), pp. 118–123. IEEE (2022). https://doi.org/10.1109/IRI54793.2022.00036
7. Tisha, T.A., Shibly, M.M.A.: Non-Functional Requirements for Blockchain: Challenges and New Directions. IOP Conf. Ser. Mater. Sci. Eng. **1110**, 012016 (2021). https://doi.org/10.1088/1757-899X/1110/1/012016
8. Kitchenham, B., Charters, S.: Guidelines for Performing Systematic Literature Reviews in Software Engineering. Technical Report EBSE 2007-001, Keele University (2007). https://www.cs.auckland.ac.nz/~norsaremah/SE750/Readings/Kitchenham_2007_GuidelinesForPerformingSLRs.pdf, Accessed 10 May 2025
9. Wohlin, C.: Guidelines for snowballing in systematic literature studies and a replication in software engineering. In: Proceedings of the 18th International Conference on Evaluation and Assessment in Software Engineering (EASE 2014), pp. 1–10. ACM (2014). https://doi.org/10.1145/2601248.2601268
10. Petersen, K., Vakkalanka, S., Kuzniarz, L.: Guidelines for conducting systematic mapping studies in software engineering: an update. Inf. Softw. Technol. **64**, 1–18 (2015). https://doi.org/10.1016/j.infsof.2015.03.007
11. Fetzer, V., Klooß, M., Müller-Quade, J., Raiber, M., Rupp, A.: Universally composable auditable surveillance. In: Proceedings of the 28th European Symposium on Research in Computer Security (ESORICS 2023), pp. 300–320. Springer, Cham (2023). https://doi.org/10.1007/978-981-99-8724-5_14
12. Huang, P., et al.: Highsimb: a concrete blockchain simulation with contract vulnerability detection for ethereum and hyperledger fabric. In: Proceedings of the International Conference on Machine Learning for Cyber Security (ML4CS 2022), pp. 553–570. Springer, Cham (2022). https://doi.org/10.1007/978-3-031-20099-1_39
13. Frauenthaler, P., Borkowski, M., Schulte, S.: A framework for assessing and selecting blockchains at runtime. In: Proceedings of the IEEE International Conference on Decentralized Applications and Infrastructures (DAPPS 2020), pp. 1–10. IEEE (2020). https://doi.org/10.1109/DAPPS49028.2020.00013
14. Vacca, A., Fredella, M., Di Sorbo, A., Visaggio, C.A., Piattini, M.: Functional suitability assessment of smart contracts: a survey and first proposal. J. Softw. Evol. Process **36**(1), e2636 (2024). https://doi.org/10.1002/smr.2636
15. Sánchez-Gómez, N., Valderrama, J.T., García-García, J.A., Gutiérrez, J., Escalona, M.J.: Model-based software design and testing in blockchain smart contracts: a systematic literature review. IEEE Access **8**(2020), 139918–139940 (2020). https://doi.org/10.1109/ACCESS.2020.3021502
16. Aumayr, L., Ersoy, O., Erwig, A., Faust, S., Hostáková, K., Maffei, M., Moreno-Sanchez, P., Riahi, S.: Generalized Channels from Limited Blockchain Scripts and Adaptor Signatures. In: Tibouchi, M., Wang, H. (eds.) ASIACRYPT 2021. LNCS,

vol. 13091, pp. 635–664. Springer, Cham (2021). https://doi.org/10.1007/978-3-030-92075-3_22
17. Didouh, A., Lopez, A., Elhillali, Y., Rivenq, A., Faruque, M.A.: Eve, you shall not get access! A cyber-physical blockchain architecture for electronic toll collection security. In: Proceedings of the IEEE 23rd International Conference on Intelligent Transportation Systems (ITSC 2020), pp. 1–6. IEEE (2020). https://doi.org/10.1109/ITSC45102.2020.9294334
18. Lu, Y., Tang, Q., Wang, G.: Dragoon: private decentralized HITs made practical. In: Proceedings of the 40th IEEE International Conference on Distributed Computing Systems (ICDCS 2020), pp. 768–778. IEEE (2020). https://doi.org/10.1109/ICDCS47774.2020.00084
19. Yadav, A.K., Mamindlapally, M., Joshi, P., Budkuley, A.J.: On commitment over general compound channels. In: Proceedings of the 14th International Conference on Communication Systems and Networks (COMSNETS 2022), pp. 593–594. IEEE (2022). https://doi.org/10.1109/COMSNETS53615.2022.9668465
20. Hashemi-Khiabani, S.S., Polónia, D.F.: Improving corporate governance using DAO. In: Proceedings of the 15th International Joint Conference on Knowledge Discovery, Knowledge Engineering and Knowledge Management (KMIS 2023), pp. 150–156. SciTePress (2023). https://doi.org/10.5220/0012164600003598
21. Gandhi, S.S., Patil, Y.N., Netak, L., Gaikwad, H.R.: Usability analysis for blockchain-based applications. In: Proceedings of the IEEE International Conference on Healthcare Informatics (ICHI 2021), pp. 460–462. IEEE (2021). https://doi.org/10.1007/978-3-030-98404-5_33
22. Laplante, P.A., Kassab, M.H.: Requirements Engineering for Software and Systems (4th ed.). CRC Press, Boca Raton, FL (2022). https://doi.org/10.1201/9781003129509
23. Six, N., Herbaut, N., Salinesi, C.: Which blockchain to choose? A decision-support tool to guide the choice of a blockchain technology, arXiv:2002.04735 [cs.SE](2020). https://arxiv.org/abs/2002.04735
24. Chondamrongkul, N., Sun, J., Warren, I.: Formal security analysis for blockchain-based software architecture. In: Proceedings of the 32nd International Conference on Software Engineering and Knowledge Engineering (SEKE 2020). KSI Research, pp. 139–144 (2020). https://doi.org/10.18293/SEKE2020-024
25. Balatska, V., Poberezhnyk, V., Opirskyy, I.: Utilizing blockchain technologies for ensuring the confidentiality and security of personal data in compliance with GDPR. In: Proceedings of the Cyber Security and Data Protection Workshop (CSDP 2024), CEUR-WS, Vol. 3369, pp. 70–80 (2024). https://ceur-ws.org/Vol-3369/
26. Michail, A.: Tackling the Challenges of Information Security Incident Reporting: A Decentralized Approach. Ph.D. Dissertation, University of East London, UK (2020)
27. Khatter K., Relan, D.: Non-functional requirements for blockchain-enabled medical supply chain. Int. J. Syst. Assur. Eng. Manag. **13**(3), 1219–1231 (2022). https://doi.org/10.1007/s13198-021-01418-y
28. European Parliament and Council: Regulation (EU) 2016/679 of the European Parliament and of the Council of 27 April 2016 on the protection of natural persons with regard to the processing of personal data and on the free movement of such data (General Data Protection Regulation). Off. J. Eur. Union **L119**, 1–88 (2016)
29. Xu, J., Wang, J., Liu, Y., Zheng, Y.: Decentralization analysis of Bitcoin and Ethereum networks. In: Proceedings of the 3rd IEEE International Conference on

Blockchain, pp. 559–566. IEEE (2020). https://doi.org/10.1109/Blockchain50366.2020.00078
30. Bano, S., et al.: SoK: consensus in the age of blockchains. arXiv:1711.03936 v3 (2019). https://arxiv.org/abs/1711.03936 (Accessed: 12 June 2025)
31. U.S. Department of Justice and Federal Trade Commission. Merger Guidelines. U.S. DOJ Antitrust Division, Washington, DC. Section 2.1: Measuring Concentration —- The Herfindahl–Hirschman Index (HHI) (2023). https://www.justice.gov/atr/merger-guidelines, Accessed 10 Apr 2025
32. European Union Agency for Cybersecurity (ENISA). Guidelines on Data Erasure in Critical Cloud Services. Technical Report. ENISA, Heraklion, Greece (2022). https://www.enisa.europa.eu/publications/data-erasure-guidelines, Accessed 15 Apr 2025
33. Health IT Benchmark Council. Clinical Software Trust Scores: 2023 Benchmark Report. White Paper. Health IT Benchmark Council, Boston, MA, USA (2023). https://hcbc.org/reports/trust-scores-2023.pdf, Accessed 20 May 2025

Remaining Agile with Hybrid Work Models

Mierhamza Rahimi(✉) and Catherine Stringfellow

Midwestern State University, Wichita Falls, TX 76309, USA
mierhamza.rahimi@gmail.com, catherine.stringfellow@msutexas.edu

Abstract. This study explores the impact of the COVID-19 pandemic and hybrid work models on Agile Software Development (ASD). By comparing pre and post-pandemic practices, it highlights shifts in priorities such as quality, communication, and organizational culture. A mixed-methods approach—surveys based on the Goal Question Metric (GQM) framework and follow-up interviews—was used to gather data from diverse software organizations. The analysis examines how hybrid work affects ASD compared to remote and in-person models, referencing challenges from Global Software Development (GSD). The goal is to offer actionable insights to enhance productivity, collaboration, and well-being in hybrid Agile environments.

Keywords: Agile Software Development · Hybrid Work Models

1 Introduction

Over the past decade, remote work has gained traction as a flexible strategy to enhance productivity. Prior to the COVID-19 pandemic, only 19.9% of employees in computer systems design and related services worked remotely [7]. During the pandemic, remote work surged to 62.5% in 2021 as organizations adapted to unprecedented constraints [7]. However, its prevalence has since declined, dropping by 5% in a single year [7], suggesting diminishing acceptance in the post-pandemic workforce. A recent article by Forbes indicates several reasons for the drive to return to office (RTO), including maintaining an organizational culture, difficulty in monitoring productivity, cost of long-term office leases, improved collaboration, more authoritarian influence, fostering morale, and to get people to quit voluntarily [3]. For all these arguments, the article also presents valid counter-arguments for such inflexibility. This study, however, focuses on Agile Software Development (ASD) trends before, during, and after the pandemic, offering informed recommendations that address evolving practices while avoiding reactionary responses to declining remote work.

This study begins by reviewing key definitions and related literature. It then outlines the data collection and analysis methods used. Results are derived from quantitative analysis and further examined alongside insights from informal forums, articles, and follow-up interviews. Finally, the study discusses these findings in context and presents informed conclusions.

K. Daimi et al. (Eds.): CSCE 2025, CCIS 2937, pp. 459–469, 2026.
https://doi.org/10.1007/978-3-032-22208-4_32

2 Background

The following literature is thematically organized to examine Agile Software Development (ASD) trends prior to the COVID-19 pandemic, its current application, and projected future directions.

Early research on agile methodologies focused on their divergence from traditional waterfall models, emphasizing iterative development, customer collaboration, and adaptability [8]. Many studies explored the challenges of hybrid approaches, where Agile was combined with plan-based methodologies. For example, a multi-case interview study in Germany examined conflicts in Agile-Plan-Based Hybrid (APH) environments, offering insights into resolution strategies and integration frameworks.

As hybrid and remote work models became more prevalent, agile practices were adapted to support distributed teams. A systematic mapping study investigated the intersection of ASD and hybrid work, identifying gaps in the literature and challenges in remote implementation [6]. Key findings emphasized the need for modified agile frameworks incorporating collaboration tools and adjusted ceremonies to maintain team cohesion and effectiveness.

Organizational climate has also emerged as a critical factor in agile success. One study introduced the TACT (Tool to Assess the organizational ClimaTe of Agile teams), developed through Design Science Research cycles [4]. TACT measures human-centric factors influencing agile performance and emphasizes continuous feedback, short evaluation cycles, and behavioral reflection among team leaders to sustain agility. Looking ahead, research increasingly focuses on the long-term sustainability of agile practices in evolving technological and managerial landscapes. Future studies anticipate the integration of artificial intelligence and automation to enhance agile work flows. The shift toward hybrid work continues to shape Agile's trajectory, driving the development of adaptive frameworks that uphold core agile principles. Refinements of tools like TACT are expected to offer more detailed insights into team performance and adaptability.

In response to the need for understanding broader ASD trends, a recent study used text mining on Scopus-indexed publications from 2001 to 2021 [11]. While the study captured trends before and during the pandemic, its early post-pandemic publication limits insights into current developments. Moreover, mapping results to eight topics based on keyword frequency may have been less effective than aligning findings with the twelve Agile principles, which could offer deeper relevance and contextual understanding.

Table 1 summarizes key studies that employed diverse methods to explore agile related questions across different pandemic phases, offering recommendations on frameworks, people-focused research, assessment tools, and key ASD trends in relation to hybrid work. The study in this paper aims to contribute to these by exploring pandemic-driven ASD trends through mixed methods.

Overall, the progression of ASD research illustrates a shift from foundational studies on agile principles to nuanced investigations into hybrid work dynamics and predictive analytics for future methodologies. The integration of systematic mapping studies, empirical case studies, and theoretical advancements continues to shape Agile's trajectory in modern software development.

Table 1. Comparison of Main Themes on Background Studies.

Study	Study Type	Question	Time Period	Recommendations
7	Interviews	How can conflicts in the combination of Agile and plan based development approaches be resolved?	During pandemic	Use recommended frames during each step of the development approach, then fill with methods and practices.
5	Literature Review	How is the scope of research on hybrid work changing and what are the emerging trends?	Before, during, and after pandemic	Shift concentration of studies focusing on "process" perspective of hybrid work into less concentrated "people" perspective.
3	Qualitative, Tertiary, Literature Review, Case Study, Survey	How can the organizational climate of agile teams be supported factoring human factors?	Before and during the pandemic	Use TACT when managing the performance of climate organizational assessments of agile teams.
10	Literature Review	Where are resources being poured into for research of ASD?	Before and during the pandemic	Team Communication, Agile Development, and Software Development are three most populartopics.
This Study	Forum Review, Article Review, Survey, Interviews	How has the pandemic impacted trends on ASD in hybrid settings?	Before, during, and after the pandemic	See Data Analysis in Results

3 Approach

3.1 Data Collection

Data from the Google Forms survey was systematically analyzed using the Goal Question Metric (GQM) approach, which involves defining goals, formulating related questions, and identifying metrics to answer those questions [2]. Survey responses were first cleaned to remove incomplete or irrelevant entries, ensuring data accuracy and reliability. Descriptive statistics—including mean, median, mode, and standard deviation— were calculated to summarize key trends and characteristics.

A comparative analysis was conducted to assess changes in Agile Software Development (ASD) practices by contrasting current trends with those from the pre-pandemic period, emphasizing the impact of COVID-19 and the shift toward hybrid work models. Relationships among variables were examined to identify factors influencing productivity, team communication, and project success in hybrid ASD environments.

Qualitative data from open-ended responses underwent thematic analysis to identify recurring themes and provide deeper insight into participant experiences. Results are presented through charts, graphs, and tables to facilitate clear interpretation.

In addition to formal survey data, insights from informal sources were systematically categorized and analyzed to capture a broader range of perspectives. This qualitative input highlighted emerging trends, common challenges, and real-time innovations discussed by practitioners. Integrating both empirical data and lived experiences enabled the development of actionable recommendations for optimizing ASD practices in hybrid work settings.

3.2 Methods

The data collected from the Google Forms survey was systematically analyzed using the Goal Question Metric (GQM) Approach that involves defining specific goals, formulating questions to achieve these goals, and identifying metrics to answer these questions [2]. Initially, the survey responses were cleaned to remove any incomplete or irrelevant data, ensuring accuracy and reliability. Basic descriptive statistics, such as mean, median, mode, and standard deviation, were calculated to summarize general trends and characteristics. A comparative analysis was conducted to identify significant changes and developments by comparing current ASD trends with pre-pandemic trends, highlighting the impact of the COVID-19 pandemic on ASD practices and the shift to hybrid work models. The data was used to understand relationships between different variables, identifying factors that significantly influence productivity, team communication, and project success in hybrid ASD environments.

Qualitative data from open-ended survey responses was analyzed using thematic analysis to identify recurring themes and patterns, providing deeper insights into participants' experiences and perspectives. The results were illustrated using charts, graphs, and tables to facilitate easy interpretation and communication of the findings. By employing these data processing and statistical treatment methods, the study aimed to provide a comprehensive and nuanced understanding of trends in ASD within hybrid work environments, informing the development of actionable recommendations for optimizing ASD practices in these settings.

By analyzing these sources, this study captured a broader range of perspectives and insights that might not be fully represented in formal survey responses. This qualitative data helped identify emerging trends, common challenges, and innovative solutions that practitioners are discussing in real-time. These informal opinions were systematically categorized and analyzed to complement the survey findings, providing a more comprehensive understanding of the current state and future direction of ASD in hybrid work environments. This approach ensured that our recommendations are grounded in both empirical data and the lived experiences of those actively engaged in the field.

4 Results

4.1 Analysis of Forum and Blog Posts

Informal sources, such as StarAgile and various Reddit communities, offered a diverse range of perspectives that helped shape the foundation of this survey. StarAgile presents a predominantly positive view of Agile implementation, citing companies like Spotify as success stories. Since adopting Agile practices in 2012, Spotify has reportedly benefited from faster decision-making and a more customer-centric approach [10]. StarAgile also highlights the enhanced team engagement enabled by Agile, noting that it fosters collaborative decision-making and promotes open communication within teams [9].

In contrast, discussions on popular Reddit forums such as r/ExperiencedDevs and r/Agile reveal more critical viewpoints. One user likens the current state of Agile to a system in need of a "Protestant reformation," arguing that while Agile was originally intended to support a communicative, feedback-driven culture, it has eroded into a rigid focus on sprints, tickets, and story points [1]. Another contributor questions whether Agile is becoming obsolete, with the respondent expressing frustration about being pressured to provide estimates based on incomplete information or assumptions [5].

4.2 Analysis of Survey

Demographics. The survey received responses from 15 individuals representing a diverse range of demographics. Figure 1 shows participants came from 12 distinct career domains, with Productivity Software, Healthcare, and Government each represented twice. Career longevity was fairly evenly distributed, with a slight skew toward mid-career professionals (see Fig. 2). This trend aligned with the majority of respondents holding leadership roles, most notably Senior Software Engineers (see Fig. 3). Figure 4 indicates that most respondents work at large companies, with the only small-company respondent having 0–2 years of experience. Despite ongoing "return-to-office" efforts, the data also show that most participants remain in hybrid or remote roles.

Responses. When evaluating the prioritization of agile values, Fig. 6 shows hybrid respondents aligned best with the value of "Responding to change over following a plan," signaling a connection with Agile's flexible nature of development and the pandemic's consistent need to pivot due to unforeseen circumstances. Meanwhile, remote respondents valued "Individuals and interactions over processes and tools," contradicting the nature of remote work inherently having more distanced individuals compared to being in-person. Finally, none of the in-person respondents favored "Working software over comprehensive documentation," again offering a contradiction, but this time from the nature of software development as a whole. However, this contradiction also speaks to the development of a Minimum Viable Product (MVP) with Agile and developing more working features with each iteration (Fig. 5).

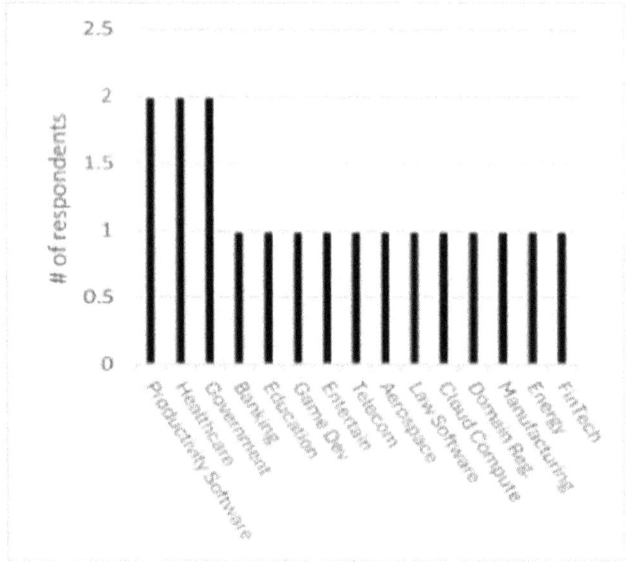

Fig. 1. Career Domain.

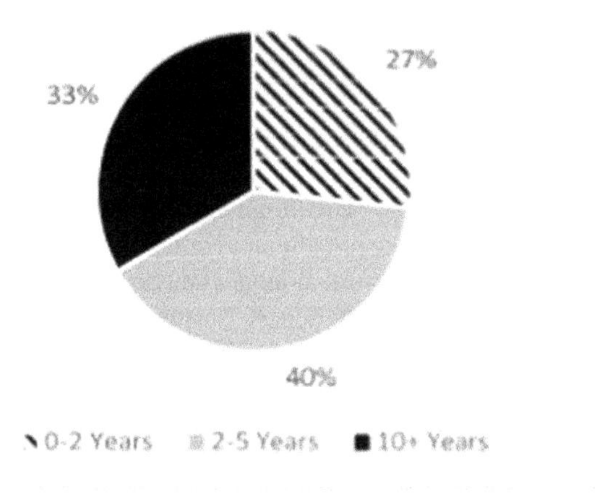

Fig. 2. Career Longevity.

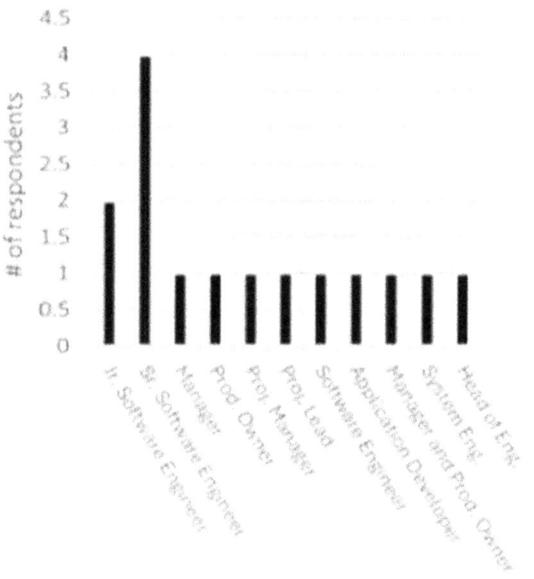

Fig. 3. Career Position.

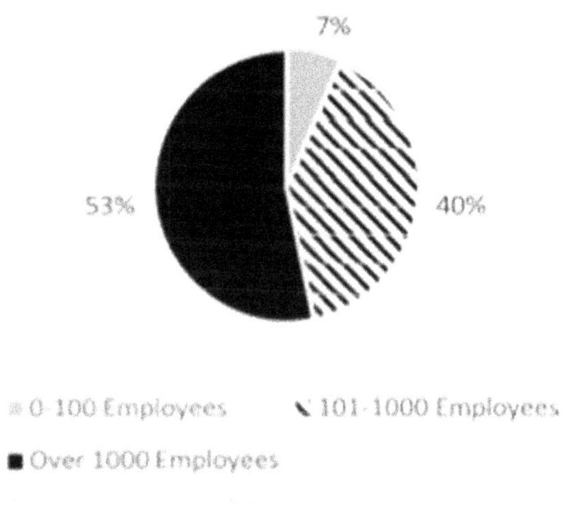

Fig. 4. Company Size by Employees.

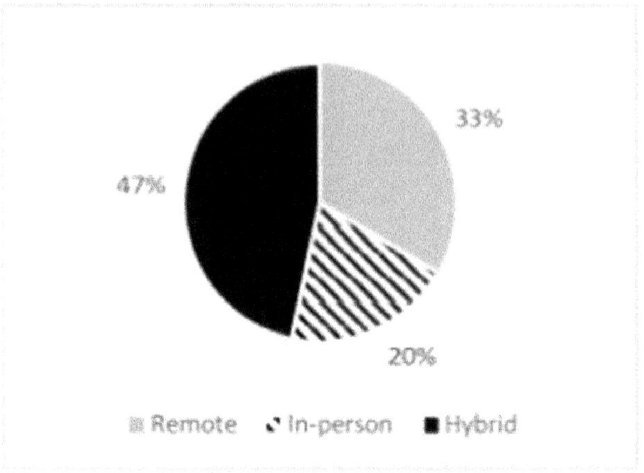

Fig. 5. Work Environment.

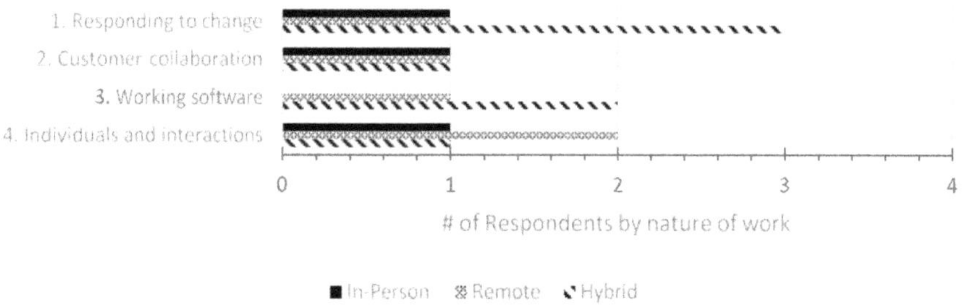

Fig. 6. Higher Agile Prioritization.

Rather than limiting the analysis to the four core Agile values, Fig. 7 presents the average ratings assigned to the expanded set of 12 Agile principles. Overall, responses show a moderately positive sentiment across all principles, with relatively uniform distribution. Notably, remote workers placed the highest value on Principle 5: "Build projects around motivated individuals," underscoring a preference for autonomy and trust in individual capability as key drivers of productivity.

Hybrid respondents, while displaying less pronounced preferences overall, also rated Principle 5 the highest. As expected, they assigned the lowest value to Principle 6: "The most efficient and effective method of conveying information to and within a development team is face-to-face conversation." This suggests that employees in hybrid environments may view in-person requirements as less efficient and favor digital communication methods.

In contrast, in-person respondents showed a slightly lower valuation for Principle 7: "Working software is the primary measure of progress." This may indicate a broader perspective on success metrics in co-located environments, where other indicators—such as team dynamics, planning, or stakeholder feedback—are considered alongside functional software delivery.

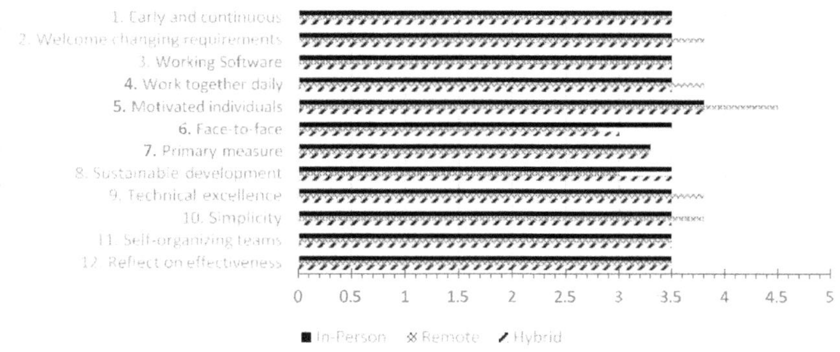

Fig. 7. Agile Principles Mean Ratings.

The data reveal divergent perspectives on which aspects of Agile Software Development (ASD) are most important, depending on the working environment. Core tensions tend to center around documentation and communication effectiveness.

For in-person employees, delivering working software is not seen as the highest priority. Instead, there is a stronger emphasis on comprehensive documentation, particularly in contexts where project development is built around motivated individuals. This perspective may be influenced by the time investment required for commuting, which employees often factor into their overall contribution. As a result, in-person workers may prioritize immediately engaging in meaningful work, with detailed documentation serving both current needs and future knowledge transfer. One respondent cited an internal restructuring that required significant documentation to ensure continuity. Although pre-pandemic workflows emphasized predictable delivery and consistent sprint cadence, these patterns were significantly disrupted during the pandemic.

Remote employees also prioritize motivation and autonomy but place less emphasis on traditional processes and tools. While in-person interaction is often regarded as superior for collaboration, remote respondents challenged this notion, stating that face-to-face communication is not essential for effective information exchange. Many high-lighted schedule flexibility as a major benefit, particularly in asynchronous work environments. One interviewee described the production of extensive asynchronous documentation during the pandemic, which allowed team members to contribute thoughtfully at their own pace. However, this approach was not without drawbacks, as it sometimes resulted in reduced depth in collaborative exchanges.

Hybrid employees expressed a more ambivalent stance. While they value the flexibility of mixed environments, they also acknowledge a lack of cohesion stemming from inconsistent in-person interactions. One interviewee suggested that r all hybrid team members to be in the office on a designated day could help establish predictable moments of team alignment without sacrificing overall flexibility. A key frustration voiced by hybrid respondents was that Agile, post-pandemic, has shifted too heavily toward performance reporting rather than true collaboration. A consistent in-person day could reintroduce a sense of cohesion while preserving the adaptability Agile is meant to support.

Limitations: This study has its limitations, the first being that only fifteen participants responded to the survey. Due to the diversity in the demographics, however, the responses still have considerable value. Second, there is also a limitation of using blogs like Reddit to collect data on agile principles is that the content is anecdotal, subjective, and may lack contextual depth or representativeness across industries. However, an advantage is that these platforms provide real-time, diverse, and candid insights from practitioners, revealing emerging trends and practical challenges often missed in formal studies.

Recommendations. Based on the opinions seen in the informal forums and articles, along with the survey results and interviews, there are a few recommendations for hybrid teams from the noted trends. The first recommendation is to reevaluate the flexibility offered by the iterative nature of Agile. In regard to the work environment, teams should be given clear expectations about how often they should divide their in-person and remote work.

However, hybrid respondents also made it clear they do not align with face-to-face expectations, so offering the flexibility in how they choose to report may need revisiting. Likewise, hybrid teams prefer responding to change over a plan, and allowing the team flexibility in time-boxed conversations before committing to a plan may be crucial. The second recommendation is to reevaluate the process of how the project is built around the team and their motivations. The chief complaint is that the reporting processes and ceremonies are redundant to a team's ability to remain productive. Hybrid employees have a secondary priority for working software over comprehensive documentation. By pivoting the processes for hybrid teams to direct their efforts into more development time over documentation time, there is more opportunity to avoid documentation of software that does not lead towards a working product.

5 Conclusion

Prior to the COVID-19 pandemic, hybrid work models were relatively uncommon. However, their rapid adoption has had a lasting influence on Agile Software Development (ASD) practices. Despite uncertainty about the future of work, current trends— reflected in both survey and interview data—highlight a shared priority across work environments: the importance of building projects around the motivation and autonomy of team members.

A recurring concern is that tools intended to support Agile processes have, in some cases, devolved into mechanisms for metric-based reporting, diminishing their original purpose of facilitating iterative dialogue and collaboration. To address this, organizations must clearly communicate expectations regarding work environments and foster a culture of trust. This will enable teams to shift their focus back to meaningful, value-driven software development.

While hybrid work continues to evolve, retaining its flexibility must be balanced with the need for clearer, more consistent processes. As developers are still adapting to hybrid models, time and intentional structure will be essential for maximizing their effectiveness. Looking ahead, the emergence of AI presents both opportunities and challenges for Agile. Its potential to streamline workflows is significant, but care must be taken to ensure it enhances—rather than replaces—the collaborative, human-centered principles at the core of Agile methodologies.

Disclosure of Interests. Authors have no competing interests to declare that are relevant to the content of this article.

References

1. Agile is in Need of Its Own Protestant Reformation, Reddit. https://www.reddit.com/r/agile/comments/17m2gew/agile_is_in_need_of_its_own_protestant_reformation/. Last accessed 2 Aug 2024
2. Basili, V., Caldiera, G., Rombach, H.: The Goal Question Metric Approach. https://www.cs.umd.edu/users/mvz/handouts/gqm.pdf. Last accessed 7 Aug 2024
3. Chamorro-Premuzic, T.: The Real Reasons Companies are Forcing You Back to the Office. Forbes (2025)
4. Dutra, E., Diirr, B., Santos, G.: On building an instrument to assess the organizational climate of agile software development teams. In: Proceedings of the XXII Brazilian Symposium on Software Quality, pp. 342–351, Brasilia, Brazil (2023)
5. Is Agile actually dying, Reddit. https://www.reddit.com/r/ExperiencedDevs/comments/1do8ehp/is_agile_actually_dying. Last accessed 2 Aug 2024
6. Khanna, D., Christensen, E., Gosu, S., Wang, X., Paasivaara, M.: Hybrid work meets agile software development: a systematic mapping study. In: Proceedings of the 17th International Conference on Cooperative and Human Aspects of Software Engineering, pp. 57–67. IEEE/ACM, Lisbon, Portugal (2024)
7. Pabilonia, S., Redmond, J.: The Rise in Remote Work Across Industries During the Pandemic. U.S. Bureau of Labor Statistics (2024) https://www.bls.gov/opub/btn/volume-13/remote-work-productivity.htm. Last accessed 9 May 2025
8. Prenner, N., Klünder, J., Schneider, K.: Defining frames to structure agile development in hybrid settings - a multi-case interview study. In: Proceedings of the International Conference on Software and System Processes and International Conference on Global Software Engineering, pp. 34–44, Pittsburgh, PA, USA (2022)
9. Reddy, N.: State of Agile 2024: Insights, Trends, and Key Findings, StarAgile. https://staragile.com/blog/state-of-agile. Last accessed 2 Aug 2024
10. Reddy, N.: Scrum Case Study: Real-world Agile Success, StarAgile. https://staragile.com/blog/scrum-case-study. Last accessed 2 Aug 2024
11. Tokdemir, G., Uğuz, S.: Research trends in agile software development. In: International Conference on Emerging Trends in Computing and Engineering Applications, pp. 1–5, Karak, Jordan (2022)

The Role of Provenance Modeling in Tracing and Reproducing Explainable AI Pipelines

Zerui Wang and Yan Liu(✉)

Department of Electrical and Computer Engineering, Concordia University, Montréal, Canada
zerui.wang@mail.concordia.ca, yan.liu@concordia.ca

Abstract. Provenance data captures and provides a detailed lineage of datasets, models, and analytical pipelines, ensuring end-to-end traceability. In the explainable AI (XAI) process, recent techniques, including LIME and Grad-CAM, provide local explanations for deep learning models. However, achieving trustworthy AI requires synergizing these local explanations with the global observability and traceability of entire XAI pipelines. Many factors introduce substantial complexity at both local and global levels, generating a vast combinatorial space for experimental tuning to improve model quality. Ensuring the reproducibility of these experiments is critical for maintaining AI performance amidst subtle variations and large-scale changes. In this paper, we propose a provenance network model for cloud-based XAI pipelines. The provenance graph data is stored in the graph database. We demonstrate our model's implementation in cloud environments, validating its effectiveness in enhancing observability, traceability, and reproducibility. Our approach is tested across multiple cloud platforms and open-source models.

Keywords: Provenance · Explainable AI · Trustworthy AI · Pipelines · Reproducibility

1 Introduction

The rapid advancement of artificial intelligence, particularly deep learning, has introduced unprecedented capabilities alongside new challenges in ensuring model trustworthiness, reproducibility, and interpretability [4]. While Explainable AI (XAI) techniques offer valuable local insights into model behavior [10], achieving end-to-end traceability across data processing, experimentation, and deployment pipelines remains a major unsolved problem [17]. The complexity of modern XAI systems arises not only from the architectures of individual models but also from the intricate development and operational pipelines that support them [12]. Empirical studies [17] show that XAI workflows typically involve data preprocessing, augmentation, explanation generation, and assessment. Each introducing parameters, dependencies, and artifacts that must be systematically managed.

K. Daimi et al. (Eds.): CSCE 2025, CCIS 2937, pp. 470–485, 2026.
https://doi.org/10.1007/978-3-032-22208-4_33

Provenance tracking offers a principled way to address these challenges [19], capturing and analyzing the lineage of AI artifacts and processes to support accountability and reproducibility. Yet, most existing provenance systems fall short in handling the metadata richness and compositional nature of XAI workflows [19], where explainability artifacts and their relationships must be explicitly modeled.

This paper presents a provenance network model for XAI cloud services, extending prior architecture [18] to manage combinatorial experiments and reproducible pipelines. The proposed research focuses on four aspects, namely (1) defining a metadata schema that captures entities and relationships across AI and XAI pipelines; (2) developing an executable provenance model that ensures data lineage under constraints; (3) introducing provenance polymorphism to derive reusable XAI pipelines from modular components; and (4) integrating the model with machine learning frameworks through open APIs for deployment and monitoring. The provenance network model supports complexity management by (1) providing quick access to data lineage across AI workflows, (2) enabling pipeline reproducibility through executable provenance, and (3) supporting cross-pipeline configuration queries for similarity analysis.

The next section details the model's design and implementation, emphasizing metadata schema design, relationship modeling, and integration with cloud-native XAI services.

2 Background and Related Work

Provenance tracking in XAI pipelines presents unique challenges beyond traditional AI systems [11]. XAI pipelines must capture complex iterative processes that include not only standard AI pipeline components such as hyperparameter tuning and model versioning but also diverse types of explanation-specific elements [4]. Recent XAI techniques, including LIME [10], SHAP [8], and Grad-CAM [13] require complex configuration of multiple parameters that significantly impact explanation quality and computational efficiency [17]. For instance, SHAP [8] requires specific sampling numbers to approximate Shapley values, while LIME needs proper iteration counts to ensure stable local explanations [10]. Grad-CAM implementations must identify appropriate network layers for generating class activation maps [13]. The selection and tuning of these parameters create additional dimensions of complexity in the experimental space [14]. Moreover, changes in these configurations can substantially affect explanation outcomes, necessitating rigorous tracking of parameter settings to ensure reproducible results.

In addition, these XAI-specific requirements include tracking feature attribution methods, explanation consistency across model versions, and the relationship between local and global explanations [4]. The inherent complexity of XAI pipelines necessitates robust provenance capture for both model behavior and its corresponding explanations. These tracking capabilities are essential for ensuring both traceability and reproducibility. Furthermore, proper provenance tracking enables validation of explanation consistency between local and global levels. Current AI provenance pipelines, such as MLflow [22] and ProvDB [9], are designed for experiment tracking and data lineage management for traditional machine learning workflows. However, they fall short in handling the intricate requirements of XAI systems. Specifically, these tools lack explicit mechanisms for tracking explanation-specific parameters such as Shapley value sampling rates or Grad-CAM layer selections. Furthermore, their inability to capture the interaction between local explanations and global model behavior impedes comprehensive traceability. Furthermore, existing tools fail to capture the intricate relationships between model training, data augmentation, and explanation generation [17].

This work addresses these gaps through a comprehensive provenance network model specifically designed for XAI pipelines. The model introduces novel capabilities for tracking explanation-specific parameters, managing cross-platform provenance, and capturing relationships between different levels of explanations. This approach enables reproducible and traceable XAI operations while supporting systematic assessment of explanation quality across diverse cloud environments.

3 The Provenance Modeling of XAI Pipelines

The foundation of our provenance network model is its metadata schema, which captures both static and dynamic aspects of XAI pipelines. The XAI pipeline software is provided in the recent study [14]. The provenance data entities are shown in Fig. 1. The proposed provenance meta model maps a typical XAI pipeline to the PROV-DM semantics. The components involved in an XAI pipeline can be categorized into `provenance data`, `pipeline steps`, `microservices & cloud platforms`, and `provenance links`.

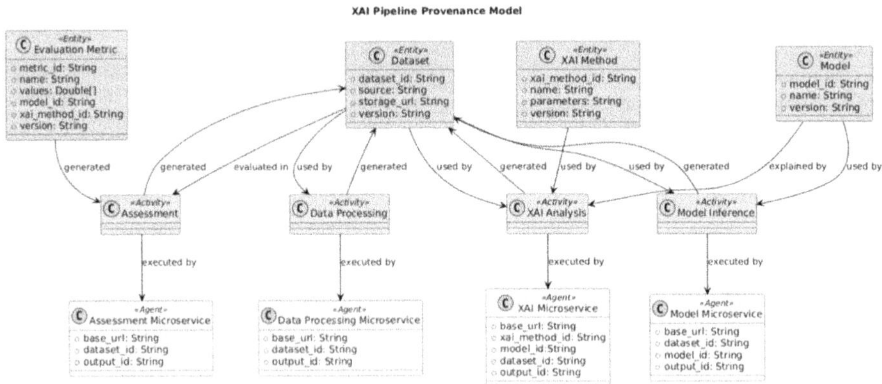

Fig. 1. The XAI provenance meta model, highlighting the interactions among entities, activities, and agents at each stage.

Provenance data are represented by PROV-DM `Entities (prove: Entity)`. Entities model things that exist over time, such as data, models, and explanations. Provenance data consists of four types, namely `dataset` that represents raw and processed datasets; `perturbation & augmentation` that track modifications applied to datasets; `model` that captures model metadata, including version and API; `XAI methods` store explainability method configurations; and `evaluation metric` stores assessment results.

The pipeline steps are represented by PROV-DM `Activities (prove: Activity)`. Activities model actions that change or generate entities. The pipeline steps involve `data processing` that includes transformations, augmentations, perturbations; `model inference` that executes model inference using AI models; `XAI analysis` that generates explanations using XAI methods; and `assessment` that evaluates models and explanations.

The microservices and cloud platforms are represented by PROV-DM `Agents (prove: Agent)`. Agents model people or systems responsible for activities. There are four types of microservices that are executed on cloud platforms, including `the data processing service` that executes data preprocessing tasks; `the model service` that hosts AI models for inference; `the XAI service` runs explainability methods; and `the assessment service` that Computes evaluation metrics. The provenance links are relationships and associations among activities and entities. Each activity "uses" relevant entities and "generates" results. Each activity is "executed by" a respective agent.

3.1 The Metadata Schema of Provenance

The provenance schema extends the provenance models by four types, namely the `data processing` provenance, the `model` provenance, the `XAI` provenance, and the `assessment` provenance.

The `XAI` provenance records the configurations and outputs of the explanation methods, detailing how the explanation summary is obtained. The `assessment` provenance focuses on evaluation metrics and quality assessments, enabling systematic comparisons of consistency, fidelity, and robustness of the explanation.

Data Processing Provenance Modelling. The `data processing` provenance tracks the lineage and transformations applied to the data sets, including transformation, augmentation, and perturbation techniques as detailed in Fig. 2. We consider each data processing operation to be callable in RESTful APIs. These APIs encapsulate the entries to the stateless cloud microservices. The APIs can be defined and published for access by tools such as SwaggerHub and FastAPI. These services are categorized into three types: data perturbation, data augmentation, and ordinary data processing.

Data perturbation introduces controlled changes, such as shot noise and defocus blur, to test model robustness. Each perturbation operation is of the type `prov: Activity` that is defined by key attributes such as `perturbation type`, `specific parameters`, and `dataset references`. The perturbation activity is executed by the corresponding microservice of the type `prov: Agent`. An API endpoint is provided by the microservice. A concrete example involves applying defocus blur at the level of three to an input dataset, generating a modified dataset, and recording the operation with a unique task identifier to ensure traceability.

Data augmentation enhances dataset diversity to improve model generalization. Methods such as CutMix [21] and PuzzleMix [6] systematically modify input datasets, creating enriched outputs that better represent varied training scenarios. These methods are encapsulated in RESTful APIs, where users specify configuration parameters such as `augmentation method` and `output dataset`. The resulting augmented datasets are tracked using unique identifiers, providing a record of the augmentation process.

Data processing focuses on ensuring the compatibility of datasets with subsequent pipeline stages by standardizing input formats. Operations such as resizing and normalization are critical for aligning datasets with model requirements. Each transformation is recorded with `dataset`, `transform parameter`, and executed by the data processing service. For example, resizing a dataset to 224 × 224 generates a transformed dataset available for model inference, with processing details logged for traceability. In addition, more data processing types can be flexibly added to this provenance with the designed RESTful APIs.

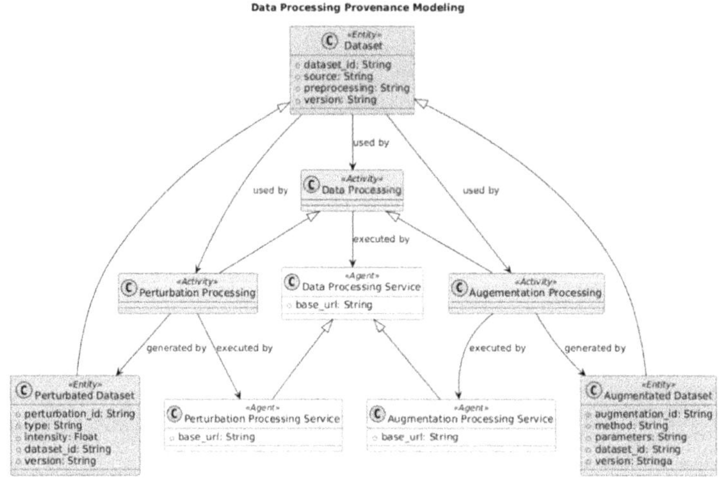

Fig. 2. The structure of `Data Processing` services within the XAI pipeline encompasses three key types: data perturbation, data augmentation, and data transformation.

AI-Model Provenance Modelling. The `model` provenance captures the configurations, inference processes, and version histories of models, providing information on the evolution of model behaviours. The provenance of AI models within the XAI pipeline is structured from the model microservices, as illustrated in Fig. 3. These services are categorized into three main types: open-source models, custom pre-trained models, and cloud-based AI services from platforms such as Azure AI, Google Vertex AI, and AWS. This categorization abstracts the deployment environment, enabling seamless integration and comparative evaluation of diverse AI models.

Each model service is characterized by a set of attributes that define its configuration and usage within the pipeline. Key attributes include the `Model name with version` and the corresponding `RESTful API endpoint`. These attributes ensure that models are invoked and managed consistently, regardless of their deployment platform or architecture. For example, a pre-trained model from Huggingface specifies the model name with version as `google/vit-base-patch16-224`. For cloud-based AI services, the configuration includes complex API endpoints that define the service region, model identifier, and required authentication. For example, an endpoint for Azure Computer Vision might be structured as: `https://<region>.api.cognitive.microsoft.com/vision/<version>/<server_id>` In this case, `<region>` specifies the service location, `version` demotes the training version given by cloud AI (for instance, v3.0 indicates the third update), `<model_id>` identifies the selected model. Authentication credentials are validated through the REST request to ensure secure access to the service. These structured endpoints ensure clear and reproducible inference setups. This abstraction facilitates integration across different deployment environments, enabling comparative evaluation of AI models.

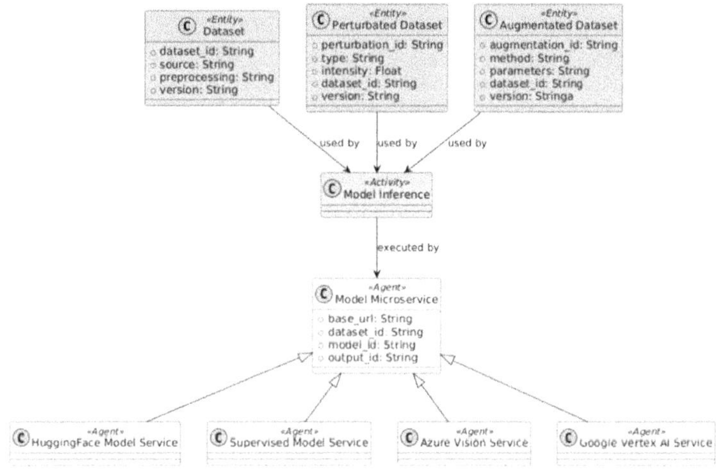

Fig. 3. REST-based `Model Service` categorized into pre-trained open-source models and cloud-based services.

XAI Provenance Modelling. The provenance pipeline for XAI methods is structured around their encapsulation as RESTful services, as illustrated in Fig. 4. These services include types of XAI methods, including SHAP, LIME, and CAM-series methods [16]. New XAI methods should be encapsulated as `XAI` service with RESTful APIs. Each XAI method in the pipeline has key attributes that include the `method type`, `parameters` (such as the number of samples for SHAP or the specific layer for Grad-CAM), `input model` that is linked to the `model provenance` of the model being explained, `dataset` that is linked to the data provenance, and the associated RESTful API endpoint.

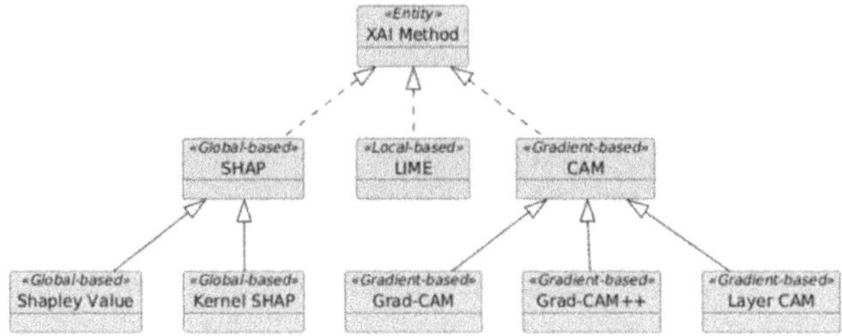

Fig. 4. The hierarchy `XAI` methods, including global, local, and gradient-based explanation methods used by XAI analysis activities.

Assessment Provenance Modelling. The provenance pipeline for assessment services in XAI pipelines focuses on capturing the metrics that define model performance and explanation quality under diverse conditions, as shown in Fig. 5. This service focuses on evaluation metrics [14] such as consistency, stability, fidelity, performance (precision, recall, F1 score), and robustness.

The assessment service is implemented as a RESTful API, where each evaluation operation is defined by attributes such as the `evaluation metric`, `input dataset`, `model ID`, `XAI method`, and corresponding `endpoint`. This modular and extensible design allows the integration of new evaluation metrics and methodologies as needed.

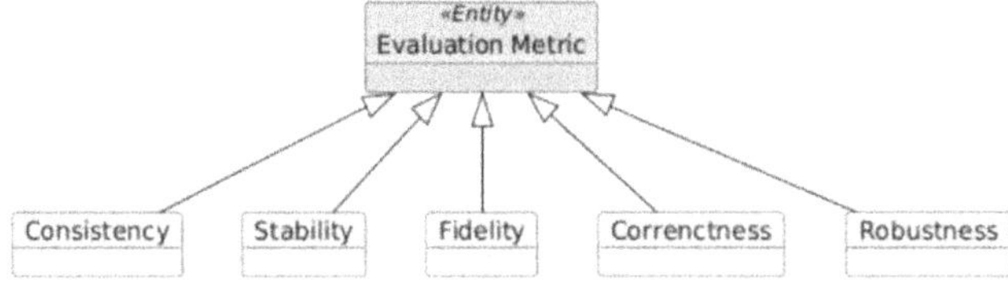

Fig. 5. `Assessment` services provide consistency, stability, fidelity, performance (precision, recall, F1 score), and robustness in XAI pipelines.

Connecting Metadata to Graph Network. The metadata schema defined earlier, comprising `Data Processing`, `Model`, `XAI`, and `Assessment` components, serves as the foundation for constructing a unified graph-based provenance network. Figure 6 demonstrates how these metadata categories are instantiated as nodes and edges in a graph database, such as Neo4j, to capture dependencies and workflows in XAI pipelines.

For the `Data Processing`, each type of data processing operation, such as augmentation or perturbation, is represented as a node in the graph. Depending on the operation type, these nodes are connected to the input dataset through the edge. This ensures that all transformations applied to the dataset are tracked in a hierarchical manner.

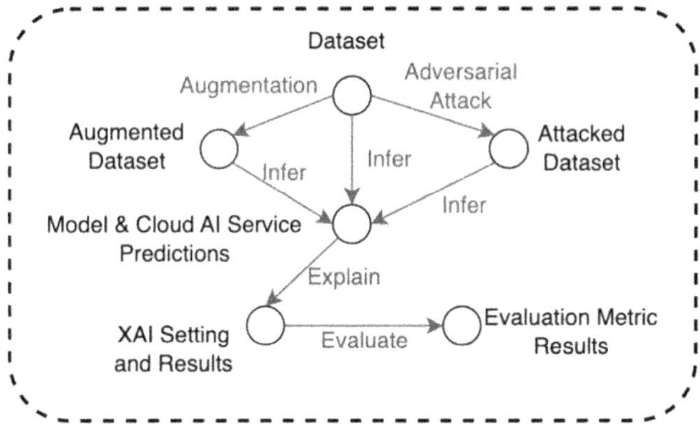

Fig. 6. Graph-based design of executable provenance data for XAI pipelines, highlighting relationships among components and enabling traceability and reproducibility.

The `Model` nodes in the graph correspond to the deployed AI services or open-source models, such as ResNet, Vision Transformer, or Azure Vision AI. Each model node has a relationship to the processed dataset, indicating which datasets are used for model inference.

`XAI` methods are added to the graph as nodes connected to the model nodes. The edge between the model and XAI captures which models are explained and the configuration parameters of the explanation method.

Each `Assessment` metric is represented as a node connected to the corresponding XAI explanation via an EVALUATE relationship. This edge ensures that the quality of explanations is tracked and linked back to the original model and XAI method.

Overall, the graph-based design of the executable provenance data, as depicted in Fig. 6, provides a representation of the interactions and dependencies within XAI pipelines.

Summary - The schema supports polymorphic behavior of diverse data augmentation techniques, XAI methods allowing for combination between different explanation methods and their corresponding model outputs. This approach enables tracking of both local and global influences on model explanations, facilitating comprehensive analysis of explanation quality and reliability. In contrast to MLflow [22], which focuses on general machine learning experiment tracking, our schema addresses the complexities of XAI, including detailed parameter tracking for XAI methods and integration across multiple cloud models.

4 Pipeline Configuration and Provenance Lifecycle

This section presents the lifecycle of the proposed provenance network model, focusing on configuration, storage, and queries. The provenance network model is represented as graph-structured data. This graph-based approach enables fine-grained traceability, allowing researchers to visualize and analyze how individual components interact and contribute to the XAI pipeline.

4.1 The Runtime Components of XAI Pipelines

The runtime components of XAI pipelines form the operational context from which a provenance model is created. Each provenance model is derived from an executable pipeline and records its composing services and configurations. These services are orchestrated by the XAI service architecture [18], which integrates data processing, model inference, explainability, and assessment modules. Centralized coordination manages service registration, metadata tracking, and capability discovery, enabling modularity, scalability, and dynamic task execution.

XAI pipelines function as blueprints, specifying task order, dependencies, and execution rules. They support both direct invocation of individual tasks and automated execution of complex workflows through provenance data, allowing the system to adapt to heterogeneous or multi-stage pipelines.

A centralized task management server orchestrates all microservices through RESTful APIs. Each microservice registers with a unique service ID and accompanying metadata such as API endpoints, supported operations, and performance benchmarks. During execution, the task manager invokes necessary services, monitors progress, and aggregates results into the provenance graph, ensuring a complete and consistent record of the workflow.

To maintain cross-platform compatibility, all APIs follow a unified interface specification, enabling seamless integration across Azure, AWS, and Google Cloud. Model inference services from these platforms are abstracted into a shared schema capturing inputs, model selection, and output formats. This design simplifies interoperability and enables direct comparison of explanation consistency across platforms. When applied to vision models offered by Azure Cognitive

Services, Google Cloud Vertex AI, and AWS Rekognition, the pipeline achieved reproducible and consistent explainability results—an essential capability for trustworthy XAI deployment in production environments (Fig. 7).

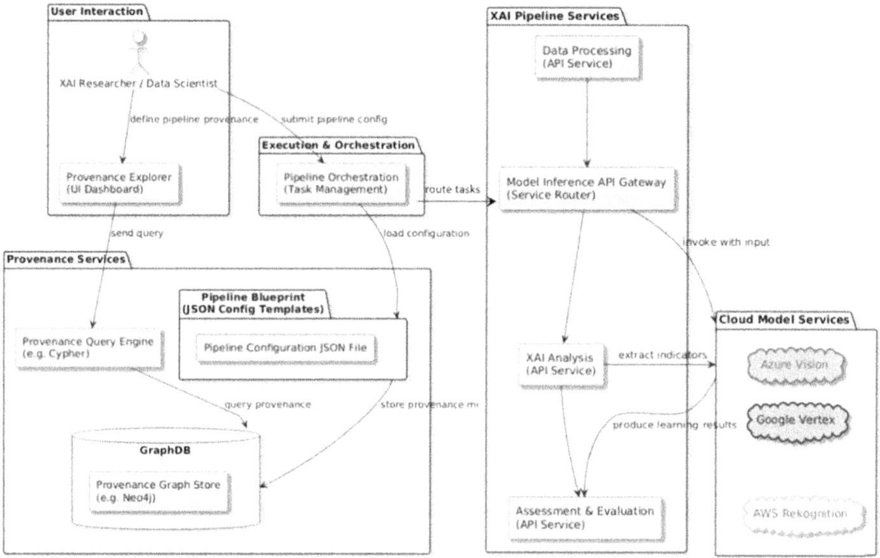

Fig. 7. The workflow of provenance and core components of XAI pipelines.

4.2 Addressing Complexity in XAI Pipelines with Provenance

XAI pipelines are highly complex due to the combination of diverse models, explanation methods, and data transformations. Augmentation techniques such as random cropping, flipping, CutMix [21], and PuzzleMix [6], together with adversarial perturbations [3], expand the input space and assess robustness, but also create a combinatorial explosion of configurations. Prior work [16] highlights this exponential growth and the corresponding challenges in reproducibility. The provenance network model introduced here addresses this issue by capturing complete metadata on pipeline components, configurations, and dependencies. We organize pipelines into three progressive evaluation layers: (1) Performance Evaluation that benchmarks accuracy, precision, recall, and latency using standardized preprocessing and REST APIs. The layer integrates Azure Vision AI, Google Cloud Vertex AI, AWS Rekognition, and six vision models (`resnet,vit,swin,segformer,convnext,cvt`). (2) Explainability Analysis that applies SHAP [8], LIME [10], and CAM-based methods [13] to generate local and global explanations, examining feature importance and decision pathways. (3) Adversarial Robustness Testing that evaluates prediction stability and explanation fidelity under perturbations such as Gaussian noise, pixelation, and defocus blur [3]. These layers collectively demonstrate the need for systematic provenance tracking to organize, trace, and reproduce complex XAI workflows.

Summary - the combination of these pipeline components generates a comprehensive assessment space. The assessment encompasses nine model configurations (three cloud services and six open-source models), five XAI methods, three data augmentation approaches, five adversarial attack variants, and two evaluation metrics. This combination yields **1350 distinct assessment pipelines**. Each pipeline processes approximately one thousand samples, generating standardized performance metrics and explanation results. Overall, more than one million data points have been processed in the XAI pipelines.

4.3 Provenance Model Initialization and Configuration

The structured configuration system enables systematic management of XAI pipeline variations. Specialized configurations define XAI-specific parameters, augmentation and perturbation strategies, and evaluation criteria. Each pipeline is specified through a JSON template that minimizes manual intervention by capturing all required parameters—perturbation types, augmentation methods, model selection, and evaluation metrics—and mapping them to corresponding service endpoints. In the provenance schema, nodes represent metadata categories such as Dataset, Model, and XAI Method, while edges encode the relationships among them.

```
{
"id": config_id,
"dataset": dataset_id,
"perturbation_config": {
    "server_url": "http://xaiport.ddns.net",
    "perturbation_type": perturbation_type},
"data_augmentation_config": {
    "server_url": "http://xaiport.ddns.net",
    "data_augmentation_type": data_augmentation},
"model_config": {
    "server_url": "http://xaiport.ddns.net",
    "model_name": model},
"xai_config": {
    "server_url": "xaiport.ddns.net",
    "datasets": {
        f"{dataset}_{perturbation_type}_
        {data_augmentation}": {
            "model_name": model,
            "algorithms": [xai_method] }}},
"evaluation_config": {
    "server_url": "http://xaiport.ddns.net",
    "evaluation_metric": evaluation_method,
    "model_name": model,
    "algorithms": [xai_method] }}
```

Fig. 8. Sample JSON template for XAI pipeline configuration.

Consider the case of adversarial robustness evaluation. The JSON configuration (Fig. 8) specifies perturbation types such as Gaussian noise or pixelation, and applies them to the dataset identified by its dataset ID. In the provenance model, the Adversarial Attack appears as a node under Data Processing, its parameters are stored as node properties, and the perturbed dataset is linked to the original dataset through the HAS_PERTURBATION edge.

This structure supports expressive provenance queries. By traversing EXPLAIN and EVALUATE edges, researchers can compare how different XAI methods behave under various augmentation or perturbation strategies and identify methods that produce more stable explanations. The utility of this configuration system is further illustrated in the next subsection, where provenance-generated graphs visualize relationships among datasets, transformations, models, XAI methods, and evaluation metrics.

4.4 Provenance Model Storage and Query

Provenance data is stored in Neo4j, an example graph database suited for managing complex connected workflows in XAI pipelines. Graph data represents the pipeline's components as nodes and their interactions as edges. This structure aligns with the interconnected nature of XAI pipelines. Graph databases' traversal and querying capabilities enable efficient analysis of pipeline relationships. Researchers can query how specific augmentation techniques influence explanation quality across different models. Additionally, execution histories can be retrieved to evaluate the consistency and stability of explanations. The graph database supports a query language for traversing graph structures. The provenance graph enables advanced queries, such as analyzing how specific data augmentations influence explanation quality across various XAI methods.

The first example provenance graph in Fig. 9 demonstrates the lifecycle of `dataset_0` within the pipeline. The dataset undergoes data processing steps, including augmentation with `Puzzlemix` [6] and perturbation with `Defocus_blur` [3]. These preprocessing techniques are systematically linked to the dataset through directed relationships (`HAS_AUGMENTATION`, `HAS_PERTURBATION`). Following preprocessing, the dataset is input into two models, Swin Transformer (`swin`) [7] and Vision Transformer (`vit`) [1] with `INFERENCE`. The inference results are subsequently analyzed using multiple XAI methods: `SHAP` [8], `GradCAM` [13], and `LayerCAM` [5]. Finally, the quality of these explanations is evaluated based on the `fidelity` [15] metric (`EVALUATE`).

The second provenance graph in Fig. 10 illustrates the pipeline applied to `dataset_1`. This dataset is subjected to multiple augmentation techniques, including `Cutmix` [21] and `Puzzlemix` [6]. These methods are linked to the dataset through the `HAS_AUGMENTATION` relationship, ensuring that the applied transformations are fully traceable. The augmented dataset is then used for inference with models such as `resnet` [2] and `segformer` [20] (`INFERENCE`). The outputs of these models are analyzed using XAI methods, including `GradCAM` [13], and `LIME` [10]. The quality of the explanations is assessed based on the `consistency` metric [4] `EVALUATE`.

The provenance graphs for `dataset_0` and `dataset_1` demonstrate the practical application of the configuration schema. The configuration schema ensures

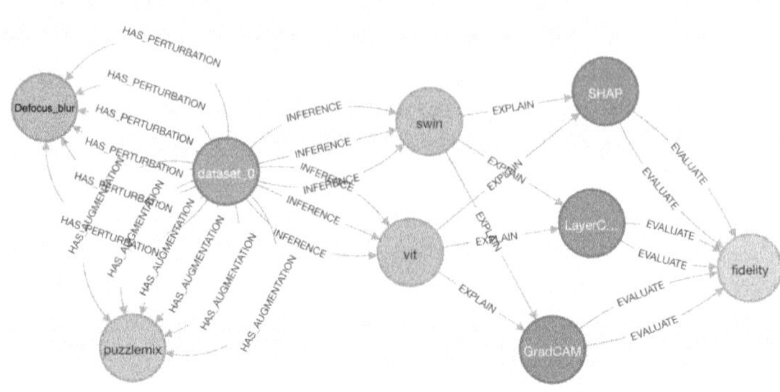

Fig. 9. Provenance graph for `dataset_0`, illustrating augmentation (`Puzzlemix`), perturbation (`Defocus_blur`), inference through models (`swin` and `vit`), explanation generation, and fidelity evaluation.

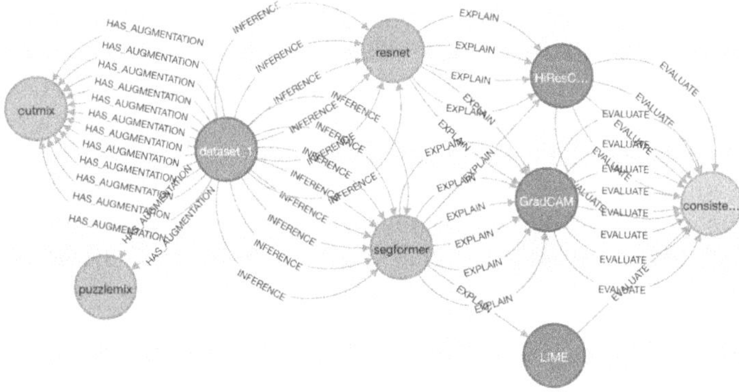

Fig. 10. Provenance graph for `dataset_1`, illustrating augmentation techniques (`Cutmix`, `Puzzlemix`), inference through models (`resnet`, `segformer`), explanation generation, and consistency evaluation.

that all pipeline components are systematically managed and tracked. The provenance graphs capture the execution flow and highlight the dependencies among components. These graphs also underscore the scalability of the pipeline in supporting large-scale XAI experiments. The structured relationships captured in the graphs allow researchers to query specific configurations, analyze the impact of different preprocessing and explanation methods, and ensure the reproducibility of results across diverse experimental setups. This capability is critical for advancing the field of XAI, where transparency, traceability, and reproducibility are essential for building trust in AI systems. By integrating the configuration schema with provenance graph visualization, this pipeline provides a powerful tool for managing the complexity of XAI pipelines while enabling systematic evaluation of their performance and reliability.

4.5 Provenance Model Execution and Reuse

The composition layer transforms our metadata schema into executable pipeline components through our microservice-based architecture [18]. This architecture enables flexible integration of diverse XAI methods with cloud AI services while maintaining the reproducibility of explanations. The pipeline composition implements three key capabilities:

First, the pipeline provides automated dependency management between XAI operations through standardized APIs. This allows seamless integration of feature contribution explanation methods as validated in our experiments across multiple cloud platforms [17]. Second, our pipeline composer implements consistent metadata validation across the XAI workflow. The validation ensures completeness of provenance data for both model predictions and explanations, enabling reproducible assessment of explanation quality [14,16]. Third, the pipeline supports configurable granularity in provenance capture through a microservice-based design. This allows the optimization of storage and computational resources while maintaining traceability of XAI operations.

The integration layer leverages open APIs to connect with existing cloud infrastructure, allowing deployment across different platforms while preserving explanation consistency. This architecture supported our systematic assessment of model performance, robustness, and explanation stability across multiple cloud providers. For real-world deployment scenarios, we provide both synchronous and asynchronous execution modes to handle varying latency requirements. Our assessment [14] demonstrates the pipeline's ability to maintain explanation quality while enabling systematic comparison of XAI services across different models and datasets.

Summary - The lifecycle of the proposed provenance model is aligned with operations of pipeline configuration, storage, and execution. By employing a JSON-based template system, the model generates and records various pipeline variations. The use of graph databases for storing provenance data enables efficient retrieval and querying of complex XAI pipeline relationships. Furthermore, the automated pipeline construction and execution are enabled based on provenance metadata.

5 Conclusion

This paper introduces a provenance network model tailored for XAI pipelines, addressing the critical challenges of traceability and reproducibility in explaining cloud AI services. The proposed model defines a systematic structure to model the complex relationships and dependencies inherent in XAI pipelines. Building upon the development of explainable AI services on cloud platforms, this provenance models are derived from modeling three major cloud vision services with

1,350 unique pipeline configurations and process over one million data samples. Our findings highlight that effective provenance tracking, encompassing both configuration and execution levels, is pivotal for achieving reproducibility and tracibility in XAI systems. This structure not only enables the precise reproduction of results but also facilitates systematic comparisons across different model architectures and explanation methods. Future research will explore automated optimization of XAI pipeline configurations using machine learning techniques and enhanced provenance data analytics.

References

1. Dosovitskiy, A., et al.: An image is worth 16x16 words: transformers for image recognition at scale. arXiv preprint arXiv:2010.11929 (2020)
2. He, K., Zhang, X., Ren, S., Sun, J.: Deep residual learning for image recognition. In: Proceedings of the IEEE Conference on Computer Vision and Pattern Recognition, pp. 770–778 (2016)
3. Hendrycks, D., Dietterich, T.: Benchmarking neural network robustness to common corruptions and perturbations. arXiv preprint arXiv:1903.12261 (2019)
4. Huang, J., Wang, Z., Li, D., Liu, Y.: The analysis and development of an XAI process on feature contribution explanation. In: 2022 IEEE International Conference on Big Data (Big Data), pp. 5039–5048 (2022). https://doi.org/10.1109/BigData55660.2022.10020313
5. Jiang, P.T., Zhang, C.B., Hou, Q., Cheng, M.M., Wei, Y.: Layercam: exploring hierarchical class activation maps for localization. IEEE Trans. Image Process. **30**, 5875–5888 (2021)
6. Kim, J.H., Choo, W., Song, H.O.: Puzzle mix: exploiting saliency and local statistics for optimal mixup. In: International Conference on Machine Learning, pp. 5275–5285. PMLR (2020)
7. Liu, Z., et al.: Swin transformer: Hierarchical vision transformer using shifted windows. In: Proceedings of the IEEE/CVF International Conference on Computer Vision, pp. 10012–10022 (2021)
8. Lundberg, S.M., Lee, S.I.: A unified approach to interpreting model predictions. Neural Inf. Process. Syst. (2017)
9. Miao, H., Chavan, A., Deshpande, A.: Provdb: lifecycle management of collaborative analysis workflows. In: Proceedings of the 2nd Workshop on Human-in-the-Loop Data Analytics, pp. 1–6 (2017)
10. Ribeiro, M.T., Singh, S., Guestrin, C.: Why should i trust you? explaining the predictions of any classifier. In: Proceedings of the 22nd ACM SIGKDD international conference on knowledge discovery and data mining, pp. 1135–1144 (2016)
11. Schlegel, M., Sattler, K.U.: Management of machine learning lifecycle artifacts: a survey. ACM SIGMOD Rec. **51**(4), 18–35 (2023)
12. Sculley, D., et al.: Hidden technical debt in machine learning systems. Neural Inf. Process. Syst. (2015)
13. Selvaraju, R.R., Cogswell, M., Das, A., Vedantam, R., Parikh, D., Batra, D.: Grad-cam: Visual explanations from deep networks via gradient-based localization. In: Proceedings of the IEEE International Conference on Computer Vision, pp. 618–626 (2017)

14. Wang, Z., Liu, Y.: Cloud-based XAI services for assessing open repository models under adversarial attacks. In: 2024 IEEE International Conference on Software Services Engineering (SSE), pp. 141–152 (2024). https://doi.org/10.1109/SSE62657.2024.00031
15. Wang, Z., Liu, Y.: Staa: spatio-temporal attention attribution for real-time interpreting transformer-based ai video models. IEEE Access **13**, 101647–101661 (2025). https://doi.org/10.1109/ACCESS.2025.3575440
16. Wang, Z., Liu, Y.: Xaipipeline: Automated orchestration of explainable AI services for cloud AI and open-source models. In: 2025 IEEE International Conference on Software Services Engineering (SSE) (2025)
17. Wang, Z., Liu, Y., Arumugam Thiruselvi, A., Hamou-Lhadj, A.: Xaiport: a service framework for the early adoption of xai in ai model development. In: Proceedings of the 2024 ACM/IEEE 44th International Conference on Software Engineering: New Ideas and Emerging Results, pp. 67–71 (2024)
18. Wang, Z., Liu, Y., Huang, J.: An open api architecture to discover the trustworthy explanation of cloud ai services. IEEE Trans. Cloud Comput. (2024). https://doi.org/10.1109/TCC.2024.3398609
19. Werder, K., Ramesh, B., Zhang, R.S.: Establishing data provenance for responsible artificial intelligence systems. ACM Trans. Manage. Inf. Syst. **13**(2) (2022). https://doi.org/10.1145/3503488
20. Xie, E., Wang, W., Yu, Z., Anandkumar, A., Alvarez, J.M., Luo, P.: Segformer: simple and efficient design for semantic segmentation with transformers. Adv. Neural. Inf. Process. Syst. **34**, 12077–12090 (2021)
21. Yun, S., Han, D., Oh, S.J., Chun, S., Choe, J., Yoo, Y.: Cutmix: Regularization strategy to train strong classifiers with localizable features. In: Proceedings of the IEEE/CVF International Conference on Computer Vision, pp. 6023–6032 (2019)
22. Zaharia, M.A., et al.: Accelerating the machine learning lifecycle with mlflow. IEEE Data Eng. Bull. **41**, 39–45 (2018)

Best Practice of Scenario-Based Modeling for Humanoid Software Validation

Sangho Lee[1], Janghwan Kim[2], and R. Young Chul Kim[2](✉)

[1] Rastech, Daejeon 34037, Republic of Korea
project@rastech.co.kr
[2] Hongik University, Sejong 30016, Republic of Korea
{lentoconstante,bob}@hongik.ac.kr

Abstract. Recent advances in adapting artificial intelligence technology have revolutionized the field of humanoid robots. The intelligence of robots is based on reinforcement learning and AI models. However, due to the nature of robot software that continuously learns and reacts through interaction with the real environment, it isn't easy to validate safety, reliability, and accuracy using only existing software testing methodologies. To address these issues, we apply scenario-based modeling in software validation to humanoid robot software, incorporating reinforcement learning models. In particular, the 'mode selection' function of humanoid robots is presented as an application case, and a systematic procedure is performed from requirement analysis to scenario creation, refined scenario-based test case creation, and scenario execution and validation using a behavior tree. This is expected to contribute to maintaining the stability of humanoid robot systems by systematically detecting unpredictable behaviors in humanoid software and enhancing efficiency and reliability by validating the decision-making process of AI models using scenario-based modeling based on behavior trees.

Keywords: Scenario-based Modeling · AI Software Validation · Humanoid Software Validation

1 Introduction

Recent advances in artificial intelligence technology have brought about revolutionary changes in the field of robotics, and humanoid robots, in particular, represent a culmination of these technologies. Humanoid robots that mimic human form are utilized in a wide range of fields, including industry, service, and entertainment, due to their potential to perform complex tasks in various environments and interact naturally with humans [1]. The intelligence of these robot systems is mainly driven by artificial intelligence models, including reinforcement learning (RL) [2].

AI models mounted on humanoid robots, especially those using reinforcement learning, are challenging to validate existing software testing methodologies due to their characteristics of continuously learning and responding through interactions with the actual environment.

K. Daimi et al. (Eds.): CSCE 2025, CCIS 2937, pp. 486–497, 2026.
https://doi.org/10.1007/978-3-032-22208-4_34

To solve these problems, this paper proposes a scenario-based modeling (SBM) mechanism to verify the safety, reliability, and accuracy of humanoid robot software equipped with reinforcement learning models. In particular, this paper presents the 'mode selection' function of humanoid robots as an application case and analyzes in detail how the proposed SBM mechanism can be applied to actual robot systems and how it can be effective. In addition, we discuss a method to trace and verify the decision-making process of an AI model by utilizing a behavior tree as a scenario execution (test) method.

In Chap. 2, we discuss validation methods for robot software, drawing on related research, and in Chap. 3, we introduce testing methods for humanoid software. In Chap. 4, we discuss scenario-based testing cases as application cases, and in Chap. 5, we discuss conclusions and future research.

2 Related Studies

2.1 Simulation-Based Testing in Robotics

Simulators are widely used to reproduce and test hazardous or repetitive scenarios in virtual environments, such as those involving autonomous vehicles, drones, and humanoid robots. Afzal et al. evaluate simulators as cost-effective and practical in automated testing pipelines but point out that their predictive power in real-world environments is limited due to the Sim-to-Real gap [3]. Huck et al. propose a Monte Carlo-based safety assessment method, but there are difficulties in configuring simulation conditions. Recent research on humanoid robots has presented techniques for reducing the Sim-to-Real gap by integrating dynamic digital twins into reinforcement learning-based walking policies.

2.2 Scenario-Based Integration Testing for Object-Oriented Software Development

The adaptive use case methodology for improving testing efficiency integrates software design, development, and testing processes through a series of algorithmic transformations and is a process of generating test plans at the design stage [4]. The Use Case Action Matrix describes executable scenarios composed of 'action units', which indicate the execution path by numerically indicating specific action steps in the scenario. Based on the list extracted in Fig. 1, the Action Matrix is created, and the Graph is verified and improved. In addition, applying the concept of Musa's operational profile to optimize the scenario execution order improves test productivity by utilizing software test metrics and effectively provides test priorities at the design stage [5].

2.3 Scenario-Based Modeling in AI Software (Fig. 2)

Scenario-based modeling (SBM) is a methodology designed to address the complexity of reinforcement learning-based AI software validation [6]. This model integrates Markov decision processes (MDPs) and scenario-based software testing approaches to explicitly model state transitions, reward structures, and depreciation rates. In particular, it divides the state of the system into initial, intermediate, goal, and failure states, and systematically expresses possible actions and the probabilistic transitions and rewards that follow

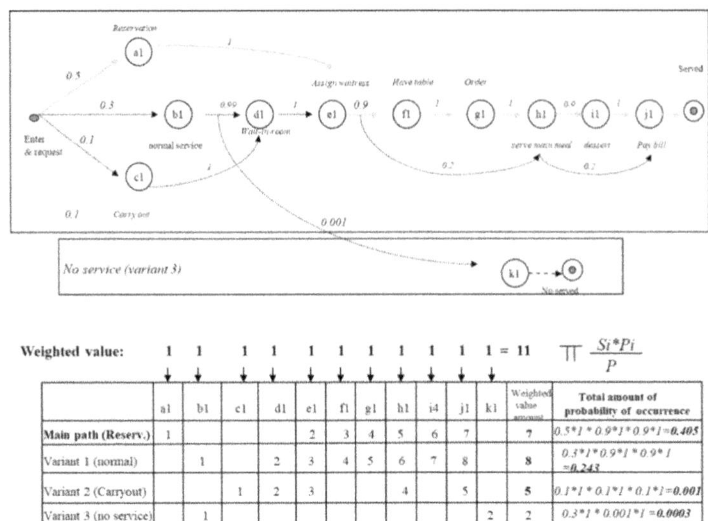

	a1	b1	c1	d1	e1	f1	g1	h1	i4	j1	k1	Weighted value amount	Total amount of probability of occurrence
Main path (Reserv.)	1				2	3	4	5	6	7		**7**	0.5*1 * 0.9*1 * 0.9*1 =**0.405**
Variant 1 (normal)		1		2	3	4	5	6	7	8		**8**	0.3*1*0.9*1 * 0.9* 1 =**0.243**
Variant 2 (Carryout)			1	2	3			4		5		**5**	0.1*1 * 0.1*1 * 0.1*1=**0.001**
Variant 3 (no service)		1									2	2	0.3*1 * 0.001*1 =**0.0003**

Fig. 1. Action Matrix on Scenario-based Integration Testing

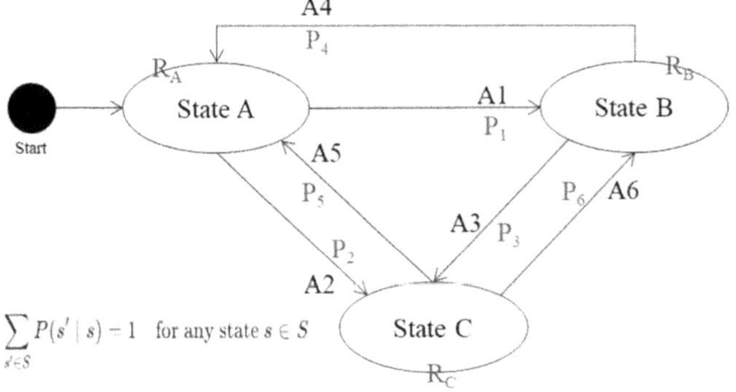

Fig. 2. Scenario Diagram

from each state. SBM defines all possible action paths of reinforcement learning agents as scenarios and reflects uncertainty and dynamic characteristics through modeling that includes probability and reward. This is connected to the concepts of state machine diagrams (SMDs), Markov decision processes (MDPs), and probabilistic scenario decision processes (SSDPs), allowing the system to be expressed visually and mathematically. These scenarios are organized in a tree form, and the priorities of each path can be set and visualized, and a test script is generated based on this, and a procedure is provided to verify the validity of the AI model in a simulation environment. Ultimately, SBM systematically detects unpredictable behaviors of AI software and contributes to increasing the efficiency and reliability of testing.

3 Humanoid Software Testing

3.1 Scenario-Based Modeling in AI Software (Fig. 3)

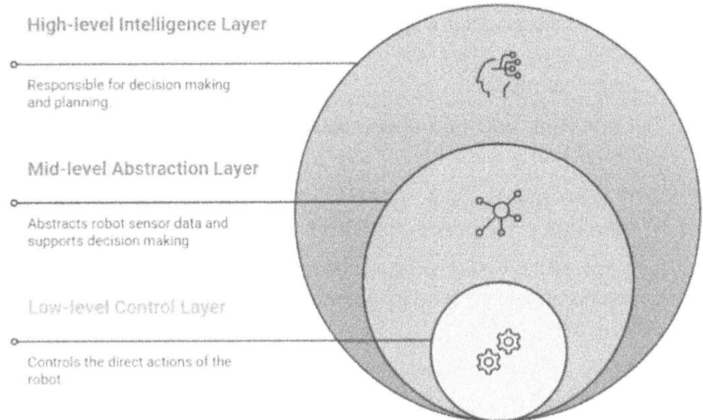

Fig. 3. Hierarchical Control Levels of Robotics System

Humanoid robots are robots with a similar body structure to humans and are designed to operate in various human-friendly environments. The software of these robots can be largely divided into three layers.

The lower control layer is directly responsible for the physical movement of the robot. This layer performs functions such as motor control, sensor data processing, and joint position control. A high level of real-time and precision is required for real-time and precise movement of the robot.

The middle abstraction layer combines commands from the lower control layers to create more complex movement patterns. For example, actions such as walking or moving arms are implemented in this layer. It also processes sensor data to perform environmental recognition of the robot. This layer may include a perception module, a planning module, and an action generation module.

The upper intelligence layer is responsible for the robot's cognitive, decision-making, and learning functions, and artificial intelligence (AI) models play a key role. AI technologies such as reinforcement learning and deep learning are utilized importantly in this layer. Interaction with users, overall task planning, and complex situation judgment are performed in the upper intelligence layer. Mode selection functions are an important part of the decision-making process that takes place in this higher intelligence layer. Humanoid robot software is characterized by complex interactions between these different layers and continuous feedback loops with the physical environment. In particular, the higher intelligence layer equipped with AI models greatly increases the autonomy and adaptability of the robot, but if unpredictable behavior or errors occur, it can have a negative impact on the safety and reliability of the entire system.

We focus on the mode selection requirements among the various functional requirements of humanoid software as shown in Table 1 and apply the Scenario-Based Modeling

Table 1. Humanoid Software Mode Selection Requirements.

Requirement ID	Requirement Description
FR-MS-001	The humanoid must support transitions between 'Standby', 'Location Guidance', and 'Conversation' modes based on user selection.
FR-MS-002	When a user selects a specific mode (e.g., 'Location Guidance', 'Conversation') from the home screen, the humanoid must immediately enter that mode.
FR-MS-003	Upon mode entry, the system must clearly indicate activation to the user, visually and/or audibly.
FR-MS-004	If a user selects 'Back' from the current mode, the humanoid must safely transition to the previous mode or 'Standby Mode'.
FR-MS-005	No system errors or delays should occur during mode transitions; if they do, an appropriate error message must display, and the system should revert to standby.
FR-MS-006	Mode selection buttons must be designed to be intuitive and clearly recognizable.

(SBM) method as a methodology to analyze and verify them. Humanoid systems provide various services, and each service is operated in a specific 'mode'. Since switching between these modes has a significant impact on the user experience and the overall usability of the system, the implementation of an accurate and efficient mode selection function is essential. We will use the SBM method to create scenarios and systematically verify them, focusing on core mode switching functions such as 'location guidance', 'conversation', and 'back'. Each scenario comprehensively considers all situations that may occur in an actual usage environment by clearly defining the initial state, specific user behavior, expected target state, and possible failure state. In this way, through the scenario-based approach, we aim to contribute to the implementation of a highly reliable humanoid system by closely verifying whether the mode selection function of humanoid software operates accurately according to the user's intention and whether the system functions stably.

4 A Case Study on Humanoid Software Validation

In this chapter, we focus on the mode selection requirement among the various functional requirements of the Humanoid Robot Nana's system in Fig. 4 and analyze it and establish a scenario-based validation procedure. Humanoid provides various services through interaction with the user, and each service is defined as a unique 'mode'. Therefore, the function of accurately and efficiently selecting and entering the desired mode by the user has a critical impact on the overall usability and user experience of the humanoid system. We create scenarios focusing on the three mode switching functions of the humanoid: 'location guidance', 'conversation', and 'back', and verify them. Through this, we verify whether the system accurately switches the mode according to the user's intention. We clearly define the initial state, user behavior, expected target state, and failure state for each mode selection scenario. This scenario-based approach contributes to systematically analyzing the functional requirements of a complex humanoid system and establishing a validation procedure by considering all situations that can occur in an actual usage environment.

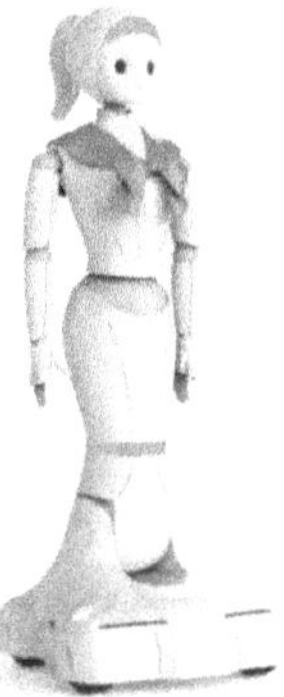

Fig. 4. Humanoid Nana

Step 1. Creation of Humanoid Software Scenario for Testing. In this step, a humanoid software validation scenario is created. The functional target environment, action unit, initial target state, and failure state of the humanoid robot to be verified are defined. These elements are the core foundation for creating an effective scenario. Information such as the environment, state, and action of the humanoid software is extracted from the functional requirements mentioned in Chap. 3. Fig. 5 shows the state table, action unit table, and scenario diagram created based on the information extracted from the requirements. The scenario-diagram diagrammatically expresses the transition process from the initial state ($S_{initial}$) to each state. Each transition branch describes the probability of the corresponding action occurring and the reward value. In this paper, the reward value is set to 1 for the convenience of calculation.

Tables 2 and 3 show the description of the state and action list extracted from Fig. 4. Organizing it in a table like this can improve the readability of the Scenario Diagram.

Step 2. Refine Scenarios with Decision Table. In this step, the initial scenario diagram generated in STEP 1 is refined through the scenario decision table as shown in Fig. 6. The decision table systematically checks the transition rules and conditions between each state to identify all possible cases and prevent unnecessary duplication. This reduces the error rate of the scenario diagram and increases reliability. The decision table defines what action the robot should take and what next state it should transition to depending on specific conditions (input, internal state of the robot, etc.). This process helps the scenario accurately reflect the complex logic of the actual robot system and consider all exceptional situations that may occur during the mode selection process. The refined scenario plays an essential role in verifying that the mode selection function of the

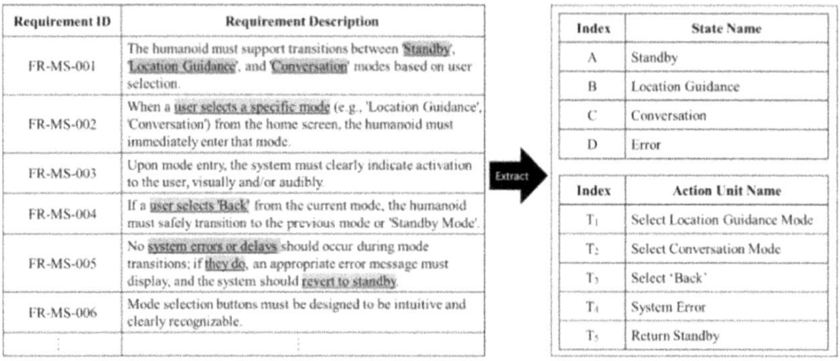

Requirement ID	Requirement Description
FR-MS-001	The humanoid must support transitions between 'Standby', 'Location Guidance', and 'Conversation' modes based on user selection.
FR-MS-002	When a user selects a specific mode (e.g., 'Location Guidance', 'Conversation') from the home screen, the humanoid must immediately enter that mode.
FR-MS-003	Upon mode entry, the system must clearly indicate activation to the user, visually and/or audibly.
FR-MS-004	If a user selects 'Back' from the current mode, the humanoid must safely transition to the previous mode or 'Standby Mode'.
FR-MS-005	No system errors or delays should occur during mode transitions; if they do, an appropriate error message must display, and the system should revert to standby.
FR-MS-006	Mode selection buttons must be designed to be intuitive and clearly recognizable.
⋮	⋮

Extract

Index	State Name
A	Standby
B	Location Guidance
C	Conversation
D	Error

Index	Action Unit Name
T_1	Select Location Guidance Mode
T_2	Select Conversation Mode
T_3	Select 'Back'
T_4	System Error
T_5	Return Standby

Fig. 5. State and Action Unit Extraction from Requirements

Table 2. State Description of Humanoid Software Mode Selection

State	Definition
Standby	A default idle state, awaiting user input
Location Guidance	An activate state providing location-related information
Conversation	An activate state engaging in conversation with the user
Error	System error encountered, displaying an error message.

Table 3. Action Description of Humanoid Software Mode Selection

Action	Definition
Select Location Guidance Button	User selects a 'location guidance button', initiating immediate transition.
Select Conversation Button	User selects a 'Conversation button', initiating immediate transition.
Select 'Back'	User selects 'back' from an active mode, transitioning to Standby mode.
System Error	System errors or delays during mode transitions
Return Standby	Represents the system's automatic recovery from the Error State, transitioning back to Standby Mode after displaying an error message.

humanoid robot operates as expected and that there are no potential defects or abnormal behaviors.

Step 3. Convert Scenario Diagram into Scenario-Based Tree. In this step, the refined scenarios from STEP 2 are converted into a tree structure that includes a common starting point and branching points. Each node of this tree represents a 'state' of the humanoid

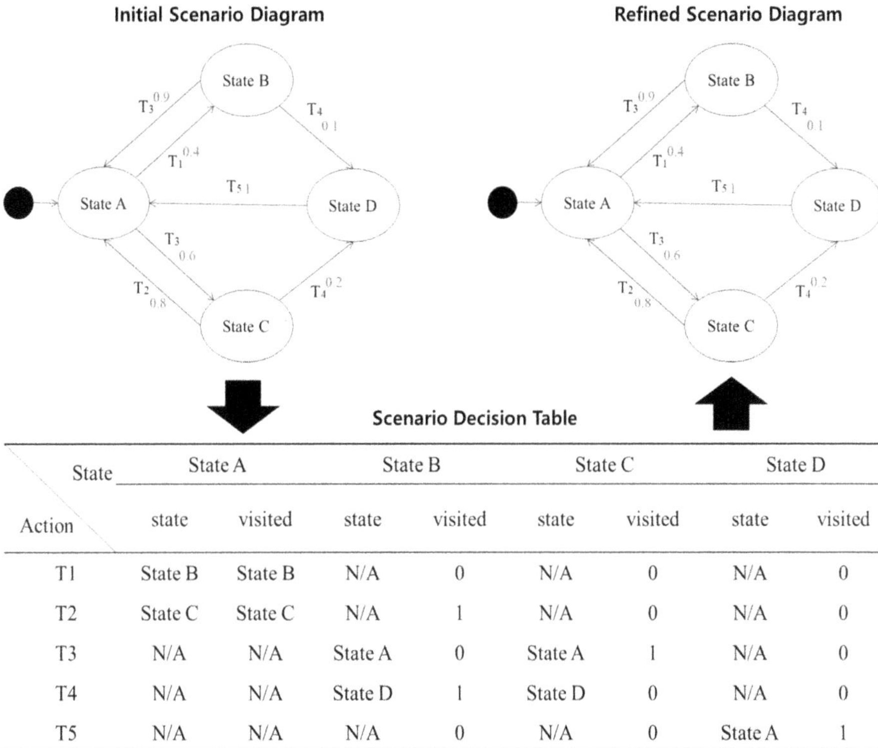

Action \ State	State A		State B		State C		State D	
	state	visited	state	visited	state	visited	state	visited
T1	State B	State B	N/A	0	N/A	0	N/A	0
T2	State C	State C	N/A	1	N/A	0	N/A	0
T3	N/A	N/A	State A	0	State A	1	N/A	0
T4	N/A	N/A	State D	1	State D	0	N/A	0
T5	N/A	N/A	N/A	0	N/A	0	State A	1

Fig. 6. Refining Scenario Diagram Process

software that composes the scenario, and the edges represent 'actions' between states. As shown in Fig. 6, the probability value based on the frequency of occurrence of 'actions' is indicated on the edges, thereby specifying the probability of the agent's action selection in an uncertain environment.

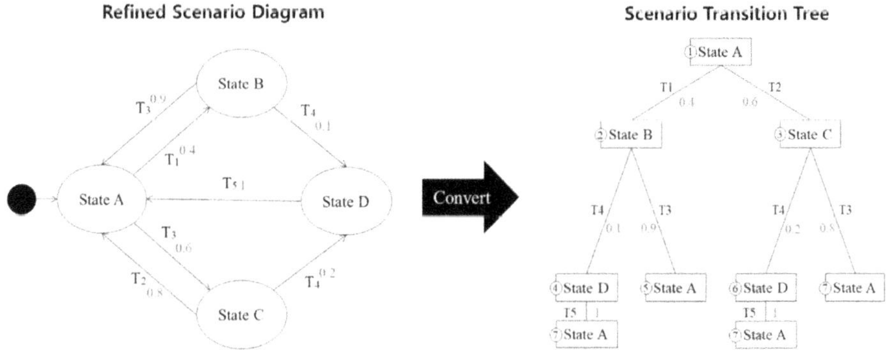

Fig. 7. Convert Scenario diagram into Scenario Transition Tree

Figure 7 shows the final form of this scenario transition tree. The refined scenario is converted into a tree structure through the decision table, and the probability value that occurs on the edge between each state is described to complete the scenario transition tree as in Fig. 8. This tree structure clearly and visually shows all possible paths that occur during the mode selection process of the humanoid robot and provides a basis for more quantitative analysis of the robustness and reliability of the system by considering the probabilistic characteristics of each path.

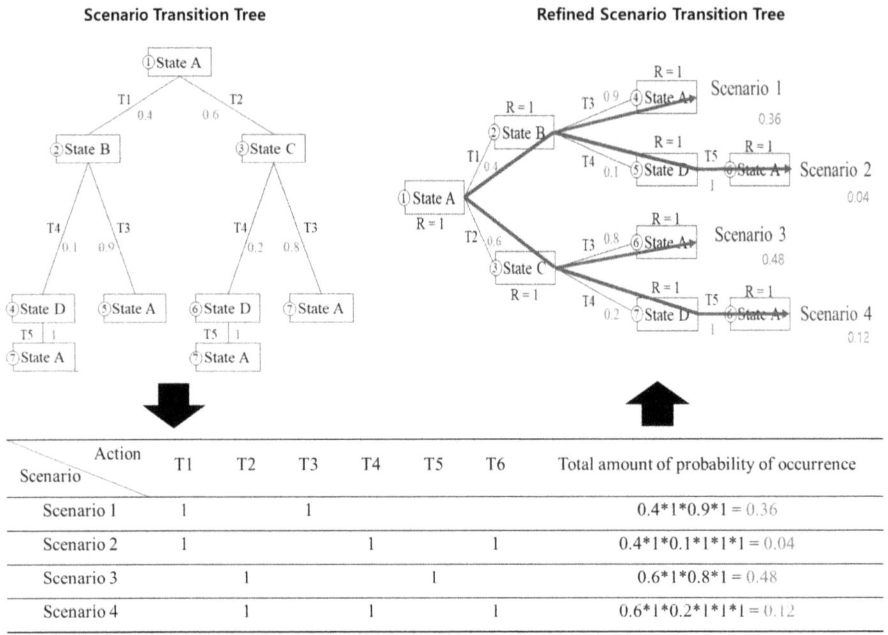

Scenario \ Action	T1	T2	T3	T4	T5	T6	Total amount of probability of occurrence
Scenario 1	1		1				0.4*1*0.9*1 = 0.36
Scenario 2	1			1		1	0.4*1*0.1*1*1*1 = 0.04
Scenario 3		1			1		0.6*1*0.8*1 = 0.48
Scenario 4		1		1		1	0.6*1*0.2*1*1*1 = 0.12

Fig. 8. Refining Scenario Transition Tree with Occurrence Probability

Step 4. Generate Scenario-Based Test Case. In this step, scenario-based test cases are generated based on the scenario transition tree generated in STEP 3. Each test case defines a specific motion sequence of the robot along the path of the tree, which is used to verify that the mode selection function of the humanoid system operates correctly in various situations. As shown in Table 4, this test case consists of Test Case ID, Initial State, Event Index, Action, and Next State. Each field clearly defines the flow of a specific test scenario and provides detailed information to verify that the robot responds as expected to a given input. This process enables systematic and comprehensive validation of the mode transition function of the humanoid robot and contributes to identifying and improving potential errors in advance in an actual operating environment.

Step 5. Generate a Behavior Tree for Performing Test Cases. In this step, a behavior tree is generated to execute the script according to each situational scenario. A behavior tree is a mathematical model of planning and execution used in computer science,

Table 4. Scenario-based Test Case

	Initial State	Action	State	Action	State	Action	Final State
TC 1	State A	T1	State B	T3	–	–	State A
TC 2	State A	T1	State B	T4	State D	T5	State A
TC 3	State A	T2	State C	T3	–	–	State A
TC 4	State A	T2	State C	T4	State D	T5	State A

robotics, control systems, and video games, and is used to effectively structure and manage complex robot behavior. The behavior of the humanoid robot operates through this behavior tree, which helps the robot to flexibly respond to various environments and user inputs. In Fig. 9, the behavior tree is generated based on the state list and action units extracted in STEP 1, as well as the scenario-based test cases generated in STEP 4. The behavior tree hierarchically defines the tasks that the robot must perform, and expresses complex decision-making logic through conditional nodes, sequence nodes, and selector nodes. The behavior tree generated through this process controls the humanoid robot to accurately and efficiently perform the scenarios specified in the test cases and makes the system's behavior predictable and stable.

Step 6. Validate Humanoid Software with Scenario-Based Behavior Tree. In this step, the mode selection function of the humanoid software is validated using the behavior tree generated in STEP 5. This step is performed by executing the scenario defined in the behavior tree in an actual robot or simulation environment. The validation process starts from the initial state specified in each test case and checks whether the robot transitions to the next state exactly according to the defined action sequence and reaches the final target state. In particular, the stability and reliability of the system are evaluated by closely monitoring cases where the robot transitions to an unintended state or enters an error state. This validation process focuses on verifying that the mode switching function of the robot operates exactly according to the user's intention and responds appropriately in exceptional situations. Additionally, the accuracy of sensor data processing and operation execution in an actual environment is evaluated to assess the system's performance comprehensively. This proves that the humanoid robot provides a stable and reliable mode selection function.

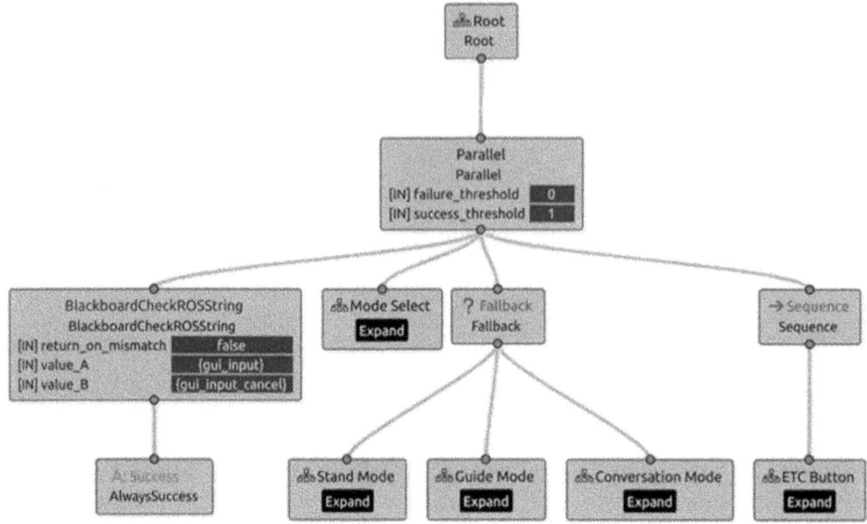

Fig. 9. The Simple case of Behavior Tree for Humanoid Software Validation

5 Conclusion

This paper is a case study on a systematic validation procedure to secure reliability and stability within the complex software system of a humanoid robot. We focus on the mode selection function in the upper intelligence layer where the AI model plays a key role. We demonstrate the efficiency of the validation method for AI-based software operating in the upper intelligence layer through relatively intuitive cases such as 'location guidance', 'conversation', and 'go back'. In future studies, we will further extend the scenario-based validation procedure proposed in this study to apply the currently fixed reward value to various reward systems in real environments, thereby performing more realistic scenario validation. Additionally, we will conduct validation directly on an actual humanoid robot, beyond simulation, to address physical interaction and real-time control issues. We will also develop and apply a scenario-based validation procedure for core robot functions (such as path planning and object recognition) other than mode selection, to enhance the reliability of AI software.

Acknowledgments. This research was conducted with the support of the Korea Creative Content Agency (Project Name: Artificial Intelligence-Based Interactive Multimodal Interactive Storytelling 3D Scene Authoring Technology Development, Project Number: RS-2023-00227917, Contribution Rate: 100%) and the Korea Research Foundation's four, Brain Korea 21 (Project Name: Ultra-Distributed Autonomous Computing Service Technology Research Team, Project Number: 202003520005).

Disclosure of Interests The authors have no competing interests to declare that are relevant to the content of this article.

References

1. Li, Y., Yang, Z., Guo, Y., Chen, X.: Humanoid: a deep learning-based approach to automated black-box android app testing. In: 2019 34th IEEE/ACM International Conference on Automated Software Engineering (ASE), pp. 1070–1073. IEEE (2019)
2. Gao, J., Tao, C., Jie, D., Lu, S.: Invited Paper: What is AI Software Testing? and Why. In: 2019 IEEE international conference on service-oriented system engineering (SOSE), San Francisco, CA, USA, pp. 27–2709 (2019). https://doi.org/10.1109/SOSE.2019.00015
3. Afzal, A., Katz, D.S., Le Goues, C., Timperley, C.S.: Simulation for robotics test automation: developer perspectives. In: 2021 14th IEEE Conference on Software Testing, Verification and Validation (ICST), pp. 263–274. IEEE (2021)
4. Kim, Y., Carlson, C.R.: Scenario-based integration testing for object-oriented software development. In: Proceedings Eighth Asian Test Symposium (ATS'99), pp. 283–288 (1999) IEEE.CONFERENCE 2016, LNCS, vol. 9999, pp. 1–13. Springer, Heidelberg (2016)
5. Musa, J.D.: Operational profiles in software-reliability engineering. IEEE Softw. **10**(2), 14–32 (1993)
6. Kim, J., Kim, K., Son, H., Kim, R.: Scenario-based modeling in AI software validation. In: The 20th Asia Pacific International Conference on Information Science and Technology, KSII, Phuket, Thailand (2025)

Cumulative Effort Estimation in an Evolving Legacy System

Lamees Alhazzaa[1], Anneliese Amschler Andrews[2], and Aiman Gannous[3](✉)

[1] Al-Imam Muhammad Bin Saud Islamic University, Riyadh 13318, Saudi Arabia
lahazzaa@imamu.edu.sa
[2] University of Denver, Denver 80208, USA
andrews@cs.du.edu
[3] University of Benghazi, Benghazi, Libya
aiman.gannous@uob.edu.ly

Abstract. Effort estimation is key in any software development organization. Over the past two decades there has been considerable activity in the area of effort prediction with approaches being typified as being algorithmic in nature such as COCOMO. However, many change request databases contain effort data for finished change requests but they do not contain data that would allow using these methods. We propose a statistical regression approach that uses cumulative effort data to predict future effort in an evolving legacy system. This method provides up to six months of effort prediction for six months in advance. It is then expanded to perform re-estimation of the prediction model to consider change-points in order to get more accurate predictions of effort.

Keywords: Effort estimation · effort prediction · evolving system · regression · change requests

1 Introduction

Estimating effort is essential to software managers to determine the cost of software development and maintenance. This helps them in making informed decisions regarding staffing, future maintenance decisions, and overall business related decisions. As critical as it is choosing the right method for estimating software effort, it is challenging to find the right method that suits a specific project. Software projects are very diverse in the amount and the type of effort they consume.

Legacy systems are software systems that are vital to an organization but due to their age may have used outdated techniques. Most legacy systems require frequent updates and maintenance to cope with changes in business [1]. Software evolution refers to the process of repeatedly updating software systems and includes requirement changes or integration of parts during development. Requirement changes could be an enhancement of features, adaption of a system to changing hardware or software, or performance improvements [2].

K. Daimi et al. (Eds.): CSCE 2025, CCIS 2937, pp. 498–511, 2026.
https://doi.org/10.1007/978-3-032-22208-4_35

Change point is a term used to refer to change in the cumulative effort during software evolution.

Traditional effort estimation approaches such as COCOMO [3], Function Point Analysis (FPA) [4] or estimation by analogy [5] require data related to function points or knowledge about code sizes and expected change in code size. However, many defect databases or change request databases while containing effort data for finished change requests do not contain enough reliable data on function points or size of code to allow using these methods.

In this paper, we examine the following research question: *RQ: Is it possible to estimate future effort through a statistical regression procedure that does not require knowledge of code size for changes?*

Our goal is to predict effort in an evolving aerospace legacy system. Alhazzaa and Andrews [6] were able to predict the number of Change Requests (CR) in an evolving legacy system using Software Reliability Growth Models (SRGMs) for cumulative CRs. This was based on Stringfellow and Andrews [7] method for predicting defects by curve-fitting SRGMs on past cumulative defect data. Alhazzaa and Andrews [6] presented a multi-staged model that predicted CR related change-points and re-estimated the prediction model after each change-point. This method requires only the availability of number of CRs over time to predict cumulative effort with the existence of effort related change-points. We developed a regression model that uses regression to select a model, and then uses the selected model to predict effort.

The remainder of the paper is organized as follows: Sect. 2 provides background on Effort Estimation methods. Then the case study in Sect. 3 followed by the proposed approach in Sect. 4 and the application in Sect. 5. Then we discuss the results in Sect. 6. Threats to validity are explained in Sect. 7. Conclusions follow in Sect. 8.

2 Background

2.1 Effort Prediction

Most of the effort prediction approaches are based on knowledge of code or function points for software development or maintenance tasks. Well known examples include COCOMO [3] and function points estimation [4]. [4,8] has developed a methodology to use function points, which is a weighted sum of the numbers of inputs, outputs, master files, and software inquiries. His work suggested the use of a two-step work-effort validation procedure by estimating (Source Lines of Code) SLOC using function points and then using SLOC to estimate the work effort. In 1997, Niessink and Van Vliet [9] used Function Points in effort prediction as well. Their experiment indicated that the performance of this method gave poor results compared to other effort estimation methods like expert estimation. Recently, Shah and Kama [10] suggested a new Software Change Effort Estimation (SCEE) model that uses a combination of Change Impact Analysis technique (CIA) together with Function Point Analysis (FPA).

This work lacks empirical results to estimate the accuracy of the new model compared to the existing FPA method.

Evanco [11] used both external and internal measures of maintainability to predict effort. A statistical analysis of fault correction effort was conducted based on those factors: fault locality in the software architecture, software characteristics of the defective components associated with the fault, and cumulative changes made to the software (i.e.,fault correction, enhancement, and adaptation).

Analogy based effort estimation uses similar projects to estimate effort. Similarity is defined as Euclidean distance. The key activities for estimating by analogy are the identification of a problem as a new case, the retrieval of similar cases from a repository, the reuse of knowledge derived from previous cases and the suggestion of a solution for the new case. Jorgensen et al. [12] added an adjustment to the analogy based estimation. When a project has an unusual high or low productivity then the estimate is adjusted towards the values of more average projects. Weiss et al. [13] used the same analogy approach to predict bug fixing. Similarity between bugs is compared using the bug description. They combine reported effort for similar bugs as a prediction for the new similar bug. Dehghan et al. [14] proposed an approach to create a hybrid model based on selected individual predictors to achieve more accurate and stable results in early prediction of task completion effort and to make sure the model is not bounded to some attributes and consequently is adoptable to a larger number of tasks. The hybrid effort model uses three independent attribute sets: early metadata based attributes, title and description of software tasks. For this study two commercial projects at IBM were analyzed, called RQM and RTC. Better effort estimation results were shown. From the historical bug-fixing data, Zhang et al. [15] proposed an empirical distribution of bug-fixing time using Monte Carlo Simulation to estimate the total amount of time required. They used a k-Nearest Neighbors (kNN) based method for classifying the bug-fixing time, which can improve the accuracy of existing methods.

Jorgensen proposed an extensive review of studies related to expert estimation of software development effort [16]. He then compared the use of expert judgment, formal models, and a combination of these two approaches when estimating software development work effort. The mean estimation accuracy of the combination based methods was similar to the best of that of the other estimation methods [17].

Several surveys and reviews have been conducted related to the body of research in effort analysis in software systems [18–21]. We found that many papers use software metrics and characteristics such as LOC, function points, defect description, etc., to compare project similarity or estimate by analogy. The COCOMO model uses LOC data for effort estimation. It has been widely used in industry. The COCOMO model uses SLOC data to estimate effort. The Basic COCOMO equation takes the form of:

$$E = aS^b \tag{1}$$

where E is effort, S refers to the lines of code, a is a coefficient and b is an exponent. COCOMO model is widely used in different forms. The three forms of COCOMO models are: basic, intermediate and detailed. The basic model uses Lines of code to estimate effort. The intermediate model takes more cost drivers into account. These drivers are attributes of the product, the hardware, the project and the personnel. These values are used to calculate the Effort Adjustment Factor (EAF), which is then multiplied with the formula for the basic model:

$$E = aS^b * EAF \tag{2}$$

The detailed model incorporates the characteristics of the intermediate model with an assessment of the cost drivers for each step of the software engineering process. These include items such as planning and requirements, system design, detailed design, module code and test [22,23].

2.2 Change-Point Analysis

When project managers and decision makers deal with software systems, changes are expected either in the form of upgrades or fixes. Changes in the system cause changes in the predicted number of change requests (CR) [6]. When such a change-point occurs, a change in the prediction model is required. A change-point is defined as "the point at which the fault detection/introduction rate is changed." [24]. Changes in a legacy system may occur due to corrective or perfective measures or enhancements. This change is reflected in the amount of effort needed to resolve CRs. Change-points are estimated using several methods and techniques such as control charts [25,26], likelihood ratio tests [27–29], or looking into the number of lines of codes added, deleted or modified around the time of the change [30].

2.3 Change-Request Prediction

Stringfellow and Andrews [7] performed a curve-fitting approach that predicted the number of future defects based on cumulative defect data in a software release. This method used Software Reliability Growth Models (SRGMs) but it was not concerned with evolving systems and did not consider change-points. Chi et al. [31] proposed a multi-stage model that segregates release times based on change-points. Whenever a change in failure rate is detected, a new modeling phase is applied as if the data after the change-point was isolated from the old data. The most recent model selected is the one used for prediction. Alhazzaa and Andrews [6] used defect prediction methods on change-request (CR) database for an evolving legacy system. The multi-staged approach used on CR data provided CR prediction with higher accuracy than the original approach proposed by Stringfellow and Andrews [7]. This approach is extended to be used on effort prediction for the same evolving legacy system. In Sect. 4, we will use a similar method for effort prediction.

3 Case Study

We use data from a release of an aerospace system. It is a legacy system that has been in use for three decades. It has over 1.2 million of lines of code, with most of the code written in C, C++, Java, and scripted code. There are over 850 components in 23 subsystems. The subject system evolved over time. Maintenance included corrective maintenance, adaptations (e.g. to a new hardware), perfective maintenance (e.g. performance improvements) and enhancements with new functionality. Enhancements happen within a single release due to contract obligations. Hence the database accounts for Change Requests (CR). This is very different than a database of failures or defects. In this case we predict a combination of defects and enhancement requests. Each CR has a submission date, and the completion date, and the number of hours recorded for CR resolution. LOC added, LOC deleted, LOC modified and LOC auto-generated for resolving the CRs are recorded as well. In addition, information about the priority of the CR, the functional area where the CR occurs is in the system and the type of the request, i.e. if it is a discrepancy or an enhancement.

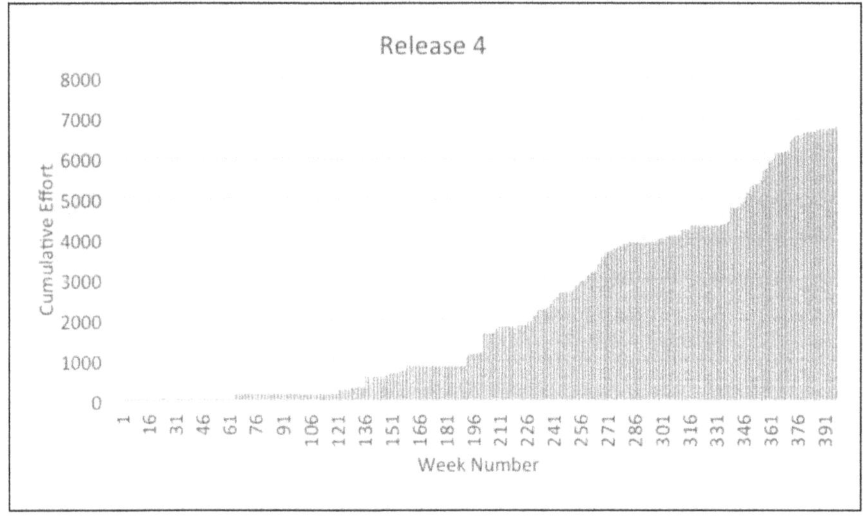

Fig. 1. Cumulative number of CRs in the software release.

Data of this study is collected "after the fact," i.e. it is an ex post facto research. The data were taken from a CR database of an operational release of an aerospace legacy system. Each CR is written to report a problem and is recorded in a CR tracking system (ClearQuest). Each CR, there are number of hours recorded. This represents the effort that the CR resolution required.

We collected effort data for four releases and grouped efforts of CRs on a weekly basis and then numbered each week. We collected effort data from

Release 4 (the most recent release). The weeks started from the 34th week of 2008 until the 15th week of 2016. The total number of weeks is 398 weeks, where a total of 211 CRs were found by the end of the release, with a total effort of 6786 h, see Fig. 1.

4 Approach

4.1 Cumulative Effort Prediction

To predict cumulative effort using past effort data using we use regression. Cumulative effort data is collected for at least ten weeks to start fitting any model to our cumulative effort data.

We follow the rule of thumb recommended by Aguinis and Harden [32]. They suggested that a minimum of 10 observations is recommended for obtaining trustworthy estimates of parameters. In statistics his rule of thumb is a benchmark on adequacy of dataset size in terms of number of observations required in regression models. Specifically, this rule suggests having a minimum of 10 observations per predictor variable[1] [33]. This is what we refer to as enough data at the beginning of a release (Fig. 2a). When data is collected regression is performed using multiple regression models.

In our application we used 11 regression models: Linear, Logarithmic, Quadratic, Cubic, Compound, Inverse, Power, S, Growth, Exponential and Logistic. For each model we measure the Goodness-of-Fit using R^2 measure. If the model fit with an R^2 of 0.9 or above, the model is then considered as a fit model. If not, then it is rejected. If more than one model fit then we select the model with the best fit. The best fit model is the model with the highest R^2 and provides a prediction value that is greater than or equal the actual value, i.e. we avoid models that under-predicts effort. If no model found that meets that criteria then we reject all models and repeat the process of collecting an additional week of effort data and then try to find a fit model. Once a model is found to be the best fit, it is then used for cumulative effort estimation for future weeks until the end of the release. After selecting a model for each stage, these models are used for predicting effort for the future. To measure the predictive ability for each model we observed future predictions from the week the model was selected for up to 6 months into the future. We compared the predicted values for each month to the actual cumulative effort. Then we calculated the relative error.

Relative error (RE) is calculated as[2]:

$$RelativeError = ((estimated - actual)/actual) \tag{3}$$

[1] Predictor variable is the independent variable used in regression analyses, which is time in this case measured by weeks.

[2] Relative error value is calculated using the absolute value of an error over the actual value. In our case we need to keep track of negative values, therefore we calculated the relative error with the real error value instead.

This process is demonstrated in Fig. 2a. For this release three change-points were identified on weeks 201, 255 and 338 using change-point estimation method using Lines of Code data proposed by Alhazzaa and Andrews [30].

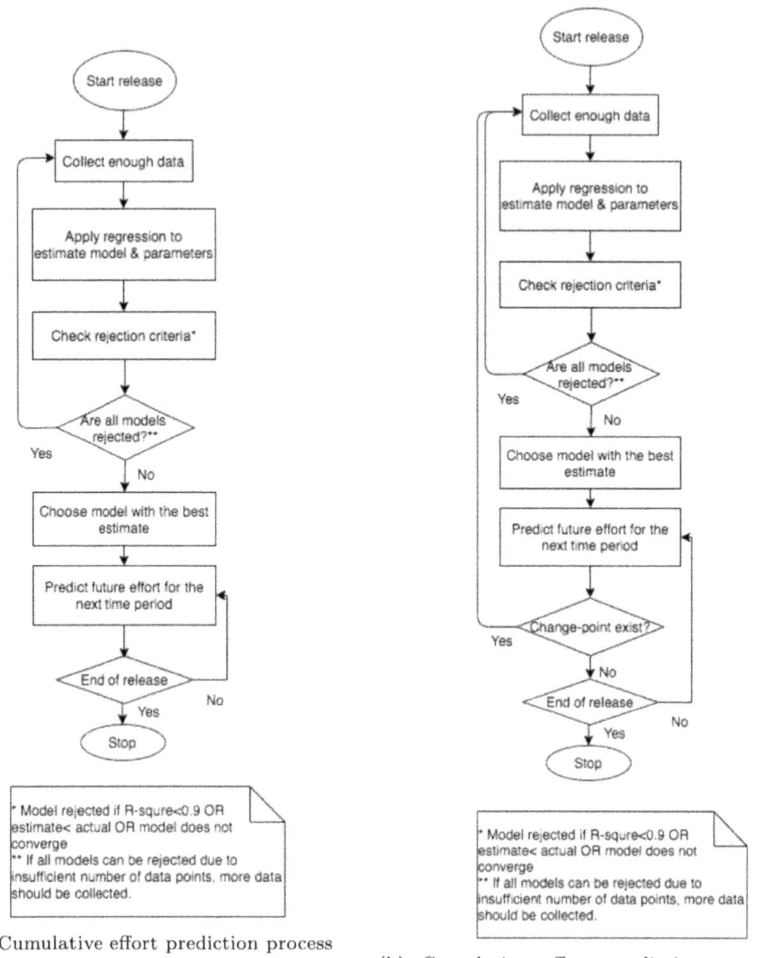

(a) Cumulative effort prediction process

(b) Cumulative effort prediction process with change-point

Fig. 2. Cumulative effort prediction process with and without change-points.

4.2 Cumulative Effort Prediction with Change-Points

Cumulative effort prediction is likely to provide descent effort predictions for the near future, but as the software release grows it is more likely to evolve and the model selected at the beginning of the release will not provide accurate predictions. Therefore, we upgrade our approach to consider evolution in a software release that might cause change-points, along the way. With the existence of change-points we develop a multi-stage model that uses regression to find a fit model, and then uses the selected model to predict effort until a change-point occurs. Change points are now defined in terms of changes in effort, rather than CRs [6]. Change-points can be estimated using likelihood ratio, control charts, or they can be expected by the software team and management if they occur due to changes in the system that might cause changes in the number of defects and change requests, which causes an increase of effort as a result.

Figure 2b shows the process of cumulative effort prediction that considers change-points. We need effort for at least 5 CRs to start model estimation and after each effort change-point we need at least 10 weeks of effort data to start prediction. After collecting effort data we check if any regression model fits the data. For a model to be considered fit, we need to measure the Goodness-of-fit of R^2 of 0.9 or greater. Also, the estimated effort should be greater than or equal to the actual effort. If a model was found to be fit then it is used for future effort prediction, otherwise more data is collected. The model is used for prediction until another effort change-point is found, at which point the whole model estimation process restarts. This whole process continues until the end of the release.

5 Application

5.1 Cumulative Effort Prediction

From the beginning of this release, cumulative effort data was collected per week. Model estimation was performed and tested if any model has an R^2 of 0.9 or greater. We also require the estimated values to be greater than or equal to the actual value for a fit model. If none of the models were found to be fit, more data was collected then model estimation was performed again until a model was found fit.

The first estimated model was in week 153, the cubic model had an R^2 of 0.92, which is the most fit model and above the 0.9 threshold. This model was then used to predict the total effort per week. This model can be used to predict effort throughout the release unless its prediction ability decreases or a change occurs in the amount of effort per week.

Table 1. Effort Predictions and Relative Errors for six months into the future for the first stage.

Model	Week	Actual Effort	Prediction	Month					
				+1 mo.	+2 mo.	+3 mo.	+4 mo.	+5 mo.	+6 mo.
Cubic Stage 1	153	680	Effort	768	848	935	1027	1126	1232
			RE	0.05	0.00	0.10	0.21	0.32	0.45

Table 1 demonstrates the prediction ability of the selected models for each stage. There are five main columns, the first column shows the model selected previously for prediction. The second column has the week number when the model was selected in the fourth release. The third column shows the actual effort by that week. The fourth column shows the predicted effort on a month-to-month basis for six months. The fifth column shows the RE value of each prediction month-by-month. After week 153, the RE value is very small in the first three months, i.e. less than or equal 0.1. After the third month RE starts increasing to 0.21 then 0.32 and 0.45. The model is applicable for the 6 months and it does not show that it under-predicts effort. The prediction ability of the model is acceptable.

Although the selected model performs well for up to six months into the future, its prediction ability decreases as the release progresses due to changes in the growth of the effort curve. Therefore, it is more useful to use different models after change-points are detected or estimated. In the following section we will demonstrate the results of model fitting of each stage after change-points and compare it with the performance of the previous models to demonstrate the magnitude of improvement in prediction ability.

5.2 Cumulative Effort Prediction with Change-Point

After week 201, a significant change was detected using the likelihood ratio method explained in [30]. The percentage of change in effort was 28 week 201 and 202. Although the cubic model selected in week 153 has a relative error of 0.7 which is still acceptable but at that point it is expected that the growth of cumulative effort has changed and this would make using the previous model for prediction less effective. From that change-point, data was collected on a weekly basis and model estimation process was performed.

Table 2 shows the results of model estimation. "Week" shows the week when the model was selected and "Actual" shows the actual cumulative effort of that week. For each model we show the R^2 value and the estimated cumulative effort for that week. The R^2 value and estimated value highlighted in Light Blue identify the selected model.

In week 247, the linear, the cubic and the quadratic models all had a valid R^2, but the linear model had an estimated value that is less than the actual value, so it is not a good fit. Both the quadratic model and the cubic models are good candidates, so we chose the cubic for this stage (second Stage). When using this model for effort prediction, we found that the relative error after one month is 0.14, while it has an RE of 0.71 if the cubic model from the previous stage was used for effort prediction. In general, the newly selected model outperforms the older model in terms of RE values. Another change-point was then detected in week 255. For the third stage, the models had an R^2 of 0.96 by week 264 and all of the estimated values are greater than the actual cumulative effort, therefore the Inverse model was chosen. Although this model under-predicted effort in the first four months but the relative error is much lower than the two previous models predictions. The final stage is the fourth that started after the change-point in week 338. By week 352 all candidate models were viable and we chose the quadratic model. The RE values for the model for the following six months provided better predictions than any of the previous models.

Table 2. Effort model estimation for Release 4.

Stage	Week	Actual	Estimation	Model									
				Linear	Log.	Inverse	Quad.	Cubic	Compound	Power	S	Growth	Exp.
1	153	680	R^2	0.68	0.37	0.05	0.87	0.92	0.87	0.57	0.09	0.87	0.87
			Est.	427	286	187	594	693	512	234	121	512	512
2	247	2694	R^2	0.90	0.89	0.88	0.94	0.94	0.89	0.89	0.88	0.89	0.89
			Est.	2567	2546	2525	2711	2718	2607	2582	2557	2607	2607
3	264	3179	R^2	0.96	0.96	0.96	0.96	0.96	0.96	0.96	0.96	0.96	0.96
			Est.	3214	3213	3212	3214	3214	3217	3216	3216	3217	3217
4	352	5331	R^2	0.90	0.90	0.90	0.90	0.91	0.90	0.90	0.90	0.90	0.90
			Est.	5335	5332	5330	5337	5371	5343	5341	5338	5343	5343

To evaluate predictions of the models estimated after each point we check the RE value of each model for long term predictions, up to six months. After week 247, the RE value of the cubic model that was selected previously increased. Due to the occurrence of change-point we estimated a different cubic model that has a better fit, see Table 2. The cubic model selected for the second stage has an RE value that ranges from 0.14 to 0.55 for the six months. Comparing the RE values of the current model vs. the previous cubic model if it was used for this stage, we found that the current model has smaller RE values, see Table 3.

Table 3. Effort Predictions and Relative Errors for six months into the future for the second stage.

Model	Week	Actual Effort	Prediction	Month					
				+1 mo.	+2 mo.	+3 mo.	+4 mo.	+5 mo.	+6 mo.
Cubic Stage 1	247	2694	**Effort**	4677	4958	5251	5555	5871	6198
			RE	0.71	0.74	0.76	0.75	0.73	0.68
Cubic Stage 2	247	2694	**Effort**	3103	3469	3908	4427	5033	5735
			RE	0.14	0.21	0.31	0.39	0.49	0.55

After week 254, the inverse model was selected for the third stage, see Table 2. Table 4 shows that the inverse model has RE values that are smaller than the RE values of the previous models. Some RE values are negative, which means that the model would under-predict effort in some weeks, but the negative values are very small and are closer to zero, which makes them acceptable.

After week 352, the quadratic model was selected for the fourth stage, see Table 5. Likewise, the last stage shows small RE but some of them are negative. In general, REs are small for up to six months of prediction, which makes effort prediction accuracy higher than the previously selected models. Table 6 summarizes the predictions of each model in the four stages using the estimated model for each stage.

Table 4. Effort Predictions and Relative Errors for six months into the future for the third stage.

Model	Week	Actual Effort	Prediction	Month					
				+1 mo.	+2 mo.	+3 mo.	+4 mo.	+5 mo.	+6 mo.
Cubic Stage 1	264	3179	Effort	5951	6282	6625	6980	7348	7729
			RE	0.67	0.70	0.75	0.79	0.88	0.97
Cubic Stage 2	264	3179	Effort	5200	5927	6758	7703	8767	9959
			RE	0.46	0.61	0.79	0.98	1.24	1.54
Inverse Stage 3	264	3179	Effort	3359	3501	3639	3773	3903	4029
			RE	-0.06	-0.05	-0.04	-0.03	0.00	0.03

Table 5. Effort Predictions and Relative Errors for six months into the future for the fourth stage.

Model	Week	Actual Effort	Prediction	Month					
				+1 mo.	+2 mo.	+3 mo.	+4 mo.	+5 mo.	+6 mo.
Cubic Stage 1	352	5331	Effort	16386	17036	17704	18388	19091	19811
			RE	2.00	1.88	1.89	1.99	1.99	2.02
Cubic Stage 2	352	5331	Effort	57157	61952	67020	72368	78005	83936
			RE	9.45	9.48	9.94	10.77	11.21	11.78
Inverse Stage 3	352	5331	Effort	5746	5827	5906	5983	6059	6133
			RE	0.05	-0.01	-0.04	-0.03	-0.05	-0.07
Quad. Stage 4	352	5331	Effort	5589	5818	6049	6284	6520	6760
			RE	0.02	-0.02	-0.01	0.02	0.02	0.03

Table 6. Effort Predictions and Relative Errors for six months into the future for Release 4.

Week	Actual Effort	Prediction	Month					
			+1 mo.	+2 mo.	+3 mo.	+4 mo.	+5 mo.	+6 mo.
153	680	Effort	768	848	935	1027	1126	1232
		RE	0.05	0.00	0.10	0.21	0.32	0.45
247	2694	Effort	3103	3469	3908	4427	5033	5735
		RE	0.14	0.21	0.31	0.39	0.49	0.55
264	3179	Effort	3359	3501	3639	3773	3903	4029
		RE	-0.06	-0.05	-0.04	-0.03	0.00	0.03
352	5331	Effort	5589	5818	6049	6284	6520	6760
		RE	0.02	-0.02	-0.01	0.02	0.02	0.03

6 Discussion

Effort estimation approaches requires the availability of data about defects and change requests. In many software systems these data are either missing, inaccurate or totally not available. Therefore, we investigate the use of previous effort data in a software release to make future prediction of effort required.

So at the beginning of the research we asked the question: *RQ1: Is it possible to estimate future effort through a statistical regression procedure that does not require knowledge of code size for changes?*

We find that the regression approach that predicts effort based on past cumulative effort data provides promising results. First, it does not require any additional data other than dates of CR submission and effort data, which makes it a more generalizable approach. The majority of the models provided prediction for up to six months with relatively low RE values. In addition to using regression, the approach changes the selected model once the growth of effort data changes or evolves. This provides more accurate prediction in the long run. Cumulative multi-stage effort prediction provides a novel way to predict effort using past effort data. It allows us to examine the fit among several models and find the most fit model.

7 Validity Threats

We follow the guidelines by Runeson et al. [34] in defining our validity threats. The results of this study may not be generalizable. This means that the success of prediction using a specific model does not guarantee that the model would be successful on different sets of data. In fact, we have seen that the cubic model make predictions with minimal RE in one part of a release, but big RE values in another part of a release, i.e. predictions of the cubic model in Stage 1 of Release 4 versus predictions of the cubic model for Stage 1 of Release 3. Our data was collected by a third party which means the researchers have less control over the quality of the data, which is a threat to internal validity. Construct validity refers to the relation between theory and observation. We observed that some models fit data better than others. This may be affected by the number of data-points used for model estimation and selection. Although we dont claim that there is a linear relationship between the amount of data and the accuracy of prediction but if the size of data used is too small we may be at risk of selecting a model that does not predict very well.

8 Conclusion and Future Work

Effort (cost) estimation is essential to any organization. It is key for management to help in budget planning, including hiring staff, managing resources, etc. Traditional effort estimation approaches rely on the availability and the quality defect and change request data including LOC and function points. Many defect or change request databases for software systems lack this data. In addition, the quality of the available data could affect the results of effort estimation.

Since we saw a resemblance between cumulative effort growth and CR growth in [6], we presented a method similar to CR prediction in using curve fitting methods. This method uses regression based on cumulative effort data to predict future effort. This approach shows predicted effort for up to six months into the future with relatively low RE values. Moreover, we found that if change-points were detected and models were re-estimated after each change point, effort predictions become more accurate.

In future work, we would like to extend our research to investigate generalizability of the cumulative effort estimation approach in an evolving software system using further releases.

Disclosure of Interests. The authors have no competing interests to declare that are relevant to the content of this article.

References

1. Bennett, K.: Legacy systems: coping with success. IEEE Softw. **12**(1), 19–23 (1995)
2. Musa, J.D., Iannino, A., Okumoto, K.: Software Reliability: Measurement, Prediction, Application. McGraw-Hill, New York (1987)
3. Boehm, B.W.: Software Engineering Economics. IEEE Trans. Software Eng. **1**, 4–21 (1984)
4. Albrecht, A.J.: Measuring application development productivity. In: Proceedings of Guide, and IBM Application Development Symposium, Joint Share (1979)
5. Shepperd, M., Schofield, C.: Estimating software project effort using analogies. IEEE Trans. Software Eng. **23**(11), 736–743 (1997)
6. Alhazzaa, L., Andrews, A.A.: Change request prediction in an evolving legacy system: a comparison. In: Transactions on Computational Science and Computational Intelligence. Springer, Chm (2020)
7. Stringfellow, C., Andrews, A.A.: An empirical method for selecting software reliability growth models. Empir. Softw. Eng. **7**(4), 319–343 (2002)
8. Albrecht, A.J., Gaffney, J.E.: Software function, source lines of code, and development effort prediction: a software science validation. IEEE Trans. Softw. Eng. **6**, 639–648 (1983)
9. Niessink, F., Van Vliet, H.: Predicting maintenance effort with function points. In: 1997 Proceedings International Conference on Software Maintenance, pp. 32–39. IEEE (1997)
10. Shah, J., Kama, N.: Extending function point analysis effort estimation method for software development phase. In: Proceedings of the 2018 7th International Conference on Software and Computer Applications, pp. 77–81. ACM (2018)
11. Evanco, W.M.: Modeling the effort to correct faults. J. Syst. Softw. **29**(1), 75–84 (1995)
12. Jørgensen, M., Indahl, U., Sjøberg, D.: Software effort estimation by analogy and "regression toward the mean". J. Syst. Softw. **68**(3), 253–262 (2003)
13. Weiss, C., Premraj, R., Zimmermann, T., Zeller, A.: How long will it take to fix this bug? In: Fourth International Workshop on Mining Software Repositories (MSR'07: ICSE Workshops 2007), pp. 1–1. IEEE (2007)
14. Dehghan, A., Blincoe, K., Damian, D.: A hybrid model for task completion effort estimation. In: Proceedings of the 2nd International Workshop on Software Analytics, pp. 22–28. ACM (2016)
15. Zhang, H., Gong, L., Versteeg, S.: Predicting bug-fixing time: an empirical study of commercial software projects. In: Proceedings of the 2013 International Conference on Software Engineering, pp. 1042–1051. IEEE Press (2013)

16. Jørgensen, M.: A review of studies on expert estimation of software development effort. J. Syst. Softw. **70**(1–2), 37–60 (2004)
17. Jørgensen, M.: Forecasting of software development work effort: evidence on expert judgement and formal models. Int. J. Forecast. **23**(3), 449–462 (2007)
18. Rastogi, H., Dhankhar, S., Kakkar, M.: A survey on software effort estimation techniques. In: 2014 5th International Conference—Confluence The Next Generation Information Technology Summit (Confluence), pp. 826–830. IEEE (2014)
19. Idri, A., Hosni, M., Abran, A.: Systematic literature review of ensemble effort estimation. J. Syst. Softw. **118**, 151–175 (2016)
20. Usharani, K., Ananth, V.V., Velmurugan, D.: A survey on software effort estimation. In: 2016 International Conference on Electrical, Electronics, and Optimization Techniques (ICEEOT), pp. 505–509. IEEE (2016)
21. Sehra, S.K., Brar, Y.S., Kaur, N., Sehra, S.S.: Research patterns and trends in software effort estimation. Inf. Softw. Technol. **91**, 1–21 (2017)
22. Boehm, B., Clark, B., Horowitz, E., Westland, C., Madachy, R., Selby, R.: Cost models for future software life cycle processes: COCOMO 2.0. Ann. Softw. Eng. **1**(1), 57–94 (1995)
23. Barry, B., et al.: Software Engineering Economics. Prentice Hall, New York (1981)
24. Deep, K., Nagar, A., Pant, M., Bansal, J.C. (eds.): Proceedings of the International Conference on Soft Computing for Problem Solving (SocProS 2011) December 20-22, 2011. AISC, vol. 131. Springer, New Delhi (2012). https://doi.org/10.1007/978-81-322-0491-6
25. Zhao, Y., Wan, C., Gao, F., Chang, S.: Change points estimation and simulation for software reliability model. In: 2013 International Conference on Measurement, Information and Control (ICMIC), vol. 1, pp. 434–438. IEEE (2013)
26. Huang, C.-Y., Hung, T.-Y.: Software reliability analysis and assessment using queueing models with multiple change-points. Comput. Math. Appl. **60**(7), 2015–2030 (2010)
27. Zou, F.-Z.: A change-point perspective on the software failure process. Softw. Testing Verification Reliab. **13**(2), 85–93 (2003)
28. Galeano, P.: The use of cumulative sums for detection of changepoints in the rate parameter of a poisson process. Comput. Stat. Data Anal. **51**(12), 6151–6165 (2007)
29. S. Inoue, S. Hayashida, and S. Yamada, “Toward Practical Software Reliability Assessment with Change-point Based on Hazard Rate Models,” in *2013 IEEE 37th Annual Computer Software and Applications Conference (COMPSAC)*, pp. 268–273, IEEE, 2013
30. Alhazzaa, L., Andrews, A.A.: Estimating Change-points based on defect data. In: The 2018 International Conference on Computational Science and Computational Intelligence (CSCI), pp. 878–883. IEEE (2018)
31. Chi, J., et al.: Defect analysis and prediction by applying the multistage software reliability growth model. In: 2017 8th International Workshop on Empirical Software Engineering in Practice (IWESEP), pp. 7–11. IEEE (2017)
32. Aguinis, H., Harden, E.E.: Sample Size Rules of Thumb. Routledge, New York (2009)
33. Troutt, M.D.: 10 k Rule of Thumb for Regression. Encycl. Stat. Sci. (2004)
34. Runeson, P., Höst, M.: Guidelines for conducting and reporting case study research in software engineering. Empir. Softw. Eng. **14**(2), 131 (2009)

The Use of ChatGPT to Teach Coding Inhibits Software Development or Supplements Coding Education

José A. Vega(✉), Juan B. Varela, and Ángel Ojeda

Department of Technology and Security, Bowie State University, Bowie, MD, USA
phdvega@gmail.com

Abstract. This study emphasizes the true driving factors behind the adoption of AI technology specifically for coding applications. We conducted a survey targeting faculty members in technology, information systems, computer science, and cybersecurity departments across all universities in the state of Maryland. For this investigation, the Technology Acceptance Model was selected as the guiding framework. Five key factors were examined as influences on the acceptance of ChatGPT use within Maryland universities:

- Inhibit software development
- Provide coding education

In this quantitative research, we identified several factors that influence the intended use of ChatGPT for coding purposes. A survey was conducted with a sample of 330 faculty members specializing in computer-related and technology fields, using Google Forms and Microsoft Forms platforms. We examined the impact of each factor on the adoption of advanced AI technologies within Maryland universities. Using SPSS and PLS statistical software for analysis, the findings revealed that faculty members in Maryland considered only one out of the two model variables to be significant. Specifically, one independent variable — serving as a valuable providing coding education — showed a positive correlation with the intention to adopt ChatGPT. The other factor — inhibiting software development was not found to be significant in influencing the decision to implement ChatGPT as a coding tool in the classroom. This study highlights that while ChatGPT offers notable advantages, it also presents certain challenges within the coding education environment. Further investigation into how students are engaging with ChatGPT could provide additional valuable insights.

1 Introduction

The integration of artificial intelligence (AI) tools like ChatGPT into higher education has significantly transformed programming instruction. ChatGPT, a large language model developed by OpenAI, offers immediate feedback, code generation, and debugging assistance, thereby enhancing students' programming skills and confidence (Ma et al., 2024). Studies have demonstrated that students utilizing ChatGPT in programming courses exhibit improved performance and a deeper understanding of coding concepts (Nie et al., 2024).

K. Daimi et al. (Eds.): CSCE 2025, CCIS 2937, pp. 512–521, 2026.
https://doi.org/10.1007/978-3-032-22208-4_36

However, the adoption of ChatGPT in educational settings is not without challenges. Concerns have been raised about students' overreliance on AI-generated code, which may impede the development of fundamental programming skills and critical thinking abilities (Yilmaz & Karaoglan Yilmaz, 2023). Furthermore, the potential for ChatGPT to provide incorrect or misleading information necessitates careful oversight by educators to ensure the accuracy and reliability of the learning process (Rahman & Watanobe, 2023).

This study aims to explore the dual impact of ChatGPT on coding education within Maryland universities, focusing on two key variables: its potential to inhibit software development and its capacity to enhance coding education. By surveying faculty members across various institutions, this research seeks to understand the factors influencing the acceptance and implementation of ChatGPT as a tool in programming courses. The findings will contribute to the ongoing discourse on the effective integration of AI technologies in education, balancing the benefits of innovative tools with the need to maintain rigorous academic standards and skill development.

2 Problem Statement

As technology continues to evolve, AI is becoming a greater presence in education. Some professors view AI as a facilitator of the learning process that supplements traditional teaching methods. Other professors are skeptical of AI, viewing it as a distraction or inhibitor of the learning process.

The integration of AI tools like ChatGPT into programming education has sparked a dichotomy of perspectives among educators. On one hand, ChatGPT offers immediate feedback, code generation, and debugging assistance, potentially enhancing students' programming skills and confidence (Ma et al., 2024). Studies have demonstrated that students utilizing ChatGPT in programming courses exhibit improved performance and a deeper understanding of coding concepts (Nie et al., 2024).

Conversely, concerns have been raised about students' overreliance on AI-generated code, which may impede the development of fundamental programming skills and critical thinking abilities (Yilmaz & Karaoglan Yilmaz, 2023). Furthermore, the potential for ChatGPT to provide incorrect or misleading information necessitates careful oversight by educators to ensure the accuracy and reliability of the learning process (Rahman & Watanobe, 2023).

Despite the growing prevalence of ChatGPT in educational settings, there is a paucity of empirical research examining its dual role in potentially inhibiting software development while simultaneously providing coding education. This gap in literature underscores the need for a nuanced investigation into how ChatGPT influences programming instruction, particularly in higher education institutions.

Therefore, this study aims to explore the dual impact of ChatGPT on coding education within Maryland universities, focusing on two key variables: its potential to inhibit software development and its capacity to enhance coding education. By surveying faculty members across various institutions, this research seeks to understand the factors influencing the acceptance and implementation of ChatGPT as a tool in programming courses. The findings will contribute to the ongoing discourse on the effective integration of AI technologies in education, balancing the benefits of innovative tools with the need to maintain rigorous academic standards and skill development.

3 Research Question

What are the perceptions of professors of the use of Chat GPT to teach coding in the university setting? (Table 1)

Table 1. Caption

The use of ChatGPT will inhibit students in their future careers as software developers.
The use of ChatGPT for coding assignments inhibits students' problem-solving and debugging skills.
ChatGPT supplements coding education without undermining the learning experience
Educators can use ChatGPT and traditional coding assignments to provide a well-rounded coding education

4 Hypothesis (See Table 2)

Table 2. Caption

H1a	The use of ChatGPT will inhibit students in their future career as software developers and problem-solving and debugging skills.
H2a	Educators can use ChatGPT and traditional coding assignments to provide a well-rounded coding education and supplements coding education without undermining the learning experience

5 Variables

This study focuses on the variables that lead to the use of ChatGPT for Coding in education, where the dependent variable is modeled through the independent variables. In this research the independent variable is the acceptance of the use of ChatGPT in the universities of Maryland. This study aims to demonstrate the positive or negative influence of all the independent variables or some of them in decision making of using ChatGPT for coding in education. This study will allow us to show if there is a correlation between the independent variables and the dependent variable. The Independent variables are listed below:

- Inhibit software development

- Provide coding education

In this framework, we aim to explore the relationship between ChatGPT usage and its associated indicators. By examining ChatGPT's role in coding from multiple perspectives, several important dimensions come to light. Our analysis will focus on ChatGPT in relation to the following factors:

1. **Inhibit Software Development**

   Potential Concerns:

- **Reduced Creativity:** If developers depend on ChatGPT to generate code, there might be a risk of stifling creativity and originality in software design.
- **Dependency:** Frequent reliance on AI-generated code might lead to a reduced ability to innovate or tackle complex problems independently.

   Counterpoints:

- **Efficiency:** For routine or boilerplate coding tasks, ChatGPT can improve efficiency and allow developers to focus on more complex and creative aspects of software development.

2. **Provide Coding Education**

   Advantages:

- **Accessibility:** ChatGPT democratizes access to coding education, providing resources and guidance to individuals who might not have formal education or mentoring.
- **Interactive Learning:** It offers interactive, conversational learning experiences that can complement traditional methods and cater to various learning styles.

   Applications:

- **Tutorials and Explanations:** It can create tailored tutorials and explain concepts in a conversational manner, helping users grasp complex ideas more effectively.
- **Practice Problems:** ChatGPT can generate practice problems and coding exercises, aiding users in honing their skills (Fig. 1).

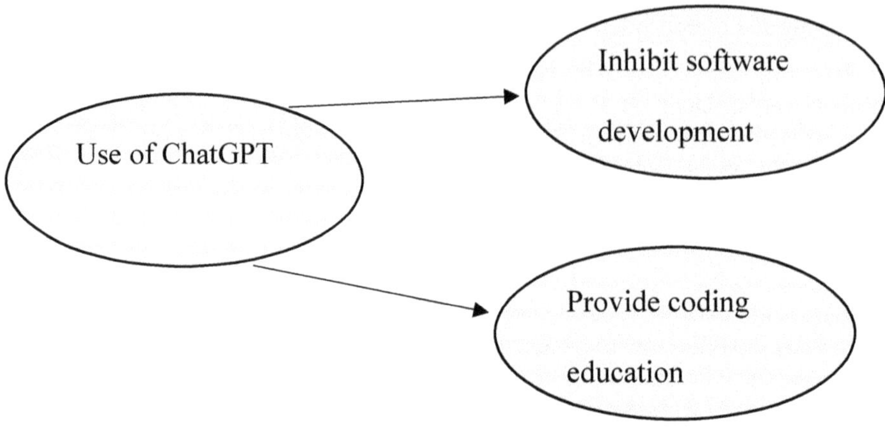

Fig. 1. Caption

6 Literature Review or Background

The integration of artificial intelligence (AI) tools like ChatGPT into programming education has garnered significant attention in recent years. While these tools offer promising avenues for enhancing coding education, they also raise concerns about their potential to inhibit the development of essential software engineering skills.

6.1 Enhancing Coding Education

ChatGPT has been recognized for its ability to support students in learning programming concepts. By providing instant feedback, code generation, and explanations, it serves as a valuable educational resource. For instance, a study by Qureshi (2023) found that students who utilized ChatGPT in programming courses demonstrated improved performance and a deeper understanding of coding concepts. Similarly, Ma et al. (2024) reported that students using AI tutors like ChatGPT learned significantly more in less time compared to traditional instruction methods.

7 Potential Inhibition of Software Development Skills

Despite these benefits, concerns have been raised about the overreliance on AI-generated code potentially hindering the development of fundamental programming skills. Firaina and Sulisworo (2023) highlighted that excessive dependence on ChatGPT can lead to a superficial understanding of coding principles, which may impede long-term skill acquisition. Additionally, Yilmaz and Karaoglan Yilmaz (2023) emphasized that while AI tools can assist in learning, they may also reduce student engagement and motivation to tackle challenging programming tasks independently.

8 Balancing Benefits and Drawbacks

The dual impact of ChatGPT necessitates a balanced approach in its integration into coding education. Educators are encouraged to guide students in using AI tools responsibly, ensuring that these technologies supplement rather than replace traditional learning methods. Further research is needed to explore effective strategies for incorporating ChatGPT into programming curricula without compromising the development of essential software development skills.

9 Methodology of the Study

This study presents a quantitative analysis of independent variables, where their relationship with the dependent variable is established and the relationship is analyzed with one or several variables to be able to present a model that serves to not-too-distant future, education can be improved with the use of GPT Chat for programming. The study presents an analysis that uses the model as a reference Davis's TAM (Davis, 1989) to investigate how the beliefs and attitudes of academics influence their intention to use Chat GPT for coding for education. It is the perception of the professors and experts at Maryland State Universities (Fig. 2).

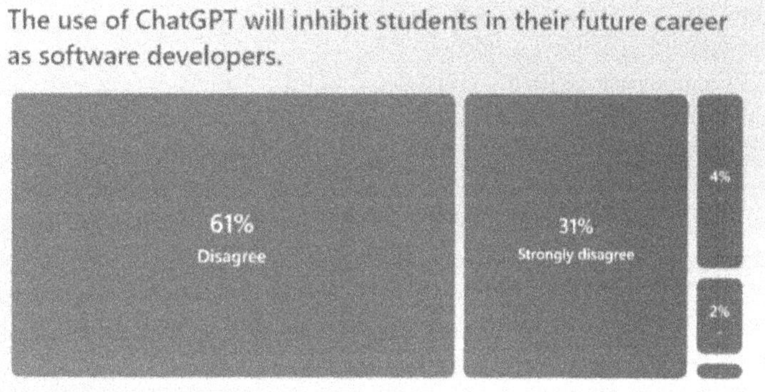

Fig. 2. Caption

The rejection of the hypothesis suggests that most participants view ChatGPT as an asset rather than a limitation for students aspiring to be software developers. Instead of inhibiting skill development, tools like ChatGPT can complement the learning process by offering diverse examples, alternative approaches to coding problems, and immediate feedback. This can accelerate skill acquisition and expose students to a broader range of programming paradigms. The overwhelming disagreement with the hypothesis indicates that the use of ChatGPT is not perceived as a barrier but rather as an enabler in the education of future software developers. As long as students continue to develop their foundational skills and use AI tools as supplements rather than crutches, their careers as software developers are likely to benefit from these technologies (Fig. 3).

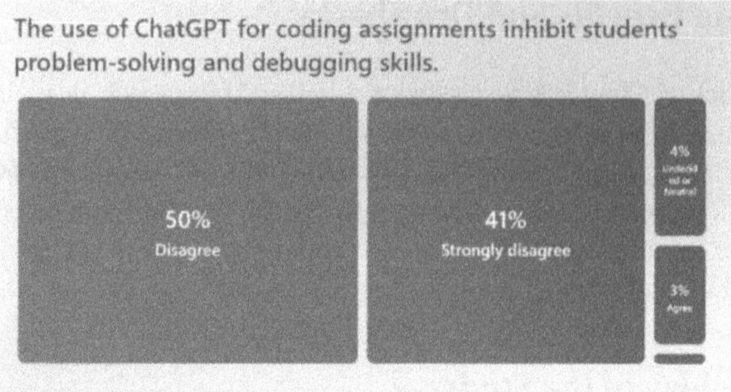

Fig. 3. Caption

Given the data that 50% of participants disagreed and 41% strongly disagreed with the hypothesis that the use of ChatGPT for coding assignments inhibits students' problem-solving and debugging skills, it indicates a strong consensus against the idea that ChatGPT is detrimental in this regard. The rejection of the hypothesis by a significant majority suggests that most participants believe ChatGPT does not inhibit but rather could enhance students' problem-solving and debugging skills in coding assignments. ChatGPT can serve as a supplementary tool that provides hints, explanations, and alternative approaches to coding problems. Instead of inhibiting problem-solving skills, it can reinforce understanding by offering students new perspectives on how to approach a problem. ChatGPT could serve as debugging is a critical skill for developers, and ChatGPT can assist by identifying potential errors and offering solutions. While it provides answers, students still need to understand the nature of the bug and the rationale behind the proposed solution, which can enhance their debugging skills over time. The substantial disagreement with the hypothesis indicates that most participants do not believe ChatGPT inhibits problem-solving and debugging skills. On the contrary, when used appropriately, ChatGPT can be a valuable educational tool that supports the development of these essential skills. The consensus suggests that the integration of AI tools like ChatGPT into coding assignments can enhance, rather than diminish, students' capabilities in problem-solving and debugging (Fig. 4).

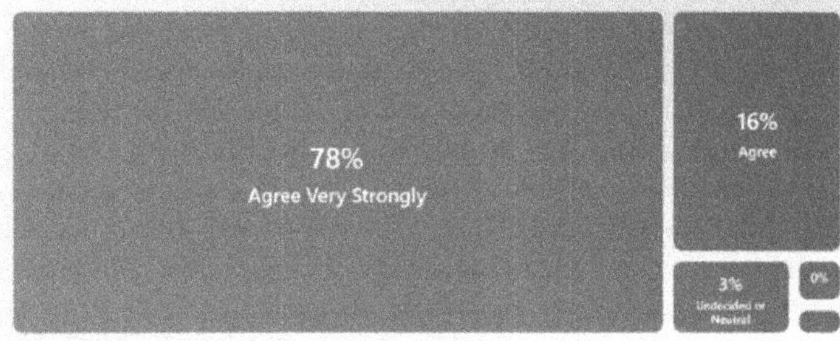

Fig. 4. Caption

The overwhelming agreement with the hypothesis suggests that ChatGPT is seen as a valuable supplement to coding education that enhances, rather than undermines, the learning experience. By providing additional support, encouraging active engagement, and promoting exploration, ChatGPT helps to create a richer and more effective learning environment for coding students. This consensus reflects the growing recognition of AI tools as beneficial aids in the educational landscape. ChatGPT can provide explanations, examples, and clarifications on coding concepts that might be difficult to grasp. This supplementary support can deepen students' understanding of complex topics, making the learning process more effective and comprehensive. This investigation suggests that one of the key advantages of ChatGPT is its ability to offer immediate feedback. When students are working on coding assignments, they can use ChatGPT to quickly check their work, troubleshoot issues, or explore different approaches. This real-time assistance helps maintain the flow of learning and prevents frustration that can arise from prolonged confusion (Fig. 5).

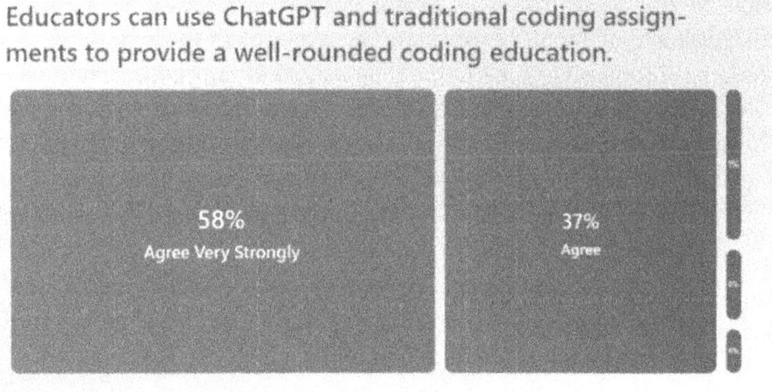

Fig. 5. Caption

The approval of the hypothesis, with 58% agreeing very strongly and 37% agreeing, indicates a strong consensus that combining ChatGPT with traditional coding assignments can offer a well-rounded coding education. This suggests that educators see value in integrating AI tools like ChatGPT into the curriculum alongside more conventional methods. The support for the hypothesis underscores the belief that a balanced approach leveraging both ChatGPT and traditional coding assignment can enhance educational experience for students. The investigation shows that traditional coding assignments are essential for building foundational skills, allowing students to practice problem-solving, algorithmic thinking, and coding syntax in a hands-on manner. ChatGPT can complement this by providing additional resources, explanations, and examples, helping students to better understand and apply these fundamentals. In the professional world, developers often use a variety of tools to aid in coding, debugging, and optimizing their work. By incorporating ChatGPT into the learning process, educators are preparing students for real-world scenarios where they will need to utilize both their foundational skills and available technological resources to solve complex problems. This blended approach can offer students a more comprehensive and effective learning experience, better preparing them for future challenges in the field of software development.

10 Alpha de Cronbach

Cronbach's Alpha shows a reliability greater than or equal to 0.68, which shows that the test applied is reliable. The normality of the data was measured using the Kolmogorov-Smirnov and Shapiro-Wilk tests, the results of which were greater than 0.5, which is the minimum acceptable, and in the five variables that were supported, there was a p-value less than 0.05 (chosen significance level) guaranteeing that the possibility of committing a type I error (rejecting the null hypothesis if it is true) is very small.

11 Conclusion

The findings of this study reveal a strong positive perception of ChatGPT's role in coding education among faculty members. The rejection of the hypothesis that ChatGPT inhibits students' problem-solving and debugging skills suggests that most participants view the tool as a beneficial supplement rather than a hindrance to developing essential software development abilities. With 50% of respondents disagreeing and 41% strongly disagreeing with the notion that ChatGPT negatively impacts coding skills, the data underscores a clear consensus: ChatGPT is not seen as detrimental to students' growth as software developers.

Furthermore, the overwhelming agreement with the hypothesis that ChatGPT enhances the coding education experience highlights its value in supporting student learning. Rather than replacing fundamental skills, ChatGPT appears to act as a catalyst for deeper engagement, offering students opportunities for immediate feedback, guidance, and practice in coding tasks. These results suggest that integrating AI technologies like ChatGPT into programming curricula can strengthen educational outcomes when applied thoughtfully.

Ultimately, this study emphasizes the importance of balancing AI tools with traditional teaching strategies to maximize their benefits while ensuring students build strong, independent coding skills. Future research should continue to explore best practices for incorporating AI in computer science education, particularly in fostering both technical proficiency and critical thinking.

12 Future Research

Future studies could explore the long-term effects of using ChatGPT on students' independent coding abilities after graduation, particularly in real-world software development roles. Comparative research across different disciplines or educational levels (e.g., undergraduate versus graduate programs) could also offer insights into how perceptions and outcomes vary. Additionally, examining students' own attitudes toward ChatGPT and measuring its impact on creativity, critical thinking, and collaborative problem-solving skills would deepen the understanding of its role in coding education. Finally, developing frameworks for responsible and ethical use of AI tools in educational settings would be a valuable contribution to both academic and industry practices.

References

Firaina, A., Sulisworo, D.: ChatGPT: Challenges and Benefits in Software Programming for Higher Education. CiteDrive. Retrieved from https://www.citedrive.com/en/discovery/chatgpt-challenges-and-benefits-in-software-programming-for-higher-education/ (2023)

Ma, B., Chen, L., Konomi, S.: Enhancing programming education with ChatGPT: a case study on student perceptions and interactions in a Python course. arXiv preprint https://arxiv.org/abs/2403.15472.arXiv (2024)

Nie, A., et al.: The GPT surprise: offering large language model chat in a massive coding class reduced engagement but increased adopters' exam performances. arXiv preprint https://arxiv.org/abs/2407.09975.arXiv (2024)

Rahman, M.M., Watanobe, Y.: ChatGPT: Challenges and benefits in software programming for higher education. CiteDrive.CiteDrive+1SpringerLink+1 (2023)

Qureshi, B.: Exploring the use of ChatGPT as a tool for learning and assessment in undergraduate computer science curriculum: opportunities and challenges. arXiv preprint https://arxiv.org/abs/2304.11214. Retrieved from https://arxiv.org/abs/2304.11214 (2023)

Yilmaz, R.M., Karaoglan Yilmaz, F.G.: The use of ChatGPT in teaching and learning: a systematic review through SWOT analysis approach. Front. Educ. **9**, 1328769 (2023)

Poster Research Papers

Branch-Commit-Validate: A Git-Inspired Workflow for Autonomous Red-Team Agents

Chinmay Shringi[1], Alon Hillel-Tuch[1](✉), and Sariya Rizwan[2]

[1] Department of Computer Engineering and Computer Science, New York University, Brooklyn, USA
{cs7810,alon.h}@nyu.edu

[2] Lubin School of Business, Pace University, Brooklyn, USA
s100399n@pace.edu

Abstract. Red-team penetration testing is critical for uncovering vulnerabilities and strengthening defenses. Automating these complex engagements requires traversing vast, dynamic attack spaces and adjusting to real-time target changes, an area where existing search-based planners and deep reinforcement-learning (RL) agents struggle due to combinatorial explosion and prolonged training requirements. This paper presents Branch, Commit and Validate, a Git-inspired workflow that orchestrates specialized agents through parallel hypothesis exploration (Branch), metadata-rich recording of CPU-hours and operator-interaction time (Commit), and automated reliability and performance validation before integration (Validate). We intend to test the framework in a multi host, multi service simulated enterprise setting, gauging gains in decision delay, exploration efficiency, and validated coverage.

Keywords: validation frameworks · autonomous red teaming · version control · penetration testing · continuous integration (CI) · deep reinforcement-learning · multi-agent systems

1 Introduction

Red-team penetration testing provides organizations with proactive insights into security weaknesses before adversaries can exploit them. According to the 2023 CyberRisk Inc. survey, more than 80% of firms perform regular red-team exercises, each requiring approximately 120 human-hours and often exceeding planned durations due to manual pivot planning and reconnaissance [1,2]. To mitigate these resource demands, researchers have introduced autonomous software agents - programs capable of perceiving network states, formulating attack plans, and executing exploits with minimal human input [3]. However, current automation techniques face three main obstacles. First, the number of potential attack paths increases exponentially with network size, causing search algorithms

K. Daimi et al. (Eds.): CSCE 2025, CCIS 2937, pp. 525–530, 2026.
https://doi.org/10.1007/978-3-032-22208-4_37

to stall and RL agents to demand hundreds of episodes to converge [4,5]. Second, static attack graphs precompute a limited set of paths and cannot adapt when target systems reconfigure mid-engagement [6]. Third, while multi-agent frameworks distribute tasks such as reconnaissance, exploitation, and privilege escalation, they often operate without formal coordination, resulting in redundant actions and conflicting outcomes [7,8].

To address these limitations, we employ concepts from Git, a version-control, shared-data system with support for concurrent development via branches, context-aware commits, and merge-gated by CI testing. Our Branch-Commit-Validate lifecycle adapts these principles to autonomous red teaming: specialized Reconnaissance, Vulnerability Analysis, and Exploitation Agents generate parallel attack hypotheses (Branch); successful findings are committed along with CPU-hours and operator-interaction minutes to a central repository (Commit); and each commit undergoes automated reliability, performance, and coverage validation before merging (Validate). We will demonstrate that this approach ensures traceability, scalability, and quality gating in red-team automation.

2 Branch-Commit-Validate Workflow

In this section, we detail each phase of our workflow proposal and ground our definitions in existing literature. From a sequencing perspective, a Reconnaissance Agent (Recon Agent) initiates campaign setup by scanning the target network to enumerate hosts, open ports, and services, and spawning distinct exploration threads called branches. Vulnerability Analysis Agents operate on these branches in parallel, formulating targeted hypotheses (for example, "Host 10.0.0.42 running SSH (Secure Shell) 7.4 may harbor CVE-2018-15473") and executing tests. This parallel frontier exploration (advancing many sibling hypotheses concurrently) resembles Monte Carlo Tree Search techniques, which improve discovery in large decision trees through concurrent path simulations [9].

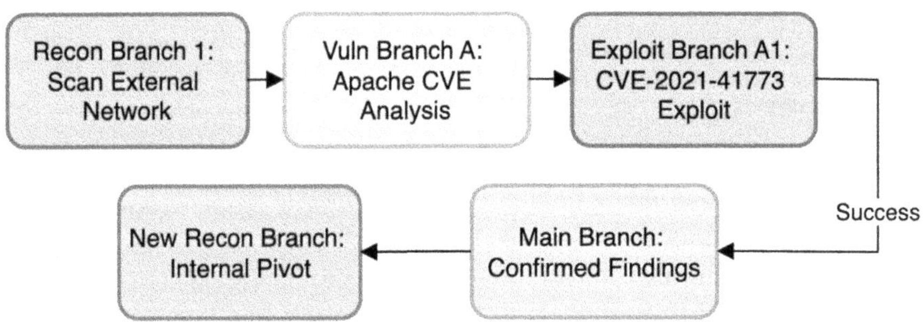

Fig. 1. Proposed Branch-Commit-Validate workflow architecture.

Figure 1 illustrates the full Branch-Commit-Validate lifecycle: the Recon Agent (red) performs host discovery and port scanning, generating branches passed to the Vulnerability Agent for Common Vulnerabilities and Exposures (CVE) analysis as well as attack graph construction. These branches are then extended to the Exploit Agent for exploit attempts and shell or data access. Validated commits from successful exploits populate the Main Branch (green). A customized Pivot Agent may be activated to start reconnaissance from the recently compromised host when a successful exploit has been verified and integrated into main, hence creating new recon branches further into the network. From this point, Pivot Agents (purple) launch new reconnaissance branches on compromised hosts.

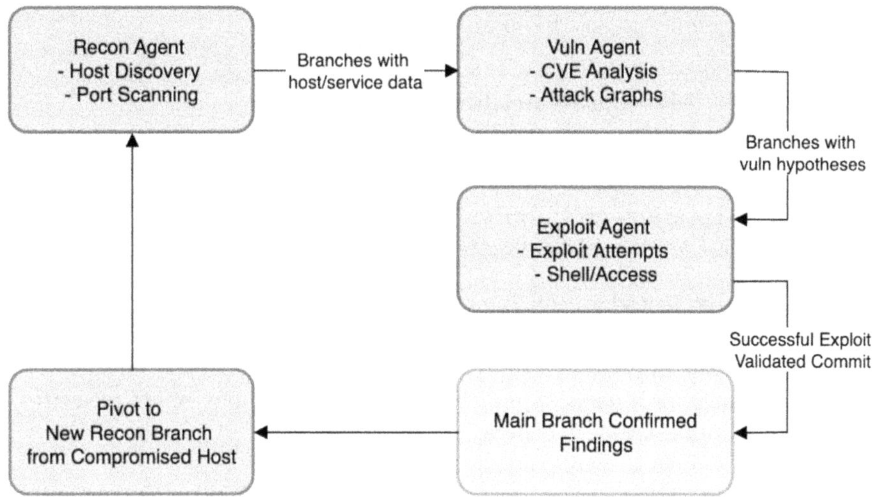

Fig. 2. Example of attack process during a penetration test.

Figure 2 presents a concrete example: Recon Branch 1 scans the external network, leading Vuln Branch A to perform Apache CVE analysis and Exploit Branch A1 to successfully leverage CVE-2021-41773, its validated findings merge into the Main Branch and trigger a pivot, spawning a New Recon Branch for internal assessment. In contrast, Recon Branch 2 probes an internal server, Vuln Branch B tests SSH weak-credential hypotheses, and Exploit Branch B1's brute-force SSH attempt fails; this branch is pruned and excluded from the main campaign. To structure our Git-inspired process, we break the lifecycle into three sequential phases:

- **Branch:** Parallel hypothesis generation and exploration by specialized agents.
- **Commit:** Metadata-rich recording of confirmed findings, including CPU-hours and operator interaction.
- **Validate:** Automated checks for reliability, performance, and meaningful coverage gain before integration.

Collectively known as BCV, each phase is described below.

2.1 Branch: Parallel Hypothesis Exploration

The process begins with a Reconnaissance Agent performing active and passive scans to enumerate hosts, open ports, and services. For every discovered target (e.g., IP address and port combination), the Agent creates a new branch, spawning a Vulnerability Analysis Agent tasked with probing specific hypotheses such as "Host 10.0.0.42 running SSH 7.4 may be vulnerable to CVE-2018-15473." This parallel exploration strategy mirrors Monte Carlo Tree Search (MCTS) methodologies, which have demonstrated superior path discovery in large decision spaces by running concurrent simulations [9]. By dividing the search space among multiple branches, we alleviate the Bellman's "curse of dimensionality" that plagues monolithic and RL-based planners [4,5].

2.2 Commit: Metadata-Enriched Recording

- **Action Trace:** An ordered log of commands and payloads deployed.
- **CPU-Hours:** Cumulative compute time consumed during branch execution.
- **Operator-Interaction Minutes:** Total human oversight time (e.g., prompt confirmations or manual adjustments).

This enhanced metadata collection builds upon best practices in collaborative security workflows, enabling reproducibility, auditability, and informed resource planning [10]. We provide a comprehensive view of automation efficiency and simplify comparisons among approaches by including human-effort measures in addition to computational expenses.

2.3 Validate: Automated Reliability and Performance Checks

Before a commit merges into the main campaign, a Validation Agent executes a three-pronged quality check. First, reliability validation replays the exploit sequence in an isolated environment to verify the consistency of shell access or payload effect. Second, performance validation measures response latency and enforces a configurable threshold (e.g., < 200 ms round-trip time) to ensure practical exploit execution. Third, coverage validation calculates the incremental reachability gain, requiring measurable incremental reachability gain (e.g., new subnets, hosts, or privilege domains) to ensure only strategically meaningful branches are integrated. Commits failing any criterion are automatically pruned or scheduled for re-examination, thereby maintaining campaign integrity and efficiency [11].

3 Related Work

Automation in penetration testing spans several paradigms. Attack-graph-based planners model network exploitation as a search problem, navigating graph nodes and edges representing hosts and vulnerabilities [6,12]. Deep RL frameworks, such as those by Hu et al., train agents through reward-driven exploration of scanning, exploitation, and lateral movement phases [4]. More recently, large language models (LLMs) power systems such as AutoAttacker, orchestrating summarization, planning, and action modules in iterative cycles to generate complex attack sequences [13]. While these methods advance the state of automation, they often lack integrated support for parallel branch management, resource-centric metrics, and gated integration. Our Branch-Commit-Validate workflow synthesizes these elements within a version-control-inspired model, offering enhanced scalability, auditability, and controlled human-in-the-loop collaboration.

4 Experimental Evaluation

We have developed a prototype implementation of the Branch-Commit-Validate framework and plan to evaluate it in a controlled simulated enterprise network environment. The testbed will consist of approximately 50 virtual hosts configured with a range of commonly exploited services (e.g., web servers, database engines, SSH). Our evaluation will benchmark BCV against a baseline monolithic penetration testing planner by comparing metrics such as the number of unique vulnerabilities confirmed, the reduction in redundant scanning and exploitation attempts, and the average time between commit creation and validation. We intend to run multiple independent trials and apply statistical tests (e.g., paired t-tests) to assess significance. These experiments will help quantify BCV's effectiveness in improving vulnerability coverage, reducing operational overhead, and accelerating the confirmation of findings.

5 Conclusion

We have presented BCV, a novel application of distributed version control and CI paradigms to autonomous red-team operations. By enabling parallel hypothesis exploration, capturing both computational and human-effort metrics, and enforcing automated quality gates, our framework delivers improved coverage, efficiency, and reliability. Future work will explore adaptive branch-prioritization heuristics based on commit metrics, integration of sandboxed CI pipelines for safe exploit replay, and scaling evaluations to larger, real-world network topologies. We also plan to examine the trade-offs between automation depth and operator oversight by analyzing detailed interaction logs.

Acknowledgments. This research was conducted as part of ongoing work in autonomous systems and cybersecurity at New York University and Pace University.

Disclosure of Interests. The authors have no competing interests to declare that are relevant to the content of this article.

References

1. Ponemon Institute and Bishop Fox: The State of Offensive Security: 2023 Benchmarking Report. Ponemon Industry Report (2023)

2. Chu, G., Lisitsa, A.: Poster: agent-based (BDI) modeling for automation of penetration testing. In: 2018 16th Annual Conference on Privacy, Security and Trust (PST), pp. 1–2. IEEE, Belfast (2018). https://doi.org/10.1109/PST.2018.8514211
3. Balaji, P.G., Srinivasan, D.: An introduction to multi-agent systems. In: Srinivasan, D., Jain, L.C. (eds.) Innovations in Multi-agent Systems and Applications - 1. Studies in Computational Intelligence, vol. 310, pp. 1–27. Springer, Heidelberg (2010). https://doi.org/10.1007/978-3-642-14435-6_1
4. Hu, Z., Beuran, R., Tan, Y.: Automated penetration testing using deep reinforcement learning. In: 2020 IEEE European Symposium on Security and Privacy Workshops (EuroS&PW), pp. 2–10. IEEE, Genoa (2020). https://doi.org/10.1109/EuroSPW51379.2020.00010
5. Abbass, H., Bender, A., Gaidow, S., Whitbread, P.: Computational red teaming: past, present and future. IEEE Comput. Intell. Mag. **6**(1), 30–42 (2011). https://doi.org/10.1109/MCI.2010.939578
6. Konsta, A., Lafuente, A.L., Spiga, B., Dragoni, N.: Survey: automatic generation of attack trees and attack graphs. Comput. Secur. **137**, 103602 (2024). https://doi.org/10.1016/j.cose.2023.103602
7. Ghanem, M.C., Chen, T.M., Nepomuceno, E.G.: Hierarchical reinforcement learning for efficient and effective automated penetration testing of large networks. J. Intell. Inf. Syst. **60**, 281–303 (2023). https://doi.org/10.1007/s10844-022-00738-0
8. Ghanem, M., Chen, T., Ferrag, M.A., Kettouche, M.: ESASCF: expertise extraction, generalization and reply framework for optimized automation of network security compliance. IEEE Access (2023). https://doi.org/10.1109/ACCESS.2023.3332834
9. Browne, C.B., et al.: A survey of Monte Carlo tree search methods. IEEE Trans. Comput. Intell. AI Games **4**(1), 1–43 (2012). https://doi.org/10.1109/TCIAIG.2012.2186810
10. Burger, E.W., Goodman, M.D., Kampanakis, P., Zhu, K.A.: Taxonomy model for cyber threat intelligence information exchange technologies. In: Proceedings of the 2014 ACM Workshop on Information Sharing and Collaborative Security (WISCS '14), pp. 51–60. ACM, New York (2014). https://doi.org/10.1145/2663876.2663883
11. Avgerinos, T., Cha, S.K., Rebert, A., Schwartz, E.J., Woo, M., Brumley, D.: Automatic exploit generation. Commun. ACM **57**(2), 74–84 (2014). https://doi.org/10.1145/2560217.2560219
12. Chen, Z., Kang, F., Xiong, X., Shu, H.: A survey on penetration path planning in automated penetration testing. Appl. Sci. **14**, 8355 (2024). https://doi.org/10.3390/app14188355
13. Xu, J., et al.: AutoAttacker: a large language model guided system to implement automatic cyber-attacks. arXiv preprint arXiv:2403.01038 (2024)
14. Skandylas, C., Asplund, M.: Automated penetration testing: formalization and realization. Comput. Secur. **155**, 104454 (2025). https://doi.org/10.1016/j.cose.2025.104454
15. Scarfone, K., Souppaya, M., Cody, A., Orebaugh, A.: Technical guide to information security testing and assessment. NIST Special Publication 800-115, National Institute of Standards and Technology (2008). https://doi.org/10.6028/NIST.SP.800-115

Author Index

K. Daimi et al. (Eds.): CSCE 2025, CCIS 2937, pp. 531–532, 2026.
https://doi.org/10.1007/978-3-032-22208-4

GPSR Compliance
The European Union's (EU) General Product Safety Regulation (GPSR) is a set of rules that requires consumer products to be safe and our obligations to ensure this.

If you have any concerns about our products, you can contact us on

ProductSafety@springernature.com

In case Publisher is established outside the EU, the EU authorized representative is:

Springer Nature Customer Service Center GmbH
Europaplatz 3
69115 Heidelberg, Germany

www.ingramcontent.com/pod-product-compliance
Ingram Content Group UK Ltd.
Pitfield, Milton Keynes, MK11 3LW, UK
UKHW020901170726
473380UK00002B/129

9783032222077